From Tin Foil to Stereo;

EVOLUTION OF THE PHONOGRAPH

by **OLIVER READ**,
and **WALTER L. WELCH**

1976   550p

Howard W. Sams & Co., Inc.
4300 WEST 62ND ST. INDIANAPOLIS, INDIANA 46268 USA

1. Sound - Recording and reproducing - History

CONTENTS

The historical events which preceded the invention. Man from earliest times has sought to imitate the sounds of nature by mechanical means.

Presents the factual sequence of Edison's experiments leading to the development of the first phonograph.

The organization of the Edison Speaking Phonograph Company, and the development of the Bell-Tainter Graphophone.

Organized under the aegis of the North American Phonograph Co., proprietors of the patents of T. A. Edison and licensee of the Bell-Tainter patents. Formation of the National Phonograph Association.

The historical account of the consolidation of the American Graphophone Co. and the Columbia Phonograph Co. A summary of the court actions between the American Graphophone Co. and the Edison Phonograph Works.

Presents the phonographic achievements of Lieut. Gianni Bettini who developed a method of reproducing the human voice emphasizing natural tonal qualities of trained musical voices.

FOREWORD

Sixteen years after its first appearance, the reprinting of *From Tin Foil to Stereo* with but modest revisions and additions and by the original publisher besides, is something of a literary oddity, especially since, in that interval, the manuscript had been returned to its authors, apparently with the thought that reprinting would probably never be warranted.

How differently things turned out! For most of that intervening period, the book was entirely unavailable from the publisher in its original binding and dust sleeves, while the going price for used copies steadily escalated, year by year, to $60, and in one known case to $200. Libraries have found it impossible to keep copies in good condition because of intensive use, and many copies have simply disappeared.

The why of all this is now obvious. *From Tin Foil to Stereo* was and still is the most comprehensive and best illustrated story of the phonograph from 1877, when Thomas Alva Edison first demonstrated his remarkable "machine that could talk," on up through the complex and confusing plethora of mechanical, acoustical, and electronic inventions that gave us the stereophonic disc process of the late 1950s. In a word, this book has become a "bible" for serious scholars of the technical and legal aspects of the development of the now mammoth audio-visual industry, as well as a boon to phonograph buffs and collectors the world over.

Moreover, *From Tin Foil to Stereo* was the first text properly to credit Edison, undisputed inventor of the phonograph, with tremendous improvements which he and his associates made, during his lifetime, toward advancement of the phonographic art. Before this comprehensive, analytical survey appeared, many physicists and chemists, to say nothing of laymen, did not fully understand the scientific basis for many of Edison's early phonographic decisions, nor the many, many contributions of the Edison pioneers to better sound-recording and reproducing techniques in the later years. Nearly everyone knew Edison as "the Wizard of Menlo Park" who had invented the phonograph, as the man who revolutionized telegraphy, who added to the success of Bell's telephone by his efficient carbon transmitter, and who was responsible for the first practical incandescent electric light and related systems for generating and distributing electric power. These aside, however, most people were relatively unfamiliar with the manifold phonographic accomplishments that resulted from Edison's work at West Orange where, having abandoned the Menlo Park works, and following his New York period, he built a second and much larger laboratory complex in 1886.

Edison was interested in literally everything, but the very catholicity of his interests, and his resulting multitudinous activities, both before and after the Menlo Park days, in a sense militated against proper recognition of his amazing insights, both early and late, in the field of natural phenomena. Vivid imagination frequently led him into channels of inquiry that never occurred to others. Being highly practical, he instinctively directed his own and his associates' efforts towards conversion to usefulness of scientific principles, often discovered by accident when in the process of solving seemingly unrelated problems. Thus, the dichotomy that had earlier existed between purely scientific laboratory research and utilization of scientific knowledge for human benefit was first closed at Menlo Park, and those two formerly divorced activities were happily wed in his later West Orange Laboratory period.

So it developed that when Edison discovered some then inexplicable phenomenon, he and his co-workers carefully observed, documented, and filed their findings for future reference. The Edison Laboratory Notebooks, now carefully preserved at the Edison National Historic Site in West Orange, and at the Edison Institute in Dearborn, Michigan, attest to the perfection of his method and to the vast resulting benefits of collaborative research and development over many long years. Indeed, it has often been remarked that Edison's original concept of the modern industrial research laboratory, as we know it today, was perhaps his greatest invention.

Because Edison not only created new devices for human use and enjoyment, but also engaged in their further development and actual manufacture, his image as an always sensitive and prescient investigator has tended to become obscured. Even in the rough-and-tumble of business, however, his policy was generally to live and let live. Thus, he became a leading proponent of fair trading and, in sequel, a target for antitrust legislation. Although he was granted 1,093 United States patents (more than awarded to any other person before or since), and hundreds of foreign patents as well, many of his inventions received protection inadequate to keep him in certain industries in which he was once a leading figure. Such was the case, for example, with his 1889 Strip Kinetograph, the original motion picture camera, which he patented only in his native land.

Similarly, in his magnificent work of inventing and developing a safe, practical, and economical system for electric power to illuminate the world's homes, factories, and opera houses, and to run its industrial machines, Edison's very successes and willingness to tolerate competition made him a controversial figure. In others' eyes, his insights seemed often more intuitive than scientific, his "cut and try" methods wasteful, even though more than one scientific luminary was later obliged to admit that by such means he often came up with what their data told them were "impossible" inventions—a highly efficient electric power generator, for instance. Conversely, this same approach, coupled with a certain stubbornness, sometimes led Edison into unfortunate paths, such as his vehement opposition, on the basis of danger to human life, to alternating versus direct current.

Edison first began commercial operation of the Pearl Street Station in New York on September 4, 1882. The move to Schenectady of the Edison Machine Works (originally at 104 Goerck Street, New York City) occurred late in 1886. This, of course, was one subsidiary company in the larger parent organization of the Edison Electric Company (founded in October 1878). The parent organization merged in April 1892 with Thomson-Houston to become the Edison General Electric Company. That consolidation accomplished, Edison was constrained to relinquish control over the industry, which in due course dropped his name and became simply the General Electric Company.

The decade of concentrated work with electric light and power behind him, Edison turned once more to his beloved invention of 1877, the phonograph. How he tried to make it practical to ship "phonograms" in place of other media of correspondence is part of the story told in *From Tin Foil to Stereo*, as is the account of the infinitely more successful improvements on his basic instrument for recording-playback of popular and classical music, contemporary wit and humor, and the voices of leading men and women of his day. Highly varied, broad in content and appeal, the Edison cylinders and discs gave to posterity an extensive repertoire of recorded sound.

When Thomas A. Edison, Inc., finally went out of the phonograph business in 1929, the hill-and-dale or vertical-cut method of recording and reproduction, which

Edison originated and championed for so long, also virtually ceased to exist. The triumph of rival companies using the more expedient lateral-cut process was assured, at least for the time being, though all were in straitened financial circumstances incident to the "Great Depression" which began that year. Today's annual two-billion-dollar industry has carried us past the "high-fidelity" period of the late 1940s, into the stereo-disc era of the 45-rpm and $33\frac{1}{3}$-rpm LPs of the 1950s and 1960s, and beyond to quadraphonics. Edison's goal of faithfully recording and reproducing what one actually heard at a live performance went largely by the board, the victim of electronic gimickry handled by technicians who tampered in all kinds of devious, questionable ways with the original sound. Many present-day phonograph enthusiasts, listening only to worn, mold-pitted, and sometimes warped recordings of the past, often played on equipment in need of repair, still think of the Edison sound as "tinny," and are seemingly unconscious either of its historical truth or of its recoverability in ways which make for pleasant contemporary listening. In the minds of such people, attuned to the blandishments of Madison Avenue advertising, anything new must necessarily be better than what has gone before.

Yet, in the basic Edison concept of the phonograph, there was embodied a prescient principle since vindicated by even the most astute of his successors, as the text of this book describes, and which seems inevitably to signal at least one more overwhelming revolution in the application of phonograph technology. On other fronts of the now multifaceted great phonograph industry, there are signs that Edison, with his vertical-cut method, was right after all. Articles on the RCA Scanning Electron Microscope, dated July 1968, offer indisputable proof, both visually and textually, that present stereo discs do not provide a durable and positive groove-stylus relationship, and that with such discs, destructive wear or demodulation begins almost immediately when they are played. Information in *From Tin Foil to Stereo* clearly shows that, by contrast, the Edison vertical-cut method answered this problem, and in the chapter on the Maxfield-Harrison electrical recording system, one notes that Western Electric had found vertical-cut much superior to lateral-cut recording.

The past several years have in fact witnessed much research and experimentation with systems for producing records by new techniques, such as EVR (Electronic Video Recording). Nearly all of these are more complex than those of old. Recent demonstrations in the United States by Teldec, a consortium of Telefunken and Decca engineers, of a process for producing video discs with both sight and sound, involved the use of vertically modulated foil in recording. Edison's 1877 phonograph also used foil and vertical modulation!

More recently, an article by Robin Lanier, associate editor of a technical journal for the broadcasting industry, appeared in the *New York Times Magazine* for May 25, 1975. Entitled "A Home TV Production," it described two other systems (RCA and Philips/MCA) likely to be employed for producing video discs in the United States. Both will make possible half-hour programs of sight and sound, reproducible through home TV sets.

The important thing to observe at this point is that none of the three above-mentioned systems use lateral modulation in any way. Of course, it may be said that neither stereo nor quadraphonic recording, involving division of signal and sound directionality, has any pertinent relationship to such TV developments, television by contrast affording point source. Nonetheless, there appears to be a growing awareness that divided directionality may not really be as important, at least not in all sound reproduction, as it seemed at first. Even today, there are high-fidelity experts and many listeners who adhere to the view that a symphony orchestra, heard naturally in the dimensions of a great concert hall, is in itself a unified source of sound, and that by using a number of speakers properly placed in the home environment, the original sound can be heard from top monophonic recordings with almost, if not entirely, as much realistic "spread" as from stereo or quadraphonic records. This is not to deny the prospect of improvements in phonographic record-ing and reproduction which are undoubtedly yet to come, simply to note once again that new is not always that much better than old, and that in Shakespeare's words, "all that glitters is not gold."

Edison's accomplishment of direct comparison of live vocal and instrumental so-loists with their recorded sound, in his famous "tone tests" made with the New Edison Laboratory Model Phonographs produced between 1912 and 1929, involved acoustical recording, vertically cut discs, and all-acoustical reproduction only. Even so, judging from unbiased reports of those tests, the results were little short of astounding.

Recent work in re-recording from Edison Blue Amberol cylinders, originally recorded on wax from 1908 to 1915, makes it clearly apparent that there were cer-tain advantages with Edison's cylinder process over discs. To make his tone tests, it had been necessary to reduce ambient reflections in the recording studio, and thus to eliminate telltale echoes from surrounding the voices or instrumental sounds that were to be compared.

Now in 1976, in his re-recording from cylinders onto cassette tape for binaural listening, Professor Welch has been able, through separate and slightly differing patterns of sound for each of the listener's two ears, via headphones, literally to re-create, with optimum historical truth, voices and music as though heard in the original Edison sound studios. The writer can personally attest to this, having listened to a number of such re-recordings made by the Welch method: one is literally transported back to the distant past, hearing such performances as if he were in the same room with the artists themselves, truly an amazing achievement!

We can be assured, furthermore, that although Edison reduced the level of studio ambience in recording for the discs, such reduction was only to a certain threshold, just enough to prevent any impairment of voices or instruments by projection into other listening environments. Through the analysis of peculiar characteristics of original studios used for disc recording, therefore, either by sub-liminal evidence in the recordings themselves, or by reconstructing the studios proper, a way seems open to re-record the discs, as well as the cylinders, with the same binaural capability as described above.

With this in mind, Professor Welch developed a way to double the strength of the music and conversely to diminish by several decibels the surface noise/signal ratio. Since many original disc and cylinder recordings are still available, and with the molds of the Edison discs that have fortunately been preserved, a new era for research and recovery of an important part of our early phonograph history is forecast.

The centennial of Edison's phonograph, December 1977, also lies close at hand. To celebrate it, a National Archives of Recorded Sound will, it is hoped, be recog-nized, planned, and eventually brought into being. Perhaps, too, it may ultimately be appreciated that, for the survival of free enterprise and the greatest possible realization of creativity, we need institutions where qualified young people may engage in classified scientific research along these lines, and thus carry the preser-vation of audio history into an even more golden future.

One final word. In his work as superintendent of the Edison National Historic Site from 1956 to 1970, and more recently through his affiliation with the Charles Edison Fund, it has been this writer's pleasure and privilege to become well acquainted with Professor Welch and his work. Comprehensive and scholarly though it is, *From Tin Foil to Stereo,* prepared in collaboration with Dr. Oliver Read, represents but part of Professor Welch's life achievement. Less well known, perhaps, but increasingly acknowledged both within the United States and abroad, have been his outstanding expertise and progress, as first and present Director and Curator of the Thomas Alva Edison Re-recording Laboratory, part of the Syracuse University Audio Archives, in developing ingenious means for optimum re-recording of Edison's records and other types of records, having always in mind their historical authenticity. In so doing, Professor Welch has opened for posterity a whole new vision of our rich audio past.

MELVIN J. WEIG
Vice President
Charles Edison Fund

ACKNOWLEDGMENTS

In genius seldom are found the combined attributes of both inventor and artist. Probably the best known exception was Leonardo da Vinci, artist, sculptor, and inventor of the Renaissance. Thomas A. Edison neither sought nor received recognition as an artist, yet his many laboratory sketches bear a striking resemblance to the analytical sketches of Leonardo da Vinci. Edison also developed a system of rapid calligraphy, which was most efficient, and at times, quite beautiful. Like da Vinci, Edison was a keen observer of nature, making copious notes of his observations and deductions, and drawing clear, vigorous sketches of his conceptions. From an historical viewpoint, it is fortunate that this was so, for the methodical Edison set an example for his colleagues in Newark, Menlo Park, and West Orange that largely accounts for the greatest collection of authentic information about the beginnings of several important industries to be found in any one place in the world. Thus, the first acknowledgment of your authors is to Thomas A. Edison, inventor of the phonograph and historian of his researches.

The continuity of corporate development of the Edison enterprises over many years, culminating in the once vast Thomas A. Edison Industries complex in West Orange, New Jersey, later to become a division of McGraw-Edison Co., also has been important in preserving much of the early industrial information. An almost continual need during the developmental period for evidence of prior concept for use in innumerable patent cases was also a potent determinant in the preserving of laboratory notes and artifacts. The personal interest of Henry Ford in keeping alive the many accomplishments of Edison led to the transfer and rebuilding of the Menlo Park buildings from New Jersey to Dearborn, Michigan, and the restoration of their contents. Accomplished during the closing years of the inventor's life, this restoration accentuated, at a critical time, a growing realization of the tremendous historical importance of the archives at West Orange.

Following Mr. Edison's death, the Edison Library, Edison's chemical laboratory, his machine shop, and the underground storage vault of the Edison archives were operated for some years as the Edison Museum by the Thomas Alva Edison Foundation, Inc., under a lease arrangement with the owners, Thomas A. Edison, Inc. On December 6, 1955, these properties, together with the inventor's former home, Glenmont, also in West Orange, were presented by the company to the United States Department of the Interior. These buildings are now known as the Edison National Historic Site, and are in the custody of the National Park Service, Gary E. Everhardt, Director. Since then, Thomas A. Edison, Inc., founded by the inventor, has been merged with the McGraw-Edison Company, Chicago.

Acknowledgment of continuing assistance is due the foregoing organizations for indispensable helpfulness to your authors. Particular appreciation is extended to

Charles Edison, deceased, a son of Thomas A. Edison, and former Secretary of the Navy, Governor of New Jersey, and Chairman of the Board of the McGraw-Edison Co., Inc. In 1952, Mr. Edison read a preliminary draft of much of this work. Mr. Theodore M. Edison, another son of Thomas A. Edison and himself an inventor, supplied much useful information, especially about the development of electrical recording. Mr. Paul B. Kasakove, of the Thomas A. Edison Industries Division, who developed the Edison high-speed disc processing system introduced in 1921, furnished other pertinent facts about Edison disc phonographs.

The long interest of John C. F. Coakley, Historian of the Edison Pioneers, in furthering this work, has been a constant inspiration. Mr. Coakley, a public relations consultant, arranged many of the more important interviews, plus access to sources of accurate information essential to this story. Early meetings were arranged by Mr. Coakley with George E. Probst, Executive Director of Thomas Alva Edison Foundation, Inc.; Vice-Admiral Bowen, then Director of the Edison Museum; and Norman R. Speiden, then Curator. The authors have since found themselves indebted to Mr. Speiden for many, many hours of research and for his unflagging zeal for establishing the unvarnished facts. Mr. Speiden fully deserves the reputation he has acquired of knowing more about Thomas A. Edison and his work than any other living person.

Melvin J. Weig, Superintendent of the Edison Laboratory National Monument after 1956, had continued the assistance always so generously offered in making the historic resources available. Mr. Speiden became Supervisory Curator and Mr. Harold S. Anderson became the Curator. Mr. Anderson was of great assistance to your authors, as was Mrs. Kathleen McGuirk, Archivist. All three have since retired. William A. (Bill) Hayes, a pioneer recording expert with Edison since 1895, until his death assisted at the Museum in furnishing information to your authors. The constant interest and helpfulness of George E. Probst, formerly Executive Director of Thomas Alva Edison Foundation, Inc., and of his Consultant, Harry L. Cherry, Jr., is also gratefully acknowledged.

Credit for willing assistance is also extended to B. L. Aldridge of RCA Victor Co., Camden, N. J., and to Columbia Records, Inc., Bridgeport, Conn., and New York City.

Second only to the Edison resources, the best kept archives of the industry are in the museum, vaults, and files of The Gramophone Co., Ltd., Hayes, Middlesex, England. This organization is now a member company of Electric & Musical Industries, Ltd. Appreciation is extended to Electric & Musical Industries, Ltd. for permission to consult the company's historian and to publish the information supplied. The authors wish to thank Miss Lydia A. Walton, A. C. I. S., Historian, for her extensive researches into the background of the E. M. I. companies, including the early Gramophone Co., later named the Gramophone & Typewriter Co., Ltd., now the Gramophone Co., Ltd.; the International Zonophone Co.; the British Zonophone Co.; Columbia Graphophone Co., Ltd.; and others. Miss Walton also edited the material referring to these companies.

Credit is also due to Mr. Anthony C. Pollard, Editor of *The Gramophone,* for his personal assistance to the authors, as well as to the ever-flowing font of inspiration *The Gramophone* has been since the acoustic days and its founding by Compton Mackenzie. Sir Compton Mackenzie is perhaps better known as a novelist, but he was also the first writer to effectively arouse public interest in the latent potential of the phonograph (or gramophone) in the creation of a recorded musical culture. In England we also wish to thank S. Arthur Renton for the timely loan of bound volumes of *The Talking Machine News,* and to our good friend, Denis H. Perry, for valued liaison.

Nearer to us, others have been most helpful, particularly Mr. Philip L. Miller, then Chief of the Music Division, New York Public Library. Mr. Miller had brought together in the Music Division one of the finest libraries of recorded music, catalogs, and general information about the world resources of recorded music to be found anywhere. The appreciation of the authors is extended to Frank A. Taylor, then Head Curator, Dept. of Engineering and Industries, Smithsonian Institution, United States Museum, Washington, D. C. Mr. Taylor and his assistant, Mr. S. H. Oliver, had been interested in the prospect of an accurate history of the industrial development of the phonograph and were most helpful. In the checking of industrial statistics, information made available by Mr. John W. Griffin, Executive Secretary of the Record Industry Association of America, New York City, has been helpful. Mr. John D. Venable, Assistant to the Chairman of the Board, McGraw-Edison Co., Inc., now retired, also furnished much information about the Edison phonograph and record production statistics.

Mr. Albert Wertheimer, long experienced in the coin-operated phonograph industry, became interested in the chapters devoted to his field and arranged for numerous contacts and for access to sources of information in this area where so little accurate history has been written. Messrs. McCann and Lupino of *Billboard* were among the earliest to offer assistance. Mr. Loren P. Meyer,[1] then Secretary of the Automatic Phonograph Manufacturers Association, with headquarters at Evanston, Illinois, was instrumental in securing the cooperation of the members of the Association in this project. The authors wish to thank Mr. Meyer and the members for their assistance, as follows:

Mr. J. W. Haddock, President
AMI, Incorporated
Mr. Carl T. McKelvy, Vice-President
The Seeburg Corporation

Mr. David C. Rockola, President
Rock-Ola Manufacturing Corporation
Mr. R. C. Rolfing, President
The Wurlitzer Company

Mr. A. D. Palmer, Jr., Advertising Manager of The Wurlitzer Company, deserves special mention for granting access to his excellent prior research into the early history of his company. (In 1974, Wurlitzer left this field of manufacture.)

Many facts were determined by checking files of popular publications and trade papers devoting all or part of their attention to the phonograph field, too numerous to mention individually. However, special credit is due to *Hobbies Magazine*, especially to the columns of Aida Favia-Artsay and Jim Walsh.

The authors are also indebted to Harold Spivacke, former Head of the Music Division, Library of Congress, and to his assistant, Mr. Edward N. Waters. We both acknowledge our indebtedness to the late Duane D. Deakins, M.D., for his genuine interest in this manuscript and his many encouraging letters, and for many valued photographs, especially of European phonographs. To Mr. Ray Phillips, serious phonograph collector, special thanks for inspiration and help, as well as his personal counsel.

Mr. Read, now retired, wishes additionally to thank his former associates at the Ziff-Davis Publishing Company, especially his secretary, Pauline Giglio, for checking historical facts and dates at the New York Public Library. Special thanks are extended to the hundreds of readers of *Popular Electronics, Hi Fi Review,* and *Radio & TV News (Electronics World)* during the 1940's and 50's who sought historical phonographs, photos, and literature from their attics and from other sources.

Mr. Welch wishes additionally to acknowledge the assistance and encouragement of many personal friends, particularly that of Richard N. Wright, President of the Onondaga Historical Association, Syracuse, N. Y.; his wife, Caroline, and Miss Violet Hostler, Archivists of the Association, for innumerable historical references

[1] Loren P. Meyer d. 1966. Some time previous to this, the Automatic Phonograph Association had ceased to function.

and clippings pertaining to matters phonographic. The extended loan by Mr. Wright of a scrapbook once belonging to Edward R. Easton of the American Graphophone Co. incited the inquiries resulting in this book. Mr. Lewis A. Clapp of the Court of Appeals Library, Syracuse, N. Y., gave valued assistance in locating references to court decisions, and the staff of the Syracuse Public Library were always helpful, especially in providing access to the files of the *Patent Gazette*.

Mr. Welch wishes to thank Mr. Victor Bettini, New York City, for facts concerning the career of Mr. Bettini's father, the pioneer recorder, Gianni Bettini. Also, thanks to Mr. William A. Maloney, Syracuse, N. Y., for thoughtfully sending informative material on many occasions.

Mr. Welch gratefully acknowledges the interest and encouragement of his former superiors in the State University College of Forestry, now the College of Environmental Research and Forestry, at Syracuse University, particularly Hardy L. Shirley, Dean; and George J. Albrecht, then Head of the Department of Landscape Architecture, both since retired.

Mr. Welch wishes to extend his appreciation to William P. Tolley, Chancellor Emeritus of Syracuse University; and Frank P. Piskor, former Vice President for Academic Affairs, now President of St. Lawrence University; Vice President Kenneth G. Bartlett, now retired; and Wayne S. Yenawine, former Director of Libraries and Dean of the School of Music, now Director of Libraries of the University of South Carolina. His successor as Director of Libraries at S.U., Warren N. Boes, was also of great help in the later work of this author. Warren is now Director of Libraries of the University of Georgia. Mr. Welch wishes to remember always his friend Dr. W. Freeman Galpin, Historian of Syracuse University, now deceased, for his encouragement and many constructive suggestions.

Mr. Welch also wishes to express his gratitude for certain preparatory instruction in Dr. Floyd Allport's event system theory to Prof. Raymond Rhine, then with the English Department of Syracuse University and a former Lexicographer with the G. C. Merriam Company.

Mr. Welch also wishes to remember many interested friends of the years past, including James Vandermark, Francis W. Dunn, John F. Adams, Elias S. Bodour, Louis E. Wallace, and Royal Coffin. Mr. Welch acknowledges his indebtedness to his former employer, mentor, and colleague, the late Melville A. Clark, collector, musician, and inventor, for his never-failing confidence and encouragement.

For the present edition, your authors also respectfully wish to acknowledge assistance by the following:

Dr. Frank S. Macomber, Professor of Fine Arts, Syracuse University.

Mr. Donald C. Anthony, Director of Libraries, Syracuse University.

Mr. Paul Christiansen, President, Charles Edison Fund, East Orange, N. J.

Dr. Robert J. Conan, Jr., Physicist, Lemoyne College, Syracuse, N. Y.

Mrs. Leah S. Burt, Museum Curator, Edison National Historic Site, West Orange, N. J.

Mr. Robert G. Wheeler, Vice President, Research and Interpretation, Edison Institute, Dearborn, Mich.

Finally, the authors are indebted to Gladys Read and Dolores Welch for their cooperation and affectionate understanding.

Your authors wish it were possible to acknowledge the many, many letters received since *From Tin Foil to Stereo* was published, especially those from researchers and libraries which sought our assistance in getting copies after the supply was exhausted. We feel that we owe special thanks to Mr. A. Nugent of Richmond, Va., an enterprising book and record dealer who assisted many persons in the years since. We hope those who were unsuccessful in getting copies will still remember us. We have our sights on the Centennial of Edison's miraculous invention only one year hence, and welcome suggestions and criticisms, favorable or otherwise.

LIST OF PLATES

(To Be Found Between Pages 246 and 247)

Other Phonographs, circa 1905—continued

Excelsior "Ruby" had a solid brass flower horn 12¼ by 10¼ inches in diameter.

Microphonograph "Henry Seymour" (1905 Model) Microphonic reproducer fitted all Graphophone types and could be fitted to the Edison machine.

"Puck," an English talking machine, had a clockwork motor.

Pathé "Coquet" reproducer.

Microphonograph reproducer, the old Pathé "Perfecta" phonograph with the improved Henry Seymour improved attachment.

Pathé "Actuelle" talking machine.

More Phonographs, Some of English Make . . . . Plate XV

"Trump" Graph-o-phone had a flower horn that came in assorted colors and was housed in an oak cabinet.

Murdoch "Sylvia C" featured a top-crank wind.

Columbia "Home Premier" Graphophone had a reduced diaphragm to soften and mellow the volume without impairing the quality of tone.

Murdoch "Angelica" had top-crank wind, sapphire styli.

New Century phonograph.

Murdoch "Pandora" had a top-crank wind, black enameled base and cover, all other parts nickelled.

Murdoch "Magnet" was mounted on imitation satin wood and had a nickel horn.

Murdoch "Excelsior" could be fitted with a green flower horn.

Pathé "Duplex" Grand Concert phonograph was advertised as a "triumph—all squeakiness and nasal twang overcome."

Unusual Talking Machines, circa 1898 . . . . Plate XVI

Talking Machine "Polyphone" featured two horns.

Dupliphone talking machine played both small and large records, combining two machines into one.

"Double Bell Wonder," like the "Polyphone," had two horns for greater volume and clarity of tone.

Talking Machine "Polyphone" used with the Edison Phonograph. Any machine could be made into a "Polyphone."

This talking machine was offered free with the purchase of three dozen Columbia records at the regular price of twenty-five cents each.

"Echophone" talking machine featured a clockwork motor and an all-glass tone arm.

Standard Talking Machine, Style X, one of two disc phonographs produced by American Talking Machine Company. Only records having a one-half inch center hole could be played on this machine.

CHAPTER 1

BEFORE THE PHONOGRAPH

FROM earliest times, man has sought to imitate the sounds of nature by mechanical means. Children often spontaneously try to do this in their play with various objects. The first serious attempt to simulate the human voice by mechanical means (as far as is known) was in the colossal statue of Memnon at Thebes. This was built in the eighteenth Egyptian dynasty, about 1490 B. C. Carved in stone with a series of hidden air chambers, Memnon was supposed to emit a vocal greeting each morning at sunrise to his mother, Goddess of the Dawn. That it did produce some sort of sound was testified to by Strabo, who visited it in 7 A. D. But it was toppled by an earthquake in 27 A. D. Although restored in 196 A. D. by Roman Emperor Septimus Severus, its alleged power of speech was gone.[1]

Questionable though the actual vocal capacity of Memnon may be, the Homeric poems attest to the belief of the Greeks in statues that spoke and later the Greeks and Persians alike consulted oracles before making important decisions. The means was probably a hidden priest. However, during the middle ages a number of talking automatons were constructed. The first that seems to have been historically well authenticated is that of a talking head made by Friar Roger Bacon, the emi-

nent medieval philosopher.[2] The culmination of automaton building seems to have been reached in 1860 by Herr Faber in Vienna, who built an intricate talking man.[3] The present tendency is to regard the building of such elaborate automatons as a great waste of time and energy. But what will the people of a future generation think of Voder, the electronic talking man exhibited by the Bell Telephone Company at the World's Fair, 1939? Voder was also keyboard-operated.

It is a far cry from the building of automatons to the application of pure science to the problem of sound reproduction, or the "storing up" of sound. However, a writer of the science fiction of an earlier day forecast as accurately the functions of the phonograph as Jules Verne did that of the airplane and the submarine. In 1649, Savinien Cyrano de Bergerac wrote his *Histoire Comique en Voyage dans la Lune*, describing a visit to the moon via skyrocket. He described in detail a talking

---

[1] *Egypt, Vol. 2,* George Ebers.

[2] *The Phonograph and How to Use It*, National Phonograph Co., New York, 1900.

[3] Idem—"A brief description of Faber's talking man may be of interest. It has flexible lips of rubber, and also a rubber tongue, ingeniously controlling vowels and consonants. In its throat is a tiny fan wheel, by which the letter 'r' is rolled. It has an ivory reed for vocal cords. Its mouth is an oval cavity, the size of which is regulated by sliding sections, rapidly operated from a keyboard. A tube is attached to its nose when it speaks French."

book, amazing in its consistency with that which has been since attained.[4]

There have been other imaginative conceptions on the part of fiction writers prior to the actual invention. These may be said to have served chiefly as entertainment, but may perhaps have stimulated the constructive thinking of others more aware of the potentials of the growing body of scientific knowledge. Certainly the thought is father to the accomplishment.

According to the statistics of world patents, the various inventions incorporated in the modern phonograph have been by Americans to quite a predominate extent. However, as shown by the

---

[4] *Histoire Comique en Voyage dans la Lune,* translated by A. Lovell 1867, Doubleday & McClure, London 1899.

"No sooner was his back turned (he speaks of his Guide, whom he terms his 'Spirit') but I fell to consider attentively my Books and their Boxes, that's to say, their Covers, which seemed to me to be wonderfully Rich; the one was cut of a single Diamond, incomparable more resplendent than ours; the second looked like a prodigious great Pear, cloven in two. My Spirit had translated those Books into the Language of that World; but because I have none of their Print, I'll now explain to you the Fashion of those two Volumes:

"As I opened the Box, I found within somewhat of Metal almost like to our Clocks, full of I know not what little Springs and imperceptible Engines. It was a Book, indeed, but a Strange and Wonderful Book, that had neither Leaves nor Letters. In fine, it was a Book made wholly for the Ears and not the Eyes. So that when any Body has a mind to read in it, he winds up the Machine with a great many little Springs; and he turns the Hand to the Chapter he desires to hear, and straight, as from the Mouth of Man, or a Musical Instrument, proceed all the distinct and different Sounds, which the Lunar Grandees make use of for expressing their Thoughts, instead of Language.

"When I since reflected on the Miraculous Invention, I no longer wondered that the Young-Men of that Country were more knowing at Sixteen or Eighteen years Old, than the Gray-Beards of our Climate; for knowing how to Read as soon as speak, they are never without Lectures, in their Chambers, their Walks, the Town, or Traveling; they may have in their Pockets, or at their Girdles, Thirty of these Books, where they need but wind up a Spring to hear a whole chapter, and so, more, if they have a mind to hear the Book quite through; living and dead, who entertain you with Living Voices. This Present employed me about an hour, and then hanging them to my Ears, like a pair of Pendants, I went to walking."

---

literature of the sciences, the purely scientific research in mechanics, acoustics, and electricity which provided the basis for the fundamental inventions had been done largely by European scientists. In other words, although the practical applications of scientific discoveries were made largely by Americans, the prerequisite acoustical and electrical science had been established principally by Europeans.

An important element in this situation was the wide difference between the viewpoints and objectives of the great school of experimental scientists of eighteenth and nineteenth century Europe and the smaller but growing group of physicists in opportunistic America. The European scientists were for the most part scholars, interested in exploring and expanding the frontiers of knowledge for its own sake. The American scientists of the time might better be termed teachers, rather than scholars, interested more in testing and demonstrating practical applications of known scientific principles than in pure research. Moreover, the latter were teaching men who were not dilettantes,[5] but who were destined for the most part to enter industry either as executives or engineers. Thus was the stage set for the great advances in applied technology in nineteenth century America, of which the phonograph was but one manifestation.

The goals of important figures in European research in electricity, such as Galvani, Romagnesi, Ohm, and Faraday; or in acoustics, such as Tyndall, Helmholz, and Lissajous; were quite different from those of the new class of practical experimenters and inventors which was then beginning to arise in the new world.

In Europe, except for England, the first reaction to the industrial revolution had been to attempt to insulate the leading schools and universities

---

[5] Derived from the Dilettanti Society, formed in England 1734 as an outgrowth of Renaissance interest in classical literature and for promotion of the arts and letters. Its members engaged in archaeology and scientific investigations purely as intellectual pursuits.

from the taint of commercialism. Scientific research was considered only as an adjunct of higher education and a leisurely pursuit reserved to gentlemen and scholars. Royalty, class distinctions, and the stratification of society contributed to the isolation of the learned class from the cycles of commercial and industrial development. Thus, quite often, men who were working feverishly to advance industrial technics were denied access to information then being revealed by extensive research going on in a higher stratum of society.

Much of European industry of the eighteenth and nineteenth centuries was operated as family affairs and often as monopolies by royal appointment, even though the corporate device of the limited stock company was coming into use. This factor further tended to restrict a competitive development of industry, retarded technological progress, and slowed the introduction of improved methods. However, the outgrowth of the apprentice system from feudalism had created a class of workmen in various trades who took pride in their work. It was principally the zeal of this latter stratum for progress and improvement, plus a trickling down of scientific knowledge from the learned class, which was responsible for vast changes in European standards of living and cultural opportunity within two hundred years.

This progress was not the purposeful result of the activities of the European scientists. They remained aloof from the work-a-day world where necessity was the mother of invention. Other men were free to make use of their discoveries, if they should happen to find out about them. There was but one American scientist important in the period just prior to the phonograph who conformed closely to the European pattern. This was Joseph Henry (1797-1878), Professor of Physics at Albany Institute, later Curator of the Smithsonian Institution. He was a singular exception to the rule of the period, that theoretical science was being advanced primarily in Europe, but applied practically principally in America. Searching carefully for the origins of the basic principles incorporated in our modern radio-phonographs and even television, one is amazed at the number of points where the pertinent relationships between electricity, magnetism, and mechanical energy were established by the experiments and recorded in the writings of Joseph Henry.

The theory of electromagnets developed by Henry was fundamental to the telegraph of Morse, to the telephone of Bell, to the speaker systems of our modern hi-fi phonographs, to our modern record changing mechanisms, or for that matter, to the electric power plants which supply the energy.[6] For this reason the story of the modern phonograph may be said to have begun not with the first machine that would talk, but more truly with the telegraph, or the experiments of Helmholtz, or the "Phonautograph" of Scott. Some might say that the story should begin with the mythological boxes that talked, or the automatons built by Faber and others which simulated speech. These tributary sources have been sufficiently dealt with in the literature of the arts, with the exception of the work of Henry, which has never received the measure of credit which it deserved.

The relationships of the various evolutionary forms of the phonograph to the cycles of activity involving what might be termed the companion acoustical inventions, such as the telegraph, telephone, and radio, have not received proper attention. The more important inventors of the first talking machines, Edison, Bell, and Berliner, had previously been engaged in telegraphic and telephonic invention. This has never been properly analyzed in respect to certain eventualities.

Some authorities feel that the invention of the tinfoil phonograph by Edison depended upon the prior invention, a short time before, of the telephone by Bell.[7] Perhaps the best way to analyze

---

[6] *American Journal of Science,* Silliman, 1831.
[7] *The Speaking Telephone, Talking Phonograph and other Novelties,* George B. Prescott, D. Appleton & Company, New York, 1878.

this would be to dissect the tinfoil phonograph and trace the origins of the components. These are: (1) trumpet, (2) diaphragm, (3) stylus, (4) moving surface, (5) feed screw, (6) wheel. The speaking trumpet is known to have been shown in a sketch by Leonard da Vinci of a tube communication system that presumably was installed in a palace of the Duke of Milan.[8] Ear trumpets are believed to have been used from ancient times as an aid to the deaf, perhaps originating in the cupping of the hand to facilitate hearing, or perhaps the conch shell. The diaphragm or tympanum had been known since the time of Hippocrates of Greece, through the dissection of human and animal ears. Its use as a sound resonator in drums and musical instruments predates written history. It was used in the Phonautograph of Leon Scott.[9] The stylus had its origin in name at least in the engraving or embossing tool used for making pictographs and hieroglyphic writing by the ancient Assyrians and Egyptians. In recording, the stylus of the phonograph was actuated by the diaphragm, indenting its vibratory pattern into the moving tinfoil wrapped around the pre-grooved cylinder. The moving surface, whether cylinder or disc, had been known in the making of lathes and other machines for years. Tapes and discs had been marked by stylii with telegraphic symbols or letters since the time of Morse. The feed screw was invented by Archimedes and the origin of the wheel is lost in antiquity.

Logic would seem to indicate that the telephone must have had something to do with the crystallization of thought

that led Edison to the phonograph. However, the elements of the first phonograph are fewer and simpler than those of the first telephone, and, it should be added, the phonograph worked much better. The telephone came about only after prolonged periods of experimentation by several independent workers who had been seeking for the most part for something quite different. Those in the forefront of this research were Thomas A. Edison, Alexander Bell, and Elisha Gray. Not one of these men prior to the actual invention had been trying to produce voice articulations over the telegraph wires, but they were all working on variations of the so-called harmonic telegraph. In the devices of these men, tuned resonators of one kind or another were employed so that multiple messages might be sent over a single wire. The dots and dashes would be sent out as musical sound of a given pitch and the receiving instrument would be tuned so that it would respond to only those messages intended for it. Charles Bourseul in France attempted to transmit speech over electric circuits as early as 1854.

Ironically, another man who tried later to transmit modulated vocal sounds over a wire, named the instrument he was trying to invent, but success eluded him. This was Philipp Reis of Germany, who in 1861 experimented with circuits which were made and broken by the vibrations of a diaphragm resulting in a similar movement of the receiving diaphragm as actuated by a magnet. Reis had worked previously on the harmonic telegraph idea and if he had followed that up he might have accidently hit upon the solution, namely, that a continuous but undulatory current is required—not an interrupted current.

Considering that Henry had established, as early as 1831, the relationships of electrical coils, currents, and mechanical energy; that the Scott Phonautograph of 1856 showed without question the nature of complex sound waves; that a certain ingenious toy called the string telephone had a wide

[8] *The Mind of Leonardo da Vinci*, Edward McCurdy, Dodd, Mead & Co., New York, 1928. *The Notebooks of Leonardo da Vinci*, Edward McCurdy, Reynal & Hitchcock, New York, 1938. References in the above show that Leonardo was familiar with the acoustical properties of tubes and trumpets. The combination of the two to design the first man-made intercommunication system may have been the first *a priori* invention in the phonographic series.
[9] Alexander Graham Bell reconstructed a telautograph using a tympanum from a human ear.

popularity in European cities as early as 1867; it is surprising that the invention of both telephone and phonograph came so much later.[10] In the case of the telephone, the missing link was the analogy of the sound waveform to an electrical waveform of continuous variability. In the case of the phonograph, the only need was to learn how to indent into an amorphous substance the waveforms of sound so that the process could be reversed by mechanical means. In retrospect, it can be seen that a great step in thinking was required between the Phonautograph (which traced sound waves for the purpose of visual analysis) and the phonograph, which had as the object the recreation at any future time, of the original sound waves.

As an example of the magnitude of a single act of disassociation involved in making a basic invention, consider the following: When the telephone was invented by Alexander Bell, there seemed to be considerable doubt about its theory as revealed by the language of his patent application.[11] Bell still wrote in the terms of the harmonic telegraph. This afforded ample opportunity for the controversy which arose almost immediately as to who really did invent the telephone. Count du Moncel wrote about this controversy in 1878, as did George B. Prescott, noted electrician and telegraph expert.[12] Both authors viewed with considerable doubt Bell's claim to the invention. It is of interest to note that Prescott saw fit to mitigate his skepticism somewhat in a subsequent book covering the same subject matter.[13] Here it should be pointed out

that Edison never laid claim to the invention of the telephone, recognizing Bell as the first to achieve the transmission of articulate sounds, or the human voice, over wires. Considering the fact that one of the devices he had made for the harmonic telegraph was later found capable of use for voice transmission, the prompt disavowal of any claim on the part of Edison is noteworthy.

But enough of automatons, fiction, the telegraph, and the telephone. The Edison tinfoil phonograph was entirely an acoustical machine. What was the knowledge of acoustics available to those men who first sought to record or reproduce sound? As has been noted, the reawakened interest in natural philosophy by the scholars of the Renaissance had set the stage for the experimental scientists of the eighteenth and nineteenth centuries of Europe. Beginning about 1822 there was made a series of notable advances in the study of acoustics. Gay Lussac, Arago, and others established the velocity of sound in air at given temperatures. Others ascertained the speed of sound through water and other media. Savart invented a toothed wheel for determining the number of vibrations per second for a given musical pitch. Helmholtz established the laws of harmonics. Lissajous, by means of a mirror attached to a vibrating body, projected light vibrations onto a screen as a series of sinusoidal curves. Tyndall investigated extensively the effects of interferences which modify the qualities of projected sounds. The writings of Tyndall had the effect of further popularizing the study of acoustics.[14] The publication in American scientific journals of articles about their work and textbooks describing their experiments and the facts revealed thereby were the principal sources of information available to American experimenters prior to the invention.

A few other, but significant early contributions to the phonograph were

[10] Now often improvised by a taut string affixed to the centers of the round ends of two tin cans or cardboard containers, held at a distance.

[11] U. S. Patent Office Gazette, Vol. 9, p. 474, Patent application file by Alexander Graham Bell, Feb. 14, 1876, granted March 7, 1876, titled "Telegraphy."

[12] The Speaking Telephone, Talking Phonograph and Other Novelties, George B. Prescott, D. Appleton & Co., New York, 1878. The Microphone and the Phonograph, Count du Moncel, Harper & Bros., 1879.

[13] Bell's Electric Speaking Telephone, George B. Prescott, D. Appleton & Co., New York, 1884.

[14] Sound, John Tyndall, England, 1867. D. Appleton & Co., New York, 1895.

Fig. 1-1. Leon Scott's "Phonautograph," an early forerunner of the modern phonograph. Could record sound but not reproduce it. (Courtesy of Smithsonian Institution.)

made by Europeans. Duhamel found that he could trace the simple, uniform vibrations of a tuning fork. Scott perfected this idea by using a sort of resonating chamber or trumpet to collect complex air vibrations, which, impinging upon a diaphragm stretched across the smaller end would convert the alternate air pressures and rarefactions into mechanical movements of the diaphragm. (See Fig. 1-1.) The diaphragm in turn actuated a bristle attached to its center, which traced the vibratory pattern as an undulatory line upon lampblack coated paper wrapped around a revolving cylinder. The cylinder was moved along by a screw as it rotated, much as in the later phonograph. Here the resemblance ends, for the movement of the bristle stylus of the Scott Phonautograph was lateral. The movement of the stylus of the Edison tinfoil phonograph, with relation to the moving surface, was vertical.

Just as the naming of the "telephone" was by an unsuccessful aspirant to the invention, Philipp Reis, so the first to coin the name "phonograph" was not the inventor, but one F. B. Fenby of Worcester, Mass. In 1863, Fenby was granted a patent on what he entitled "The Electro Magnetic Phonograph." However, the device did not embody the essentially simple registering of the waveform, a feature of all successful sound recording and reproducing systems; hence, except for the name, it did not contribute to the phonographic development.

Perhaps the closest (both in time and concept to Edison's phonograph) was the idea of M. Charles Cros, who deposited a sealed packet with the Academie des Sciences des France in April, 1877. It was about three months

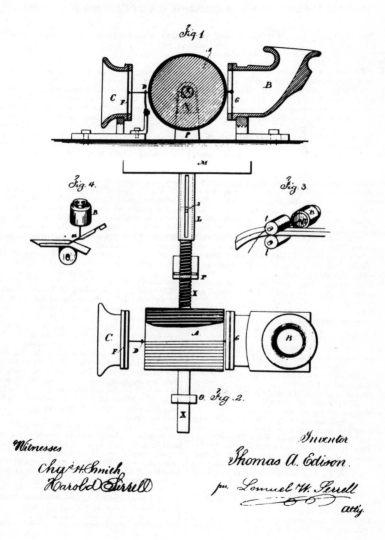

T A. EDISON.
Phonograph or Speaking Machine.

No. 200,521. Patented Feb. 19, 1878.

Fig. 1-2A. Thomas A. Edison patent for his Tinfoil Phonograph. (Courtesy of Edison National Historic Site.)

UNITED STATES PATENT OFFICE.

THOMAS A. EDISON, OF MENLO PARK, NEW JERSEY.

IMPROVEMENT IN PHONOGRAPH OR SPEAKING MACHINES.

Specification forming part of Letters Patent No. 200,521, dated February 19, 1878; application filed December 24, 1877.

To all whom it may concern:

Be it known that I, THOMAS A. EDISON, of Menlo Park, in the county of Middlesex and State of New Jersey, have invented an Improvement in Phonograph or Speaking Machines, of which the following is a specification:

The object of this invention is to record in permanent characters the human voice and other sounds, from which characters such sounds may be reproduced and rendered audible again at a future time.

The invention consists in arranging a plate, diaphragm, or other flexible body capable of being vibrated by the human voice or other sounds, in conjunction with a material capable of registering the movements of such vibrating body by embossing or indenting or altering such material, in such a manner that such register-marks will be sufficient to cause a second vibrating plate or body to be set in motion by them, and thus reproduce the motions of the first vibrating body.

The invention further consists in the various combinations of mechanism to carry out my invention.

I have discovered, after a long series of experiments, that a diaphragm or other body capable of being set in motion by the human voice does not give, except in rare instances, superimposed vibrations, as has heretofore been supposed, but that each vibration is separate and distinct, and therefore it becomes possible to record and reproduce the sounds of the human voice.

In the drawings, Figure 1 is a vertical section, illustrating my invention, and Fig. 2 is a plan of the same.

A is a cylinder having a helical indenting-groove cut from end to end—say, ten grooves to the inch. Upon this is placed the material to be indented, preferably metallic foil. This drum or cylinder is secured to a shaft, X, having at one end a thread cut with ten threads to the inch, the bearing P also having a thread cut in it.

L is a tube, provided with a longitudinal slot, and it is rotated by the clock-work at M, or other source of power.

The shaft X passes into the tube L, and it is rotated by a pin, 2, secured to the shaft, and passing through the slot on the tube L, the object of the long slot being to allow the shaft X to pass endwise through the center or support P by the action of the screw on X. At the same time that the cylinder is rotated it passes toward the support O.

B is the speaking-tube or mouth-piece, which may be of any desired character, so long as proper slots or holes are provided to re-enforce the hissing consonants. Devices to effect this object are shown in my application, No. 143, filed August 28, 1877. Hence they are not shown or further described herein.

Upon the end of the tube or mouth-piece is a diaphragm, having an indenting-point of hard material secured to its center, and so arranged in relation to the cylinder A that the point will be exactly opposite the groove in the cylinder at any position the cylinder may occupy in its forward rotary movement.

The speaking-tube is arranged upon a standard, which, in practice, I provide with devices for causing the tube to approach and recede from the cylinder.

The operation of recording is as follows: The cylinder is, by the action of the screw in X, placed adjacent to the pillar P, which brings the indenting-point of the diaphragm G opposite the first groove on the cylinder, over which is placed a sheet of thick metallic foil, paper, or other yielding material. The tube B is then adjusted toward the cylinder until the indenting-point touches the material and indents it slightly. The clock-work is then set running, and words spoken in the tube B will cause the diaphragm to take up every vibration, and these movements will be recorded with surprising accuracy by indentations in the foil.

After the foil on the cylinder has received the required indentations, or passed to its full limit toward O, it is made to return to P by proper means, and the indented material is brought to a position for reproducing and rendering audible the sounds that had been made by the person speaking into the tube B.

C is a tube similar to B, except that the diaphragm is somewhat lighter and more sensitive, although this is not actually necessary. In front of this diaphragm is a light spring, D, having a small point shorter and finer than

Fig. 1-2B. Application filed December 24, 1877, and granted February 19, 1878.

the indenting point on the diaphragm of B. This spring and point are so arranged as to fall exactly into the path of all the indentations. This spring is connected to the diaphragm F of C by a thread or other substance capable of conveying the movements of D. Now, when the cylinder is allowed to rotate, the spring D is set in motion by each indentation corresponding to its depth and length. This motion is conveyed to the diaphragm either by vibrations through a thread or directly by connecting the spring to the diaphragm F, and these motions being due to the indentations, which are an exact record of every movement of the first diaphragm, the voice of the speaker is reproduced exactly and clearly, and with sufficient volume to be heard at some distance.

The indented material may be detached from the machine and preserved for any length of time, and by replacing the foil in a proper manner the original speaker's voice can be reproduced, and the same may be repeated frequently, as the foil is not changed in shape if the apparatus is properly adjusted.

The record, if it be upon tin-foil, may be stereotyped by means of the plaster-of-paris process, and from the stereotype multiple copies may be made expeditiously and cheaply by casting or by pressing tin-foil or other material upon it. This is valuable when musical compositions are required for numerous machines.

It is obvious that many forms of mechanism may be used to give motion to the material to be indented. For instance, a revolving plate may have a volute spiral cut both on its upper and lower surfaces, on the top of which the foil or indenting material is laid and secured in a proper manner. A two-part arm is used with this disk, the portion beneath the disk having a point in the lower groove, and the portion above the disk carrying the speaking and receiving diaphragmic devices, which arm is caused, by the volute spiral groove upon the lower surface, to swing gradually from near the center to the outer circumference of the plate as it is revolved, or vice versa.

An apparatus of this general character adapted to a magnet that indents the paper is shown in my application for a patent, No. 128, filed March 26, 1877; hence no claim is made herein to such apparatus, and further description of the same is unnecessary.

A wide continuous roll of material may be used, the diaphragmic devices being reciprocated by proper mechanical devices backward and forward over the roll as it passes forward; or a narrow strip like that in a Morse register may be moved in contact with the indenting-point, and from this the sounds may be reproduced. The material employed for this purpose may be soft paper saturated or coated with paraffine or similar material, with a sheet of metal foil on the surface thereof to receive the impression from the indenting-point.

I do not wish to confine myself to reproducing sound by indentations only, as the transmitting or recording device may be in a sinuous form, resulting from the use of a thread passing with paper beneath the pressure-rollers *t*, (see Fig. 3,) such thread being moved laterally by a fork or eye adjacent to the roller *t*, and receiving its motion from the diaphragm G, with which such fork or eye is connected, and thus record the movement of the diaphragm by the impression of the thread in the paper to the right and left of a straight line, from which indentation the receiving-diaphragm may receive its motion and the sound be reproduced, substantially in the manner I have already shown; or the diaphragm may, by its motion, give more or less pressure to an inking-pen, *n*, Fig. 4, the point of which rests upon paper or other material moved along regularly beneath the point of the pen, thus causing more or less ink to be deposited upon the material, according to the greater or lesser movement of the diaphragm. These ink-marks serve to give motion to a second diaphragm when the paper containing such marks is drawn along beneath the end of a lever resting upon them and connected to such diaphragm, the lever and diaphragm being moved by the friction between the point being greatest, or the thickness of the ink being greater where there is a large quantity of ink than where there is a small quantity. Thus the original sound-vibrations are reproduced upon the second diaphragm.

I claim as my invention—

1. The method herein specified of reproducing the human voice or other sounds by causing the sound-vibrations to be recorded, substantially as specified, and obtaining motion from that record, substantially as set forth, for the reproduction of the sound vibrations.

2. The combination, with a diaphragm exposed to sound-vibrations, of a moving surface of yielding material—such as metallic foil—upon which marks are made corresponding to the sound-vibrations, and of a character adapted to use in the reproduction of the sound, substantially as set forth.

3. The combination, with a surface having marks thereon corresponding to sound vibrations, of a point receiving motion from such marks, and a diaphragm connected to said point, and responding to the motion of the point, substantially as set forth.

4. In an instrument for making a record of sound-vibrations, the combination, with the diaphragm and point, of a cylinder having a helical groove and means for revolving the cylinder and communicating an end movement corresponding to the inclination of the helical groove, substantially as set forth.

Signed by me this 15th day of December, A. D. 1877.

THOS. A. EDISON.

Witnesses:
GEO. T. PINCKNEY.
CHAS. H. SMITH.

2

after this date, on July 30, 1877, that a provisional specification was filed with the British patent office by Thomas A. Edison, covering a telephonic repeater device. This was the same device which a few months later in *Scientific American* was to be hailed as the first machine which would store up and repeat at will the human voice—the first talking machine. Curiously, Edison seems to have had exactly the same difficulty in taking the complete step of disassociation between his telephonic experiments and the invention of the phonograph as Bell did between his quest for multi-channel telegraphy and the invention of the telephone.

On December 24, 1877, Edison filed application with the U. S. Patent Office for a patent covering the first phonograph to be built exclusively for the purpose of sound recording and reproduction at will. He received his patent No. 200,521 issued Feb. 19, 1878. (See Fig. 1-2.) This was the tin-foil phonograph built for Edison by his colleague, John Kruesi, and which first repeated Edison's voice reciting "Mary had a little lamb . . . ."

There have been periodic attempts to dim the lustre of Edison's phonograph achievement—even to the extent of taking away the credit for the first conception and giving it to Cros, even though the latter never built a machine.[15] Actually, there was not the

---

[15] *The Sewanee Review*, article by R. D. Darrell, January-March, 1933. *The Reproduction of Sound*, Henry Seymour, W. B. Tattersall, Ltd., London, 1918. *The Fabulous Phonograph*, Roland Gelatt, Lippincott, 1955.

slightest resemblance between the proposed talking machine of Cros and either of the Edison phonograph concepts. It has been reported that it was at the insistence of Cros that the sealed packet he had left with the Academie was opened, after he had somehow learned of "successful experiments" in America. This was hardly necessary, for a complete description of Cros' idea had been published in the October 10th issue of *La Semaine du Clerge* by Abbe Lenoir, who described it as a "phonograph." Edison's adoption of this descriptive term is in itself pointed out as a very suspicious circumstance, despite the fact that it had been coined in 1863 by F. B. Fenby, of Worcester, Mass., in connection with a patent granted upon "The Electro Magnetic Phonograph," a complicated device which was never built.

There was also little similarity between the Cros concept and the cylinder and disc phonographs built in later years by Edison. If anyone may be said to owe credit to Cros, it would be Emile Berliner, who after several years of fruitless endeavor was forced to abandon the photoengraving idea. Meanwhile, the phonograph was an accomplished fact. Moreover, both laterally and vertically actuated methods of making sound records were described in the foundation patent of the phonograph industry, issued to Thomas A. Edison, February 19, 1878. This patent was granted by the U. S. Patent Office without a single reference and its validity was never challenged.

CHAPTER 2

THE EDISON TIN-FOIL
PHONOGRAPH

THE successful transmission of articulate speech by the telephone of Alexander Graham Bell in 1876 may have provided the stimulus which resulted in the invention of the phonograph by Thomas A. Edison the next year. It must have been a jolt to Edison to have come so close to the secret of the telephone and the securing of what has been often since described as "the most valuable single patent in the world." It seems natural to suppose that he would re-think all of his many experiments in harmonic telegraphy which, to a considerable extent, had paralleled those of Bell. Certainly it is but a consecutive step in thought from the transmission of the vibrations of a diaphragm over an electrical circuit to the recording of those vibrations so that they may be repeated at will. Edison had already taken such a step in his telegraph repeaters.

Edison did not lose interest in the telephone because he had not been the first to achieve voice transmission. He characteristically set to work with his seemingly inexhaustible energy to make it the practical instrument of communication it has since become. Within a few years he was granted upwards of forty patents dealing with telephonic improvements, including not only the vital carbon button transmitter, but also several basic types of microphones still used in improved forms in radio, television, and sound pictures today. These include the dynamic and electro-static microphones. The importance of the Edison contributions to the success of the telephone in its earliest days is well exemplified in the story of the carbon transmitter as told by Alfred O. Tate, at that time private secretary to Mr. Edison.[1] He stated that the transmitter patent was first sold by Edison to Jay Gould for $150,000 payable in equal installments over a period of fifteen years. Gould later sold this key patent to Western Union, then in competition with the Bell interests. In one year alone, according to Tate, the Western Union income from this patent was $900,000.

A letter announcing the phonograph published in the *Scientific American,* November 17, 1877 seems further to tie the conception of the phonograph to the telephone. Despite the laboratory evidence to the contrary, many have thought that Edison had been forced to invent the phonograph to make good the boasts of his press representative, Edward H. Johnson, the writer of the letter. Both he and the editor of *Scientific American* were warm personal friends of Edison and so it was no surprise that the letter from Johnson was made the subject of an enthusiastic editorial which was headlined

**"A Wonderful Invention—Speech
Capable of Indefinite Repetition
from Automatic Records"**

[1] *Edison's Open Door,* Alfred O. Tate, E. P. Dutton & Co., New York, 1938.

The editor then proceeded to extoll the marvels of the latest Edison device as follows:

"It has been said that Science is never sensational; that it is intellectual, not emotional; but certainly nothing that can be conceived would be more likely to create the profoundest of sensations, to arouse the liveliest of human emotions, than once more to hear the familiar voices of the dead. Yet Science now announces that this is possible, and can be done. That the voices of those who departed before the invention of the wonderful apparatus described in the letter given below are forever stilled is too obvious a truth; but whoever has spoken into the mouthpiece of the phonograph, and whose words are recorded by it, has the assurance that his speech may be reproduced audibly in his own tones long after he himself has turned to dust. The possibility is simply startling. A strip of paper travels through a little machine, the sounds of the latter are magnified, and our grandchildren or posterity centuries hence hear us as plainly as if we were present. Speech has become, as it were, immortal.

"The possibilities of the future are not much more wonderful than those of the present. The orator in Boston speaks, the indented strip of paper is the tangible result; but this travels under a second machine which may connect with the telephone. Not only is the speaker heard now in San Francisco, for example, but by passing the strip again under the reproducer he may be heard tomorrow, or next year, or next century. His speech in the first instance is recorded and transmitted simultaneously, and indefinite repetition is possible.

"The new invention is purely mechanical—no electricity is involved. It is a simple affair of vibrating plates, thrown into vibration by the human voice. It is crude yet, but the principle has been found and modifications and improvements are only a matter of time. So also are its possibilities other than those already noted. Will letter writing be a proceeding of the past? Why not, if by simply talking into a mouthpiece our speech is recorded on paper, and our correspondent can by the same paper hear us speak? Are we to have a new kind of books? There is no reason why the orations of our modern Ciceros should not be recorded and detachably bound so that we can run the indented slips through the machine, and in the quiet of our apartments listen again, and as often as we will, to the eloquent words. Nor are we restricted to spoken words. Music may be crystallized as well. Imagine an opera or an oratorio, sung by the greatest living vocalists, thus recorded, and capable of being repeated as we desire.

"The invention, the credit of which is due to Mr. Thomas A. Edison, should not be confounded with the one referred to by us in a previous number, and mentioned in our correspondent's letter. That device is illustrated on another page of this issue, and is of much more complicated construction. Mr. Edison has sent us sketches of several modifications and different arrangements of his invention. These we shall probably publish in a future number."

As intimated by the editor, the device illustrated on another page of the same issue had little in common with the phonograph. This was the invention of a Dr. Rosapelly and Professor Marey, of France. Its purpose was to record graphically the movements of the lips, veil of the palate, and the larynx, for the purpose of teaching deaf mutes to speak. It had been remarked in a previous article that it might be possible with the apparatus for the words of a speaker to be taken down by telephone wire at a distance. There was no more thought of voice reproduction than in the conception of the Phonautograph.

The editorial was followed immediately by the letter from Edward H.

Johnson which because of its importance will also be given completely, as follows:

"To the Editor of
the Scientific American
"In your journal of Nov. 3, page 273, you made the announcement that Dr. Rosapelly and Professor Marey had succeeded in graphically recording the movements of the lips, of the veil of the palate, and the vibrations of the larynx, and you prophesy that this, among other important results, may lead possibly to the application of electricity for the purpose of transferring these records to distant points by wire.

"Was this prophesy intuition? Not only has it been fulfilled in the letter, but still more marvelous results achieved by Mr. Thomas A. Edison, the renowned electrician, of New Jersey, who has kindly permitted me to make public not only the fact but the *modus operandi*. Mr. Edison in the course of a series of extended experiments in the production of his speaking telephone, lately perfected, conceived the highly bold and original idea of recording the human voice upon a strip of paper, from which at any subsequent time it might be automatically re-delivered with all the vocal characteristics of the original speaker accurately reproduced. A speech delivered into the mouthpiece of this apparatus may fifty years hence—long after the original speaker is dead—be reproduced audibly to an audience with sufficient fidelity to make the voice easily recognizable by those who were familiar with the original. As yet the apparatus is crude, but is characterized by that wonderful simplicity which seems to be a trait of all great invention or discovery. The subjoined illustration, although not the actual design of the apparatus as used by Mr. Edison, will better serve to illustrate and make clear the principle upon which he is operating.

"A is a speaking tube provided with a mouthpiece C—, X is a metallic diaphragm which responds powerfully to the vibrations of the voice. In the center of the diaphragm is secured a small chisel-shaped point. D is a drum revolved by clockwork, and serves to carry forward a continuous fillet of paper, having throughout its length and exactly in the center a raised V-shaped boss, such as would be made by passing a fillet of paper through a Morse register with the lever constantly depressed. The chisel point attached to the diaphragm rests upon the sharp edge of the raised boss. If now the paper be drawn rapidly along, all the movements of the diaphragm will be recorded by the indentation of the chisel point into the delicate boss—it, having no support beneath, is very easily indented; to do this, little or no power is required to operate the chisel. The tones of small amplitude will be recorded by slight indentations, and those of full amplitude by deep ones. This fillet of paper thus receives a record of the vocal vibrations of air waves from the movement of the diaphragm; and if it can be made to contribute the same motion to a second diaphragm, we shall not only see that we have a record of the words, but shall have them re-spoken; and if that second diaphragm be that of the transmitter of a speaking telephone, we shall have the still more marvelous performance of having them re-spoken and *transmitted by wire at the same time to a distant point.*

"The reproductor is very similar to the indenting apparatus, except that a more delicate diaphragm is used. The reproductor, B, has attached to its diaphragm a thread which in turn is attached to a hair spring, H, upon the end of which is a V-shaped point resting upon the indentations of the boss. The passage of the indented boss underneath this point causes it to rise and fall with precision, thus contributing to the diaphragm the motion of the original one, and thereby rendering the words again audible.

Of course Mr. Edison, at this stage of the invention, finds some difficulty in reproducing the finer articulations, but he feels quite justified by results obtained, from his first crude efforts, in his prediction that he will have the apparatus in practical operation within a year. He has already applied the principle of his speaking telephone, thereby causing an electromagnet to operate the indenting diaphragm, and will undoubtedly be able to transmit a speech, made upon the floor of the Senate, from Washington to New York, record the same in New York automatically, and, by means of the speaking telephone redeliver it in the editorial ear of every newspaper in New York.

"In view of the practical inventions already contributed by Mr. Edison, is there anyone who is prepared to gainsay this prediction? I for one am satisfied it will all be fulfilled, and that too, at an early date."

(signed)

Edward H. Johnson, Electrician

Evident in this first published story of the phonograph is the influence of the embossing telegraph on the form it was to assume. It is rather interesting to note that, from the first, separate recording and reproducing styli were envisioned as well as separate diaphragms and diaphragm assemblies for recording and reproducing, of definitely different characteristics. This proves one thing conclusively, that this first published concept of the phonograph had been based on experiment. In no other way would the fact that quite different qualities are needed in recording and reproducing diaphragms have been known. Also, most important from the viewpoint of the modern phonograph was the fact that the use of a form of electrical amplification was contemplated. This was based on the then recently completed Edison invention of the loud-speaking telephone, based on his electro-motograph principle.[2] This principle rested on the discovery that

the resistance between a pad moistened with acid and an alkali surface was reduced by the passage of a weak electrical current. It was made an actuating device for the telephone diaphragm by a lever from its center to the pad which rested on a slowly revolving cylinder of chalk which was partially immersed in a container of acid, much as are the cylinders of envelope moisteners today.

That this was indeed a pregnant thought with great possibilities even though never commercially developed is attested to by the fact that the Edison loud-speaking telephone was used in England for a number of years, a completely successful achievement technically. The reason it was discontinued was the desire for privacy by subscribers in their telephone conversations. Listeners were sometimes quite embarrassed by indiscreet remarks suddenly and loudly blatted out by the person at the other end of the wire, who could not know what persons might be present in the room of the listener. Lest we tend to become too smug about our vaunted progress in this respect, we may recollect that we still have a great many party lines in America!

The very first evidence which exists of Edison's thinking prior to the announcement in *Scientific American* is in the form of a sheet of paper containing notes and sketches made by him and dated July 18, 1877. (See Fig. 2-1.) The sketches are of a cylinder device with batteries, diaphragms, membranes and contacts arranged to act as a telephone repeater, or amplifier of telephone voice vibrations. The function was similar to that of a telegraph repeater, to receive and reinforce signals and send them on to the next station. The sheet at the top was captioned "Speaking Telegraph," but this was also true of other such sheets which have no direct bearing on our subject, the

---

[2] Patent on the loud-speaking telephone, embodying the electro-motograph principle was sold by Thomas A. Edison, March 20, 1880, to the Western Union Telegraph Co. for $100,000.

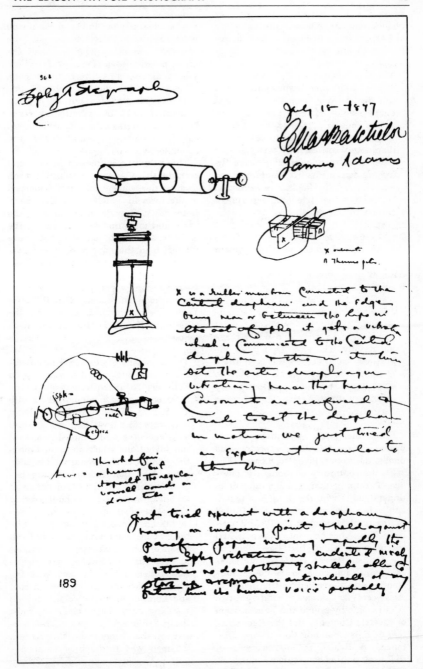

Fig. 2-1. *Experiment with diaphragm having an embossing point held against moving paraffin paper. (Courtesy of Edison National Historic Site.)*

phonograph. In this case the notes are of particular significance. The note referring to one of the sketches was as follows:

"X is a rubber membrane connected to the central diaphragm at the edge, being near or between the lips in the act of opening it gets a vibration which is communicated to the central diaphragm and then in turn sets the outer diaphragm vibrating hence the hissing consonants are reinforced and made to set the diaphragm in motion —we have just tried an experiment similar to this one."

The consecutive development of his thought leading to the next experiment was described, but not illustrated by a note at the bottom of the sheet, as follows:

"Just tried experiment with a diaphragm having an embossing point and held against paraffin paper moving rapidly. The spkg (speaking) vibrations are indented nicely & there is no doubt that I shall be able to store up & reproduce automatically at any future time the human voice perfectly."

From the later application of the principle to a telephone repeater, and finally the sketch given to Kruesi (Fig. 2-2), the continuity of thought is obvious. The thing that is a bit difficult to understand is why the filing of a patent application was delayed in the United States until December 24, 1877. It may have been because of a provisional specification which had been filed in the British Patent Office on July 30, 1877, which had covered the device substantially as described in the *Scientific American* by Johnson and entitled "Controlling by Sound the Transmission of Electric Currents and the Reproduction of Corresponding Sounds at a Distance." A British patent was granted to Edison on this conception January 30, 1878. It may also be possible that Edison and his associates were not fully

aware of the true importance of the invention until the editor of the *Scientific American* pointed out its great potentialities. Perhaps Mr. Edison, realizing this, may have been shocked to find that in view of this publicity he was far out on a limb without benefit of patent protection. This is the course of events which preceded the actual making of the first machine that would talk.

There are two conflicting stories concerning the manner in which Edison derived the concept of the phonograph in the form in which it was first built. Both received wide circulation in the press and magazine articles during the early years. Both, surprisingly, were published in the handbook of the Edison phonograph published by the National Phonograph Co. in 1900. One of these versions was copied from a news story which had appeared in the *New York Sun* of March 1, 1899, upon the occasion of the death of John Kruesi, as follows:

"The man who made the first phonograph was buried at Schenectady on February 25, 1899. He was one of the little band of men who worked with Thomas A. Edison at Menlo Park, and through whose skill and faithful assistance were developed many of the inventions which gave to Edison the name of 'The Wizard'. It was in those days that Edison used to become absorbed in the development of an idea, work at it without rest or sleep for two or three days and nights and keep all those about him busy at the same time. He would call in an organ grinder from the streets to keep his men awake, or resort to some other such device, and when the strain was finally over, charter a boat and take all hands down the bay on a fishing excursion. Among the most tireless of the men about 'The Wizard' at that time was John Kruesi, the man who made the first phonograph. The idea came to Mr. Edison as an inspiration a few days before, while he was experimenting with a

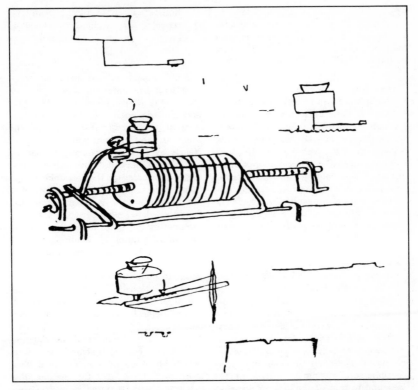

Fig. 2-2. The above copy of the original sketch given to John Kruesi is authentic; however, as originally given to your authors, it bore the inscription "Kreusi (sic) Make This—Edison Aug. 12/77," which was discovered by subsequent research to have been added years later for some publicity purpose, and has been deleted. (Courtesy of Edison National Historic Site.)

telephone disc. The disc was not enclosed and there was a sharp, pointed pin on the back of it.

"As Mr. Edison spoke against the face of the disc its vibrations drove the pin into his finger. 'If the disc has power enough to prick my finger,' thought 'The Wizard,' 'it has power enough to make a record which can be reproduced.'

"A few days later he called Kruesi to him, and putting into his hands a rough sketch of the Phonograph, explained what the thing was to do, and told him to make it. It was a roll machine, the roll covered with tin foil to make the record. Kruesi made the machine and brought it to Mr.

Edison. Edison set it going and spoke into it:

'Mary had a little lamb,
Its fleece was white as snow;
And everywhere that Mary went,
The lamb was sure to go.'

"Then he started it to repeat his words, expecting at the best but a hoarse murmur in answer. He was almost awed when he heard his words actually repeated in clear tones by the little machine. That machine is now in the Patent Museum at South Kensington, London, England."

In later years, Edison denied the finger pricking incident time and again.

The wonder is that it ever appeared in an official Edison publication, especially as Edison's own authenticated version had been given in the text just before, as follows:

"The story of the invention is best told in Mr. Edison's own words. In an article on 'The Perfected Phonograph' which he wrote for the *North American Review* in 1888, Mr. Edison calls attention to the well-known effects of certain musical notes and chords upon sand, when loosely sprinkled on a sounding board; in response to the sound waves, the sand sifts itself into various curves, differing according to the pitch and intensity. He speaks also of the fine line of sand that is left high up on an ocean beach, as each breaker spends its force in its uttermost ripple, and then recedes. He draws the following parallel:
'Yet, well known though these phenomena are, they apparently suggested until within a few years, that the sound waves set going by a human voice, might be so directed as to trace an impression upon some solid substance, with a nicety equal to that of the tide in recording its flow upon the sand beach.

— — —

'My own discovery that this could be done came to me almost accidentally while I was busy with experiments, having a different object in view. I was engaged upon a machine intended to repeat Morse characters, which were recorded on paper by indentations that transferred their message to another circuit automatically, when passed under a tracing point connected with a circuit closing apparatus.
'In manipulating this paper, I found that when the indented paper was turned with great swiftness, it gave off a humming sound resembling that of human talk heard indistinctly.
'This led me to try fitting a diaphragm to the machine. I saw at once that the problem of registering

human speech so that it could be repeated by mechanical means as often as might be desired, was solved.'—T. A. Edison."

If the reader will compare this version with the notes on the laboratory sheet (Fig. 2-1) dated July 18, 1877, and the first published story of the invention in *Scientific American,* he will see that they are mutually consistent. Nearly every one of Edison's numerous biographers have provided other interesting variants to the oft-told story. Some have it that there was a bet of a box of cigars as to whether the device would work or not, between Carman, foreman of the shop, and John Kruesi, the latter being of the opinion it would not. Others have said that Kruesi did not know what the machine was supposed to do until he brought it to Mr. Edison. Obviously, if one story is true, the other is not! In any case, it seems rather illogical that Kruesi would have been expected to build a successful machine for a function which he did not understand, especially from the crude sketch which we know he received. The price paid to Kruesi for making the machine has been stated in various accounts as $8, $18, and $30. However, all these matters are inconsequential as compared with establishing the facts of the inventive process. There seems to be general agreement by all authorities that Edison did recite "Mary Had a Little Lamb" and that the machine (Figs. 2-3 and 2-4) promptly and clearly repeated Edison's words, to everyone's great surprise. Edison later stated this to have been his own reaction:

"I was never so taken aback in my life —I was always afraid of things that worked the first time."[3]

The time for embellishing the story of the invention is past. The purpose of presenting the story in this manner is to allow the reader to sift the evidence for the essential historical facts.

---

[3] *Thomas Alva Edison, Inventor,* Dyer and Martin, p. 208, 2nd. Ed. 1929, Harper & Brothers. *North American Review,* June, 1878.

Fig. 2-3. *Edison's original tinfoil phonograph patented in 1878. (Courtesy of Edison National Historic Site.)*

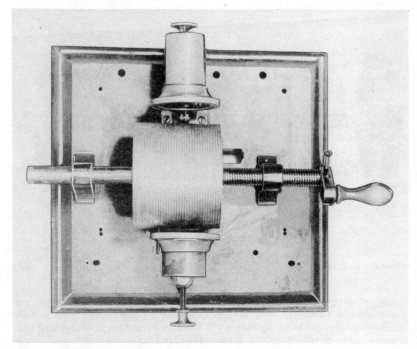

Fig. 2-4. *Constructional details of Edison's tinfoil phonograph are shown including both "speaker" and "reproducer." (Courtesy of Edison National Historic Site.)*

Fig. 2-5. *Experimental apparatus for illustrating the principle of Edison's speaking phonograph, patented February 19, 1878. Manufactured by S. Bergmann & Co., New York.* (Courtesy of *Smithsonian Institution.*)

Fig. 2-6. *A tin-foil phonograph of 1878. About 600 of these were made to demonstrate the principle of the phonograph.* (Courtesy of *Edison National Historic Site.*)

Approximately 600 tin-foil machines were made and distributed early in 1878 to illustrate the principle of Edison's speaking phonograph. One of these (Fig. 2-5) was made by S. Bergmann & Company of 404 Wooster Street, New York City. The model produced by the Edison people is shown in Fig. 2-6.

Edison apparently was eager to have his tin-foil machine receive widest possible publicity. Several small shops went to work to turn out their own versions of Mr. Edison's phonograph. One of these is shown in Fig. 2-7.

Fig. 2-7. A very small quantity of this tinfoil phonograph was produced by an independent maker in New Jersey in 1878. It uses a combination recorder-reproducer.

Demonstrations followed and were attended by notables and the press. *Harper's Weekly* reported as follows: [4]

"If it were not that the days of belief in witchcraft are long since past, witch-hunters such as those who figured so conspicuously in the early history of our country would now find a rich harvest of victims in the Tribune Building. Here are located the head-quarters of two marvels of a marvellous age. The telephone, which created such a sensation a short time ago by demonstrating the possibility of transmitting vocal sounds by telegraph, is now eclipsed by a new wonder called the phonograph. This little instrument records the utterance of the human voice, and like a faithless confidante repeats every secret confided to it whenever requested to do so. It will talk, sing, whistle, cough, sneeze, or perform any other acoustic feat. With charming impartiality it will express itself in the divine strains of a lyric goddess, or use the startling vernacular of a street Arab.

[4] *Harper's Weekly,* March 30, 1878.

"A few days ago a reporter for Harper's visited the phonograph for the purpose of ascertaining, so far as an unscientific person might, the peculiar characteristics of the marvellous little instrument. Prepared for an elaborate system of weights, pulleys, levers, wheels, bands, such as abounded in the case of Barnum's talking machine, whose utterances, by-the-way, were confided to some half dozen inarticulate sounds that no man living could understand, it was rather startling to find in the famous phonograph a simple apparatus, which, but for the absence of more than one cylinder, might have been a modern fluting machine. This single cylinder of hollow brass is mounted upon a shaft, at one end of which is a crank for turning it, and at the other a balance-wheel, the whole being supported by two iron uprights. In front of the cylinder is a movable bar or arm, which supports a mouth-piece of gutta-percha, on the under side of which is a disk of thin metal, such as is used for taking tin-types. Against the centre of the lower side of this disk a fine steel point is held by a spring attached to the rim of the mouth-piece, as shown in our illustration. . . . (See Fig. 2-8.)

"An India-rubber cushion between the point and the disk controls the vibration of the spring. The cylinder is

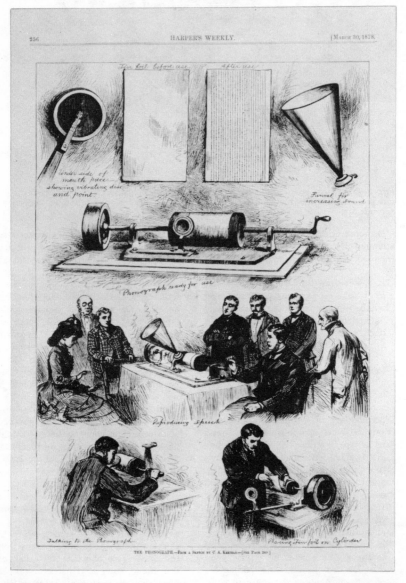

Fig. 2-8. Reproduction of an early plate from Harper's Weekly, March 30, 1878, showing recording and reproducing process of the tinfoil phonograph. (Courtesy of Harper's Weekly.)

covered with a fine spiral groove running continuously from end to end. In using the phonograph the first operation is to wrap a sheet of tin foil closely around the cylinder. The mouth-piece is then adjusted against the left-hand end of the cylinder so closely that the vibration of the voice on the disk will cause the point to press the tin foil into the groove, making minute indentations resembling, on a very small scale, the characters of the Morse telegraph. The cylinder is moved from right to left by the screw crank, so nicely adjusted that the steel point is always against the centre of the spiral groove. While turning the crank the operator talks into the mouth-piece in a voice slightly elevated above the ordinary tone of conversation. Every vibration of his voice is faithfully recorded on the tin foil by the steel point, the cylinder making about one revolution to a word. "In order to reproduce the words— that is, to make the machine talk—the cylinder is turned back, so that the steel point may go over the indentations made by speaking into the mouth-piece. A funnel, like a speaking-trumpet is attached to the mouth-piece, to keep the sounds from scattering. Now turning the crank again, every word spoken into the mouth-piece is exactly reproduced, with the utmost distinctness.

"Thus the disk is either a tympanum or diaphragm, as the case may be, the first when it listens, and the second when it talks. Herein the phonograph seems actually to have got ahead of that other marvellous construction, the human body. In our anatomical economy the contrivances by which we are enabled to hear and talk are not only separate and distinct, but are also much more complicated than the method by which the phonograph accomplishes the same results.

"While comparing this remarkable machine to the race whose characteristic attribute it has stolen (it is, we be-

lieve, habitually asserted by people who have no means of knowing any thing whatever about the matter that man is the only animal that talks), it may not be unfitting to allude to the admirable example it sets many garrulous and wearisome individuals. The phonograph never speaks until it has first been spoken to. Herein it also offers a worthy admonition to many ambitious but inexperienced writers. It has no original ideas to advance, or else is possessed of that spirit of modesty which precludes the possibility of its annoying the public with unripe fancies and crude speculations. The phonograph only consents to astonish the world at the instance of some dominant and controlling mind. When it is about to exhibit itself, an operator must be on hand to put it through its paces. On the occasion in question this gentleman was Mr. William H. Applebaugh, General Superintendent of the Telephone Company of New York.

"Seating himself before the instrument, Mr. Applebaugh confided to the disk names, numbers, scraps of poetry, comic songs, and various other bits of information calculated to amuse the phonograph, but not improve its mind. These were faithfully recorded upon the foil, which was made to revolve by turning the crank. Then the disk was sent back to the original starting-point, the crank again set in motion, and the metallic point brought into contact with the foil. Presently the phonograph began, in clear, distinct tones, to count, to call names, to describe its own peculiar talents, to give its own address, and finally to sing:

'There was an old man whose name
    was Uncle Ned,
    And he died long ago, long ago;
And there wasn't any wool on the
    top of his head,
    On the place where the wool
    ought to grow.'

"This dropping into poetry apparently gave a sentimental turn to the thoughts of the phonograph, for presently, in spite of the fact that it was discoursing to a mixed and probably unsympathetic audience, it began to long for

'the touch of a vanished hand,
And the sound of a voice that is still.'

"As yet the phonograph is in its infancy. Its discovery was the result of an accident, and so far but little idea can be formed on the development of which it is susceptible. The gentleman who has the honor of being its inventor is Professor Thomas A. Edison, the famous electrician, who, in experimenting with the telephone, happened to notice the manner in which the disks of that instrument vibrated in accordance with the breath used in speaking. Believing these vibrations could be recorded so as to be reproduced, he set to work to manufacture a machine for the purpose, and the result is the phonograph. In a short time we shall, no doubt, have the curious little contrivance worked up to its highest perfection. And then, possibly, there will follow a revolution in all departments of public singing and speaking.

There is no reason why we should not have all the great men of the age, as well as all the brilliant singers and actresses, taken possession of and driven off the course by the phonograph. Let them sing or speak once in any place, their words and tones will be captured by the phonograph. The tin foil, whereon all they have said is duly recorded, will be electrotyped, and copies sold at so much a piece. We shall all waste a portion of our substance on these little instruments; and then we have only to turn a crank, or set a kind of clockwork in motion, in order at any time to hear the great ones of the earth discourse in our own parlors."

And indeed a "revolution in all departments of public singing and speaking" did develop—but not with electrotyped tin foil!

However, in England a quite serious effort was made to develop the tin-foil phonograph. The London Stereoscopic Company had been made sole licensees of the phonograph and developed a model with a gravity-driven motor, with a Swiss fan-type speed governor. One of these is in the Museum of E.M.I. at Hayes, Middlesex.

CHAPTER 3

THE NORTH AMERICAN PHONOGRAPH COMPANY AND THE BELL-TAINTER GRAPHOPHONE

ON April 24, 1878, the Edison Speaking Phonograph Company was organized under the laws of Connecticut to exploit the tremendous popular interest which had been created by the announcement of the invention of a machine that could talk.[1] Edison was paid ten-thousand dollars for his tin-foil phonograph patent and a guarantee of twenty percent of the profits. The five stockholders of the company were George L. Bradley, Hilbourne L. Roosevelt, Uriah H. Painter, Charles A. Cheever, and Gardiner G. Hubbard. Painter was a Washington reporter who came from Westchester, Pennsylvania. Gardiner G. Hubbard was the father-in-law of Alexander Graham Bell, eminent jurist, financier, and the chief organizer of the Bell Telephone Co. Without Hubbard's assistance and encouragement, Bell might never have reaped the rewards of his invention and quite possibly might never have received even the credit due him as the creator of the first articulating telephone. George L. Bradley was a metallurgist and financier, organizer with Hubbard of the New England Telephone Co. and the National Bell Telephone Co. of New York City. Charles A. Cheever was a most unusual man. He had been severely crippled when an infant as a

result of being dropped by a nurse. As a result his legs never developed and he had to be carried about on the arm of an attendant. Despite his deformity, Cheever had an indomitable will, engaged himself actively in business, making and spending fortunes. While still a young man, he secured an option on the New York City rights to the Bell telephone, but his father refused to loan him the necessary funds, so the option was dropped. Cheever was so certain of the success of the telephone enterprise that he persuaded Hilbourne Roosevelt, a cousin of Theodore (later President of the U.S.), to back him and together they secured the New York City rights from Hubbard. From this it can be seen that some of the men closest to Alexander Graham Bell were also associated with Thomas A. Edison and sponsored the commercial introduction of the phonograph. This is how the two budding enterprises, the telephone and the phonograph, came to share the same offices at 203 Broadway, New York City.

At the time of the introduction of the phonograph, the telephone business had yet to show its first dollar of profit anywhere, so it was an economic convenience for the two embryonic industries to share office expenses as well as certain officers and backers. During the first year of the Edison Speaking Phonograph Co., Hilbourne Roosevelt, who was a manufacturer of pipe organs as well, arranged demonstrations of the

---

[1] This was the same day on which an important patent was issued in England to Edison covering numerous projected improvements on the phonograph, but this patent was not assigned to this new company.

phonograph in and around New York City. These were attended by thousands, to which admissions were charged. James Redpath, of later Lyceum fame, divided the country into territories and leased demonstration rights. The phonographs at first were leased to the demonstrators, not sold, which accounts for the very few which have survived from this period.

The elemental phonograph, using tinfoil for the recording surface, was a simple and crude affair and the reproduction was generally poor. Yet contrary to the telephone, the phonograph was a commercial success from the first, paying its own way handsomely for the first few years. However, it was inevitable that people would tire of the novelty of hearing the human voice reproduced and it eventually became evident that there would have to be a further technical development of the instrument if it was to continue to be profitable. Edison had intended to do this from the first but now had his time committed to other projects of more immediate importance. So just as the telephone began to show promise of eventually becoming a paying proposition the phonograph had worn out its initial welcome and had no place to go.

Criticism has often been leveled at Edison for his failure to develop the phonograph during the decade from 1877 to 1887. The particular reason was that during these years Edison was very busy with the electric light. He felt that it was more important to perfect the means for the factory production of his incandescent lamp and to create community-wide electric power and distribution systems essential for their use, such as the one he was about to install in New York City. Who today would quarrel with his decision as to the relative importance of the two? For a period of five years beginning November 1878, Edison's services were placed under exclusive contract to the Edison Electric Light Co. When it became apparent that the demonstration phase of the phonograph was about over, Edison bought the assets of the

Edison Speaking Phonograph Co. so as to prevent loss to the stockholders and to facilitate the resumption of development work when time permitted.

In the meantime, while Edison was busy with the electric lighting problem, word came that the United States Patent Office had disallowed his 1878 phonograph patent application—identical with the British patent which had been promptly granted him covering numerous important improvements—for the then novel reason that the English patent covering the same claims constituted prior publication. However, before this time other devices had often been covered by identical patents issued by both these and other countries— many of Edison's inventions both before and after were so covered. The decision was appealed, but the patent examiners were adamant, holding that Edison's interests were adequately protected under the international agreements covering patents and copyrights. Edison always felt that this decision was most unfair. Perhaps the Edison attorneys protested too much, for on other occasions portions of other patent claims had to be abandoned by Edison because the examiners held that the subject had been already covered broadly by his 1878 patent (British).[2] On the other hand, learned judges of the American courts sitting in trials of certain important phonograph patent cases failed utterly to deal objectively with this British

---

[2] In the Edison file of patents in the Edison Library, Edison National Historic Site, West Orange, N.J., there is a marginal note pointing to No. 259,896 U. S. Pat. which reveals the Edison viewpoint as follows:

"Note, the broad application on duplications, filed Jan. 5, 1888, was abandoned. Edison's English patent No. 1644 of 1878 was acknowledged as covering a 'part' of the invention. The application was abandoned apparently under the doctrine of Fuller v. Eagle Co., since the specification was the same as patent No. 484,582.

" It is difficult to see now why this was done since patent 484,582 covers the specific vacuum process, and the broad application was comprehensive enough to include graphite, and silver salts and gold leaf chemically reduced. Possibly the doctrine of double patenting was not clearly understood."

patent, one even betraying his emotional prejudice in his opinion.[3]

One of the great mysteries of the history of the companion industries, the telephone and the phonograph, is that with a collaborative beginning and cordial relationships between the principals such a schism should have developed between them. The common sponsors have already been noted. That the Edison and Bell family relationships were initially cordial is indicated by a letter in the vault of the Edison National Historic Site from Mrs. Alexander Graham Bell to Thomas A. Edison congratulating him upon the invention of the phonograph.

There is another such congratulatory letter from Gardiner Hubbard, Bell's father-in-law and chief backer, who was one of the original stockholders of the Edison Speaking Phonograph Co. On the other hand, Edison's vital carbon transmitter patent had been recently delivered to the up-and-coming telephone rivals of the Bell Telephone Co.—Western Union. This was nothing new, for Edison had sold many telegraphic patents to Western Union in prior years. It may be that Bell thought that Edison should have desisted from continuing his work with the telephone, or that he should have discontinued his

_____

[3] American Graphophone Co. v. Leeds et al., June 18, 1898, a decision was handed down in a key case involving the Bell-Tainter patents in which the Edison British patent of 1878 was cited by the defense as evidence that the work of the Bells and Tainter had been anticipated by Edison, although Edison was not a party in the case. Many precedents damaging to Edison were established by such court decisions in which the Edison interests were not represented. In this case the presiding Judge said,

"A recording cylinder for a graphophone, consisting of a blank made of a pliable substance, covered with tin or metal foil, on which indentations are made by a rigid indenting point, is not an anticipation of a cylinder of a waxy substance from which the metal foil is omitted, and upon which an engraved record is made."

"When a patentee has made an actual living invention, which the public are able to use, the court is not called upon to struggle to decipher an anticipation in the unfinished work and the surmises of earlier students of the same subject."

association with Western Union when it became evident that this company was going to set up competition to the Bell interests. Perhaps these considerations may have influenced Bell to see what he could do with the phonograph, inasmuch as Edison was not doing anything with it at the time.

It was at this crucial point that a decision made some years before by Emperor Napoleon III, of France, was to play a decisive role in the molding of the future of the phonograph. While a reigning monarch, the Emperor had created an award for scientific achievement in honor of the distinguished French scientist, Andre Volta. In 1880, a committee of the French Academy of Science granted this award to Alexander Graham Bell in recognition of his invention of the telephone. With the twenty-thousand dollars which he received as the monetary part of the award, Bell organized the Volta Laboratory Association for the purpose of engaging in electrical and acoustical research and opened a research laboratory in Washington, District of Columbia, the following year. To assist him in his work he brought from England his brother Chichester and Prof. Charles Sumner Tainter, the three henceforth were known as the Volta Laboratory Associates.

It must be emphasized that up to this time Bell had not received a cent of profit from the telephone. So the benevolence of a former Emperor of France was posthumously to exert a most powerful influence on the future methods and form of the phonograph. Moreover, the results of this series of events was to profoundly affect what Edison was able to do with the instrument subsequently.

The greatest need of the Bell Telephone enterprise at the time Bell established the Volta Laboratory Association was a successful telephone transmitter. The patent rights to the Edison carbon button transmitter had been delivered by Jay Gould to the rival Western Union interests which were opening telephone exchanges in many cities. For a short time the attention of the Volta associates was directed towards that end. Among other devices, Alexander Bell with Charles Tainter invented a photophone transmitter which produced a voice-modulated current by means of a light-sensitive selenium cell activated by a variable beam of light reflected from a small mirror attached to the speaker diaphragm. However, the associates failed to develop this or other devices into practical commercial instruments—all were manifestly too costly or complex to compete with the simple, inexpensive carbon button transmitter of Edison. There were a total of eleven patents on telephonic devices issued to the Bells and Tainter in 1880 and 1881. There were no patents issued to any of the three during the next four years and no telephone patents were ever again issued to any of the associates. On the other hand, Edison was granted no less than twenty-five patents on telephonic improvements subsequent to 1880, most of which received commercial application.

The laboratory notebooks of Charles Sumner Tainter, given in later years by his widow to the Smithsonian Institution, reveal that very early in the work of the associates their attention became diverted almost exclusively to the phonograph. Rather significantly, Tainter's first recorded notes are upon experiments with the phonograph, rather than the telephone. Moreover, the laboratory notes and the various disc and cylinder experimental devices show very clearly that the associates began with the information and sketches contained in Edison's British patent of 1878, covering some sixty-seven technical drawings embodying many improvements, but which had not been carried to any practical stage by Edison, for reasons already given. The importance of Edison's British patent warrants reproduction in its entirety. (See Fig. 3-1.)

From the notes of Tainter and other evidence in the Smithsonian Institution, it appears that it was Tainter who was largely responsible for the change of direction of the research of the associates. If the circumstances surrounding the founding of the Volta Laboratory Association may fairly be described as dramatic, the steps taken by the associates to protect the results of their phonographic researches may be characterized only as fantastic. On February 28, 1880, Alexander Bell and Sumner Tainter deposited a sealed envelope with the Smithsonian Institution containing hand-written copies of notes on their first phonographic experiments and a statement of conclusions, with what appears to be a declaration of intention to invent, similar to a caveat. More than a year later, October 20, 1881, there was deposited with the Smithsonian Institution a sealed wooden box, containing two Washington newspapers of a day or two previous; a roll of about forty-seven pages of notes and sketches traced and copied from the laboratory notebook of Tainter; an eight-page statement by Tainter and Chichester A. Bell describing their invention of a method of reproducing sound from a phonogram record by means of a jet of compressed air; and a device which later was to be described as the first "Graphophone."

The reason we know these things is that in 1937 the box was opened at the request of an official of the Dictaphone Corporation, presumably with the acquiescence of Mrs. Tainter, who made a gift to the Institution of the original notebooks of Mr. Tainter. Attached to the base of the instrument contained in the box was a yellowed card affixed with sealing wax, with the following typed statement:

"The following words and sounds are recorded upon the cylinder of this graphophone:—

'G-r-r-G-r-r- There are more things in heaven and earth Horatio, than are dreamed of in our philosophy-G-r-r-I am a graphophone and my mother was a phonograph.-'

Speaking mouthpiece and length of tube. Deposited Oct. 20, 1881."

A.D. 1878, 24th April. N° 1644.

Recording and Reproducing Sounds.

LETTERS PATENT to Thomas Alva Edison, of Menlo Park, in the State of New Jersey, United States of America, for the Invention of " IMPROVEMENTS IN MEANS FOR RECORDING SOUNDS, AND IN REPRODUCING SUCH SOUNDS FROM SUCH RECORD."

Sealed the 6th August 1878, and dated the 24th April 1878.

PROVISIONAL SPECIFICATION left by the said Thomas Alva Edison at the Office of the Commissioners of Patents on the 24th April 1878.

THOMAS ALVA EDISON, of Menlo Park, in the State of New Jersey, United States of America. " IMPROVEMENTS IN MEANS FOR RECORDING SOUNDS, AND IN
5 REPRODUCING SUCH SOUNDS FROM SUCH RECORD."

My present improvements are for more fully developing and perfecting the device heretofore invented by me, and known as the " phonograph."

By extensive experiment and research I have been enabled to obtain very perfect articulation and to produce a record in a convenient form for preservation.
10 The sound vibrations are made to move a point that by preference is a diamond or other very hard substance and of a peculiar shape. The sound vibrations in the atmosphere act upon a diaphragm or other body capable of motion, and the same moves the indenting point, and acts as a phonograph. The indented material is properly designated a phonogram, and it is preferably metallic. Sometimes tin-
15 foil is used upon a grooved surface; sometimes a thin sheet or leaf of metal is placed upon a piece of paper having a surface of parafin or similar material.

Sometimes the metallic surface is copper, and where a matrix has been made of steel or iron by electrotype deposit, or otherwise, upon the phonogram it may be hardened and used for impressing a sheet or roller of metal, and thereby the original
20 phonogram can be reproduced indefinitely in metal that may be hardened and used for any reasonable length of time to utter the sentence, or words, or sounds phonetically.

[Price 10d.]

Fig. 3-1. Thomas A. Edison's British Patent No. 1644, dated April 24, 1878.

2   A.D. 1878.—N° 1644.   Provisional
                                                                      Specification.

Edison's Improvements in Recording and Reproducing Sounds.

The instrument or portion of the instrument that reproduces the sound from the
phonogram I term a " phonet."

In order to facilitate production, use, and preservation of the phonograms I
employ a ring or margin of thick paper or pasteboard, caused to adhere to the
foil or sheet by resinous substance ; this is used as a gauge in placing the sheet in   5
the instrument or replacing the same in the phonet. I find that a disc revolved by
gearing, and a weight or spring, and the movement regulated by a fan or governor,
is a convenient device for presenting the surface to be indented to the phonograph,
and the phonograph is on an arm that swings towards and from the centre of the
disc, and is guided by grooves or other convenient mechanism.   10

The phonet device takes the place of the phonograph device when the sounds are
to be reproduced.

When the sheet of material is wrapped around a cylinder its edges are passed
down into a slit and held firmly. Either the cylinder may be moved endwise by a
screw, or the phonograph or phonet devices be moved along the cylinder, and where   15
the same sound is to be reproduced periodically, as calling out the hours of the day
in a clock, or reproducing the sounds of animals in toys, the phonet is to be brought
to the place of beginning automatically.

The phonographic devices employed by me are preferably a diaphragm of metal,
against which the sound vibrations act. Sections of rubber tube applied to the   20
surface act as dampers to prevent false vibrations ; pieces of felt or similar yielding
material may be used for the same purpose, and a small delicate hoop of spring
metal between the diaphragm and the indenting point renders the phonogram more
perfect than it would be if the diaphragm acted upon the point direct. A similar
effect is produced by a disc upon the arm that carries the point, said disc being so   25
close to the diaphragm that the atmosphere will produce the vibrations.

It is often advantageous to use a case between the mouth of the speaker and the
diaphragm to gather or hold the sound, and in some instances the head of the
speaker should be inserted into this case, up through a hole in the bottom. The
mouth-piece is sometimes slotted or perforated, and has irregular edges to re-inforce   30
the hissing sounds, and sometimes a membrane of rubber or gutta percha is fitted
to the teeth, and forms a bag between the lips and the diaphragm.

The disc upon the arm that carries the point as aforesaid may be acted upon by
a magnet, and the current through a helix from a diaphragm, or the motion of the
arm and points may serve to set up a secondary current through such helix in con-   35
sequence of the motion given by the phonogram to the point. The arm carrying
the point in this latter case should be magnetised.

The phonogram may be produced by the direct action of air concentrated to the
spot by a funnel terminating with a small hole, the end of the funnel being almost
in contact with the moving surface to be indented.   40

When the foil is perforated instead of indented it can be rolled up in the form of a
horn or cylinder, and revolved, and the articulation result from air blown from the
end of a small tube passing through the perforations as they are presented in
succession.

Leverage is sometimes employed between the diaphragm and the phonogram,   45
either to lessen or increase the motion of the phonographic action in recording, or of
the phonetic action in speaking, and for recording quartette, trio, and other
characters of singing, two, three, four, or more phonographic devices are employed
upon one cylinder or plate, and the sounds will be reproduced by corresponding
phonets ; or where singing is conveyed through tubes to one diaphragm the phono-   50
graphic record will be the combined tones, and the reproduction by the phonet will
be complete and correct.

I find that an arm at right angles to a diaphragm, with a point resting upon the
phonogram, will reproduce the tones by the weight and leverage of the arm moving
the diaphragm.   55

The phonogram may be in the form of a disc, a sheet, an endless belt, a cylinder,
a roller, or a belt, or strip, and the marks are to be either in straight lines, spiral,

Fig. 3-1. Edison's British Patent No. 1644 (Cont'd.)

Provisional
Specification.

A.D. 1878.—N° 1644. 3

Edison's Improvements in Recording and Reproducing Sounds.

zig-zag, or in any other convenient form, so long as the apparatus is adapted to bringing the same into contact with the phonet or speaking part of the apparatus, and the reproduction of the phonogram from a matrix or copy in relief of an original phonogram may be made upon a belt, roller, cylinder, plate, or other convenient
5 surface.

For amusement and instruction this phonograph is capable of extended use. For instance, a revolving cylinder containing phonograms of the letters of the alphabet and phonet keys, with corresponding letters on them, can be used in teaching the alphabet; and phonogram sentences, speeches, and other matters can be spoken by
10 the phonet and repeated by the learner without the eyesight being called into use.

For amusement or instruction the phonogram can be of a dog's bark, a rooster's crow, a bird's song, a horse's neigh, a lion's roar, and the like, and the phonogram can be used in a toy animal with a single phonet for the reproduction of the original sound.
15 This phonograph or speaking machine applied to a mask produces a semblance of vitality if the phonogram is made to operate upon moveable lips by levers, and in the production of such a phonogram a portion of the surface is to be indented by delicate levers and points, receiving motion from the lips during articulation; thereby a correct reproduction of the motion of the lips is obtained.
20 In connection with the phonet it is important to avoid the sound that usually results from the rubbing action of the phonogram upon the point. I am enabled to prevent this by an electric action between the point and the phonogram. In this case the phonogram should be of iron, and the point of steel and the parts magnetised so as to slightly repel each other; the point will follow the undulations and reproduce
25 the sounds by the phonet.

It is important that the point used in the phonet correspond in shape to that of the phonograph, but slightly smaller, so as to follow the bottom of the depressions without contact upon the sides.

The diaphragm or other body employed in the phonet to receive motion from the
30 phonogram is connected with a funnel of paper or other resonant substance that acts as a sounding board to render the phonet louder and more distinct.

Fig. 3-1. Edison's British Patent No. 1644 (Cont'd.)

Edison's Improvements in Recording and Reproducing Sounds.

SPECIFICATION in pursuance of the conditions of the Letters Patent filed by
the said Thomas Alva Edison in the Great Seal Patent Office on the 22nd
October 1878.

THOMAS ALVA EDISON, of Menlo Park, in the State of New Jersey, United
States of America. " IMPROVEMENTS IN MEANS FOR RECORDING SOUNDS, AND IN 5
REPRODUCING SUCH SOUNDS FROM SUCH RECORD."

This Invention consists in means for recording in permanent characters th
sounds made by the human voice in speaking and singing, those made by musical
instruments, birds, animals, or any sound whatever, and in means for reproducing
those sounds at any desired time.   10

The sound vibrations act upon a diaphragm or other body capable of motion
this diaphragm is at the back of a chamber provided with an opening or mouth-
piece, and to this diaphragm an indenting point is secured. This instrument I term
a "phonograph." The phonograph is adjusted to position with its indenting point
contiguous to a moving surface covered with a thin sheet of metal foil or other 15
suitable material, or else the surface with the metal foil is stationary, and the phonograph movable.

The surface upon which the metal foil is secured is by preference grooved
spirally, and this indenting point indents the foil in the line of this groove as the
diaphragm is moved back and forth by the sound vibrations; these indentations 20
are a record of the sound waves, and form the characters for reproducing the sounds.
This indented sheet I term a "phonogram."

The instrument or portion of the instrument that reproduces the sound from the
phonogram I term a "phonet." It is similar in construction to the phonograph,
being provided with a diaphragm and point, but the mouth-piece is by preference 25
funnel-shaped to render the sound loud and distinct. The sounds are reproduced by
the phonet being adjusted to place so that the point of its diaphragm is at the
beginning of the spiral line of indentations, and as the surface containing the
indented foil is moved the diaphragm of the phonet is vibrated by the point passing
from one indentation to the next, hence the diaphragm receives the same movement 30
from the indentations as when making those indentations, consequently the sounds
made by the phonet will be the same as those that operated upon the diaphragm
of the phonograph.

In the Drawing Fig. 1 is a section of the phonograph and sectional elevation of
the mechanism for presenting the surface to be indented: and Fig. 2 is a plan of 35
the same.

The phonograph is made of the body portion a, diaphragm b, and indenting
point c. The body portion a has a central opening forming the mouth-piece into
which the person speaks, or through which opening the sound vibrations pass to act
upon the diaphragm, and the diaphragm is secured at its edges to the body a, 40
leaving a space between the body and diaphragm in order that the diaphragm
may vibrate freely. The indenting point should be a diamond or other very hard
substance.

The diaphragm is made of a thin sheet of iron or other material, and it is preferable to place the indenting point upon a delicate spring arm e², and to employ a 45
short piece of rubber tubing e³ between the spring and diaphragm ; this rubber acts
as a damper to prevent false vibrations of the diaphragm.

The phonograph is upon a lever arm i pivoted at 5 to the vertical stud 6, so that
the phonograph may be raised or lowered vertically, or moved horizontally for a
purpose hereafter explained.   5

It is now to be understood that if a person speaks with his mouth near the
mouth-piece of the phonograph the sound vibrations will act upon the diaphragm,
and vibrate it, and communicate to the indenting point a similar movement, and
that if a piece of metal foil or other material susceptible of being indented is placed

Fig. 3-1. Edison's British Patent No. 1644 (Cont'd.)

Specification.   A.D. 1878.—N° 1644.   5

Edison's Improvements in Recording and Reproducing Sounds.

beneath or behind the indenting point and caused to move regularly, or the indenting point moved over the material; that said material will be indented and form a perfect record of the sound vibrations.

I will now describe the means for sustaining the sheet to be indented, and the
5 mechanism for moving the same :—d is a disk or plate secured to and turning with the shaft e, and hinged to this disk is a ring frame f; this disk d has two spiral grooves 3, 4, in its surface. There are pins 2, 2, upon the surface of the disk, and holes at corresponding places in the ring frame; the sheet to be indented is of a size and shape to correspond with that of the disk d and frame f, and said sheet
10 has holes in it corresponding to the position of the pins 2, 2, and these holes form register marks in placing or replacing the sheet upon the disk d, and after the sheet is so placed the ring frame f is brought down upon the sheet and holds it firmly in place. There may be a central opening in the indented sheet of a size slightly larger than the space occupied by the spiral 3, and the outer edges of the sheet are
15 stiffened by a ring of thick paper or pasteboard caused to adhere by glue or other adhesive material. The surface of the disk d is made with two spiral grooves 3 and 4 as aforesaid; the groove 3 is a guide for a pin that is upon an arm g on the phonograph, and the groove 4 is for the indenting point c. As the disk and sheet are revolved the groove 3 causes the indenting point to occupy a position imme-
20 diately over the line of the spiral 4, and the indentations will be made upon the sheet of foil in a line corresponding to that of the spiral 4, shown in Fig. 2. The indentations made in the foil are a complete record of the sound vibrations that acted upon the diaphragm b, and from this indented sheet, which I term a " phono-gram," the sounds are reproduced. The phonograph is carried outwardly by the
25 spiral 3, and in so doing the parts swing upon the vertical stud 6. By depressing the outer end of the lever i the phonograph is raised so that it can be swung aside from the disk d to allow of the ring frame f being thrown back and the indented sheet or "phonogram" removed from the disk.

The shaft e is revolved by a weight, or spring, and gearing at h, and the spring
30 is wound up by moving the lever k back and forth, which acts upon a ratchet and pawl of ordinary construction; l is a lever provided at its outer end with an inclined groove, in which is a pin on the lever m, and the other end of this lever m is con-nected with the coupler m¹ by moving the lever l one way or the other, the shaft e will be connected to or disconnected from the gearing h, and hence the disk d
35 stopped or started at pleasure without interfering with the motor.

As it is necessary that the shaft e should be revolved with uniformity I provide a governor at n to prevent the apparatus revolving too rapidly; and this may be made as in Figs. 1, 3, & 4, in which there are metal blocks o at the ends of spring arms from a cross head on a shaft that is driven by the gearing h, said blocks
40 swinging radially and acting against the interior of a stationary cylinder p if the speed becomes too great, thereby checking the speed by the friction of the blocks against the cylinder. These spring arms may be secured at one end to a prismatic block as shown in Fig. 5. It is preferable to cover the surface of the blocks o next the cylinder p with felt or similar material that will slide upon the interior
45 surface of the cylinder p, but produce more or less friction, according to the centri-fugal action.

The guide spiral 3 may be dispensed with, and either of the devices shown in Figs. 6, 7, 8, or 9, made use of,

In Figs. 6 and 7 the shaft e projects above the surface of the disk d, and there
50 is a tooth upon the shaft contiguous to a rack bar extending from the phonograph, hence each revolution of the shaft, the rack bar, and phonograph will be moved the space of one tooth, consequently the lines of indentations will be parallel and con-centric to the shaft e, excepting at the places when the tooth acts to move the rack bar and phonograph outward or inward. In this case the spiral grooves are
55 cut to correspond to the feed.

In Fig. 8 a worm upon the shaft e acts upon a worm pinion to revolve the shaft e⁵, and the worm at the other end of this shaft e⁵ acts upon teeth around the base of

Fig. 3-1. Edison's British Patent No. 1644 (Cont'd.)

C   **A.D. 1878.—N° 1644.**   *Specification.*

Edison's Improvements in Recording and Reproducing Sounds.

---

the lever *i* on the stud 6. By this device the phonograph will be moved outward gradually, and the line of indentations will be in a spiral corresponding to the continuous spiral groove in the plate *d*.

In Fig. 9 the shaft *e* is made with a fusee at p^1, and one end of a swinging arm connected to the phonograph takes against the same. The spirals of the fusee 5 gradually move outward the phonograph, as the disk and shaft are revolved, and the line of indentations will be spirally the same as that made by the spiral 3.

In Fig. 10 the shaft *e* is provided with a screw pinion meshing with teeth upon a cam wheel 7. This gives the same movement to the phonograph as the spiral groove 3.   10

In Fig. 11 the guide groove 3 for the arm and pin *g* is upon a disk d^1 upon the shaft *e*, but the groove 3 occupies the same relative position upon the disk d^1 as the groove 4 upon the disk *d*, so that the phonograph is moved outwardly by the groove of the disk d^1, swinging both the arms *g* and *i* upon the vertical pivot 6.

Instead of the sheet of metal foil being upon the disk *d* it may be wrapped upon 15 a cylinder *q*, as in Fig. 12. In this case the cylinder is upon a shaft e^1 revolved by the gearing at h^1, and upon said shaft there is a right and left hand screw at k^1, and there is a corresponding double spiral groove in the surface of the cylinder *q*. The phonograph is secured to a sliding shaft l^1, and said shaft is moved endwise back and forth by the screw k^1 acting upon an arm m^3 that is secured to the said 20 shaft l^1. As the phonograph is moved in one direction the line of indentations is made spirally in the foil on the cylinder *q*, and when the arm m^2 reaches the end of the screw it will be moved in the other direction by the reverse screw thread, and the phonograph will make a second spiral line of indentations that will cross the first spiral line. This feature is especially available for a phonet where the 25 surface of the cylinder *q* is formed of an electrotype or other copy of the phonogram, so that the words or sounds may be reproduced automatically and at intervals if desired.

It is preferable to make use of a thin metal plate n^2, see Figs. 13 and 14, pivoted at one end and fitting within a longitudinal groove in the surface of the cylinder *q* 30 for securing the edges of the metal foil and holding it securely upon said cylinder. The top of this plate n^2 is flush with the surface of the cylinder, and grooved to correspond with the groves in the cylinder, so as not to interfere with the indenting point. A wire may replace this device, such wire being secured by arms at each end of the cylinder, and raised and lowered in and out of the groove by a cam or 35 otherwise. I find that an interruption of one-eighth of an inch space where there is no recording is not detected by the ear.

The apparatus shown in Figs. 13 and 14 is similar to that shown in Fig. 12, except that the phonograph is stationary and the cylinder moves horizontally, and the shaft e^1 is only provided with a screw thread in one direction, hence the 40 cylinder will have to be moved back by hand to bring it to place if desired to reproduce the sounds from the phonogram, or to position the phonograph if a new sheet of foil is to be indented after the first one has been removed. This is readily accomplished by raising the arm o^1 and its tooth from the screw k^1, which leaves the shaft e^1 and cylinder free to be moved back and forth.   45

In Fig. 15 the phonograph is fitted to move horizontally instead of the cylinder *q*, as in Fig. 12, but the shaft e^1 is provided with a screw thread in one direction only, hence the phonograph has to be positioned by hand after the arm o^1 has been raised from the screw k^1.

In Figs. 12 and 15 the phonograph can swing upon the shaft l^1 to raise the 50 indenting point from the cylinder *q*, and allow for the removal or insertion of a sheet of foil, and there is a stop at 8 for adjusting the position of the phonograph when brought down to indent the foil.

In Figs. 13 and 14 the phonograph is upon an arm pivoted at 9, so that it can be swung horizontally away from the cylinder *q* for the purpose aforesaid, and the 55 adjustable stop 8 is also provided.

Thus far I have described the " phonograph " or instrument upon which the

Fig. 3-1. Edison's British Patent No. 1644 (Cont'd.)

Specification.   A.D. 1878.—No 1644.   7

Edison's Improvements in Recording and Reproducing Sounds.

sound vibrations act, and which instrument acts to indent the sheet of foil and produce the "phonogram" or record of such sound vibrations.

Mechanism has also been described for presenting the sheet of foil to be indented by the phonograph.

5   I will now describe how the sounds are reproduced from the phonogram.

If it is desired to reproduce the sounds from the phonogram in the same instrument in which the phonogram was produced it is only necessary that the indenting point c be made to traverse the line of indentations in the phonogram, and that a funnel-shaped mouth-piece, shown by dotted lines in Fig. 1, be added to the phono-
10 graph to aid in increasing the loudness and distinctness of the sound. The instrument in this form I term a "phonet."

In the instrument shown in Figs. 1, 2, 6, 7, 8, 9, 10, 11, 13, 14, and 15, the phonet requires to be positioned by hand, as before explained, in order that the point c may be placed at the beginning of the spiral line of indentations. As
15 the point c passes from one indentation to the next, either by the foil being moved beneath said point, as in Figs. 1, 2, 6, 7, 8, 9, 10, 11, 13, and 14, or by the point moving over the foil, as in Figs. 12 and 15, the diaphragm b receives a movement corresponding to the depth of the indentations, and corresponding also with the same movement it received from the sound vibrations when making those
20 indentations, hence air waves will be produced by the movement of the diaphragm that will make sounds by passing through the mouth-piece of the phonet that will be exactly the same as the sounds that acted upon the diaphragm of the phonograph.

The material upon which the record is made may be of metal foil, such as tin,
25 iron, copper, lead, zinc, cadmium, or a foil made of composition of metals.

Paper or other materials may be used, the same being coated with parafine or other hydrocarbons, waxes, gums, or lacs, and the sheet so prepared may itself be indented, or the material, say paper, may be made to pass through a bath of hot parafine and thence between scrapers. Thin metal foil is now placed on the
30 material, and the sheet passed through rollers, which give it a beautiful smooth surface. The indentation can now be made in the foil, and the parafine or similar material, and the indenting point, does not become clogged with the parafine in consequence of the intervening foil.

If the copper foil, or tin foil with copper surface is used, and a matrix of iron or
35 steel made by electrotype deposit or otherwise upon the phonogram, such matrix may be hardened and used for impressing a sheet or roller of metal as hereafter mentioned; thereby the original phonogram can be reproduced indefinitely in metal that may be hardened and used for any reasonable length of time to utter the sentence or words or sounds phonetically.
40 I will now briefly describe some modifications in the construction and operation of the phonograph and phonet.

In Fig. 16 the indenting point c is upon a spring arm e^2, as in Figs. 1 and 2, but there are short sections of rubber tube e^3 at each side of the diaphragm b to dampen the diaphragm and prevent false vibrations.
45 In Fig. 17, the rubber of the diaphragm acts against the outer end of the arm e^2 to increase the leverage and lessen the depth of indentations in the foil and allow of the record being made in less yielding material than tin foil.

Fig. 18 shows a modification of the last-mentioned device, the pressure being
50 applied to the arm e^3 between the indenting point and the support for the arm so as to increase the depth of the indentations.

Fig. 19 shows the arm e^2 made as a lever with a spring.

Fig. 20 shows the indenting point upon the center of a spring bar that is firmly held at each end; the bar is connected at its center to the diaphragm b by a string
55 or otherwise.

Fig. 21 represents the diaphragm b as of concave form instead of flat.

Fig. 22 shows the indenting point upon a spring secured to the diaphragm.

Fig. 3-1. Edison's British Patent No. 1644 (Cont'd.)

S   A.D. 1878.—N° 1644.   Specification.
_____

Edison's Improvements in Recording and Reproducing Sounds.
_____

Fig. 23 shows a disk upon the spring e^2 of the indenting point; this disk is
placed quite close to the diaphragm and is moved by the air as the diaphragm is
vibrated, the disk being so close to the diaphragm that the two will vibrate
together, as air cannot pass between or escape as rapidly as the vibrations take
place.   5

Fig. 24 shows the diaphragm vibrated by electro-magnetism; in this case the
diaphragm is to be of iron, and the power of the electro-magnet will be varied by a
rise and fall of electric current passing through the helix of the electro-magnet; this
rise and fall of electric tension is to be produced by the action of sound upon a
diaphragm and connections in an electric circuit.   10

Fig. 25 shows the method of vibrating the indenting spring and point by the
direct action of an electro-magnet without the use of a diaphragm, the electric
tension in the helix being varied by sound vibrations upon a diaghragm.

Fig. 26 shows the spring arm e^2 connected to one end of a permanent magnet so
as to highly magnetize the reproducing point; the foil should be of iron. When   15
the point passes an indentation there will be less attraction than when passing no
indentation; this will give good articulation free from the scraping noise of the
point on the foil, for in this case it does not touch the foil, but is worked by
magnetic attraction.

Fig. 27 represents two instruments in connection with the cylinder q; in this case   20
the phonet and the phonograph are separate. The phonograph records in the usual
manner, but the phonet has its diaphragm set in motion by the rise and fall of the
lever e^2. This reduces the scraping noise of the foil and acts by leverage, and a
slight tension to move the diaphragm as the phonogram is moved beneath the
point c.   25

Fig. 28 shows an arrangement whereby four persons may speak simultaneously
and have records made in separate parallel lines upon one cylinder, and the phonogram will reproduce the sounds the same as though it contained the record of but
one voice.

Fig. 29 shows a single phonograph adapted to receive the voices of three persons   30
as in singing; the sounds made by the three voices are conveyed through flexible
or other tubes to the diaphragm, and will be recorded in a single line of indentations, but when reproduced by the phonet the sounds uttered will correspond to
the three voices.

In Fig. 30, the foil is sustained upon a hollow cylinder with a funnel-shaped end.   35
The record is made upon the foil in the usual manner by the phonograph, excepting
that holes are made entirely through the foil. A nozzle with a small opening is
placed so that it will always be opposite the line of perforations as the cylinder is
revolved. This nozzle is connected to a source of compressed air or other fluid, and
every time a perforation comes opposite the nozzle, a puff of air passes into the   40
cylinder and a sound is produced upon the principle of the siren. The nozzle may
be placed on a spring to keep the end of the nozzle in contact with the line of perforations.

Fig. 31 shows the phonograph as made with a large chamber between the
diaphragm and the mouth-piece; this is especially useful in collecting sound when   45
the person speaking or the sound to be recorded is made several feet from the
instrument.

Fig. 32 shows a device whereby the indenting point may be dispensed with in
the phonograph. The funnel forming the phonograph is made with a diaphragm
at the larger end or mouth-piece, and a very small hole at the pointed end adjacent   50
to the foil on the cylinder q; this foil should be very thin so that the indentations
will be made by the direct action of the air waves as concentrated by the funnel
without the interposition of the indenting point.

Fig. 33 shows a phonet in which the phonogram or sound record has been made
upon an endless belt; this is a convenient arrangement for toys, as the same may   55
be made to imitate the bark of a dog or other noise made by an animal; and this

Fig. 3-1. Edison's British Patent No. 1644 (Cont'd.)

Specification.   A.D. 1878.—N° 1644.   9

Edison's Improvements in Recording and Reproducing Sounds.

belt may be of steel or other hard material that allows the same to be used for a
long period of time.

    Fig. 34 is a perspective view showing a double phonet, there being a spiral line
of indentations on each side of the revolving disk d, one phonet coming into action
5 as the other finishes ; in this case the spirals should be in opposite directions, so
that the disk continuing to revolve in the same direction moves one phonet from
the center outwards, and then the other phonet is connected and moved back
towards the center ; this may be used as a toy.

    Fig. 35 represents a phonet in which the phonogram containing a sentence,
10 speech, words, or other sound record is upon a belt or strip wound upon a reel ;
this belt is drawn along gradually and wound upon the second roller by any
suitable mechanism, and as the phonogram is thus moved it actuates the
phonet c, b.

    Fig. 36 shows a phonograph or phonet similar to that shown in Fig. 12, the
15 cylinder q is revolved, but remains in one positson, and the phonograph or phonet
is movable back and forth over the cylinder. In this instance the arm m^3 is
extended beyond the screw k^1, and passes beneath the inclined spring guide m^5,
when the screw is carrying the arm and phonograph towards the right ; as the
arm m^3 passes from beneath the end of the guide m^5 it is no longer held to the
20 screw, and the arm m^2 and phonet are lifted by the guide m^2 as the springs m^6
draws the shaft, phonograph, and arm, along to the place of beginning, at which
place the arm m^3 drops off the end of the inclined guide m^5 into the thread of the
screw, and as this revolves it carries the arm along beneath the guide m^5 as
before.

25   Fig. 37 represents the phonograph or phonet upon a pivoted arm, so that it may
swing across or at right angles to the line of movement of the intended material or
phonogram. In this case the line of indentations may be lengthwise of the belt, or
across the same in the arc of a circle.

    Fig. 38 shows a phonograph similar to that shown in Fig. 31, except that the
30 sound chamber is of a different shape.

    Fig. 39 shows a mouth-piece with an orifice of soft rubber to fit the mouth or the
lips of the person speaking, so that all sound waves will be confined to the chamber
and diaphragm.

    Fig. 40 shows the mouth-piece of the phonograph made with cross slots with
35 irregular edges.

    Fig. 41 shows the mouth-piece as perforated with numerous holes.

    Fig. 42 shows but one opening in the mouth-piece ; the edges of this are irregular.
These irregular edges reinforce the hissing sounds and cause a more perfect phonogram to be produced.

40   Fig. 43 represents a mouth-piece of mica with a central opening protected at its
edges by a wooden ring.

    In Fig. 44, the diaphragm b is of wire gauze with a backing of paper connected
to it by any suitable cement, and there is a ring of stiff paper at the edges of the
gauze disk to strengthen it.

45   Fig. 45 represents a diaphragm b of parchment or similar material stretched
tightly within the frame b^6 by cords and screws. The cords may be of different
lengths and tension, and respond to and reinforce certain sounds.

    Fig. 46 shows a mouth-piece for the phonet made in imitation of the human
mouth.

50   Fig. 47 represents the body portion of the phonograph or phonet made triangular,
and the diaphragm is of corresponding shape.

    Fig. 48 represents three cylinders, each provided with a phonograph or phonet ;
this is useful in recording and reproducing three-part singing or music.

    Fig. 49 represents a phonet made as a tube, with flaring or trumpet-shaped ends,
55 and with two diaphragms 15, 16, placed crosswise of the tube so as to form an air
chamber. There is a third diaphragm b, which is vibrated by the movement of the
reproducing point c, and said diaphragm gives motion to the air in the chamber,

Fig. 3-1. Edison's British Patent No. 1644 (Cont'd.)

Edison's Improvements in Recording and Reproducing Sounds.

and vibrates the diaphragms 15, 16, which latter produce air waves, and the sounds issuing from the two trumpet-shaped ends will blend and increase the volume of sound.

Fig. 50 represents a device whereby deep indentations are made in the metal foil. Two diaphragms are employed, the first (b^2) is vibrated by the sound vibrations, 5 and controls a valve b^7 in a tube connected with a source of compressed air or other fluid ; this valve b^7 allows more or less air to pass to the diaphragm b, according to the vibration of the diaphragm b^2, hence the diaphragm b will vibrate in harmony with the diaphragm b^2, but it will be acted upon by greater force, and consequently the indentations will be deeper in the foil than if the diaphragm b was acted upon 1 simply by the sound vibrations of the voice.

Figs. 51 and 52 represent a device that may be used with a phonet to increase the loudness of the sounds reproduced. The sound vibrations from the phonet are conducted by a tube shown by dotted lines in Fig. 51, to the diaphragm b^3 that controls a valve b^7 in a tube connected with a reservoir of air or other fluid under 1⅗ pressure, and the air as it escapes by the valve passes into the trumpet-shaped end of the tube, and produces sounds that are very loud and clear, and are a reproduction of the sounds resulting from the use of one of the phonets before described.

This same apparatus may be used to reproduce with louder utterances a person's voice, the the sound from the voice being used to vibrate the diaphragm b^3, and 20 thereby regulate the air waves escaping from the valve b^7 into the trumpet.

Fig. 53 shows the speaker's head within a box or case ; in this instance nearly all the sound vibrations act upon the diaphragm.

Figs. 54 and 55 illustrate how the movements of the lips in speaking may be recorded and reproduced. In this instance, a lever applied to the diaphragm carries 25 the indenting point c, Fig. 55, and the end of this lever is placed in the mouth of the speaker, and the movement of the lips regulates the indentations in the foil.

A similar apparatus shown in Fig. 54 within a case is connected to the movable lips of a mask, so that these lips open and close as in articulation, at the same time that the sound vibrations are given by the phonogram to the phonet. 30

Fig. 56 represents a toy phonet in which the phonogram strip 35 is secured at one end to a cylinder upon which it is wound. By pulling upon the strip it is unwound, and a rubber cord 37 is wound upon the shaft of the cylinder. When the hand is removed from the indented strip, the rubber cord rotates the shaft and winds up the phonogram upon the cylinder, and the sounds are reproduced in the 35 phonet by the phonogram acting upon a point and diaphragm a. The movement of the shaft is regulated by the fan, worm, and pinion 38.

In Fig. 57, the cylinder for moving the phonogram strip is shown as provided with pins that enter holes in the edges of the strip ; this causes the strip to be fed along very regular. 40

In Fig. 58, the cylinder with pins is shown as made with heads to act as guides for the strip.

Fig. 59 shows a re-indenting device for amplifying or increasing the size of the indentations. There are two rollers, one of which a^4 travels faster than the other a^3, and there is a lever 40 pivoted at 41, and provided with a point c for each 45 cylinder. One point follows the indentations in the cylinder a^3, and the other rests upon a^4, and as this travels the fastest, the indentations made therein will be longer and also deeper by the point being at the outer end of the lever.

In Fig. 60, one roller 42 of the pair is made of hardened metal with the sound record in relief. This is obtained by electrotype or other process from an iron foil 50 or other metal phonogram, and this roller is used to indent strips or sheets of foil or rollers to produce copies that can be used with the phonet.

Fig. 61 represents a roller 42 of hardened metal with the record in relief, and arranged so as to knurl or indent the phonogram in a roller 43 of soft metal that is to be pressed against the roller 42 by a screw or other suitable means. 55

The cylinder having a spiral groove in its surface may be made by placing the mould shown in Fig. 62 around a cylinder or shaft, and filling the space between

Fig. 3-1. Edison's British Patent No. 1644 (Cont'd.)

Specification.   A.D. 1878.—N° 1644.   11

Edison's Improvements in Recording and Reproducing Sounds.

the cylinder and mold with plaster of Paris or other suitable material. The mold is of metal with a screw or spiral rib projecting therefrom, and it is made in two parts and hinged so that it can easily be removed when the plaster of Paris is dry.

For amusement or instruction, the phonograph is capable of extended use ; for
5 instance, a revolving cylinder, see Fig. 63, containing rows of indentations representing the letters of the alphabet, and provided with keys containing corresponding letters, can be used in teaching the alphabet, and sentences, speeches, and other matter can be spoken by the phonet, and repeated by the learner without the eyesight being called into use.

10 Clocks may be provided with phonogram cylinders or wheels to call off the hours, to give alarms, &c.

The phonogram may be upon a strip, sheet, belt, or roller, and it can be of a dog's bark, a rooster's crow, a bird's song, a horse's neigh, and these can be used in toy animals with a simple phonet for reproducing the sound.

15 In copying phonograms, or making duplicates, an original phonogram may receive a deposit of copper or iron in a plating bath ; and, if of iron, may be carbonized to convert it into steel and hardened, and then the same should be backed up with type metal, and used for impressing strips or pieces of metal.

A bed of gutta percha, or similar material, may be used to sustain the sheet
20 metal while being pressed. Numerous copies of the original phonogram can thus be reproduced.

A plaster cast can be used for producing a copy by pressure.

The governor to regulate the speed of the instrument may be made of a pendulum weight 61, see Fig. 64, hung at the lower end of a rod that is provided
25 with a universal joint at 62, and the upper end of the rod is moved around by a crank 63 that is revolved by the train of gearing. As the speed increases the weight will describe a circle of larger diameter, and thereby increase the resistance.

The universal joint may be displaced by a spring wire, Fig. 65, that allows of
30 the movement.

A magnet 64 upon the crank arm 63, Fig. 66, may be used to revolve the pendulum by attracting an armature at the upper end of the pendulum rod, and thereby avoid the friction resulting from the contact of the surfaces of the pendulum rod with the crank.

35 In Fig. 67 the diaphragm b is represented as connected to a pair of delicate piston valves within a tube 68 that has three ports ; one, 69, is connected to a reservoir of compressed air, the others, 70 and 71, are connected to a chamber 72 at opposite sides of a diaphragm, so as to vibrate the same in harmony with the diaphragm b, but there will be greater amplitude given to the same by the pressure
40 of the air, and by a connection to the phonet diaphragm b^2 the sound produced will be greatly increased.

What I claim as my Invention is,—

First. The combination with the diaphragm and point of a flat receiving surface and means for revolving the receiving surface, and causing the point to follow
45 a volute or spiral line, substantially as represented in Figs. 1, 2, 6, 7, 8, 9, 10, and 34.

Second. The combination with the revolving plate phonograph or phonet of a propelling weight or spring and a governor to regulate the speed, and ensure uniformity of movement, substantially as set forth.

50 Third. A revolving disk provided with a clamping frame to secure the foil or other material in combination with the swinging arm, diaphragm, and point, substantially as specified.

Fourth. In a phonograph or phonet, a spring introduced between the diaphragm and the point, substantially as set forth and shown in Figs. 16, 17, 18, 19, 22,
55 and 26.

Fifth. In a phonograph or phonet a rubber spring, or similar device, to dampen

Fig. 3-1. Edison's British Patent No. 1644 (Cont'd.)

12   A.D. 1878.—N° 1644.   Specification.

Edison's Improvements in Recording and Reproducing Sounds.

the vibration of the diaphragm, and prevent false vibrations, as set forth and shown in Figs. 16 and 21.

Sixth. The combination with the diaphragm in a phonograph or phonet apparatus of a lever to modify the relative action of the diaphragm and point, substantially as described, and shown in Figs. 17, 18, 27.   5

Seventh. The combination with the diaphragm and point of a permanent or electro-magnet, substantially as described, and represented in Figs. 24, 25, 26.

Eighth. The method of recording and reproducing two or more sounds or speeches simultaneously, substantially as described, and as illustrated by Figs. 28, 29, and 48.   10

Ninth. A phonet composed of a perforated sirene and a jet tube, substantially as described, and represented in Fig. 30.

Tenth. The mechanism for producing a phonogram, and employing the same in a phonet, substantially as described, and illustrated in Figs. 32, 33, 35, 36, and 37.

Eleventh. The combination with the phonograph, diaphragm, and point of a 15 sound chamber, substantially as described, and illustrated in Figs. 31, 38, 39, and 53.

Twelfth. The diaphragm and mouth-pieces for speaking phonograph, substantially as described, and as illustrated in Figs. 41, 42, 43, 44, 45, and 46.

Thirteenth. The combination with a diaphragm and its point of two diaphragms 20 for the purposes, and substantially as shown in Fig. 49.

Fourteenth. The combination with a diaphragm and valve actuated by sound vibrations a source of compressed fluid and a trumpet, as in Figs. 51, 52, or a phonograph as in Fig. 50, substantially as set forth.

Fifteenth. The combination of two diaphragms with a valve and a source of 25 compressed fluid, as represented in Fig. 67, for increasing the volume of the voice or other sound, as set forth.

Sixteenth. The combination with two or more phonograms of phonet keys for selecting letters or utterances as described, and illustrated in Fig. 63.

Seventeenth. The means for duplicating or reproducing phonograms from an 30 original phonogram, substantially as set forth.

Eighteenth. The combination with the phonograph or phonet of the revolving crank and pendulum governor, substantially as described, and shown in Figs. 64, 65, 66.

Nineteenth. The combination with the phonograph of a lever moved by the lips, 35 and of a lever and phonet to move the lips of a mask, substantially as described, and illustrated by Figs. 55 and 54.

Twentieth. The combination with a phonogram of a clock movement or toy and a phonet for reproducing sounds for clocks or toys, substantially as set forth.

In witness whereof, I, the said Thomas Alva Edison, have hereunto set my 40 hand and seal, this 17th day of September, A.D. 1878.

                              THOMAS ALVA EDISON.   (L.S.)

Witnesses,
    CHAS. H. SMITH,
        76, Chambers St., New York,   45
    HAROLD SERRELL, 76, Chambers St., New York.

LONDON: Printed by GEORGE EDWARD EYRE and WILLIAM SPOTTISWOODE,
        Printers to the Queen's most Excellent Majesty.
            For Her Majesty's Stationery Office.

                            1878.

Fig. 3-1. Edison's British Patent No. 1644 (Cont'd.)

A.D. 1878. APRIL 24. N.º. 1644.
EDISON'S SPECIFICATION
(5ᵗʰ Edition)

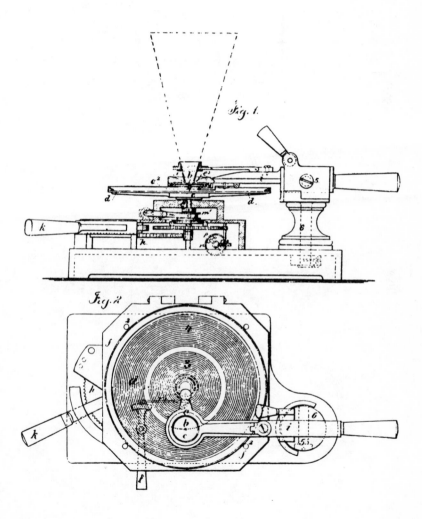

Fig. 3-1. Edison's British Patent No. 1644 (Cont'd.)

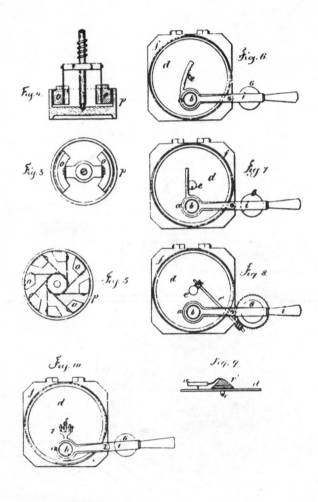

Fig. 3-1. Edison's British Patent No. 1644 (Cont'd.)

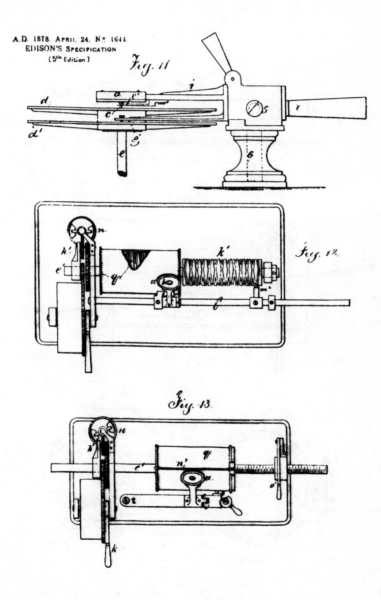

Fig. 3-1. Edison's British Patent No. 1644 (Cont'd.)

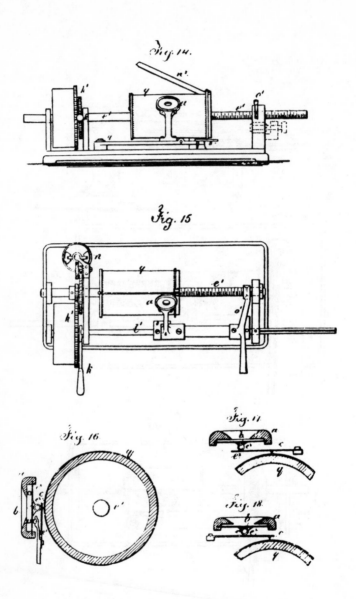

Fig. 3-1. Edison's British Patent No. 1644 (Cont'd.)

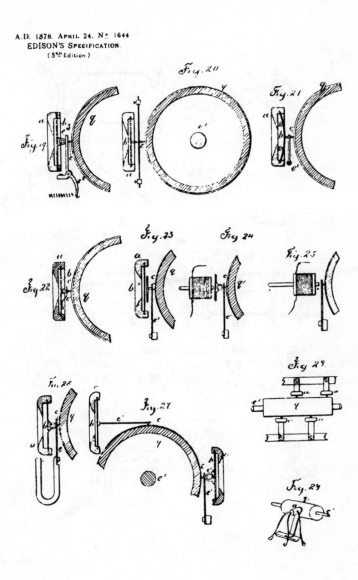

A.D. 1878. April 24. N.° 1644
EDISON'S Specification.
(5ᵗʰ Edition)

Fig. 3-1. Edison's British Patent No. 1644 (Cont'd.)

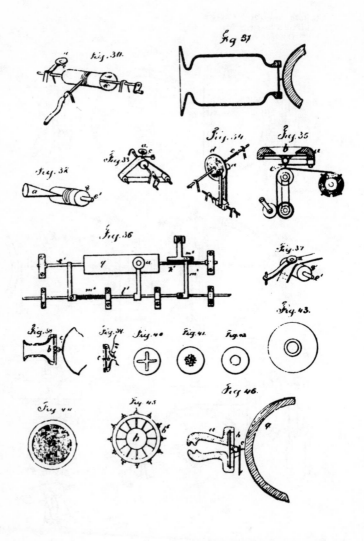

Fig. 3-1. Edison's British Patent No. 1644 (Cont'd.)

A.D. 1878. April 24. N.° 1644.
EDISON'S Specification.
(5th Edition)

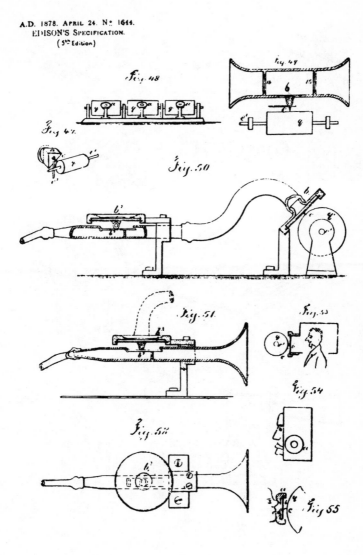

Fig. 3-1. Edison's British Patent No. 1644 (Cont'd.)

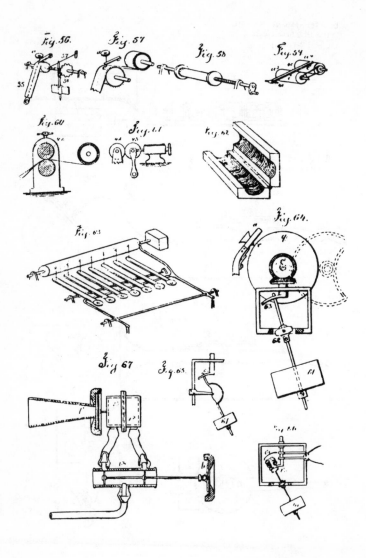

Fig. 3-1. Edison's British Patent No. 1644 (Cont'd.)

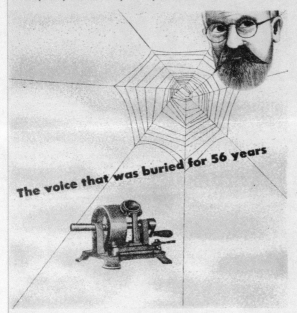

Fig. 3-2. The original "Graphophone"—almost identical to the $15.00 Edison tinfoil phonograph, but with wax in the grooves of the metal cylinder to receive the recording.

Fig. 3-3. *This Edison tin-foil phonograph in the Museum at West Orange, N. J., is identical with that illustrated (see Fig. 3-2) in the New York Tribune, March 23, 1878, in connection with the publication of a lecture on "The Phonograph" by Prof. J. W. S. Arnold. It may be compared with the "Graphophone" deposited by C. S. Tainter and Chichester Bell at Smithsonian Institution on October 20, 1881.* (Courtesy of *Edison National Historic Site.*)

Fig. 3-4. *Experimental phonograph (graphophone) with recording in wax-filled grooves of metal drum. This machine was removed from a box marked as having been deposited in the Smithsonian Institution, October 20, 1881, by Chichester Bell and Sumner Tainter. The card on the base reads "G-r-r G-r-r- There are more things in heaven and on earth Horatio than are dreamed of in our philosophy-G-r-r-I am a graphophone and my mother was a phonograph."* (Courtesy of *Smithsonian Institution.*)

After the opening of the sealed box in 1937, in advertisements of the Dictaphone Corporation (Fig. 3-2) and in newspaper stories and publicity it was claimed that the recorded message on this first "graphophone" had been perfectly reproduced on that occasion. Examination of the machine fails to indicate how this could have been accomplished in view of the condition of the air jet reproducing mechanism.[4] Is it possible that the message was simply taken from the yellowed card attached so long ago by sealing wax? Or was special equipment brought in to play it? In any case, the instrument and reproductions of it which appeared in advertisements of the Dictaphone Corporation under the heading "The voice that was buried for 56 years," may be identified easily as the 1878 Edison tin-foil phonograph. (See Fig. 3-3.) The only change which had been made was that instead of using tin foil, wax had been imbedded in the grooves of the iron cylinder and into this wax the voice vibrations had been incised, rather than indented. No reproducing mechanism was shown in the advertisements, nor any mention made as to the method of reproduction used on the celebrated occasion of the opening.

Although this but slightly modified Edison (Fig. 3-4) instrument had been deposited in 1881, it was June 27, 1885 before the first applications for patents were made by the Bells and Tainter. The reason for the long delay may only be conjectured. It may be that the associates at first had decided to wait until the original Edison patent had expired, depositing their notes and experimental apparatus in order to prove priority of conception in case others came along later with similar ideas, or it may have been only that they wished to forestall a possibly adverse decision by the patent examiners on the basis of the Edison British patent of 1878. At least the delay did apparently serve to give the examiners an opportunity to forget the parallel of the Edison United

States patent application of 1878 which had been refused.

Of the five patents applied for by the Bells and Tainter on June 27, 1885 and granted May 4, 1886 the only one (Fig. 3-5) to become important in the later patent litigations was no. 341,214.[5] This substituted for the indenting stylus of the Edison tin-foil phonograph an incising stylus for recording, and for the tinfoil recording surface substituted a wax-coated cardboard cylinder. (See Figs. 3-6 and 3-7.) The unique contribution of this patent was in clearly defining in the specifications for the first time the difference between incising and indenting. Edison had done experimental recording with wax-coated surfaces from the earliest days as is attested to by laboratory notes, published accounts and in his patent specifications. A recording stylus that would only indent tin foil under the same operating conditions would automatically cut a groove of variable depth in a wax surface, due to the differing characteristics of the two materials. As this was as obvious to physicists then as now, it should not seem strange that Edison should have then failed to see anything of patentable value. That Chichester Bell and Sumner Tainter did not themselves realize the importance that their later attorney, the astute Philip Mauro, would attach to this matter of semantics, is indicated by the long delay in filing application when from Tainter's notes it may be seen that they were incising from the beginning. If, as later was maintained in the

---

[4] A tag attached to the machine indicates that the glass nozzle is missing.

[5] U. S. Patents granted May 4, 1886, applied for June 27, 1885, as follows: to Alexander G. Bell, Chichester A. Bell and Charles Sumner Tainter

No. 341,212—Reproducing sounds from phonograph records

No. 341,213—Transmitting and reproducing speech and other sounds by radiant energy

to Chichester A. Bell and Charles S. Tainter

No. 341,214—Recording and reproducing speech and other sounds

to Charles S. Tainter

No. 341,287—Sounds, recording and reproducing

No. 341,288—Sound apparatus for recording and reproducing.

(No Model.)   4 Sheets—Sheet 1.

C. A. BELL & S. TAINTER.

RECORDING AND REPRODUCING SPEECH AND OTHER SOUNDS.

No. 341,214.   Patented May 4, 1886.

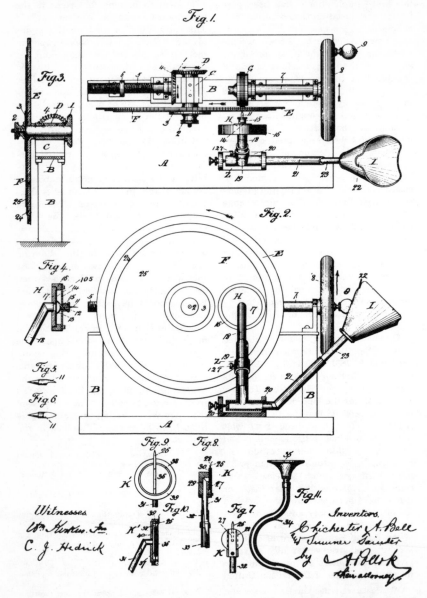

Fig. 3-5A. The Bell-Tainter patent No. 341,214, patented May 4, 1886, sheet 1.

(No Model.)   4 Sheets—Sheet 2.

C. A. BELL & S. TAINTER.

RECORDING AND REPRODUCING SPEECH AND OTHER SOUNDS.

No. 341,214.   Patented May 4, 1886.

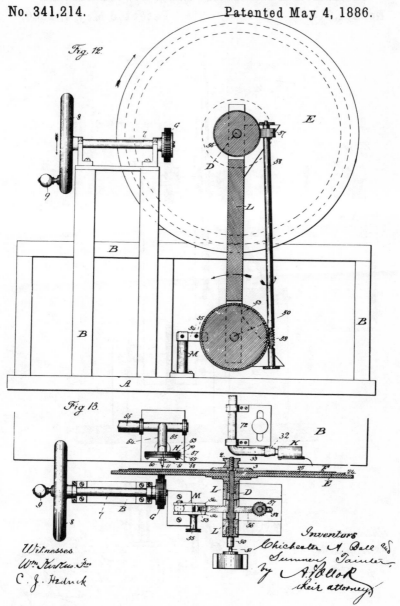

Fig. 12.

Fig. 13.

Witnesses
Wm. Kirtles Jr.
C. J. Hedrick

Inventors
Chichester A. Bell &
Sumner Tainter,
by A. Pollok
their attorneys

Fig. 3-5B. The Bell-Tainter patent No. 341,214, patented May 4, 1886, sheet 2.

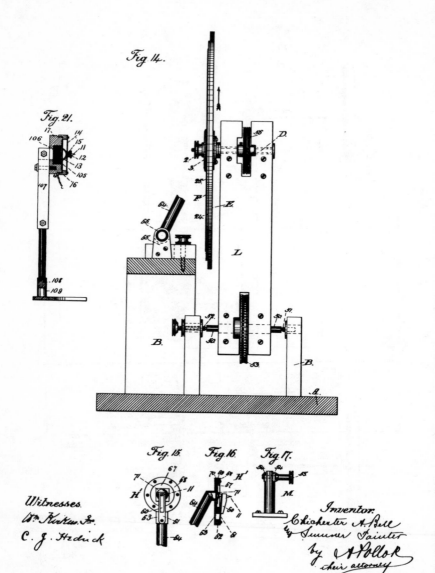

(No Model.)   4 Sheets—Sheet 3.

C. A. BELL & S. TAINTER.

RECORDING AND REPRODUCING SPEECH AND OTHER SOUNDS.

No. 341,214.   Patented May 4, 1886.

Fig. 3-5C. The Bell-Tainter patent No. 341,214, patented May 4, 1886, sheet 3.

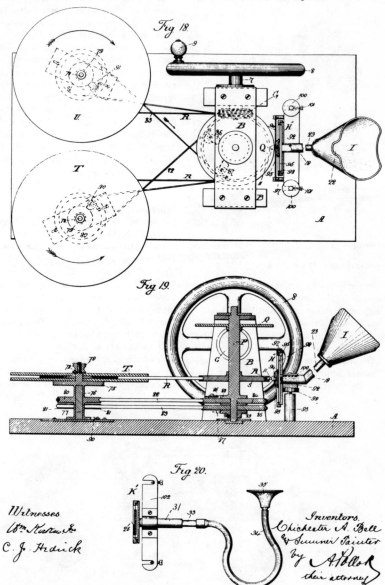

C. A. BELL & S. TAINTER.

RECORDING AND REPRODUCING SPEECH AND OTHER SOUNDS.

No. 341,214.   Patented May 4, 1886.

Fig 18.

Fig 19.

Fig 20.

Witnesses.

Inventors.

Fig. 3-5D. The Bell-Tainter patent No. 314,214, patented May 4, 1886, sheet 4.

courts, this patent embodied the one important concept that made possible the establishment of the commercial phonograph industry; why was application for a patent delayed for four years?

Fig. 3-6. The graphophone of Sumner Tainter patented in 1886. (Courtesy of Smithsonian Institution.)

The implication certainly cannot be avoided. The importance of the subtle difference between indenting and incising was much more apparent to certain attorneys and jurists than it had been to the original inventors! In any case, with this one exception, all of the Bell-Tainter improvements to be later used in the industry in any way had been anticipated by the Edison British patent of 1878, including the method of amplifying the sound in reproduction by means of a jet of compressed air.

The one real contribution resulting from the Bell-Tainter research has been completely overlooked by posterity. This was a continuously variable rpm speed turntable for recording and reproducing disc records, turning slowest when the stylus was at the outer circumference and progressively more rapidly as the stylus approached the center. This permitted a constant speed for the surface passing under the stylus. The failure to adopt and perfect such a method is perhaps one of the chief failures of present technics. As mentioned previously, the type of moving surface is not in itself patentable and both cylinder and disc types were represented in both the Edison British patent of 1878 and the Bell-Tainter patents of 1886.

Upon the issuance of the 1886 patents, Bell and his associates organized the Volta Graphophone Co. at Alexandria, West Virginia. Undoubtedly this was done because of the restrictions on manufacturing in Washington, and the District of Columbia. Headquarters were still maintained in Washington and by reason of a chance demonstration of the graphophone to various men then engaged in the reporting of the proceedings of the congressional bodies

Fig. 3-7. Sumner Tainter's graphophone with accessories for recording and reproducing sound from a coated cardboard tube. (Courtesy of Smithsonian Institution.)

and the Supreme Court, certain men became interested who were to have a great deal to do with the future of the industry. One of these men at this demonstration, Andrew Devine, Reporter of the United States Supreme Court, was destined to later become president of the American Graphophone Co.

In a deposition filed in a phonograph patent case in February of 1896, Devine said that he was immediately impressed with the potential of the machine for dictating. At that time (late 1886 or early 1887) according to Devine, the attention of the Volta Graphophone Co. associates seemed directed towards exploiting it for the reproduction of music, and that these men rather doubted whether the machine could be used successfully for business purposes.

There has never been any question as to the enthusiasm of Mr. Devine for the graphophone and it was he who interested another Supreme Court reporter, James O. Clephane, in the possibility of developing it as an aid to men in their profession, as well as for general business purposes. Clephane was the right sort of person to talk to, for he was already involved in financing development work on the typewriter, later commercially produced as the Remington. He was also interested in the Linotype of Mergenthaler and as his organizer and chief backer was gradually assuring success to that project. A demonstration was arranged of the graphophone to which it was proposed to bring others who might be interested. One of these was John H. White, one of the corps of reporters of the House of Representatives, who later proved to have considerable inventive ability, contributing a number of minor improvements which were patented in his name.

At the time of this demonstration and for some years after, the graphophone employed removable cylinders of cardboard coated with ozocerite, the dimensions six inches long and one and five-sixteenths inches in diameter. A separate speaker was required for recording and reproducing. The motive power was a hand crank and the listening was done with stethoscopic ear tubes. (See Fig. 3-8.) A feature which may perhaps have attracted the favorable attention of Devine was the ease with which any passage of a recording might be located. Due to the extremely small diameter of the record cylinder as compared with the prior tin-foil cylinder, or even the later wax-type cylinders, the lateral displacement was much greater for a given number of

Fig. 3-8. A heavy drive wheel served to stabilize rotation of Tainter's cylinder when rotated by hand. Hearing tubes were used for reproduction. (Courtesy of Smithsonian Institution.)

words recorded. The ease of replacing the record was also important, for in the prior phonograph the tin-foil record was often damaged or destroyed in removing or attempting to replace.

Andrew Devine was a competent and cautious man. Knowing that the Edison patents were basic and the Bell-Tainter patents had not yet been tested in the courts, he proposed during the summer of 1885 that some of those interested in the project pay a personal visit to Edison to see if he might be amenable to the joining of forces, with the object of organizing an entirely new company to manufacture and market the new graphophone as a commercial dictating and transcribing instrument. So Devine, Clephane, and Tainter made arrangements to visit Mr. Edison at Orange. However, according to an article which was published in *Electrical World*, July 1, 1888, Edison was ill and unable to see them. Tainter said, however, that he had exhibited the graphophone to several members of the Edison Speaking Phonograph Co. in New York. Tainter further said that the graphophone which he exhibited to them was " . . . a machine on which records of sound were engraved and reproduced from cylinders of wax, in substantially the same manner as the so-called improved Phonograph of Mr. Edison." At that time, Edison could not have consummated an agreement with the men from Washington, for the Edison Speaking Phonograph Co. was the owner of the Edison patents of 1878. That the stock of this first company was still outstanding is proven by an Annual Certificate and the original phonograph contracts which were found in Edison's desk in 1947. The certificate was dated February 14, 1888, and contained the following items of information:

1. paid in capital stock $600,000.
2. cash value of real estate $0.
3. cash value of its personal estate, *exclusive of patents* about $5,000.
4. amount of debts $0.
5. amount of credits $0.

It appears from these facts that Edison may have felt that his first duty was to his own stockholders who still retained their rights even though the enterprise had been dormant for some time. In any case a review of the patents issued to Edison before and after the attempt of the graphophone promoters to call upon him in the summer of 1885, leaves little doubt that this event incited him to renew his efforts to improve the phonograph. Whether in the interests of his stockholders, or because he felt that the graphophone was a deliberate infringement of his British patent of 1878 is not known. Since the original patent, Edison had been granted two additional United States patents on phonographic improvements (one in 1878 and the other in 1880), both of minor importance. Edison may have been irked to find so many of the improvements which he had projected in his 1878 British patent now incorporated in the Bell-Tainter devices and now patented by them in the U. S. The broad scope and vision of the Edison British patent has never been fully appreciated in this country because the application for a similar patent in the U. S. was denied. Moreover, as far as is known, the specifications (see Fig. 3-1) and rather completely detailed drawings have never been published heretofore. The existence of this important patent, covering numerous suggested improvements, has been quite completely ignored in the fragmentary literature of the industry prior to this work.

Such were the circumstances at the time Edison was able to resume work on the development of the phonograph in the latter part of 1886. In 1888, there were seventeen U. S. patents issued to Edison on phonographic devices, in 1889, nineteen others.[6] By an interesting and fateful coincidence, it was just at the height of this activity that Jesse Lippincott, former Pittsburgh glass magnate, approached Edison with a proposal to merge the rival grapho-

[6] *Edison, the Man and His Work*, George S. Bryan, Alfred A. Knopf, N. Y., 1926.

phone and phonograph forces through a combined sales agency. About the only things the opposing camps had in common by this time were mutual feelings of distrust and suspicion. Naturally under these circumstances, each side hedged in negotiating with Lippincott, fearful of being "sold out" to the other. The amazing thing is that an agreement was finally reached. Undoubtedly the fact that he had millions to invest had something to do with his success!

Lippincott's decision to approach Edison was the result of the suggestion of a friend and partner in some mining ventures, Thomas Lombard, who was also to play a part in the future of the phonograph companies. The approach came at a crucial moment, for a new company had just been formed by Edison and his associates to manufacture the improved Edison phonograph. Now it seems that Lippincott was somewhat of a "gay blade," chartering special trains to New York, throwing lavish parties at the Waldorf and backing Broadway musical shows.[7] If this sort

of conduct be deemed reprehensible and worthy of retribution, Jesse Lippincott did not need to go to hell, for he met several Nemeses right here on earth! One of these was in the person of Ezrah T. Gilliland, an inventor whom Edison had met in his roving days as a telegraph operator and who was now temporarily associated with Edison at the latter's invitation. Gilliland, in the latter part of 1887, made the first working model of the new type of Edison phonograph at a shop furnished for him on Bloomfield Avenue in West Orange. The new instrument was based largely on the concepts of the 1878 British patent and other suggestions offered by Edison.

Edison was forever running out of cash as a result of the great expense of running his research organization. To the credit side of the patent system, it must be admitted that it was largely from the sale of patents, or money advanced in anticipation of patents, that Edison was enabled to carry on the first organized research laboratory of industry. So, as President of the Edison Phonograph Co., Edison gave to Gilliland a contract for exclusive sales rights for

[7] *Edison's Open Door*, Alfred O. Tate, E. P. Dutton & Co., Inc. N. Y., 1938.

Fig. 3-9. Gilliland's development, a so-called "spectacle" device, permitted the recorder to be immediately switched into place instead of the reproducer, or vice versa. (Courtesy of Smithsonian Institution.)

the United States, in return for services rendered. By the terms of this contract, Gilliland would receive a commission of fifteen per cent on all phonographs sold. In Tate's account, much is made of the fact that there had been no performance under this contract by Gilliland up to the time of its surrender by him to Lippincott. Nevertheless it was a valuable contract and both Edison and Gilliland knew it. Moreover, just three weeks to a day before the sale of his rights to Jesse Lippincott, Gilliland had applied for a patent on a most valuable phonographic device. This was the so-called "spectacle" device (Fig. 3-9), which permitted the recorder to be immediately switched into place of the reproducer, or vice versa. This was to become of great importance in the use of the phonograph as a business machine, because for the first time it permitted a quick and convenient means for the user to check back on what had just been recorded, or for recording and transcribing with one machine. The value of the "spectacle" invention is attested to by the fact that it was used on later Edison Business phonographs until well into the 1900's. Under his contract, Gilliland had formed a sales company and had set the price of the stock in his company, as was his right. On June 28, 1888, two companion agreements were drawn up by Edison's attorney. One, between Thomas A. Edison and Jesse Lippincott, provided for the purchase of the Edison Phonograph Co. stock held by Mr. Edison for the sum of five-hundred thousand dollars, to be paid in installments over four months. Included was a stipulation that Edison would try to repurchase 150 shares which he had previously sold to Mrs. Mary Hemenway,[8] of Boston, for which she had paid $22,500. The other agreement was between Ezrah Gilliland and Jesse Lippincott, providing for the purchase of the stock of Gilliland's sales company for two-hundred fifty thousand dollars,

to be paid in five equal monthly installments.[9] The Edison-Lippincott contract provided that the stock involved would be placed in escrow until paid for in full. It is only reasonable to assume that the same course was followed in the case of the Gilliland Sales Co. stock. However, Edison evidently felt that Gilliland should have turned back some of the $50,000 cash he received into the development work. Instead, he and the Edison attorney sailed for Europe on a holiday, both terminating their association with Edison. Tate stated that Gilliland had paid the attorney $75,000 cash, which obviously cannot be true.

By these contracts, Jesse Lippincott's North American Phonograph Co. became the sole proprietor of the Edison phonograph patents in the United States, with manufacturing and development to be carried on by the Edison Phonograph Works. He then returned to his negotiations with the Graphophone Co. officials. In Col. Payne, he met his second Nemesis as a trader, for Payne then shrewdly refused to make anything other than a personal, non-transferable agreement with Lippincott, by which the latter was made exclusive sales agent in the United States for the graphophone, but with the proviso that he agree to purchase a minimum of five thousand grapho-

[8] Mary Hemenway (1820-1894), philanthropist, born in New York of old New England ancestry; daughter of a shipping merchant, Thomas Tilet-

son. Married Augustus Hemenway, merchant of Boston, Mass., who died 1876. Mrs. Hemenway promoted education and physical culture for girls, introducing gymnastics and Swedish system in Boston schools. Interested in civic affairs, organized movement to preserve Old South Meeting House. Also promoted scientific research and archaeology.

[9] Alfred O. Tate, one time Edison private secretary, in *Edison's Open Door*, E. P. Dutton & Co., New York, 1938 stated that this sales contract had been sold by Gilliland to Lippincott for $250,000 cash. That he was mistaken in this is proven by the contracts which were discovered in Edison's desk in the library at Orange in 1947. The implications which he made in his account of a connivance between Gilliland and Edison's attorney do not seem justified by the facts. Tate said that later "Edison instituted an action at law to have the transaction adjudicated but his complaint was answered by a demurrer and the litigation never was carried further. It probably involved nothing more than a breach of ethics."

phones a year. Payne drove a hard bargain, for before the papers were signed, Lippincott had also given the American Graphophone Co. an option to purchase at any time within five years the stock of the Edison Phonograph Co. for what Lippincott was paying Edison for it. The basic Edison phonograph patents were still owned by the old Edison Speaking Phonograph Co. and Lippincott also agreed to try to purchase control of that company. This was never done, for reasons which will become apparent. By these involved transactions, Lippincott's North American Phonograph Co. became the sole sales agent for the Edison phonograph in the United States, and Lippincott, personally, agent for the graphophone in the United States, except for the District of Columbia, Virginia, and Delaware. The graphophone rights for this area had been earlier granted by the American Graphophone Co. to a group of men in Washington, some of whom were also officers and stockholders in the Graphophone Co., and who had organized the Columbia Phonograph Co. These men had set up a tentative scheme of organization in February, 1888 and the Columbia Phonograph Co. was incorporated in January 1889, as its name implies, to also operate as a local company licensed by the North American Phonograph Co., thus also securing sales rights to the Edison phonograph in their territory. The Columbia organization was carried out principally by two United States Supreme Court reporters, Edward D. Easton,[10] and R. F. Cromelin. The predominance of men who were Washington reporters and lawyers in the American Graphophone Co. and Columbia Phonograph Co. organizations may possibly have had something to do with the phenomenal success of these companies later in the jungles of patent law and jurisprudence. It is not surprising, however, that these bright young men had envisioned a great opportunity for the useful employment of these machines for stenographic work in the courts, in the offices of congressmen, and for general business purposes.

But in this maze of corporations and legal agreements, Jesse Lippincott was not destined to find a basis upon which a great industry might be built, but only a monstrous web from which there was to be no escape—save for that which is vouchsafed the unwary fly.

---

[10] Edward Denison Easton, later president of the American Graphophone Co., born Gloucester, Massachusetts, 1856. LL.B. Georgetown University, LL.M. 1889. Became prominent as a shorthand reporter, reported Guiteau trial and Star Route trials. Died 1915.

CHAPTER 4

THE LOCAL PHONOGRAPH COMPANIES

THE plan of operation by which the phonograph and the graphophone were to be launched in the United States was obviously patterned after that of the American Bell Telephone Co., which leased rights to local companies in the various states, or metropolitan areas, such as New York City. Considering that the intent of Jesse Lippincott was to promote the use of these instruments as business machines, the plan was not so outrageously impossible as some of the industry historians would have us believe. Other enterprises than the telephone have both before and after been based on the state's rights distribution plan and many have been successful. It was also thought that ownership of the machines should remain with the companies and that they should be leased and serviced for an annual fee. As the performance (under actual business conditions) of the phonograph or the graphophone had not been proven, it would seem that the leasing of the machines with service provided under contract by the lessor was a sensible means of overcoming an understandable reticence to the outright purchase of machines which would very likely be high priced in the beginning stages of manufacturing.

The fact that within two years of the time of the organization of the North American Phonograph Co. there were organized thirty-three state or regional companies to operate under license in-

dicates the confidence that the men who financed these companies must have had in Jesse Lippincott. Of course one of the considerations which led many to invest in these phonograph companies was a faith in the genius of Thomas A. Edison, who was known to be in the background of the united effort. In retrospect, it seems extremely unlikely that Edison would have been willing to have had his name associated with the enterprise unless he felt that it had a good prospect of complete success. That Edison was jealous of his good name and confident of his ability to produce satisfactory instruments is indicated by certain provisions which were included in a second contract between Lippincott and himself which was executed shortly after the contract covering the sale of the stock of the Edison Phonograph Co. These were, first, that the name of the company to be organized by Lippincott was to be "The American Phonograph Co."; second, that the instruments the Edison Phonograph Works were to supply should be called "phonographs" and that the instruments to be supplied by the American Graphophone Co. should be called "phonograph-graphophones." (See Fig. 4-1.) Another provision was that the phonograph and the phonograph-graphophone should be placed before all prospective users as a free choice. To effectuate this provision and to prevent unauthorized changes, Edison also required that official models of both the phonograph and the phono-graph-graphophone be deposited with him. Of course this may be construed as an effort by Edison to circumscribe the graphophone in its then existing state and to prevent changes which would be needed to make of it a successful instrument of commerce. On the other hand, tacitly recognizing the validity of the Bell-Tainter patents as he was doing by the signing of the agreements, it might be construed as a legitimate precaution to prevent the illegal use by the American Graphophone Co. of the latest improvements which Edison had recently applied to the phonograph.

These were the final conditions preparatory to the setting into operation of the great plans which had been prepared by Jesse Lippincott. The Certificate of Organization of the North American Phonograph Co. carried the names of Lippincott, Thomas R. Lombard,[1] George S. Evans, George H. Fitzwilson and John Robinson. The capital stock of 66,000 shares was given a par value of $100 each. The beginning capitalization was stated as $4 million, covering forty thousand shares at par. Surely this was no shoestring venture to be virtually ignored by later historians of the industry!

The work of organizing local companies was immediately undertaken with great enthusiasm by Lippincott and his associates and within two years there were thirty-three local companies to operate under the aegis of the North American Phonograph Co. It became apparent early that many problems of inter-company relationships would arise and that a need existed for exchanging useful information gained from experience in arranging demonstrations, promoting sales, and methods of servicing. For these reasons the National Phonograph Association was formed by representatives of the thirty-three local companies. The first annual convention was

held at Chicago, May 28th and 29th, 1890. As this sequence of events really marked the inception of the commercial phonograph industry, there were no trade papers devoted especially to it. In fact, many well-established industries of those days operated without the aid of the trade papers which play such an important role in disseminating information concerning activities within most industries today. Such news stories concerning the early activities of Lippincott and the local companies as appeared infrequently in the press were fragmentary and often inaccurate. Therefore, the proceedings of this and the following conventions are the best sources of information as to what actually occurred during those troubled years.

Fig. 4-1. This Tainter Graphophone operated by means of a treadle similar to the early sewing machines. The reproducer is in position and connects to hearing tubes. The recorder (in upright position) may be swung down after reproducer is lifted clear. (Courtesy of Oliver Read collection.)

The first convention of the National Phonograph Association was called to order by Edward D. Easton, president of the Columbia Phonograph Co., of Washington, District of Columbia. Mr. J. H. McGilvea of Roanoke, Virginia, official of the Volta Graphophone Co. was designated as temporary chairman. Mr. R. F. Cromelin became secretary and Henry D. Goodwin, of Milwaukee, treasurer. The first topic of discussion was how to overcome the widespread opposition which the phonograph was receiving from stenographers, similar to the problem that was then also confronting the pioneers of the typewriter

---

[1] Thomas R. Lombard, a mining prospector, had been associated with Jesse Lippincott in some mining ventures while the latter was owner of the Rochester Tumbler Co., Pittsburgh, Pa.

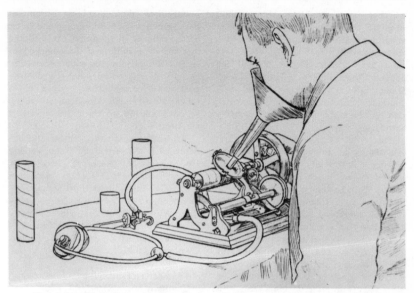

Fig. 4-2A. "Talking to the Graphophone." (Courtesy of Harper's Weekly.)

industry. Many persons then employed as secretaries or clerks were fearful that the introduction of these machines would endanger their jobs—creating technological unemployment it was later called! A typical minor question before the convention was as to which company the sales of supplies should go in the case of traveling men who might wish to carry a business phonograph from one territory to another. Especially important was the question as to

Fig. 4-2B. "Listening to the Graphophone." (Courtesy of Harper's Weekly.)

whether more portable machines might supplant the heavier ones. The lighter machines were the graphophones which operated with a foot treadle (Fig. 4-1) or a hand crank (Fig. 4-2), and the heavier machines were the Edison phonographs (See Figs. 4-3 and 4-4) operated with electric motors, which also required heavy storage or primary batteries.

The rental of all machines was first established at forty dollars per year, which in terms of purchasing power was of course much greater than it is today. Mr. Easton proposed that the rental of foot treadle machines (Fig. 4-5) be increased to fifty dollars per year, but that the hand power graphophones be retained at forty dollars. He also proposed that the rental of the Edison electric motor phonographs be increased to sixty dollars per year. In view of certain later developments, this proposal seems significant, for Easton was one of the founders and president of the Columbia Phonograph Co. which had been originally planned to deal in graphophones even before Lippincott had organized North American. Easton was destined later to become president of the American Graphophone Co. This proposal was not carried, however, and in any case the association had no powers over prices.

A resolution was proposed and carried to the effect that the North American Phonograph Co. be requested to permit the member companies to drop the mandatory franchise provision which required that each company carry on its letterhead and in all advertising the following phrase:

"Acting under the authority of the North American Phonograph Co. and Jesse H. Lippincott, sole licensees of the American Graphophone Co."

Easton stated that at the time there were sixty machines in use by congressmen. He also stated that the capital stock of his company was a quarter of a million dollars. This would seem to indicate that as this was but one of thirty-three member companies, the

half-million dollars which Lippincott had agreed to pay Edison for the stock of the Edison Phonograph Co. and the quarter of a million dollars agreed to with Gilliland for his valuable patent and sales rights had not been disproportionately large. The eventual capitalization of North American had been set at $6,600,000, so the expectations of all were high.

Mr. James Clephane, one of the organizers of the American Graphophone Co. and also of one of the local companies, the Eastern Pennsylvania Phonograph Co., brought forward some comments indicative of the existing situation. After stating that his company then had out under rental in Philadelphia between 150 and 170 machines, Mr. Clephane said;

"The Eastern Pennsylvania Phonograph Company spent $3,000,000 on improved phonographs. Mr. Macdonald, at the expense of the Eastern Pennsylvania Phonograph Company got up an improved machine which did away with all adjustments; a machine which I am happy to say received the earnest endorsement of Mr. Easton. He wrote us that he had put aside his graphophone and was then using the Macdonald phonograph and liked it very much. When Mr. Edison returned from Europe this machine was called to his attention and of course he was not to be outdone and the result was the phonograph which you now have. Now we propose to start forth upon the basis which Mr. Edison has given us of a mailing cylinder and give you here a machine in that phonograph which combines every single qualification which you gentlemen can possibly desire."

It is evident from the testimony of this important figure in the Graphophone Co. that the graphophones were not giving satisfactory performance. It is evident also that Edison was ever willing to adopt suggestions for improving the phonograph, no matter whence they came.

Fig. 4-3. The Class M Edison Electric phonograph first produced in 1889 by North American employed a wax cylinder and was powered by a 2½-volt DC motor.

Fig. 4-4. Edison's Class M Electric phonograph, 1889, equipped with spectacle type recorder-reproducer. Power was furnished by a Grenet cell. The speaking tube was used for recording. (Courtesy of Edison National Historic Site.)

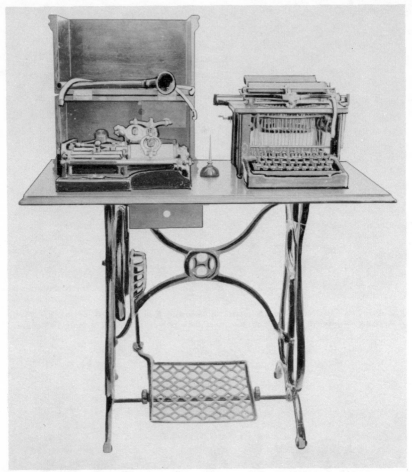

Fig. 4-5. Photograph taken September 24, 1889 shows Edison's foot-powered model mounted on treadle stand. Typewriter shown was of current design. (Courtesy of Edison National Historic Site.)

A need for more sensitive recorders was a chief topic of discussion at the convention. Quite often it was necessary to shout to secure a satisfactory record. Mr. Louis Glass introduced a resolution of importance in assessing the reasons for the eventual disaster. His resolution, in part, was as follows:

"that all parties, that is, the American Graphophone Co., the North American Phonograph Co. and Mr. T. A. Edison, shall direct all their efforts

to that end; that they give us one instrument for correspondence, stenographic work and for amusement."

Mr. Chadbourne of the Minnesota Phonograph Co. said that he was heartily in favor of Mr. Glass' resolution, but he added,

"If these two companies which are fighting each other like Kilkenny cats, can't be made to come together and use a little sense in this thing, I think it is time the subcompanies instructed them what to do."

Mr. Easton then arose and asked Mr. Chadbourne where he had received his information that the two companies were fighting like "Kilkenny cats." Chadbourne replied,

"I was told so by Mr. Tainter, himself, a year ago."

This statement was greeted with cheers, which brought Samuel Insull,[2] Edison's personal representative, to his feet. Mr. Insull said,

"Might I be permitted to make a remark? It takes two to make a fight in any case. If the two interests are fighting like Kilkenny cats, all I can say is, the fight is all on one side, because I know on our side, the Edison side, there is no fight at all."

Col. Payne, the president of the American Graphophone Co. then arose and said,

"We have never had any fight with Mr. Edison, a year or two ago or any other time, and I doubt whether Mr. Tainter ever said so in this world."

Mr. Chadbourne replied to this,

"I will give you the words of Mr. Tainter, if you will allow me to explain just a moment. I took dinner with Mr. Tainter at the Graphophone factory. I said to Mr. Tainter that the cylinder of the graphophone was a superior one, and that I would like to have him make some to go on the Edison machine. He got mad at once and said, 'Thomas A. Edison can go to hell! (great laughter) He hasn't got anything that he didn't steal from me. I would like to see him use that cylinder or any part of my machine.'" (great laughter).

Mr. Clarkson, of the Florida Phonograph Co. then arose and corroborated what Mr. Chadbourne had said, stating

that he had been present at the dinner at the Graphophone factory.

This amusing but significant episode was followed by the adoption of Glass' resolution that all of the companies desired one machine. Two other statements of some importance were made at this convention. One was the announcement of the availability of 6" × 2¼" diameter cylinders for the Edison phonographs. The former Edison cylinders had all been 4" × 2¼", the same size as the later standard musical cylinders. The new six inch length became the standard size for dictating machines until the 1940's, when acetate discs replaced cylinders. The graphophone cylinders were 1⁵⁄₁₆" in diameter by 6" long. The other important statement was made by Louis Glass of the Pacific Coast Phonograph Co., who stated that all of the money his company had made was through the use of the nickel-in-the-slot phonograph, upon the coin mechanism of which he had secured a patent. Then Mr. Gottschalk of the Automatic Phonograph Exhibition Co., which had been operating in the Glass territory, complained of having had to pay Glass "blood money" to use the multiple tube listening device, as he found that Glass had it patented. He announced that in retaliation the Automatic Phonograph Co. was buying up patents on all coin operating mechanisms and that it would "step on the toes of all infringers."

Thus at the very first convention of the phonograph companies these things were apparent:

1. Edison was continuing to improve the phonograph.
2. The graphophone was showing weakness in performance.
3. The demand was for one standard instrument.
4. A trend was under way towards use for entertainment purposes.
5. Tainter was the source of the rift between the parent companies.

If these matters were to be seen from the proceedings of the first convention

---

[2] The later well-known utility magnate.

they were conclusively proven by the second, held in New York City in June, 1891. At this meeting there were represented only nineteen companies as against the thirty-three of the previous year. Despite the difficulties that had been encountered during the first full year since the prior meeting, good relations existed between the local companies and North American. This was reflected in the rising vote of welcome extended to Jesse Lippincott by the assembled representatives. At this meeting A. W. Clancy was elected president of the association; Edward D. Easton, vice-president; K. McClellan, secretary; and James L. Amden, later to play an important role in the legal tangles of the industry, was elected treasurer.

One of the parent companies was conspicuous because of the absence of a representative. So a resolution was introduced extending such an invitation and directed to Col. Payne, president of the American Graphophone Co.; Thomas A. Edison, President of the Edison Phonograph Works; Samuel Insull, Mr. Edison's personal representative; and also to the North American Phonograph Co. The resolution was amended to omit the names of persons, inviting representatives of the three companies to attend. Subsequently, by phonogram (record) from the Edison Phonograph Works at nearby West Orange, New Jersey, a message was received inviting the representatives of the companies to visit the Edison plant the following afternoon to witness a demonstration of a new super-sensitive diaphragm and other improvements soon to be made available on the Edison machines. It was decided to accept.

At this convention there were a number of coin slot phonograph operators and the problem of securing suitable musical cylinders was discussed. These men were to be particularly interested in the demonstration at the Edison Plant. James Amden, whose Ohio Phonograph Co. like others had turned to exploitation of the phonograph for entertainment, stated that there were then eighteen interference cases pending in the patent office on coin operating devices, one of the parties being the Automatic Phonograph Exhibition Co. Other of the representatives stated that they had received letters from that company warning all infringers. The fact is that the companies had been forced to turn to the entertainment field in order to stay in business.

Historically, the most important information to be derived from the proceedings of the second convention of the National Phonograph Association was contained in a poll taken of the number of machines in each of three categories which the member companies then had out on rental.[3] This poll definitely discloses the motivation for the later bitter speech of Col. Payne, president of the American Graphophone Co., as well as the answers to many of the untruths and false accusations against Edison and the Edison interests which were given such wide circulation in newspapers and trade papers by clever publicists subsequently employed by the Graphophone Co. The poll proved conclusively, even to those men whose interests were inseparably identified with the American Graphophone Co., that the graphophones had not proved acceptable, neither as a business machine nor as an entertainment device. For every graphophone in use, there were approximately fifty phonographs. Incidentally, as the poll showed that there were then out on rental only something over three thousand machines of all types, how could Lippincott be expected to buy five thousand graphophones a year when only one user out of fifty was choosing that instrument? The trend towards use of the phonograph for entertainment was emphasized by the fact that more than one out of three were coin operated.

In response to the request from the convention that his company be represented at the convention, Col. Payne, president of the American Graphophone Co. appeared and was introduced. In his opening remarks he reminded his

---

[3] Complete poll in appendix.

listeners that his company had been organized in 1887 to undertake the exploitation of the Graphophone in the United States and Canada under license from the Volta Graphophone Co. He stated that in 1888 Jesse Lippincott had made a proposition to undertake the introduction of the Graphophone in the United States, and after considerable negotiation a contract was entered into, the terms of which were known to all of the members present. Col. Payne referred to the demand for a single machine but said that he was not going to discuss it, as he felt that it was a matter of secondary importance, even though he conceded that it might be desirable.

Col. Payne said that wisely, or unwisely, the Graphophone had been practically withdrawn from the field by the action of the North American Phonograph Co. and that last summer it had been proposed to enter into a new contract. It seems obvious that Payne was trying to lay the blame for the failure of the Graphophone to Lippincott, even though the poll showed that in Washington, where his own colleagues of the Graphophone Co. were the founders and managers of the Columbia Phonograph Co., of four-hundred machines out on rental only twelve to fifteen were graphophones! Despite these facts which were well known to all present, Payne made it clear that the American Graphophone Co. intended to hold Lippincott to his contract to purchase five thousand graphophones per year.[4] The Graphophone Co. was flatly refusing to acknowledge that the poor performance in service of the graphophone should have any effect on the contract.

The phonograph was also far from a complete success as a business machine. One reason was that the machines had not yet been equipped with some of the foolproof starting and stopping devices, as well as the locating and resetting contrivances which made the later Ediphone such a convenient instrument to use. Other objections, such as cumbersomeness and the opposition of stenographers have already been mentioned. Some representatives stated at the convention that the slot machines were proving very profitable, others stated that they had dropped them because of service difficulties. Amden of the Ohio Phonograph Co. said that he found the secret of the service problem was in the grouping of a number of machines in one location. This also provided the patrons with a choice of selection. Here was the origin of the penny arcade, in modified form still in existence. Even through the darkest days ahead, there was never to be a time for more than fifty years when the musical cylinders would not be turning somewhere! Amden also told of having some very handsome and expensive slot machines made to his order by the Standard Locomotive Works of Cincinnati. These must have been the first deluxe juke boxes. The tradition has been well carried on, for today some of our juke boxes from the front have been said to resemble more a diesel locomotive than a musical instrument!

As planned, the representatives of the companies visited the Edison factory. There they watched phonographs and record blanks in the process of manufacture. The new, more sensitive recording diaphragm was demonstrated, among other improvements which had been developed. Most important to those interested in the entertainment field were two developments in the manufacture of musical records. The first was the supplying of musical cylinders to the companies through North American. A sample lot of six was to be sent out to each company with lists of records available, the price each to be fifty cents. The second was a service of duplicating records made by the companies at the same price, North American to receive a royalty of eight cents per record. However, there were two classes of duplicated records which had been demonstrated, those by a transcribing method and others which apparently involved a molding method.

---

[4] Payne's speech complete in appendix.

There seemed to be some confusion about the difference and Walter Miller of the Edison Phonograph Works at the meeting next day was asked by President Clancy to clarify the matter. Mr. Miller proceeded to do so by referring to the second type, as follows:

"He (Mr. Edison) would have to have a guarantee before he would go ahead with that, but as to these duplicates, we are willing to furnish them at fifty cents each. The cylinders, by the more expensive process, are absolutely perfect; and you can get as many as a million duplicates from one master; whereby, by the other process you cannot get over two-hundred, although we are not prepared to say positively how many duplicates we can furnish under this process of which we are now speaking."

Mr. McClellan then said,

"Mr. Miller, I suppose all the musical records you send will have the title on the end of the cylinder, as we saw arranged at the laboratory yesterday?"

Mr. Miller replied,

"Yes sir, they will be fixed up in that way."

This is important, for the inscribing of a title into the end of a record, as well as the much larger number of high quality copies indicates molded, rather than a transcribed record. Now Edison had applied for a patent June 30, 1888 on a process of duplicating phonograms involving the vaporizing metal in a vacuum as a means of rendering the record surface conductive, which would then be plated and when backed by heavier metal, used as a mold for making duplicates. (See Fig. 4-6). This patent was granted October 18, 1892. Apparently this was the process which Edison was offering to develop to a commercial basis if suffi-

Fig. 4-6. Original mold used by Dr. Schulze-Berge and C. Wurth in 1889. (Courtesy of Edison National Historic Site.)

cient interest was shown. This seems to be indicated in a statement by Mr. Clephane in summing up the situation, as follows:

"As I understand from Mr. Miller, there is a class of cylinders that Mr. Edison will furnish without having the exclusive right to do so; but that the more perfect cylinders he cannot undertake to furnish unless the gentlemen agree to support the manufacturer altogether themselves and give their orders to him. Here is an opportunity, it seems to me, to obtain a very fine cylinder at a very low price, if the gentlemen themselves feel like suspending their manufacture."

However, sufficient interest was not forthcoming and so the introduction of molded records was not achieved for another decade. According to Mr. Will Hayes, sole surviving member of the Edison staff of those days, a great deal of experimental work by Walter Miller and Jonas W. Aylesworth was done before the first commercially produced gold-molded records were issued by the later National Phonograph Co. in 1901. The principal difficulties concerned the fact that the shrinkage in cooling made it necessary to have differently dimensioned styli for recording and playback, as well as a different number of threads per inch in the lead screws of the recording and reproducing mechanisms. Also, the early records were cut so deeply that it was not possible to withdraw the molded cylinders—the shrinkage in cooling was insufficient.

One of the important factors that was responsible for the almost total collapse of the musical entertainment field was inherent in the lack of quality control of the records, as every machine could also be used to record. Consequently, all of the local companies were record manufacturers, as well as most of the operators of coin machines. Almost from the first it had been found possible to copy records by rerecording, or by use of pantographic devices, but always with a loss in quality from the original. Good recorders were scarce and each of the local companies jealously guarded secrets which they had discovered for getting better records. Amden remarked, for instance, that his company was being paid five dollars each by operators for records of an entertainer by the name of Brady. Amden raised the question as to what protection the local companies would have against the misappropriation of such valuable records sent in for duplication. Actually, although a resolution was passed recommending that the companies cooperate with the Edison Phonograph Works in the matter, nothing came of it.

As a last bit of business, a committee of three was appointed to investigate the relationships of the parent companies. The net result of this as far as securing a more lenient attitude on the part of the American Graphophone Co. was concerned was nil. The Graphophone Co. from this time forward attempted to win its fight for financial success through the courts, rather than in trying to compete technically with Mr. Edison. The Graphophone Co. immediately sought to prevent the companies from doing business with Lippincott, but despite the obstacles placed in their way many of the local companies

persisted. In fact, at the 1893 convention of the phonograph companies there were twenty-two companies represented as against the nineteen of 1891.

Men of ability and vision had been attracted to the phonograph industry as well as the sharpies and get-rich-quick promoters who received so much attention in the press. The better class was well represented on the program of the 1893 convention. A. W. Clancy was re-elected president of the association and gave a talk on "The Phonograph in the Schools." During the course of his talk Clancy quoted Mr. Edison as having said,

"I will yet live to see the day that phonographs will be almost as common in homes as pianos and organs are today."

Prophetic indeed and a quite complete refutation of the attitude later attributed to Edison by his former secretary. A paper was presented by Mr. Harry P. Godwin on "The Phonograph in Musical Education" and R. T. Haines gave an address on "The Phonograph for Social Progress." Dr. R. S. Rosenthal, one of the first pioneers in the use of the phonograph for language instruction, spoke on his work. Rosenthal in later years sent out thousands of sets of foreign language courses, with blanks for the return of recitations by students. This set the example for others, including the International Correspondence Schools.

By this time there had been an extensive, but little publicized development of the potential uses of the phonograph in the study of acoustics, phonetics, voice training and in the preservation of sound for scientific, ethnological and educational purposes. For these reasons there was a definite need for a light weight machine like the graphophone if equipped with a spring motor and certain of the Edison improvements. The proceedings of this meeting disclosed that Edison was willing to push ahead as rapidly as the status of the industry would permit. The failure of the companies to take advantage of the plan of Edison to develop the molding process was due to the high prices that some of the expert recorders with popular talent were able to get for original records from the coin slot phonograph operators. These men worked through various territories, specializing on the securing of good "locations," even as now, but generally securing their supplies and records from the local companies. It is well known that some of the companies were producing somewhat risque cylinders for use in certain locations, as this problem was discussed in the 1893 meetings, also.

Thus, the facility with which cylinder recordings might be made anywhere actually became a block in the development of the cylinder phonograph as a musical instrument of cultural value. The disc machines, even of the earliest period never afforded this opportunity for making records here, there, and everywhere. This overlooked fact may seem overweighted in these days of 45's and LP's. Consider, however, that in those days there was no positive way to identify the source of cylinder records—all blanks looked pretty much alike. As blanks could be secured without restriction anywhere, there was little possibility of tracing the origin of a given recording. Under these conditions there was a great deal of pirating of desirable recordings by unauthorized copying. Some years later an abortive attempt was made to restrict the manufacture of musical records to the original parent companies by selling blanks for export only. Actually, local manufacture of records continued right up to 1902 when the obvious superiority of studio recorded and molded records to the locally recorded "original" and duplicated records made the latter obsolete and unsaleable.

Although the molding process was not at this time developed for use, the North American Phonograph Co. continued the issuance of directly recorded, or "original" cylinders to the member companies. There were fifteen supplemental lists to September of 1892, the last one listing twenty-four military band numbers, indicating the improvement of recording technics. By March 30, 1893, there had been twenty-five supplements. The latter two listed cornet solos by the great Jules Levey, piccolo solos by R. K. Franklin, songs by tenors Ed Francis and Will Nankerville, and baritone solos by Ed Clarence. The recording of those days was done by arranging tiers of recording phonographs on shelves, with the several recording horns directed to the performers.

Some of the local companies also developed improved recording technics in the making of musical records. Calvin G. Childs, later with the Columbia Phonograph Co. and eventually recording director of the Victor Talking Machine Co., gained his early experience with the Ohio Phonograph Co. These were the days when Fred Gaisberg played piano accompaniments while his brother Will supervised the intricacies of recording. Both later became recording experts for the Gramophone Co. Victor Emerson, Walter Phillips, Thomas Macdonald and others who were to become renowned in the later days of disc recording, were now learning the tricks of capturing voices and instruments in the wax with no other force than the voice or instruments themselves. In this connection, it should be noted that the lateral disc process of Berliner did not become a complete success until after the adoption of solid wax blanks for recording—initiated by Edison as cylindrical tablets in 1888, plus the incising concept of the Bell's and Tainter.

As time went on it became apparent that the leasing plan, which might have eventually been successful if the function of the phonograph had been confined to the business machine field, was not suited to the entertainment field involving the manufacture and sale of records. Lippincott, broken in health, had been forced into bankruptcy by his creditors, but chiefly by the American Graphophone Co. Samuel Insull assumed presidency of North American for a short time, succeeded by Thomas R. Lombard prior to the 1893 convention. Thomas A. Edison, as a chief creditor of North American, broached a plan to Lombard whereby all manufacturing of phonographs and blanks might revert back to the parent companies, North American and the Edison Phonograph Works, to take care of the situation presented by the shift from the business to the entertainment field. At this time the American Graphophone Co. was itself in the process of reorganization, having produced no machines for more than two years. Tainter, no longer with the Graphophone Co., was in Washington trying desperately to convert his unsuccessful small diameter cardboard cylinder machine into a coin-operated machine for use at the World's Fair of 1893.

The plan which was presented to the companies by president Lombard was that each of the local companies should return all sales rights in their territories to North American in return for a straight ten per cent royalty on all sales made in each of the territories. This was a most liberal offer and if it had been effectuated would have made the stockholders of the local companies wealthy. But the industry was in a state of anarchy—threats and false accusations were being hurled against the Edison people by the men who were trying to resuscitate the Graphophone enterprise—many did not know whom to believe. According to Tate, Lombard believed the plan could be consummated only if Edison would agree to assume the presidency of North American. This was agreed to and a special meeting of representatives was called to be held in Detroit. The plan was approved by all of the companies except the Columbia Phonograph Co., of Washington, District of Columbia, which had by this time received exclusive rights to the graphophone for the United States.

Alfred O. Tate, in *Edison's Open Door*,[5] lays a great deal of the blame

[5] E. P. Dutton & Co., New York, 1938.

for the failure of the North American enterprise to what he alleges was Edison's aversion to the use of the phonograph for entertainment. He stated in his book that early in 1894 Edison had left a note on his desk to this effect;

"Tate—I don't want the phonograph sold for amusement purposes, it is not a toy. I want it sold for business purposes only."

However, it is known that Tate was interested in the talking doll enterprise, which also caused Edison many headaches, so it may have been in reference to this that the note had been left, and as to the note, we have but Tate's word. Also, by Tate's own account, it was over the phonograph business that he and Edison had parted company. On the other hand, we know that North American continued to produce musical records until it ceased functioning. It is also well known that the company which Edison organized to take its place designed its products primarily for the entertainment and home phonograph market. As a bit of rather conclusive evidence that Tate was wrong, a picture of the North American display at the World's Fair of 1893 shows a phonograph with the words on it "Edison Household Phonograph." This was published in the proceedings of the 1893 convention. This seems to indicate that Edison had his eye on the potential of the home phonograph market and that it was no secret kept from the local companies. In this there is no intimation that Edison was then preparing to scuttle the ship, as Tate intimates, but was continuing to press forward, following any course that seemed to offer a reasonable promise of success. This had been stated by President Clancy of the National Association of Phonograph Companies at the Detroit meeting who quoted Edison as having said to him,

"I desire every man to have an equal chance with me to get back his share of the profit, who in any way put a

single dollar into the phonograph interests."

As further evidence that he was trying
to effectuate his program, North American prepared a series of records especially for demonstration at this great
fair.

But it was not to be. In 1894 suit
was brought by the American Graphophone Co. against the Edison Phonograph Works on the basis of alleged
infringement of the Bell-Tainter patents. The defense, instead of being predicated on the superiority of the Edison
patents, was based on the premise that
the Edison Phonograph Works had secured the right to use the patents
owned by the American Graphophone
Co. by reason of the agreements which
that company had made with Lippincott and between Lippincott and North
American. That this was a tactical error
of the first magnitude became apparent
from the verdict which was reached
only after a considerable delay due in
part to the death of the judge before
whom the case was first scheduled to be
tried. Judge Green of the Circuit Court
of New Jersey, his successor, rendered
the following verdict:

"I am unable to discover that the
agreements of August 1 and August
10, 1888, purport to invest the defendant with a perpetual license to manufacture and sell under the complainant's patents. Nor do I perceive that
Lippincott had authority to so deal
with the complainant's patents. His
rights with respect to the graphophone patents are to be found in the
two agreements between him and the
complainant,—one original, and the
other supplemental,—dated respectively March 26, and August 6, 1888.
Plea of defendant overruled, with
leave to file an answer within 30
days."

Although appealed, the decision was
later upheld by Judge Acheson, on
June 24, 1895.

Contrary to the version given by
Tate, who admits to having left the

employment of Edison on the first of
May, 1894, it seems evident that it had
been the bringing of the suit which revealed to Edison the bungling of his
advisors and which brought him to the
inescapable conclusion that he should
promptly take steps to get back the
ownership of his own patents. Consider
these facts. The score thus far, as to
the actual introduction of improvements, was heavily on Edison's side.
The Bells and Tainter had long since
made their first and last contributions to
the science of sound recording and reproduction. Eight years had elapsed
without a single patent being issued to
any of the three. The score stood, for
the Bells, Tainter, and Thomas H.
Macdonald, who had joined the Graphophone forces, a total of ten graphophone patents; for Thomas A. Edison
alone, eighty-one phonograph patents!

The Graphophone Co. had secured
but recently the services of Macdonald,
who had earlier attracted the favorable
attention of Edward Easton, the latter
in process of reorganizing the graphophone enterprise and effecting a virtual
amalgamation with it of his Columbia
Phonograph Co., as sales agent; with
a view of re-entering the market.
Edison knew of this, yet here he was
being stymied by the same stupidity
and ineptitude on the part of his own
associates which had so recently cost
him the leadership of the lighting industry which he had established.

Today it seems an unfathomable mystery as to why Edison's attorneys never
saw fit to make a test with either the
American Graphophone Co., or with the
later Gramophone Co., of the superior
patents which he now sought to reclaim. Even at that moment, in graphophones then being prepared for the
market, Macdonald without leave had
incorporated the Edison tapered mandrel, the Edison solid metallic wax
blank, the Edison sapphire cutter and
other Edison improvements. From this
time forward the records of the two
companies were interchangeable.

Edison, as chief stockholder and creditor of the North American Phonograph

Co. decided to petition North American into bankruptcy in order to regain control of his patents against the advice of his personal secretary, Mr. Tate, and of his legal counsel. In view of the tactics of the Graphophone Co. affecting other companies in a similar position to that of North American a little later on, the wisdom of Edison in making this decision must be admired. Unquestionably, with the adverse decision standing against his own Edison Phonograph Works, it would be a simple matter for the Graphophone atttorneys to secure an injunction and an accounting against North American as a prelude to acquiring title to the Edison patents. This was prevented by Edison's swift and unexpected decision and the result is best summed up by a short story which appeared in the *New York World*, January 12, 1896, as follows:

"Litigation in which inventor T. A. Edison, Edison Phonograph Works and John R. Hardin, receiver for the North American Phonograph Co. have been involved for a long time, ended yesterday. Vice-Chancellor Emery in Chancery Chambers in Newark, signed a compromise offer by Edison and agreed to by Receiver Hardin and creditors, stockholders, and counsel. Receiver Hardin receives patents on all phonographs applied for since August 1, 1888, Edison to receive $65,000 with interest, total $75,000 on a note, deducted for reason of a sale."

This cleared the way for a sale of the assets, which were put up for auction on February 5, by order of the court. Twelve thousand shares of Edison Phonograph Co. stock was put up as one lot, and all other assets as the other. For each of the lots there was but a single bid of $50,000 for each, and on the property as a whole, a single bid of $99,500. Edison thereby became for the first time sole proprietor of his phonograph enterprise.

By Tate, this is painted as a somewhat shady deal which in some sense defrauded the local companies of rights for which he states that they had paid more than one million dollars. But to anyone who makes a thorough study of the phonograph industry, it will be apparent that Edison moved just within the nick of time. Within a year, North American and the Edison patents would have become the property of the avaricious Graphophone Co. Thomas A. Edison truly loved the phonograph, he still had a great deal more to contribute to it. He had withstood the shock of the monetary loss and loss of control of his multi-million dollar Edison General Electric Co. stoically, but he had determined not to lose the phonograph —at least not entirely. Perhaps final judgment should rest with what he was yet to do with it.

Jesse Lippincott, organizer and first president of North American Phonograph Company; b. Mount Pleasant, Pennsylvania, Feb. 18, 1842, d. Newton Center, Massachusetts, April 18, 1894.

CHAPTER 5

THE NEW GRAPHOPHONE

In 1893, after the Detroit convention of the local phonograph companies had tentatively approved Lombard's plan for restoring all sales rights to the North American Phonograph Co., about a year was required to straighten out difficulties and to put through contracts with each of the companies. The Columbia Phonograph Co. was the only company to refuse to sign an agreement. This was because of the unique position of this company by reason of its having acquired sales rights for the graphophone for the District of Columbia, Maryland, and Delaware *prior* to the organization of North American and the resulting acquisition by Lippincott by personal contract of the graphophone sales rights for the rest of the United States. This situation enabled the Columbia Phonograph Co. to claim that these rights, which had been conceded to Lippincott when Columbia was functioning under the local company plan in exchange for equal sales rights for the Edison phonograph in the same territory, now reverted to the Columbia Phonograph Co.

Edward D. Easton, shrewd President of Columbia, could see that here was an opportunity of a lifetime. He gathered together his associates, among them R. F. Cromelin, Andrew Devine, and James Clephane and they agreed upon a plan, which if successful, would put them in control of what everyone could see was eventually to be a great industry. To assist them in their scheme, Easton enlisted the aid of a brilliant young Washington attorney, Philip Mauro, who was to justify his confidence time and again.

Briefly, the plan was this. If these men, some of whom already possessed stock in the American Graphophone Co., could gain control of that company and its Bell-Tainter patents, they might well be able to take advantage of the demoralized state of the industry and as Edison was not in possession of his own patents on phonographic patents they might be able to drive him from the phonograph field, just as he had been driven so recently from the electric lighting industry by others.[1] As the stock of the American Graphophone Co. was then practically worthless due to the inability of the management to produce a successful machine and the consequent inability of Lippincott to fulfill his contract, it was fairly simple to execute the first step of the plan. On May 1, 1893, the new group assumed control of American Graphophone, with Edward D. Easton as president.

The next step was the appointment of Thomas H. Macdonald as factory manager, who had attracted the favorable attention of Easton by improvements which he had been able to make to the earlier Edison phonograph, and which Edison had adopted. There were thousands of the inoperable Bell-Tainter graphophones in the fac-

[1] *Edison's Open Door,* Alfred O. Tate, E. P. Dutton & Co., New York, 1938.

tory and these were promptly scrapped. By the greatest economy and borrowing a few dollars from a few friends of the company, it was found possible to put together a new type of machine which would work satisfactorily.[2] To do this, Macdonald adopted the tapered mandrel, solid metallic wax blanks, sapphire recording and reproducing stylii as developed and patented by Edison. These new machines were equipped with spring motors and a hand-to-mouth production was begun. For the first time cylinders were employed which were interchangeable with those of the Edison phonograph and the recorded cylinders were cut to the Edison established standard of 100 threads to the inch.

Undue emphasis has often been placed on the part that patent law and the adjudication of patents has played in the development of the phonograph industry. It is true that many minor companies which might have become large were put out of business because they had no patents, but in the frequent litigations between the few leaders, or those who had patents, the true relative merits of those patents as essential contributions to the art were seldom weighed objectively, logically, or even consistently by the courts. Perhaps this was because the jurists were not technicians or scientists and were often swayed more by the effectiveness of presentation of a case than by the material evidence, which under these circumstances was often quite imponderable, as far as the presiding jurist was concerned.

The proposition that the voluminous histories of court cases are an accurate guide as to what occurred in this industry, or any other, is a great fallacy. Many important patents never came before the courts, and further, the frequent reversals of decisions point up the fact that the eventual victor is most frequently the one who has the most money. However, a fairly accurate picture of the progress of the art is to be gained from a study of the patents issued year by year, as published in the *Patent Gazette.* As anyone who has taken the trouble to do research on this subject will know; a very different and distorted picture is obtained by reviewing the testimony and decisions handed down in the court cases year by year. In many cases, the bias of the jurists in favor of one side against the weight of the evidence can now be seen unmistakably. In many such cases, various questionable legalistic devices had been resorted to, such as bringing a suit in a court remote to the defender, or of attacking a company which had previously been bought off so that a consent verdict might be acquired.[3] Yet, to read the testimony and decision rendered in these cases, it would seem to those who read only the compendia of case histories available in the law libraries, that complete justice had been done. It is only by understanding the context of the situation under which a certain suit has been brought that the historian is in some cases able to prove that justice is indeed blind.

The very first case of a suit for infringement of the Bell-Tainter patents by the new legal battery of the American Graphophone Co. is an instance of the above. This was brought in the District of Columbia against the North American Phonograph Co. just after Lippincott's death and before a reorganization could be effected. Did the court take cognizance of this? It did not, but granted a verdict to the plaintiff by default. This established a precedent and immediately after Edison had bought back his patents from the receiver, the Graphophone Co. brought suit against the receiver before the United States Circuit Court for New Jersey, as it would have to under bankruptcy laws, so even though defended by Dyer of the Edison legal staff, a similar verdict was granted to the American Graphophone Co. This was obtained by consent, as the bringing of action by the Graphophone Co.

---

[2] *Annual Report of the American Graphophone Co.,* New York, 1900.

[3] This practice is no longer permitted.

had prevented the receiver from distributing the property of North American. This then, represented but a financial settlement of the claims of the two companies against North American.

However, in publicity releases issued to the newspapers by the Graphophone legal counsel, this was not presented as a settlement but as a victory which proved the superiority of the Bell-Tainter patents over those of Edison.[4] The next step in the Graphophone campaign was to institute a suit against the Edison Phonograph Co. and the United States Phonograph Co., a subsidiary Edison distributing company, for an injunction on the basis of alleged infringement of the Bell-Tainter patents and an accounting for damages. As the Edison attorneys were busy with the task of settling affairs with the local companies, as well as many legal matters having to do with other Edison enterprises, they chose to delay bringing this suit to trial. This was perfectly agreeable to the attorneys of the Graphophone Co. as this particular case pending against The Edison Phonograph Works gave the graphophone salesmen plenty of ammunition. The campaign thus far had worked perfectly. The American Graphophone Co. in its advertising was able to point out that its Bell-Tainter patents had been sustained by the courts and that they had brought suit against Edison (as President) and the Edison Phonograph Works.

This long delay in defending the Graphophone suit gave the Graphophone Co. time to gain strength. By 1895 sales had picked up to the point where the next step in the campaign could be undertaken. By an ostensible purchase of the stock of the Columbia Phonograph Co. by the American Graphophone Co. a virtual consolidation of the two companies was effected. Except for a block of Graphophone stock held by Tainter, the ownership of both companies was practically held by the same men. By this the Graphophone Co. was enabled to confine itself

to development and manufacturing and the Columbia Phonograph Co. to distribution and sales. But this was not the primary purpose, as we shall see.

In the meantime, another unforeseen incident delayed the Graphophone Co. —Edison Phonograph Works trial. Just as decision was about to be given, Judge Green of the United States Circuit Court in Trenton died. But Philip Mauro had not been idle. Knowing that it would be easier to roll up an imposing record of validity for the Bell-Tainter patents against people who had no patents than those who had, he had brought suit against a number of firms which had been manufacturing machines or blanks elsewhere, without benefit of patents. One of the more important of these precedental cases was that of the American Graphophone Co. versus Edward H. Amet of Waukegan, Illinois. Amet had been making and selling a machine allegedly for reproducing graphophone records, thereby infringing upon the Bell-Tainter patents. Amet claimed that he was not infringing because he did not make cylinders or sound records, but merely reproduced them, and that the art to this extent was open to the world. Judge Grosscup in the United States Circuit Court for the northern District of Illinois granted a permanent injunction and ordered an accounting of his profits and the Graphophone Co. damages.

The ironic fact, of course, is that Amet was making a machine to reproduce records of a type which had never been produced by Bell and Tainter, this type had been designed, patented and made by Edison and only shortly before had been adopted without leave by Macdonald in the new graphophone. Nevertheless, this case was to be cited in case after case to be brought by the Graphophone Co. against other infringers. Here it should be brought to the attention of our readers that although Alfred O. Tate,[5] former Edison private secretary, said in

4 *Washington Evening Star*, August 31, 1886.

5 *Edison's Open Door*, Alfred O. Tate, E. P. Dutton & Co., New York, 1938.

his biography that Edison had decided to put North American out of business, it was the actions of the Graphophone Co. which forced him to this decision and which Tate failed to state. Moreover, it was not Edison who forced the

Realizing rather late that the Graphophone Co. had been stealing a march on him, Edison organized the National Phonograph Co. as exclusive sales agent for the United States and opened a sales office in New York, offering dis-

Fig. 5-1. The Edison Spring Motor phonograph, 1896, first of the spring-driven phonographs.

local companies to suspend their recording and coin-operated phonograph business, but the American Graphophone Co., which picked them off one by one on the basis of infringement of the Bell-Tainter patents.

tributorships and dealerships on the order now generally obtained in many industries. Since the reorganization of the Graphophone Co. the new Macdonald graphophones had been designed primarily for the home market, although models were made for dictating purposes and coin operation somewhat later. To compete, Edison put out in April of 1896 his first spring-motored phonograph. (See Fig. 5-1.) A description of this was given in the *New York Electrical Review* of April 8, and is quoted because it reflects very well the attitude of those close to the scene at the time:

"The recent announcement that Mr. Thomas A. Edison had bought back from the receivers of the North American Phonograph Company his own property and rights is followed by the placing on the market of the new Edison phonograph, here illustrated. This machine is being built at the Edison Phonograph Works at Orange, N. J., and will be handled by the National Phonograph Co., which is now establishing agencies everywhere for its sale.

"The new machines conform in a general way to the older type, but it has two decided elements of novelty. One is that it is operated by a spring motor, the other is that it is to be sold for about $40., thus placing the instrument within the reach of everyboby, as a formidable rival to the music box.

" . . . The thread on the main shaft is 100 to the inch, so that standard music cylinders, of which there are now thousands, can be used. It is so arranged that multiple tubes can be employed, enabling several persons to listen at once, and it is also furnished, when desired, with a large horn and stand, answering the needs of a large audience. . . . The machine is fitted for reproducing only, but for a small extra charge it is built also to record, or to do both."

The sale of the new spring motor Edison phonographs was very good and so the Graphophone attorneys and publicists decided that it was time to call a halt, so a circular was prepared for wide distribution to the trade warning against buying Edison goods, as follows:

"*American Graphophone Company*
    Washington, D. C., Oct. 15, 1896
"The American Graphophone Co. owns the fundamental patents which created and cover the talking-machine art as it is known and practiced today; and every so-called 'Edison Phonograph,' unless it indents in tinfoil, infringes these patents. All of the so-called improved Edison Phonographs manufactured in 1889 were made under a license from the Graphophone Co. and paid the Graphophone Co. a royalty until Jesse H. Lippincott, President of North American Phonograph Co. became bankrupt. Since then suits for infringement, injunction, accounting etc. have been vigorously pressed against the Edison Phonograph Works, the United States Phonograph Co., the Ohio Phonograph Co., the Kansas City Phonograph Co., the New England Phonograph Co., and others. Already, several judgments have been entered in our favor, the latest being against the Receiver of the North American Phonograph Co., who voluntarily submitted to an injunction and paid damages.

"The suit against Edison, the United States Phonograph Co., and others was argued in Sept., 1896, before Judge Green in the United States Circuit Court in Trenton, N. J., although the defendants did everything in their power to retard trial, and for a time succeeded in postponing a hearing by urging upon the court that no phonographs had been made since 1889, and that they were doing substantially no business.

"Shortly after final hearing Judge Green died suddenly, leaving the case undecided. This delay has emboldened the infringers, and they are now re-embarking in the business with a hastily-constructed type of phonograph, some of which they hope to market before another judge can rehear and act upon our suit, leaving the purchasers of these machines to settle with us. We are pressing the matter with all possible haste in the courts, and meanwhile give public notice that every individual, firm or corporation who sells or uses the so-called Edison Phonograph, or appliances therefor, does so unlawfully and will be *legally accountable* to this company in damages."

American Graphophone Co.
E. D. Easton, President

Naturally, the Edison camp had to reply, which they did in the following words:

"*National Phonograph Co.*
Orange, New Jersey
"Our attention has been called to a circular letter dated Oct. 15, 1896, and signed and distributed by the American Graphophone Co., warning the public against the use or sale of Edison phonographs and appliances.

"It is generally known beyond dispute that Mr. Edison, and not the Graphophone Co., invented the phonograph. Most persons and concerns interested in the talking machine enterprise understand the controversy between the two interests too well to be misled by the Graphophone Co.'s reckless statements.

"As to the Graphophone Co.'s claim that its 'fundamental patents' created and cover the talking machine art, it seems sufficient to call to mind the dismal failure which met the graphophone, made some years ago under those patents—a failure which continued up to the time the Graphophone Co. appropriated the Edison improvements which made the phonograph a success.

"The entry of the 'several judgments' in the Graphophone Co.'s favor, as referred to in the circular letter, was upon consent and in no wise affected the merits of the Graphophone Co.'s patents. Particularly is this true as to the decree against the Receiver of the North American Phonograph Co., which was consented to in order to expedite the distribution of the assets in the receiver's hands. The Graphophone Co. has never yet obtained a judgement at final hearing and upon

a full showing of the facts. It did obtain, in Chicago, a final decree upon two of its claims, but this case was tried upon affidavits, and not on the customary oral evidence, and the case was manifestly so incomplete that on Nov. 10, 1896, the United States Circuit Court for the Southern District of New York, refused to follow the Chicago decision, and denied a motion made by the Graphophone Co. for a preliminary injunction under the same claims.

"The Graphophone Co. has never sued Mr. Edison, nor the Edison Phonograph Co. as stated in its letter to the public. One of the suits argued before Judge Green in September has been pending nearly four years. If the Graphophone Co. had any confidence in its patents this case would have been tried and decided long ago.

"Suits are now pending against the Graphophone Co.'s factory and selling agents for infringements of the Edison patents ' on the phonograph improvements which the graphophone was forced to adopt to keep before the public. We believe that a decision on these suits will set the present controversy at rest for all time. Then the only persons or concerns 'legally accountable' will be the handlers of of graphophones who have invaded our patent rights in the Edison Phonograph."

National Phonograph Co.
W. S. Mallory, President

Hereafter, the story of the battle may be followed fairly well by reading the files of the *Phonoscope*,[6] the first independent publication to be devoted primarily to the phonograph field. At this time the motion pictures were coming along also, which accounted for the name chosen for the publication. Strangely, the *Phonoscope* was launched

---

[6] *The Edison Phonograph News,* published for a time after 1893 by James L. Amden, was actually an Edison house organ, devoted to the Edison Phonograph and the interests of the local companies and operators. Amden also wrote an official service manual of the Edison Phonograph.

at the time when this exchange was at its height—November 15, 1896, was the publication date of the first issue. Evidently the editor didn't know which way to jump, for it was not until the April issue of 1897, that he took cognizance of it and then very neatly avoided the necessity of taking sides by publishing both letters, with the following comment:

"We have had many inquiries relating to the cause and result of the late legal trouble between the Phonograph and Graphophone Companies. We print the claims of both concerns as put forth in circulars issued by their parent companies of the rival parties during the recent controversy. We are pleased to say, however, that the trouble has been amicably settled, and both concerns are now working for the general interest of the talking machine."

The editor must indeed have been an incorrigible optimist if he believed the last sentence of his statement! However, it is true that an uneasy truce had been agreed upon, but it was to prove not more than a lull in the more or less continuous warfare between the two companies, neither of which seemed to be willing to risk an all out court decision as to the superiority of the patents which they held. With respect to the two statements which had been issued by the companies prior to this settlement, and statements which were later made by counsel and in advertisements in later years referring to the terms of this settlement, it is important to get a clear point of view as to not only what these terms were, but the Graphophone Co.'s official attitude in accepting them. As statements concern-the settlement were issued by the Graphophone legal staff to the press, numerous stories were printed in the newspapers the following day. As these news stories are in substantial agreement with the known terms of the settlement and it is the Graphophone Co.'s interpretation of these terms as of that date which is important, one of these news stories based on the Graphophone press release is quoted, as follows, from the *Brooklyn Eagle*, Dec. 19, 1896:

"The litigation which has been proceeding for several years between the American Graphophone Co., of Washington, D. C. and Thomas A. Edison and the Edison Phonograph Works relative to the talking machine patents, has been brought to an amicable conclusion. Edison, *it is stated by counsel for the Graphophone Co.*,[7] admits the fundamental character of the graphophone patents, and that they control the commercial art of sound recording and reproducing as it is practiced today, and agrees to a decree of injunction in the principle case pending in the United States Circuit Court for the District of New Jersey. The American Graphophone Co., on the other hand, admits the validity of patents for various improvements which Edison has taken out since the issuance of the graphophone patents, and consents to decrees in favor of Edison on those patents."

Shortly before this, determined not to let Edison get a foothold in the home talking machine market, Columbia offered a spring-wind graphophone (Fig. 5-2) at the then unheard of low price of twenty-five dollars, with discounts to the trade as high as forty percent. Now, with the settlement of the court cases making legal for the first time the adoption of the Edison improvements, the Graphophone made use of another stratagem. As the Columbia Phonograph Co. had not surrendered its contract with North American, it could maintain that the provisions of the contract were still enforceable upon Edison and the Edison Phonograph Works. It could still represent itself before the public as agents for the Edison Phonograph and to demand that it be sold merchandise under its provisions.

---

[7] Italics added.

In January 1897, the Columbia Phonograph Co. moved its main offices from Washington to New York City, where its chief sales activity was then centered, evidently anticipating the terms of the settlement and recognizing that the objective of driving Edison from the field must be given up, for the time being, at least, a three-story building prominently located on Broadway had been secured. Offices and recording studios were located on the upper floors

The Columbia, Price $25.

Fig. 5-2. This early Columbia Graphophone sold for $25 complete with recorder, reproducer, speaking and hearing tubes. It played the 2-minute wax cylinder record.

and the main floor was given over to a large salesroom for machines and records. Large, electrically lighted signs the entire width of the building were placed above each of the three floors, as follows:

EDISON PHONOGRAPHS
THE PERFECTED GRAPHOPHONE
THE COLUMBIA PHONOGRAPH CO.

The stock of the Graphophone Co. was soaring. Charles Tainter, who had not been with the company since the collapse, now secured himself a job in a rather interesting manner. On July 9, 1897, be brought suit for twenty-thousand dollars against a former stockbroker, whom he alleged had loaned him money on stock of American Graphophone Co. he had deposited with the broker the year pre-

viously. Tainter alleged that when he tendered repayment, the stock could not be produced. Perhaps it was sheer coincidence, but a few days later, on July 30th, it was announced in the daily newspapers,

"Prof. Charles Sumner Tainter, who with Prof. Alexander Graham Bell and Prof. Chichester Bell, invented the Graphophone, has entered the service of the American Graphophone Co. to conduct experiments looking to improvements in sound-recording and sound-reproducing apparatus. Prof. Tainter since the original invention has contributed much towards the improvement and perfecting of the talking machine. The talking machine as it is represented in the graphophone, was invented and improved in Washington and as a business enterprise the graphophone has been developed largely by Washington capital and energy."

(Washington Star, July 30, 1897)

The finesse of Philip Mauro in pulling chestnuts out of the fire, turning an adverse situation into a favorable one and at the same time salving the local press is well illustrated with many such classic examples of his consummate skill, not only as an attorney, but as a public relations expert extraordinary.

It can be seen that the campaign of the Washington reporters was succeeding handsomely, at least in a financial sense. Meanwhile the Edison cause was in a bad way. In October, 1897, Edison was forced to mortgage the Edison Phonograph Works for three-hundred thousand dollars to take up demand notes for money which he had secured from other sources to finance operations. The contrasting prosperity of the Graphophone enterprise is emphasized that just about the same time Andrew Devine, headlined as "Noted House Stenographer," in the newspapers of Washington and elsewhere, was announced as leaving his remunerative post to accept the vice-presidency of the American Graphophone Co., of which he had been a founder and director, and to which he would henceforth devote all of his time.

Philip Mauro and his staff were now so busy with the business of narrowing competition by eliminating the many opportunists who had entered the talking machine field that he felt an advertising department should be organized. This was done and outstanding men in the newspaper business were brought in to prepare advertising and publicity, headed by Harry P. Godwin, then editor of the *Washington Star*.

However, Mauro's ability to translate technical information and the legal phraseology of the courts into simple and meaningful English was never to be transcended by his hired publicity experts, as good as they were. From this time forward, the success of the Graphophone seemed assured.

It was not until 1898, with the introduction of the "Edison Home Phonograph" (see Fig. 5-3), that the National Phonograph Co. began to compete successfully with the graphophone in the home market. An extremely interesting

Fig. 5-3. First of several models known as the Edison Home phonograph. It was a spring-motor type and produced sufficient volume to be heard through a 14-inch horn. A shaving knife permitted erasure of sounds for cylinder reuse.

facet of this situation was that as the Columbia Phonograph Co. had gained its early successes through the opening of showrooms in the larger cities, such as Boston, Chicago, Philadephia and St. Louis, much of the distribution was in urban areas. However, the National Phonograph Co., finding the big city competition more difficult because of the lower prices of the graphophone, concentrated on securing outlets in the smaller cities and towns and through farm mail order houses, such as Babson Brothers, Chicago. Two other influences assisted in establishing a strong trend towards predominance of the Edison phonograph in rural areas; first, the isolation of farmers in the more remote areas, which it is hard to appreciate in these days of the automobile and radio, made for ready acceptance of the rugged, dependable Edison phonograph as filling a long felt need for entertainment; second, the admiration of rural people for Thomas A. Edison, the great inventor, knew no bounds. The maga-

zines and papers which went into rural homes carried but little of the anti-Edison propaganda, now almost continuously being ground out by the publicists of the graphophone. When a luckless graphophone salesman did venture into the farmhouse and attempted to follow the line then being followed as a sales opener by saying, "Did you know that Edison was not the inventor of the phonograph?" he was fortunate to escape without bodily injury. The country folk would have none of it. These influences which shaped the growth pattern of the cylinder industry also later affected the disc talking machine industry. For similar reasons the disc gramophone and its successor, the Victor talking machine, were to make their initial successes in the urban areas, while the phonograph was continuing to expand in the rural areas. The Graphophone Co., in trying to ride both horses, almost dropped between, but that is a story to be told in a succeeding chapter. '

CHAPTER 6

THE BETTINI STORY

IN seeking to provide entertaining reading, there is an understandable tendency of authors to seize upon the more fascinating or dramatic episodes of a period and to develop them out of proportion to their actual importance. This has happened with respect to the reporting of the phonographic achievements of Gianni Bettini, one time Lieutenant in the Italian cavalry, who came to the United States in the mid 1880's. Bettini was born in 1860, in Novara, Italy, to a family of the landed gentry. As was the nineteenth century custom for young men of his class, Gianni was given a gentleman's education, stressing languages, classical literature and a grounding in the arts and music. Not being particularly scholarly in his tastes, he ultimately gravitated towards an army career. A dashing and handsome young man, with a turned up military mustachio, he made a striking figure in his uniform as a Lieutenant in His Majesty's Cavalry.

The life of an Italian cavalry officer in those days offered considerable opportunity for travel and social life. While on a visit to Paris Bettini met a vivacious young American socialite, Daisy Abbott, of Stamford, Connecticut, a descendent of the Pomeroy Abbott branch of the well-known New England pioneer family. Lieutenant Bettini so fell in love with Miss Abbott that he gave up his military career, followed her back to New York and persuaded her to marry him. For a short time the newlyweds settled in Stamford, the home of the parents of the bride. Perhaps Bettini grew bored with the somewhat stilted existence as a country squire, for he soon began to evidence a great interest in mechanical contrivances and turned to inventing. However, the first product of his efforts reflected his musical background in that it was a mechanical page turner, upon which he applied for a patent September 5, 1888.[1]

Sometime during the latter part of 1888, Bettini secured somehow one of the improved Edison phonographs. As Jesse Lippincott had organized the North American Phonograph Company in June of that year and the local companies were only then in the process of organization, it seems unlikely that he could have secured one earlier. There is some little mystery as to just how Bettini secured one at all, for by the terms of the contracts between North American and the local companies both phonographs and graphophones were to be offered by lease only and were not to be sold outright. Sales of machines were not permitted until a considerably later date. The phonographs then produced were designed to serve as business machines. Consequently, when Lieutenant Bettini tried to use the Edison phonograph, which had been equipped for use only for office dictation, he quite understandably found it

---

[1] *U. S. Patent Gazette,* Vol. 45, p. 895—issued August 13, 1889.

unsuited for the purpose of recording and reproducing the singing voice and music. The present day telephone instruments are similarly unsuited for the purpose of transmitting music and song. Today it would be economically feasible to substitute sensitive, wide frequency range, piezo-electric crystal microphones for the comparatively deaf carbon grain transmitters of our telephones. Why is it not done? Because so much extraneous background sound and both high and low frequencies out of the narrow range needed for speech transmission would be picked up as to make conversation more difficult, rather than facilitating it.

When the licensed companies found a prospect of financial salvation in the use of the phonograph for entertainment, they had only to request that the "speakers" be equipped for the making or reproducing of musical records, rather than "phonograms," as they were then called. The origination of the term "phonogram" by Edison, underlines the fact that the Edison machine of the time, with its heavy chassis and electric motor with battery, was intended to be a business machine, rather than an entertainment device. Perhaps it may be inferred that Bettini may have obtained his phonograph through an unauthorized channel. If so, this would explain why he chose to design recording diaphragms and reproducers suited to his purpose, rather than by appealing to Edison. Bettini was the first "fan" of the phonograph, in the sense that it has since been applied to amateur photographers. From the beginning his purpose in recording was to get realistic and pleasing "pictures," so to speak, of the voices of accomplished singers, so that he might play them over for their pleasure and his. It was a worthwhile, if expensive, avocation; and finding the pursuit of it fascinating, he determined to move to New York where there were many great singers whom he might persuade to "pose" before his recording horn.

In analyzing the reasons for the poor quality of the vocal records he had been

able to secure with the original Edison recording diaphragm, Bettini came to the conclusion that the chief difficulty lay in the single point of contact of the cutting stylus with the diaphragm. Conversely, he reasoned that this was also a fault in the reproducing diaphragm assembly. Bettini therefore designed a more flexible diaphragm made of mica, instead of the thin French glass used in the Edison "speaker," and attaching four radial spurs from the stylus to the diaphragm at points on a circle equidistant from the stylus and the center of the diaphragm. He did this both for the recording stylus and the reproducing stylus assemblies. These devices became the subject of his first phonographic patent and the operation was described in the specification, in part, as follows:[2]

" . . . taking vibrations off a vibratory body at several points or places, communicating them to a common or central point or place by independent conductors, causing a record to be made from this common point or place, and then causing this record to act at the common or central point or place, communicating vibrations to a vibratory body at several points or places."

It is necessary to look elsewhere to find out exactly what Bettini was trying to accomplish and the theory in back of his method. In an article written in French in June, shortly after the filing of his application, Bettini stated that he had found it was difficult to get an audible impression in the cylinders and that when a good impression was secured the quality of the reproduction lacked the clarity of timbre that permitted the distinguishing of one voice from another. He stated also that he thought it unpleasant to use the ear tubes and that when a metal horn was substituted the reproduction was even poorer and lacking in musical quality.

[2] *U. S. Patent Gazette*—Vol. 48, p. 921 "Recording and Reproducing Sounds" filed April 11, 1889, issued Aug. 13, 1889.

This was undoubtedly true, especially as we know that Bettini must have secured one of the earliest commercial instruments produced, and equipped with the thicker glass diaphragms intended for dictation.

Both Bettini's purpose and theory in respect to his invention are better explained by the author of an article which appeared in the *Scientific American* of April 26, 1890, from the text of which the following is quoted:

"Any reader of the daily papers must have noticed within the last few months frequent mention of a new instrument of the phonograph type, invented by Lieut. Gianni Bettini, an officer in the Italian navy (sic), at present residing in this country. This gentleman conceived the idea of constructing a phonograph so as to be exceedingly sensitive to the different qualities of the tones of the human voice, and to reproduce those tones with the original qualities, so that the voice of the speaker could be easily recognized; and furthermore to produce uniformly good records without regard to the quality of the speaker's voice, also to secure a volume of sound which would compare favorably with that of a voice engaged in ordinary conversation, so that the words could be heard and understood without the necessity of employing stethoscopic ear tubes.

"Every student of acoustics knows that vibrating membranes, strings, rods, columns of air, and thin plates of various kinds have active points and neutral points, and Lieut. Bettini has taken advantage of this fact in the construction of his instrument. He connects his recording stylus with the diaphragm at various points, to insure contact with one or more of the actively vibrating parts or centers of the diaphragm, thus avoiding the points of rest or nodes where little or no vibration occurs."

With what Bettini was trying to accomplish as conveyed by the reporter of

Scientific American there can be little quarrel, but his theory does not conform to certain facts even then quite well known. The statement which the author attributes to Bettini that "vibrating membranes, rods, columns of air, and thin plates of various kinds have active and neutral points" is true now as it was then. But this law applies only to the free, or natural modes of vibration of these media when in a rectilinear conformation of some sort, and of uniform diameter or cross section, as in cylinders and prisms. It did not and does not apply to the mode of vibration of a thin and more or less flexible diaphragm of circular shape. The mode of vibration of such a flexible disc, whether the edges are free, or clamped more or less tightly and uniformly, is always in concentric waves. The bar, cylinder, confined air columns, or thin plates, do not respond to all air vibrations, but only to certain tones, or the harmonics thereof. There are neutral points in this case. The usefulness of the diaphragm is its capacity for responding to a wide range of vibrations, and conversely, by setting it into vibration by appropriate mechanical means that it is possible for it to emit a wide band of tones. The fact that it has always been possible to secure the reproduction of a sliding tone from as low a fundamental as the air loading of the diaphragm and its area and stiffness will permit, to as high a tone as the inertia of its mass will permit, is ample evidence that there are truly no "dead," or neutral points. It is true that there are resonant peaks due to faults in material and design, but this is not the phenomenon to which Bettini was referring.

What Bettini did accomplish with his first quadruped-shaped spider, with its legs attached to the diaphragm of mica, was to lower the emphasis upon upper register response and to increase the relative bass register response. In modern parlance, Bettini had altered the recording and reproducing characteristic. The "cross-over" was at the pitch at which the principal node of vibration would be in the circle in which the legs of the spider were attached. This will explain his success in recording the upper registers more smoothly, as in the soprano voice, which could be taken with much greater facility and less danger of "blasting." However, the placing of the four legs in a thin, flexible diaphragm at any other point than the center sets up eddy currents— tending to vibrate the diaphragm in concentric circles around each of the legs, whether in recording or reproducing. This is the fact which makes the spider of questionable value and is perhaps the reason it was not adopted by others. Later in the development of the art, the same result of de-emphasizing the upper register and increasing the lower register response was achieved by laminating the diaphragm in concentric layers, thickest at the center. Just to set the record straight, with respect to certain misleading sketches which have been published, the legs of Lieutenant Bettini's "musical spider" were generally placed concentrically and not placed haphazardly and of various lengths. Only one of his models shows such a random disposition of the legs. He made also multiple diaphragm units, in each of these cases the spider came from the center of each diaphragm to a point centered between the diaphragms, where the cutting or reproducing stylus was affixed.

Now why is this important? If Bettini had indeed fashioned something of outstanding merit, it would seem as though one of the leading companies would have adopted it—with or without leave. Will Hayes of the Edison staff (now deceased) said that they had one of the Bettini attachments there but the experts there considered it weak, though producing results of good quality. On the other hand, the editor of *Phonoscope*, Russell Hunting, himself a prolific recorder, had these good words to say about the Bettini micro-phonograph method in response from an inquiry from a reader, that the Bettini-microphone attachment would make a better record than the standard Edison

recorder. In his column "Trade Notes" in *Phonoscope* of November 1896, he said,

"The records taken with the Bettini Micro-phonograph Diaphragms are wonderful for their solidity of tone and resonant carrying powers. Records of the female voice taken with the attachment are truly marvelous."

Just for perspective, the following is quoted from the same issue by another commentator whose offering was headlined "Voices from the Dead." The writer had evidently attended one of the rare occasions upon which some of the early wax cylinders sent to Thomas A. Edison by his European representatives, Dr. Wangemann in Berlin, and Col. Gouraud in London, had been played. This correspondent said,

"Recently the writer had occasion to attend a phonograph recital. Among the cylinders used that night were some whereon Hon. W. E. Gladstone and the venerable Bismark had recorded their voices. . . . I have read the speeches of Gladstone and Bismark, but I did not know their spirit until I heard their voice on the cylinder of a phonograph. The body, the strength, the soft modulation, the emphasis, so faithfully reproduced by the delicate mechanism, the life thus imparted to the words, made them sink indelibly into my soul, showing to me the fulness of their power, the men whom till then I had only known vaguely."

Of course, this referred only to the speaking voice. However, there was one important vocal coach and surgeon who utilized both the Edison phonograph and the Bettini micro-phonograph attachments (Fig. 6-1) during these years and who wrote about his experiments. This was J. Mount Bleyer, M.D., Surgeon to the New York Throat Infirmary and Editor of the *Electrical Review*. Dr. Bleyer was employed as consultant by many of the famous vocal artists of the

Fig. 6-1. Reproduction of an early ad illustrating Bettini's micro-reproducer which was later made available as an accessory for Edison and other phonographs.

time, and collected recordings of their voices much as had Bettini, but with a somewhat different purpose. Dr. Bleyer utilized the records of the voices of his illustrious patients as a means of studying the functioning of their vocal cords and singing technics. Collectors have avidly sought to find some of the Bleyer recordings, but they are now believed to have been destroyed. But Dr. Bleyer did leave important comparative information in a paper which he wrote entitled "The Edison Phonograph and the Bettini Micro-Phonograph—The Principles Underlying Them and the Fulfillment of their Expectations."[3]

The following significant comments are quoted from the Bleyer paper:

"It is a known fact that in instruments made in exactly the same way there is still perceptible a certain difference in the shade, the quality, or the timbre of their tones. So we find it with the human voice. A certain standard is necessary in order to judge of the proper timbre, pitch and quality in a tenor, a baritone, and a basso voice, as well as in a soprano, a mezzo-soprano, an alto, and a contralto. By bestowing some further

experimental study on this subject, I am certain that shortly I can bring forward a standard as well as an additional new art to aid the learning of singing, etc.

"Some of the records which served me for my purpose were taken from celebrated tenors of the Metropolitan Opera House, as Julian Perotti, Andreas Dippel, Carl Streitman, Mr. Koppel etc. Also singers Theodore Reichmann, Emile Steger, Conrad Behrens, Felicia Koshofska, F. C. Nicolini, Nina Bertini, Helen Mora, Bertha Ricci, and many others less educated in the several arts." - - -

"Mr. Thomas A. Edison has interested himself in my behalf regarding these studies, and has specially built for me a phonograph which has many new attachments, besides a number of fine diaphragms on a new principle; with its recorder I shall be able to receive the fine tones and reproduce them."

Contrary to Tate and others who have incorrectly stated that Edison was opposed to the development of the phonograph as a musical instrument at that time, Dr. Bleyer's testimony indicates conclusively that Edison was very much aware of this potential and desirous of encouraging it.

Perhaps the best way to arrive at an impartial judgment today, as to the comparative merits, would be through

---

[3] Read by Dr. Bleyer before the Section on Laryngology, 43rd Annual Meeting of the American Medical Association, Detroit, June 1892, also before the American Electro-Therepeutical Association later.

resort to the three dimensional evidence that is left. However, this sort of evidence, the records and machines of Edison and Bettini of that time, are getting extremely hard to find, particularly of the latter, to say nothing of getting sufficient quantities together in one place to make direct comparisons! A former columnist of *Hobbies Magazine*, Stephan Fassett, who in his writings claimed to have looked forward with great eagerness to hearing some of these rarest of the rare Bettini cylinders, expressed great disappointment when some were found and played for him. A cache of fifteen of the Bettini cylinders had turned up in Mexico City in 1945. Mr. Fassett's disappointment may have stemmed from the fact that these records were principally of the less important artists. A contributory factor may have been the fact that they were played for him by means of an improvised electric pick-up made partially of an old Edison reproducer equipped with a crystal cartridge and connected to an amplifier and speaker of undetermined characteristics. This could have resulted in a positive mismatch, for the Bettini records were quite different in quality from the regular commercially produced musical records of the time. As is now becoming well recognized, the acoustically recorded records of any period or type of manufacture have a recorded "characteristic" that may be as clearly defined as those of modern electrical recordings. All too often the assumption has been made that playing acoustic records by any type of electrical equipment must necessarily result in improved reproduction over anything that was possible during the acoustic era.

Another factor is that all of the records offered for sale by Bettini were duplicates, and not original recordings. All records were transferred from the one original "master" cylinder which Bettini kept in his studio at 115 Fifth Avenue. On March 14, 1892, he applied for a patent on his method of duplicating cylinders. This involved the use of opposed cylinders, similar in principle

to the device for recording both sides of a sound wave, one side on each of two parallel cylinders, with a double pointed stylus between as patented by Hall in 1899. However, Bettini's device was so arranged that gravity assisted in the cutting of the cylinder which was located diagonally below the mandrel holding the master record and which was of course traced with a smooth stylus. Very likely Bettini did not offer copies of his growing repertoire of records until after he had perfected this transcribing device.

Lieutenant and Mrs. Bettini were popular with the musical people of New York and especially the great opera stars of the 1890's and often entertained them. Naturally, they would play the Edison phonograph with the Bettini micro-diaphragm attachment, and their distinguished visitors, pleased to hear themselves as others heard them, would willingly consent to record a song or two. In this manner Bettini gradually built up over a period of three or four years a fabulous archive. Without question his technic of recording improved with the passage of time. In developing this talent, Bettini was greatly assisted in his work by two of his best friends, one of whom was destined himself to become one of the most famous of recording directors. This was Emilio de Gogorza, the distinguished baritone, who sang so many selections for Bettini that they decided it would be best to adopt a pseudonym for some of them and that is how "Signor Francisco" was originated, a practice which de Gogorza carried into his prolific latter day recording with later companies. The other friend was Rosa Chalia, South American soprano, who sang for him many solos, as well as duets with de Gogorza, de Bassini, and others. The constant demonstrations and the taking of duplicates may well also have served to reduce the quality of many of the Bettini cylinders. It is not known how efficient the Bettini copying device was, but this much may be gleaned from the article by the reporter of the *Phonoscope* who visited the Bettini studio in 1896. He said,

"Signor Nicolini has a cylinder to which he sang on his last visit to this country with Mme. Patti three years ago. Nicolini was never much of a singer and the phonograph of today does not give him even justice, as it has been considerably worn from repetitions given to those who wanted to hear Mme. Patti's husband sing."

Bettini filed an application for an improved duplicating machine in April, 1897. This seems to indicate that the former device left something to be desired. The new model provided means for adjusting the pressure on the cylinder being cut to match the volume of the master cylinder being copied.

Another factor in this situation was that by reducing the emphasis in the upper registers in order to achieve a more pleasing "original" record, the number of satisfactory copies which could be secured must have been reduced. Very likely this is the drawback which prevented other companies from seeking to use it. It should be also emphasized that until the late 1890's, Bettini had not designed or made a complete phonograph—nor did he make blanks. He made the records to order on the standard commercial blanks and he made the micro-phonograph attachments for the phonograph and graphophone, but he did not revolutionize the phonograph industry.

Calvin G. Childs, Victor Emerson, Frank Capps, Will and Fred Gaisberg, Walter Miller, and the others who were about to begin the job of capturing in more permanent form the voices of the greatest singers on earth, were also learning. They were learning that the secret of getting brilliant and lifelike recordings lay in selecting the right thickness of diaphragm, of adjusting the damping of the edges just so, of selecting the right horn, of the proper design and polishing of the cutting stylus, the proper composition and conditioning of the wax and in controlling many other variables. By experience and careful judgment in these matters these experts soon learned how to get the best results from each recording session, which was to become an important matter in the days of large fees to come. But these men were still using glass diaphragms and the conventional phonographs or graphophones. And more importantly to the assessing of credit, when most of these men switched to disc recording, they took with them the experience gained in making cylinder "masters." Even de Gogorza, Bettini's good friend, had his voice registered by a glass diaphragm with a single arm from the cutting stylus to its center. Who can say that the Bettini micro-diaphragm contributed to the superior results thus achieved?

This is not being said wholly without reference to the third dimensional evidence in the form of the records. The large number of recordings made by de Gogorza from Bettini through to the electrical recording era and for several companies, has offered a rare opportunity to make comparisons. Always bearing in mind the variables caused by wear, the necessity of securing a proper matching and the changing voice of the singer, comparisons are still quite revealing. No less than three authentic Bettini cylinders of de Gogorza have been compared with those taken of the same singer by Columbia (probably by Victor Emerson) and others; also discs by Berliner, Eldridge R. Johnson, Victor, and Zonophone (as Ed Franklin). There is no question but that the Victor records are the best. There is considerable doubt as to whether the electrical recordings are as faithful as some of the acoustic recordings, at least as far as the voice is concerned. The important thing is that all of these discs were taken, as far as is known, with the exception of the electrical recordings by the means of glass diaphragms with a stylus making a single contact with the center of the diaphragm.

"But," some critic will say, "didn't the Orthophonic Victrola employ a spider in the reproducer?" The answer is yes, but the center portion of the Duralumin diaphragm was bowl shaped, so that it would tend to vibrate as a unit and the remainder of the area was concentrically corrugated to eliminate as far as possible the eddy currents, which was not true of the design of the Bettini diaphragm.

The larger number of the Bettini cylinders were probably made after 1896 and the development of the improved duplicator. For these reasons there is a hope that additional caches will be discovered which will reveal better quality than those found in Mexico City.[4] To be fair to Mr. Bettini, it is rather amazing that he was able to persuade so many of the greatest artists to record for him. The cost of such talent if he had to pay for it would soon have terminated his recording activities. Very likely it was the venturing of the enterprising Gramophone Co. into the recording of celebrities for fees in 1900 which brought this phase of Bettini's career to a close. Meanwhile, to gain a better picture of the galaxy of stars which Bettini had fixed in wax as early as 1896, the following is quoted from the *Phonoscope* article of 1896:

"The collection is unequalled anywhere. There are songs by Yvette Guilbert, who sang into the phonograph on her recent visit to this country. When the writer visited the studio lately, Yvette's voice sounded from the phonograph, one of her English songs, 'I Want You, My Honey.' Then the voice gave 'La Soularde' and an imitation of Bernhardt's style of delivery in a favorite character. Then followed a selection from 'Izeyl,' by Bernhardt herself, with all the passion in which the passage was recited on the stage.

---

[4] A more promising find of Bettini cylinders was found near Syracuse, N. Y. in 1952, some of them in a barn. Included were records by the Metropolitan tenor Thomas Salignac, Emilio de Gogorza, Frances Sayville, Dante del Papa, Giuseppe Campanari and other opera artists, totalling twenty-two. Some are excellent recordings, others poor.

" . . . The next cylinder was one labelled 'Melba,' which was truly wonderful; the phonograph reproducing her wonderful voice in a marvelous manner, especially on the high notes which soared away above the staff and were rich and clear. . . . Among them were Victor Maurel, the well-known baritone singer, . . . Tomaso Salvini, who rolled out a grand passage from 'Otello' in the Italian translation; M. Coqelin, the famous French actor, whose visit to this country will be remembered; Pol Plancon and Mme. Saville, the beautiful Frenchwoman, who warbled a bit from the opera of 'Rigoletto,' and another from 'Carmen' . . . Sigrid Arnoldson's voice was heard in a cylinder to which the artist sang three years ago."

Despite all of the publicity and free talent, there is considerable doubt as to whether he actually made money, even though he must have had an enjoyable and rich experience. He dabbled in other things than the phonograph. In 1893 he invented a nickel-in-the-slot machine, not for playing phonograph records, but for dispensing gum or candy balls! In 1897, he was issued a patent on an acetylene lamp. This latter year he published a twelve-page catalog of cylinders for sale. The next year Bettini ventured also into the field of popular songs and issued a catalog over twice the size listing over four-hundred selections, about evenly divided between popular and classical.

By 1899, Bettini was offering for sale at from two to six dollars each records by such world famous artists as the sopranos Nellie Melba, Frances Sayville, Sigrid Arnoldsen and Marie Engel; the tenors Dante del Papa, Albert Saleza, Ernest Van Dyke; the contralto Eugenia Mantelli; and the noted bassos Pol Plancon and Anton Van Rooy. He also advertised for sale dramatic recordings by Bernhardt, Rejane, and Salvini. It seems quite likely that some artists who had recorded for him wished to have him refrain from advertising their names, for in his 1899 catalog the following paragraph appears:

"We have in our collection many records from celebrated artists, not mentioned in this catalog, and we are constantly adding new ones."

From newspaper stories, articles in the trade papers and elsewhere, it is believed that Bettini also had records by both Jean and Edouard DeReszke, Italo Campanini, Emma Calve, Francesco Tamagno, Lola Beeth, Ellen Terry, Mark Twain, John Drew, Lillian Nordica, and Lillian Langtry.

The handful of Bettini cylinders that are known to exist are but a mockery of an opportunity lost, for Edison had created in 1890 the large cylinder to small cylinder transcribing mechanism providing means by which Bettini might have been able to preserve so much that now seems irretrievably lost. The irony is that if Edison had used the device himself in the interim between the time of application and the granting eight years later (just the period in which Bettini was most active), very likely the courts would have perversely ruled that his patent was invalid for prior publication as they had his celluloid molding patent! It is true that during this same period Edison was not particularly concerned with the finer aspects of recording. He had his hands full with the troubles of the North American debacle and in somehow regrouping for a fresh start. In Europe, however, Pathe was about to begin its own great saga of recording the famous artists of Europe, using the large cylinder recording method of Edison, which permitted transcribing with greater fidelity to smaller sized cylinders and with much less wear to the master cylinder.

How much better it might have been with his splendid opportunity to serve posterity, if Bettini had consulted with Edison about his problem just once! But enough of crying over spilled milk. In 1897, Bettini had filed a patent on a small spring-motor phonograph, evi-dently with the intention of going into the manufacture of machines. This was the year the hand-wind phonographs and graphophones really began to open the home phonograph market. For this reason there were many eager to get into it and Bettini sold the patent to the Lyraphone Co. of West Virginia, which introduced a modified version of it on the market. Subsequently Bettini designed two other chassis for small spring-motor phonographs which he also patented and which were not assigned. Some of these he had made up were advertised for sale. Not many can have been sold as they are as scarce as the Bettini cylinders, if not more so.

Of some interest is the fact that in 1897 Bettini had also filed an application for a patent for copying records involving an electrical method. The specification shows a coil and an armature attached to the recording stylus and refers to the "transmitter." No information seems to be available as to whether it was used commercially. Meanwhile in the March 1898 issue of *Phonoscope* a letter from F. M. Prescott, export and import dealer in phonographs and supplies stated that Pathe in France were manufacturing the Bettini micro-phonograph attachment. The next month Bettini placed a notice warning purchasers against infringements being offered for sale in the European market. Evidently Bettini followed up this alleged infringement by making a trip to France to look into it, for in August an item appeared in *Phonoscope,* as follows:

"Mr. G. Bettini, has sold his patent rights for France and the French Colonies to a newly organized company in France, called Compagnie Micro Phonographes Bettini, with a capital of 1,200,000 francs. Mr. Bettini is to remain in France some time in order to organize the company and take charge of the establishment of the manufacturing plant."

Lieut. Bettini's last application for an American patent was filed May 2, 1900, and was on a small spring-motored phonograph. By the time the patent was awarded to him in 1902, he apparently realized that in America he was lost in battling with the giants which had grown up around him in every sense—whether in the acquiring of recording talent, maintaining continued research, or the ability to organize and operate a business enterprise on a large scale. It is said that he sold his microphonograph patents to Edison, if so, Edison never made them, although prior to this time he had used mica for diaphragms—not a patentable feature in itself. Bettini sold his business name to a newly organized American company. Lamentably, he did not part with his priceless collection of great voices, but chose to take them with him to France, where they were destined to be destroyed during World War I. The company bearing his name continued until 1905 when it was advertising a disc machine called the "Hymnophone," which was made in Germany. This was a table model with a horn which came down in back and under the motor with the flange of the oval shaped horn protruding from the cabinet in front. In June of this year the American company was reorganized as Bettini Company Ltd. with a capital of only $20,000, and in December of 1907 retired from business.

In Paris, Bettini had meanwhile continued his practice of making his attachments, phonographs, and to personally record and to sell duplicate records of great artists. Shortly before the death of Pope Leo XIII in 1903, Bettini secured records of his voice. Columbia issued a special brochure featuring cylinder recordings of the Pope after his death, but whether these were duplicates of the Bettini recordings has not been established. Bettini also embarked in the making of disc machines and records toward the end of his recording career, but they were not particularly successful.

After 1908, Bettini went into the motion picture business. He invented a motion picture camera, but this also failed to impress the trade to any considerable extent. Later, he was a war correspondent for a Paris newspaper. In 1917, he returned to the United States as a member of a military mission from the Italian government. He never returned to Europe and died in 1938. As far as the phonograph was concerned, Bettini had been at least its foremost dilettante. Like that other man of wealth who had been fascinated by its attraction, Jesse Lippincott, Bettini lost a great deal of money, but unlike Lippincott, he had a grand and glorious time doing it. However, Lippincott had gotten into and affected the main stream of phonographic development while with all the glamour of his activities, Bettini scarcely affected it.

CHAPTER 7

THE CONCERT CYLINDERS

THE compromise which permitted the graphophone and the phonograph to continue a now somewhat parallel and peaceful period of development gave no such peace to others who had entered, or were to try to enter the industry. Other inventors had made contributions, or wished to make contributions, but if they sought to work independently, their path was to be a thorny one due to the vigilance of the legal staff of the Graphophone Co. The one important exception to this general rule was Gianni Bettini.

Many others were not so fortunate. Some had made a start in the business by having the Edison phonograph copied by local machine shops. Complete instructions as to how to make both the Edison tinfoil phonograph and the later electric-motor wax cylinder Edison phonograph had been published in England and distributed in this country.[1] This manual was very complete with working drawings, even to the details of the electric motor and the making of molds for molding cylinder blanks. (See Fig. 7-1.) Other service handbooks published in the United States for users of the Edison phonograph contributed everything that was needed on the later improvements.[2]

The experience of Edison in having his improvements "lifted" by Macdonald in the new graphophone resulted in a period when a certain class of discoveries no longer were patented, such as improved recording technics, differing compositions of recording blanks, and the methods of grinding and polishing styli. This was a period of "trade secrets" and Edison henceforth applied for patents on major and definitive changes only, which were more amenable to protection in the courts. Edison was always very meticulous in the keeping of laboratory notes and despite this alteration of policy, it can be seen that it would have been very inconsistent of him to allow major improvements to go without patent registration. Perhaps in view of the rather unsatisfactory performance of the patent system on his behalf, Edison realized that at least it would permit posterity to place credit where it was due.

The phonograph-graphophone story of the mid-nineties forward until well in the 1900's is one of continuous espionage. Both the Edison interests and the Graphophone Co. had spies in each other's plant. Every change in formula of the blanks being produced by Edison at Orange was reported promptly at Bridgeport. Survivors of those hectic days at Orange, New Jersey, will testify that this is true! Employees of one plant would suddenly turn up missing, later found to be employed at a nice advance of salary at the other.

---

[1] *The Phonograph and How to Construct it,* W. Gillett, E. & F. Spon, London 1892.

[2] *A Practical Guide to the Use of the Edison Phonograph,* James L. Andem, C. J. Krehbiel & Co., Cincinnati, Ohio, 1892.

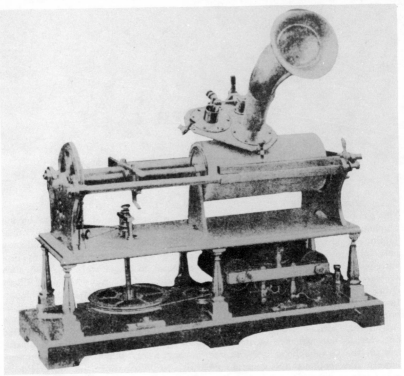

Fig. 7-1. W. Gillett's phonograph of 1892 operated from a direct-current motor and used an attachment based on Edison's spectacle device for recording and reproduction. (Courtesy of "The Phonograph and How to Construct It.")

Sometimes employees were practically kidnapped, it is said, and when important men left the Edison fold for any reason, there were agents from the Graphophone Co. on hand to hire them to go to Bridgeport. Among these was Victor Emerson, later founder of Emerson Phonograph Co.

Owing to the fact that a molding process had not yet been made commercially practical, both Edison and Macdonald were working feverishly upon it, which was one of the reasons for the secrecy and cloak and dagger tactics. Writers about this period generally assume that because of the known practice of recording cylinders by the "round," in which a singer might sing the same song over and over again into the recording horns of a bank of phonographs, that duplicating methods were seldom used. This was not true. In the absence of a molding method many experimenters had developed quite satisfactory methods of copying records one from another, or "dubbing," as it is now called. The third patent issued in the United States upon phonographic devices embodied the principle involved in some of these, although it was patented for a different purpose.[3] Edison,

[3] *U. S. Patent Gazette, Sept. 23, 1879,* pat. No. 219,739, to A. Wilford Hall. "This invention consists in certain improvements in the phonograph which is the subject of letters patent No. 200,521, dated Feb. 19, 1878 to Thomas A. Edison." The device described was a dual cylinder recording machine which utilized both sides of the sound wave, one half being indented in the recording surface on the two opposed cylinders. A lever arm from the diaphragm had two stylii at the other end which, when at rest, would just touch the recording surface of the two cylinders.

Macdonald, and a number of others patented various forms of transcribing machines employing two cylinders, one to receive a recorded cylinder and the other a blank. Between the two cylinders would be a lever with a smooth reproducing stylus bearing on the record, on the other side of the lever a cutting stylus bearing on the blank. Even the Hall device covered by the third patent could be adapted to make wax duplicate records, though these were not known at the time of the invention. The use of a single lever arm, applied in various ways by various inventors, would produce a waveform in the second record that was inverse to the original record, but sounded the same. Other devices were based on the principle of the pantograph, which produced identical copies. Of course there was some loss in dubbing from one record to another—there still is today, even though reduced to an infinitesimal amount. The matter which restricted its use to the extent where it could not completely displace the recording by "rounds" was the softness of the so-called wax records, which were a nonsoluble metallic soap that varied in composition and qualities from time to time.

Knowing this, there was also a continual search for a material for blanks which could be hardened after recording. A hard playing surface would have permitted a large number of duplicates through the use of any one of a half dozen transcribing devices already in general use. The surprising thing is that with duplicating methods known almost from the first, the fiction that most commercial records of that time were "originals" should have received such credence. One explanation may be that the same psychology existed with respect to "copies" as we now know exists in the preference for "live" broadcast performances over recorded performances, even though the latter most often are more technically perfect.

Actually, it was almost impossible with the playing equipment then in use to distinguish many of the "dubbed"

records from the originals. There was a great deal of variation in the recording qualities of blanks, and recording diaphragms of identical thickness and appearance would often record quite differently. This applied also to the recording styli which would wear and consequently there was sometimes a great deal of variation in volume and quality of records taken from phonographs in a bank from the same performance. For this reason, copies of some of the better "takes" would often sound better than some of the original records. Of course, as more and more copies were taken from a given original, it would deteriorate and the copies would also be poorer.[4] Nevertheless, presumably because of the psychological factor mentioned, the salesmen and publicists of the various companies would invariably insist that all of *their* records were "originals."

How well this deception was carried out is well illustrated by the story that Russell Hunting used to tell as to how he discovered that unauthorized duplicates were being made of his records.[5] According to his story, Leeds and Catlin, one of the pioneer companies in making entertainment records, had engaged him to take ten rounds of his specialty, "Cohen at the Telephone," at five dollars per round. He stated that he had just finished the fourth round when a boy crossed the end of the studio with a tray of twenty-four cylinders. He was curious, and upon investigating, found that these were all records of himself

[4] A letter from the North American Phonograph Co., dated May 12, 1890 sent out to all local companies announced reductions of price on all musical cylinders. Band records were reduced to $1 each, vocal quartets to $1.20 and instrumental solos to 75¢ each. The letter stated that there would be a further reduction on those not quite perfect, including those *not so loud*.

Another letter dated August 31, 1891, signed by Thomas R. Lombard, president of the North American, to all companies stated that Edison had not the right to sell the local companies *duplicate* records as promised in the proceedings, but that it would be permitted for the present. (Letters in the files of the Edison National Historic Site.)

[5] *The Music Goes 'Round,* Fred Gaisberg, The Macmillan Co., New York, 1943.

reciting "Cohen at the Telephone." Well, he had only completed four rounds reciting into four recording funnels, which made a total of but sixteen cylinders! So, according to Hunting, he accused Leeds and Catlin of scheming to defraud him and when he threatened to expose them, they offered to make good. What is the matter with this story? Just this—four records at five dollars (the contract price) meant that Hunting was to be paid $1.25 for each cylinder. At that time the price of blanks alone was seventy-five cents each. Even at wholesale, Leeds and Catlin could not have sold the recorded cylinders for less than $1.65—even without making a profit. Obviously, someone was doing some "leg-pulling," to use an expression popular in those days. Some years later an exception to the general rule of secrecy regarding the duplicating of records was made in one notable instance. The importance of this practice to the commercial development of the industry was revealed on the occasion of a visit to the American Graphophone Co. plant of a group of recording artists. These were George Gaskin, Russell Hunting, Len Spencer, Dan Quinn, George Schweinfest, George Graham, and the recording director of the Columbia Phonograph Co. New York studio, Victor Emerson. The following account of the visit was published in the *Bridgeport Connecticut Farmer*, March 26, 1898.

"The company arrived at the factory about noon, and were met by Assistant Manager W. P. Phillips. They were first treated to a lunch and then made an inspection of the plant. Of course, the visitors took occasion to make some 'master' records. Huntington (sic) made a Casey speech to the G.A.R.; Gaskin sang 'On the Banks of the Wabash'; a trio and other records were also made.

"The 'master' record is made in just the manner one having a graphophone at his home would employ; the company, of course, has a special machine for the work, in which the recording of sound is quite pronounced, so much so that one hearing the 'master' records is often surprised to hear the human voice in such strident tones in the upper register. All the harshness is eliminated in making the duplicates. From each record 25 to 100 duplicates are made, the number depending on the quality of the 'master' record. The company turns out an average of 12,000 records a day from the 'master' records sent them, and yet are unable to keep up with the demand."

While on the subject of stories, nearly everyone is acquainted with the well-known story of the Sorcerer's Apprentice, in which the apprentice takes to monkeying around with the master's magic, bringing down a torrent of water around himself, eventually being saved by the timely arrival of the master. In this parable, Edison is the sorcerer and Macdonald the apprentice. Only in this case the ensuing flood changed the entire course of an industry! The master as long ago as December 3, 1890 had applied for a patent on a device for receiving cylinders of different diameters. What was the purpose of this? Edison had discovered that the higher frequency sound waves could be captured with less distortion on cylinders of larger diameter, traveling at a higher surface speed, thus spacing out more the finer undulations of the harmonic range vibrations. By this device the recording could then be transferred (at less troublesome speeds) to cylinders of smaller diameter with less loss of the delicate overtones. This was done on a recording phonograph operating at a corresponding relative speed.

Unfortunately for the progress of the industry, this patent was not granted until September 13, 1898. Unlucky day indeed! This may have been when the "apprentice" first learned of it, perhaps by reading the *Patent Gazette* of that date. Or he may have observed that a fellow by the name of Leon Douglass in Chicago had been reported as having been using a large size cylinder with dual tandem reproducers. In either event, the "apprentice" reasoned this way, if the use of a larger cylinder and higher speed assists in securing a better record, why not go all the way and also reproduce the music from the larger cylinders? The catch was that ever since 1895, Emile Berliner had been putting out more and more of those little seven inch hard rubber disc records, of which fifty could be placed in virtually the same space occupied by one of the large concert size cylinders which Macdonald prepared to place on the market.

There will always be a question as to whether Philip Mauro realized what the end result would be of what Macdonald proposed to do. It does not seem consistent with Mauro's keen judgment in most matters. However, Mauro went along with the proposal and in launching the Graphophone Grand (Fig. 7-2) made one of the most brilliant intellectual forays of his career. The American Graphophone Co. late in 1898 introduced this deluxe new graphophone designed to play exclusively the new large cylinders. These were so unwieldy

that it was found necessary to build a tape lifting device into the cartons for removing them, whereas the standard size cylinders could be withdrawn by spreading the fingers on the inside. If Mauro had ever in later years gone over to the Victor Talking Machine Co., the successors of Berliner in the United States, it might have been suspected that Berliner had paid him to go along with the gag!

Here it might be emphasized that the size of the cylinder, or the size of a disc, for that matter, is not a patentable feature in itself. It is only "in combination" that known basic elements form patentable inventions. In this case the purpose of the Edison device was to utilize the principle which he had discovered of spacing out the higher frequency undulations by recording on a larger cylinder at a relatively high surface speed which could then be re-recorded at a slower speed by a lever system or other means to the more convenient standard size cylinder for use by the public. That Edison was fully aware of the importance of this concept is attested by the unusually large num-

The Graphophone Grand
The long-looked-for Talking Machine
The Greatest Achievement of the Art

THE GRAPHOPHONE GRAND WITH A 56-INCH SPUN HORN

Fig. 7-2. The Graphophone Grand played the large Concert-sized wax cylinders. Increased volume and improved high-frequency response was obtained due to increased surface speed under the stylus. (From an early catalog.)

ber of countries in which applications for patents were filed. Although the majority of these patents were delivered promptly, for the most part within two years, the application lay dormant in the United States Patent Office for nearly eight years. The value of the principle discovered, aside from his own use of it, was best exemplified in the experience of Pathe-Freres, who for many years made all master records on large diameter cylinders, transferring to smaller diameter cylinders and even later to discs as late as the 1920's.[6]

Edison was a practical man and without question realized that the sale to the public of cylinders of large size was not desirable, even though his National Phonograph Co. was forced soon to produce them as a matter of competitive necessity. One of the persons responsible for the course of events to follow was Leon Douglass, a former associate of Edward Easton in Washington. Douglass in 1892 had applied for a patent on a method of rerecording from one cylinder to another by means of connecting tubes between the reproducer and recorder of two mandrels located upon the same shaft. He assigned this patent to Easton who later granted Douglass a license to manufacture records under patents of the American Graphophone Co. Douglass later moved to Chicago, where he became associated with Babson and others in the manufacturing of large quantities of cylinders for the growing midwestern market. Records were also merchandised through Sears, Roebuck & Co., and eventually he and his colleagues engaged in the manufacture of machines also, which eventuated in a court conflict with Easton and the Graphophone Co.

On February 4, 1898, Leon Douglass applied for a patent on a phonograph

which used dual reproducers in tandem, so that the stylus of the second followed closely in the same turn of the groove path of the first. By recording and reproducing at a fairly high rate of speed, the slight delay in response of the second reproducer was not particularly noticeable, in fact, the volume was seemingly more than doubled, probably because of the synthetic effect of reverberation thus introduced. Here as in Edison's concept, high surface speed for recording was important, but so also was a high surface speed for reproduction. Douglass apparently almost immediately realized that a larger size cylinder was required for the best functioning of his "Polyphone," as the dual reproducer instrument was named, for the *Phonoscope* for March told the story of the Douglass invention and that he was already employing experimentally wax cylinders five inches in diameter.

Whether Macdonald was inspired by this or the belated issuance of the patent to Edison on October 18, 1898, is immaterial. It seems more likely that it was the latter, for it was the November *Phonoscope* which carried the first announcement of a private exhibition at the New York Bowling Green offices of the American Graphophone Co. of the new instrument to be called the Graphophone Grand. As the *Phonoscope* was then published a month or two later than the nominal date, this was quite possible. The story stated that the demonstration was conducted by Philip Mauro who introduced the Graphophone Grand as the result of a miraculous new discovery in sound recording and reproduction by Thomas H. Macdonald. The December *Phonoscope* carried on its back cover a full page advertisement of the Graphophone Grand at $300 by F. M. Prescott, jobber and exporter who had theretofore dealt in Edison goods and had also, peculiarly, been closely associated with Hawthorne & Sheble, manufacturers of phonograph accessories in Philadelphia.

On December 24, 1898, an Associated Press dispatch to member newspapers

---

[6] Patents issued to Thomas A. Edison on this device as follows: England, Sept. 8, 1891; Belgium, Sept. 8, 1891; Spain, Oct. 16, 1891; Norway, Oct. 24, 1891; Austria-Hungary, Feb. 14, 1892; Cape Colony, March 31, 1892; New South Wales, April 28, 1892; Victoria, April 29, 1892; South Australia, May 4, 1892; Tasmania, May 4, 1892; Portugal, Nov. 23, 1892.

announced that a suit had been filed against Hawthorne & Sheble by the American Graphophone Co., seeking to have that firm enjoined from allegedly converting Edison phonographs into Grands, as authorized by Edison's National Phonograph Co. The fact is that to this point, neither Thomas H. Macdonald nor any other person of the Graphophone Co. had applied for any sort of a patent on a device utilizing large diameter cylinders! The only U. S. patent on such a device issued to that date was the one granted to Edison in October. The cleverness of Philip Mauro and the many astute publicists who had been gathered into the Graphophone employ was never more evident than in this coup in which the true inventor was made to appear as the pirate and which eventually forced Edison to produce a similar product (the Concert and the Class M Concert) just to prove that he had the right to do so! The following story as published in the Pittsburgh Dispatch of December 23, 1898, is typical of those printed throughout the United States and in many foreign countries:

"Not An Edison Invention"

"Associated Press Dispatch
Philadelphia, Pa. Dec. 24

"The American Graphophone Co. has entered suit in the U. S. Circuit Court here against Messrs. Hawthorne & Shebley (sic), to enjoin an alleged infringement of the graphophone patents. The American Graphophone Co. has recently developed a new model of talking machine known as the Graphophone Grand, whereby, it is claimed, acoustical results are obtained far exceeding in volume and quality anything heretofore obtained.
"It is alleged that Messrs. Hawthorne & Shebley have arranged to unlawfully construct graphophones of this type by reconstructing phonographs, making the necessary changes in the mechanism. The defendants, it is said, claim to be acting under the authority of the National Phonograph Co.,

which manufactures the so-called Edison Phonograph.
"The National Phonograph Co., it appears by the averments in the complaint, manufactured its machines under certain restricted rights under the graphophone patents, but these rights, it is claimed, were not transferable, and also do not include the right to make machines of the type known as the graphophone grand.
"The suit brings out the interesting fact that what is known as the Edison phonograph is manufactured under a license from the Graphophone Co. and is not an Edison invention. The Graphophone Co. patents, which cover every successful device for recording and reproducing sound, have recently been firmly established by court decisions."

Many of these stories bearing the Associated Press dateline were printed with such headlines as "The Phonograph Not an Edison Invention," or "Graphophone Grand Patent Infringed." Pushing their publicity campaign to the utmost, the Graphophone officials arranged a demonstration of the new Graphophone Grand before the Washington Academy of Sciences on January 31, 1899. No less a personage than Alexander Graham Bell introduced the speaker of the evening, Philip Mauro. Surrounded by notable men of science, Mauro delivered a brilliant paper entitled "Development in the Art of Recording and Reproducing Sound." The undeniable ability of Philip Mauro to deceive even the most intelligent people was never more in evidence than in his admirable exposition of the scientific principles involved. It was so successful that it was later repeated before the Franklin Institute of Philadelphia, for which Mauro later received a citation. The free publicity which resulted was worth a fortune.

To understand what a hoax had been perpetrated upon the Associated Press and the scientific societies it is necessary to note the way in which Mauro was able plausibly to attribute every constructive development in the science of sound reproduction to his associates and their predecessors. He opened his speech with the following statement:

"The Graphophone had its inception in the Volta Laboratory, in this city, of which Professor Bell was one of the founders, but the perfection of the instrument in the form of the Graphophone was due to Thomas H. Macdonald of Bridgeport, Connecticut."

In his second paragraph, Mauro stated that the invention of the phonograph had been quite dependent on the prior invention of the telephone the year before by Bell, who of course was on the platform. This was not true, for Bell had not achieved successful speech transmission until 1876, instead of 1875, as stated by Mauro.[7] The public demonstration that proved Bell had succeeded did not occur until June, 1876 at the Philadelphia Centennial Exposition. Moreover, the quality of reproduction obtainable from any of the Bell instruments made prior to the invention of the phonograph was not nearly as good as that of the first tin-foil phonograph.[8] Just a few years ago, a tin-foil recording made on a replica of the first Edison phonograph was broadcast with complete success over a radio network. This experiment was later repeated on television in connection with the Diamond Jubilee of Light.

Mauro also said in referring to the Graphophone Grand,

" . . . . a notable result has recently been produced"

rather than "invented," or "discovered." Truthful, but entirely misleading in its implication.

[7] *Journal of the Franklin Institute* also published complete in *The Household Journal*, April, 1899.

[8] *The Telephone in a Changing World*, Marion M. Dilts—Longmans, Green and Co., New York-Toronto, 1941, p. 3.

In the fourth paragraph, Mauro indulged in another sly deceit in order to deprecate the importance of the original invention of the phonograph by Edison. He said,

"So far there is nothing original in his thought, for Leon Scott had, many years previously, devised an instrument (known to all physicists as the 'phonautograph') whereby graphic representations of sonorous vibrations could be traced by means of a stylus in a film of lampblack."

Scott's method described a *laterally* undulating line without depth. Edison's first phonograph indented, or embossed, a *vertically* undulating groove of variable depth, which could be used to recreate sound—an entirely original conception.

Later on in his speech, in paragraph eight, Mauro stated,

"The failure of the phonograph was so pronounced as to discourage effort in the same direction for a long period of time."

The fact is that the phonograph made money in even its most primitive state while the telephone was yet attempting to demonstrate enough capability to warrant financial backing. As is now well known, Edison had shelved the development of the phonograph to perfect the electric light, certainly a decision the wisdom of which can hardly be questioned. In the meantime, by the publication of his British patent in 1878, covering large numbers of projected improvements to the phonograph, he had pointed the way for Bell and the Volta Laboratory Associates, as anyone who takes the trouble to read it may see.

Mauro in considerable detail outlined the work of the Bell's and Tainter as having provided the essential basis upon which Macdonald had built. As has been pointed out elsewhere, the graphophone had just one element left from the original graphophone of the Volta

Graphophone Co. and that was the admittedly important idea of incising. The methods and the materials then in use in the graphophone at the time Mauro was speaking had been developed by Edison in 1887 and 1888, and had been incorporated into the graphophone in 1893 without permission, and therefore had been illegal until the agreement of 1896, which was virtually a cross-licensing agreement.

With respect to the large diameter cylinder and what it would accomplish in the Graphophone Grand, Mauro said in paragraph ten,

"But within a few months a new development has taken place, which produces results in volume of sound and fidelity to the original far exceeding the limit of what was previously, and by those best able to form an opinion, deemed possible."

Here again, it is noteworthy that Mauro does not use the words "invention," or "discovery." Needless to say, the essential feature, the recording on a large diameter cylinder as a means of spacing out the closer sound vibrations so essential to what some now call "high fidelity," had within a few months received a belated patent awarded to Thomas A. Edison.[9] The principle involved and cylinders of identical size had been used in manufacturing machines and records by Douglass in Chicago, months before the appearance of the Graphophone Grand. Edison's later use of the principle was practical. Recordings on large size cylinders were transferred to cylinders of smaller diameter by means of a button-shaped sapphire, situated so that the major axis of the button was transverse to the groove. The advantages of the large cylinder were made available on cylinders of a size suitable for use by the public. This same principle had, in fact, been made available to the lateral field by the elliptical stylus designed

by the well known English inventor, Williamson, for use in the Ferranti moving-coil pickup with 78 rpm records. The reduction of the stylus tip for LP records from 1 mil to 0.7 and 0.5 mil was to meet the same problem.

In paragraph fourteen of his speech, Mauro emphasised the importance of the jewel recording stylus in achieving the results to be demonstrated. Here only the skeptic would perhaps have noted that he failed to credit the Bell's or Tainter, or even Macdonald with this essential feature. Why? Because it had been patented by Edison in 1892, applied for in 1890.[10]

Aside from questions of ethics, the ability of Philip Mauro to make a lucid explanation of the principles incorporated in the Graphophone Grand must be conceded. No better exposition of the scientific basis of a phonographic development has ever been given. However, in summing up in reference to the principle of the large cylinder, Mauro said,

"It seems strange indeed, that with so strong an incentive to increase the volume of sound, this simple law has not sooner been discovered."

The truth is, that it had been the publication of the patent belatedly awarded to Edison on September 13, 1898, which had taught Macdonald just enough of the Master's magic to launch a device which was to serve within a year or so only to emphasize certain superiorities of the disc to the cylinder —ease of handling, lower cost to the consumer, and economy of storage space!

The cleverness of Mauro in verbalizing the Edison concept and in foisting a perversion of it upon a learned scientific society as a new achievement for which the genius of Thomas H. Macdonald was responsible would be rather admirable, if it were not also so despicable. Not only had the Graph-

---

[9] Apparatus for receiving cylinders of different diameters, application filed by T. A. Edison, Dec. 30, 1890, granted Sept. 13, 1898.

[10] U. S. Patent Gazette, No. 484,583, issued Oct. 18, 1892, applied for May 27, 1890, jewelled point cutting tool, issued to Thomas A. Edison.

Fig. 7-3. The Edison Concert phonograph was spring-driven and was designed to play the Edison Concert records exclusively. Speed was about 160 rpm. Sound could be heard throughout a large auditorium.

ophone Grand principle been pirated from Edison, but also practically the entire list of contributory improvements which Mauro had cited, with the lone exception of the incising idea. The jewelled incising tool, the sloping mandrel, the solid wax blank, the jewelled reproducer, all were Edison patented improvements used by the American Graphophone Co. under the cross licensing agreement of 1896 and from which Edison never received a dollar. Macdonald and Mauro were both intelligent men and if they had devoted the same intensive effort to sincere research and constructive invention as they did to the securing of undeserved credit, their names perhaps now would be heralded by their posterity. Nor was this an isolated case. The year previously Macdonald had sought to steal from Edison the credit due him for the invention of the motion picture camera and the companion viewing machine called the Kinetoscope. Macdonald, with the assistance of a Bridgeport photographer by the name of Farini, built a machine infringing on the Edison patents which he called the "Graphoscope," again, as in the case of the Graphophone Grand, without having a single patent on the device at the time it was being announced to the public as his invention.[11] Nor did Macdonald ever receive a patent upon a motion picture device!

The only patent ever issued to Macdonald on a concert size graphophone was applied for on March 14, 1901 and granted on July 23, 1901. This was a graphophone which would permit the playing of both the standard size and concert size sylinders upon the same machine by means of one mandrel telescoping within the other. In retrospect, it was the introduction of the

[11] *Bridgeport Standard,* Aug. 24, 1897, article describing the Graphoscope as the invention of Macdonald and Farini.

Graphophone Grand and the accompanying campaign of misleading publicity which forced Edison to also manufacture the Edison Concert Phonograph (Fig. 7-3) in self-defense. This created the situation which gave the Berliner disc its great opportunity. The advantages of the concert size cylinders over the standard cylinders were volume and quality of sound. The first little hard-rubber discs had plenty of volume, but not much quality, and they were inexpensive and easy to handle. By 1898, the quality of reproduction from the discs was improving, because of the substitution of wax for zinc in the recording and shellac for rubber in the records. Now the difference between the space required by the concert cylinders as compared to the discs became an important consideration. Four standard cylinders could be stored in the space occupied by one concert cylinder, but fifty of the thin improved Berliner discs could be kept in the same space as has been noted. The concert cylinders were also much more expensive. The earliest ones sold for five dollars each, which would be equivalent to ten dollars or more today. Most of the Graphophone Grands were sold for exhibition purposes. Phonograph exhibitions and concerts to which admission was charged were given well into the 1900's. This temporarily lucrative business may have seemed to offer a sufficient incentive for the production of concert type machines and records.

This one patent issued to Macdonald on a concert cylinder instrument was later adjudged by the courts to be an infringement of the Edison patent.[12] Yet in 1899 the impression to be gained from the press and monthly publications was that Edison was the infringer and that Hawthorne & Sheble had been stopped from converting Edison phonographs to Grands on the basis of a patent issued to Macdonald on the Graph-

ophone Grand. The patent under which Hawthorne & Sheble had been rather willingly enjoined was the Bell-Tainter patent, under which Edison was licensed, to be sure, but only in the same way that the American Graphophone Co. was licensed under a much greater preponderance of Edison patents. This sort of publicity and frequent litigation centered around a very few of the many thousands of patents issued on phonographs and phonographic improvements during these crucial years in the development of an industry made a mockery of the patent system and the working of the courts, as well as fools of the newspapers and their readers.

In this episode, the smart Mr. Mauro knew that he could not stop Edison from producing concert type machines and cylinders, but he knew how to secure a million dollars worth of free publicity and convince a great many people that Edison had stolen the idea from Macdonald, instead of vice-versa. Meanwhile the competition went on to see who would be the first to introduce a practical molding process. Regardless of its glamour as a demonstration instrument, the large cylinders were unwieldy, fragile, and expensive. They offered to the manufacturer little more control over the record market than had the standard size cylinder. On the other hand, the inexpensiveness, convenience and minimum space requirements of the new discs, which meant so much to the user, carried a corresponding advantage to the producer.

Disc records from the beginning were all pressed, or molded duplicates. The company which made the Berliner Gramophone controlled completely the making of records for it. The advent of the discs therefore redoubled the intensity of a search for a process which would do for the cylinder what Berliner had done for the disc. Very early there had been a search for a different kind of recording surface, one which would be soft when recorded upon, but which could be hardened and used for making duplicates. Also envisioned almost from

---

[12] Macdonald vs. Edison, 21 APP-527, Court of Appeals, Washington, D. C. confirming finding of lower court that Macdonald's patent was invalid.

the first was making the surface of the wax somehow electrically conductive and then to make a mold by plating. Edison had been following the latter approach, having a number of patents on making the surface of the wax master conductive by dusting on finely divided graphite or plumbago and also by electrostatically depositing gold and then plating with baser metals. He also received patents on various types of molds, some one piece and others of two or more pieces. The multiple piece molds were unsatisfactory because of the virtual impossibility of casting without a seam. The one piece mold failed because of the lack of sufficient shrinkage to permit withdrawal on account of the depth of groove then employed. A different screw thread feed was necessary in recording in order to compensate for lateral shrinkage, as well.

There were so many "bugs" involved in the cylinder molding processes that it was not until 1901 that Edison was at long last enabled to market molded records in commercial quantities.[13] The gold-molding process which had been patented in principle as early as 1892 did not become a commercially useful method until after almost a decade of constant experimentation involving more than a score of contributory patents. The final link in this chain of inventions necessary to the final result was dated February 5, 1901, No. 667,662. Macdonald, who had been feverishly working towards the same goal, apparently was informed of this and very shortly found a way to circumvent this particular patent. At about the same time, the American Graphophone Co. began the production of molded records which they called Columbia High-Speed XX records. Both companies adopted 160 rpm as the standard speed, instead of the former 120 rpm speed which had been gradually arrived at as the standard speed of the earlier non-molded musical cylinders.

The harder composition which could be employed for the molded cylinders, plus the button-shaped stylus of Edison which permitted the accurate tracking of the more closely spaced undulations of the higher frequencies, made these new cylinders superior to the concert cylinders and consequently the large cylinder machines were obsolete. But the damage had been done. By early 1902 the discs were on the march. The Victor Talking Machine empire had begun its phenomenal growth. Molded metallic soap cylinders for certain technical reasons were impractical in the concert size, although Edison in 1912 made molded blue Amberol celluloid cylinders in that size for providing the sound for his kinetophone—talking pictures. Greater volume could now be obtained from the harder molded standard size cylinders than the softer concert cylinders, as well as longer life and better quality. From this time forward the concert cylinders were made only to order. By 1902, Columbia was claiming the world's record in cylinder production—two million per month, and these were the standard size cylinders as established by Edison in 1888. It is rather noteworthy in respect to the squabble that later arose as to who did develop the first successful molding process that Columbia did not call their records gold-molded until a year or two later, when an infamous decision was handed down in a district court of Connecticut. The American Graphophone Co. never owned a patent on gold-molding.

With respect to the technical importance of Edison's original device for transcribing a recording from a large diameter cylinder to a smaller one, this should be said. Pathe-Freres who operated under Edison licenses in Europe, for years used this device or an adaptation of it in all of its European studios. Master records were made on large diameter cylinders and then transcribed on smaller diameter cylinders in three different sizes for sale to the public. Even after the introduction of molding methods, Pathe re-

[13] The first molded cylinder records on the market were the pink celluloid cylinders produced by the Lambert Co., of Chicago, in 1900.

corded the originals on the large size cylinders and reduced them to the smaller sizes for processing. Pathe even recorded on cylinders for transferal to discs into the 1920's. Many French and other European opera artists had their voices recorded by this means by Pathe in France and other countries. Edison and Columbia also recorded opera and classical vocal artists on cylinders in European cultural centers, most of which were never offered for sale in the United States.

Meanwhile, by 1902, Columbia and its parent company had contrived to also enter the disc talking machine business by the back door. This proved to be yet another story of intrigue, corporate manipulations, and devious methods. Is it possible that Mauro foresaw this eventuality in 1898?

CHAPTER 8

THE CELLULOID CYLINDER AND MOLDING PATENTS

THE search for a record surface which would harden, or which could be hardened after recording, had a very early inception, although not quite as early as the effort to find a satisfactory molding method. As news stories and the specifications of his earliest patents tell us, Edison from the first, had envisioned making molds, beginning with the idea of plating the tinfoil and copper sheets used for the recording surface after recording for use as a matrix for making duplicates. Offhand, it would seem this would be feasible and it is rather surprising that nothing commercially was done with it. Many experiments were made along this line, as Edison's notebooks tell, also in backing up the recorded foil with plaster of Paris, or asphaltum compounds. Undoubtedly the lack of a suitable plastic material for the making of useful duplicates was a contributory reason for many of the early failures.

The first record surface to be found that would harden after recording was covered in a patent granted to George H. Harrington of Wichita, Kansas, February 12, 1889. It had been applied for June 18, 1887. Harrington assigned the patent to himself and Edward H. Johnson, Edison's friend who had heralded the invention of the phonograph in a letter to *Scientific American* a decade before. This too, like Edison's first telephone repeater using paper as the recording medium, was a moving strip idea—what we would now call a

tape recorder, although neither involved magnetism as do those of today. The composition of the tape in the Harrington invention was the important element. Two different formulas were covered in the specification, one of celluloid mixed with molasses and beeswax, the other of glue, molasses, and wax. Smoothly surfaced tapes of these compounds could be temporarily softened by application of a solvent, such as alcohol, recorded upon while soft, than allowed to harden. This was the prototype of the later acetate type recording surfaces, although it was never introduced commercially as far as is known.

In France, M. Lioret a little later also experimented with methods for softening celluloid for receiving the impressions of sound waves. More important, his particular method of softening celluloid preparatory to recording, pointed the way to the eventually successful method of molding recorded cylinders of this material. By plunging a celluloid ring of the proper diameter into hot water, M. Lioret found that the surface was rendered soft enough for recording. This led directly to his later concept of a molding method on which he was granted a patent in the United States, No. 528,273, October 30, 1894. The method was to soften a celluloid ring by plunging it into hot water, then removing and inserting it into a mold. The pliant celluloid ring was then forced into the recorded undulations

93

of the mold by forcing a tapered mandrel lightly inside the ring. Then, by plunging mold and all into cold water, the shrinkage of the celluloid would permit withdrawal from the one piece mold.

As with many of these early molding patents, this sounded very plausible, but M. Lioret evidently had difficulty in perfecting it into a satisfactory process, for in November, 1897 an article appeared in *Scientific American* telling of the phonograph of M. Lioret, but making no mention of a record molding process. The making of the records was described only as the result of "a secret softening process." However, it was stated that the Lioret phonograph

was provided with a large trumpet and had been used for demonstrating in large halls very successfully. This was one of the advantages to be gained through the record material which would harden after recording. It was possible to impose more weight on the record, thus to generate more physical energy and thereby increase the volume of the reproduction. (See Fig. 8-1.)

In 1901 in the United States there was a legal case resulting from a patent interference involving a very similar idea. This was the suit of Frank J. Capps versus A. N. Petit of Newark, New Jersey, both former employees of Edison. It was claimed by Petit in his action that while employed at the

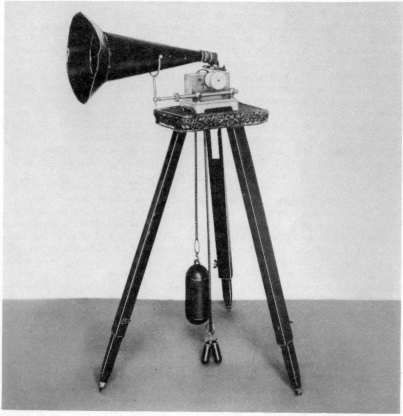

Fig. 8-1. The Lioret phonograph. (Courtesy of *The Science Museum, London England.*)

Edison Phonograph Works in 1896 he had conceived the possibility of recording on celluloid softened by a solvent and that he had conducted experiments at that time with only fair results. He claimed that later he discovered that by using acid of oil with an alcohol solvent that excellent results could be obtained and that patents on his process had been taken out all over the world, also that a company had been formed in England to exploit it. Capps had entered a claim in interference which was the subject of review by the court, which decided in favor of Petit.

Although this celluloid recording method seems to suggest spheres of usefulness similar to that filled by the acetate discs of today, it was really the need for a harder reproducing surface to permit the making of more and better copies by rerecording that provided the chief stimulus, for this was the only method of making duplicates then in commercial use. There was also a need for a harder surface for producing more volume, to compete with the discs, which from the beginning had considerable volume even though lacking in quality.

At this time the manufacturers of cylinder machines considered the ability to record anywhere to be a great advantage in the selling of these instruments in competition with the new disc talking machines which could not so be used for recording. Experience was soon to show that this advantage was more than offset by the lack of control over the record market. A laboratory processed record would have been of great assistance to the manufacturers of the cylinder machines, and Lioret had this in mind in 1897, for according to the *Scientific American* article, his thought is indicated by the reporter as follows:

"The apparatus, it is true, is not reversible, that is to say, it is impossible, as in the old phonographs, for a person to register songs and speeches for himself. The rollers have to be procured already prepared, and none of these can be in the

apparatus. The difficulty might be overcome if the inventor desired it, but it is very evident that he does not care to do so. He prefers to sell his rollers, and it is thus certain that they can be properly registered."

"Bought and paid for, too," it might be added, which was the Achilles heel of the cylinder industry in the United States.

Edison had not been trailing the procession in his efforts to achieve the same end results. As early as 1888 he had filed a caveat on a method he proposed to develop for molding celluloid records. A caveat is a formerly used device of filing an intention to invent. It was not an application for a patent. Numerous "snags" had to be eliminated in order to make the process he had in mind commercially applicable, as Lioret undoubtedly had discovered. So it was a decade later and after countless experiments before Edison filed a patent application. In the meantime, his former employees, Capps and Petit, having seen the celluloid experiments in progress, had independently conceived the idea of recording directly on celluloid blanks, as already noted. As with the similar Lioret process, these developments were useful and of interest, but still left unsatisfied the need for a mass producible, molded cylinder with a hard surface.

In the meantime a patent was applied for by Thomas B. Lambert of Chicago, on August 14, 1899, upon a process for making a copper mold by electroplating a graphite-dusted master wax cylinder and then using this mold for making "cellulose" or similar plastic duplicate records. The Lambert Record Co. was organized as a result and early in 1900 began the production and sale to the public of molded musical cylinder records of celluloid for use on the standard Edison and Columbia machines. A patent was granted to Lambert on December 18, 1900. Meanwhile, an Edison application for a patent on a celluloid record molding process had been gathering dust somewhere in the files of the patent office since March 5, 1898 —more than six months before the filing of the Lambert application. This was finally issued to Edison, November 11, 1902, No. 713,209. This together with another patent issued to Edison on an improvement to his gold deposition or "sputtering" process, completed the series essential to carry out the intention of his caveat. This was No. 713,863, applied for June 16, 1900, issued November 18, 1902.

But the first records to be molded in commercial quantities by Edison's National Phonograph Co. were not celluloid, but a metallic soap compound, somewhat denser and harder than that used for recording. The method was substantially the same, however. The first Edison molded records were made in 1901. However, Edison was not the first to manufacture molded cylinder records for the trade, the first were the "pink" Lambert celluloid cylinders, now collectors' items of great rarity. A suit was filed by the National Phonograph Co. for infringement of its Edison patents. The case was brought before the Circuit Court of the Northern District of Illinois. The decision in this case and the subsequent appeal were both adverse to the plaintiff.

The first decision, briefly, was to the effect that a patent for a process is not infringed by the sale of a product. It was held that the proof offered by the plaintiff that the defendant sold an article a month or two after the patent had been issued to the plaintiff was not sufficient to establish that the article had been made after the date of issuance of the patent. So the motion of the plaintiff for an injunction was denied and the defendant continued to infringe. In August, 1905, the Circuit Court of Appeals of the 7th Circuit handed down the decision that the Edison celluloid patent of 1902, applied for in 1898, was void, because he had used the process described therein for nine years before the patent was issued. The basis for the decision of the court was apparently in the testimony of Dr. F. Schulze-Berge and Charles Wurth of

the Edison staff, who had explained in great detail a series of seemingly endless experiments which had preceded the obtaining of results reliable enough to justify the application for a patent. The judge in his decision stated that the production of a great many matrices and a great many copies in this manner constituted public use and thereby disqualified the patent. The essential facts are and were that Edison had filed a caveat as permitted at that time by law on October 26, 1888; but it had not been found possible to overcome a multitude of technical difficulties until March 5, 1898, when application was filed—more than a year before that of Lambert, upon which action was then delayed for nearly five years in the patent office. Those records were experimental and were not sold to the public. Nevertheless, the decision of the Judges Grosscup, Baker, and Seaman, with the opinion written by the latter, was that Edison patent number 713,209, dated November 11, 1902, filed March 5, 1898, for a process of duplicating phonograms was void, by reason of prior publication of the invention.

Thus, one of the most costly and important inventions of the cylinder phonograph was taken from its originators and given to others. The sequel to this story is that in July, 1906, the Indestructible Record Company was organized under the laws of Maine, to operate under the Lambert patents and others which it acquired, including one issued to W. F. Messer, July 29, 1902, which had been applied for February 1, 1902.

Edison could not now use celluloid as a record surface. He had step by step, patent by patent, built up the several and constituent elements of a complete process. He had lost the keystone patent because he had found it necessary to actually make molds and mold records in order to perfect a commercial process, further complicated by the dilatory performance of the patent office. The National Phonograph Co. actually made one more attempt to stop the Lambert Co., this time on the basis of the Edison tapered bore patent. But as the Lambert cylinder made contact with the mandrel only at either end of the cylinder, where the celluloid was turned in for about a quarter of an inch, this patent was held not infringed. In other words, even though the Lambert cylinders were made to fit upon the Edison tapered mandrel, because the Lambert cylinders only had a bearing surface for about one-half inch of the interior, it was decided that it did not have a tapered bore! This again was a most specious interpretation, typical of cases with which our patent history is replete.

The unjust decisions in these patent cases alone altered the entire course of the industry, for it was several years before Edison was legally able to again return to the inevitable superiority of the expanded plastic film impressed into the now perfected molds which he was able to produce through the other essential elements of his process. Instead, he was forced to fall back on a metallic soap composition, fragile and much less durable. This placed a limit on the volume of reproduction just at a time when this was a critical factor in the competition with the rapidly improving discs in late 1901 and 1902.

Meanwhile, another series of patent cases involving the molding methods arose between the National Phonograph Co. and its old arch enemy, the American Graphophone Co. The latter had begun producing molded records almost simultaneously with the former. One of these cases involved the same celluloid molding patent as the one in litigation with Lambert. In Circuit Court District of Connecticut on March 17, 1905, in two cases in which the National Phonograph Co. was plaintiff, Judge Platt handed down decisions adverse to the Edison patents. In the one, Judge Platt held that the patent was limited in its application to the process of expanding the blank within the mold, and was not infringed by a casting process. In the other, he held that Edison patent No. 667,662 for a process of duplicating cylinder phonograph records was entitled

only to a narrow construction in view of the prior art and so was not infringed by the process of the Macdonald patents, Nos. 682,991 and 682,992.

The necessity of bringing suit in the court district where the infringement allegedly occurs was one of the factors which served to make a mockery of the patent laws in the United States, as it does to some extent yet today.[1] In a given district, the local industrialists, lawyers, politicians, and the district court judges are invariably well known to each other and are often inextricably involved in the same general cycles of activity which mutually involve them economically, socially, and politically. Under these circumstances a suit brought against a local manufacturer by an outside inventor often has as much chance as the proverbial snowball in Hades. The findings of the judge in these two cases were so inconsistent as to be fantastic. In fact his prejudice against the complainant shines forth through his legalistic phraseology in more than one place, as in the following example,

"And now let us step, as best we can into the patentee's shoes, (Edison's) and find whether, in the particular branch of the art at which he aimed, he did, by the exercise of inventive genius, add anything to the then existing common stock of knowledge. The graphophonic art may be said to have fairly begun with the invention of Bell and Taintor (sic), letters patent No. 341,214, dated May 4, 1886. This taught the public how to produce the commercial and transferable sound record. It led at once to an anxious search for a mold and material for producing a large number of satisfactory duplicate records of unvarying and excellent quality. On the same day Tainter told how records could be duplicated by so using plum-

---

[1] However, this is also sometimes a much needed protection for a poor defendant. Actually, it can usually be avoided by bringing suit against a customer, whom the manufacturer, as a practical matter, is forced to defend.

bago as to make an electroplated matrix, and then copying the master record by mechanism."

Judge Platt chose to ignore the Edison British patent of 1878 and also the pertinent fact that neither Edison nor Tainter "by the existing common stock of knowledge" had been able until 1901 to produce "a large number of satisfactory duplicate records of unvarying and excellent quality." Elsewhere in his decision Judge Platt blandly admitted the fact that it was the invention by Edison of the curved edge scoop recording stylus which had made the withdrawal of the record from a single piece mold possible, because of the shallower grooves. For some reason the Edison attorneys had not seen fit to bring action on this particular patent, but Judge Platt in mentioning it admitted his knowledge of it, while at the same time attempting to justify his assertion that Edison had abandoned the attempt to use a single piece mold! As the literature of patent law so often affirms, the act of invention consists most often of the combination of several known elements to accomplish a new purpose. In the long search to complete a practical molding method, Edison had acquired no less than twenty-five different a priori combinations leading to the eventual success which crowned this persistent and costly effort. As against this, Thomas Macdonald to the time of the litigation had received but two patents dealing with the molding process. The one which consisted of pouring molten material into a one piece mould was described by Judge Platt in his decision as a process well known to the other arts and hence devoid of invention. So it was and the question might well be asked as to how then the patent office could possibly have granted Macdonald a patent upon it. Also, this being true, why did not the judge hold that the molding of cylinder records was now an art open to the public? All that he held was that the Edison patent was not infringed by the Macdonald patent, thus still restricting the produc-

tion of molded records to the two companies. Judge Platt knew full well that the molding was but one constituent part of a complete process. He also admitted in his opinion that he knew of the vital importance of another Edison invention to the operation of the molding method as used by Macdonald. As long as the patent on the scoop recorder was not before the court, the judge could ignore it legally, if not morally, instead he chose to brazenly flaunt it before the Edison attorneys, as though challenging them to bring suit for infringement of that patent. As it involved "incising," the brilliant Graphophone Co. attorney, Philip Mauro would have probably loved to have had an action brought into the local district court on that issue!

The other Macdonald patent involved in this case covered the case hardening of the molded record surface by the introduction of cooling water in the outer jacket of the mold, displacing the steam which filled it during the pouring. This was also a phenomenon well known in the arts. It was so well known that in the method of the competing Edison patent, which differed only in that the molten material was drawn into the mold from the bottom in order to avoid bubbles and in which the record was hardened in precisely the same way, the idea of claiming "case hardening" probably never occurred to the Edison patent attorneys. This latter case is very similar to that of the famous Jones lateral disc patent which was granted on almost precisely identical process as had been developed and patented earlier by Berliner and Johnson by means of clever re-wording of the specifications and claims. This had served to permit the Graphophone Co. to get into the disc business in 1902, just as this dual decision by Judge Platt permitted the Graphophone Co. to continue to use processes of molding records developed at great expense by Thomas A. Edison on the basis of but two patents by Thomas Macdonald which had contributed absolutely nothing new to the art.

Edison's firm belief in the technical superiority of the cylindrical surface with its uniform speed beneath the stylus is well indicated by the persistency with which he attacked and eventually overcame the multiplicity of problems which had plagued the development of the molding method. The Graphophone Co., on the other hand was already in the disc business, into which it had been trying to crash since 1899 and which had been made finally possible by the infamous Jones patent. The initiation of the later famous red seal series of Victor in 1902—all ten inch imported recordings, followed by the Grand Opera series of Columbia ten inch discs recorded in this country issued in 1903, somehow failed to stimulate Edison to do likewise. The Columbia discs, poorly recorded and with a poor surface, received but a slight acceptance. The Victor discs recorded in Europe by the Gaisbergs and other recording teams of the Gramophone & Typewriter Co. Ltd., were much better and prompted a change of policy of the Victor Co. shortly after Calvin Childs

began consistently to record the great opera stars appearing in the United States for Victor, engaging them whenever possible on an exclusive basis.

A factor affecting the disc versus cylinder competition was the introduction of the twelve inch disc by Victor in 1903 which increased the playing time to about three and one-half minutes, as against the two minutes of the cylinders. Edison delayed putting out a grand opera series until 1906 and by this time both competitors were putting most opera selections on the longer playing discs. In their fragile form and restricted playing time, the cylinders could not begin to compete in the field of serious music with the discs.

As has been mentioned elsewhere, Columbia's early strength had been in the urban areas, as Edison's had been in the rural areas. Consequently, with Victor gaining the attention of opera lovers and city folk by its success in enrolling the great opera artists and top flight entertainers, Columbia's cylinder business began to fade early. In

Fig. 8-2. The Twentieth Century Graphophone type BC, also called the Premier, sold for $100 without horn. (From a 1907 catalog.)

an attempt to stem the decline and to stimulate interest in cylinders again, the American Graphophone Co. purchased the rights to a new mechanical amplifying system which had been earlier invented by Daniel Higham, of Boston, Massachusetts. By means of a simple little amber friction wheel device, the mechanical pull upon the diaphragm from the stylus was augmented by power from the spring motor. By this, much greater volume could be secured from the cylinder than formerly. The technical flaw was that, as in the use of the floating weight by Edison, the wear upon the record was increased proportionately, as well. By combining Higham's contrivance with a longer mandrel, the playing time could also be increased. This was named the Twentieth Century Graphophone, Fig. 8-2, and was introduced in 1905. Records six inches long were cut with the then standard one-hundred grooves to the inch, thus increasing the playing time by a little more than half. This was probably the chief stimulus to the premature decision to launch the Amberol four minute wax Edison record. As a competitive expedient, it was decided to go the Twentieth Century Graphophone one better and to double the playing time by increasing the number of grooves to the inch from one hundred to two hundred. The difficulty lay in the fact that virtually the same comparatively soft, fragile metallic soap compound was to be used for the new records. The closer spaced smaller grooves also necessitated the sale of special reproducers and a new feed mechanism for existing phonographs. Because of the smaller groove it was necessary to impose a much greater unit area pressure on the record surface to produce the same volume as the prior standard cylinders. This soon caused difficulty. Just at the time when faced with the job of selling attachments and introducing the four minute Amberol record to the thousands of Edison users through trade channels, jobbers began to report that dealers and customers were complaining that the new records would not stand up. This was where the adverse decision in the 1902 celluloid patent battle with Lambert was to prove most costly.

The Edison Grand Opera Series had been continued consecutively numbered into the Amberol four minute records where it was thought the increased playing time would be most useful and welcome. Instead, the advantage of the longer playing time was quite lost on the purchaser when he found that the beautiful high notes of Leo Slezak singing Celeste Aida were being cut off after a few playings. Even for Slezak, a two dollar record that played a few times only was considered too expensive. In September, 1908, announcement was made in the *Talking Machine World* that in Cleveland, Ohio, the U. S. Phonograph Record Co. capitalized at $300,000, had been organized to produce indestructible cylinder records. These soon appeared on the market as the U. S. Everlasting records. Two-minute cylinders were made in 1908, four minute in 1909. At the same time the Columbia Phonograph Co. announced that it was taking over the sales of the celluloid cylinder records made by the Indestructible Record Co. of Albany.

The National Phonograph Co. was in a dilemma. What had been intended as a challenge to the longer playing Twentieth Century Graphophone and the discs had boomeranged. The effort to provide longer playing time had only served to focus attention on the chief drawback of all of the Edison cylinders—their fragility. Edison called together his associates Jonas W. Aylesworth and Walter H. Miller who had assisted in solving the shrinkage problem which had so long delayed the introduction of molding and put it up to them to find a new record composition. An intensive drive was organized and experiments began which eventually resulted in the ultimate decision to manufacture an entirely new type of disc record. However, the experiments failed to disclose a more practical material than celluloid for cylinder records.

Great damage was done to the Edison potential classical record market by this situation which existed for four critical years. When the solution to the four minute Amberol impasse was found by buying the rights to the celluloid process now owned by Philpot in England, it was too late for Edison to make any sort of real competition for Victor which had solidified its bid for the domination of the classical market during those same years. The irony of this bitter experience for Edison was that the Philpot process had been developed from patents originally issued in the United States to A. N. Petit, former Edison employee. Philpot had acquired additional information as trustee for the bankrupt Lambert Co. which had, a decade before, thwarted Edison in a contest over molding method patents. Now there was little difficulty in the perfecting of a factory system for producing celluloid records—Edison and his colleagues had been through all that before. It was found possible to even use the same molds previously used for the wax Amberol records. The exterior of the new celluloid records was a rich, glossy blue, with a plaster of Paris core. They were designated as Blue Amberol records. The playing time, as with the prior wax Amberols, was four minutes or more, revolving at 160 rpm. The records were unbreakable and among the most durable records ever made. Later a celebrity series was introduced in a brilliant, reddish purple color. A new, larger volume reproducer (Fig. 8-3) was designed for use with these records utilizing a cork stiffened diaphragm. A greatly improved air tight tone passage was developed with a constantly increasing cross section from the apex of the neck of the reproducer to the outermost rim of the horn. This then highly advanced design may now be recognized as the prototype of the modern "exponential" horn. As happened so many times, Edison conceived improvements in terms of functional performance, others later erected the verbal and theoretical explanations and wrote learned scientific papers. With

the higher priced Edison phonographs the reproduction was much more accurate than in the other machines then before the public. Following the lead of Victor with its Victrola, phonographs were designed with internal horns (Fig. 8-4) and were labelled "Amberolas." The high point in the development of the acoustic cylinder phonograph was reached with the "Concert" models (Fig. 8-5) which were made in both the in-

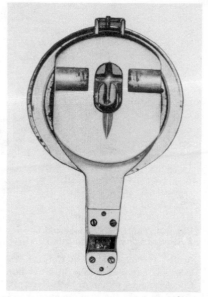

Fig. 8-3. Edison's improved reproducer had a cork-stiffened diaphragm and spring-loaded weight.

ternal and external horn types. These had a fixed and air-tight tone passage with constantly expanding bore from diaphragm chamber to the flare of the horn. The record moved horizontally beneath the stylus on the principle of the lathe. The earlier Concert Amberolas, prior to the introduction of the blue Amberol records, played both two and four minute wax records by an ingenious turn-over reproducer, prototype of the turn-over cartridge of today. Later models were made to play the Blue Amberol cylinder only. Acous-

Fig. 8-4. The Edison Amberola 6, one of a series of Amberola types. (Courtesy of Edison National Historic Site.)

tically, the external horn Concert, Fig. 8-5, was superior to the internal horn Concert model although both were produced to meet the same general specifications. Functionally, the open horn was and is always inherently superior to the enclosed horn. In England, open horn machines for disc records were made for connoiseurs until well into the 1940's.

In the search for a better record surface for the cylinders, a material was discovered which had the desired properties, but was applicable only to a disc process. The extensive and important research made by Edison and his associates in the field of chemistry of plastic materials at this time not only resulted in the decision of Edison to make a disc phonograph, but also marked the beginning of our modern synthetic thermo-setting plastics industry. Coin-

cidentally only a few miles away, another group of men working entirely independently were seeking for a similar material for other uses and had come up almost simultaneously with a similar answer. Named after its chief inventor, Leo Baekeland, the product "Bakelite" was a phenolic plastic as was the Condensite used for the Edison disc record. Multitudes of other uses for phenolic resin plastics have been discovered since.

The decision to develop a disc record really marked the end of the long, progressive development of the cylinder process which first began in 1887.

Following the introduction of the four-minute wax Amberol record in November 1908, the U. S. Phonograph Co., Cleveland, Ohio, the following year began molding four-minute "Everlasting" cylinders in celluloid. In 1910, the

Fig. 8-5. The Edison cylinder Concert phonograph featured a moving mandrel and a shut-off attachment. (Courtesy of Edison National Historic Site.)

Indestructible Record Co. of Albany also began producing four-minute celluloid cylinders.

The last two-minute metallic soap-type cylinders made by Edison were issued in September 1912. A few two-minute Edison cylinders were molded in the Blue Amberol celluloid shortly afterward, and the first of the four-minute Blue Amberol cylinders were issued in October 1912.

Edison had a dependable rural area trade which stuck by him through thick and thin. The adoption of the celluloid process and the conversion of many thousands of machines in homes to play the new cylinders, together with the sales of new Amberolas, again accelerated the Edison cylinder business even after the disc machine was introduced. Although by this time the discs had already fairly well pushed out the cylinders on the continent, there was also a large sale of Edison Blue Amberol records in England until World War I. This may also be said to mark the beginning of the decline of Edison cylinder sales in the United States.

However, due to the situation which existed with respect to the markets, the Twentieth Century Graphophone actually had aroused but mild interest. It was advertised until 1909 when Columbia filled its still diminishing demand for longer playing cylinders by taking over the sales for the Indestructible records. These were made in both two and four minute types, but generally the four minute Indestructible records were inferior in recorded quality and surface to the Blue Amberols. Within a few years Edison had the cylinder field virtually to himself.

Edison's biggest year to this time was 1907, with gross phonograph, record and accessory sales of over 7 million dollars. Sales had dropped to about 2¼ million dollars by 1913, when the Edison disc machine was introduced. Strangely, although the sales of Edison disc machines and records increased year by year, as might be expected, to a peak of over 20½ million dollars by 1920, the sales of cylinder machines and records first decreased to a low of something over a million dollars a year by 1915 and then began to rise again. In 1920 over 2½ million dollars was spent by the public for Blue Amberol cylinder machines and records. In the United States, most of these cylinder machines went to the rural trade.

CHAPTER 9

THE COIN-SLOT PHONOGRAPH INDUSTRY

COIN-IN-THE-SLOT machines are nearly as old as coinage. An Egyptian priest is said to have devised a mechanism that would deal out a small amount of a magic potion for warding off the powers of evil upon the deposition of a coin of the proper weight. This was presumably contrived so that he might pursue uninterrupted his experiments in alchemy by which he hoped to transmute lead into gold. Since those days of the Pharaohs it has become recognized that if this wise man of old had developed the full potential of his coin-slot device he would have wound up with all the gold in the kingdom anyway! Today, it is estimated that in one year in the United States alone, the coins that pass through coin slots are worth more than all of the gold at Fort Knox.

Of course, it was not until the development of minted coinage of precise diameters and weights that it was possible to make reliable coin-operated devices suitable for commercial use. Even so, from medieval times there have been coin-operated automatons, toys, and primitive mechanical banks. But the great incentive towards the development of such devices for commercial use was the rising costs of labor and the extension of the principle of the division of labor resulting from the industrial revolution into merchandising methods.

Considering the mechanical skills which had been developed, it is rather surprising that more practical use of

coin-in-the-slot devices had not been made before 1889, which marks the beginning of this use with the phonograph. Prior to this time there were in use generally only such devices as weighing machines and gum dispensing machines. To the younger generation, it will seem strange also that these primitive "juke boxes" were in use before there were any home phonographs.

In 1888, Jesse H. Lippincott had organized the North American Phonograph Co. to operate as sales agent for the improved Edison Phonograph and he had personally contracted to distribute the Graphophone in the United States, except for the territory which had prior to this been given to the Columbia Phonograph Co. of Washington, D. C. The original intention was to promote the use of both machines for office work, a free choice to be given the lessors of the instruments as to which type they were to use.

Although the organizers of the Columbia Graphophone Co. were themselves court reporters and therefore fully conversant with the needs of stenography, they were unable to make a success of the business of renting machines for that purpose. This was true even after substituting the Edison machines for the Bell-Tainter type graphophones, which had proven entirely impractical. If these men could not do it, it was quite obvious that others less familiar with the field in which the phonographs were to be used would be even less successful.

Louis Glass, general manager of the Pacific Phonograph Co., was up against this situation in common with the rest of the local phonograph companies. But Glass was a resourceful fellow. He equipped one of his electric motor operated Edison phonographs with a nickle-in-the-slot operating device so that it might be used as an entertainment machine. On November 23, 1899, Glass installed it in the Palais Royal Saloon in San Francisco. It was equipped with four listening tubes and a coin slot for each tube. Thus for each playing of the record the machine would take in from five to twenty cents. Within a few months it was apparent to Glass and his associates that here was the way to "coin" money, and more than a dozen of the other idle Edison phonographs were converted and placed in other locations. Glass also designed a multi-tube attachment and applied for a patent on his coin-controlled mechanism.

Meanwhile, in New York City, Felix Gottschalk, secretary of the Metropolitan Phonograph Co., had arrived at the same brilliant conclusion by a somewhat different route. He had decided that a coin-operated phonograph working on the principle of the weighing machine would be a profitable idea. In February of 1890, Gottschalk organized the Automatic Phonograph Exhibition Co., of New York, with a capital of one million dollars, for the purpose of making the mechanisms, leasing them to others on a profit sharing basis and in operating them in their own territory. However, about this time Louis Glass met Gottschalk in New York and a deal was consummated by which the Automatic Phonograph Exhibition Co. acquired the rights to Glass' multi-tube coin-slot mechanism, pooling it with others.

The Automatic Exhibition Co. began operating with a glass-topped cabinet which would hold a single cylinder Edison machine in the top and a space for the storage battery in the bottom. Listening tubes protruded from the front for the listeners. The original coin device operated on the principle of making or breaking the electrical circuit from the storage battery to the motor. Central station current was not then available everywhere as it is now, even in metropolitan cities like New York, so storage battery operation was a quite expedient means, although primary batteries also might be used.

At this time the phonograph and the graphophones were quite different instruments. As the graphophones were not electric motor equipped generally, but employed a foot treadle, the phonograph was used predominately for entertainment purposes. This posed a thorny dilemma for Lippincott, for he had personally contracted for the delivery of five thousand graphophones per year. Moreover, the graphophones used a different size and kind of cylinder than that used on the phonograph.

As a means of exchanging useful information and settling problems of inter-company relations, the National Association of Phonograph Companies had been organized. The first convention of representatives was held in Chicago, May 28th and 29th, 1890.

The advantages of standardization were quite obvious to all, as well as the predicament of Lippincott with respect to his contract with the Graphophone Co. Regardless of what occurred later, these pioneers of the phonograph felt kindly towards Lippincott and stuck with him to the end. With this background the reasons for the resolution to be requested by Louis Glass are apparent. This resolution was as follows:

"Be it resolved
    that all parties, that is, the American Graphophone Co., the North American Phonograph Co., and Mr. T. A. Edison, shall direct all their efforts to that end; that they give us one instrument for correspondence, stenography work and for amusement."

At this convention, one of Automatic's first machines was exhibited by Gottschalk. He offered the independent companies contracts by which Automatic would supply the cabinets and operating mechanisms and the companies could use their own Edison machines obtained through their contracts with North American. To secure the right to do business with the independent companies on this basis, Gottschalk had given North American fifteen thousand shares of Automatic Phonograph Exhibition Co. stock. By the contract offered to the companies, the machines were not to be sold, all servicing was to be done by the local companies and profits were to be shared with Automatic.

The opposition of Thomas A. Edison to the use of the phonograph for entertainment purposes has been greatly exaggerated in some accounts, and this opposition has been largely held responsible for the collapse of the Lippincott enterprise. To set the record straight it is necessary to deal with the source of the stories of this opposition. Samuel Insull, of later utilities fame, was the personal representative of Thomas A. Edison at this first convention of the local companies. Knowing of Mr. Edison's profound conviction in the ultimate usefulness of the phonograph as an efficient aid to business, and that he was loathe to see this aspect of its utility neglected, Insull stated that Edison was not too enthusiastic about the slot machines and felt that their use might tend to discourage acceptance of the phonograph as a business machine. In line with this, Mr. Insull warned the local company men that they should not neglect the original purpose of the organization of the companies—the promotion of the phonograph as an adjunct to business—its employment as a dictating and transcribing machine. How far sighted Edison was may be seen in the fact that this was also the last branch of the phonographic art abandoned by the Thomas A. Edison Industries Division of McGraw-Edison Co.

That Thomas Edison was not opposed to the use of the phonograph for entertainment purposes, per se, is evidenced by the fact that North American as early as this convention of 1890, or before, was recording and selling musical records to the local companies. This is proven conclusively by a letter in the files of the Edison museum dated June 19, 1890, reducing the prices on band and orchestra records to one dollar each. The month previously a letter had gone out to all companies showing that sapphire had been adopted by Edison as standard equipment for recorders and speakers. This removed the last obstacle to securing better records and better wear in service. The constant effort of Edison to have his machines "make good" in service must be given consideration in view of later events.

The impression seems to exist quite generally among the "authorities" of the recorded music industry that the Columbia Phonograph Co. was actually the first in the field of commercial recording. This has been fostered by the published recollections of some of the famous popular artists who recorded there first and consequently remember the experience quite vividly. But this false impression was nurtured mostly by the arrogant publicity of that company in its later campaigns, which as usual paid little heed to the truth. Even as distinguished and disinterested an observer as Fred Gaisberg fails to define how and when the changeover took place in that studio which marks the inception of commercially useful recording, as differentiated from the struggling and fruitless experimental stage. The first stage was when the enterprising *reporters,* Edward Easton and R. F. Cromelin were pursuing their will-o-the-wisp in futilely trying to introduce the Bell-Tainter graphophone as a dictating machine. The second stage was when *businessmen,* Edward Easton and R. F. Cromelin seized on the phonograph and the entertainment potential to save themselves from a most certain bankruptcy.

The failure of the graphophone in the hands of its best friends is conceded by

Gaisberg, who said, referring to Easton and Cromelin:

"Their purpose was to exploit it as a dictating-machine for office use. In this respect, however, it proved a failure. I remember some hundreds of the instruments being rented to Congress and all being returned as impracticable. The Columbia Company seemed headed for liquidation at this failure, but it was saved by a new field of activity which was created, almost without their knowledge, by showmen at fairs and resorts demanding records of songs and instrumental music. Phonographs, each equipped with ten sets of ear-tubes through which the sound passed, had been rented to these exhibitors. It was ludicrous in the extreme to see ten people grouped about a phonograph, each with a tube leading from his ears, grinning and laughing at what he heard. It was a fine advertisement for the onlookers waiting their turn. Five cents was collected from each listener so the showman could afford to pay two and three dollars for a cylinder to exhibit."

The machines which were returned from the congressmen were the Bell-Tainter graphophones, employing the one and five-sixteenth inch ozocerite coated cardboard cylinders eight inches long. The musical cylinders which Columbia then began making for the phonographs were the standard Edison solid wax type, 2⅛ inches in diameter and four inches long.

Gaisberg jumps from this to 1893, when he went to work for Charles Sumner Tainter to do some recording for him on the ozocerite cylinders. As noted in a prior chapter, Tainter was no longer working for the Graphophone Co., since it had ceased production.[1]

---

[1] *Manual of Industrial and Miscellaneous Securities—1900*
American Graphophone Co.
"From January, 1891, until May 1, 1893, the Company endeavored to establish a business by selling graphophones in competition with the

Tainter had turned to the designing of a coin-slot machine which he was readying for demonstration at the World's Fair at Chicago that year. Gaisberg says that the entire repertoire consisted of "Daisy Bell" and "After the Ball was Over." But this is the balance of this incident in his own words:

"His slot-controlled automatic phonograph was a truly remarkable achievement for that period but proved too delicate to stand the rough handling at the Chicago Fair Grounds. It was withdrawn and shipped to Washington where, acting on Tainter's instructions, I installed some dozens in the local saloons, restaurants and beer gardens. They were not infallible and sometimes would accept a coin without giving out a tune. In carrying out my job of collecting the coins in the early morning and reloading the machines with cylinders, I would at times be badly handled by an irate bartender who accused me of taking money under false pretenses. With the failure of the World's Fair venture, I was free to work for the Columbia Phonograph Company which had begun to make musical cylinders on a large scale."

This must have represented the last attempt to use the Bell-Tainter graphophone commercially, for by this time the American Graphophone Co. had ceased operations and was in the process of reorganization by Easton and others of the Washington group. Tainter had evidently been working independently for some time and the distinction which Gaisberg makes between working for Tainter and the Columbia Phonograph Co. is important. The records which Columbia "had begun to make on a large scale" were for the phonograph—not the Bell-Tainter graphophone, nor the Macdonald graph-

---

phonographs of the North American Phonograph Co. During this period of twenty-eight months the total receipts from agents and the public for machines and supplies amounted to about $2,500."

ophone, which had yet to make its appearance. But in establishing priority in the music recording industry, correspondence in the files of the Edison museum proves that North American Phonograph Co., sales agents for the Edison Phonograph Works had been issuing lists of musical records of this type regularly since early in 1890. At least a few of the *earlier* North American cylinders and the *later* Columbia phonograph cylinders are in the hands of collectors. The few musical cylinders which Gaisberg states he made for Tainter have apparently vanished.

The poll of the phonograph companies made at the June 1891 convention showed that of an estimated four-hundred machines which the Columbia Phonograph Co. had out on rental, only twelve to fifteen were graphophones. The men who managed this company were closest to the American Graphophone Co. and were the men who were within two years of the convention to take it over lock, stock, and barrel.

So that there will be no further confusion about it, and to anticipate the suggestion that Columbia made the records North American distributed, it should be noted that the roster of artists is quite different. Gaisberg mentions the pioneers who were recording under his direction at Columbia in 1893 as Dan Quinn, Johnny Meyers, George Gaskin, Len Spencer, and Billy Golden —all of whom made records later for Edison and other companies. However, the lists sent out by North American in 1893, include Thomas Butt, Tom Wooly, Ed Francis, Ed Clarence, Will Nankerville, R. G. Wilson, and R. K. Franklin.

That the Columbia singers were better known at a later date must be admitted, but in the earliest period talent was a minor consideration, the novelty of hearing reproduced voices or music was enough. As time went on it was found that the patrons would not waste their nickels on poor records. As the Automatic Phonograph Exhibition Co. stated in one of its early letters to the trade,

"Receipts increase or decrease in various machines as the records, which are changed daily, are good or mediocre, and the different localities require different attractions."

In general the preferred fare seemed to have been comic songs, monologs, whistling and band records. However, in some saloon locations, hymns were quite popular!

By the time of the second convention of the phonograph companies held in New York City, June, 1891 all but three of the remaining nineteen local companies were in the coin-slot phonograph business. The New York Phonograph Co. had 175 machines on location and the Old Dominion Phonograph Co. of Virginia 142. Many of the companies were reluctant to pay the fifty per cent of gross demanded by the Automatic Co. in its contracts, especially as the local companies had to do all of the servicing. The machines were placed usually without paying a percentage to the owners of the locations, as they were considered to be business boosters. Despite the stern warnings to infringers by the Automatic Co., there were several new types of nickel machines offered for outright sale, averaging about fifty dollars each, creating considerable competition for Automatic with its stiff percentage deal. These new machines generally had a square, or slanting glass top on a base cabinet of oak, cherry, or mahogany, with the ear tubes hanging from the front, to be used with the standard Edison phonograph and battery. In general, these machines were equivalent to the machines offered by the Automatic Co.

The receipts from some of these early slot-machines were amazing, especially in view of the mediocre quality of entertainment offered and the fact that there was no selection offered, except in the case of the phonograph parlor. But contrary to the erroneous opinion now held which has been built up by generations of looking down the nose at the products of a prior time, many of the cylinder records of the time when heard through the ear tubes had surprising clarity and musical quality. This may be demonstrated today with aged records made sixty or more years ago! Hearing the same records through one of the crude early horns, however, reveals a shocking loss in quality.

The Louisiana Phonograph Co. reported that one of its machines had taken in one thousand dollars in two months following April of 1891, which then represented three times the purchasing power compared to today. The location is suspected to have been one of those rather illegitimate types of establishment from which the latter day "juke" box derived its name. The Missouri Phonograph Co. reported that it had about fifty machines on location at the time, one of which took in one-hundred dollars in a week. This company then serviced each machine twice daily, changing the record each time.

Although Edison is said to have been not too enthusiastic about the coin-slot business, it is noteworthy that the Edison Phonograph Works, of which he was President, began the manufacture of musical "phonograms" as early as 1890.[2] To begin with, the Edison Phonograph Works also made all of the blanks which were used by the companies, as it was entitled to do by the contracts between all concerned. But human nature being what it is, many of the operators sought to keep a larger part of the profits by molding their own blanks, even though this violated the patent rights of Edison. The Columbia Phonograph Co. and the American Graphophone Co. which its chief executives had reorganized, were the chief offenders. The New York, New Jersey, and Ohio Phonograph companies also produced recordings for other companies and supplied operators far and wide. It was not illegal for the companies or anyone to make records, but it was illegal to make records on blanks made to fit on the Edison mandrels

[2] Letter in files of the Edison Museum from North American Phonograph Co. to the New Jersey Phonograph Co.

which were not made by the Edison Phonograph Works.

Under this situation many of the original records of exceptional drawing power would sell for from two to six dollars each. Even as today, operators with good locations could make money while others were losing their shirts. Machines were bootlegged, altered, imitated and soon the industry was in a virtual state of anarchy. It was impossible, as Tate later said, for Edison or the North American Phonograph Co. to police the entire country to see that territorial restrictions were not violated and that the terms of the leasing contracts were being adhered to. The fact is that the leasing plan originally adopted for exploiting the phonograph as a business machine had utterly failed to meet the needs for its promotion as an entertainment device.

In 1892, Thomas R. Lombard, one of the original stockholders of North American, was elected President. Jesse Lippincott as a result of his ill-advised contract with the American Graphophone Co. had been pushed to the wall, suffered a paralyzing stroke and had died. That Lombard had the confidence of the local companies and also of Edison was attested to by A. W. Clancy, President of the National Association of Phonograph Companies at its 1893 meeting. By this time, however, the American Graphophone Co. was being reorganized by the officials of the Columbia Phonograph Co. It was well understood by all that the latter company was to be the exclusive sales agents for the new graphophones which would be patterned after the Edison instrument, except for the motive power. While mention was not made directly of this ominous new threat, President Clancy reminded the representatives of the twenty-two companies that two years previously Mr. Charles Swift of the Michigan Phonograph Co. and he had championed the cause of unification of the phonograph interests. He stated that Mr. Edison was in sympathy with the efforts of Mr. Lombard to re-establish a sound basis for future operation. He quoted Edison as having said:

"I desire every man to have an equal chance with me to get back his share of the profit, who in any way put a single dollar into the phonograph interests."

Students of the Edison saga will recognize the characteristic forthrightness of this attitude expressed towards those who had invested in his enterprises. Present when this statement was read was Mr. Alfred O. Tate, who had succeeded Samuel Insull as Mr. Edison's personal representative. There was little love lost between Tate and Insull, as Tate somewhat naively reveals in *Edison's Open Door,* published in 1938. The important matter is that Tate throws much of the blame for the failure of the cylinder phonograph industry at this time upon Edison's alleged opposition to the use of the phonograph for entertainment purposes. In his story, Tate says that one day about this time Edison had left a note on his desk saying,

"Tate—I don't want the phonograph sold for amusement purposes. It is not a toy. I want it sold for business purposes only."

Tate said that either Edison was unable to visualize the potentialities of the amusement field or that he had made up his mind to combat it. The fact that at this convention, the Edison Phonograph Works exhibited multitube phonographs does not seem to bear out Tate's statement. It seems rather, that Edison was willing to do anything that he felt was desired by the local phonograph companies that would assist them in being financially successful. It is known that Tate was interested in the Edison Talking Doll Co., and from the wording of the note, it is quite possible that it was this use of the phonograph to which Edison was referring, if such a note was written. Both multi-tube instruments and a new

"Edison Household Phonograph" were featured in the Edison Exhibit at the Chicago World's Fair later in the year of this convention. As noted previously A. W. Clancy in his opening speech of the convention had also quoted Mr. Edison having said,

"I will yet live to see the day that phonographs will be about as common in homes as organs are today."

How completely prophetic! But Edison undoubtedly realized that the phase of use in the home was yet to come and that the circumstances of the present had to be faced. In respect to the implications of Tate to the contrary, a careful examination of all of the acts of Edison indicate that he did his best to make his expressed wish for success for all those who had invested in his phonographic enterprises come true. At this convention, beside the twenty-two surviving companies of those organized by Lippincott, there were five annex members, as they were called, consisting of battery manufacturers who had become interested in the business being developed for their products by these prototypes of the "juke" box.

In his somewhat bitter reminiscences, Tate attributed some of the difficulties of the phonograph companies to Edison's slowness in development of a spring motor phonograph. Obviously this would have meant little to the amusement field. As in the 1930's, electric motor operation was an essential to it.

After the 1893 phonograph convention, the plan was instituted by which sales might be made by North American to operators or others anywhere in the United States and the commission on such sales credited to the account of the local companies in whose territories the merchandise was sold. For a time it seemed that this new plan might work. But the operators, and not the local companies or North American, were really in command. Irresponsible and lawless elements, even as in the later juke box industry, were to "cut themselves in." The illicit manufacture of machines and blanks without regard to patents or territories continued and it soon became apparent that neither the parent companies nor the local companies were going to be able to regain control of the situation. An element in this was the location of the Edison Phonograph Works at Orange. Shipping costs to the mid-west, far west and the south were high and added stimulus to the continuation of illegal manufacturing. However, the decisive factors were the lack of control over the record manufacturing inherent in the cylinder phonograph before the perfection of record molding processes, and the lack of control over activities within their territories by the local companies.

Meanwhile, Easton was known to be reorganizing the American Graphophone Co., Macdonald was already putting out a few graphophones employing the Edison mandrel and other improvements, and Columbia was beginning to develop a business based on store demonstrations and direct sales to the public. It was obvious that the Edison business could no longer be allowed to dwindle in the face of this new threat. So, according to Tate, one morning early in 1894, he found a terse note from Mr. Edison stating that he wanted to put the North American Phonograph Co. into bankruptcy and intended to sell phonographs direct from the factory regardless of the local companies.

Tate in his account states that he was appalled at this decision and at some length explained to Mr. Edison why he felt he could not go through the ordeal of facing the representatives of the local companies with this decision, and so resigned his posts with the Edison enterprises. The facts as previously given were certainly well known to Mr. Tate although he failed to clarify the existing situation to his readers. Tate in his discussion of the issues makes a rather obviously futile effort to condone as an expedient business decision what he is intimating in a not too subtle way was an unethical breach of contract by Edison. He stated that Edison had no

thought of doing anyone an injustice but wanted to recover the territories that had been sold and was ready and willing to pay for them, but that if he attempted to recover them by negotiation he would be met with exaggerated demands. His object therefore, according to Tate, was to have the value of the short remaining period of these contracts established by court action. However, it is not satisfactorily explained by Tate why he felt impelled to resign from all of his posts from Edison when this matter concerned only the phonograph companies, if he really believed what he said of Edison's motives. Because it was over this matter that Tate broke with Edison, Tate becomes a party to the historic controversy of which he sets himself up as arbiter. In this connection it should be noted that Tate makes several misstatements, as well as omitting essential facts. For instance he states:

"I knew that these companies had paid more than one million dollars for their rights in the territories which Edison now proposed to invade."

Actually, in a statement later made by counsel for the "phonograph companies" (and who by the oddest coincidence was one Philip Mauro of the Graphophone Co.) the total amount claimed as paid in by the local companies for their rights was given as $724,000, which had been collected by Lippincott, not by Edison.

Mr. Tate neglected also to state that although Lippincott had agreed to buy the controlling stock of the Edison Phonograph for $500,000, only a part of this had been paid in and that even this payment had been more than offset by phonographs and supplies which had been sold to North American and which had not been paid for. Nor did Tate reveal that most of the local companies were heavily in debt to the North American Co., which in itself constitutes an abrogation of contract, as any businessman knows. Edison, as the largest creditor of North American, had the legal right to pursue the course he did and in view of the existing situation he had to do it whether distasteful or not.

Tate stated the case this way:

"The territorial companies in turn organized a combined attack to vindicate their rights, and for fourteen long years this litigation was prosecuted. When a final decision was reached in the form of the judgment to which I referred and whose satisfaction and dissolution involved the payment of a sum closely approximating my original estimate, Edison settled in cash over night without a murmur of complaint. The litigants on both sides were satisfied."

The fact is that ten years had elapsed before Philip Mauro and James L. Andem, former President of the Ohio Phonograph Co., were able to get together enough evidence that they represented the stockholders of the long defunct local companies in order to make a case in court. That Andem, himself, had earlier considered Edison's course just and inevitable is clearly shown by a news item which was published in the *Phonoscope* of May, 1897, as follows:

"The Ohio Phonograph Co., of Cincinnati, Ohio, has been succeeded by the Edison Phonograph Co. with offices at Cincinnati, Cleveland, Chicago and Indianapolis.—Mr. James L. Andem, formerly President of the Ohio Phonograph Co. is General Manager."

The "final action" to which Tate referred was that of the New York Phonograph Co. versus National Phonograph Co., in which decision was handed down by Judge Hazel in 1908. The defendants were fined $2,500, with $1,500 additionally to be paid the complainant for expenses. Quite obviously this total amount would not have paid for fourteen years of litigation for even one of the companies and represented a shallow victory for the small group of men who had engineered it. The nature of

the alleged fourteen years of litigation was this; Andem had left the employ of Edison's new local distributing company as general manager after a little more than two years of service, Mauro met him and the discussion can be pretty well inferred from subsequent events. A rump so-called "Fifth Annual Convention of the National Phonograph Association" was held in Cincinnati, Ohio, September 25, 1900. This was the blackest hour of infamy, when a few of the men who in a time of honest endeavor and mutual respect had praised Edison, now revealed that they had sold their souls to his enemies for what was to prove to be a pittance. Henry D. Goodwin was Chairman and James L. Andem secretary. A. M. Clancy was one of the few actual executives of the former companies to take part.

Thomas A. Edison had lost his financial interest in the electrical industry of which he had been the chief creator through the chicanery and greed of ambitious rivals. He has been disparagingly referred to as a stubborn man who became less and less inclined to listen to the advice of others. What would have been the result if he had listened to Mr. Tate? Might he not have lost his phonograph enterprise too?

Althought Tate's book appeared in 1938, he does not mention the sweeping decision in favor of the National Phonograph Co. in its suit against Davega, which had resulted from an endeavor by the New York Phonograph Co. to prevent the National Phonograph Co. from doing business in its territory. This put a final end to the efforts of the American Graphophone to push Edison out of the phonograph business. During the years Amden alone had filed some three hundred suits against one or another of the Edison companies on some pretext or another, but none of which were prosecuted simply because they had been instituted for propaganda purposes with the wily Philip Mauro always hovering in the background. Finally in his zeal, Andem overstepped himself and was indicted by a grand jury in Trenton, New Jersey for forgery in connection with one of the true bills he had presented, this one on behalf of the New England Phonograph Co., to which he had falsely signed his name as secretary.

Fig. 9-1. The Edison "M" coin-slot phonograph powered from a storage battery and was usually operated by a nickel.

The status of the industry at the time of Tate's break with Edison was roughly this; most of the local companies were bankrupt; the original intention to promote the phonograph as a business machine was forgotten; the only profitable business was with the slot machines in phonograph parlors and in locations with the profits going largely to operators and not to the local companies or North American Phonograph Co. There

is no reason why any of the local companies could not have continued in business if they were able to pay for their purchases. Most of the executives were absorbed in the new distributing agencies, as Andem had been in Cincinnati. Shortly after acquiring the assets of North American, the Edison Phonograph Works began the production of a new and improved line of coin-slot machines for the entertainment field. See Fig. 9-1. Operators could buy them as they had before, but now the Edison Phonograph Works was going to be paid for them. The only thing which had been lost by the companies was the unenforceable right to an exclusive territory which had not been justified on the basis of the business produced and in nearly every case already abrogated by the failure to pay for merchandise delivered.

Now the American Graphophone Co. re-entered the field, with the Macdonald graphophone equipped with the Edison sloping mandrel and employing solid wax blanks which were now interchangeable with those of the Edison phonographs. It must be recognized that a principle object of the re-organized parent companies was to develop the home market, in which the local companies had manifested but slight interest. Both companies in 1896 began the manufacture of spring-motored machines for use in the home. The American Graphophone Co. also introduced a new line of spring-motored coin-slot machines. Despite the troubles of the manufacturing and distributing companies, the phonograph parlor idea continued to grow, not only in the United States, but throughout the world. In Paris, Pathe probably had the most unique establishment of this type, employing about forty people. On the spacious street floor there were many desks equipped with listening tubes, with a chair before each desk. There was also a speaking tube at each desk. All the customer had to do was seat himself, order the selection he wanted played by speaking into the tube, deposit his coin and the record would be played on the phonograph in the room below which was connected to his particular pair of ear tubes. The customers had a choice of fifteen hundred cylinders—truly the first musical library!

How well the phonograph parlor idea was going in the United States is illustrated in the planning of the first "deluxe" motion picture theater. This was Vitascope Hall in Buffalo, New York. The vestibule of the theater was designed to be what was described as "a palace of pleasure itself." Twenty-eight of the latest Edison Phonographs were placed for "the diversion and instruction" of the visitors, as well as a number of kinetoscopes, Edison "peephole" motion picture machines.

The introduction of the coin phonographs was probably responsible for the development of coin-operated music boxes, which made their appearance about this time. In 1893, the manufacturers of the Polyphon, a German music box, sent a representative to the United States to look into the prospects for opening a factory. This resulted in the organization of the Regina Music Box Co., Rahway, New Jersey. The representative invented a fool-proof coin mechanism which closed the coin chute while the box was playing, which prevented jamming. By 1898, the Regina Co. was producing both penny and nickel operated types. The success of Regina inspired others to enter the field, such as the Criterion, made by M. & J. Paillard Co. of New York, and Symphion, another German designed box, made at Asbury Park, New Jersey.

The first nickel-in-the-slot Peerless Player piano was put on location in 1908. This immediately became so popular that it threatened the business of the coin phonographs and music boxes. Regina this year had developed a Deluxe automatic music box with a piano type sounding board, which gave it a rich, full-bodied tone. It also offered selectivity, giving a choice of a dozen or more of the huge twenty-seven inch punched metal discs. The mechanism was housed in handsome, tall cabinets of carved oak or rosewood, with plate glass in the front so that the operation of the record changing mechanism and the playing of the record might be watched. These finely finished music boxes sold for around five-hundred dollars and dominated some of the best locations against all comers for years. In elegance of appearance, workmanship and opulence of tone, these Reginas filled the position occupied by the best automatic phonographs of today quite adequately.

In order to compete successfully with other types of coin machines, the operators of non-selective coin phonographs were forced to resort to the employment of gadgets. One method resorted to was in the combining of changing pictures with the sound. The Mills Novelty Co. of Chicago, a name still known in the "slots," developed a machine which periodically dropped cards illustrating the song being played. Another of these picturized phonographs was the Illustraphone, made by Hawthorne & Sheble of Philadelphia, who also made cylinder records and later discs, until forced out of business by the Victor Talking Machine Co. for infringement of patents. Other machines of this type were the Cailophone and the Scopephone, both made by the Caille Brothers, Detroit; and the Illustrated Song Machine, made by the Rosenfeld Co. of New York. Later the Valliquent Novelty Co. of Newark, New Jersey, made the first illustrated machine to be sold in the United States using disc records, called the Discophone. A coin-operated disc machine had earlier been made in the United States by the Universal Talking Machine Co., but it was not advertised nor sold here, but in Germany!

Although the best locations had been taken over by the automatic pianos and the music boxes, the phonograph parlor had persisted, and by the addition of other nickel and penny catching devices was gradually transformed into the "penny arcade," which in evolutionary form still exists. The reason the phonograph did not remain permanently in the picture was the lack of selectivity.

If the idea of the Multiplex had been carried further earlier, it might have given a continuity to the use of the phonograph in some form or another from the early period of public entertainment to the juke box era of the 1930's. The Multiplex was a five mandrel attachment made to fit over the standard Edison chassis, first put on the market in 1896. It was fitted with the customary ear tubes and while the customer could push a lever to push the cylinders ahead so as to play the next one, a free choice could not be made. This attachment sold for $150, but was not widely sold.

The Automatic Reginaphone, made by the music box manufacturers of Rahway, New Jersey, was a similar machine but designed as a complete unit, with a glass in front so the operation of the mechanism could be viewed. This held six cylinders on mandrels around a wheel, with the cylinders parallel to the center shaft of the wheel, as in the Multiplex. When a coin was deposited the wheel would move so that the next cylinder was in position for playing. Therefore for each coin deposited a different record would be played to the extent of six, but there was still no preselection possible. However, this machine was equipped optionally with ear tubes or a speaker horn. It was first produced in 1905. Another early interest of the Regina people in the phonograph was in the production of a combination instrument that would play both the Regina music box discs and disc phonograph records.

Also in 1905 there was developed the first truly selective automatic phonograph. This was the Multiphone, utilizing the same wheel principle but a much larger one holding twenty-four cylinders. It looked something like a ferris wheel in a china cabinet. Each of the cylinders was numbered and an accompanying chart gave the titles. With an external crank, the patron could deposit his nickel and then turn the crank to the selection he wanted played. The patron also supplied the motive force, winding the crank of the standard Edison spring motor machine which was supplied. The machine had a huge overhead horn which was masked by a grille in the top of the rather grotesquely bulging mahogany cabinet, which had plate glass in the front and sides. Quite understandably, the customer was really being asked to work too hard for his entertainment and the company was bankrupt in 1908. If electrical operation had been retained from the earlier period and the Multiphone had been more attractively designed it quite conceivably might have been successful. As it was, large sums were poured into the organizing of operating companies. Long after the failure of the company some of the machines were still in locations, some being converted later to play the Edison four minute Blue Amberol records. (See Fig. 9-2.)

An unusual cylinder machine was the Concertophone, provided with a carrier which held twenty five of the then new six inch long Columbia 20th Century Graphophone cylinders. This also employed the 20th Century Graphophone loud speaking mechanical amplifier, invented by Higham of Boston. It was operated by setting a dial at the side of the cabinet and manipulating a sliding bar to maneuver the desired record into place. This was first announced in the September 1906 *Talking Machine World*. A later model shifted the records automatically. With the plate glass front and a mirror to reflect the machinery in operation, this was the most spectacular of all of the cylinder record players developed. In its original locations, the Concertophone earned up to ten dollars per day. This mechanism was also sold for home use without the coin mechanism, so it was probably the first home automatic record changer as well as being the last new coin-slot cylinder phonograph.

By 1908 coin-operated disc machines were becoming fairly numerous. As mentioned briefly elsewhere, one of the first attempts to market a disc machine for coin operation had been by the Universal Talking Machine Co., which

Fig. 9-2. The Multiphone was a monstrous coin-operated "jukebox" and contained 24 cylinders mounted on a large wheel. (Courtesy of C. Y. deKay.)

had been organized as a result of the strange hassle between Seamon, Berliner, and the Graphophone Co. Oddly, this first coin machine was not offered for use in the United States, but in Germany, where it met with comparatively little success.

Similar to the course of evolution of the cylinder machines, Julius Wilner of Philadelphia invented a coin-operated phonograph that played twelve 10-inch discs in sequence, but with no preselection, which limited its usefulness. In 1906, the Automatic Machine and Tool Co. of Chicago produced John Gabel's Automatic Entertainer. This held twenty-four 10-inch records, twelve on either side of the turntable. Any record could be played by the turning of a knob. Although powered by a hand-wound spring motor, the operation otherwise was entirely automatic. A forty-inch long horn protruded from the top of a five-foot tall cabinet of oak,

glassed in on three sides so that the mechanism might be viewed. A magazine holding 150 needles was positioned directly above the sound-box. The handle which wound the motor changed the needle and the record all in one turning. The coin device was also very advanced, being equipped with a magnetic coin detector and so in the trade, which is very sensitive to the word "slugs," the Gabel Entertainer is looked up to as the progenitor of the modern juke boxes.

Although years passed since the zenith of the coin-operated phonographs of the 1890-1908 period (Fig. 9-3) there were practically no new devices placed on the market until the 1920's, although a number of patents were issued. Lack of suitable methods of amplification was a principal deterrent, but the emphasis on the highly profitable home phonograph market was probably more responsible. After the talking machine

Fig. 9-3. The Edison Excelsior phonograph was a simple spring-wound type, containing only one selection, made in 1900. (Courtesy of Edison National Historic Site.)

was to be found in nearly every home there was little reason to suspect that ever again people would become avid in dropping their coins into a slot to hear phonograph records. With the advent of broadcasting in 1920, even the phonographs in the home gradually came to be looked upon with disdain. Soon, with the development of loudspeakers, a radio became a fixture in many popular places where coin operated pianos and other automatic musical instruments formerly had been profitable.

The introduction of electrical recording brought about the introduction of the Automatic Orthophonic Victrola, used in the home, but not adaptable for coin operation. Hit hard by the popularity of radio, the manufacturers of coin-operated pianos were among the first to sense a future profit potential in the new kind of musical quality and

sound volume made possible to the phonograph by electrical means. In 1927, the Automatic Music Instrument Company of Grand Rapids, one of these piano manufacturers, placed on location a selective, coin-operated juke box which played either or both sides of ten records, producing nearly 3,000 of these machines the first year. Other makers of coin-operated pianos and other automatic musical instruments, such as J. P. Seeburg and the Rudolph Wurlitzer Co. were producing selective, coin-operated phonographs in the early 1930's. During the depression years when economic conditions and the consuming interest of the public in radio combined to push over-the-counter record sales to the lowest levels since 1900, the electronically jazzed up juke box was creating a market which became a most important factor in the rehabilitation of the recording industry.

CHAPTER 10

ADVENT OF THE DISCS

THE idea of disc records was by no means new at the time of their commercial introduction in 1895 by Emile Berliner. Nor was the use of a disc as a moving surface a patentable feature in itself. Edison had made experimental discs in 1878, the Bells and Tainter in 1885. The Phonautographs of Scott had utilized both cylinders and discs as the moving medium upon which was traced the sinuous, but mute, wave patterns of sound. The phonautograph operated on the precise laterally undulatory action later made use of by Berliner in his invention. Cros had carried the Scott concept forward to the point of describing a method by which a photoengraved laterally undulating groove might be used to actuate a sound reproducing mechanism.[1] The method employed by Edison in the first phonograph indented a vertically undulating groove of variable depth, which concept originated with him. Both the lateral and vertical methods were equally applicable to cylinder, disc or tape—all well known forms of moving surfaces.

M. Charles Cros, the Frenchman, had deposited with the French Academie des Sciences a sealed packet describing his conception a short time before the filing of the Edison patent application upon a telephone repeater in July, 1877, the latter being the earliest concept of the vertical recording principle.[2] When the Cros packet was opened in December, 1877, it was discovered that Cros had described an idea for a talking machine along lines which we now recognize as very similar to those followed later by Berliner in his Gramophone. The important fact is that it was 1887 before Berliner was able to reduce to a patentable form the essentials of the Cros proposal and another eight years before even a crude commercial instrument resulted. Within a month after Edward Johnson had let the cat out of the bag with his letter to *Scientific American,* revealing the more important significance of Edison's telephone repeater, Edison had produced the first phonograph. It should not be overlooked that Edison also covered the laterally undulatory groove as well as the vertically undulatory groove in his first United States patent, thus being the first to receive official recognition of invention in both fields. Berliner experimented with both cylinders and discs, one of his first patents describing a cylinder machine. On the other hand, the Bell-Tainter specifications of 1886 describe disc machines and records, although not brought by them to a commercial state. The Bells and Tainter utilized the Edison vertical method only, their most important contribution consisting of the concept of cutting, rather than indenting the groove. In view of subsequent events it is important to remember that Bell-Tainter patents never covered any aspect of lateral recording,

---

[1] *Le Natur,* article by Abbe Lenoir, October 1877.
[2] British patent issued to T. A. Edison, January 30, 1878.

with the possible exception of the applicability of the incising idea.

A patent covering a large number of projected phonographic improvements had been granted to Edison without question in 1878 in Great Britain. Detailed drawings and specifications for many of these improvements were submitted with the application and form an irrefutable part of the patent document. In England to that date no talking machine patents had ever been issued to anyone else. Application had been filed at the same time on an identical specification by Edison with the United States Patent Office. However, as the British Patent Office had acted so promptly, the United States Patent Office examiners for some reason ruled that the issuance of a British patent to Edison constituted prior publication and that under the international agreements governing copyright and patent procedures he would receive ample protection in the American courts under his British patent. Therefore, a United States patent was not granted to Edison, although the French Government, operating under the same international covenants, issued Edison a similar patent without quibbling or delay. Yet less than a decade later letters patents were granted by the U. S. Patent Office to the Bells and Tainter which not only embodied the Edison vertical recording principle, but also many of the improvements covered in the Edison British patent of 1878.[3] It should be observed that the Bell-Tainter method was entirely dependent upon the hill-and-dale modifiable groove which had been to that time exclusively the concept of Mr. Edison and upon which presumably he had been granted a seventeen year period in which to develop and improve by his original phonograph patent.

The markedly different appearance of disc and cylinder mechanisms is re-

sponsible for the popular impression that these are patentable features, which is not so. All of the inventors were free to use any type of moving surface. The Bell-Tainter patents show a disc machine almost identical to the one illustrated in the Edison British patent of 1878 and the experimental model was deposited by Tainter with the Smithsonian Institution. Also in the exhibit is an experimental waxed-tape machine, the tape being fed by three wooden wheels. The first published story on the invention of a machine that would "talk" by Edison, had described a tape machine involving electrical recording and reproduction and the first Berliner Gramophone patent shows a cylinder. However, each form of moving surface presents certain advantages and disadvantages. One of the chief advantages of the cylinder was that it provided a constant rate of travel of the recorded groove beneath the stylus. In the conventional disc record with which we are familiar, the speed of the groove under the stylus varies markedly from the outer turns of the spiral to the inner. This represents an inherent fault present yet today, even though the difficulties have been minimized by compensatory measures. Undoubtedly this factor was largely responsible for the original decision of Edison to develop the cylinder rather than the disc.

Credit for recognizing the importance of this factor must be extended to Charles Sumner Tainter for in 1887 he applied for a patent on a variable rpm disc recording apparatus which would give a uniform surface speed beneath the stylus, although he too continued commercially to develop the cylinder form.

Edison, soon after the invention of the phonograph, became engaged almost exclusively with problems of the electric light. In the three years from 1881 through 1883, he had alone been granted 199 patents, mostly upon various elements of the complex generating and distributing systems and he also directed the research and experiments

---

[3] Some patent authorities justify this issuance of patents on similar devices to the Bells and Tainter by reason of their having "reduced to practice" the ideas embodied in the Edison British patent.

of scores of others. Some of the Edison patents were upon telephonic improvements, especially various kinds of transmitters which in a much later era contributed importantly to the phonographic development. While Edison was thus engaged at Menlo Park, there was feverish activity also being directed towards the securing of an efficient and practical telephone transmitter in Washington, District of Columbia. This competitive effort was in two parts, the Volta Laboratory Associates, founded by Alexander Graham Bell; the individual efforts of Emile Berliner, by daytime a clerk in a store, by night an experimenter.

An unexplained mystery is why these men chose to locate in Washington to do scientific research. Manufacturing was practically non-existent in the District of Columbia. The materials necessary for experiments were hard to get. There were few facilities for the making of parts and few skilled artisans. The headquarters of the sprouting American Bell Telephone Co. organized by Bell and his associates was in Boston, where there were ample stocks of materials and facilities for the manufacture of experimental apparatus. This mystery is heightened by the fact that about this same time other telephone inventors such as Gilliland, Blake and others were being brought to Boston to assist in development work. The reason for the removal of Berliner to Washington from New York is given by his biographer as the securing of a job as a clerk. The coincidences with respect to certain succeeding events have also never been satisfactorily explained. For instance, how was it that Emile Berliner, " . . . with the aid of two physics books, patched up a telephone transmitter from a child's drum, a needle, a steel dress button and a guitar string" [4] and shortly after by using some pieces of carbon and other odds and ends was able to apply for a patent upon a transmitter utilizing the same principle as

the carbon button transmitter upon which Edison had already applied for a patent, but not yet granted? It was twenty-five long years later before a Federal court finally adjudged the patent granted to Berliner void as anticipated by that of Edison.

There was a certain pattern of consistency in the way in which Berliner operated. Just as many forms of prior experimental transmitters of Edison, Blake and others had preceded the makeshift device upon which Berliner was eventually granted a patent,[5] so there were fairly well developed ideas of others upon which he based his Gramophone. The principle prototype was the improved phonautograph of Scott, which traced the waveforms of sound in a spiral, laterally undulating line upon a lampblack coated glass disc. Another chief source was the method described by Cros of making a metallic reproducible record by photoengraving. This Berliner later abandoned for a method which involved the tracing of the sound wave pattern through a thin film of fat or wax, and then etching the record wave pattern into the glass or metal disc by immersing in acid. Berliner acknowledges this in part in describing his process in his first patent specification as "phonautographic recording."

After considerable experimentation, Berliner finally arrived at the use of zinc discs for recording. He discovered that by placing a second, protective layer of wax over the first, it was possible to handle the discs better for processing. After recording, the wax coated zinc discs were immersed in a chromic acid bath, which etched the wavy lines exposed to the action of the acid by the recording to the desired depth. The volume of sound reproduced from these zinc discs was good, but was accompanied by a great deal of hissing noise, for the acid not only ate downward into the zinc, but laterally as well. Impurities in the zinc also pro-

---

[4] *The Telephone in a Changing World,* Marion May Dilts-Longmans, Green and Co., New York, 1941.

[5] Berliner applied for a patent on a carbon button transmitter in June, 1877, but it was not granted until fourteen years later.

Fig. 10-1. Emile Berliner's original hand-driven Gramophone, 1887.

duced irregularities in the etching. However, by playing the record over two or three times it was found that the reproduction became smoother. After a time, Berliner was able to make stampers by electrotyping from the original record, so that duplicates could be pressed from heated plastic materials. Vulcanite, or hard rubber, was the first material used commercially by Berliner and provided the necessary basis for exploitation of his Gramophone.

Berliner was far from an expert mechanic. Although he received his first Gramophone patent in 1887, it was 1895 before he was able to develop records and reproducing machines for sale. Even then the Gramophone (Fig. 10-1) was exceedingly primitive, with a hand-turned disc and no motor. The reproducing part of the mechanism consisted of a stubby conical horn, pivoted near the larger end, and with a sound-box with diaphragm and stylus at the small end which was propelled across the record by the spiral groove of the record. To maintain a proper perspective, neither the phonograph or the graphophone were very highly developed by 1895 from the standpoint of music reproduction, in fact both of the latter still employed listening tubes for listening, as did also the first Gramophones. However, it must be remembered that the cylinder instruments had been primarily designed for purposes of office dictation and not as amusement instruments. The Berliner machine was designed to reproduce speech and music for home entertainment only, and could not be used for dictation.

Compared with the Berliner method, the recording process then employed by the phonograph and graphophone was unable to compete with the Gramophone in volume. Due to the necessity of having a sufficiently dense and hard material for the cylinders (to stand up under successive playings) the resistance of the material to the cutting stylus was considerable. Each cylinder record sold was an original or a transcribed record—a practical process of molding recorded cylinders had not yet been developed. On the other hand, as the resistance to the lateral movement of the stylus by the thin film of wax on the zinc master Berliner record was slight, its movement was but slightly impeded. In other words, the actual groove was cut by the acid bath, rather than by the acoustical energy of the sound waves. Therefore, the sound volume from the Berliner discs was much greater than that from the contemporary cylinders, thus permitting the use of a reproducing funnel instead of ear tubes. It may have been in part due to the introduction of the Berliner Gramophone that shortly thereafter the incising methods used in making cylinders were improved so as to also permit the use of horns for reproduction.

Another means of recording discs somewhat comparable to the Berliner method was patented in the United States and England by Rev. A. C. Ferguson, a Baptist minister of Brooklyn, New York. In his recording device a diaphragm-controlled shutter varied a tiny beam of light directed along a spiral path directed to a seven inch glass plate coated with photographic emulsion. The plate was then developed and then transferred by photoengraving to a metal plate. In this manner a groove of required depth could be etched so that it could be used for reproducing the sound by means of a stylus-diaphragm-horn assembly similar to that of the Gramophone. A matrix could be made for pressing duplicate discs, although as far as is known this was not done commercially. Articles on Ferguson's Lightophone were published in the *New York World, New York Herald* and other newspapers in June of 1897. Ferguson claimed that as there was no friction in the recording, there was no distortion, although the volume was said to be not as great

as that obtained by the Berliner method. Without doubt, if the use of wax disc recording blanks had not superseded the zinc plate acid etching process about this time, it is conceivable that the Lightophone might have been commercially developed, as the idea was practical and the processing simple. This was made evident at a later time by the use of the diaphragm-controlled shutter principle in recording sound on motion picture film. Other photographic methods were developed experimentally by others in France, England and the United States, but none were commercially employed, as far as is known.

Considering Berliner's limited background and facilities, it is amazing that he was not only the first to produce disc records commercially, but was also the first to commercially produce stamped, or molded records. Edison had molded and demonstrated experimental wax musical cylinders in 1891 to representatives of the local phonograph companies.[6] The Bells and Tainter had molded experimental vertical cut discs in 1885, which may be seen at the Smithsonian Institution, but they were never able to bring the process to a commercially practicable state. Edison had equipped an experimental disc machine with a spring motor as early as 1878. However, although Berliner had been working on the Gramophone to the exclusion of everything else for almost eight years, he had not yet provided it with a motor.

If Berliner had been a more practical experimenter, he might possibly have been able to refine his original carbon button transmitter to at least a demonstrable form before applying for a patent. That this Berliner transmitter was actually inoperative, Berliner, himself, admitted in a statement given in interference, March 4, 1887[7] when he said, "a person heard sounds, but could

---

[6] Proceedings of the 2nd Annual Convention of the National Association of Phonograph Companies, 1891.

[7] Amer. Bell Tel. Co. vs. Nat. Tel. Mfg. Co. at Circuit Court D., Mass., June 27, 1901.

not generally make out the words I spoke" and concerning which the person to whom he was speaking testified he heard no words.

Certain historians of the telephone and even supposedly impartial and well informed cyclopedists are still perpetuating the monumental historic error of citing Berliner as the inventor of the "microphone" and the carbon button transmitter.

The hopelessly inadequate and non-performing mechanism upon which Berliner had applied for a patent on March 4, 1877, and which was not granted because of alleged interferences until November 17, 1891, is important in the history of the talking machine industry by reason of the facts to follow. This transmitter patent after its delayed issuance, was used by the Bell legal staff as a means of extending the life of the monopoly which had been granted under the original Bell patents. Connivance with the patent examiners was alleged by the Attorney-General in a famous suit of the United States versus Emile Berliner, instituted to have the patent set aside as having been purposely delayed in date of granting by the United States Patent Office. However, the United States Supreme Court upheld the right of the patent office to grant the patent. The Supreme Court decision is what misled many "authorities" into asserting that Berliner's claim to have invented the carbon button transmitter had been sustained by the Supreme Court. Actually, the question before this court had to do only with the right of the patent office to issue the patent after what was alleged by the attorneys for the United States to have been an abnormally long delay and suspicious circumstances. The decision of the Supreme Court had absolutely nothing to do with the priority or validity of the patent! The Bell attorneys knew full well during the epochal struggle with Western Union that it would have been fatal to have permitted the Berliner patent to have been subjected to a test on those grounds. The Berliner patent was not finally adjudicated as to its priority until June 24, 1901, by the District Circuit Court D of Massachusetts. The decision was that the invention of Berliner had been anticipated by that of Edison and that the Berliner patent was invalid. Thus Edison may be said to have had three Nemeses in Washington, the Volta Laboratory Association, Berliner, and the Patent Office!

These circumstances are important to the course of development of the phonograph industry, for it was this controversial telephone transmitter which had almost immediately caused the Bell interests to engage the services of Berliner on a retainer basis, and which gave him the time and money to develop the Gramophone. As has been stated, Berliner worked upon the Gramophone almost continuously from 1887 to 1895 before producing any machines or records for sale. Fred Gaisberg, one of Berliner's early associates, a few years ago wrote a fascinating story of the development of the lateral disc industry entitled, *The Music Goes Round*. In this he stated that he had opened the first professional recording studio in Philadelphia in 1897. A small store was opened nearby, with Alfred Clark in charge of sales. Gaisberg was referring to Berliner discs, for there were by this time many cylinder recording studios all over the United States and Europe. However, there are in existence in the hands of collectors, including ourselves, some of the hard rubber discs bearing etched recording dates as early as 1896, bearing the familiar type-faced etched title, "Berliner Gramophone Co., Washington, D.C."

Gaisberg was undoubtedly of considerable assistance to Berliner in becoming established commercially, for he had prior experience in the cylinder recording studios. Both Fred Gaisberg and his brother Will were well acquainted with many of the popular vocalists and entertainers of the cylinders and this may explain why so many of these were soon recording for the discs. According to Fred Gaisberg's story, Berliner had put him to work rounding up talent so that evidence of a basis for further development would assist in attracting capital. In 1895, singing for the cylinders was by the "round," with up to twenty cylinders being recorded at a time. This was hard work for the entertainers and their income was limited quite obviously by the few records which could be secured from each performance before the recording horn. Thus, the Berliner method, which would permit an indefinite number of duplicates from one master and with volume surpassing that of even the best cylinders of the time, was given its great opportunity for commercial success by that earlier failure of the local companies to accept the offer of Edison in 1891 to develop molding methods for their use.

Gaisberg said that when he first went to work for Berliner he searched the highways and byways of Washington for entertainers suitable for recording. Among the first, he recalled, was George Graham, a negro member of an Indian Medicine troup and John O'Derrel, an Irishman who played the banjo and sang songs with the same company. Later many of the artists already popular in the phonograph parlors were also induced by the Gaisbergs to make Berliner records. Fred Gaisberg says in his account that it was he who was chosen by Berliner to represent him in introducing the Gramophone to Europe and so he became the first to record upon discs many of the great vocal artists of the operatic world, including Enrico Caruso, Sigrid Arnoldson, Adelina Patti, and Mattia Battistini. However, according to Will Hayes, a veteran cylinder recording expert and European representative for Edison, it was Will Gaisberg who was business agent for Berliner and not his brother Fred, who then played the piano accompaniments. Hayes, moreover, is of the opinion Will Gaisberg deserves the larger share of the credit for the phenomenal success of this initial Gramophone recording tour. Be that as it may, it was the zeal of these two particular converts to the discs which gave initial impetus to the popularity of the Gramophone throughout the world.

It was largely a result of the work of the Gaisbergs that Europe quickly adopted the disc Gramophone as a cultural medium—a means of bringing into the home the voices and art of great singers. In America there had been but

Fig. 10-2. Berliner disc Gramophone operated by a direct-current motor. Speed was controlled by a two-ball governor, 1896. (Courtesy of Smithsonian Institution.)

slight recognition of the potential of the various phonographic inventions for preserving and making continuously available great performances of vocal art. Before Will and Fred Gaisberg had come along, Berliner had been in a rut, with a good idea but unable to work it out. In 1895, the Gramophone was still hand-driven, appeared to be a toy and was largely sold on the basis of that appeal. Consequently, when Berliner produced a motor-powered gramophone late in 1896 (Fig. 10-2), those invited to invest in its commercial development dismissed it with scant consideration. The Gaisbergs and Clark together with William Barry Owen, another graduate from the cylinders and the Bell-Tainter school, were largely responsible for the success of the English Gramophone Co. Ltd., which by sponsoring the recording of great artists in Europe, set the precedent for similar activities by its Victor affiliate in America.

So, strange as it may seem, the award of the Volta Prize to Alexander Graham Bell, which had directly resulted in the formation of the Volta Laboratory Association and the formation of the American Graphophone Co., now had a secondary regenerative effect in the cycles of the Gramophonic development. Without the catalyst of the Gaisbergs and Owen, which had been developed through their experiences in the Volta Laboratory, it is extremely doubtful that a certain key event which led to the formation of the Victor Talking Machine Co. and the English Gramophone Co. ever would have taken place. Bell's invention of the telephone paid for the initial cost of development of both the Graphophone and the Gramophone. The Bell Telephone Co. in 1879 paid Berliner twenty-five thousand dollars for the rights to his telephone transmitter patents, when and if issued, plus a retaining fee of five-thousand dollars per year. Even with this financing, the Gramophone was far from being a practical musical instrument at the time the Gaisbergs and Owen became interested in it. Because of Ber-

liner's prior success in getting money from the backers of the Bell telephone, Gaisberg quite logically thought these men might be persuaded to back the commercial introduction of the Gramophone. So with a special exhibit, Fred Gaisberg and an assistant went to Boston to attend a meeting of the board of directors of the telephone company. However, as Gaisberg relates in The Music Goes Round, the financiers were amused but were not in any way inclined to invest. Little did the directors realize the keen interest that the Bell Telephone Company would one day be exhibiting in the sound recording field!

However, largely through the enthusiasm and efforts of the Gaisbergs, twenty-five thousand dollars was raised by the sale of stock to a group of Philadelphia investors, the United States Gramophone Co. was organized and the work of fitting a clock-work motor to the Gramophone was begun. Gaisberg in his account stated that while engaged with this problem he happened to see an advertisement of hand-wound spring motors for use with sewing machines, which indirectly led him to the machine shop of Eldridge R. Johnson in Camden, who was destined to play a powerful part in shaping not only the future of the Gramophone, but also the entire course of development of the industry. The first order to Johnson was for two hundred motors, an advance being given to him from the funds which had been raised. The first lot failed to operate properly and Fred Gaisberg reported it was necessary for him to advise Johnson the governors of the motors would not function as they should unless a change was made to the flat type of spring, such as Edison was using in his spring-motored phonograph. The change was made, Gaisberg said, with complete success. (See Fig. 10-3.) At the time Gaisberg opened the Philadelphia studio, all discs were seven inches in diameter, stamped from vulcanite by matrices made by electrotyping from the acid-etched zinc originals. Some were later made from Durinoid, a semi-

Fig. 10-3. The Improved Berliner Gramophone featuring Eldridge Johnson's spring-wound motor.

flexible composition, by the Durinoid Corp. of Newark, N. J. button manufacturers. The average playing time was about two minutes as against the approximately three minutes for the slow speed cylinders then in use. Gaisberg succeeded in rounding up more and more of the popular recording artists and soon had a considerable stock of recordings which Clark was able to dispose of as more machines were sold. One day while at Atlantic City, Gaisberg met the then handsome and popular tenor, Ferruccio Giannini, who was then travelling with a small opera company. Gaisberg persuaded Ferruccio to accompany him back to the studio, where he recorded La Donna e Mobile and Quest o Quella, from Rigoletto. Gaisberg said that these were highly successful, as well as being the first operatic records to be made upon discs.

Many years later in Berlin, Fred Gaisberg drew up a recording contract with Dusalina Giannini, daughter of this pioneer operatic recording star!

Both the acid etching process and the hard rubber from which the records were pressed had serious faults. The spreading of the acid in all directions into the zinc from the smoothly sinuous surface line in the surface wax created excessive surface noise and loss of quality. The vulcanite, or hard rubber, gave much trouble because of uneven shrinkage in cooling, causing warping. Impurities in the mixture and gas bubbles also ruined many of the pressings. Gaisberg had heard of the Durinoid Company in Newark, New Jersey, button manufacturers, who were said to be using a substitute for hard rubber in making buttons, with considerable success. He investigated, and the company officials agreed to make some sample pressings from matrices which Gaisberg was to furnish. The test records proved to be amazingly superior to the hard rubber. The patented button composition, was largely composed of shellac, lampblack, byritis, with cotton flock as a binder—practically the same composition (but flexible) used for standard 78 rpm records well into the 1950's.

The problem of securing smoother original recordings still existed. Faced with the threat of the discs, wax cylinder recording had been improved to a point where musically the results were superior to the zinc discs of Berliner, although not quite equal in volume. Experiments were begun with solid wax disc blanks of a composition similar to that being used for the improved cylinders. Methods of making wax conductive for electroplating had been patented by Edison (the gold electrostatic deposition process) and other methods had been suggested by Edison in his patent specifications and experimentally used by Bell and Tainter. One hazard involved in the switch to wax recording was that the incising into wax might be construed as violating the Bell-Tainter patents, even though the groove pattern was laterally undulating instead of vertical.

There is some confusion as to who did first discover that wax could be rendered conductive by simply brushing with finely powdered graphite, but that was the process first commercially adopted. Several years later, in the case of the American Graphophone Co. versus Emerson Phonograph Co., Eldridge R. Johnson testified that he had found in September of 1896 that wax blanks could be copper plated by this method and that it was first done for him by a friend by the name of Dubois. From this it seems obvious that Johnson, as well as Berliner, had been experimenting with wax-blank recording, even though Johnson at that time was not a partner with Berliner and was operating on a contract involving the production of machines only. Johnson, in his sworn testimony, stated that

duplicate records were not actually produced commercially under this process until April of 1898. He said that a number of persons had seen them in the interim and that he had reproduced them for a number of persons, but always in the strictest confidence. It was derived from his testimony that he had made every effort to keep his work secret until 1900, which is perhaps understandable in view of the tangled situation arising about this time in his relationships with Berliner and Frank Seamon. The latter meantime had been exclusive sales agent for Gramophone products in the United States by contract with the United States Gramophone Co.

By 1898, the sales of Gramophones and records were zooming. Eldridge R. Johnson was quoted in the Camden, New Jersey *Telegram* in October as having said that he had been putting out six hundred machines per week for some time and that he was planning to increase production to fifteen hundred per week by operating his shop twenty-four hours per day. Now, with commercial success seemingly assured to Gramophone, the avaricious proprietors of the Graphophone Co. began to lay plans for getting into the disc market which would inevitably result in testing relative value of certain key patents.

Regardless of the question of the applicability of the Bell-Tainter incising patent to the use of a cutting stylus, as adopted by Berliner in 1898, there was invention in the idea of incising a groove of different relationship to the plane of the record than that produced by the Bell-Tainter devices. These had produced a groove of varying depth, as had Edison's original tin-foil phonograph. The Berliner method produced a groove with laterally undulatory form and of non-variable depth. The basic patent was number 564,586, issued to Emile Berliner July 28, 1896, applied for November 7, 1887. A sentence of the specification reads:

"The original record, as well as the copy of the same, is thus obtained as an undulatory line of even depth, as distinguished from a line of varying depth, obtained from the ordinary phonograph and graphophone."

However, this principle had not originally been combined with the incising method in the recording of blanks. The possibilities of such a combination had occurred to Berliner and Johnson and it is known that they were engaged with experiments with wax blanks at the time of the issuance of the patent. However, it was virtually impossible to frame an application for the combination of these principles without tacitly admitting the priority of the Bell-Tainter patents over that of Berliner.

Thus the battle lines were drawn between the proprietors of the Bell-Tainter incising patent and the proprietors of the Berliner patent covering a method of producing a laterally undulating groove of unvarying depth, with neither side daring a frontal attack. Now it is apparent that the executives of the American Graphophone Co. had mapped a carefully planned campaign to break into the lateral disc talking machine business early in 1899, coupled with a scheme to trap Edison, as well. In August, 1899, there appeared in the *Phonoscope* a half-page advertisement of a new horn-type machine similar to the Gramophone, called the "Vitaphone." This advertisement carried the statement "Manufactured under the basic patents of the American Graphophone Co."

In the next issue of *Phonoscope* a notice was published by the Berliner Gramophone Co. that the Vitaphone machines and records were being made in violation of its patents. The Gramophone Co. further alleged that the bright red Vitaphone records were actually copies of Berliner records, as well. In this same issue appeared a story which told that another disc machine similar to the Gramophone was being offered for sale by a New York company affiliated with the National Gramophone Co., the latter being the exclusive sales agents in the United States for the Gramophone. This affiliated company turned out to be the Universal Talking Machine Co., which by a strange coincidence had been organized in February 1888 in Yonkers, New York, where Seamon's National Gramophone Co. the authorized Gramophone distributing company, had also been organized.

The most conclusive instance of the identity of these two corporations is not to be found in the examinations of court testimony but as moulded irrefutably into the first Zonophone records to be issued. These were seven inches in diameter and similar to the Berliner records in appearance. Above the hole for the spindle in a shield-shaped panel was the following caption:

"Zonophone Record—National Gramophone Corp.—All Rights Reserved."

The title and number was under the hole. On the back of the record, in relief, was the following:

"Universal Talking Machine Co.
   All Rights Reserved
Condition of Lease
This record is leased upon the express condition that it shall not be copied or duplicated, and that the full right of property and possession immediately reverts to the *Universal Talking Machine Company* upon violation of the above contract."

As the records were thus leased and not sold, perhaps the conspirators felt that the courts would not be able to construe the subsequent use as a violation of the Berliner patents, or of the exclusive sales agreement which Seamon had with Berliner. The absence of patent information on the record itself, is significant. The product, (Fig. 10-4), of the Universal Talking Machine Co. was named the "Zonophone" and shortly it was announced that F. M. Prescott had been appointed sole export agent. To make the tangle more complete, Prescott had been until then

Fig. 10-4. The Zon-o-phone Improved Gramophone, made by the National Gramophone Corp. in the year 1900.

the export agent for the United States Phonograph Co., of Newark, New Jersey—also to this point the exclusive exporters of Edison cylinder machines and supplies.

Prescott suddenly sued Edison, the Edison Phonograph Works, and its business manager for diverting his formerly profitable export business which he had enjoyed with the United States Phonograph Co. to a new distributing company which had been organized by Edison, called the National Phonograph Co. However, by another interesting coincidence, the United States Phonograph Co. suddenly consented to a decree in a suit which had been brought against it by the American Graphophone Co. alleging infringements of a Bell-Tainter duplicating patent. Undoubtedly the skids had been well greased for this maneuver, for Edison's attorneys made no attempt to defend his former export company and announced that its former manager,

George E. Tewksbury, no longer had any relationships with the Edison Phonograph Works.[8] The American Graphophone Co. magnanimously announced to the trade that it was making a shipment of blank cylinders to the United States Phonograph Co. so that it could wind up its business.

In November 1899, a story criticising the apparent duplicity of certain individuals was carried in the *Phonoscope*. Particularly attention was drawn to the fact that Seamon's National Gramophone Co. was issuing circular letters calling favorable attention to the Vitaphone made by the American Talking Machine Co., but not to the Zonophone made by the Universal Talking Machine Co. of which C. H. LaDow was President and financial backer. This article pointed out that this same

[8] In 1897 Tewksbury had written *A Complete Manual of the Edison Phonograph,* for which Edison had written the Introduction, in which he refers to "friend Tewksbury's book."

LaDow was also at the same time Secretary and General Manager of the
National Gramophone Co. Suit was
brought against the American Talking
Machine Co. by the Berliner Gramophone Co. on the basis of the Berliner
patents. Aware now of what was going
on, the Berliner Gramophone Co. stopped shipment of machines and supplies
to the National Gramophone Co., alleging that its President, Frank Seamon,
had been assiduous in betraying the
Berliner interests to its competitors.
Seamon replied with a petition to have
the Gramophone Co. enjoined from
using the name "Gramophone" on its
products, on the basis of his exclusive
contract. As the American Talking Machine Co. in another court action was
enjoined from infringing on the Berliner patents and the Berliner Gramophone was enjoined from using its own
name on its own products, the result
was a complete tying up of the disc
industry. For a considerable time the
American Graphophone Co. was stymied in its efforts to break into the disc
business and Berliner in the United
States had to confine himself to the
export business, although Eldridge R.
Johnson continued to market machines
and records under his own name.

Now the scene of battle shifted and
another concern which also heretofore
had been close to Edison became involved. It was Hawthorne & Sheble of
Philadelphia. A patent had been granted
to Horace Sheble on December 11, 1899
upon a device which he had invented
for playing the new concert size cylinders upon the standard Edison phonograph. Edison had intended to manufacture these attachments for Hawthorne & Sheble according to later
court testimony, but for some reason
had failed to do so, bringing out the
Edison concert Grand, instead. Edison
apparently had been well advised to
change his mind, for suddenly another
surprise consent decree was entered in
the case of the American Graphophone
Co. versus Hawthorne & Sheble for
violating the Bell-Tainter patent number 341,214, and an injunction was also

granted! In February of 1900 Hawthorne
& Sheble introduced the "Discophone"
licensed under the patents of the American Graphophone Co. In view of the
closeness of dates, it seems rather obvious that this had been another carefully laid plan to trap Edison. Hawthorne & Sheble, together with Prescott,
organized the American Record Co.,
and a record manufacturing plant was
opened in Springfield, Mass. These discs
were a rich blue with a colorful label
with a white background.

The machinations of 1899 and 1900
were nothing less than fantastic. Back
of a gigantic conspiracy to gain control of the entire recording industry
throughout the world were the legal
batteries and financiers of the American
Graphophone Co. The prime movers
were Andrew Devine and the sagacious
Easton. In the field at the close of every
legal battle, as the smoke cleared, would
be seen the inscrutable countenance of
major strategist Philip Mauro. These
clever, unscrupulous men had agents
everywhere who sought out and bought
off key men in every branch of the industry. These included Amden, Sheble,
Tewksbury, Seamon, F. M. Prescott,
LaDow, and others. As an instance of
the chicanery then so prevalent, Fred
Gaisberg in *The Music Goes Round*
tells of a young man by the name of
Joe Jones who spent one summer working in Berliner's laboratory where he
witnessed experiments in recording on
wax blanks. Later, Gaisberg avers,
Jones drew up the specification from
memory to apply for a patent which
was to become the most famous, or infamous, depending upon the viewpoint,
of all of the phonographic patents ever
to be issued by the United States Patent
Office. Who was the eventual purchaser
of this patent? Let us see.

The *Wall Street Journal* of June 2,
1900 stated that the Berliner Gramophone Company of Philadelphia and the
United States Gramophone Company of
Washington had filed bills in equity in
the United States Circuit Court for the
Eastern District of Pennsylvania to re-
strain the National Gramophone Com-

pany from infringement of the Berliner patents and to compel an accounting. The instrument the manufacture and sale of which was alleged to be an infringement was sold under the name "Zonophone." In a prior action the Gramophone interests had been able to have the National Gramophone Company enjoined from using the name "Gramophone" on its products, just as the Gramophone Co. also had been enjoined from using its own name on its products by another court. The Berliner interests won this contest and the ultimate result was that in September, 1901, the National Gramophone Corporation was adjudged bankrupt and a receiver was appointed. In July of the same year, the injunction previously granted to Seamon restraining Berliner from the use of the word "Gramophone" had been continued on a technicality. Thus, the disc business had been thoroughly tied up except for Eldridge R. Johnson, who had continued to produce a limited number of machines and records, but eliminating the name "Gramophone" from his products. At first the records bore the label "Eldridge R. Johnson Record;" later adding to his own name "Victor Record." It is significant that the Johnson records never bore any reference to patents. Nor did the Victor or Victor Talking Machine Co.'s records until after the eventual settlement which may indicate there was not complete understanding between Johnson and Berliner.

Fred Gaisberg for some reason attributes the stalemate which occurred as a result of the events described to an opportune patent issued to J. W. Jones —the same Joe Jones who worked one summer in Berliner's laboratory. This was United States patent number 688,739. It was not issued until December 10, 1901, and had not been invoked in any legal proceedings prior to the settlement so it could not have been a cause of the two-year legal stalemate, which Gaisberg says was resolved in 1902. However, it was the Jones patent which brought the matter to a head. As we have seen, it was really Berliner

and to a lesser degree Johnson who had been put on the spot and the terms of the 1902 settlement tend to prove it. This was contained in a review of prior litigation in the case of Victor Talking Machine Co. versus American Graphophone Co. filed March 27, 1911.

Joe Jones, who had seen the wax recording experiments in the Berliner laboratory in 1896, decided that he could write a specification upon which he might be granted a patent. That his source of inspiration was the Berliner Gramophone experiments is indicated by a minor invention consisting of a bevelled steel talking machine needle (patent applied for in February, 1897 and granted in April of 1898). The sketch shows a Berliner Gramophone and the needle is described as a "Gramophone Needle." However, the application for a patent on "Production of Sound Records" which he filed on November 19, 1897 was presented as an entirely original conception, whereas it was in reality quite devoid of invention, representing only a reverbalization of the principle of the Berliner lateral groove, plus the method of making duplicate records which he had seen used experimentally in the Berliner laboratory. Uninhibited by any fear of conflict with the Bell-Tainter incising patent, which may be understandable in view of later developments, Jones in his specification provided the simplest and most logical description of the improved lateral recording method as it had been developed by Berliner and Johnson. One of the judges who later gave an opinion sustaining its validity summed up as follows:

"The Jones patent 288,739, for a method of producing sound records for use in a talking machine of the disc type, which consists in cutting or engraving a record groove of uniform depth, by means of the lateral vibration of a suitable stylus, upon a disc of wax-like material, and then forming a matrix thereon by electrolysis, from which duplicate records are made by impression, was not anticipated by the prior act and discloses a patentable invention."

However, the patent examiners must not have been quite as easily convinced of his originality for the patent was not issued to Jones until December 10, 1901. It was originally assigned to himself and to J. A. Vincent, of Philadelphia. Before the current issue of the *Patent Gazette* was cold, representatives of the American Graphophone Co. were calling on these gentlemen. The result was that the Graphophone Co. agreed to purchase the Jones patent for twenty-five thousand dollars and agreed to hire Jones as a recording and research engineer. This was the key by which the Graphophone Co. was able to enter the lateral disc talking machine business.

In the 1911 patent case of Victor Talking Machine Co. versus the American Graphophone Co., by which the Jones patent was finally declared invalid, Eldridge R. Johnson was interrogated by counsel as to why the Victor Talking Machine Co. had agreed to take license under the Jones patent. He replied:

"At the time the Jones patent was issued the Victor Company had a large quantity of goods on the market. We had no opportunity of avoiding this patent because we did not know of its existence. I therefore sought a license as a matter of insurance. I felt that such a course was necessary because of the great value of the goods in question. I never infringe a patent or run the risk of an adverse patent decision where any other course is possible."

Prior to the issuance of the patent to Jones, Eldridge R. Johnson during the time of the enforcement of the injunction against the use of the word "Gramophone" had organized a small concern in New York City for the manufacture of disc sound records. This company was known as the Globe Record Company and the records were

designated as "Climax" records. Suit was brought on the basis of the recently acquired Jones patent by the Graphophone Co. against the Globe Record Co. and Eldridge R. Johnson. Johnson, realizing that he was over a barrel, agreed to turn over the Globe Record Co. and all of its assets and also to give the Graphophone Co. all details of the system of making records which had been developed by English, of the Johnson staff, provided the litigation be dropped. From the historical sense, this latter provision is important, for, if Jones was indeed the inventor of the process, one thing that is hard to understand is why should it be necessary for someone from the Johnson side to show the American Graphophone Co. how to make lateral disc records! This important and self-incriminating detail was furnished by Edward D. Easton of the American Graphophone Co. in his testimony in this famous trial of 1911. It is perhaps of interest to note that some of the numbered series originally produced as "Climax" records were carried over into the first "Columbia" black and silver label series indicating the continuity of process development.

The background of English and how he came to be associated with Johnson is also of more than casual importance to the proper unravelling of this tangled skein. An item in the *Phonoscope* of November, 1899, throws light on this, as follows:

"Mr. English, well-known in the earlier Edison Phonograph Laboratory work, has taken charge of the new laboratory of the Universal Talking Machine Co. on 24th Street, and is manufacturing a full line of flat indestructible records, same as the Berliner Gramophone records. The new Company expect to have a full line of records in the field shortly. Mr. Orville LaDow is said to be the President and financial backer of the Universal Talking Machine Co., and is also largely interested in other talking machine enterprises, being secretary and general manager of the

National Gramophone Corporation of this city."

Actually, the Universal Talking Machine Co. had been created in anticipation of a possible adverse decision against Seamon and his National Gramophone Co. as a result of the introduction of the Zonophone, which did occur. The capitalization of the National Gramophone Co. had been increased shortly before the introduction by it of the infringing Zonophone machine and the corporate name changed to National Gramophone Corporation. By these corporate manipulations, production of machines and records competing with the Gramophone products had been continued after Seamon had been stopped. Seamon had been enjoined from using the word "Gramophone" early in 1901. This was shortly before Eldridge R. Johnson filed the name "Victor" as a trade mark with the United States Patent Office in March of 1901. Actually the famous "His Master's Voice" trademark already had been registered in the United States Patent Office by Emile Berliner in July 1900. The painting of little Nipper (the dog) had originally been painted by an Englishman by the name of Francis Barraud for exhibition at the Royal Academy. However, the hanging committee refused it space and Barraud endeavored to sell it to the talking machine manufacturer whose product he had portrayed. This manufacturer refused to avail himself of the opportunity to purchase what came to be generally considered the most valuable trademark in existence. Barraud then painted out the original cylinder machine and painted in the Gramophone, with the result that William Barry Owen of the newly-formed English Co., The Gramophone Co., Ltd., purchased it for one hundred pounds. Later, Barraud made other copies for the company, but according to Owen in a story in the *Talking Machine World*, July, 1906, the original then graced the office of Eldridge R. Johnson at Camden. Although Nipper was an English dog, the astute Eldridge R. Johnson made

early use of "His Master's Voice" trademark, which he adopted even before the formation of the Victor Talking Machine Co.[9] although the use of the word "Gramophone" in the United States was never revived.

Johnson is given credit by Gaisberg for having brought the various conflicting interests together, that is, the American Graphophone Co., Berliner, and Edison. However, from the study of the court cases it seems that Berliner had already been stopped by the chicanery of Seamon and that with the Jones patent in the hands of the Graphophone Co., Johnson knew his turn was next, as indicated by his deal in which he turned over the Globe Record Co. Very likely the situation enabled Johnson to talk Berliner out of the exclusive rights to the Gramophone patents for the Western Hemisphere, excepting Canada, in return for certain improvements which Johnson had made to the Gramophone.

But this was an uneasy truce, the Globe transaction merely having been used by Johnson to buy enough time to find a legal basis for retaliation. On October 24, 1902, the Victor Talking Machine Co. brought suit against the American Graphophone Co. for alleged infringement of the Berliner patents, and on July 13, 1903, another suit alleging infringement of a reproducer patent, number 670,896, which had been issued to Johnson. The American Graphophone Co. and its sales agents, the Columbia Phonograph Co. had been continuing to do business with the Universal Talking Machine Co. and the Zonophone and had been adopting Johnson's improvements without leave. When Johnson returned to the fray with these two suits, the Graphophone legal experts realized he had a strong case. But they had the Jones patent, so a compromise was arranged. The Universal Talking Machine Co. and its assets were turned

---

[9] This trademark was used in advertising of Johnson's "Consolidated Talking Machine Co." which appeared in nationally circulated magazines several months before the organization of the Victor Talking Machine Co.

over to Johnson and the American Graphophone Co. exchanged licenses with the Victor Co. so that both the American Graphophone Co. and the Victor Co. were permitted to manufacture lateral disc talking machines and records. Actually, Columbia disc records had previously been manufactured by the American Graphophone Co. since 1902, always bearing in the shellac in raised letters "Patented December 10, 1901"—the date of issuance of the Jones patent.

It is significant that on December 12, 1902, Frank Seamon, who had previously applied for a writ of certiorari against the Berliner Gramophone Co., had his appeal dismissed by his counsel —Philip Mauro. From this time forward until well into the era of electrical recording, the lateral disc market was to be controlled by two forces, the American Graphophone Co.—Columbia Phonograph Co. and the Victor Talking Machine Co.—Berliner Gramophone Co. and their affiliated companies.

CHAPTER 11

THE INTERNATIONAL SITUATION

IN addition to the basic cylinder phonograph patent of 1877, granted in Great Britain as well as in the United States, Edison had also received promptly and without question the comprehensive patent (with 65 detail drawings), including 'a disc phonograph method, in 1878. Theoretically, his position with respect to the subsequent patents of the Bells' and Tainter, or of Berliner, should have been much stronger in Britain than in the United States. In this second patent, Edison had indicated the possible use of wax, or yielding substances other than tin foil, as well as the use of copper and sheet iron for record making purposes. He also covered the use of electro-typing for the making of duplicates and the utility of diamond for styli.

Both of the Bells and Tainter were Englishmen. Chichester Bell and Sumner Tainter, whose names appear on the more important basic graphophone patent, had not been brought over from England by Alexander Bell until after the issuance of these Edison patents in England. It may be recalled that this was a direct result of the fortuitous granting of a fund to Alexander Bell by the French Government for his invention of the telephone by reason of a prize award which had been set up by the former Emperor Napoleon III.

So, although there was plenty of European influence, the actual roots of the talking machine were sprouted in America. The first of these, the phono-

graph, by a native born American; the second, the graphophone, by three Englishmen; and the third, the gramophone, by a German emigrant, Emile Berliner. Quite naturally, the three types of machines had offshoots in Europe, but all were not destined to appear immediately after their introduction in America.

As in the United States, the tin-foil phonograph had its day of successful demonstration as a curiosity in European countries. It failed of sustained interest as in the United States because of the impermanence of the foil records. The Bell-Tainter graphophone of 1887 promised to make good that deficiency, but before the promise was fulfilled Edison contrived his own answer to the need. Reasons other than the strength of his British patents favored Edison in the face of threatened competition as far as the European scene was concerned. Following the successful introduction of his incandescent lighting system in various places in Europe and his telephonic achievements in England, Edison's prestige was at its peak. There were Edison representatives in most of the larger countries to look after the Edison interests. One of the most influential of these was his chief European representative, Col. George E. Gouraud of London, who had successfully engineered the introduction of Edison's speaking telephone in England and had a part in organizing the Edison lighting industry there.

Tate in his reminiscences states that in 1887 Col. Gouraud was approached by unnamed persons who asked him if he would accept the Chairmanship of a British Graphophone company. He is said by Tate to have communicated with Edison about the proposition, and had been advised by him not to have anything to do with the Graphophone people, that they were pirates trying to steal his invention, and that he had started improving the phonograph.[1] Whether true or not, no such company was formed at that time. Nor was there a serious effort made to introduce the original Bell-Tainter graphophone anywhere in Europe. As from the beginning, on its home grounds and in the hands of its friends and colleagues of the Columbia Phonograph Co. of Washington, District of Columbia, it was proving to be an impractical instrument.

As soon as Edison's improved phonograph made its appearance commercially in 1888, demonstration models were sent to Col. Gouraud and the attempt to introduce it as a business machine paralleled the similar effort in America. But in Europe there was to be no serious competition for nearly a decade. Although not meeting with the expected acceptance, the new phonograph had a modest success in England, due principally to the sincere interest of Col. Gouraud in the enterprise. His personal belief in the potential of the phonograph was as staunch as it was realistic. He experimented with it constantly, demonstrating it and making records of the voices of all the important people with whom he came in contact. Gouraud invented several improvements, one of such importance that it was referred to in some of the many court cases in the United States.[2] In 1890, Col. Gouraud recorded the voices of Florence Nightingale, Prime Minister Gladstone, and others which he

sent to Thomas A. Edison on "phonograms."[3] Edison had envisioned direct vocal communication, as afforded by the telephone, but in more permanent form, by "phonograms." To this end, he devoted a considerable amount of time in trying to develop a flexible, unbreakable phonogram, but without practical results. However, the phonograph received considerable acceptance in Europe by scientists, for acoustical research and the collection of ethnological data; and by educators for the teaching of languages. Although the "phonograms" were used for interoffice correspondence between Edison, Gouraud and others, this field of use would hardly have been commercially practical in Europe because of the language barriers. Today we know that there are certain other psychological reasons why it would never become a universal means of communication, but this could hardly be expected to have been apparent at that time, especially in the light of the success of the telephone.

It was several years before the modified graphophone made its appearance in Europe. Meanwhile the entertainment potential of the phonograph had become recognized as it had in America. The travelling exhibitor and the phonograph parlor had become European institutions as well. The need of reliable machines and musical records for this field helped as in America to offset its lack of substantial success as a business machine. Consequently by the time the modified graphophone came into the market in most European countries there were companies operating as licensees of Edison's United States Phonograph Co., his export agency. Other companies had sprung up also as operators and manufacturers of records, some legitimate and some not.

As soon as the Columbia Phonograph Co., Ltd., began the selling of the new graphophones and records in England, it was attacked by Edisonia Ltd., the

---

[1] *Edison's Open Door,* Alfred O. Tate, E. P. Dutton & Co. Inc., New York, 1938.

[2] American Graphophone Co. vs. American Record Co., Circuit Court S.D., New York, Feb. 19, 1906.

[3] Some of these 1890 cylinders were re-recorded on a Decca LP record, "Hark, the Years" in 1950.

official distributors of the Edison products. Thus the legal battle in England began just about the time that a temporary truce had been reached in November of 1896 between the Edison and the Graphophone interests in the United States. There was never any clear-cut definition of the respective merits of the basic Bell-Tainter patents and the Edison patents in the courts of the United States, nor in England. After a virtual stalemate of two years the problem was resolved in England by a merger of the conflicting interests, early in 1898. The Edison-Bell Consolidated Phonograph Co. was organized with a total capital of 110,000 pounds. By the agreements which were signed, rights were acquired to the patents of T. A. Edison, A. G. Bell, C. A. Bell, C. S. Tainter, and others for the United Kingdom, Australia, South America, China, and Japan. This pattern estab-

lished the precedent for the division of the world into territories by the disc industry in later years.

A calm and peaceful period of development seemed in prospect. But, in the meantime one of the other roots had sprouted, received nourishment and had begun to bear fruit, made possible by a sort of cross-pollination with the older branches of the industry. Emile Berliner had secured the technical assistance of Will Gaisberg, who had prior experience with Tainter in the Volta Graphophone laboratory, and Alfred Clark, who had been previously working in the Edison laboratory. Clark had invented an improved hand drive for the gramophone, which eliminated a great deal of the uncertainty of pitch which had afflicted Berliner's first commercial model. This was in 1896. The next year Eldridge R. Johnson supplied from his Camden machine shop the first

Fig. 11-1. First of the spring-motored Gramophones using Eldridge Johnson's motor supplied from his Camden machine shop.

spring-motored gramophones. (See Fig. 11-1.) Will Gaisberg opened the first recording studio in Philadelphia, with his brother Fred to play the accompaniments. Alfred Clark opened the first retail store nearby. These three men were to play an important part in the European industry.

Just at this point there began that series of devious maneuvers the true motivations for which were to remain obscure to the public for years and the results of which were to vitally affect the future of the industry throughout the world. In Yonkers, New York, to operate as exclusive distributors of the Berliner Gramophone for the United States, there was organized a company called the National Gramophone Co., with a capital of fifty thousand dollars. There were three organizing directors, Frank Seaman, of Yonkers; Henry Boutz and William Barry Owen, of New York City. Shortly after the organization of this company, Owen was sent to England by Berliner to attempt to sell the European rights to the gramophone for cash, in order to finance the furtherance of development and production in this country. This Owen found impossible, but after about a year of effort he found men willing to underwrite a credit of fifteen thousand pounds to finance the importation of gramophones from the United States and the setting up of recording facilities in Europe.

Both Berliner and the producer of his spring-motor gramophones, Eldridge Johnson, were working on a hand-to-mouth basis, but they agreed to the proposal. It was recognized by all that the making of records suitable for the English market was the chief immediate problem, for the gramophone did not offer the opportunity to make records anywhere, as had the phonograph, for it was necessary to set up special recording and processing equipment to make the master records and also machines for pressing the records. Therefore, it was decided to send Will and Fred Gaisberg to set up a recording studio in London and that Berliner's brother Joseph in Hanover, Germany, would set up a processing and pressing plant. These momentous decisions also played a great part in the future of the European industry.

These developments had not escaped the attention of Philip Mauro, Edward Easton, Thomas Macdonald, and others. No one associated these men with the quiet formation of another new talking machine company in February of 1898. By the sheerest coincidence, this one was also organized in Yonkers, New York, by three men—although not the same ones. The capitalization was a modest twenty thousand dollars and the organizing directors were Orlando J. Hackett, Edward A. Reser, and William Mayse, all of New York City.

The company was named the Universal Talking Machine Co. In July, the Gaisbergs were on their way to London to begin recording for the new English Gramophone Co. In October, 1898, the American Graphophone Co. brought suit against the National Gramophone Co., the sales company organized by Frank Seaman of Yonkers, for selling machines and records infringing upon the Bell-Tainter patents. The next month a preliminary injunction was issued against the National Gramophone Co. to take effect in January, 1899. Seaman, putting up a straight front, appealed the decision, but apparently to get around the difficulty he reorganized the National Gramophone Co. in March into the National Gramophone Corporation, increasing the capitalization to $800,000. Frank J. Dunham was elected president, Seaman treasurer and one Orville de LaDow, secretary. Conspicuous by their absence were the former directors, with the exception of Seaman, and particularly missed was the name of William Barry Owen.

Now it becomes apparent that the two American disc talking machine enterprises had more things in common than the place of origin. O. L. LaDow, who was acting as both secretary and general manager of the reorganized National Gramophone Corporation was also now the general manager of the Universal Talking Machine Co. But these facts escaped general observation at the time and it was not until the November 1899 *Phonoscope* (actually published about two months later) that the editor called attention to the apparent duplicity involved, as has been stated previously.

Not aware of this situation, three of the most important Gramophone people had sailed for England in April of 1899, ostensibly to organize a Gramophone Co. for France. These were Cleveland Walcutt, A. E. Footman, W. Barry Owen, organizer of the English Gramophone Co. and Emile Berliner. Alfred Clark, another of the principals, had preceded them in January. While in Europe a bombshell struck. A disc machine strangely like the gramophone, if somewhat heavier and more ornate, made its appearance in London, offered by an American exporting company which prior to this time had dealt only in Edison goods. This machine was called the Zonophone. Soon it was learned that these were being manufactured and exported by the Universal Talking Machine Co., with a line of records similar to those of the gramophone. Undoubtedly William Barry Owen would have taken the first plane back to America, if such had been available. In any case the discussion which must have taken place in America later between himself and Frank Seamon would probably have made most interesting listening, if anyone would dared to have recorded it!

The immediate result was that the supply of gramophones and supplies to Seamon's National Gramophone Corporation was suddenly cut off and Seamon's exclusive sales contract cancelled. But this was not the entire extent of the ramifications of the plot. The former export distributor of Edison goods was involved in a big way, as were the heads of a number of companies which formerly had done business with Edison and were now finding it expedient to permit consent decrees to be brought against them by admit-

ting that they had been infringing the Bell-Tainter patents for one reason or another. The stage had been cleverly set for this part of the operation by the Graphophone master strategists. By indirect contacts they secured the tacit consent of the Edison forces to co-operate in an endeavor to put a stop to some of the flagrant unlicensed competition which had sprung up, particularly with respect to the duplication of cylinder records. In Chicago there were several companies making complete machines. In the March, 1899 *Phonoscope,* under "Legal Notices," it was observed that even the number plates and patent notices of the genuine Edison phonographs were being copied on some of these machines. Whether this notice was part of the campaign it is hard to say, but the Edison forces apparently went along. Shortly thereafter suits began to be filed thick and fast and injunctions with accountings, as well. Although the Graphophone Co. bore the costs of the litigation, it also collected the awards.

Later in the year the Edison legal staff was chagrined to find they had been taken in by this ruse, when the Graphophone legal experts began to pick off the former Edison allies by the "consent decree" routine, as well as the true infringers, often using the precedents of similar cases to establish a case. One of these was Hawthorne & Sheble, of Philadelphia, mentioned in connection with the concert cylinder story. The most important one, however, was the case of the Graphophone Co. versus the United States Phonograph Co., of Newark, New Jersey, which had been the chief exporting company for Edison goods and which had been the supplier of F. M. Prescott. This had been preceded by a suit by Prescott against Edison, the National Phonograph Co. and others alleging a conspiracy to wreck his export business. In the court testimony it had developed that Prescott had taken in as a partner in his business Charles B. Stevens who was in the employ of the National Phonograph Co. and that he had turned over confidential information as to the customers of National Phonograph Co. and United Phonograph Co. to Prescott, who in turn had offered Stevens a partnership. Rather understandably, the National Phonograph Co. had blacklisted Prescott and refused to sell him goods. Whether these events preceded or followed Prescott's contacts with National Gramophone Co. doesn't really matter—the results were the same. Prescott's was not the only export company, but it was probably the largest. Now, perhaps with the idea of making their adversaries scatter their shots, the Graphophone Co. launched other disc talking machine enterprises, including the American Talking Machine Co. and the Vitaphone Co., boldly announcing that they were licensed under the Bell-Tainter patents and under the legal protection of the Graphophone Co. Now it could be seen that a frontal battle between the legal forces of the parent companies must be imminent. It was also becoming very apparent that the control over the manufacture and sales of records was the chief advantage to the manufacturers of disc machines over those of the cylinders. The cylinder experts now began to leave Edison and the smaller companies like rats from a sinking ship. The prevailing situation is well symbolized by two little news items from the September 1899 *Phonoscope,* (published in November), as follows:

"Rumours of patent litigation are flying thick and fast. A suit is pending between two of the most important talking machine companies which will undoubtedly prove very interesting. The lawyers are all rubbing their hands in anticipation of fat fees. In matters of this kind success generally waits on the one with the largest purse. . . ."

"From rumors which have come to us it would appear that the parent wax cylinder companies anticipate the failure to no longer control the duplicating of records. Several suits are now being fought strenuously with apparent success so far to the defendants. Neither the Orange nor the Bridgeport companies will now sell blanks in the United States unless they are guaranteed for export and they are shown the shipping documents to prove the shipments. By refusing to supply blanks in the United States can the companies alone hope to shut off the duplication of records other than in their own factories."

The prediction of the first quotation was fulfilled by the bringing of suits by one or another of the patent-holding parent companies now in the disc business against each one of the disc producing or distributing companies in the United States, thus resulting in a tangle of injunctions which effectually tied the retail disc business of the United States in a knot by the end of 1899. Eldridge R. Johnson was the sole exception. By dropping the name "gramophone" from his machines and records, he carried on alone. This lull also gave the cylinder business a break and accelerated the competition for a practical molding method. The imperative need for it was emphasized by an ad which had appeared on behalf of a New York dealer offering $5,000 cash for a permanent master phonograph record. The word "phonograph" at that time was applied only to the cylinder type machine.

In England, a similar stalemate had been reached in the litigation between the Edison-Bell Consolidated Co. and the Gramophone Co., but elsewhere in Europe the process of recording and the selling of talking machines and records went on unimpeded. So with nothing to do in the United States except to record for export, most of the disc experts went to Europe. On Jan. 27, 1900, Joseph W. Jones sailed for Europe with recording apparatus to make Zonophone records of coster songs and music hall novelties for the English trade, according to the news story in *Phonoscope.* In view of the spate of recordings by Zonophone of opera singers made in various European music cen-

ters and issued under the International
Zonophone label in 1900 and 1901, it
seems more likely that Jones had been
instructed to beat the Gramophone Co.
in its bid for supremacy in the field of
classical recording through the recording trips of the Gaisbergs.

Edison also attempted to gain some
sort of control of the European cylinder
market. Branches of the National
Phonograph Co. were established in the
various countries, with headquarters in
London, Paris, Berlin, Brussels, Vienna,
and Milan. Will Hayes of the Orange
staff was sent abroad in 1899 to organize recording studios in these centers.
Successful introduction of the cylinder
molding method may have been anticipated, for after 1901, a considerable
amount of molding was done by the
European branches of National Phonograph Co., as well as by some of the
licensed survivors of the earlier companies, such as the "Compagnie Americaine du Phonograph Edison," in Paris
the Pathe-Freres Co., of France (who
had branches in various European
countries) and the Anglo-Italian Commerce Co. of Genoa, Italy—the only
cylinder company to record Caruso.
These Caruso cylinders were later
transferred by Pathe to the hill-and-
dale center-start discs. Many important
artists were recorded on cylinders in
Europe, particularly by Pathe-Freres
and its subsidiaries.

During the time of its legal difficulties with Edison-Bell, the Gramophone
Co. decided to manufacture electric
clocks and typewriters. It only actually produced the latter, but this accounts for the change in corporate
name to the "Gramophone and Typewriter, Ltd." The typewriter was not
a success and eventually the name
was again changed. In the meantime,
an agreement was reached in the
United States which also resolved the
situation in England. Both Berliner in
Europe and Eldridge Johnson in the
United States had been recording ten
inch disc records during 1901. The resumption of open competition for the
English market was marked by the in-

troduction of the now famous series of
red label celebrity records by famous
artists. These included the cream from
a recording trip by the Gaisbergs including the ten songs obtained from
Caruso for the terrific total fee of one
hundred pounds! These were recorded
in March of 1902. A copy of one of these
records was sent to Heinrich Conried,
manager of the Metropolitan Opera in
New York and resulted in the offering
of a contract to Caruso for the next
season. The rest is musical as well as
phonographic history.

From this time forward, copies of
many of the masters of records by
famous European artists were exported
to the United States for pressing there.
Many other artists were first to become
known to the American public through
their recordings. Many times their fame
and the invitation to sing in America
was to be founded on a prior reputation based upon their recorded performances. Even the "red seal" idea was
European in its origin and was not
copyrighted by the Victor Co. until
several years later for its exclusive use
in the United States. The initial celebrity series of recordings on discs was
such an outstanding success that both
of the major disc producing companies,
International Zonophone Co., and the
Gramophone & Typewriter, Ltd., redoubled their efforts and even organized recording expeditions to India and
China in search for musical novelties.
The enrolling of the famous opera and
concert artists for the Victor roster
was begun in New York by Calvin
Childs, who also had received his training in the cylinder recording business.
Incidentally, many of the cylinders recorded in Europe were reproduced by
the molding method for the American
market, but by and large, the patrons
of the Edison phonograph were neither
opera fans, or lovers of classical music.

The ten inch records were soon followed by the longer playing twelve inch
discs. As far as Europe was concerned,
in respect to both talent and playing
time, the cylinders were too late with
too little. The early seven inch Berliner

and Zonophone discs were about on a par with the cylinders as far as playing time was concerned—about two minutes, even though the surface was noisy. But with the improved results obtained from the switch to the use of the wax blanks for disc recording and the longer playing time of the larger diameter discs the balance was altered. Operatic arias and concert songs especially benefited by the extension of playing time to three and one-half minutes or better on the twelve-inch discs.

This was not quite as evident in England as elsewhere in Europe. Perhaps the average Englishman was a little less interested in opera and the classics, or perhaps he was more sensitive to the rasping surface noise of the discs. Or perhaps it may have been the result of the more capable efforts of Col. Gouraud and his successors. Whatever the reason, the English people had welcomed the cylinder records from the first and the story of that branch of the industry is most interesting.

As early as 1901, a brilliant young entertainer and pioneer recordist had gone to England to employ the valuable experience he had gained in working in all of the recording laboratories of America. He was well known even then to owners of all kinds of talking machines as "Michael Casey." He was as well known in a way, as "Bing" Crosby is today. He was so well known that his endorsement of a product was considered an advantage. In the 1899 catalog of the Talking Machine Co. of Chicago, Russell Hunting gave his endorsement of the Polyphone, a dual reproducer phonograph, as follows:

"I consider that it gives three times the volume of tone that could be originally attained from any other reproducing machine. The tone it produces is marvelous.
"I never realized how wonderful the talking machine could be until I heard your Polyphone."

Hunting until shortly before this had been the Editor of the *Phonoscope*. In

any case, he was well known and respected in the field and shortly after his arrival in England was made the recording director for Edison-Bell.

Another emigre from the United States about this time was to become an even more famous person eventually —in fact to the extent of being knighted for his accomplishments in the industry —Louis Sterling. But Sterling was already on the side of the discs. The International Zonophone Co. had been organized in 1900 as a subsidiary of the Universal Talking Machine Co., both in reality were originally satellites of the American Graphophone Co. Gramophone & Typewriter, Ltd. in 1903 obtained a controlling interest in the International Zonophone Company and its American affiliations. Mr. Louis Sterling was then on the staff of Gramophone & Typewriter, Ltd. Early in 1904 the British Zonophone Company was formed to channelize the British zonophone trade and to develop the market for a cheap disc. Mr. Sterling became manager in October of 1904, and employed Russell Hunting to supervise recording activities for Zonophone. Mr. Sterling resigned from British Zonophone in November of 1904, and in December registered the Sterling Co., Ltd., to manufacture and deal in phonographs, gramophones, talking machines, etc. The result was that both Sterling and Hunting reverted to the cylinders. The following announcement was made in the *Talking Machine News*, of London, in the February 1905 issue:

"The Sterling Record Co., of which Mr. Louis Sterling is managing director, have taken extensive premises for the manufacture of gold molded records at Bishop Road, Cambridge Heath E. - - - the recording department to be under the management of Mr. Russell Hunting. Mr. Charles Stroh, well known inventor of the Stroh Violin, has joined the board."

In view of the breadth of their past experience this switch of Sterling and Hunting back to the cylinders would seem to indicate their doubt as to the ultimate supremacy of the disc over the cylinder. That Hunting was not a silent partner, or a shrinking violet, may be gleaned from the following announcement made only two months later:

"The Sterling Record Co. has changed its name to Russell Hunting Co. Ltd., but the new gold molded record will be known as the Sterling Record."

By the following January, an advertisement of the new company in the *Talking Machine News* stated that one million records had been sold in twenty-two weeks. A short time later it was announced that retail outlets had been created in Canada, Australia, and New Zealand.

The legal entanglements of the three major patent holding groups in the United States and England offered an opportunity for a few newcomers to become established sufficiently well to be able to defend themselves on the basis of minor or contributory improvement patents. One of these was the Odeon Co. of Germany, which produced the first regularly issued double faced records in 1904. The American Graphophone Co. had made a few on an experimental basis the same year, but there was not a regular series of double disc Columbia records until 1908. Odeon established branches in some other countries, such as France. In Italy, an affiliate of Odeon was known as Societa Italiana di Fonotipia. This group soon were offering strong competition to the Gramophone and its sister companies. At first this competition was confined largely to the mainland. Strange as it may seem now, the most intense competition at this time in England was between the cylinder manufacturers. There were now three major producers of cylinder records in England, the National Phonograph Co., the Edison-Bell Consolidated Phonograph, and the Russell Hunting Co., Ltd.

The London *Talking Machine News* of February, 1906, reported that a "well-known" cylinder manufacturer would soon reduce prices. Although the name of the firm was not mentioned in the story, the publisher was immediately sued by the National Phonograph Co., which cancelled its advertising contract forthwith. No advertising by this company appeared again in the *Talking Machine News* for several years, in retrospect as neat a job of slicing off one's own nose as was ever done, considering that this was the only trade paper that covered the entire United Kingdom.

As predicted, the National Phonograph Co. reduced the prices of its cylinders to one shilling. The selling price of the three leading brands to this time had been one shilling and six pence. Illustrative of the lack of business sense on the part of the National Phonograph management, it was announced that the price reduction would not take place until August—five months away. Naturally the business of all Edison dealers dropped to practically nothing. One dealer placed a bitterly sarcastic ad in the *Talking Machine News,* inviting the public to hurry in and buy his stock of records before the price should drop!

Although the English public were not appraised of it, the price war had actually been touched off by Russell Hunting Co. Ltd. on the other side of the Atlantic. An advertisement had appeared in the *Talking Machine World,* published in New York in January, 1906, offering Sterling gold-molded records to the American trade to be sold at twenty-five cents each, then roughly equivalent to the English shilling. In this way Edison and the National Phonograph Co. were wrongly condemned for having started what proved to be a disastrous price war, although this is not any excuse for the incredibly stupid bungling which followed. Edison-Bell and Russell Hunting immediately met the price reduction announced by the National Phonograph Co., the former none too cheerfully, as this company entered an ad in the shape of a tombstone in the London trade paper with copy inscribed as follows:

"To the memory of One-and-six
He shuffled off
Existence here
Still joyful, he roams
Another (hemi) sphere
Where Cents of Duty Guard Him
  GONE BUT NOT FORGOTTEN
He suffered long through lacking
  the sense
To know he couldn't sell here for
  18 pence
In the land of dollars he still may
  sell—
Import duty protects him from
  Edison-Bell."

The result of this was a blacklisting of Edison-Bell by the National Phonograph Co., which refused henceforth to sell them machines. According to a later news story, they managed somehow through devious connections to get hold of Edison phonographs to tide them over the period of the ban. But even though National Phonograph still got the phonograph business, by a circuitous route, the blacklisting cost them the cylinder business. In August, 1906, Edison-Bell introduced a slightly longer cylinder to give a little longer playing time and which did not require the use of a special mandrel—obviously not an Edison product. To add to the turmoil in the cylinder industry in England, an independent manufacturer by the name of General Phonograph Co. this same month introduced a new line of "White" cylinders. It was about this time that John McCormack was engaged by Hunting to make Sterling records. He also made records for Edison-Bell, National Phonograph Co., and the Gramophone and Typewriter Co. McCormack received then about five pounds for each song he recorded. He was not as yet a world famous artist but was coming along rapidly, to a considerable extent his popularity growing from his records.

Nor should it be overlooked that in England celluloid cylinders very early had scored a considerable technical and financial success. Instead of the stalemate caused by incompetent handling

of contributory patents in the United States, Edison-Bell early was enabled to make use of the celluloid molding method, whereas Edison, the inventor of the phonograph had been enjoined against doing so. The Lambert Co., first producers of commercial celluloid cylinders in the United States, were similarly handicapped though able to stop Edison on the basis of a single patent. In England, The Lambert Co. made both phonographs and records for a number of years. In 1905 it had a factory covering over a half-acre of ground with a capacity of 100,000 records a week. It produced the Lambert celluloid cylinders using the Edison Gold-molded process, as well as a companion, lower-priced wax-type cylinder known as the Rex. In the later period it also made the Lambert cylinders in a three-minute, six-inch length—a much more practical record than the comparable wax-type Twentieth-Century cylinders then being produced by Columbia in the United States.

Meanwhile, the interest and competition was also building up in the disc industry. A new unbreakable disc was demonstrated at the offices of Henry Seymour, Ltd., in London, invented by a Dr. Michaelis. This was the product of the Neophone Co., who were making celluloid coated vertically recorded discs, in nine-, ten-, and twenty-inch diameters and were introducing a grand opera series. They produced a recording attachment as well, a unique feature in the disc market. Without doubt Russell Hunting was well aware of these developments, as well as others abroad, for also in this fateful month of August, 1906, he announced that his company had acquired sole distribution rights for England and Australia of the Odeon and Fonotipia disc records from the International Talking Machine Co.

The headquarters of the International Talking Machine Co. was in Berlin. In December, 1906, an interview with F. M. Prescott, President and General Manager of the company was published in the American *Talking Machine World*, relative to the European business situation. Prescott said that there were no trade restrictions in Europe, that competition was strong but there was plenty of business for everyone. As to the patent situation, he stated that in Europe there were no fundamental patents, only constructive patents. He said that on the continent the only important cylinder manufacturers were Edison, Columbia, and Pathe-Freres, the local manufacturers having ceased to exist. He said that this was not true in England, where the cylinder business was fully equal to, if not greater, than that of the discs.

In Germany, Prescott reported that there were no less than twenty manufacturers of discs and that prices were better (higher) than in the United States. Four sizes of discs were manufactured, he stated, 7″ at 60¢ each; 10″ at $1.20 each; 12″ at $1.80 each, and 14″ at $2.40, as manufactured by the Gramophone and Typewriter Ltd. From the standpoint of understanding the world competitive situation, Prescott made a revealing statement, as follows:

"You know, the world, in so far as the sale of their products is concerned, has been divided between the Gramophone & Typewriter, Ltd. of London, England and the Victor Talking Machine Co. of Camden, N. J., the latter controlling South, Central and North America and that part of Asia not included in the British Colonies. The Edison, Columbia and Zonophone are well known in these countries. We, however, operate everywhere and with a catalog of 14,000 titles do a splendid business at our prices. We have only been in business three years. The European Gramophone catalog represents 23,000 selections. Prices of recording labs in America ranges from $2., the lowest, to an average of $5., sometimes reaching $10. In Europe, singers are paid $20. to $25. for a song, and that not for the so-called celebrity artists!"

So according to F. M. Prescott, business and patent conditions were gener-

ally more favorable than in the United States. However, he was in the disc business now and it seems likely that operating largely in Europe with its different languages, patent structures and court procedures that his company was in a temporarily advantageous position because of being remote from the home offices of the big three of the United States and their ever busy patent attorneys. It was in February and March of this year that Victor and the American Graphophone Co. had conducted a heated advertising contest in the *Talking Machine World* to show the trade who was the boss of the disc industry. Looking back, it seems that the cylinder industry had always been hectic, both in the United States and England. As a result of the price war and the switch in the type of cylinders being sold, the National Phonograph Co. tried to have the Edison-Bell Consolidated Phonograph Co. restrained from further use of the name "Edison" in its name, or upon its products. Stemming from this and an alleged loss of business, the Edison-Bell Co. sued the National Phonograph Co. for damages and a verdict in favor of the plaintiff was reported by the *Talking Machine World* in April, 1907, with damages to be assessed by a referee. Regardless of ethical considerations, National Phonograph had blundered badly again, for the original contract to the Hough Brothers, who had founded Edison-Bell, not only conveyed the right to use the name "Edison" for which a large stipulated payment had been made, but also contained a clause which insisted that the name "Edison" should appear on all of the products to be manufactured!

The battle of the cylinders again spread across the Atlantic. In the June issue of the *Talking Machine World* an ad was headlined "GENUINE BRITISH MANUFACTURE," accompanied by the slogans "Better than America's" and "Cheaper than German's." But the advertising staff of Edison-Bell pulled out all stops the next month with a full page ad on the record situation, as follows:

"The Edison-Bell Records have at last brought *all* down to one level price in Great Britain and the Colonies.

"In Great Britain, the Free Market
EDISON-BELL, 1/- EDISON, 1/-
ALL OTHERS, 1/-

"How are the mighty fallen ! ! !
"What price in the tariff-ridden U. S.?
"No reason why records should be made in the States and sold at home for 35¢, and carriage paid, warehoused and distributed in England for 24¢.
"*Any How*—if there is a dealer or factor in the U. S. with pluck enough to handle *Edison-Bell Products* we'll help him to pay duties and sell better Records—particularly for a large number of British residents—and better phonographs than America knows.
"You experts, just consider—America and America's great *man* have not improved the Phonograph one iota in 12 years."

The singular "man" in the last sentence was corrected to "men" in the next issue, whether because it really was an error, or because of possible legal repercussions, was not made clear. Perhaps it would not be "cricket" to point out that it was an American made Edison Concert Grand which Edison-Bell had recently presented to King Edward for use on his yacht!

Despite the low prices, another new cylinder called the Clarion, manufactured by Premier, was introduced to sell for nine pence, thus adding even more pressure to the price war. But the balance began to swing to the discs. For a time, almost monthly, new types of disc talking machines and records were announced. A double disc called the Melograph was manufactured in Liverpool. The General Phonograph Co. Ltd. announced a White disc phonograph for playing both the hill-and-dale and laterally recorded discs, the first of an eventual long line of such combination instruments. These were also offered in the American market through a full page ad appearing in the September,

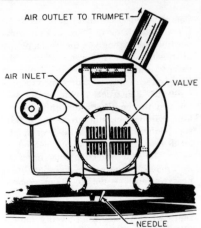

AIR OUTLET TO TRUMPET

AIR INLET

VALVE

NEEDLE

Fig. 11-2. Construction details of Parson's Auxetophone designed for intensifying sound by means of air pressure.

1907 *Talking Machine World.* Another new manufacturer was the British Sonogram Co. which made an initial offering of eighty double disc records (160 titles), also offered in the American market.

These events reveal two things rather definitely; first, that it was apparently much easier to become a phonograph or record manufacturer in England than in the United States; second, that a trend had set in towards the discs. That the cylinder industry still had plenty of vitality was indicated by a statement towards the close of the year by Russell Hunting Co. that it now had recording laboratories in France, Spain, Holland, and Denmark.

This year, the Hough brothers, founders of Edison-Bell, had left this company and engaged in producing Electric cylinder records. These records were electric in name only and it was disaster by fire that put an end to the enterprise, rather than the competition of either discs or cylinders. As a result, William Ditcham, their chief recording expert who had been with them at Edison-Bell, became chief recorder for the Russell Hunting Co. He is particularly noted for having recorded excerpts of the entire "Pinafore" on the Sterling cylinders, a feat not equalled elsewhere in the cylinder industry.

Meanwhile, apparently not satisfied with their virtual freedom from molestation by the legal bloodhounds of the big three of the United States, various of the disc and cylinder manufacturers of England and the continent began to cast avaricious eyes at the juicy American market. Soon determined efforts were being made to break through the tariff barrier. The ads of the Neophone Co., General Phonograph Co., Edison-Bell, International Talking Machine Co., British Sonogram Co., and others appeared with increasing frequency in American trade papers. In addition the Auxetophone (Fig. 11-2), a compressed air amplifying disc phonograph invented by an Englishman by the name of Parsons, was marketed in the United States through the Victor Co. This utilized the "aerophone" principle first patented by Edison. Another disc instrument called the Hymnophone manufactured in Leipzig was advertised by Bettini, Ltd. of New York. The Clarion cylinder machine, made in England, was also offered on the American market. In September, 1907, there was a full page ad in the *Talking Machine World* of the Devineau Biophone, an attachment by which disc records could be played on a cylinder machine, selling for fifteen dollars.

Victor had from time to time released recordings made from imported masters although the policy was to replace European recordings whenever possible by domestically recorded records by the same artist. Usually the astute C. G. Childs would attempt to secure such artists on an exclusive contract henceforth, as he had the great Caruso, thus making the sister companies dependent upon Victor, rather than vice versa. Columbia had made rather ineffective efforts to compete with this sound and consistent policy established at Victor. Columbia introduced a "banner label" series to compete with Victor's now famous "red seals," but was somehow unable to line up talent of equal public appeal. It was partially an

act of desperation when in 1908 Columbia announced that it was to issue the Fonotipia series of recordings by famous European opera and concert artists in the United States bearing a special Columbia-Fonotipia label.

The international situation at this point seems to indicate that the only areas in which the existence of patents really hampered the development of business were in the United States, where most of the fundamental patents were held, and in England, where the only consistent attempt to impartially enforce them had been made. In the United States, the multiplicity of jurisdictions in which actions could be brought, and if brought, defended, meant only those with unlimited funds were able to protect the rights presumably acquired by the granting of letters patent. In England, with a more centralized system of courts, the inevitable result was the creation of combinations and monopolies. For about a year, it had been proposed to amend the English patent law to end the abuse of monopolies, largely as the aftermath of the cylinder war. The law was amended in 1908 and it was predicted in the trade papers that this would have a serious effect on American export trade. This was followed by the announcement of the National Phonograph Co. that it was closing its European factories, but not its recording studios and sales agencies. Henceforth it was stated that all Edison machines and records would be made in the United States.

As Edison was then preparing to issue the Amberol records, which doubled the playing time, this is perhaps the major reason for the withdrawal of all manufacturing to Orange. Virtually every improvement he had made to the phonograph year by year, almost immediately had been adopted by competitors without regard to patents. It seems most likely that the decision was to rely on the keeping of the processing of the new records a trade secret for as long a time as possible. Unfortunately, the new Amberol records, made with virtually the same composition used formerly for the two-minute records, cut very easily. By the time celluloid was adopted great damage had been done to the Edison cause in England and America.

The peak of the cylinder business in England had been reached in 1907. Up to July of that year, three million Sterling records had been sold in the prior twelve months, according to Russell Hunting Ltd. But 1908 failed to follow the expected pattern of increasing sales. Both cylinders and discs were hit in a general business recession. The Neophone Co., pioneer manufacturers of hill-and-dale discs went out of business, as also did the British Sonogram Co. and the General Phonograph Co., which made White machines and cylinders. The regular announcement of new Sterling records failed to appear in July of 1908. In May it had been announced that "Sterling and Hunting, Ltd." had taken larger quarters due to the demand for Odeon and Fonotipia records and Odeon machines. It was announced also that Sterling and Hunting were no longer connected in any way with Russell Hunting Co., Ltd. This represented a switch back to the discs by two of the men who had been leaders in the British cylinder industry.

Evidently the new set-up did not last, for in October, the *Talking Machine News* carried a story that Russell Hunting, who had been in charge of the recording department of Pathe-Freres was now appointed Director General of all the recording departments of the company, located at Paris, London, Milan, Brussells, Amsterdam, St. Petersburg, Moscow, Odessa, and Rostoff. It was stated that he would visit each of them in turn to reorganize them and to install a new method of record-

ing. It was announced that a new eleven inch Pathe disc was to be manufactured and that Hunting was to supervise the extensive Pathe cylinder business as well.

The December, 1908, *Talking Machine News* contained the information that Mr. Sterling, Hunting's former partner, was now managing director of the Rena Manufacturing Co., Ltd., and that this company was going to put out a new double disc record. Later this company was consolidated with the English Columbia Co. and records issued under the Columbia-Rena label. Sterling's accomplishments with the English Columbia Co. are well known and his ascent to the top was constant from this time forward.

The stock securities of the defunct Russell Hunting Co. had been sold at auction by court order and in this manner the corporate name continued for a time. A new line of Sterling records was advertised as made by a new molding process and were on sale for a few years. Control of the company was secured in the interim by Edison-Bell and in 1912 the affairs of the company were completely liquidated. In a news account of the career of Russell Hunting and of the brilliant promise of his company, blame for its downfall was attached to the reduction in price from 1/6 to 1/-. Ignored in the story was the fact that Hunting had touched off the price war, himself. Russell Hunting, famous "Michael Casey" of the halcyon cylinder days in America had done as much to build up the cylinder business as any popular entertainer of his day. He pushed the cylinder industry in England to an unprecedented peak by his business ability and then brought it crashing down by a single tactical mistake.

CHAPTER 12

DISCS VERSUS CYLINDERS

PERHAPS the most difficult fact of phonograph history for the layman to accept is that the method of recording involving the more serious technical compromises was the one destined to win. A basic reason is one of economics, for in a commercial venture the first concern necessarily is for profits rather than technical perfection. This means that when a choice is offered between an inexpensive expedient and a more costly but more perfect method, the expedient is usually adopted. The biological law of the survival of the fittest simply did not apply to the field of phonographic development any more than it has in so many others wherein "cheaper" has vanquished "better."

The reasons for the technical superiority of the large concert cylinders over the prior standard diameter cylinders as compared with the disc methods still in use will serve to illustrate this point. The principle behind the use of the large diameter cylinder was that the higher overtones could be recorded with greater facility and fidelity if the speed of the surface beneath the stylus was high enough so that the minimum wave lengths produced by the higher frequency sounds would not be shorter than the width of the groove. This principle is as important today as when first discovered. It was a rather belated recognition by some of our later day recording experts which made the Columbia LP record commercially acceptable, whereas a former Victor at-

tempt to accomplish precisely the same thing, but neglecting this factor, had been an ignominious failure.[1]

But a still neglected corollary principle, as far as the discs are concerned, is that there is always an optimum surface speed for recording and reproduction, depending on certain other variables in materials and methods employed. Edison believed that the essential superiority of the cylinder over the uniform rpm disc lay in this inherent ability to record at a constant, optimum surface speed under the cutting stylus. He apparently also felt that this advantage and the corresponding advantages in reproduction technics would offset the conveniences offered by the discs in handling, filing, and economy of space. In this we know that he was wrong. However, the confidence of Edison in the technical superiority of the cylinder over the disc was such that his company continued the development of the cylinder method long after most others had dropped it. This attitude was also responsible for the belated development of an Edison disc instrument.

The important overtone recording principle had been discovered by Edison and incorporated by him in a machine for recording upon a cylinder of large diameter and then re-recording upon smaller diameter cylinders for use by the public.

[1] This series was first listed in the 1931 Victor catalog, but only nine of these 33⅓ rpm records remained in the 1940-41 catalog.

Fig. 12-1. The Edison Concert phonograph played 5-inch wax records. Stepped-up surface speed produced higher frequencies.

The placing of the Concert Grand type instruments (see Fig. 12-1) upon the market, with the cumbersome and fragile 5-inch diameter wax cylinders, eventually emphasized the disadvantages of the cylinders as compared with the discs. As was then the practice with the smaller diameter cylinders, the cartons were made somewhat larger in diameter than the record, so as to leave an air space around. The concert cylinder cartons occupied a space six inches in diameter and five inches high. In about the same space, increased but an inch in diameter, fifty of the comparatively unbreakable little Berliner discs could be stacked. The cost of these large cylinders was another unfavorable factor of comparison. Each had to be an original recording, as no molding method was ever developed successfully for larger wax cylinders, although some were undoubtedly duplicated by transcribing. Thus, for but one selection, the cost was five dollars, although later decreased to two-fifty. Even the latter figure would buy five of the seven-inch discs. Edison was well aware of these facts and as he found time devoted his attention to the development of means by which the increased volume and improved quality of the larger cylinders might be transferred to the more convenient and inexpensive standard size cylinders. Experience had shown that only a portion of the improvement could be carried to the smaller cylinders by the transcribing method of 1890. Edison finally accomplished this by the invention of a cup-shaped cutting stylus which permitted the incising of wavelengths shorter than the width of the groove and in the designing of a button-shaped sapphire playback stylus, to replace the ball-shaped stylus then in use. As the long axis of the button stylus was transverse to the groove, it would also track the undulations of the shorter wavelength vibrations.

This development was also responsible for the increase in rpm of all standard cylinders from 120 to 160 rpm. About the same time the multiple difficulties in the way of molding were surmounted and all of the gold-molded Edison cylinders were recorded at this new speed. Columbia introduced its line of XP high speed cylinders also. The only drawback was the playing time was reduced conversely to the increase in speed, as the number of grooves to the inch still remained 100. The use of molding methods permitted the use of much harder metallic soap compounds than could be used for the directly recorded cylinders. This facilitated the employment of the button stylus, which of course had less bearing area on the record than the spherical stylus. More weight could be sustained on these harder surfaced cylinders, which permitted the increased use of "amplifying" horns as they were often incorrectly described, thus bringing the cylinder machines up in sound volume to a point where they were able to compete on almost even terms with the disc talking machines of Berliner, Johnson, and Seaman. Actually, with a cylinder machine of the best quality and freshly molded records, the reproduction was cleaner, contained less surface noise, and was much more accurate, even though the volume level was reduced somewhat, than that obtainable from the best discs.

The fact is that the cylinder method from the first was more scientific than that of the disc. With the constant rpm disc there has never been the opportunity to adhere to the optimum recording or reproducing speeds. The groove speed beneath the stylus of a standard ten-inch disc becomes diminished by more than fifty per cent in travelling from the outermost turns of the groove spiral to the innermost. It is true today

of the microgroove records and the 45's, regardless of the tremendous improvement achieved despite these inherent limitations. On an advertising disc of the early Orthophonic period, Milton Cross asserted with great conviction, "With Victor, there is no compromise with tone." There is, always has been and always will be, as long as the lateral recording method with constant rpm speed turntable is employed.

Fred Gaisberg, veteran recording expert of the English Gramophone Co. had this to say in *The Music Goes Round*:

"Scientists of the Bell and Tainter school had promptly rejected the Berliner process of disc recording as fundamentally wrong. Their criticism was that the surface speed of the outside of the disc was greater than that of the inside. This was wrong in 1890 and so it is today, fifty years later, but it was practical and simple; further, the gramophone record could be manufactured cheaply enough to bring it within the means of the poorest families."

Actually, Gaisberg errs in thus excusing his important role in winning the commercial triumph over science, for cylinders were made to sell for as little as the disc and eventually for less. Phonographs and Graphophones were made to sell for as little as $7.50 and $5.00. This was, of course, not true of the concert size cylinders, which never became competitive, for reasons already discussed.

After 1903, Victor abandoned the seven-inch record size, inaugurating a new policy of recording the same popular selections on eight-, ten-, and twelve-inch discs. The matrix of the earlier seven-inch discs had been prefixed with the letter "A," the ten-inch with "B" and the twelve-inch "C." Very likely "D" had been reserved for the short lived fourteen-inch Victor series. In any case the new eight-inch series matrix numbers were prefixed with "E." With the larger discs the customer received proportionately longer playing time and usually somewhat better tone quality and durability, for reasons with which the reader is now doubtless fairly familiar.

At first the standard molded cylinder records sold for fifty cents each. During this same competitive period the seven-inch discs had also sold for fifty cents. The new eight-inch discs were priced at thirty-five cents, the ten-inch popular music discs at one dollar and the twelve-inch at a dollar and one-half. The same selection, recorded by the same artist or artists would have the same matrix number with the appropriate prefix letter on each of the sizes. The same catalog number was used for the eight- and ten-inch records of the same selection, although not for the twelve-inch. Columbia discs were also made in seven- and ten-inch sizes, using the same catalog number for the same selection.

One of the most successful and continuous advertising campaigns of all times had its inception shortly after the formation of the Victor Talking Machine Company by Eldridge R. Johnson in October of 1901. President Johnson was from the first a firm believer in the business potentials of national advertising and distribution. The campaign began with rather small ads in the more popular American magazines, but with a consistent regularity. Johnson and his advertising men not only abided by the formulas used since for creating a market for consumer goods through well-planned schedules involving properly estimated proportional expenditure of income for space, copy preparation, art work, and layout —they established many of the principles of advertising since followed by others!

At first this advertising was centered around the Victor Talking Machine, its capability as a home entertainer and popular records. From the first, the famous trade mark with "Little Nipper" began to make its appearance, identifying each ad as that of the Victor Co.

In fact, Johnson had used the dog trademark in ads of his Consolidated Talking Machine Co. in 1900 prior to the organization of the Victor Talking Machine Co.; therefore, although he was an English dog, he was well known to Americans for several years before he came to be used by the Gramophone and its sister companies. They were using the recording angel trademark during this period.

Within a year, Victor was asserting to the trade that it had ten-thousand dealers and had sold two million dollars worth of goods. When the first group of Victor Imported Red Seal records were offered for sale in 1902, through arrangement with its European affiliate, the Gramophone & Typewriter, Ltd., the astute Johnson realized that he had the right combination for building prestige and volume sales for his company. This first release included records by Maurice Renaud, famous French baritone; Mme. Kristmann of the St. Petersburg Opera; Pol Plancon, noted French basso; Ada Crossley, soprano; Jean Delmas, baritone; Antonio Scotti; Mattia Battistini, baritone; and tenor Enrico Caruso. Caruso had shortly before recorded ten ten-inch selections for Gaisberg in Milan, one of which when played for Heinrich Conried, impresario of the New York Metropolitan Opera Company, was to result in the engagement of Caruso for the following season. In turn, this resulted in the opportunity which was offered Calvin Childs, recording director for Victor, to secure a contract from Caruso to record exclusively for Victor for a long period of years.

Full page ads on the Imported Red Seal Records, with pictures of the artists were featured in *Harper's Weekly* and other popular magazines during 1903. The acceptance of these celebrity records at prices considerably advanced over those of the popular records was phenomenal considering the comparatively few disc machines that had been sold by this date. The success of this initial offering undoubtedly inspired the inauguration of the Victor Red Seal series, from which the first releases were made in 1904. Particularly in the metropolitan areas, sales of Victor Talking Machines began to increase rapidly as a result of the availability of operatic and celebrity recordings. By 1906, when Edison belatedly began to issue his Grand Opera series on the two minute wax cylinders, he was too late and the playing time too little.

Victor did not issue red seal records in the eight-inch size. More and more weight was being imposed upon the records and as the smaller radius turns towards the center of the smaller discs cramped the steel stylus unduly, excessive wear resulted, as well as fuzziness in reproduction. Around 1908 Victor discontinued the eight-inch records. These are factors still important and troublesome with small diameter laterally recorded discs, even though minimized with the use of permanent styli and smoother surfaces.

One reason for the excessive wear experienced at that time was in the abrasive that was mixed in the material of the record for the purpose of making the variable steel needles conform to the groove. This caused particles of steel to be ground from the stylus and dropped behind in the groove. With successive playings, these steel particles scoured the sides of the grooves, especially toward the center of the disc, where the higher-frequency sound undulations were also finer and more susceptible to damage. This method of making the more or less irregular steel needles conform to groove patterns which were also quite variable often resulted in a quite rapid flattening of the sides of the rounded conical point, reducing its ability to track the finer

Fig. 12-2. The Columbia type AH Disc Graphophone produced in 1902. Cheapest model sold for $20 complete. (From an early advertisement.)

undulations. At the same time the slower groove speed beneath the point and the cramping action of the smaller diameter turns on the stylus also became effective in reducing the higher-frequency response. Often the needles would "shoulder," riding partially on the ridge between adjacent grooves, resulting in unsatisfactory reproduction and damage to the record. The wonder is, considering the many quite irreconcilable and inherent limitations of the lateral method, that it should have ever been developed to the present comparatively high standards of performance. How this came about is of course a principle theme of this story.

Meanwhile the chief competition centered between Victor and the American Graphophone Co. The ever greedy Graphophone executives, now with one foot in each of the two fields of records, realized the threat and decided to institute a red seal series under the Columbia label. With the opportune Jones patent and the skill of Philip Mauro, the Graphophone Co. had broken the stalemate created by conflicting court decisions and injunctions and forced the compromise permitting them to enter the disc field. Early in 1902 they were producing two styles of disc graphophones (Fig. 12-2) selling for twenty and thirty dollars respectively. Under the Columbia label there was being offered two series of popular disc records, seven-inch diameter at fifty cents and ten-inch at one dollar each, or ten dollars per dozen, all with the black and silver label.

Perhaps in anticipation of Victor's venture into celebrity recording, in 1903 Columbia announced a red label Grand Opera series. The first issue featured records by Marcella Sembrich, Soprano; Anton Van Rooy, baritone; Ernestine Schumann-Heink, contralto; Suzanne Adams, Soprano; Giuseppe Campanari, baritone; and Edouard De-Reszke, bass. Three titles were offered by DeReszke, the only commercial records ever to be made by this renowned singer. However, the Columbia Grand Opera Series was poorly recorded and

the venture was comparatively unsuccessful. It seems that Victor must have threatened prosecution for the use of the red label, for later copies were given other labels. Some of these ten-inch records, with some subsequent additions to the series, were carried in Columbia catalogs until 1908, some, including two of the DeReszke recordings, even appearing on double discs.

The merchandising policies of the two disc companies differed in certain important particulars. Columbia for a number of years adhered to its original method established with the cylinder business of opening its own branch salesrooms and warehouses. Victor appointed already well established commercial houses in various centers of distribution as jobbers and distributors. As early as mid 1903 Victor had by this policy secured three times as many wholesale outlets as Columbia had been able to open. Victor was never bitterly competitive with Edison as was the Graphophone Co. and so several important jobbers in various areas carried both Edison and Victor merchandise. One factor in this situation that should not be overlooked is that in this period, as well as quite consistently through the succeeding years, Victor produced generally better disc machines and records and Edison better cylinder machines and records. Both were in competition with the Graphophone Co. and its Columbia ally.

Now that the chief battleground for a time was to be in the marts of trade, rather than in the courts of law, the sagacity and business sense of Eldridge R. Johnson was given full opportunity. In April, 1904, Victor used the entire back cover of the *Saturday Evening Post* to announce its exclusive contract to record the voice of Enrico Caruso. Conscious of the superiority of their goods, the Victor executives entered the latest Victor Talking Machines and records in the premium awards competition of the St. Louis Exposition of 1904. The Columbia Phonograph Co. did likewise, and both installed large exhibits. Both companies profited greatly from the great public interest and both prepared to get the most advertising value possible from it. That perhaps some chicanery was involved in the conduct of the premium award contest may be gathered from the first issues of the *Talking Machine World,* which for many years to come was the most influential trade paper of the industry. The first number was January of 1905 and came in the middle of a hot controversy between the leading talking machine companies over the awards made at the exposition. This was undoubtedly responsible for the paper taking the position that it should not comment editorially upon such matters. A battle therefore was waged in the form of paid advertisements, which perhaps assisted the *Talking Machine World* in getting off on a sound financial basis!

The advertisements of Victor and Columbia in the *Talking Machine World* revealed a complete difference of opinion as to which had won the grand prize at the World's Fair. In the second issue, Victor had a large ad claiming,

"Victor wins the Grand Prize, highest possible award over all talking machines at the Exposition."

Columbia also had an ad stating,

"The Graphophone and Columbia Records win highest honors—Double Grand Prize, three gold medals."

Columbia's ad stated that the Victor ad was based on the *recommendation* only of an inferior jury, which had been empowered to make recommendations, but that the decisions as to awards was actually in the hands of two superior juries. Eventually the Columbia Graphophone Co. sued the exposition authorities and the Victor Co. and won the verdict. This gave Columbia the opportunity to create a new celebrity label, the famous banner label, carrying the awards won. Very likely Victor officials thought the decision was in the bag on the basis of the recommendation of the inferior jury but the misrepresentation is inexcusable. How could they have expected to win with an official of the Columbia Phonograph Co. as Chairman of the Exposition Talking Machine Exhibit Competition?

About this time there was a tremendous spurt in the popularity of the talking machines, both cylinders and discs. This accelerated competitive efforts both in this country and abroad, attracting capital, promoters and inventors to the industry which seemed to offer opportunity much as television does today. Following the St. Louis Exposition there was a constant succession of new devices, some of very promising potential, but few were brought into the proper financial or patent environments to survive. One new company named Talk-O-Phone began the production of a lateral disc machine and records in March of 1904 and within a year claimed to have sold over 25,000 machines. Even the music box manufacturers began to eye the talking machine field and the Regina Co., of Rahway, New Jersey, makers of high quality disc type music boxes for many years previously, announced the Reginaphone, a combination music box and disc type phonograph for playing the lateral records. Another smaller company also brought out a combination music box and talking machine. These music box companies did not make records, but the Talk-O-Phone Co. engaged in record production on a large scale, which naturally brought it into court with the companies holding the key patents.

Many inventors worked on improvements for the cylinders. A man by the name of Dunton, of Grand Rapids, invented the Multiphone (see Fig. 9-2), which would hold and play automatically twenty-four standard cylinders. He stated that a model would be made which would take cylinders up to twenty-five inches in length, for reproducing entire lectures or operas. Considering the popularity which player piano rolls achieved subsequently, Dunton's idea was not as far fetched as it may now seem. A company was organized and a considerable number of the Multiphones were made and sold as coin-in-the-slot machines. A new type machine and record was introduced in England called the Neophone. The record was a strawboard disc with a surface coating of celluloid. This was the first hill-and-dale type disc record actually commercially produced and a sapphire stylus was used for reproduction. It was patented in England, Austria, Italy, Russia, and Germany by Dr. Michaelis and its manufacture assumed quite large proportions.

The original wire recorder, the Telegraphone, had been invented by Valdemar Poulsen, Danish scientist, in 1898. This worked very similarly to the wire and magnetic tape recorders of today. However, as there was no means of amplification, the playback was through telephone earphones. A previous recording could be erased simply by recording right over, just as with the improved instruments of today. But without amplification, the potential of the Telegraphone seemed to be in its use as a business machine, where the phonograph and the graphophone had encountered such great difficulty in becoming established. During the early 1900's considerable research was done in the United States by Poulsen and his associates and funds were raised by stock subscription to finance development. Poulsen also developed a method of recording magnetically on iron discs four and one-half inches in diameter, about one-twentieth of an inch thick. Relatively few of the Telegraphones were sold and as far as is known none of the disc machines were sufficiently well developed to be marketed.[2] Now it may be recognized that the lack of an adequate method of electrical amplification was the chief obstacle to the development of these ideas at that time, just as it was to the talking pictures in a somewhat later period.

A somewhat parallel approach, but utilizing acousti-mechanical recording, was the making of a ribbon tape with a groove as in phonograph records, but which would permit a continuous re-

cording of any length. Aside from technical difficulties to be found in making duplicates, the great drawback is the lack of convenience, which is responsible yet today for the failure of home motion pictures to gain anything like the popularity which has been accorded the phonograph record. The average person, at the time simply would not bother with the winding and unwinding of wires, tapes, or films. It is failure to recognize this simple fact which has broken the financial back of many otherwise feasible and commendable audio-visual devices. This factor was potent in the battle for public favor between the cylinders and the discs, the discs having always had an obvious edge in ease of handling, identification, and playing to say nothing of the problems of care and storage.

One of the more fascinating devices to be launched in this creative period was the Auxetophone, invented by C. A. Parsons, of London, England. This employed a compressed air amplifier based on the principle of the Aerophone, invented as a means of amplifying the voice for out-of-doors communication by Edison some years previously. In the Auxetophone, a stream of compressed air was modulated by a valve actuated by the reproducing stylus. The rights to the Parsons' patent were bought by Gramophone & Typewriter, Ltd. and the instruments were placed on the market. The machines were capable of great volume, but were not of much use in the home, because of a hissing sound. They were offered for sale in the United States by the Victor Talking Machine Co., but at the modest price of five hundred dollars, not many were sold.

Another interesting machine developed for the purpose of producing greater volume was based on the principle of a friction valve, invented by Daniel Higham, of Boston. Rights were bought by the American Graphophone Co. and a machine was marketed in August of 1905 as the "20th Century Graphophone." This was a cylinder machine (Fig. 12-3) with a larger than

---

[2] Oxide of iron coated discs and other magnetic discs have been produced by others, as well.

Fig. 12-3. The Twentieth Century Graphophone type BC produced substantial volume due to 4-inch diaphragm augmented by a frictional coupling. (From an early catalog.)

usual diaphragm to which amplified vibrations were delivered by means of a variable tension device involving a cord running over an amber wheel, augmenting the pull from the stylus bar by force supplied by the motor turning the amber wheel. The length of the mandrel was also increased to six inches to permit increasing the playing time about one-third. Some models were made to play concert size cylinders, but were soon discontinued. In the advertisements it was claimed that the 20th Century Grand would produce sixteen times the volume of the standard machines. Whether true or not, it was not as simple and foolproof an amplifying device as the Edison floating weight principle, which was a type of mechanical advantage amplifier. By mounting a stylus bar of unequal length

arms upon the side of the floating weight toward the record (Fig. 12-4), more pressure could be exerted upon the record and greater amplitude given to the diaphragm movement. The amount of amplification depended on wear limitations and a feature of the entire course of development of the Edison method was a constantly greater pressure on the record even continuing into the period of the Edison disc and electrical recording. The use of the floating weight principle exclusively by Edison was an important factor in the industrial development.[3]

In the United States, the purchase of improvements conceived by independent inventors was the exception, rather

[3] In 1912 Edison purchased rights to the Higham amplifier for use with the Kinetophone (talking pictures).

than the rule, however. The course of development was pretty well controlled by the big three companies. However, abroad, the situation occasionally got out of hand. By 1905, cylinder machines manufactured in Germany and Switzerland were offered for sale in the United States. Bettini, Ltd., a New York company which had purchased the business created by the pioneer recorder Lieutenant Bettini, introduced a disc machine called the Hymnophone, made in Germany. This had a tone arm

Fig. 12-4. Edison Model C reproducer used sapphire stylus with an 8 mil radius. It was shaped like a door knob.

carrying the reproducer, with a swivel joint connecting the tone arm to a horn which emerged from the front under the turntable. It may be that it was this machine that suggested to Eldridge R. Johnson the idea of the Victrola, with the entirely enclosed horn and hinged covered cabinet, which was introduced later. Other companies also exported machines to America including the Clarion and Denham. The Germans also made miniature machines and post-card records for sale as novelties. Machines with aluminum horns and an all glass horn also came to this country from Europe. But means to deal with these sporadic efforts to invade the home market were evidently ade-

quate, for these incursions seldom lasted long.

Victor, as early as 1904, was making twelve-inch records, as well as a little known series of fourteen-inch discs, which meeting with little success, were supplied on order only for about a year and then dropped. Only popular music appeared on these now very rare outsized discs. They were very bulky, weighing better than a pound apiece and tended to nullify the advantage of the usual size discs over the equally cumbersome concert size cylinders. In Europe, some of the Gramophone affiliates and Fonotipia later produced celebrity records on discs of this approximate size, but not as heavy. Later Pathe sold vertical cut discs of this diameter in the United States and of course radio transcriptions have been made up to twenty inches in diameter.

After the final litigation resulting from Seaman's manipulations, the assets of the Universal Talking Machine Co., including the corporate name, had been acquired by Eldridge R. Johnson for the Victor Talking Machine Co., which by the judgment and accounting granted by the court had become the principle creditor. Thus the Universal Talking Machine Co., which heretofore had really been a creature of the American Graphophone Co. became a subsidiary of the Victor Talking Machine Co. In June of 1905 the first advertisement of a new series of Zonophone records appeared under the corporate name of the Universal Talking Machine Co. The advertising of the two companies was kept entirely distinct and there was no general knowledge of the identity of ownership on the part of the general public, although it was well known to the trade. This advertisement also announced four models of Zonophone Talking Machines, with tapered tone-arms (Fig. 12-5) ranging from $27.50 to $55. The tapered tone-arm had been invented by Johnson to relieve the weight and inertia of the entire horn assembly from the record. As horns had become larger and heavier, counterbalancing them failed to suffice, as the outer groove wall of the record spiral still had to work against the inertia of the horn-sound-box assembly in order to propel it across the record. Slight eccentricities in the centering of the records resulted in frightful wear as well as producing distressing effects in the reproduction.

This improvement of Eldridge R. Johnson was now to become the focal point in the patent conflicts with the other disc talking machines, then and for some years to come. The conception of the tone arm as a portion of the amplifying horn and not just as a sound conduction tube was original with Johnson, as well as the method of providing a horizontally revolvable joint of sufficient air-tightness to be practical. Others seeking to evade the Johnson patent were forced to use a straight tube, which caused undue distortion.

Even though the Johnson idea was correct in one respect, his failure to reconcile its design with certain other factors of good horn design already known, imposed a straight jacket on lateral disc reproduction practice that was effective until the sweeping nature of the changes brought about by the introduction of the Western Electric process made all of the old patents valueless. During the Johnson reign it was possible to vastly improve the reproduction from the current lateral disc records by improving the design of the tone arm and horn and a number of inventors attempted to do this, but the courts stood firmly behind Johnson and his right to malform his invention. This was in strange contrast with the treatment accorded by prior courts to Edison with respect to some of his basic patents.

In the meantime, other manufacturers, some with experience in the cylinder field, such as Leeds & Catlin, attempted to get in the disc business. This company had been almost continuously in the courts, having been attacked for various infringements by each of the big three. Despite innumerable setbacks, Leeds & Catlin had per-

sisted and in 1905 had large plants in Middleton, Connecticut and New York City. However, now fortified with the Jones patent, the American Graphophone Co. was enabled to force them out of business. For several years to

Fig. 12-5. The Tapering Arm Zonophone made by Universal Talking Machine Manufacturing Co., New York. (From an early advertisement.)

come, the most important patents in the lateral disc field were the Jones patent and the Johnson tapered arm patent. Johnson had also invented an improved sound box which he named the "Exhibition" which for a considerable time was not improved upon. Johnson's claims to the advances were reinforced by court decisions, especially against his traditional rivals of the Graphophone Co., who were better lawyers than inventors.

A trend towards increased complexity due to competitive inventiveness has ever been a feature of American industrial development. Despite the high mortality rate of phonographic inventions, this phenomenon was evident a few years ago in the necessity of combining automatic record changing mechanisms with devices which would play records in three sizes, of four

Fig. 12-6. This Graphophone was furnished with a standard mandrel and a large adapter mandrel for playing Grand records. Height of reproducer is adjustable. (Clark-Welch Collection.)

speeds (including 16⅔ rpm for talking books) and with a minimum of two styli diameters. During the early 1900's attempts to combine the advantages of one type of instrument with another had resulted first in the combination Graphophone (Fig. 12-6) invented by Thomas H. Macdonald which by means of two mandrels, one which would telescope within the other, enabled the playing of both standard and concert size cylinders on the same machine. Some of the later Twentieth Century Graphophones, such as the Peerless also played two types of cylinders, the standard and the six-inch long cylinders made for them. (See Fig. 12-7.) However, it remained for an Englishman to invent a combination cylinder and disc machine, which was on the market for a short time. (See Fig. 12-8.)

But in these years, while there was much activity in the cylinder field in England and the United States, elsewhere the disc was already in the ascendancy. In Germany, in 1904 the Beka Co. announced the first double discs of the industry, which multiplied the former advantage of the disc in handling and storage by two. A seemingly reactionary note in America at about the same time was the announcement by Rosenfield, a New York manufacturer of automatic entertainment devices, of an illustrated song machine for use in the penny arcades which was provided with ear tubes for the listeners! On the other hand there was a new wave of interest in the cultural uses of the phonograph, both cylinders and discs. Williams College adopted the use of the phonograph for language instruc-

Fig. 12-7. The Columbia Peerless Graphophone, similar to that shown, had an extra long mandrel for playing 6-inch records. (From an early catalog.)

tion in 1905. Cornet technic was taught by phonograph at an institute in Chicago. It should be noted that the International Correspondence Schools had used the Edison phonograph for language courses as early as 1897 and Rosenthal even before that. The teaching of languages continued later with the Blue Amberol cylinders; and on discs, has persisted to the present time. In America, this is one of the bright spots in an otherwise lamentable lack of appreciation of the cultural possibilities of sound recording.

An article appearing in a magazine mentioned the fact that Edison had in his personal collection hundreds of metal sheets (tin-foil records) of the voices of famous persons who had visited his laboratories. What became of them? The trustees of the British Museum once announced that it would be willing to receive carefully selected phonographic recordings of distinguished living men. As far as is known, no American museum curator ever raised a hand to see that the priceless souvenirs of the great collected by Mr. Edison should be preserved for posterity. Mr. Edison was an inventor, for which the world may be thankful, but he was no historian, and the model of an earlier invention of great scientific importance was as likely as not to be robbed for some part that he might use in a new experiment.

Ironically enough, curators of museums generally welcomed the capacity

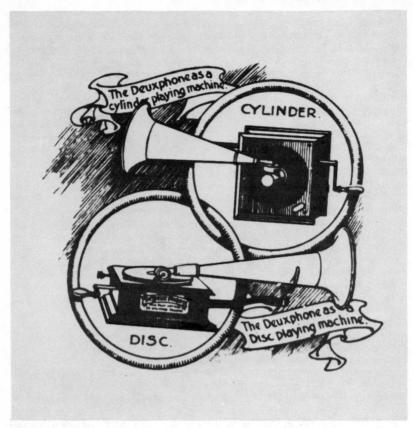

Fig. 12-8. The Deuxphone, an English product, played both disc and cylinder records. (From an English catalog.)

of the phonograph for preserving the voices of the living and as a means of immortalizing historic performances of great musicians, but the musicians and music educators generally ignored it. Undoubtedly this was in part due to the inadequate tone range and lack of fidelity of the early machines. It could not be appreciated, as it is now, that there was much more truth in the records than could then be brought out, but which one day it would be possible to reveal to a remarkable extent. In part this aversion to the phonograph was perhaps psychological—an uneasy fear of the direct comparisons between performances which for the first time was made possible. Mistakes in timing,

or technic are fleeting and lost in the performance in a crowded hall, but once indelibly engraved into the wax are always available for repetition, comparison with others and critical analysis —the same factors which should have made the phonograph an invaluable aid to music instruction. Even today, most music schools and fine arts colleges are yet in the experimental stages of toying with the greatest asset for implementing the teaching and appreciation of music that has occurred since the invention of the printing press.

Until the 1940's, space to any considerable extent has never been devoted by national magazines or newspapers to the phonograph, as compared to that devoted to such things as photography, for instance. Largely the fault for this neglect was in the apathy of the musicians and music critics, who with an aloof attitude, refused to recognize the cultural potential of the phonograph, much as the early painters refused to admit that there was a place for photography. That there was a genuine hobby interest in phonographs and records, is illustrated by the fact that phonograph and talking machine parties were popular in the late 1890's and early 1900's, very like the television parties within easy recollection.

Nearly all of the publicity of the early days came from direct advertising, demonstrations at the fairs, phonograph concerts, and the talking machine parties. The three major companies competed hotly for the business and one result was a price war. On December, 1905, Victor announced the following price reductions:

> 7" records reduced from 50¢ to 35¢
> 10" records reduced from $1 to 60¢
> 12" records reduced from $1.50 to $1

These were for the popular series. Columbia met the cuts the same day and Leeds & Catlin reduced the prices of their Imperial records. Columbia also now offered double disc records for $1. The fact that these double discs were being made ready for the market may have been the primary reason for the precipitation of the price war by Victor. Zonophone, now a Victor affiliate, announced a temporary price reduction, "until a policy decision had been reached," according to its ads. This was probably a shrewd tactical maneuver on the part of Johnson so as to be prepared for any possible reaction from the Graphophone Co.

Although the Graphophone Co. possessed the best lawyers, the Victor Co. began to prove that it had the best business men. At the close of 1906, Columbia and the American Graphophone Co. had been in business seventeen years and had acquired an earned surplus of something less than $1,250,000. Victor had been in business but five

years and had already almost $3,000,000 in its cash and surplus account. Edison was also doing a tremendous business, particularly in the rural areas.[4] These facts naturally whetted the interest of other entrepeneurs.

The January, 1906 issue of *Talking Machine World* carried a full page advertisement by the Talk-O-Phone Co. featuring a new mechanical feed phonograph. Up to this time all cylinder machines were mechanical feed instruments; that is, the reproducer or "sound-box" was carried across the record by a feed screw. In the disc machines produced commercially, the reproducer was carried across the record by the sound groove of the record. In the ad of this new mechanical feed disc machine, the attention of the trade was directed to "The Fearful Grating Sound" of machines in which the sound-box was propelled by the record groove. This feature of lateral disc record practice was one of the basic claims of the Berliner patents, so it was quickly averred by the Victor Co. that the Talk-O-Phone device was merely a pretext to avoid the Victor owned patent. Victor immediately sued this company and on April 25th was granted a decision. It was 1909, however, before the litigation was finally closed and the Talk-O-Phone and records were withdrawn from sale. For a considerable time these records carried the announcement, "Warning, for Use with Machines Equipped with Mechanical Feed Only," although the records were of the conventional lateral disc type, playable on any of the standard instruments.

All independent disc manufacturers in the United States, whether in possession of patents or not, were sure to be brought into court by either the Victor Talking Machine Co. or the American Graphophone Co. The Victor suits at this time were usually brought on the basis of alleged infringement of the Berliner patent 434,543, and the Graphophone Co. on the basis of the Jones patent 688,739. A comparative

---

[4] Edison phonograph and record sales for 1906 were over 6 million dollars.

analysis of court opinions as to the validity of these two important key patents will serve to illustrate the completely unscientific nature of the system of judicial review of patents in the United States, and will be given a bit later. Although there were several alleged infringers of the Jones patent which were put out of business with the loss of millions of dollars to investors, the Jones patent was, in 1911, finally adjudged to have been anticipated by the work of others, and therefore invalid. This reversal of prior decisions did not serve to reinstate those who had been forced out of business—not even to give them a cause for action against anyone, regardless of how arbitrary or capricious the earlier decisions may have been.

From the viewpoint of the three leading companies, the patent situation was not altogether bad, as they were enabled to keep the field pretty well closed to independent inventors or opportunistic interlopers. Quite often, a carefully selected group of opinions culled from the many court cases would be brought to the attention of a prospective entrepreneur by legal counsel of one of the companies with the result that usually he could be persuaded to sell out at a reasonable figure, or would just agree to drop plans to enter the field to avoid the almost certain prosecution. Many cases were begun and consent decrees obtained on just such a basis, especially by the Graphophone Co.—all of which helped to present an even more convincing picture to the next hapless victim. But this procedure did not apply to the relationships between the big three. The court records are filled with suits and appeals for decisions, but one looks in vain for evidence that the verdicts had any considerable monetary effect. The actual amount of money that changed hands between the three companies in any decade was infinitesimel and probably would not have paid the attorneys' fees of any one of them for a year! *The purpose behind most of these suits was publicity and ammunition to use on anyone who might have*

the temerity to try to enter the field of phonograph or record manufacturing. The almost constant succession of suits served to notify prospective record or machine manufacturers that they would have to be prepared to spend a large share of their time and money in the courts if they should persist, regardless of whether they had patents or not.

The advertising pages of *Talking Machine World* for February and March of 1907 illustrate the truth of this. The Victor Talking Machine Co. had just sued the Duplex Phonograph Co., of Kalamazoo, Michigan, then established for several years. This company made, as the name may intimate, a two-horned monstrosity with a two way reproducer between (Fig. 12-9), but they also were making a good record which was achieving a considerable sale and was being used on other machines. By a coincidence, the National Phonograph Co. had notified jobbers that they were no longer to be permitted to carry other lines of talking machine goods, calling attention to a long non-enforced clause in their contract to this effect. It seems that some of the Edison jobbers had been carrying the Duplex records. But, perhaps a more important motivation lay in a recent decision of the Court of Appeals, 2nd District, which reversed a prior decision by Judge Hazel in favor of the defendant in the case of the American Graphophone Co. versus the Universal Talking Machine Co. and the American Record Co.

Thus, the Victor cause seemed to need bolstering, as current publicity was favoring Edison and the Graphophone Co. Having no better way to do it, Victor utilized a full page in the *Talking Machine World*, to expound to the trade the strength of its patent situation. The ad stressed the importance of its possession of the basic Berliner patent 534,543 and summarized its position as being in full control of the industry, as follows:

"1. That the Victor Co. controls the
    disc reproducing machine and disc

Fig. 12-9. The Duplex made in Kalamazoo, Michigan, had twin brass horns coupled to a single reproducer.

record, where the reproducer is vibrated and propelled by the record.

2. That the Victor Co. controls this method of reproducing sound.

3. That the Victor Co. controls the disc records for use on these machines."

The ad giving the claims of the Victor Co. regarding the strength of its patent situation continued with the following:

"The U. S. Courts have sustained this Berliner patent broadly (claims 5 & 35) in following decisions: Victor et al, vs. American Graphophone Co., decision of U. S. Circuit Court S.D., New York, filed Sept. 28, 1905. Victor et al vs. Leeds & Catlin Co., same court, April 26, 1906. Victor et al vs. Talk-O-Phone Co., same court, April 26, 1906. Victor et al vs. Leeds & Catlin Co.,

U. S. Circuit Court of Appeals, 2nd Circuit, Oct. 12, 1906. Victor et al vs. Talk-O-Phone Co., U. S. Circuit Court of Appeals, 2nd Circuit, Oct. 12, 1906. "The U. S. Circuit Court for the Southern District of New York on decision by Judge Lacombe filed Jan. 5, 1907, in contempt proceedings has held these claims of the Berliner patent include records as well as machines in the combination, and that a sale of such disc records for use in these disc machines was an infringement of the patent."

Then came one of the most astounding lines of the ad, which read:

"The Victor Co. hesitates at anything like bragging, but - - - the Victor Co. is on top. We have issued a license to the Universal Talking Machine Co. and to the American Graphophone Co."

168   EVOLUTION OF THE PHONOGRAPH

This put the fat in the fire with a vengeance and the American Graphophone Co. replied with four full pages in the next issue of *Talking Machine World*.

The first page started off with a feature headline, as follows:

"WHO'S WHO IN THE TALKING MACHINE INDUSTRY, WITH A FEW ILLUSTRATIONS BY U. S. JUDGES"

To students of dialectic, of patents, or of advertising, or even of the often alleged aloof and impersonal nature of corporations, this controversy should be of particular interest, so the more relevant comments of the Graphophone Co.'s anonymous spokesman will be quoted verbatim, as follows:

"Thomas A. Edison was one of the first persons to recognize that an industry could be built upon the basic foundation which the Graphophone afforded, and the so-called Edison Phonograph IS A LICENSED GRAPHOPHONE, which would be of no commercial importance without the principles first given to the world with the invention of the Graphophone and which had lawful existence only when the Graphophone Co., after prolonged litigation granted the National Phonograph Co. the rights to use its patents.

"Judge Shipman in the U. S. Circuit Court in New York, in American Graphophone Co. vs. Leeds, et al., referring to the earlier work of Mr. Edison, characterizes most of the descriptions as 'confusedly vague' saying: 'It is confessedly difficult to know the interpretation which the writer placed on some of the words which he uses.'

"But, said Judge Shipman, 'Bell and Tainter made an actual, living invention, and a court is not called upon to decipher an anticipation in the unfinished work and surmises of earlier students of the same subject.' 87 Fed. 873"

Other court decisions referred to in this four page spread are as follows:

"Judge Platt in the U. S. Circuit Court, Conn., in National Phonograph Co. vs. American Graphophone Co. said; 'The Graphophonic art may be said to have fairly begun with the invention of Bell & Tainter, Letters Patent No. 341,214, dated May 4, 1886. This taught the public how to produce the commercial and transferrable sound record.' 135 Fed. 809

"Judge Grosscup in U. S. Court in Illinois, in American Graphophone Co. vs. Amet, said, 'Bell and Tainter lay no claim to having conceived the idea of a mechanism whereby speech or sound could be recorded and reproduced. Much thought and experimentation, before their patents were completed, were expended upon the general conception of such an instrument. BUT THE FACT REMAINS THAT, PRIOR TO THEIR GRAPHOPHONE, THE CONCEPTION OF A PHONOGRAPH HAD NEVER BEEN MECHANICALLY WORKED OUT TO THE EXTENT OF MECHANICAL PERFECTION. THE GRAPHOPHONE, INDEED SEEMS TO HAVE TAKEN THE PLACE OF ALL PREVIOUS MECHANISMS, AND TO HAVE ADVANCED BY A VERY LARGE SPACE, THE ART OF RECORDING AND REPRODUCING SOUND.'

"And speaking of the Graphophone and its record, he said, 'SUCH COMBINATION IS THE MECHANICAL MEANS WHEREBY THE ART OF REPRODUCING SOUNDS IS MADE PRACTICALLY EFFECTIVE.' 74 Fed. 789"

Then, in the advertising text, the writer claimed for the Graphophone the first spring motor, as used in the Graphophone "Baby Grand." He also claimed the first mechanical duplicating machine as having been invented by Thomas H. Macdonald, as used for producing the first commercially duplicated cylinders. Other claims were listed as follows:

"The Graphophone Grand - - - created a sensation and was widely copied by Mr. Edison, who finally admitted the validity of the patent and became a licensee on payment of substantial royalty.

"The moulded cylindrical record, invented by Macdonald, and sold in large quantities more than one year before a competitor put out its moulded records on the market. In the case of National Phonograph Co. vs. American Graphophone Co. already referred to before Judge Platt in Conn., the testimony showed conclusively that Edison, notwithstanding the oft-repeated claim that he is the inventor of the so-called Gold-Moulded record, had never up to that date, 1905, succeeded in making a practical and successful moulded sound record. By his own testimony it was proven that the records extensively advertised as his own are made by a process which was really the invention of two of his employees years after our process, invented by Macdonald, had been perfected."

Summing up was a list of claims with specific references to the Victor ad of the prior month, as follows:

"1. The first disc talking machine was a Graphophone.
2. The first disc talking machine record was a Graphophone record.
3. Before Berliner conceived his uncommercial process of etching them, disc records had been made by others.
4. Long before our boastful competition were ever heard of we had licensed their predecessor, the National Gramophone Co., who admitted they were using Graphophone patents in order to make their product commercial, and who paid us substantial royalties up to the time of their dissolution.
5. The Victor Co. used our patented process to manufacture their records. They are licensed under our

patents, and are absolutely dependent upon them in order to make a saleable record.

"In American Graphophone Co. vs. Universal Talking Machine Co. & American Record Co., U. S. Circuit Court of Appeals, N. Y., re. #688,739, (Jones Patent) Wallace, Lacomb and Townsend said,

" 'The disc produced by this patented process RESPONDS TO THE TEST OF SUCCESS WHERE OTHERS HAVE FAILED.'

'The patentable novelty of the process of the patent is not only indicated by large sales, but also by the unassailable evidence of that most sincere form of flattering recognition: IMITATION AND APPROPRIATION BY RIVAL MANUFACTURERS.'

'In short, it has so far supplanted all other methods previously used that apparently all disc records are now made by said process, and COMPLAINANT'S CHIEF COMPETITOR (referring to Victor Co.) ADMITS THAT IT DISCARDED ITS OWN PATENTED ETCHING PROCESS (referring to Berliner patent) AND HAS SUBSTITUTED THEREFORE THE PROCESS OF THE PATENT IN SUIT.' "

The advertisement then closed with this modest statement:

"IF ANY BRAGGING HAS BEEN INDULGED IN, THE U. S. CIRCUIT COURT JUDGES HAVE BEEN OUR MOUTHPIECES, AND WE ONLY HAVE TO QUOTE FROM A FEW DECISIONS TO USE THEM TO SUSTAIN EVERY CLAIM WE MAKE."

This is, indeed, what any of the big three could have said. By selecting the opinions from the right court cases they were enabled to prove anything they wished to anybody—except to each other!

In comparison with the Graphophone Co.'s reply, the Victor advertisement was a model of reserve and accuracy.

However, the point of the Victor Co. having issued a license to the Universal Talking Machine Co. was quite academic, as it now was a wholly owned subsidiary. The tables had now been completely turned since mid-summer of 1900 when the National Gramophone Corporation was advertising that it, the Universal Talking Machine Co., the American Graphophone Co., and the Columbia Phonograph Co. "had made an agreement between themselves for legal protection and commercial advantage." For a different reason, the issuance of a similar license to its arch competitor, the American Graphophone Co., was also academic. From the first, cross licensing existed among the big three as a necessity resulting from the defects of our patent system and had little financial significance between them, although it permitted any one of them to put newcomers out of the game almost at will. Only in the rare instances of court orders directing the payments of usually trivial sums, did the payment of money between the big three ever take place. To all intents and purposes, the cumulative results of all the patent litigation was to enforce the division of the talking machine world between the big three and to provide them with the ammunition to drive off all others.

The claims made by the Graphophone Co. in its advertisement to have been the first in every element of phonographic, or as stated, "graphophonic" progress, have been dealt with elsewhere sufficiently. Altogether it comprises a fiction that would do credit to the writer of a modern "whodunit." It is comparable with arctic explorer Cook's capsule story on "How I Discovered the North Pole" as recorded for Victor by him while the world yet believed him, but which was hastily withdrawn from circulation by Victor within a month or two of its issuance when the fraudulency of his claim had been exposed by the Danish Geographical Society.

The court cases cited in the Graphophone advertisement were largely the product of the diligence and legal acumen of Philip Mauro, chief legal counsel and a director of the company for many years. Many of the honorable Federal Judges were as putty in his hands, although the occasionally incredible stupidity of opposition counsel was a frequent contribution. However, it would seem almost a certainty that Mauro had nothing to do with the writing of this four page ad, nor that he approved it, for it was altogether too bold and too brassy to have been the product of his logical and subtle method. In selling the scientific societies an old lamp for a new one, in introducing the Graphophone Grand (Fig. 12-10) he spoke as a scientist, presenting his alleged facts in a thoroughly convincing and logical sequence and without referring to a single court decision! He undoubtedly recognized that scientists are quite apt to question our court procedures as often at variance with the scientific method of ascertaining facts. To the scientist, the fact that a certain decision has been made in a patent case does not necessarily prove anything, but that the results may either hinder or facilitate the application of certain discovered principles to useful commercial applications. The distaste of the so-called "pure" scientist for commercial research, or even commercially sponsored research, may in part stem from his inherent distrust of what he knows often to be the unscientific procedures of our patent system and law courts.

There is nothing changeable about the discoveries or devices contrived by inventors. Whenever there is a question about what a certain device will do, one may again test the procedure or equipment which the inventor used, provided the three dimensional evidence yet exists. Thus it would seem that as close to the scene as the District Courts of the time were, with the same body of facts available to each, the judges of those courts should have reached quite uniform decisions with respect to a given patent question. Instead, it was exceptional when a series

Fig. 12-10. The Graphophone Grand designed to play the 5-inch wax cylinder.

of court cases in various jurisdictions reviewing the same controversial issue would result in the same decision.

To convince one's self that by and large court decisions in patent cases mean nothing, one needs only to read the series of decisions rendered by the Federal judges involving any one of the patents of sufficient importance to be worth fighting over. To illustrate, a few quotations from a few of the decisions involving the infamous Jones patent, which is of especial interest, are as follows:

July 9, 1904—American Graphophone Co. vs. Leeds & Catlin, et al.

"A bill for the infringement of two patents, though one is for a process, and the other for a product, is not multifarious, where both relate to the same article and are capable of being jointly infringed as is alleged in the bill they are by the defendant."

Feb. 19, 1906—Victor Talking Machine Co. vs. American Graphophone Co. Judge Hazel

"The Jones patent, No. 688,739 for a

method of producing sound records for talking machines, is void for anticipation in the prior art." (Held anticipated by Adams-Randall patent of 1899; Gouraud nos. 12,593 & 15,206 of 1894, British; Edison no. 382,419 of 1888; Young no. 1,487, British; Bell & Tainter, no. 341,214 of May 6, 1886 and Berliner, no. 548,623 of 1895.)

Jan. 14, 1907—American Graphophone Co. vs. Universal Talking Machine Co. Judge Townsend

"The Jones patent 688,739 for a method for producing sound records for use in talking machines of the gramophone type, which consists in cutting or engraving a record groove of uniform depth, by means of the lateral vibrations of a suitable stylus, upon a disc of waxlike material, coating the same with a conducting material, and then forming a matrix thereon by electrolysis, from which the duplicate records are made by impression, was not anticipated by anything in the prior art, and discloses patentable invention."

June 11, 1907—American Graphophone Co. vs. Leeds & Catlin Co., Judge Lacombe

"The mere making of duplicate copies of fully finished, commercial foreignmade records for talking machines does not constitute infringement of the Jones patent no. 688,739, for a process of producing sound records. - - - Preparation or threats to infringe a patent shown by ex parte affidavits only are not sufficient to warrant the granting of a preliminary injunction."

June 11, 1907—American Graphophone Co. vs. International Record Co., Judge Lacombe

"Patent sustained and construed by the Court of Appeals upon voluminous records and after a long hearing on exhaustive briefs. Complainant may take order for preliminary injunction." (re. Jones pat. 688,739.)

Sept. 1908—Judge Hough
"Anything narrower than this I find it difficult to conceive" (re. Jones patent 688,739. He held it anticipated by British patent of Charles AdamsRandall of nine years priority.)

April 31, 1909—American Graphophone Co. vs. Leeds & Catlin, Judge Coxe
"The Jones patent 688,739 for a Process of Making Commercial Sound Records was not anticipated by the AdamsRandall British patent no. 9,996 of 1888, and is valid, also held infringed."

March 27, 1911—Victor Talking Machine Co. vs. American Graphophone Co.
" - - - while there is no evidence that Jones got his ideas from Johnson, he did not seem to appreciate, and certainly did not claim, that he had made any discovery in cutting his groove into, not out of, the wax-like tablet." (The Johnson patent 896,059 patented Aug. 11, 1908, for a laterally undulating groove of constant depth, was held not to infringe the Jones patent 688,739.)

Aug. 4, 1922—Victor Talking Machine Co. vs. Starr Piano Co.
"We think it reasonable to infer, as Judge Learned Hand did in the court below, that this court in the case of American Graphophone Co. vs. Universal Talking Machine Co. supra, sustained the Jones patent over the Bell & Tainter patent because of the novelty and usefulness of the combination of the former, and not because any single element thereof was pattentable." (re. the Jones patent. He held that the Jones patent had been anticipated in part by the Edison British patent no. 15,206 of 1891 and the Bell-Tainter patent no. 341,214 of May 4, 1886. The latter patent, he said, showed that Bell & Tainter were familiar with lateral cutting!)

The Alice in Wonderland feeling that one gets in reading these conflicting decisions may be lessened somewhat by studying the circumstances which had

permitted Eldridge R. Johnson to secure a belated patent upon precisely
the same claims as had been embodied
in the Jones patent specification, differing but slightly in terminology.

There are distinct prohibitions against
the issuance of patents on devices or
processes which have been kept secret,
not patented and which have been
commercially used over a period of
time. Such use had been admitted in
court by Johnson.

However, it was claimed by Johnson
that the concept covered by the Jones
patent had been a part of a patent
application which he had filed Aug. 16,
1898, and which after the issuance of
the Jones patent had been divided and
refiled Nov. 12, 1904. A similar case
involving patent office delays and such
alleged public use with but little evidence had provided the basis upon
which Edison had been deprived of use
of the celluloid cylinder a few years
earlier. Yet by the questionable procedure of granting Johnson a patent
upon a process he admitted in court he
had invented before 1900 and had used
during all of the succeeding years, the
Victor Co. was given an extension of
its monopoly for another period of
seventeen years!

During the course of the 1911 trial
of Victor Talking Machine Co. vs.
American Graphophone Co., Johnson
made this admission of the process on
which he belatedly received a patent.
By the 1911 decision the Johnson 1908
patent displaced the Jones patent as
the keystone of the lateral disc industry
patent structure. This is well illustrated
by the closing statement of the Judge
of the 2nd Circuit Court of Appeals
in the case on Jan. 23, 1912 as follows:

"It now appears that complainant - - -
had made agreement with defendants
waiving all past damages and profits
and granting a license for the future.
Everything is settled, except the demand for injunction relief, etc. - - -
decree is affirmed without costs, and
without passing upon the validity of
the patent."

The status quo was maintained between the two companies until 1922 in
the case of the Victor Co. vs. Starr
Piano Co. By 1912 many of the more
aggressive personalities of the Graphophone Co. were gone, which perhaps
may account for the long truce. The
Graphophone Co. was not actually a
party to the case, but interesting is
what Justice Augustus N. Hand had to
say about the Jones patent as well as
the Johnson reverbalization of it which
was in question. With respect to the
Johnson patent he said that the keeping of a process secret for years by the
inventor constituted abandonment under
the patent laws and declared the Johnson patent 896,059 void for lack of invention and abandonment. In referring
to the Jones patent, Judge Hand said
that it had been anticipated by the
Edison owned Gouraud British patent
no. 15,206 of 1891 and the Bell-Tainter
patent no. 341,214 of 1886, as had his
namesake Judge Learned Hand had
found in the case of American Graphophone Co. vs. Universal Talking Machine Co. years before. Judge Augustus
Hand went one step further than his
illustrious predecessor in stating that
the Bell-Tainter patent no. 341,214
showed that Bell and Tainter were
familiar with lateral recording. A close
study of this patent and its specification fails to reveal any basis for this
supposition.

As the foregoing shows, there was
but slight consistency in the widely
variable decisions of these most important patent cases involving the
rights of many inventors and upon
which material success or failure depended. A statement made by the premier of Iran during the Anglo-American
oil crisis with respect to the world
powers seems applicable to the court
and patent situation. He said,

"They handcuff the weak and hasten
to the assistance of the strong."

The one man, to whom more patents
were issued than any other, was well
qualified to comment on the workings

of our patent system. This, of course, was Thomas A. Edison.

He said:

"In England, when a case is finally decided it is settled for the entire country, while here it is not so. Here a patent having been once sustained, say, in Boston, may have to be litigated all over again in New York, and again in Philadelphia, and so on for all the Federal circuits. Furthermore, it seems to me that scientific disputes should be decided by some court containing at least one or two scientific men—men capable of comprehending the significance of an invention and the difficulties of its accomplishment,—if justice is ever to be given an inventor. And I think also, that this court should have the power to summon before it and examine any recognized expert in the special art, who might be able to testify to facts for or against the patent, instead of trying to gather the truth from the tedious essays of hired experts, whose depositions are really nothing but sworn arguments. The real gist of patent suits is generally very simple, and I have no doubt that any judge of fair intelligence, assisted by one or more scientific advisors, could in a couple of days at the most examine all the necessary witnesses; hear all the necessary arguments, and actually decide an ordinary patent suit in a way that would more nearly be just, than can now be done at an expenditure of a hundred times as much money and months and years of preparation. And I have no doubt that the time taken by the court would be enormously less, because if a judge attempts to read the bulky records, and briefs, that work alone would require several days.

"Acting as judges, inventors would not be very apt to correctly decide a complicated law point; and on the other hand, it is hard to see how a lawyer can decide a complicated scientific point rightly. Some inventors complain of our Patent Office, but my own experience with the Patent Office is that the examiners are fair-minded and intelligent, and when they refuse a patent they are generally right; but I think the whole trouble lies with the system in vogue in the Federal Courts for trying patent cases, and in the fact, which cannot be disputed, that the Federal judges, with but few exceptions, do not understand complicated scientific questions. To secure uniformity in the several Federal circuits and correct errors, it has been proposed to establist a central court of patent appeals in Washington. This I believe in; but this court should also contain at least two scientific men, who would not be blind to the sophistry of paid experts. Men whose inventions would have created wealth of millions have been ruined and prevented from making any money whereby they could continue their careers as creators of wealth for the general good, just because the experts befuddled the judge by their misleading statements."

Elsewhere has been mentioned the Edison carbon button telephone transmitter which although it had made the Bell telephone a commercial practicality, was not conceded by the courts to have been prior in conception to the inoperable Berliner carbon transmitter until 1902, or twenty-five years after the application for a patent had been filed by Edison. Edison's fundamental incandescent lamp patent was not completely adjudicated until 1892, or more than twelve years after the date of issuance. Then, the very next year, it was back in the courts because of an alleged anticipation by one Henry Goebel, whose claims had presumably been thrashed out and disposed of years previously. Edison may have been inclined to tread a bit lightly on the toes of the patent examiners, in view of the failure of the Patent Office with respect to his important application of 1878, and the suspicious delay in issuance of a patent to Berliner upon an inoperative device, as well as a few other things of this nature. Perhaps he felt that he should be cautious in view of the fact that he still had to do business with them! Indicative that he may have repressed his feelings somewhat was a story in the *Talking Machine World* for August of 1907, in which he was quoted as advising young inventors to keep their inventions secret and to manufacture without benefit of patents, in order to secure a return upon their efforts. However, it is noticeable that he did not follow his own advice, thereafter!

The complex patent situation and the necessity of continually fighting innumerable and costly suits in defense of his rights while at the same time carrying on the task of development and commercialization of his inventions in several divergent fields at once is perhaps in itself sufficient explanation of Edison's delayed entrance into the disc field. The conflicting decisions with respect to the Jones patent and certain others were probably potent influences which resulted in Edison's decision to build a machine which in no way could be construed as infringing upon any of the numerous patents on sound recording and reproducing instruments which were yet in effect.

By a continuing of this reasoning, the structuring of the patent issuing and reviewing system was in reality responsible for the necessity which Edison faced of having to design an exclusive system and which, consecutively, resulted in the situation in which he would have no truck with the granting of licenses to others and which deprived

many of the greater artists and posterity of the values which might have obtained from having their voices recorded by the best possible means. This will be analyzed in a later chapter.

To sum up the commercial conflicts between the cylinders and the discs, the following are the more important factors:

1. The cylinder method was commercialized first because of its basic simplicity.
2. The Edison patent application of 1878 covering important improvements to the phonograph, including a disc machine, was not acted upon by the U. S. Patent Office.
3. Bell & Tainter chose to adopt the Edison hill-and-dale cylinder method, rather than the disc.
4. The ease of duplicating discs by molding or pressing, as compared to cylinders gave the discs an advantage to offset the earlier start of the cylinders.
5. The control over the record market inherent in the fact that discs could not be made everywhere.
6. The convenience in handling and storage of discs.
7. Edison's belief in the essential superiority of the cylinder with its uniform surface speed beneath the stylus.

Although musical cylinders were sold by Thomas A. Edison, Inc. until it retired from the field in 1929, the ultimate doom of the cylinder had been sounded with the announcement of the Edison Diamond Disc Phonograph in 1912.

CHAPTER 13

INTERNAL HORN TALKING MACHINES AND THE PHONOGRAPH

DURING the first decade of the century a considerable number of inventors and entrepreneurs attempted to get into the burgeoning talking machine industry. One of the most persistent of these had begun even before the turn of the century. This was Loring L. Leeds who first had engaged in the manufacture of cylinder records. Decrees were handed down by the courts that he was guilty of infringing patents owned by the American Graphophone Co. as early as 1896, and again in 1898. Thus prevented from continuing profitably in the cylinder business, Leeds, together with Catlin, turned to the manufacture of disc records. However, in 1904, a decree was found against the new firm of Leeds & Catlin in another suit brought by the Graphophone Co. Undaunted, Leeds & Catlin in advertisements in the *Talking Machine World* in 1906 announced a new talking machine. The year following in another suit instituted by the Graphophone Co. on the basis of both talking machine and disc record patents, Leeds & Catlin received another adverse decision.

In 1908, Victor also sued Leeds & Catlin and as a consequence of an ordered accounting and the costs of litigation, the company was forced into bankruptcy in the following year. At the close, Edward F. Leeds was president and Henry Leeds treasurer. This was the longest continuous assault upon the patent citadels of the big three by any one group in the United States.

Meanwhile other prominent entrepreneurs sought to invade the upward zooming disc market, among them Hawthorne & Sheble, American Record Co., Talk-O-Phone, Duplex and the International Record Co.—all names to be found on early discs. Each of these was set upon by the attorneys of one or the other of the two leading disc companies, and kept in the courts until they either acceded to a consent decision and an accounting because of the costs of litigation, or until some judge would render the eventual decision compelling the same result. Even if the parent companies had not a superior patent position, the fact remains that in the long run only companies with a financial position strong enough to afford unlimited expenditures would have the final decisions in their favor. Because the American Graphophone Co. had been organized by men familiar with law and several of its officers were lawyers of exceptional ability, this company held a decisive edge in any court contest.

Under these circumstances, it is amazing indeed that one or two manufacturers were able to wheel up trojan horses and get within the citadel. One of these was the Sonora Chime Co. of New York City, which announced in the latter part of 1907 its intention of producing a talking machine. The Victor Co. responded with an immediate suit, on the basis of infringement of the Berliner patent 534,543. The defense of the Sonora attorneys was that this Berliner patent was no longer in effect, as it was dependent on the Suess Canadian patent 41,901, which had expired. Suess had been an assistant to Emile Berliner at the time of the original Washington research and had assigned this and other patents to Berliner, which were subsequently transferred to the Victor Talking Machine Co. Although the methods developed by Berliner were acknowledged to be dependent on the collateral Suess improvements, the court found that the Berliner patent in question had not expired with the Suess patent and was still valid for its life, which had about a year to go. This was in the Circuit Court of the Southern District of New York, which, although affirming the validity of the patent, refused an injunction to the plaintiff. So the Sonora Chime Co. was reorganized as the Sonora Phonograph Co., a name to become familiar to the public for many years. The origin of the company is self explanatory of its still remembered trademark "Clear as a Bell."

As originally the word "phonograph" had a connotation of the hill-and-dale method, there was considerable speculation as to whether the new machine and records would use this process, in view of the name chosen for the company. As a matter of fact, a few hill-and-dale records were produced with the Sonora label and the machines were designed to play either type of discs, being equipped with a universal tone arm, which permitted the soundbox to be turned to the front for playing the vertical cut records. Two circumstances of possible significance may be observed; first, the Sonora sapphire ball disc record was without patent information, such as was usually found on labels; second, the fact that neither major disc company continued to attack after 1911 suggests that perhaps an agreement was eventually reached to let the newcomer in provided it would desist from the manufacture of records. At any rate, no records bearing a Sonora label were again issued until

sometime in the 1940's, even though the company became a major producer of machines during the latter part of the acoustic period.

It was not until about the year 1908 that the place of the phonograph in the home really began to seem assured. The early phonograph had made an obtrusive appearance as a sort of visitor, who was not expected to stay. Yet the coming of the phonograph was a definite influence in the transformation of the nineteenth century formal parlor into a room where visitors and friends might be entertained, instead of a place reserved for state occasions only, such as the visit of the minister, weddings and funerals. The way had been paved however, by the melodion and the music box which with their dulcet tones seemed to fit the sombre formality of the parlor of the period. It can be appreciated today that the designers of the early phonographs and graphophones had little conception of a suitable enclosure for their machines to promote acceptance in this fashion. It is well enough to excuse Edison and Macdonald on the grounds that they were inventors and not furniture designers, but we must also concede that the designers of the many beautiful melodions and music boxes of the time were also inventors. It is only to our nostalgic senses that the early phonographs with ear tubes, or the later ones with horns, seem to be appropriately Victorian!

Our modern proponents of a strictly "functional design" should somehow be forced to contemplate for long periods in their own living rooms one of the early phonographs, with a long horn suspended from the ceiling! The first successful invasion of the Victorian home by what we would now term a "functional" machine had been made by Elias Howe and Singer with their sewing machines. The re-design of the phonograph and the graphophone for the home market had been accomplished by the mistaken course of patterning the example of the sewing machine, rather than by following the lead of some of the music boxes, which had been designed more appropriately for the parlor. This is rather easily explained however, in the case of the graphophone, for these were made in the old Howe sewing machine factory in Bridgeport and the earlier business machines used the same foot treadle mechanism and tables. Many of the same cabinet makers and finishers continued on when the factory had been taken over by the Graphophone Co. and so it is quite obvious as to how the home graphophones came to be made of similar materials and finishes—even to the removable wooden covers!

Why Edison also chose to follow virtually the same procedure for the Edison home phonograph as to materials and finishes, as well as design, is not so easily explained. It may be that the removable, rounded top, attachable to the base by various latching devices, with a carrying handle at the top, was the simplest solution at the time. The early phonographs were for the most part also recording machines, and this feature, as in home recording disc or tape machines of today, implies design for portability. Then, as now, the portable instrument of whatever type never seems to appear "at home" in the living room.

The initial awkwardness of the cylinder machine in the home environment was not as obvious as later—it was the advent of the altogether too obtrusive horn which prejudiced the bid of the phonograph for acceptance as a permanent fixture in the domestic scene. Despite this, the advantages of the horn over the ear tubes as a means of entertainment became so apparent that the more avid phonograph devotees soon were demanding bigger and better horns. Several concerns sprang up to fill the demand for special horns, horn cranes, cabinets for records and other accessories. Hawthorne & Sheble had been one of the pioneers in the manufacture and sale of these items. Among other makers of patented types of horns was the Searchlight Horn Co. Horns were made of wood, brass, aluminum

and even glass. Although the Edison Gem, one of the cheapest phonographs came equipped with a short horn, most models were sold without horns until November, 1907, when the National Phonograph Co. announced its first complete outfit of phonograph, large horn and stand at one price.

Contrasting with this practice in the cylinder business, Victor from its founding in 1901 had sold its talking machines as a complete unit, although special horns were supplied by others to fit the Victor models. More importantly, the Victor machines from the beginning were designed to be placed somewhere in the home and left there. They were not equipped for the making of records so there was little need of providing for portability. Victor also exhibited remarkable restraint in not plastering florid decalcomania scrolls across the front of its machines as had their competitors who had emblazoned "Edison Home Phonograph" and "Columbia Graphophone Grand" in large letters on these respective instruments.

Victor used an inconspicuous etched brass or aluminum plate, instead. The earlier method also seems to have emulated the example of the sewing machine manufacturers, who likewise had made the most of their advertising opportunities in the home. But the cylinder manufacturers had gone them one better! Not satisfied with the billboard effect of the decalcomanias, each cylinder opened with the announcement of the title of the selection and artist, followed by the statement that this was an "Edison Record," or "Columbia Record, made by the Columbia Phonograph Co., New York, London and Paris."

Indicative of the influence of precedent, the title and artists of the earlier Victor Discs were also announced, even though this information was printed in full upon the labels—which was not true of the cylinders of the same time, which had the titles printed on a separate slip of paper very easily misplaced. Even after the name of the selection was later pressed into the thicker edge of the cylinders, there was seldom room for inclusion of full information, often omitting the name of the artist, which may account for the fact that the vocal announcements were not discontinued for several years after the introduction of the molded cylinders.

The shape of horns progressed from the earliest ones of conical form, first in adding a flaring bell at the outer end, often of brass, and then finally to the securing of a constantly expanding cross section from the reproducer end to a broad flare at the orifice. It was soon found more economical to build up horns of this shape by making the larger part of pieces cut out of sheet metal, brazed or soldered together, thus being polygonal in cross section. This led to the rounding of the outer end of the segments and ultimately developed into the familiar "morning glory" horn. In the final stages of development these morning glory horns were guilded, or hand painted with gay colors with flowers in the petals. Actually, fancifully decorating the already too conspicuous horn served only to further point up its essential discordance with the home environment.

Fig. 13-1. The Victrola IV, first Victor machine featuring an enclosed horn. (Courtesy of RCA Victor.)

Quite possibly it was the Hymnophone, a German built disc machine offered for sale in this country in 1905, which gave the alert Eldridge R. Johnson the idea of the completely internal

horn machine (Fig. 13-1) which he christened the "Victrola." The Hymnophone had the horn cleverly brought down in back of the machine and under the turntable and motor so that only the bell of the horn protruded in front. It may be that Johnson was also stimulated by the cabinets which were being sold by other manufacturers for the storage of records for both cylinder and disc type machines and which served also as a table for the machine. By 1906, the sales of these cabinets and other accessories were reaching large proportions. As the selling price of the Victor machines at that time ranged from $22 to $100, with the average sale about $50, it must have been quite obvious that a lot of the important business being created by Victor advertising was going elsewhere. It may be also that the marketing in the United States by Victor of the British Auxetophone, a compressed air amplified talking machine which came enclosed in a massive cabinet at the modest price of $500, may also have suggested the building of standard type machines with the horn enclosed.

In 1906, Victor announced the Victrola, with internal horn and record storage space, meeting with immediate public acceptance. The chief mechanical obstacle to the building of an internal horn disc machine had already been solved by Johnson in his invention of the ball bearing, swivel-pointed tone arm, with a goose neck joint for turning back the reproducer to facilitate the changing of needles. This had already been used on the open horn machines. It was only necessary that the back end of the tone arm be turned down instead of up. However, the successful designing of a horn to fit in the limited cabinet space was not so easily dealt with and caused acoustical difficulties never completely solved to the end of the acoustic period. Johnson mounted the re-designed tone arm on a cast iron section of horn at the bend, with the remaining part of the horn made of wood. The bell, or outermost part of the flare characteristic of the better

Fig. 13-2. Victor VI, last of the outside horn models produced in 1906. The machine came in oak or mahogany.

Victor external horns had to be sacrificed and as a consequence the tone reproduction was adversely affected. Actually, as it is still possible to demonstrate, the open horn Victor Model VI of 1906 (Fig. 13-2) or any of the larger open horn machines made by Victor were better reproducing instruments than any of the internal horn Victrolas made right up to the period of electrical recording. In further evidence of this point, it should be observed that the Victor school machine utilized an open horn right up to 1925, in service where articulation, tone range, volume and quality were the decisive factors, rather than style trends or conformity to the home environment. (See Fig. 13-3.)

In England, long after the inception of electrical methods, custom built open horn gramophones were made by two or more prominent makers for the use of record connoisseurs. But in 1906 in the United States, the concept of the Victrola as a piece of furniture had caught on—tone quality became secondary. Others tried to get into the act,

such as Schroeder Hornless Phonograph Manufacturing Co., which advertised in the *Talking Machine World* in 1907. Probably Victor lost, no time in informing its officers of the futility of so doing!

Fig. 13-3. The Victrola XXV was commonly called the Victor School Machine. This model did much to spark great interest in the talking machine. (From an early Victor brochure.)

A prominent factor in the unquestioned acceptance of the Victrola was the preference shown for them by the music dealers. The average unit sale was at a higher figure and by making the open horn machines seem obsolete, favorable trade-ins could be arranged. Many of the persons who bought the new Victrolas never had heard one of the better open horn Victor machines and thus had no criterion for evaluating the comparative reproducing qualities of the two types of instruments. Stylistically and financially, the Victrola was a tremendous success; technically, it represented retrogression rather than progress. Nevertheless, by the end of 1906 Victor had an earned surplus of six million dollars, while Columbia had not quite two and a half million.

This same year of 1906, Giulemino Marconi, the famous inventor of wireless telegraphy, paid a visit to the American Graphophone Co. plant at Bridgeport. Shortly after, it was announced that Marconi had been retained as consulting physicist. Upon his departure for England he stated that he intended to make a thorough study of sound recording and reproducing technics. At the time it must be conceded that the Graphophone Co.—Columbia Phonograph Co. alliance was in need of expert help. Victor was running away with the the disc business, and the introduction of the Victrola had brought sales of Columbia Graphophones almost to a standstill. Despite the introduction of the long mandrel, loud volume Twentieth Century Graphophone cylinder machine, Edison was now capturing the lion's share of the cylinder business. Marconi must have done a phenomenally quick job of research—or else he had the idea in mind before approaching the Graphophone Co., for the first announcement of the new Columbia Marconi Velvet-Tone records were made in July of 1906. These were thin, flexible laminated records, with a paper core and a plastic surface which were surprisingly similar in appearance and texture to those of the black plastic records of today. These new records were pressed by the Graphophone Co. from the standard stampers at a slight advance in price, a policy comparable to the special editions of 78 rpm records made available by Victor in red Vinylite some years ago. While available the Marconi Velvet-Tone records were manufactured in both single and double faced records, carrying the same catalog numbers as the regular editions.

Probably it was the influence of Marconi's method that resulted in the laminated process later used for the standard Columbia discs, which had an inflexible core of coarser materials between two layers of paper, which was coated with a surface of finer shellac and other ingredients. In later years the name "Velvet-Tone" was used by Columbia and successor companies for records made for the so-called ten cent store trade.

Columbia also became more and more concerned with the astounding success of the Victor red seal series of celebrity recordings, which had caught both Columbia and Edison with little to offer in competition. Eldridge R. Johnson and his director of repertoire, Calvin Childs, had from the first instituted a firm policy of signing the greater artists on exclusive, long term contracts, wherever possible. Even as early as 1907, Columbia found it difficult to find available operatic singing stars to even make a respectable showing against Victor's all star aggregation. For Victor's exclusive list included in addition to the great Caruso, his baritone friend Antonio Scotti; sopranos Marcella Sembrich, Nellie Melba and Johanna Gadski; contraltos Louise Homer and Ernestine Schumann-Heink; the two leading bassos Pol Plancon and Marcel Journet, as well as many others of the other names from now fabulous casts. Moreover, by placing what was then a colossal advertising budget behind the exploitation of these well-known names, Victor further inflated their reputations and its own. In a desperate attempt to compete, Columbia signed the famous Wagnerian soprano Lillian Nordica on an exclusive contract. Nordica was by this time considerably past her prime, but so also were several of the artists of the Victor Co. However, the records of Nordica were also poorly recorded and although thousands were ultimately sold, the net result was not to increase the public estimate of the Graphophone Co.'s products, or its capacity for choosing talent. Perhaps nothing could have served to stem the Victor tide. The high-water mark had been set by the initial stroke in securing Caruso, who was the greatest salesman Victor ever had and well worth the millions it was to pay him. Caruso records were exported all over the world by way of masters delivered to the several affiliated European companies and of course are being sold in large quantities yet today.

The desperation of Columbia in meeting this competition was fully revealed in its method of handling a fortuitous opportunity to introduce records by Allesandro Bonci, an Italian tenor who was brought to New York in 1907 by the Manhattan Opera Co. impresario, Oscar Hammerstein, to offset Caruso at the Metropolitan. Thinking to exploit this break to the limit, Columbia announced at one fell swoop a gigantic list of no less than forty-six titles by Bonci, including three fourteen-inch discs! Very few men experienced in the industry then or since, would consider it sound judgment to issue so many records at one time of an artist whose appeal to the public was untested. These records had been recorded in Europe by the Societe de Fonotipia. Bonci also later made records at the Graphophone studio, but the quality of these recordings was inferior both artistically and tonally to those produced in Europe. This contrasts decidedly with Victor's procedure with respect to Nellie Melba, who had recorded first in Europe for the Gramophone & Typewriter, Ltd. Victor first issued pressings made from imported masters, providing them with a special mauve label bearing the caption "Victor Melba Record." These records were also put in a special container with a glassine window the size of the label on one side, so that as the record was withdrawn a picture of the famous diva appeared in the opening. The price of the Melba records were five dollars each, as was also a similar series of Tamagno records. However, as soon as Victor could arrange to secure Mme. Melba's signature to an exclusive contract, work was begun on re-recording most of the titles previously imported and with considerable technical improvement in the recording. Then to withdraw from circulation the earlier records, Victor offered a special trade-in offer of new Melba records for the old—the new, better Melba records were priced at three dollars, but minus the special packaging. The Victor men were shrewd students of sales psychology!

Victor also had another thorn in the side of the Graphophone Co. The new Zonophone open horn talking machines and records made by the Universal Talking Machine Co., now a subsidiary of Victor, were selling well and at prices intentionally competitive to Columbia's disc line. The Zonophone machines now embodied the Johnson tapered tone arm, were superior in reproduction to the Columbia machines and lower in price than the Victor's. Zonophone issued the first records in America by the great Tetrazzini in January, 1908. These had been recorded in Europe by the International Zonophone Co. and were nine-inch discs. Tetrazzini had also been recorded in Europe by the Gramophone & Typewriter, Ltd. and in March, Victor issued some of these in twelve-inch discs and immediately announced the acquisition of this artist on an exclusive basis. Shortly after Tetrazzini came to the United States, these records pressed from English masters were replaced by domestically recorded discs, following the now familiar pattern.

Meanwhile, Columbia's bid of Bonci to balance off Caruso had been to no avail. To American ears, Caruso was the only, the ideal type of Italian tenor. No erudite discussion of Bonci's alleged superior mastery of the art of bel canto would serve to equate him in the eyes (or ears) of the American opera lovers with Caruso. Nor did the announcement this year by Columbia that it was offering the choicest of the Fonotipia and Odeon recordings by famous European artists to the American public serve to meet the power of the Victor line-up. It may have been true that many of the Odeon and Fonotipia artists were equal in fame to others on the Victor roster—in Europe, but not in America. The initial market for operatic recordings in America had been largely created by Victor advertising based on a canny appreciation of the prestige of Caruso and the association values of the Metropolitan Opera Co. and its highly publicized casts. Victor easily met the challenge of the Columbia-Fonotipia series by instituting as a regular feature of its catalog selected records by "Famous European Artists," which were pressed from masters supplied by its European affiliates.

Neither Marconi's magic nor his name seemed to assist in balancing the scales for the Graphophone Co. in its effort to catch up technically with Victor. The flexible, unbreakable Marconi Velvet-Tone record was a forward looking development which failed perhaps because of the lack of a permanent stylus, or perhaps because a special playing non-permanent needle was required. The standard Columbia double disc records were introduced this year, also laminated, but considerably heavier, inflexible and surfaced with shellac. Difficulty was experienced for years in that the fiber bonding materials would rise up in the pressing, causing undue surface noise. The Columbia recording experts devoted much effort to record the difficult bass registers and the resonance of the recording studio, often at the expense of the more important higher registers and overtones. But the chief technical nemesis of the Graphophone was Johnson's tapered tone arm, which had made the Victrola acceptable whereas the Grafonola without it became audibly inferior. The results of all of these competitive factors may be read in the fact that Victor had been able to pay its stockholders dividends totalling $750,000 in the first ten years and had total assets of $8,000,000, more than double the assets of the Graphophone Co.

On the cylinder front, the picture was also shifting. The Indestructible Record Co., having secured the Lambert and other celluloid record patents, in 1907 had acquired a large factory in Albany, N.Y., and opened a recording laboratory in Brooklyn. This company was amply financed and its production was confined to the manufacture of high quality popular cylinders at low prices. From the viewpoint of the cylinder machine manufacturers, this operation was completely parasitical. After the reorganization of the cylinder industry following the Lippincott debacle, the emphasis became placed on developing the home phonograph market. With the perfection of molding methods the capacity to control the market for records had been placed back in the hands of the parent companies. Then there had developed a competition between the two to see who could put out the most machines to assist in securing the greater share of the record business. Consequently both the National Phonograph Co. and the American Graphophone Co. had come to expect the greater profit to come from the sales of records rather than machines. Thus, when Indestructible began flooding the market with high quality, unbreakable records, even the normally imperturbable Edison began to sit up and take notice, especially as the Indestructible Co. was furnishing a new, heavier reproducer enabling the production of more volume with the new records with existing types of machines.

It would seem that the announcement of the first four-minute wax Amberol records in September, 1908, was Edison's answer to the Indestructible challenge. However, these new cylinders, with double the playing time of the old, were molded of the same fragile, metallic soap compound as the standard two-minute cylinders. It also became necessary to supply adapter kits for the existing Edison phonographs in order to create a market. These kits contained a gear reducer, reproducer, and a set of ten specially-recorded demonstration records selling as a unit from five dollars to eight-fifty, depending on the model to be equipped. Obviously, there was no money made on these kits; but by the end of a year, thousands of the older Edison phonographs were equipped to play the new (200 grooves per inch) longer playing records. This did not prove to be an ideal answer in every respect, however. When the records were fresh and new, the recorded quality and reproduction from the new cylinders of longer playing time were excellent, but they were fragile and easily damaged. As with the standard wax cylinders, accidentally dropping the sapphire reproducing point upon the record would make a hole, producing an annoying click in successive playings, even affecting several adjacent turns. The finer grooves were also more subject to wear and to cutting due to the lack of what would now be called tracking compliance due to the mass of the moving parts of the stylus-diaphragm assembly. These considerations led to frequent break-down of the side walls and repeating.

Despite these technical difficulties, the National Phonograph Co. pushed ahead. The Edison Grand Opera Series initiated in 1906 in the standard two-minute records with a 'B' prefix to the catalog number, had the titles embossed in light blue in the edge of the cylinder and with deluxe cartons were sold for seventy-five cents each. This series was extended into the new four-minute Amberol records, similarly packaged, with prices up to two dollars. Within the next year or so many fine operatic selections were recorded by first rank singers, such as the sopranos Blanche Arral and Bessie Abbot, and tenors Leo Slezak and Riccardo Martin. The difficulty was that the records were not durable enough for the cost involved; consequently, these records did not receive wide circulation.

To further plague Edison, in 1908 another manufacturer of cylinders had also entered the competition. This was the Cleveland Record Co. which was incorporated with a capital of three hundred thousand dollars with the object of supplying principally the mail order market, which had been developed by Babson and other distributors

to large proportions. Probably the last company to enter the field of cylinder machine manufacture was the United Talking Machine Co., which announced the Echo-Phone. However, also in December, 1908, Regina, the music box manufacturer announced the Regina Hexaphone, an automatic coin machine phonograph offering a choice of six cylinders. The year of 1909 was an eventful one in the history of the phonograph. Columbia this year gave up the production of cylinder machines and records. It then made a deal with the Indestructible Record Co. to market their records under the Columbia label. By this move Columbia became enabled to put out four-minute cylinder records to compete with those of Edison, although never producing a machine upon which they were to be played. To curtail the expected effects of this and the other new competition mentioned, the National Phonograph Co. in July had notified all dealers and jobbers that henceforth they were not to be permitted to carry other makes of cylinder records or machines, in accordance with the clause in their contracts to the effect, which had never been rigorously enforced. To emphasize that it meant business, National sued another company engaging in the manufacture of cylinder records, Donnelly and Fahey, on the basis of the Edison owned Aylesworth patent for duplicating records. However, for reasons which are described in proper context, the battle of the cylinders versus the discs was being lost in Europe and the National Phonograph Co. announced that it was closing its European branches and would confine all future recording activities to the United States.

The switch from the cylinders to the discs in the United States became evident this year in more ways than one. The Multiphone Co., manufacturers of the coin machines offering a choice of twenty-four cylinders went into bankruptcy and Gable's Automatic Entertainer, which offered a choice of twenty-four discs was introduced. This somewhat resembled the Multiphone in

Fig. 13-4. The Columbia Grafonola was a popular table model using an inside horn with adjustable louvers.

that it had a large horn protruding from the top.

Some of the attempts to compete with Johnson's internal horn Victrola were quite ludicrous. One was the Orchestraphone, which had a large squarish horn coming out over the top like a kitchen wall cabinet, with doors upon it. The American Graphophone made its earliest bid early in 1907 with the Symphony Grand Graphophone, which had the general appearance of one of the upright pianos of the time, but with little discernable design derived from its function. A cabinet manufacturer by the name of Herzog advertised a line of tall cabinets with folding doors for containing the various standard open horn disc and cylinder machines. This was provided with a shelf for holding the machine, with a grilled aperture above through which the horn, like good children, could be heard but not seen. The space under the shelf was provided with shelves or racks for holding records. Another company by the name of Star made an internal horn talking machine as early as 1908, but for the most part it was 1910 and after before other manufacturers began to

catch up with Johnson's Victrola and began the production of their "olas." [1]

The philosophy that Eldridge R. Johnson sought to apply in the creation of an unique and new kind of furniture design appropriate to the function of the Victor in reproducing all kinds of music in the home was perhaps correct in itself. The music box industry had done much the same thing years before, but not on a mass production basis. The point which must be re-emphasized with respect to what Johnson did, is that the acoustical problems involved in putting the more adequately designed tone passages then available inside the Victrola cabinets were not solved, neither were they ever solved by Johnson nor his technicians.

How then, one may well ask, did the Victor Co. manage to have its greatest financial successes in the years yet to come? The answer is to be found in three important facts; first, Victor's monopoly of the leading Metropolitan stars, and of leading concert and stage celebrities; second, the smartest advertising staff ever assembled anywhere; third, the possession of the Johnson tapered tone-arm patent.

Although the Victrola tone reproduction suffered by the truncating and malformation of the horn in the squeezing of its design into too small a compass, particularly in the lower registers, the tapered tone-arm as an integral part of the total tone-passage design did assist in properly developing the middle and upper register response to at least an acceptable extent. However, prevented from using a tone-arm of expanding cross section by the Johnson patent, the introduction of the Columbia Grafonola (Fig. 13-4) was delayed until 1911 and its reproduction quality was effectively throttled by the necessity of using a tubular tone-arm.

It was the establishment of a style trend through the power of Victor advertising and prestige that forced the other companies to abandon the use of external horn machines. Technically,

[1] Earlier Columbia had introduced a table model advertised as "The Hornless Graphophone."

but two functions were served by the internal horn Victrolas, to transform what had been theretofore considered a "talking machine" into a musical instrument with greater compatability with the home environment and to provide a storage place for records. But another function came to be equally important, that of "conspicuous consumption." It soon became desirable to be the owner of a Victrola, even if one seldom listened to it, much as in the filling of the bookcase with impressive looking books which were never read. So popular was the name "Victrola" to become within a decade that it replaced the use of "phonograph" and "talking machine" in popular use and became almost a generic.

Only Edison was able to effectively circumvent the Johnson tapered tone-arm patent. This was because in Edison reproducing instruments the groove of the record was not required to supply the force to carry the reproducer mechanism across the record. However, it would be a mistake to assume that it did not have any effect on the design of the Edison diamond disc phonograph which was still to come, and which will be dealt with in proper context.

As late as 1920, the Victor Talking Machine Company had secured a court verdict and an injunction against the Brunswick-Balke-Collender Company for infringement of Eldridge R. Johnson's patents on the tapered tone arm and the internal horn talking machine. It seems there had been pending a sub rosa interference proceeding before the U. S. Patent Examiners to determine whether John B. Browning or Eldridge R. Johnson was the true inventor of these features. The Patent Examiners

had upheld Johnson's claim, but the case was finally brought into court by Brunswick, who had bought the Browning patents. On April 4, 1921, the Court of Appeals of the District of Columbia not only held that Browning was the prior inventor of the enclosed horn talking machine with doors; but also that the evidence overwhelmingly indicated that Johnson had not only derived this idea from Browning, but the important tapered tone arm concept as well.

A prominent exhibit in the case was a sketch and description of Browning's machine penciled on the back of a printed dance program dated May 3, 1897. The sketch bore Browning's signature and was witnessed by two ladies, who presumably were at the dance. Evidence was also introduced showing that Browning had subsequently submitted other drawings and a crude model of his instrument to Johnson and that he (Browning) had later been employed by the Victor Talking Machine Company. The sketch dated May 3, 1897 unmistakably shows the tapered tone arm, horizontal louvers, and sound-controlling doors—all features of the internal horn Victrolas made from their introduction in 1906 to the advent of the Orthophonic Victrola in 1925.

The important fact concerning the Victrola is that it enabled the establishment of a style trend backed by the power of Victor advertising and prestige. It was this style trend and not technical excellence that forced the other companies to abandon the use of external horn machines. In the naming of the Columbia "Grafonolas" and the Edison "Amberolas" is to be found the sincerest tribute to the accomplishments of Eldridge R. Johnson!

CHAPTER 14

THE EDISON DIAMOND DISC PHONOGRAPH

RUMORS circulated from time to time in trade circles that Edison was contemplating the manufacture of a disc machine and records. That he could have done so at any time he wished cannot be doubted in view of the patent situation which existed in any year prior to his decision to do so, despite contemporary popular belief to the contrary.

In the first patent of the industry, applied for December 24, 1877, Edison had said:

"It is obvious that many forms of mechanism may be used to give motion to the material to be indented. For instance, a revolving plate may have a volute spiral etc."

Also in his important British Patent No. 1644 of April 24, 1878, which had been applied for and granted before any other phonographic patent to any other person, Edison had said:

"The phonogram may be in the form of a disc, a sheet, and endless belt, a cylinder, a roller, or a belt, or strip, and the marks are to be either in straight lines, spiral, zig-zag or in any other convenient form."

It is evident, therefore, that contrary to the popular impression prevalent for so many years, Edison could have engaged in the manufacture of disc phonographs and records whenever he

wished. Another common misconception is that he was limited by his patents to the use of tin foil. Not only is the British patent referred to above in evidence to the contrary, but a Caveat filed in the U. S. Patent Office on March 8, 1878 stated:

"The material for recording upon may be various metallic foils or sheets, such as tin-foils of various compositions, iron, copper, brass, lead, tin, cadmium, zinc; also, paper and various absorbent materials may be used and coated with paraffine and other hard hydro-carbons, waxes, gums, lacs, and these may be used to record on directly, or they may have a metallic surface; - - -"

Moreover, in one of his later patents which had been granted, Edison had claimed:

"- - - a graphic sound record on a disc-like or cylindrical blank formed of a sinuous groove of substantially uniform depth and width, as distinguished from a phonograph wherein these dimensions of a record groove are not uniform."

A direct comparison of the wording of this claim and that of the Jones patent or the Johnson patent which displaced the latter, after a strange lapse of nine years, reveals no essential difference in meaning, even to a semanticist!

As has been observed previously, Edison had built an experimental spring-motor disc phonograph in 1878. A completely designed disc machine was included in his British patent of that year. However, for many years Edison was firmly convinced that the technical superiority of the cylinder as a moving surface would ultimately result in public preference for it, insuring as it did a constant speed beneath the recording and reproducing styli.

By 1907, some of Edison's business associates had begun not to share his confidence in the eventual supremacy of the cylinders. The spectacular gains made by Victor had not gone unnoticed. However, Edison often said that because someone else was making money was not a sufficient reason for making a change. So it was with considerable trepidation that his advisors began once more to urge action to meet competition. An important factor in this situation was the fragility and short playing time of the standard Edison cylinders. To quiet the complaints of his phonograph associates, Edison finally agreed to make certain immediate changes.

To meet the competition of the longer playing time of the larger discs, 3½ minutes for the 12″ disc as against the 2 minutes for the standard cylinders then in use, Edison introduced the Amberol record with 200 grooves per inch which would play for 4 minutes. The patent application upon this record was filed January 3, 1907 and the first records were issued in 1908, so it may be seen that not much time was lost in tooling up for producing feed device attachments for various types of Edison machines in order to play them. This necessitated gear reducing mechanisms and new reproducers. (See Fig. 14-1.)

The new Amberol cylinders were molded from a somewhat harder metallic soap compound than had been used previously for the standard 2 minute cylinders. Also, being harder, they were more brittle and because the unit area pressure from the stylus was greatly increased, these records were more easily cut in playing, or otherwise damaged. As the Indestructible Record Co. was now introducing a special heavier reproducer for use with its celluloid records for use on the Edison machine, the shortcomings of the fragile wax-like Edison cylinders were becoming quite obvious.

By 1910, some of Edison's associates were so concerned by the competitive situation that they decided to initiate a secret project in experimental disc recording, hoping to convert Edison if the results were promising. However, the experiments were hardly well under way when the ubiquitous Mr. Edison discovered them. Instead of opposing the project, Edison enthusiastically endorsed the program of developing disc records and the creation of a new disc phonograph. Somewhat to the dismay of some, Edison also assumed full and complete leadership. Moreover, he also expanded the objectives to include a search for better materials for the manufacture of cylinder records, as well. A result was that instead of possibly resorting to the lateral recording method, emphasis was directed by Edison towards adapting the more highly perfected vertical method to the flat disc surface, plus the development of suitable recording and reproducing

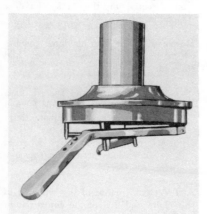

Fig. 14-1. Edison Model H reproducer had sapphire point with a tip radius of .0047 designed to play the new 4-minute records.

Fig. 14-2. An early Edison recording machine for vertically-cut records. (Courtesy of *Edison National Historic Site.*)

mechanisms. An early Edison recording machine is shown in Fig. 14-2.

It should be observed that to this time and for many years to come only the vertical-cut method employed two important requisites which are now acknowledged as indispensible to correct sound reproduction from phonograph records, grooves of uniform dimensions, and accurately ground permanent styli. In 1899 Edison had made experimental wax-type cylinders with 400 threads per inch—considerably finer than the microgrooves of today.[1] But the molding method had not yet been perfected and the wax blanks were not hard enough to permit the commercial employment of such a fine groove. Now Edison was producing the new Amberol cylinders with 200 threads per inch, using a somewhat harder me-

tallic soap compound than used for the 100 thread per inch standard cylinders, for he had been denied the use of celluloid for molding records since 1903 by an adverse decision in the case of National Phonograph Co. vs. Lambert Co.

The year of 1909 was to be the year of decisions for Edison and his associates. On the one hand, the Amberol cylinders were fragile and easily damaged, something had to be done to provide a better cylinder record surface. On the other hand, the Victrola and the discs were sweeping the country. Especially in the city stores and homes, the open-horn phonographs and talking machines were being rapidly supplanted by the Victrolas. Thomas A. Edison was now quite aware of the need for drastic action.

The first progress from the new experimental project came in improved recording technics. Heretofore, the damping of the glass diaphragms used

[1] One of these 400 thread per inch grooved cylinders is in the vault of the Edison National Historic Site at West Orange, New Jersey.

in the recording heads had been accomplished by the use of rubber rings. Now it was discovered possible to use viscous damping, the edges of the diaphragm floating in a semi-fluid—a principle now used for damping ribbon type pick-ups, tone-arms, and moving-coil devices. The improvement in quality was especially pronounced in the recording of what are now called transients, ambience, and in capturing the elusive sibillants. So spectacular were the tests when reproduced by means of the improved Edison Triumph phonograph with the cygnet horn (Fig. 14-3) that it was decided to immediately start recording disc masters with this cutter, in anticipation of the develop-

Fig. 14-3. Edison Triumph phonograph with Cygnet horn. It had a triple spring motor and speed regulator.

ment of a machine to be commercially produced to play them. There was no particular difficulty in making wax blanks for recording purposes in either the cylinder or disc form, nor was there any great obstacle to the setting up of a recording lathe for either type of recording.

Early in 1910, Edison's recording expert Thomas Graf and an assistant by the name of Bocchi were sent to Europe to make cylinder and disc masters. The same recorder, made a bit heavier, was used for the discs. The same wax was used for both cylinders and discs, with test playbacks with the same lightweight reproducer. These facts explain, according to Will Hayes, veteran Edison recording expert when interviewed prior to his death in 1958, why the vaults of the Edison National Historic Site contain scores of 12″ disc waxes by famous European artists which were never processed, as well as a number of others which had been converted to test pressings only after a lapse of several years, but none being made available to the public.[2] It seems that technical difficulties, perhaps having to do with the gold-sputtering process, prevented the successful processing of the 12″ diameter discs for a number of years. As a matter of fact, 12″ Edison discs were not sold to the public until 1927 and then only in the form of the Edison forty-minute long-playing record. However, after the introduction of the High-Speed process in 1921, which involved the abandonment of gold-sputtering, 12″ sampler discs for circulation to dealers only were made for some time. However, this limitation on diameter in the earlier years was not as serious as it may appear, for the 10″ Edison disc played for better than four minutes. The groove spacing of the new discs was 150 threads per inch, midway between that of the standard cylinders and the new Amberol cylinders.

[2] A 10″ LP Vinylite rerecording of six of these 12″ discs was released for promotional purposes by the Voicewriter Division of Thomas A. Edison, Inc., in 1956.

The new facility in cutting records with the viscous-damped recording heads had two important effects. First, the increased breadth and volume now incised into the records made it imperative that an improved material be found for molding the four-minute cylinders, for the metallic wax compound was not standing up well in service. Second, due to the variation in surface speed beneath the reproducing stylus in reproducing the discs, it was even more imperative that a new and harder material than heretofore used for any records should be discovered for the surfacing of the contemplated new discs.

Some of the two-minute Indestructible celluloid cylinders then in use on Regina Hexaphones and other early period "juke boxes" had rolled up indisputable evidence of durability. However, prior attempts to use celluloid for discs had proven unsuccessful. One of these was the Neophone disc, made in England beginning in 1904. Pathe was now producing vertical-cut discs in Europe. The Pathe discs were pressed in a shellac composition differing but little from the lateral disc Victor records. Pathe discs were played by a sapphire ball stylus of rather large diameter, so the grooves were shallow and wide; consequently, there was less playing time for a given diameter than even with the conventional lateral disc, which then had about 90 threads per inch. To offset this, Pathe records were regularly issued in diameters up to 14". (Neophone discs had been made up to 20" diameters.) [3] Due to the difficulty of securing and maintaining a permanently flat plane in a plastic molded disc record, the sapphire ball used to play them would often bounce out of the groove, either for lack of what would now be called "compliance" in the diaphragm-stylus assembly, or from the vibration of someone walking across the floor. This would send the tonearm and sound-box skittering across the record, alarming the listeners, but usually without damage to the disc! To avoid such difficulties, it was determined from the beginning by the Edison experimenters to use a stylus of smaller diameter, to impose more weight upon the record and to use precision ground diamond styli. The tip diameter was to be about .0075 mil. The maximum depth of groove was determined by the minimum land to be left between the grooves. In this way the same diameter cutting and playback styli could be used for both the 200 groove per inch cylinders and the 150 groove per inch discs. However, the greater weight envisioned as necessary for disc reproduction imposed a considerably greater unit-area pressure on the discs than on the cylinders.

For these reasons a special crew of expert chemists was brought together to develop the best possible materials to be used with each type of record. This part of the project was placed in charge of Jonas W. Aylesworth under the over-all direction of Walter Miller, both of whom had been with Edison for many years and had been largely responsible for the successful development of the molding method. The intensity of the drive is indicated by the number of patents issued to these men and Mr. Edison within the next three years. The phonograph project was but one of several then under way. In 1909, Edison was still a factor to be reckoned with in the motion picture industry. The recent improvements in recording technics were also tangent to this important Edison activity and renewed his long dormant interest in talking pictures. To illustrate the diversity of Edison's interests at this time, in the four year period from 1909 through 1912, Edison received some 72 patents, of which only 23 were phonographic improvements! Edison was the active director of all of his research projects and closely observed the progress of all experimentation. He would circulate from place to place, making pertinent suggestions and comments which often bore fruit in patents issued to others. It was about this time that he

---

[3] The approaching invasion of Pathe-Freres was undoubtedly an important factor in the decision of Edison to enter the disc market.

organized the New Jersey Patent Co. as a means of pooling patents and arranging for the payment of royalties.

Not all improvements were patented, however. The machines for grinding and polishing the cutting styli, the reproducer styli, and the methods for mounting the styli were kept secret. Mr. Theodore Edison, son of the inventor, recently disclosed that the diamonds were mounted to the shanks by electroplating with nickel which plates under tension. The competitors never did solve that one! Virtually the same process then used with the cylinders was adapted with the disc waxes. They were rendered conductive by the electrostatic gold deposition process (or sputtering) then plated with other metals, in the case of discs, with nickel.

Experiments with various surfaces for the cylinder records resulted in the adoption of a brilliant blue celluloid composition, around a rigid supporting core of plaster of Paris. Later, a royal purple color was used to designate the celebrity and grand opera series. As a reacting surface for actuating the reproducer stylus assembly, this new celluloid composition was about as smooth and, if anything, harder than the vinyl compounds used for discs today. However, it was not deemed hard enough for the new discs. It was also considered necessary to provide a rigid, non-warping core for the discs, for an absolutely plane surface was required where the recording action was perpendicular to that plane as was also the tracking force. A core was developed for the new discs by compressing under great pressure a compound of wood flour, china clay, and an asphaltic binder.

For the surface Aylesworth and his associates developed a phenolic resin varnish which he named "Condensite." Unbeknownst to Edison and Aylesworth, not far away up on the Hudson, Baekeland and another group of chemists had been equally hard at work seeking for virtually the same thing for other purposes. They also developed a material similar to Condensite which they named "Bakelite." Thus Edison and his associates came to share the honor with Baekeland and his colleagues for the founding of the modern thermosetting plastics industry.

That Edison still considered the cylinder record the ideal surface is indicated by the fact that he chose it for the Kinetophone—the first theater talking pictures, introduced in 1912. For this he used 5½-inch diameter cylinders 8 inches long, which were really giant size blue Amberol cylinders, with a similar plaster of Paris core.

However, the perfection of molding mechanisms for the new disc records required a considerable amount of time and much fruitless experimentation before all of the "bugs" had been eliminated. The first experimental disc machines for playing them were evolved quite directly from the improved Amberola cylinder machines which had been developed for playing the Blue Amberol cylinders with greater volume. The improved cylinder reproducer, Fig. 14-4, employed a laminated diaphragm made of some 20 layers of rice paper impregnated with shellac, with a stiffening cork disc on the side towards the woven silk cord which connected it to the stylus lever. The new disc reproducer, Fig. 14-5, was of similar design, with a slightly larger diaphragm and a heavier floating weight. A stock Herzog cabinet, such as was sold to the trade

Fig. 14-4. Edison reproducer designed to play the blue Amberol cylinder records.

Fig. 14-5. Heavily weighted Edison disc reproducer had a diamond point. (Courtesy of *Edison National Historic Site.*)

for concealing the overhead horn cylinder and disc machines, was equipped with a spring-driven disc turntable and an overhead horn made of sheet iron. The tone arm was propelled across the record by a feed-screw device. Like the internal horn table model Amberolas which were introduced about this time, the reproduction suffered from air leaks in the slip-joints in the tone-arm assembly, just as had the lateral disc talking machines.

Edison solved this problem in his Concert model cylinder phonographs, made both with external and internal horns. This mechanism was also equipped with a built-in gear shift to enable the playing of both the two- and four-minute wax records and a combination reproducer with a turn-over stylus assembly for playing the two types operated by turning a button at the front (Fig. 14-6) very similar to the turn-over cartridges of today. The in-

ternal horn machine was named the "Concert Amberola" and sold for $200. In the bottom of the well-built cabinet were four drawers for records.

Unquestionably, Edison's National Phonograph Co. had been losing ground rapidly to the competition of the discs and Edison, personally, is often held responsible by uninformed critics for this situation. Not only was Edison busy with other research and industrial ac-

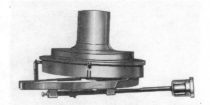

Fig. 14-6. Edison Model O reproducer had two styli selected by means of the knob extending to the right. Could play either 2- or 4-minute cylinder records.

tivities of equal or greater importance during these years, but it should be remembered that since the breakdown of Lippincott's local phonograph company plan due to the machinations of the Graphophone Co. executives, his phonograph enterprise had been the target of a seemingly unending series of lawsuits. It was 1908 before the last of these was settled by the decision in a case of National Phonograph Co. versus Devega, of New York City, involving the New York Phonograph Co., one of the original phonograph companies. These opposition-inspired suits cost Thomas A. Edison and the National Phonograph Co. many millions of dollars and diverted much money and effort which otherwise might have been devoted to research and product improvement during the critical years of phonographic development.

Many of the basic United States patents were about to expire and consequently another European invasion loomed. The decline of the cylinder industry in England had resulted in the acceptance by Russell Hunting of the post as director of all recording activities for the French firm of Pathe-Freres, who had recording laboratories in the principal European countries, and were now manufacturing both cylinders and discs. Hunting's successful work with this company culminated with a decision to attempt a conquest of the American market. To do this Hunting was sent to New York City in 1910 to outfit a factory and recording laboratory preparatory to launching Pathe disc machines (Fig. 14-7) and records. For a time, the records were made much as the Pathe discs in Europe; that is, center-start, with the

Fig. 14-7. A Pathe spring-wound phonograph using a diaphragm type reproducer responding to vertically cut records.

groove beginning at the label and spiralling outward. There were good technical reasons for this. One was that centrifugal force naturally tends to throw a gliding weight resting upon a revolving horizontal surface outward; hence, center-start records offered less resistance to the passage of the sapphire ball. Another reason was that owing to the shallowness of the grooves, at peak volume the undulations tended to throw the reproducing ball out of the groove. This tendency was lessened with the center-start records. This was always one of the drawbacks of the Pathe method, however. Records which were slightly warped gave trouble also. Believing in the technical superiority of the vertical method, Hunting and his men were smart in designing the Pathe machines with a universal tone arm, so that they might be used to play either lateral records or the new Pathe discs. This set the example for other companies which were to enter the field during the next decade, such as The Aeolian Co. and the Brunswick-Balke-Collender Co.

Acoustically, the Pathe machines were unable to demonstrate the superiority of the Pathe records. With the tapered tone-arm patents firmly held by the astute Mr. Johnson, the design of the tone-arm system of the new Pathe suffered in precisely the same way as did that of the Grafonola. In other words, the possession of a superior internal tone passage system by Victor served to offset quite completely any superiority which inhered in the Pathe record. The advent of Pathe again served to stir up conjecture in the trade as to the possibility of Edison entering the disc field. All was silence at the Edison plant however, except for continual sounds from recording studios and the testing of cylinders and machines.

As soon as the last ghost of the Lippincott debacle had been laid in 1908, there had begun at the Edison laboratories one of the most intensive drives for improvement in the history of the art. Up to this time most of the phonographic patents in the portfolio of the National Phonograph Co. had been granted to the "old man," himself, as he was known to his associates. In 1910 a reorganization of the Edison companies was effected. All of the several manufacturing enterprises controlled by Edison and which had been organized as separate corporations, such as the National Phonograph Co., were brought into one corporation and named Thomas A. Edison, Inc. and the former corporations dissolved. The phonograph business was continued as the "Phonograph Division" and the dictating machine business as the "Ediphone Division." There were also separate divisions for the storage battery, cement manufacturing, and others.

Prior to this reorganization, another corporation had been organized as a patent holding corporation as a means of pooling the patents of Edison and his associates. In 1909 a series of patents were issued to J. P. Ott, one of Edison's key men in phonographic research, which were assigned by him to this company. In 1910 a patent was issued to W. F. Messer on a phonogram reproducing apparatus, but this was assigned by him to the new Thomas A. Edison, Inc. This was the same Messer who had been granted a celluloid cylinder patent in 1902, after Edison's prior patent had been held invalid and anticipated by his own experimental use of it. This earlier Messer patent had supplied the basis for both the Lambert and the Indestructible Record Co. operations and this patent date appeared on all of the cylinders of the latter company.

In 1910 and 1911, other phonographic improvements were patented by Walter Miller, veteran recording expert of the Edison laboratory, and E. L. Aiken, another Edison associate. Stephen Porter, more familiarly known as "Steve" Porter, the recording comedian, also invented a laterally recorded disc of constantly varying depth to compensate for needle wear, then the bugaboo of the lateral record method. Porter assigned a half interest to Walter Miller, indicating that both were toying with the idea of a lateral disc record at that time. That Edison had no intention of abandoning the cylinders seems proven by the fact that until after the Edison Diamond Disc phonograph was actually produced in 1912, the larger number of patented improvements were on cylinder records or devices.

Because of the failure of the wax-type Amberol records to stand up in service, Edison reverted to the use of

Fig. 14-8. Edison Amberola Model B mechanism had a moving mandrel and starting lever. (Courtesy of Edison National Historic Site.)

celluloid for the molding of these records only.[4] These Edison "Blue Amberol" records, as they were named, were brilliantly smooth, with the titles indented clearly in white in one end, contrasting beautifully with the rich blue. Among certain collectors these records are prized because of their clarity and naturalness. Rerecordings have been made from the best copies of these blue Amberol cylinders and which excel in brilliance. The diamond was used for the stylus of an improved reproducer employing a much heavier floating weight enabling the extraction of more energy and therefore greater volume than was feasible with the metallic soap records. As in introducing

the earlier wax four-minute records, kits were supplied for equipping most of the standard Edison machines, including the necessary feed gear mechanism, a reproducer, and a set of special records—all at a nominal cost. Here again, as so many times in the Edison saga, a development of technical importance was introduced commercially too late. Aside from Pathe-Freres, Edison was virtually the only manufacturer of both cylinder machines and records left in the world at that time.

The Edison Amberola phonograph (Fig. 14-8) previously mentioned as having a mandrel which moved, rather than the reproducer, played these new records when equipped with the new, heavier reproducer, with excellent tone quality. An open horn machine of the same type played them even better! The reproducer developed for these models became the prototype of the later diamond disc reproducer; in fact, the stylus diameter remained the same, 0.0075 mil at the tip. After the introduction of the Blue Amberol records, a line of internal horn Amberolas was developed, using slip-joint reproducer arms to connect the horn with the reproducer which was fed across the record in the usual manner by means of a feed screw. (See Fig. 14-9.) Although less expensive to manufacture, none of the later models of this type were as good as those with fixed reproducer and air-tight horn assembly.

In 1912, there was a veritable flood of phonographic patents issued to the Edison associates. Among the most notable were those in the name of Jonas W. Aylesworth. Titles indicating the sphere of his research include "Forming Phenolic Condensation Products," "Fusable Phenolic Resin and Forming Same," "Electrotyping," and "Phonograph Record Molding Apparatus," the latter of which he was co-patentee with E. L. Aiken. One or two patents on "Talking Machines" were issued to Frank L. Dyer, Edison's attorney and his personal biographer.[5] Other inven-

---

[4] This involved the purchase of rights from Philpot in England.

[5] *Thomas Alva Edison, Inventor*, Dyer and Martin.

Fig. 14-9. The Edison Amberola Model 75 with storage cover open. Regular feed-screw drive moved the reproducer across the cylinder. (Courtesy of Edison National Historic Site.)

tors who at this time assigned patents to either the New Jersey Patent Co. or to Thomas A. Edison, Inc. included Leslie A. Brown of Bedford, Indiana; Charles P. Carter, Kingston, N. Y.; Herbert L. Dyke and Charles L. Hubbard, East Orange, N. J.; Newman H. Holland, East Orange, N. J.; Frank D. Lewis, Elizabeth, N. J.; Alexander N. Pierman, Newark, N. J.; Charles Schiffl, Peter Weber and Albert F. Wurth, of the Edison staff.

Although the Edison disc phonograph was first produced in the later part of 1912, the amazing fact is that virtually all of the thirty or more patents by associates or assignors were upon cylinder machines or cylinder record improvements. Nor was the perfection of the Edison phonograph largely due to the work of others with Edison getting the credit, as has sometimes been alleged. In 1912 Edison alone received nine patents on phonographic devices, some of which were upon essentials of the forthcoming Edison disc phonograph. In the two years prior he had received ten other phonographic patents, mostly applicable to cylinder machines and records. During the three years of this intensive drive to improve the phonograph, Edison had personally received a total of forty-eight patents on inventions ranging from mining and ore crushing machinery to storage batteries. Edison was the first master of collaborative research and pointed the way for the great research laboratories of the present.

Edison was more than the director of the world's first great research laboratory, he was also an industrialist and an organizer of factory production methods. From the first, the manufacture of parts for the Edison cylinder phonograph mechanisms were to high standards of materials and workmanship. After 1889, parts were standardized to extremely close tolerances and made to be interchangeable. It has often been said that Edison learned of precision manufacturing and mass production methods from his friend Henry Ford. Actually, while the latter may have been true to a very limited extent, Edison was practicing precision manufacture before the model T was born!

Efficiency in using up existing materials was also a characteristic of Edison design and production practice. Cabinets which had been originally designed for the large cylinder Amberola phonograph for the National Phonograph Co. were also later used for enclosing the early air-tight horn reproducer assembly disc mechanisms, typical in acoustical design of all acoustic Edison disc machines from this time forward. Even the space below the mechanism, which formerly just neatly held four sliding drawers for cylinder storage, now was rearranged to accommodate two drawers for the vertical filing of the ten-inch Edison discs. Some will say that this kind of efficiency is achieved at the expense of the best possible results. However, it must be borne in mind that the theory which has been so often cited as governing the lowest fundamental frequency which an acoustic horn will reproduce, has seemingly been violated by the Edison horn for many years. In the Edison method, the reproducer diaphragm was loaded by a floating weight which compelled it to follow the longer sinusoidal undulations in a manner akin to the powerful action of a voice-coil dynamic

speaker. Thus, much lower fundamental bass notes could be reproduced than could be expected from a lateral disc talking machine with a horn of equal length and orifice diameter, just as a dynamic speaker would reproduce a lower note without a baffle than a magnetic speaker with equal diameter cone.

This fact may in part explain the uncanny fidelity eventually achieved after another of those protracted periods of intensive experimentation so typical of Edison. One only has to read a few of the specifications of the many patents issued from 1912 to 1915 to Edison and his associates to realize to some extent the colossal proportions of the research and development program which was instituted at this time. Laboratory notebooks covering thousands of carefully tabulated experiments still exist to attest to the exhaustive research and minute detail lavished upon every component of the new disc phonograph.

Visitors to reconstructed Menlo Park, as relocated at Dearborn, Michigan, by Henry Ford, may see many of the models of the inventions of the earlier days. At the Ford Museum, also at Dearborn, may be seen many of the later, evolutionary forms of the phonograph and the graphophone. However, it was at West Orange, New Jersey, that the Amberol record, the Blue Amberol record, and the Edison Diamond Disc Phonograph had been created. Here, in the keeping of the Edison National Historic Site, is to be found the bulk of the experimental data and the most convincing evidence concerning one of the industry's most idealistic accomplishments—the precise re-creation of the human voice.

This admirable result was achieved through the purely empirical methods of Edison, similar in every way to the prior search at Menlo Park, 35 years before, for a suitable material for the filament of the incandescent lamp. Some may recall that even a hair from the red beard of Mackenzie was tried and that Japanese bamboo, brought back by an emissary from a world-wide hunt for the best fibre for carbonizing, finally provided a commercially employable solution. So now it was in the search for record materials, for compositions of diaphragms, of materials and designs for horns, and of governors and driving mechanisms. The size and shape of grooves, the number of threads per inch, optimum recording and reproducing speeds, maximum and minimum number of vibrations per second were the considerations to be decided by test after test, results tabulated and checked off methodically. The design, therefore, of the Edison disc phonograph was evolutionary and empirical, with changes determined largely by the process of trial and error, with little attention to academic theory.

There is an unfortunate tendency on the part of many of our contemporary theoretical scientists and science writers to look down upon the empiricism of the work of Edison. Yet there is not a scientist alive today who has been able to advance the useful store of human knowledge by a tenth of that contributed through his own and the collective efforts which he guided.

During the height of the development period, fate again stepped in and dealt a powerful blow. On December 9, 1914, a fire broke out in a film inspection booth. Before it could be subdued, six buildings of brick and wood had been destroyed, as well as the flammable contents of seven reinforced concrete structures. Although in his usual indomitable fashion Edison had ordered reconstruction begun immediately, much valuable material was irretrievably lost. Many priceless master records were destroyed, both cylinder and disc, as well as a great deal of experimental apparatus. Production machinery and supplies of raw materials were also lost, hastening the effects of war shortages which were already beginning to hamper industry. The British blockade of Germany had cut off machine tools and essential chemicals from the United States, then quite dependent upon Germany for many important items. As the British required all of their own

limited production of phenol, the supply sources for the United States were entirely cut off. At this time none was produced commercially in the western hemisphere. Large quantities were already required for the production of the new Edison disc records . By this time Thomas A. Edison, Inc. was reputedly the largest consumer of phenol in America. Another important chemical used in the manufacture of the Edison discs was paraphenylenediamine, also imported from Germany.

Faced with the necessity of stopping record production, Edison contacted various chemical manufacturers of the United States to see if they would undertake the production of synthetic phenol. The most favorable reports were that it would take from six to nine months before deliveries could be promised. Edison then set to work to study all existing formulae and methods of manufacture and perfected a new process. Within eighteen days after the building of a new plant was begun, a quantity of half a ton per day, enough to supply the disc records needs, was being produced right at West Orange. Within a month the plant was turning out a ton per day and the surplus was being sold to other hard-hit manufacturers. This was but typical of the Edison reaction to adversity!

By 1915, it was variously estimated that from two to three million dollars had been spent in the development of the Edison disc phonograph, aside from the losses incurred from the fire and the shortage of phenol. This is not to say that all of Edison's decisions were wise ones in the light of the knowledge we now have. For instance, for some unfathomable reason he decided that the labels of the new disc records should not carry the name of the artist. It is true that the record sleeves did sometimes divulge this information. After paying large sums to first-rank operatic stars, including Alessandro Bonci, Lucrezia Bori, Aino Ackte and Emmy Destinn, it is difficult to understand why their names should have been omitted from the discs. The early labels contained the Edison trade-mark, a photo of Edison, title of the selection, composer, and was pressed into the glossy black surface of the record itself by means of a half-tone electrotype. This produced a self pattern similar to that produced by acid-etched designs in glass, very attractive, but difficult to read. It is a question as to which killed the most sales, the monotonous descriptions of the arias given on the reverse sides of most of the celebrity records by elocutionist Harry E. Humphrey, or the mistaken policy of not providing readable labels with complete information. To make matters even more confusing, especially to the clerks at the music counters, the catalog numbers were stamped in three places around the edge of the record. Often one had to look at all three to find one that was completely legible!

At this time all of the Victor red seal records were single sided and had a maximum playing time of about 3½ minutes. By hindsight, it is easy to see that it would have been much better to have capitalized on the longer playing time of the Edison discs, and to have placed a musical selection on each side. This would have more than offset the double thickness of the Edison discs, which was necessitated by the need for an absolutely plane surface for reproduction vertically.

The ten-inch Edison discs weighed ten ounces as against an average of perhaps eight ounces for the twelve-inch Victor record of that period. The Columbia records were laminated, in that sense similar to the Edison discs. These discs were stronger than the Victor records and were also thicker, the twelve-inch discs being fully as cumbersome as the Edison discs. However, these were errors of manufacturing judgment and salesmanship, rather than technical faults as far as reproduction of sound was concerned. Regardless of these initial mistakes, the intense striving to produce a more perfect reproducing instrument went on.

Just how successfully the Edison research activities had been conducted

was revealed publicly on October 21, 1915, through an event having a rather remote connection with the Panama-Pacific Exposition in San Francisco. It seems the exposition authorities had named this "Edison Day," for the reason that it was the thirty-sixth anniversary of his first successful incandescent lamp. Mr. and Mrs. Edison were guests of the Exposition for the occasion.

Meanwhile, in the library of the Edison laboratory at West Orange, New Jersey, another distinguished group of visitors had gathered to witness the first demonstration of the new Official Laboratory Model Edison phonograph. The beautiful opera soprano, Anna Case, who had recently scored a great success at the Metropolitan was also present. To make a long story short, Miss Case sang for the assembled guests in the library. More than this, she sang in direct comparison with her recorded voice as reproduced on the new Edison instrument. The first selection was the aria "Depuis le Jour" from Charpentier's "Louise." To the amazement of all, they were unable to detect any difference between the voice of the singer and that coming from the phonograph. The recorded voice of Anna Case was carried to Thomas A. Edison at the Panama-Pacific Exposition in San Francisco by long-distance telephone.

Transcontinental telephony was inaugurated this same year through the use of vacuum tube amplification. What irony that the devices which one day were to doom the Edison phonograph should have been used to convey to the inventor the proof of a successful consummation of his long time goal—to be able to exactly re-create the human voice!

Christine Miller, contralto, also sang on this occasion in direct comparison with her recording of "Ah, Mio Son" from "Prophete." The result was the same, the audience found it impossible to distinguish between the voice of the singer and the phonographic reproduction. Miss Case, when interviewed some time later about this first audacious tone-test said,

"Everybody, including myself, were astonished to find that it was impossible to distinguish between my own voice, and Mr. Edison's re-creation of it."

The following year on the 28th of April, Marie Rappold, dramatic soprano of the Metropolitan, sang before an audience of 2,500 in Carnegie Hall in New York. Again the precision of voice reproduction attainable with the New Edison phonograph was demonstrated. Eminent music critics acquiesced in the expressments of amazement on the part of those who heard this new comparison test. The music critic of *The New York Tribune* said, "- - - Edison snares the soul of music," and the critic of *The New York Globe* described the instrument as "The phonograph with a soul."

Within the next year or two, hundreds of similar tone-tests were conducted in scores of cities over the United States and Canada, in which a number of vocal and instrumental artists participated. Among the more well-known artists who at this time, or later, permitted public comparisons to be made were the following: sopranos Frieda Hempel, Claudio Muzio, Yvonne de Treville, and Alice Verlet; contraltos Carolina Lazzari, Merle Alcock, and Margarete Matzenauer; tenors Jacques Urlus, Karl Jorn, Giovanni Zenatello, and Guido Ciccolini; and bassos Henri Scott, Arthur Middleton, and Otto Goritz. Instrumentalists also played in direct comparison with their recordings on some occasions, including the noted violinists Albert Spaulding and Vasa Prihoda.

In giving these tone-tests, the artist would play or sing in unison with the phonographic reproduction, stopping from time to time permitting the phonograph to carry on alone. From time to time the singer or instrumentalist would sing or play in obbligato to the recorded melody. Thus, a most critical and direct comparison could be made of the timbre and nuances of the voice and the reproduction of it. A startling climax was

provided when during the latter part of the program the stage would be darkened, ostensibly so that the auditors could guess as to when the artist was singing and when not. Suddenly the lights would come on, revealing that the singer was no longer on the stage. Invariably, each person in the audience would give an involuntary gasp, as he realized that he had been utterly unable to tell when the artist had actually ceased singing.

Understandably, there were many skeptics who were not prepared to believe. During one of the later tone-test recitals given by Miss Case, Roy T. Burke of the Edison staff sat in a box with one of New York's best known advertising writers and a well-known artist. When Miss Case was about to sing her first number with the New Edison, the artist said, "I'll show you that I can detect a difference. I'll sit down on the floor, so that I cannot see the stage, then when Miss Case stops and the phonograph sings alone, I'll press your foot; when Miss Case starts to sing in unison with the instrument, I'll press your foot again."

Miss Case stopped singing and the phonograph continued alone, but no signal came from the critic seated on the floor of the box. Again Miss Case resumed singing with the phonograph, but again no signal. Twice she sang with the instrument, twice it sang alone, but never a pressure on the foot from the artist. Upon completion of the song, the artist arose and said, "She sang with it all the time, you can't fool me." Even though the others in the box assured the artist he was wrong, he steadfastly refused to believe it.

Not only in New York but all over the United States prominent music critics from leading newspapers attended similar tone-tests and were uniformly generous with their praise of Edison's great accomplishment. *The Boston Herald,* for instance, said of Christine Miller's recital;

"Just how true and faithful is this Re-creation of the human voice was best illustrated when Miss Christine Miller sang a duet with herself, it being impossible to distinguish between the singer's living voice and its Re-creation by the instrument that bears the stamp of Edison's genius,"

The phonograph withstood the test of direct comparison with the voices of male singers equally well. Of a tone-test given by Thomas Chalmers, then leading baritone of the Boston Opera Company, the critic of the *Pittsburgh Leader* said;

"Unless one watched the singer's lips it was quite impossible to determine from the quality of tone whether Mr. Chalmers was singing or whether he was not, the tone of the re-creation being exactly like his own living voice in every shade of tonal color."

Of another tone-test given in London, Ontario, by tenor Hardy Williamson, the *London Advertiser* said, in part;

"The most sensitive ear could not detect the slightest difference between the tone of the singer and the tone of the mechanical device. Both were equally liquid, flexible, and vibrant."

However, not only did the general public sit up and take notice of these remarkably convincing tone-tests,—so also did the opposition leaders of the talking machine industry. No applause was forthcoming, but their actions bespoke their concern. For many years past there had been a virtual truce between the Victor Talking Machine Co. and the Edison interests. Knowing the attitudes and policies of Eldridge R. Johnson and Thomas A. Edison, this is quite understandable. As long as a clear cut demarcation was possible, Edison adhering to the cylinders and Johnson to the discs, there was little inclination on either side to incite open and costly hostilities. In fact, for many years the products of both companies had been handled in several territories by the same jobbers. But now the Edison disc was arousing tremendous popular interest and the Victor executives began to worry, and for good reason. R. H. Macy in New York dumped Victrolas and Victor records on the market at cut prices. Other dealers followed suit. To plug the break in the price dyke Victor sued Straus, owner of Macy's on the basis of the price agreement embodied in the sales contract. At first the case against Straus was dismissed, but Victor won upon appeal. During this litigation other Victor dealers became frightened and though not many dared to cut prices, they refrained from buying except on a hand-to-mouth basis. This accounts for the comparative scarcity of certain Victor records issued during this period.

This was an unprecedented situation for Johnson. To meet it the Victor Talking Machine Co. sued Thomas A. Edison, Inc. for infringement of its Johnson patents 814,786 and 1,060,550. The former was the famous tapered tone-arm patent with a total of 42 claims and the other a late patent upon an idea which had been used earlier upon open horn machines. However, the Edison method involved the swinging of the entire reproducer-horn assembly from a single pivot, the reproducer being carried across the record by a feed screw device. This permitted an absolutely air-tight tone passage from the diaphragm to the outer periphery of the horn. This was a concept which originated in the Edison research program. The screw feed was inherent to the Edison technology from the first, in which the groove had never been used to propel a tone arm across the record. There was nothing even remotely resembling the Edison means fundamental to either Johnson patent. Unquestionably the sole purpose of this suit was to bolster the wavering morale of the Victor jobbers and dealers. On appeal, the Edison disc phonograph was found not to infringe these patents, which was also the decision of the lower court. Costs were asessed against the plaintiff.

Chapter 15

The Tone-Tests and the Vertical-Cut Bandwagon

THE fact that the laboratory model of the Edison phonograph was able to successfully withstand repeated public comparisons with living vocal and instrumental performances using stock phonographs and records is quite likely to be greeted with skepticism by most of the high-fidelity enthusiasts of today. Yet in the files of newspapers from coast to coast may be found the reports of newspaper writers and critics attesting to that accomplishment, with but few expressing even the slightest doubt or reservation. Were all the millions of persons who attended these memorable tone-tests mesmerized? Were all of the newspaper critics subsidized?

Actually, there is no more scientific procedure available to prove a certain claim as valid than repeated public performance. Today leaders in electronics and sound reproduction find themselves unable to agree upon a definition of "high fidelity." Edison in his development of the phonograph bothered little with either theories or definitions. Very early he had set for himself the goal of exact reproduction of the original sounds. Sometimes, seemingly on the threshold of accomplishment, Edison advertising had claimed too much. Up to the time serious work began on the disc phonograph, Edison had sought to achieve his goal by making the recording process more efficient, therefore, more sensitive to the slightest sounds. Collaterally he had sought to make the molding process more perfect,

with the least possible loss of the delicate overtones and the subtler nuances. Constantly the endeavor was to extend the range of vibrations per second which could be recorded and reproduced. The design of reproducing instruments involved continuous research to find the best materials for diaphragms, better motors and horns which would bring out more fully everything that was captured in the record. Understandably, this was never completely successful, nor is it yet today.

In the striving towards the goal of precise reproduction of the voice, it was found that the more sensitive the recording diaphragm became, and the more fully what was captured became utilized in the reproduction, the farther away the objective seemed to recede—like a mirage. The difficulty was that the more sensitive the methods became in the registering of sounds, in the processing to records, and in reproduction technics, the more room resonance or reflected sound was picked up and reproduced along with the originating sounds. Obviously, the reproduced sound from the phonograph became less like the sound of the singer as more and more reflected sound became added to the directly recorded voice.

Consequently, in perfecting the Edison disc recording system to permit the direct comparisons between voice and instrument, it was found necessary to employ a dead studio. Thus, the sounds issuing from the phonograph were the close-up sounds as they issued from the singer's mouth, or as heard from a few feet away from the violinist —not as heard in the concert hall. When an artist performed in a tone-test the recorded vocal or instrumental sounds were not surrounded by the sound pattern reflections of another room or auditorium, as are most of such recordings of today. Much stress is now laid upon the necessity of broad front, or sound diffusing enclosures, for most enjoyable listening. True perhaps where orchestral ensemble is most important, but it should be evident that in the case of solo voice and many instruments that the originating sounds come from a point source. Should a singer's voice seem to be coming to you from all sides? Just how correct is it in theory to superimpose the acoustical qualities of one room upon that of another?

The philosophies of the various recording engineers of the acoustic era may now be better understood in retrospect. Victor always strove for brilliance in voice reproduction. Hence all of the reflected sound which it was possible to gather was utilized to enhance the brilliance, which to some extent covered up a lack of true overtones. However, due to the fact that the recording horns and recording diaphragms would not respond to all frequencies equally well, the result was a series of peaks or resonances in the recordings which are obvious even when played by the best equipment now available.

Columbia records suffered similarly, but generally the bass reproduction was more adequate, as a general statement. No matter how good the records, all were at the mercy of the temporary steel and fibre needles. The lateral disc industry suffered principally for two reasons, the lack of suitable damping means in the limited higher frequency range then attainable and in the lack of laboratory standard instruments for evaluating reproduction. Victor's reaction to the reality of the competition offered by the Edison tone-tests has been cited previously.

Others reacted to the sensational Edison accomplishment in other ways. The great Aeolian Company, then a principal manufacturer of pianos and pipe organs, entered the lists with a line of phonographs and vertical-cut shellac records. It is notable that the cut of the grooves of the new Aeolian disc was precisely that of the Edison disc, also the same number of threads per inch, 150. The Aeolian-Vocalian, as it was named, was equipped with a universal tone-arm, so that both lateral- and vertical-cut discs could be played by changing the reproducer stylus and the position of the reproducer. In England, where these machines and records were also manufactured, the Edison idea of a description on the reverse side was also employed for a time. Whether voluntarily or because of certain unsolved technical difficulties, the hill-and-dale records were replaced with laterally-recorded discs within a year or so.

Other well-informed persons with access to the various recording studios also attempted to climb on the bandwagon. Henry Burr, popular recording tenor who made records for all of the companies, apparently was equally impressed with the results obtainable by the new Edison methods. He organized a recording company of his own called Par-O-ket. These records, strangely enough, also had the same groove cut and number of threads per inch as the Edison discs. The Par-O-ket records were made only 8 inches in diameter, but it is understood that this company also put out a 10″ disc of the same type with another label. These and the Aeolian-Vocalian records could be played on the Edison diamond-disc machines by putting two discs on at the same time, to raise the playing surface of one to the requisite height. The only difficulty was that the shellac base records were not hard enough to stand up to the reaction of the Edison reproducer. At this time it would have been a wise move on the part of the Edison executives to have licensed their complete process, including the harder condensite record surfacing material for the use of other manufacturers. The failure to do so was certainly a most important factor in the triumph of the technically inferior, but more easily adaptable, lateral disc.

Another company jumped on the vertical-cut bandwagon. The Starr Piano Co. of Richmond, Indiana, in 1918 brought out a line of hill-and-dale discs also with the Edison cut which was named the Gennett Art-Tone series. However, as had occurred also with the Aeolian-Vocalian vertical-cut records, these also were shortly replaced with lateral recordings. There were factors other than the lack of hardness of the record materials responsible for the shift to the lateral record; one was the poor design and excessive inertia of the sound-box and tone-arm assemblies of the machines designed to play them. The lack of sufficient compliance in the diaphragm stylus assembly was also a critical factor. One of the inherent disadvantages of the vertical-cut method is that the reactive forces generated by the stylus tracking the groove are superimposed in one direction upon the weight required to insure the tracking. Even with the carefully balanced Edison reproducer which did not depend upon the groove for carrying it across the record, the shellac discs would not stand up. A licensing plan permitting the use of the Edison developed materials would have easily obviated this difficulty and would have extended the repertoire of the vertical-cut branch of the industry at a time when it might have become an important consideration.

These things are admittedly easy to see by hindsight. The Edison lesson seems not to have been lost on Columbia Records, Inc., when in introducing the microgroove records in 1948, it immediately offered licenses to all of its competitors, with results which have exceeded all expectations.

One of the best known recording experts of the time was Victor W. Emerson, who had early been in the employ of Edison and later the United States Phonograph Co. He and his brothers, also employees, had left after a dispute over some missing cylinders around 1900, and had been immediately hired by the Graphophone Co. Emerson also became greatly impressed with the technical success of the new Edison process and set to work to find a way to circumvent the patents involved. He soon came up with the idea of a record that was universal, rather than another machine that would play either type of record. To accomplish this Emerson designed a cutter that would record on a bias, producing a record groove that was partially vertical and partially lateral; therefore, they could be reproduced on the Edison machines, which were designed to play only one type of vertical discs, or on the Victor or Columbia machines, which were designed to play only laterally-recorded discs. This was the first 45° cutter.

The fallacy in the Emerson idea lay in the fact that his record would play even less well on the Edison phonograph than the other shellac discs with the requisite 150 grooves per inch, for due to the bias cut, the vertical bearing surface was reduced by approximately one-half. Emerson resigned from his position with the Graphophone Co. and founded the Emerson Phonograph Co., which, in altered corporate form, functioned for many years in the radio and television field. The unique concept of a universal record served to protect Emerson from the legal clutches of his former employer, however, which as the reader will realize by now was better than par for any one patent! How touchy the lateral disc people were about this climbing onto the vertical-cut bandwagon was indicated by the suit which was immediately brought against Emerson by the American Graphophone Co.

Emerson later did some quite interesting things, though some might be considered a bit unethical. One of these was to put out a series of 7″ discs to be played with a sapphire ball, at low prices. Some of these were dubbed from Pathe records by great artists and are now great rarities. The voice of Enrico Caruso, as recorded originally upon cylinders by the Anglo-Italian Commerce Co. was one of these, but the label did not carry his name.

Probably the introduction of vertical-cut discs and machines by Pathe and Edison gave independent inventors and entrepreneurs the opportunity they had been seeking. Most of the new phonographs were universal with various ways of making the accommodations for playing the Pathe sapphire ball records, the Edison-cut records, and the lateral discs. Now there were several instruments designed to play all types of records including Pathe, Aeolian-Vocalian, Emerson, and Gennett. The basic superiority of the hill-and-dale record had been proven by the Edison tone-tests and the attempts of artists, inventors, and entrepreneurs to utilize it shortly after these demonstrations began is ample affirmation.

However, events in world history as well as the simple laws of economics seemed to be moving against the sanguine Edison enterprise. Less than a week before the first memorable tone-test, Edison had been summoned to Washington to act as head of the Naval Advisory Board. Strange as it may seem to us today, up to that time there had been no organized research in the Navy Department. The threat of unrestricted submarine warfare was upon us and it was imperative to implement the sudden demand for preparedness. Already, war-created material shortages were impeding production in the Edison industries as in many others. The phenol and other materials required for surfacing the new Edison discs were not of the requisite high quality that the sensitivity of the recording and reproductive process demanded. Consequently during the World War I years, the Edison disc records became inordinately noisy, and the "old man" was in Washington, with more important matters occupying his attention.

After the failure to license the process, the failure of the Edison Co. to set up adequate advertising budgets was probably next most important in the swing away from the vertical-cut discs. To illustrate how important this was and the pressures involved, consider the following. The first time around, the sensational tone-tests made the headlines everywhere; but repeat performances, even though as successful or more so than the previous ones, seldom drew the same attention from the newspapers. This is partly understandable as, of course, the novelty had worn off. But of perhaps greater influence was the fact that the large advertisers in the newspapers were Edison's competitors, particularly Victor and Columbia. Edison spent large sums for the tone-tests, but not for newspaper advertising. By subtle hints, the advertising managers of some newspapers were able to prevail on the good judgment of their music critics and to persuade them to stay away from the tone-tests. Perhaps the eventual outcome might have been different if the Edison advertising men had been given appropriate budgets for advertising these recitals. The newspapers were later faced with a somewhat similar situation in the early 1930's by the competition of radio advertising. By united action they forced radio advertisers to use space in their competitive medium by abruptly curtailing the large amount of free space that formerly had been given to the listing of radio attractions.

The salesmen of the opposition forces also found it possible to suggest in devious ways to prospective purchasers that the Edison tone-tests were faked, that the singers simulated the reproduced voices, that the violinists also imitated the recorded violin tones. That top flight artists would stoop to such a thing is incredible, but not everyone paused to consider whether it was likely that an established singer would be likely to risk his reputation in that way. To meet this sort of snide competition, Edison officials encouraged popular artists in vaudeville also to use the phonograph in connection with their acts. Numerous comparisons were given on the Keith and other circuits, not only by singers but by Hawaiian guitarists, banjoists, and players of the marimba and xylophone. The impossibility of mimicing these instruments was of course quite obvious to anyone, as there is no control over the quality after the string has been plucked or the hammer used. To anyone who had heard the magic of hearing the banjo of Joe Roberts, or the xylophone of Friscoe perfectly reproduced by a stock laboratory model Edison phonograph from the stage, there was no possibility of suggesting such a thing.

Outside of the uncanny accuracy in the reproduction of solo voices and instruments, or of small ensembles, the Edison phonograph did have some serious faults. One was the surface noise previously mentioned, which was particularly aggravating from 1917 through 1920, just when the opportunity to realize upon the wide acceptance engendered by the tone-tests was greatest. Another was the comparative "deafness" of the Edison dead studio recording technic. Essential to facsimile reproduction of instrument or voice alone, this method limited the size of orchestras that it was possible to record satisfactorily. Edison personally believed that one should be able to hear each individual instrument in the band or orchestra. As this was before the successful development of microphonic recording and broadcasting it was not nearly so obvious then as today that to satisfy the ear in the recording of large instrumental or choral groups that it would be necessary to record some reflected sound, or room resonance, with the source sounds. The partially deaf Edison would often bite into the cabinet of the phonograph to judge as to whether each instrument had been individually registered. Utmost fidelity and definition was his goal. The chief reason Edison orchestral recording proved unsatisfactory was that a room of live acoustical properties was required for proper development of the ensemble effect. Reproduced in the home, where upholstered furniture,

drapes, and rugs quite often prevented such an acoustical development of ensemble through multiple reflections, the Edison orchestral recordings were often singularly unappealing.

Although Victor and Columbia were hardly more successful in the recording of large orchestras, it was not a matter of avoiding room resonance, but chiefly the limitations of tone range that made the acoustical records of these companies so pitifully inadequate. Yet Victor from 1918 on had advertised recordings by the Boston Symphony Orchestra, directed by Muck and by the Philadelphia Orchestra with Leopold Stokowski as conductor, at a time when it was impossible to get one third of the men of either organization within registering range of the recording horns. Columbia later did the same with Ysaye and the Cincinnati Orchestra. Yet Edison never descended to such flagrant misuse of the reputation of great orchestras and conductors. However, by 1918, Edison was able to record orchestras of thirty-five men, with each instrument individually registered, but as the number of instruments was increased the proportional volume of each was decreased, with those farthest from the recording horn being diminished most. Every effort was made to achieve a proper balance. In the best of these, a feeling of placement, or three dimensional quality was achieved. But, as the average volume of individual instruments was diminished, the abominable surface noise of the period became more obvious, seemingly limiting progress in the direction of increasing the number of men in the orchestra. One of Edison's costly but futile attempts to solve the problem of securing good recordings of large orchestras involved the construction of a huge recording horn two blocks long, (about 200 ft.) built of sheet brass, which was not dismantled until World War II, when it was sold for scrap.

About this time, a very important tangential event occurred which was to have far-reaching repercussions. This was the publication in the *Proceedings* of the *National Academy of Science* in 1919 of a theoretical treatise by A. G. Webster entitled, "Acoustical Impedance and Theory of Horns and Phonograph." He outlined the functions of a logarithmic horn and suggested corresponding relationships in electrical circuits. He originated a considerable amount of the phraseology subsequently employed in the development of theories and ideas of others, such as that of "impedance" in an acoustical system, which could be balanced by a corresponding "electrical impedance" in an electrical circuit. It was undoubtedly as a result of this basic concept that

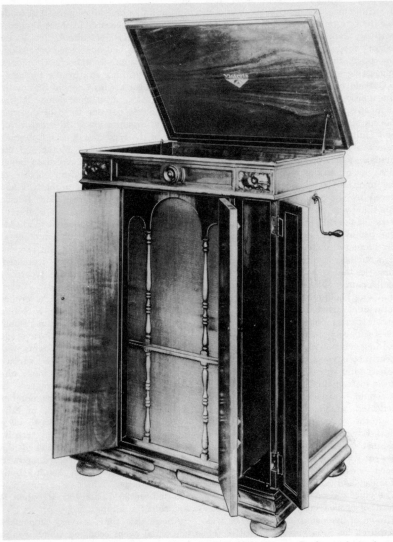

Fig. 15-1. *The Victor Orthophonic Victrola 8-30, first to use the logarithmic horn.* (Courtesy of *RCA Victor*.)

actual research was begun by a variety of investigators into the possibilities of electrical recording. Hanna and Slepian in 1924 published "The Function and Design of Horns for Loud Speakers," but it was the work of J. P. Maxfield and H. C. Harrison which resulted in the introduction of the Western Electric system of recording and the Orthophonic Victrola (Fig. 15-1) and Viva-Tonal Columbia Phonograph in 1925. The results of their work was summed up in "Methods of High Quality Recording and Reproducing of Music and Speech Based on Telephone Research," published in a transcript of the *Proceedings of the American Institute of Electrical Engineers* in 1926. These developments will be dealt with in proper sequence and in the Appendix.

However, there are a few remaining developments in the acoustic period prior to the actual commercial introduction of electrically recorded records which should be covered. One of the more important of these is the story of how the Brunswick-Balke-Collender Co., well-known manufacturers of bowling equipment, happened to come into the phonograph and record business. Rumors claimed Edison cabinets had been supplied by this company. A disagreement occurred supposedly about certain standards of manufacture. At any rate, a large shipment of cabinets intended for Edison was refused. The Brunswick executives then decided to make a talking machine themselves, to use up these cabinets. In 1920, the Brunswick phonograph was introduced, as well as the Brunswick record. The phonograph featured a universal tone arm, but the records were conventional lateral-cut shellac discs. Unquestionably, this was another potent factor in the now obvious swing towards a situation in which the rest of the industry became to all intents and purposes arrayed against Edison. However, deluxe models employed what the Brunswick advertisements termed the "Ultona" reproducer, which was the best device provided by a competitor for playing the Edison discs, equipped

with a permanent diamond point with an independent stylus-diaphragm assembly for these records and an ingenious sliding weight for providing the proper pressure upon the disc, lateral or vertical. In comparison with other contemporary lateral discs, the Brunswick records were well recorded, brilliant in the higher register, and with a good surface. The Brunswick records of pianist Leopold Godowski and others were considered sensationally good at the time.

Perhaps this was one of the reasons for the decision of the Edison executives to secure Rachmaninoff for a series of Edison records. These were also issued in 1920, but were first issued with the wartime, noisy surfaces which detracted very considerably from the excellent fidelity and volume of the records. There is no question but what the Edison men also did their best to persuade Rachmaninoff to agree to a tone-test appearance, which doubtless would have created a sensation. However, he evidently refused, so the Edison advertising men did what they thought was the next best thing. They had Rachmaninoff pose for a picture at a piano with a jury behind a screen, the test being as to whether these men could tell the difference. An advertisement on this privately conducted tone-test with the picture appeared in *Etude* for December, 1920 and other national magazines. As at this time Rachmaninoff was also recording for Victor, the implications of this ad were obvious. Under the picture was this caption: "Hear Rachmaninoff on the New Edison" and the following statement, "Now you can make a straightforward comparison and find out which is the best phonograph. Rachmaninoff himself, the great Russian pianist, gives you this opportunity. He has made recordings for one of the standard talking machines. We are very glad he has done so. For now you can compare." At any rate, Rachmaninoff failed to make other Edison records thereafter. One factor in this may have been that one of the duplicate masters of one of Rachmaninoff's own compositions contained a technical pianistic error, yet thousands of pressings from this defective recording were issued to Edison dealers throughout the country. This particular master was not used, however, when within a short time these Rachmaninoff Edison records appeared with the white labels, with the improved surfaces, when they again had wide circulation.

In 1922, Columbia introduced a new silent surface record developed by its affiliate, English Columbia. Had it been found possible in the decade before to have solved the noisy surface so long associated with the Columbia laminated records, Columbia also might have given the Victor Co. much more competition. Even as late as it was, it was undoubtedly a factor in the Victor decision to double all of the red seal series and to withdraw from the market thousands of their own rather noisy surfaced single discs which had been piling up in warehouses and on the shelves of dealers since before the war. Unsold record return allowances had been a policy of all companies, but these allowances were insufficient. So Victor for the first time in its history permitted dealers to sell at reduced prices—half price, to be exact—on all single-face, red-seal records.

In England, radio did not have the immediate and unqualified public acceptance manifested in the U. S., in part due perhaps to the lack of commercial competition as there were no commercially sponsored programs. Consequently, the gramophone did not seem to be threatened with the serious inroads that early became apparent in the U. S. Immediately following the war, great strides were made by English recorders in improving the quality of acoustical lateral disc recordings and in developing better sound boxes and horns. In 1922, a machine was placed upon the market in England called the World. The inventor reverted to the principle of the constant speed beneath the point that had been covered in the original Bell-Tainter patents of 1886. This allowed the production of records which had a playing time of several minutes. Reports were that the reproduction quality was excellent. But by this time the preponderance of machines and records in England had been also standardized as lateral, and lack of artists and other considerations prevented the success which the idea merited. This, as with a number of other industry developments through the years, was an example of a correct principle being introduced at the wrong time, or under the wrong auspices.

There was also another factor of vital importance to the successful merchandising of phonographs, particularly in the United States. This became of more and more consequence as time went on; namely, the design of the cabinets in relation to the increasingly rapid shift in trends of interior decoration.

Style played a much greater part in the building and crashing of the phonographic dynasties than most people realize. The largest upswing in Victor fortunes began after the introduction of the internal horn Victrola in 1906. As pointed out, this represented not an improvement in reproduction but an endeavor to adapt the form of the machine to the home environment. In other words, it was largely a stylistic development. However, by 1918, the Victor Co. had grown sleek and fat—as corpulent as its leading tenor, Enrico Caruso.

Eldridge R. Johnson had been smart in envisioning the Victrola as a musical instrument and in endeavoring to style it in such a manner as to induce its acceptance into the best homes. However, there was a subtle distinction between the concept which he held and that attached to it by the public at large. This subtle distinction was in the concept of Johnson that the Victrola was a unique musical instrument, rather than a reproducing machine. He therefore thought that it should have a unique format growing out of and expressing its function, somewhat as that of a harp, cello, or piano. However, the purchasers of Victrolas missed this point and looked upon these instruments as items of furniture—not being particularly concerned with the appropriateness of their design in a philosophic sense. This differing viewpoint eventually resulted in the loss of the whole-hearted acceptance that the Victrola had achieved in a few short years and which had been so clearly shown by the adoption by a large share of the public of the term "victrola" as the generic term for "talking machine." This success actually had grown to such an extent that it proved embarrassing and it became necessary for the Victor advertising men to use the redundant term the "Victor Victrola."

For a number of years while Victor was setting the upward pace, other companies had confirmed the "rightness" of Victor design by copying its general character and outward appearance. There is no more sincere tribute than imitation! The first Amberolas, the first diamond disc phonographs, the Sonoras, Pathes, Aeolian-Vocalians, and even the Columbias, were patterned more or less openly after the style trend that had been established by Victor with the first upright internal horn Victrola. This unquestioned style leadership had been strongly reinforced by advertising, which as in all other fields, exerted an undeniably strong influence upon public taste. The glorification of the Victrola in full-color advertisements in nearly all popular magazines month after month was a potent element in molding popular desires and finally in convincing many who cared little about music that they should have an expensive Victrola, because it was the thing to do. It became a symbol of cultural attainment of the same order as that supplied by enterprising book salesmen who filled bookcases with imposing leather bound volumes that were seldom opened. The curvi-linear corner posts and heavily molded tops of the Victrolas became almost as symbolic as the famous Victor trademark.

Having established the trend and set the pace for so many years, it is not surprising that the executives and directors of the Victor organization be-

Fig. 15-2. Edison Disc phonograph Model A290 in mahogany Sheraton inlaid marquetry. (Courtesy of Edison National Historic Site.)

came eventually somewhat overconfident and insensitive to changes in public taste. The first step taken by a competitor that resulted in the eventual overthrow of what might be termed the "ola" style cycle was taken by Edison. In 1915, it had been decided that the new line of Edison instruments should be considered, not as machines, the prior Edison concept, nor as musical instruments, the Johnson concept, but as furniture housing a sound reproducing instrument. Its function was not to be concealed, but it was to have cabinets designed by foremost cabinet designers and supplied in a sufficiently wide number of styles so as to fit properly into any home environment. At that time it would have been impossible for any smart furniture designer to have bucked the trend towards the so-called "period" styling in home furniture design. "Modern" was almost as far away as TV. In view of that fact, the cabinets designed by Elsie de Wolfe for Edison were provided in various woods and finishes in designs founded on furniture motifs of the famous eclectic designers of the late Renaissance. Among these were the original line of upright cabinet models called the Chippendale, William and Mary, Sheraton, and Jacobean. (See Figs. 15-2 and 15-3.)

There is no doubt but that the careful styling of these cabinets was responsible for acceptance by many who rebelled against the non-traditional conventionalism of Victor cabinet styling. Edison differed from the other leading manufacturers by placing but three different qualities of reproducing equipment in a wide variety of cabinets. One was the so-called "laboratory model," which was the standard Edison disc reproducing equipment for which the records were designed. The others had a somewhat smaller horn and shorter spring-wind motors, for installation in the smaller cabinets at a lower price. Victor's only notable reaction at the time to this style trend was the introduction of a special series of eight period models (similar to the Victor XI shown in Fig. 15-4) intended for limited distribution, as shown in a double page spread in the 'Voice of the Victor' for November, 1917.

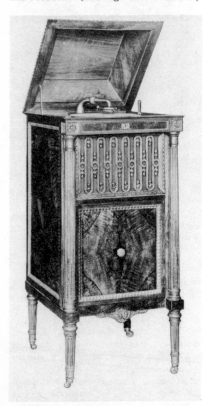

Fig. 15-3. A popular model of the Edison Disc phonograph manufactured in 1915. (Courtesy of Edison National Historic Site.)

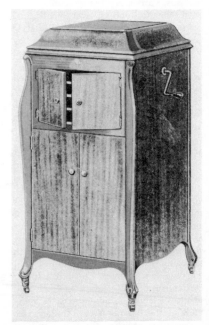

Fig. 15-4. The Victrola XI first made in 1917 reached considerable popularity. It sold for $110. (Courtesy of RCA Victor.)

In 1918 articles began to appear in popular publications denoting the failure of phonograph manufacturers to keep pace with new trends in interior decoration. One of special interest appeared in "Country Life." A fad developed of taking the functioning mechanism out of the manufacturer's cabinet and installing it in a special cabinet. This evolved into quite a profitable business by small furniture factories making special deluxe period model cabinets for the trade. Other companies were not as insensitive as Victor to this trend and soon phonograph manufacturers such as Cheney and Sonora were putting out models with custom-built cabinets at high prices—some of which are probably serving as liquor storage cabinets today! This trend led to the famous DeLuxe hand-made Sonora phonographs with all wood tone-arms and tone-chambers. Some of these Sonoras sold for as much as $1,500. When the Brunswick-Balke-Collender Co. entered the field in 1920, it also put out a line of period models and custom-built cabinets for the higher-priced units. Sonora was one of the first of the regular manufacturers to market the so-called console models, which were horizontal, rather than vertical. Even the Edison executives, for once alert, also soon had companion console models design patterned after their upright period models.

Here it must be noted that style again was overcoming function. All reproducing instruments sound better if the sound comes from a position above ear level. This phenomenon may be checked and verified easily under widely varying conditions. It is partially due to the fact that higher registers and overtones travel in more or less straight lines more or less parallel to the central axis of the horn or cone reproducer and are easily absorbed, or reflected by obstructions. This phenomenon years later accounted for the use of the inclined sounding board for the mounting of the dynamic speaker in Philco radios, and again is being used in some hi-fi speaker enclosures.

Among the leaders of the industry, only Victor resisted the trend towards the consideration of the phonograph primarily as a piece of furniture and later, the trend towards consoles. It was said by one writer that the Victor directors "had clung to the upright Victrola as stubbornly as Edison had clung to the early cylinder." [1] However, there is this to be said for both Johnson and Edison: they both had tenacity in clinging to concepts that they personally firmly believed to be fundamentally correct.

In 1923, when the console craze had reached its height, Victor sales dropped $10,000,000, or 20%. Victor representatives and jobbers all over the country were astounded to find Victor dealers extremely resentful of the fact that Victor was not preparing to meet this strong consumer demand. Many dealers, especially in metropolitan areas, felt obligated in self-defense to take on competing lines who had for years been exclusively Victor. This naturally resulted in the establishing of dangerous competition for the Victor lines in places where before there had been little. Many of these dealers, freed from the idea that they ought to restrict their loyalties to one company, never again went back to an exclusive basis. This situation finally forced the directors to action, they persuaded Mr. Johnson that it was essential to design a line of console Victrolas. However, he insisted in adhering to his conception and would not agree to eliminating the stylisms and curvatures which had become so thoroughly identified with Victor design. Actually the design of the new console Victrola from the "modern" point of view was a success, but from the standpoint of the housewife of that time who wished to use the console as a table when not in use as a Victrola, it was a failure. The new models had curved top surfaces on either end, with the conventional Victor lift top rising yet higher in the center. These were promptly labelled "humpbacks" by some irate dealers.

[1] *The Rise and Fall of the Phonograph—American Mercury,* Sept. 1932, by Dane Yorke.

By 1924, total capitulation to the demands of dealers and public had to be made. A series of cabinet consoles with flat tops was made ready, but hardly in time. Sales had declined to $37,000,000 and net operating income had fallen off more than 80% in the two years through 1924—this despite the fact that in that year Victor was the largest single advertiser of any American corporation. The advertising budget for 1924 was $5,000,000, or 14% of sales.

As evidence that this myopia of the Victor directors had not been confined to trends in home decoration, it should be cited that in the same two-year period just discussed the sales of radios in the United States had leaped from $60,000,000 to $350,000,000. Yet at the end of this time it has been stated that not a director or major official of the great Victor organization had a radio in his home. Considered objectively, this can be understood, but not necessarily excused. Naturally enough, with the greatest talent in the world at their beck and call, why should a director of the Victor Company have to go elsewhere than their own resources for entertainment? Moreover, the mean cultural level of radio at the time was as puerile as the average TV program today. However, when sales began to slough off, it is rather surprising that some of them did not begin to study radio broadcasting and its possible impact upon the phonograph industry. The thought that radio was about to "take over" probably never occurred to them. Certainly, when the radio magnates wheeled up the trojan horse of "Bell telephone research" letting in the technologists of the radio industry in the guise of telephone repair men, they were either too far gone to object, or didn't suspect the eventual outcome.

To give the reader a brief financial picture of the latter days of the acoustic phonograph industry, a few of the highlights of the two leaders, Columbia and Victor, may not be amiss. Edward Easton, president of the Graphophone Co., had died in 1915, leaving an estate of about $1,000,000. The assets of the Columbia Graphophone Co. were then about $14,000,000, or about $2,000,000 surplus. Victor's assets that same year were about $21,000,000, with about $14,000,000 surplus, of which $7,000,000 was cash. By 1917, the American Graphophone Co. assets had grown to $19,000,000, but still the surplus remained at about $2,000,000. Meanwhile, Victor's assets had leaped to $33,000,000, with a surplus of $23,000,000, with $5,000,000 in cold cash. Edison's total phonograph and record sales in 1917 was something over $9,000,000, but jumped to $22,600,000 by 1921, its largest year.

Phonograph stocks were not listed on the New York Stock Exchange until 1919 when a New York financier bought control of the American Graphophone Co. stock. He changed the capitalization from 150,000 shares of $100 par value to 1,500,000 shares of no-par value. He then had this new stock listed on the New York exchange. The list price moved steadily upward until it was quoted at $65 per share. On that basis the new capitalization was over $90,-000,000, although the actual assets of the company were less than a third of that.

To create an income picture corresponding to this inflated capitalization, production and sales promotion were expanded. However, the product was not sufficiently improved to create the requisite demand and much merchandise remained unsold. The situation became observed by the investing public and the price of the shares dropped to below $5 per share. The financier who started this cycle of activities retired with a handsome profit on his initial investment, but the oldest company in the phonograph industry was ruined. The bankers kept it going a year or two, but in 1923, receivers were appointed.

Victor in the meantime had purchased a half interest in the English Gramophone Co. in 1921, for $9,000,000. This year Victor sales had exceeded $51,000,000. The year before sales had been more than $50,000,000. Years before, Johnson had sold the controlling interest in the English Gramophone Co. for $50,000,000.

In the first 20 years, the Victor Company had earned assets of $43,000,000, of which $31,000,000 was surplus and undivided profits. In 1922 $30,000,000 was distributed by means of a six-for-one stock dividend. That year Victor's net operating income was over $7,000,000. The next year, however, as stated previously, Victor's gross sales dropped by about $10,000,000 to approximately $37,000,000. Meanwhile, radio sales were zooming to astronomical heights with even greater acceleration than the converse drop in sales of phonographs and records. To assist in getting a true perspective, record sales alone of the industry in 1955 totalled approximately $300,000,000.[1]

---

[1] Gross sales of phonograph records in the U.S. in 1974 were over $2,000,000,000.

January 1, 1924, Victor gave its first great broadcast party, with John McCormack and Lucrezia Bori. In more ways than one this event epitomized the victory of radio. Historically it marked the day when Victor celebrated the arrival of its Trojan horse!

Meanwhile Thomas A. Edison, Inc. plugged along, paying no attention to radio, but slowly and continually improving the white label disc record. The strange reluctance of Edison and his associates to interest themselves in the latter day development of electronics in which they had played such a vital part in the telegraph and telephone days still remains to be satisfactorily explained.

CHAPTER 16

WIRELESS TELEGRAPHY,
WIRELESS TELEPHONY,
AND RADIO

TELEGRAPHY, telephony, wireless telegraphy, and wireless telephony all contributed to the modern art of electrical recording and sound reproduction. The theory of electromagnets written by Joseph Henry in 1843 not only laid the foundation for Morse's telegraph, but for our transducers and transformers. The work of Bell and Edison in telephonic research gave us our basic forms of earphones, microphones and loudspeakers. Edison and Hertz demonstrated the possibility of wireless communication, Lodge and Marconi demonstrated its practicality. Reginald Fessenden almost alone and quite early proved that wireless telephony was just around the corner and was the first man to actually broadcast music over the airwaves.

Edison, Fleming, and DeForest contributed the three constructive elements of the vacuum tube that converted wireless telegraphy and telephony into the radio. Fessenden, Armstrong, and Williamson developed circuits that were milestones in the tortuous progress towards relatively distortion-free amplifiers—a prerequisite for high fidelity.

The science of electronics may be said to have begun with the theories of a Britisher, Clerk Maxwell, a mathematician who investigated electromagnetic phenomena. During the period beginning in 1863, he proved by mathematical formulas that energy was radiated from electrical circuits and that this energy which escaped into space would have to obey the laws which apply to light. This information he published in 1873. Two years later, Edison made the first known device for detecting this vagrant form of electrical energy.

In the December 25th issue of *Scientific American* for 1875, a complete description with pictures was given of the experiments and apparatus used to demonstrate the then inexplicable phenomenon which, for want of a better name, was called "etheric force." Pictured was the very first wireless detector, or detector of what are now known as electromagnetic or radio waves. This consisted of a little black box containing two carbon electrodes which could be delicately adjusted to a very fine gap by means of micrometer screws, which Edison had devised as a means of detecting the presence of the new force. Experiments proved this to be, indeed, a new form of energy, obeying none of the usual laws governing electric currents, voltaic or static, for it would not charge a Leyden jar, would not register on either the electroscope or the galvanometer, and had no respect for insulation. Although its presence was detected by a spark, it was a spark different from that of galvanic cells or from the electrostatic machine. In the same month, Edison gave a demonstration with his apparatus before the members of the Polyclinic Club of the American Institute.

Immediately after these events a great furore arose among the electrical experts. A majority scoffed, few were impressed sufficiently to try experiments of their own, or to withhold judgment. The next issue of *Scientific American* carried a lengthy editorial entitled "Etheric Force and Weak Electric Currents." It seems that Prof. Philip Reis, the eminent German inventor of later telephonic fame, had attempted to duplicate Edison's experiment by use of an electrostatic machine and a pair of Leyden jars and had confused the usual "brush" discharge with what Edison was demonstrating as a new force. In respect to this the editor stated:

"Thus far all attempts to generate the Edison 'etheric force' by means of such an apparatus as Professor Reis employed have been fruitless. It has been produced only by means of an interrupted current from several electropoin cells, using a vibrator magnet or an electromagnet operated by an ordinary telegraph key, the current following a wire connected with the core of the magnet or with a piece of metal within the magnet's sphere of influence. The force manifests itself as a spark when the wire is rubbed against a piece of metal; when a body of metal, such as a stove or gas pipe, is connected with the wire and touched by a piece of metal, as a knife blade; or when two carbon points are brought in contact in a dark box, one carbon being connected with the wire leading to the magnet, and the whole apparatus being carefully insulated to exclude inductive electricity.

"Sparks are also obtained when the conducting wire is rubbed by a lead pencil or a piece of metal held in the hand, and even when the wire is rubbed by its own free end. The conducting wire does not require to be insulated. It may be lead through water, wound around large bodies of metal, or trailed along the ground, yet the sparks appear. One rainy night Mr. Edison led the wire from the vibrator out of doors, across the sidewalk, up and down the block in the gutter, through which a torrent of water was pouring, thence by an alley way to the rear of his laboratory, and thence up stairs to the floor above, where the sparks were distinctly seen between carbon points in a dark box. (This box was illustrated in our last number.) On another occasion the vibrator was connected by means of a wire with the general system of gas pipes of Newark, whereupon signals were transmitted, without other connection, to his house in a distant part of the city.

"- - - Enough has been said to show that Professor Reis and Mr. Edison are pursuing two widely different lines of investigation. So far from being identical, the phenomenon are at variance in every particular; the cause of the one being statical electricity of low tension, and the cause of the other,—etheric force, as Mr. Edison calls it,—being, if not a new and distinct kind of force, as he suspects, at least a new and hitherto unstudied phase of electricity. In either case, Mr. Edison will rank with the most fortunate and eminent of scientific discoverers."

In the January 15th *Scientific American* it was further stated that Edison had discovered that it was not necessary to have any connections to the black box, if it is brought within a short distance from any electromagnetic spark, such as that of the operating electric telegraph equipment.

Thus, according to the editor of the *Scientific American,* Edison had demonstrated the existence of a previously undiscovered form of energy which we now know was identical with what Hertz a short time later was to call "Hertzian waves" and which are now termed electromagnetic or radio waves. If you will carefully note that by this means and according to the testimony of the editor that "signals were transmitted" from one place to another without a completed wire circuit, that constitutes the first demonstration of wireless telegraphy just as certainly as Henry demonstrated electromagnetic wire telegraphy before Morse.

Some modern writers upon electronics purposely or otherwise choose to minimize the importance of this discovery by Edison. Several have stated in one way or another that it was a pure accident and that he did not have an appreciation of its importance. Although he was then only a young man of twenty-eight, he was very busy with several other pressing matters, including multiplex telegraphy, which had led him to the idea of the harmonic telegraph and telephony. That he did understand quite fully its importance is shown by his prophetic words as quoted in "The Operator," a telegrapher's journal in January, 1876, as follows:

"The cumbersome appliances of transmitting ordinary electricity, such as telegraph poles, insulating knobs, cable sheathings, and so on, may be left out of the problem of quick and cheap telegraphic transmission; and a great saving of time and labor accomplished."

This incidentally, was just a matter of two months before the issuance of the patent to Alexander Graham Bell on his "speaking telegraph," which, because of Edison's relationship with Western Union, probably had considerable to do with his inability to find time to follow up his experiments in communicating with "etheric force."

Before he was able to return again to this line of research, he became involved in the race to produce the first successful electric lamp, and in which we all know he was eminently successful. Who can say which is the greater gift to the world?

And who, but Thomas A. Edison, carrying on routine experiments with the incandescent lamp, would have noted the associated phenomenon of the emission of electrons from the heated filament and the fact that this stream of electrons could be used to carry currents of electricity in one direction only —or to perceive that by putting another receiving element in the lamp that it would serve as a voltage indicator—the basic radio tube! It was identical with the tube patented later by Fleming, the English physicist, who simply revised the external circuit for use as a detector of high frequency, or electromagnetic waves, which Edison had first termed "etheric force."

But this development came later and much work by others intervened. Many other men made important contributions—some have received altogether too much credit, however, such as Marconi, who is known as the "father of wireless" chiefly because of his successful demonstration of trans-Atlantic wireless communication. Our intent is to focus attention on some of those who have not received proper recognition.[1] One of these is Reginald Aubrey Fessenden, who was chief chemist of the Edison laboratories from 1887 to 1890. He later accepted a position with the Westinghouse Electric & Mfg. Co. of Newark, N. J. In 1893 he became professor of electrical engineering at the Western University of Pennsylvania. Fessenden made many inventions in electrical and chemical engineering and also wrote numerous scientific papers. From 1900 to 1902 he was special agent of the U. S. Weather Bureau in charge of investigations in wireless telegraphy, which led him into the researches into wireless telephony with which we are primarily concerned. During the next six years Fessenden became occupied with intensive experimentation which resulted in his establishing basic principles essential to radio-telephony, radio broadcasting, and even to television. Before the employment of electromagnetic waves, various other types of "wireless" telegraphy had been experimented with.

---

[1] It is essential to trace the course of development which led to commercial broadcasting in order to properly credit the basic work of the men who were indirectly responsible for the introduction of electrical recording.

In 1842, Professor Morse had established telegraphic communication between two stations on the opposite banks of a river, with no wires between. Along one bank he laid a wire with sending battery and key in circuit, with the ends terminating in widely spaced metal plates in the river. A similarly widely spaced pair of plates were placed in the water off the other shore which were connected with a receiving galvanometer by another wire. Thus, although only a small portion of the current differential was effective upon the receiving galvanometer, "wireless" telegraphy was a demonstrable fact, even though this was hardly a commercially practical means. However, not knowing of Morse's experiments, in 1859, Lindsay in Dundee, Scotland had been working on the same principle. He suggested that if two large plates were inserted in the ocean, one off the northern coast of Scotland, the other off the southern tip of England, that it would be possible by the employment of similar plates on the American side to have trans-Atlantic wireless telegraphy. Further investigation showed, of course, that this principle was capable of only extremely limited application, and in no way applicable to trans-Atlantic communication. However, similar experiments were carried out as devices for ship to shore signaling and for use as warning devices between ships, with considerable promise.

A second early means of accomplishing "wireless" telegraphy was the use of the induction principle. It had early been discovered that two wires, or plates, parallel to one another, would have a charge induced in them of opposite polarity, if the other were charged. In 1885, Edison and Gilliland devised an induction system for signaling to moving trains by using the telegraph wires paralleling the track. Stevenson in England in 1892 established a working induction wireless from the mainland to an island half a mile distant, by using at either end large horizontal coils 200 yards in diameter. Utilizing this same idea, Dolbear described in 1893 a scheme for wireless communication in which he used at either station an elevated wire grounded at one end and in series with transmitter and receiver, respectively. Communication was established up to one-half mile.

However, it was the theoretical research of Clerk Maxwell in the period from 1860 to 1870, published in 1873, and before Edison's laboratory experiments, which showed that energy may be radiated from an electrical circuit, and that this radiated energy then follows the same laws as does light. Edison's discovery, "etheric force," of course was the same phenomenon to which Maxwell previously referred. Maxwell was a pure scientist and perhaps had little thought of the probable future utility of his concepts. In general, the English scientists were quick to grasp the significance of Maxwell's electromagnetic wave theory, but there was considerable lag in other quarters, particularly in Europe. However, one of the exceptions, von Helmholz, the well-known German physicist, persuaded Heinrich Hertz to take up experimentally the relationships between radiated electrical energy and light. This was several years after Charles Batchelor, Edison's technical assistant, had demonstrated "etheric force" using the black box at the Paris Electrical Exposition of 1881.

During the course of his experiments, Hertz detected the evidence of electromagnetic radiation by means of a minute spark-gap which as we know was demonstrated by Edison and Batchelor previously. Before April, 1888, he demonstrated the feasibility of wireless communication by use of these electromagnetic waves. For sending he used a spark-gap with one side attached to a radiating conductor, a similar receiving conductor at a distance was connected to a tuned receiving circuit and the minute spark-gap detector.

Hertz altered the frequency of the radiated waves by changing the capacity of his radiating conductor, or antenna, and succeeded in reflecting and focusing the radiating electromagnetic waves, thus proving the correctness of Maxwell's electromagnetic theory of light, and vindicating Edison's prediction of a tremendous usefulness in communications.

Hertz' experiments were of tremendous scientific importance and after the publication of his "Electric Waves," in 1888, it became realized that he had laid the foundation for the future development of electromagnetic wireless communication as assuredly as had Henry for wire telegraphy. This was reflected in the almost immediate projection by a large number of experimenters of the possibility of using the "Hertz" waves, as they were then called, for penetrating fog and material objects for electrical signaling purposes.

Professor Elihu Thomson in 1889, in a lecture at Lynn, Massachusetts, suggested their use for this purpose and Sir William Crookes in the *Fortnightly Review* for February 1892, quite completely canvassed the possibilities and problems to be overcome in making practical application of the Hertzian waves for wireless telegraphy. Among several scientists who repeated the experimental work of Hertz and expanded upon it was Professor David E. Hughes, who reported his work in *Electrician*, of May 5, 1890. Professor Dolbear, who had been granted a patent on the principle of induction for wireless telegraphy in 1882, and who had been active in telephonic and acoustical research—inventor of the opeidoscope—also became interested in the possibilities of the electromagnetic waves.

The principle of the coherer, in which tubes containing conducting powders were used to detect the waves had been established by Munck in 1835 in experiments using Leyden jars. He discovered that the resistance of the powder was changed after a Leyden jar was discharged nearby, without of course having a true appreciation of its significance.[2] However, it was not until 1890 that Branley showed that such a tube would respond to electrical discharges at a distance. In 1893, Professor Minchen demonstrated the use of a coherer with a battery and galvanometer shunted around the tube to detect electromagnetic waves at a distance.[3]

On June 1, 1894, Sir Oliver Lodge delivered a lecture before the Royal Institution on "The Work of Hertz."[4] In this lecture, Lodge describes the filings coherer, the automatic tapper for loosening the filings to make continual detection possible, a metallic reflector for focusing the Hertzian waves, the connection of the coherer to a grounded circuit, and other variants. Professor Lodge stated that in his estimate the apparatus then used would respond to signals at a distance of half a mile.

Early in 1895, Professor Alexander Popoff of Cronstadt, Russia, now heralded by the Soviet authorities as "the father of radio," also was experimenting with the coherer with the automatic back-tapping mechanism (similar to an electric bell tapper). However, he substituted for the galvanometer used by earlier experimenters an ordinary telegraph relay. Popoff apparently was the first to use the high, external antenna. He used a mast 30 feet high connected to one side of the radiating spark-gap, the other side of the gap being grounded. On the receiving end, one terminus of the coherer circuit was attached to the antenna, the other grounded.[5]

Several others experimented along similar lines, including Captain Jackson of the British Navy, A. C. Brown and Guglielmo Marconi of Italy. Marconi filed a provisional specification in England on June 2, 1896 showing two forms of the apparatus, one similar to that described by Lodge two years before for an ungrounded system and another almost identical with Lodge's 1894 and Popoff's 1895 apparatus—all

---

[2] "Coherer Action," Guthrie, *Transactions of the Electrical Congress*, St. Louis, 1904.

[3] *Proceedings Physical Society*, Minchen, London, 1893.

[4] *Proceedings Royal Institution*, June 1, 1904.

[5] *Journal Russian Physics—Chemical Society, Apparatus for Detection and Registration of Electrical Vibrations*, A. S. Popoff, December, 1895.

three incorporated a coherer and tapper, but in Marconi's provisional specification only the receiving antenna was
grounded.[6] It was not until March 2,
1897 that Marconi filed the complete
specification in which was included a
statement that the transmitting antenna could also be grounded. Thus,
here again we have the spectacle of the
pure scientists pointing the way and
the fruits being gathered by the opportunists!

In the meantime, in July of 1896,
Marconi had arrived in England and
made a number of demonstrations for
the English post-office. Using ungrounded aerials and parabolic reflec-
tors, he succeeded in communicating
nearly two miles. On May 10, 1897, Sir
Oliver Lodge filed a complete specification showing both the antenna grounded
and also the use of an inductance
wound in the form of a coil for the purpose of diminishing the rate of damping
of the waves.

At this time little work was being
done in America. Fessenden made some
experiments with the assistance of two
of his students, Messrs. Bennett and
Bradshaw, in the fall of 1896 and the
spring of 1897, which were reported
in a thesis.[7]

Inspired by the possibilities, Fessenden then began quite intensively to investigate, with the result, as we have
stated that he was made special agent
of the U. S. Weather Bureau in 1900, to
do research in wireless telegraphy.

After the termination of his contract
in 1902, he moved his laboratory to
Brant Rock, where he continued his
research, but now with the definite
goal of wireless telephony; a field in
which he was quite alone for several
years.

The story of his experimental work
was well summed up in a paper which
Fessenden presented before the American Institute of Electrical Engineers on
June 29, 1908. In this paper, Fessenden

quite meticulously recounted the development of wireless telegraphy to that
date, giving due credit to the various
contributors to the sum of knowledge
then available. He then presented an
analysis of the trends in development
along various lines then in evidence.
In conclusion, Fessenden gave an account of his own experiments in wireless telephony, with specific descriptions of the apparatus used. In introducing his lecture, Fessenden called
attention to the fact that to assure
accuracy in describing the progress of
research he was referring to published
results such as scientific articles, theses,
and patent specifications.

It is interesting that the opening reference of his text was to Joseph Henry,
to whom so much credit is due for the
establishment of the principles of the
electromagnetic telegraph. Fessenden
said of Henry:

"Joseph Henry, to whose work the
development of wire telegraphy owes
so much, was the first (1838-1842) to
produce high frequency electrical oscillations, and to point out and experimentally demonstrate the fact
that the discharge of a condenser is
under certain conditions oscillatory,
or, as he puts it, consists 'of a principle discharge in one direction and
then several reflex actions backward
and forward, each more feeble than
the preceding until equilibrium is attained.' "[8]

Fessenden stated that Henry's view of
this phenomenon was later adopted by
Helmholz and that the mathematical
demonstration of the fact was first given
by Lord Kelvin in his paper on "Transient Electric Currents."[9]

From these beginnings, Fessenden
traced onward the successive additions
to the information on these mysterious
oscillations, including contributions by
von Bezold in Germany, Prof. Elihu

[6] *British Patent,* No. 12039, issued to Guglielmo
Marconi, 1896.
[7] *Thesis,* Western University of Pennsylvania,
May, 1897.

[8] *Scientific Writings of J. Henry,* Smithsonian
Institution.
[9] *Erhaltung der Kraft,* Helmholtz, Berlin, 1847;
Philosophical Magazine, Kelvin, June, 1853.

Thomson and E. J. Houston in the U. S., and Prof. Fitzgerald in England, with references to publications of their researches. He summed up the preliminary stages of the laying of the factual basis for wireless development through the use of electromagnetic waves by stressing the importance of the experiments of Hertz, which we have described.

Fessenden said of Hertz:

"Great interest was excited by the experiments of Hertz, primarily because of their immense scientific importance. It was not long however, before several eminent scientists perceived that the property possessed by the Hertz waves of passing through fog and material obstacles made them particularly suitable for electric signalling."

Fessenden reviewed briefly the experiments of Hertz, crediting him with the first demonstration of the practicality of using the electromagnetic waves for communication at a distance. He also reviewed the work of Sir Oliver Lodge, Popoff, and Marconi, substantially as we have given it, but in considerable more detail.

Fessenden then analyzed the progress of the art to that time. He described the limitations of coherer detection and the more or less futile attempts by the various experimenters to break these limitations. Lodge and Braun among others, he stated, attempted to solve the problem by the use of damped waves. Fessenden described the stalemate in the following words:

"The fact that no coherer-damped wave system could ever be developed into a practically operative telegraph system, and the fact that it was necessary to return to first principles and initiate a new line of development along engineering rather than laboratory lines was perceived in America in 1898 and a new method was advised which may be called the sustained oscillation-nonmicrophonic re-

ceiver method as opposed to the damped oscillation-coherer method previously used.[10]

Fessenden then compared the two methods and by a tabular exposition demonstrated his reasons for believing that a new approach was essential. He describes the period of the development of the sustained oscillation-nonmicrophonic receiver method as between 1898 and 1902. In the new method, instead of a spark-gap producing the oscillations, an arc or high frequency generator is used. For a receiver, nonmicrophonic, or contact receivers are employed, instead of the coherer, or imperfect microphonic-contact method. There were other collateral differences, but these were the important ones.

Fessenden described several types of current-operated receivers as developed by several experimenters with the new method. Among these was the Boy's radio-micrometer, which consisted of a light thermo-couple suspended in the field of a permanent magnet and heated by radiation from a wire, which was in turn heated by the current to be detected.[11] This device was succeeded by Prof. Elihu Thomson's alternating current galvanometer, as modified for telegraphic work.[12]

Another detector described by Fessenden was the hot-wire barretter, consisting of a minute platinum wire a few hundred-thousandths of an inch in diameter and approximately one one-hundredth of an inch in length, which he invented.[13] The following year he developed and patented a liquid barretter, which he stated was compared to various electrolytic detectors somewhat erroneously, for the barretter operated by heating of the fluid, with the depolarization caused by the heating, rather than by rectification, as in

[10] *Electrical World*, July 12, August 12, Sept. 16, 1899; and *Proceeding American Institute of Electrical Engineers*, Nov., 1899, and Nov. 20, 1906.
[11] *Electrician*, June 24, 1904.
[12] U. S. Patents, No. 363,185, Jan. 26, 1887, Nos. 706,736 and 706,737, Dec. 15, 1899.
[13] U. S. Patent, No. 706,744, June 6, 1902.

the case of the electrolytic detectors.[14] Tests to authenticate this were made, Fessenden stated, by Dr. L. W. Austin, of the U. S. Bureau of Standards.

Among the electrolytic detectors mentioned was the Neughschwender-Schaefer, patented in Germany in 1898 and in England in 1899, which operated by the rupturing of minute filaments produced by electrolysis by the wave-produced oscillations, thus increasing the resistance. These were, in fact, extensions of the coherer principle. Another was the liquid coherer of Captain Ferrie, which operated by the production of the electrolytic action of a thin film of gas, which was ruptured by the electromagnetic waves.

Next, Fessenden turned to the methods then employable for producing the sustained oscillations essential for the new methods. He stated that Prof. Elihu Thomson discovered that by using a transformer without an iron core, (employing a spark-gap and condenser in the primary circuit) suitably tuned, that great resonant surges of potential could be obtained, giving sparks up to 64 inches in length. These air-core transformers of Elihu Thomson were described in *Electrical World,* Feb. 20 and 27, 1892.

However, essentially the same device was patented by Nikola Tesla under U. S. patent No. 645,551, Sept. 2, 1897. So here once again, we see the work of the first inventor being patented by another. In 1898 this principle was expanded upon so as to give, instead of a continuously cumulative rise in potential, an initial rise in potential followed by a gradual feeding in of the energy from the local circuit to replace the energy lost by radiation. Fessenden stated that he used this method in his original installation at Brant Rock, where he had removed his laboratory from Allegheny, Pennsylvania.

Fessenden credited Elihu Thomson with the discovery of the method of producing high-frequency oscillations from an arc and continuous current,

patented by Thomson July 18, 1892 (No. 500,630). Fessenden stated that by following the specification it was possible to obtain frequencies as high as 50,000 cycles per second, and which he employed in his experiments in wireless telegraphy and telephony between 1900 and 1902. Even before this, in 1889, however, Thomson had built the first high-frequency alternator which converted electrical energy into the high-frequency currents necessary for wireless work. This was described by Thomson in the *Electrical Engineer,* July 30, 1890 and the *London Electrician,* Sept. 12, 1890. In experimenting with this alternator in later years, Doctor Tatum made the interesting discovery that such high frequencies could be passed through the body without injury.

From these and other experiments it was concluded by Fessenden and others that the construction of alternating current dynamos with high-frequency output for wireless telegraphic purposes was practical and in 1900 such a dynamo was planned, being built the following year.[15]

It should be noted that here was being laid the essential groundwork that made radio broadcasting stations possible in 1920—not in the laboratories of the Bell Telephone Co.

Considerable time and effort went into improving the dynamo. By 1906, Fessenden said that many difficulties had been overcome and by the fall of that year the dynamo was working regularly at 75,000 cycles, with an output of half a kilowatt and was being used for telephony to Plymouth, a distance of approximately 11 miles. He also stated that in the following year, dynamos were constructed having a frequency of 100,000 cycles per second and with outputs of 1 and 2 kilowatts.

Fessenden said, "The credit for the development of this machine is due to Messrs. Steinmetz, Haskins, Alexanderson, Dempster, and Geisenhoner, and

[14] U. S. Patent, No. 727,331, April 9, 1903.

[15] U. S. Patent, No. 706,737, May 29, 1901.

also to the writer's assistants, Messrs. Stein and Mansbendel."

This then is the story of the exhaustive work which went into the designing of motor-generator equipment upon which the broadcasting industry was initially dependent, and for which the General Electric laboratories often mistakenly are given all of the credit.

Fessenden pointed out that it was early discovered in the new field of experimentation that closed tuned circuits were an improvement over the earlier open tuned circuits and that greater selectivity was promised by placing the condenser in shunt to the inductance instead of in series with it. He also stated that it was also early realized that the number of stations would be limited if selectivity was controlled solely by tuning to wave frequencies and that as early as 1900 a new method was developed by which stations were tuned to both the wave frequency and to the independent, or group frequency. In this way, selectivity could be greatly increased by varying either or both, providing an almost unlimited number of combinations and thus vastly increasing the possible number of stations.[16]

Marconi was still using the improved Lodge open-circuit receiver in 1898 and in a test for the U. S. Navy achieved wireless communication over a distance of 35 miles. About this time a variety of new detectors were being introduced. Fessenden mentioned favorably the magnetic detector patented by Marconi in England in 1902 (No. 10,245). He also points out that Marconi also patented in Great Britain a version of his (Fessenden's) tank circuit, which served to increase the range of transmission. Fessenden observed that after 1902 most better informed experimenters gradually abandoned the elements of the damped wave-coherer method for the sustained wave non-microphonic method.

That Fessenden's estimate of the comparative merits of the two systems was

correct was verified later by Marconi, himself, for in a paper to the Royal Institution of June 1911, he called attention to his (Marconi's) discovery of the advisability of tuning to group frequency as well as periodicity. This was a belated discovery, indeed, for Fessenden had thoroughly explained the necessity for this procedure in 1908!

At this point, the slow development of the vacuum tube by others becomes important to an unfolding of the progressive development of the wireless technics. The a priori importance of the invention of the incandescent lamp to the vacuum tube is seldom recognized. How did the incandescent lamp come into being? Who were the contributors towards it?

Americans generally are aware that into the development of the first successful incandescent lamp by Edison, he and his associates, financed by a group of New York financiers, had engaged in the most costly and concentrated search for the answers to a challenging problem in the history of scientific investigation to that time. The highly organized, intensive day and night saga of Menlo Park is familiar to almost every schoolboy. The worldwide search for suitable filament materials, of a seemingly endless series of unsuccessful experiments, of desperate efforts to secure a more perfect vacuum, of many promising types of lamps patented and then discarded, is a story often told in texts and memorialized in Ford's Edison Institute and the reconstructed Menlo Park at Dearborn, which thousands visit each year. Eventual success, in the lamp with carbonized cotton thread and the one-piece all glass globe, built on October 21, 1879, was the crowning effort of that heroic achievement.

The search for an incandescent electric lamp actually had begun not long after the discovery of the principle of the arc lamp by the famous English chemist, Sir Humphrey Davy, about 1802. As early as 1820, De la Rue made a lamp with a coil of platinum wire for a burner which was enclosed in a piece

---

[16] U. S. Patents, No. 727,325, June 2, 1900 (also subsequent patents).

of glass tubing from which the air was partially evacuated, with the ends sealed by brass caps. The first incandescent lamp patented was that of De Moleyn, in Great Britain, in 1841. Lamps of varying types were devised by numerous experimenters, including Grove (inventor of the Grove cell), Starr, Staite, Shepard, M. J. Roberts, De Changy, Farmer (of arc light fame), Swan, Lodyguine, Kosloff, Konn, Boulegine, Sawyer, and Maxim—all of them well known and competent inventors. Many patents were issued in various countries upon their lighting devices.

To illustrate the kind of competition Edison was facing in stepping into the race to produce a practical incandescent lamp, consider the fact that in 1874, the Russian Academy of Sciences awarded Lodyguine (a Russian scientist) fifty thousand rubles for his invention of an incandescent lamp and a company was organized with a capital of 200,000 rubles to manufacture it. Lodyguine had already installed 200 of his lamps about the Admiralty dockyard at St. Petersburg. Jablochkoff, another Russian inventor not mentioned previously, had illuminated the boulevards of Paris with his "electric candles" which were, however, really a form of arc light rather than incandescent lamps. In this country, Wallace and Farmer produced complete arc lighting systems as did Weston of Newark, of later electric instrument fame; so also did Charles Brush of Cleveland and Prof. Elihu Thomson, the latter a partner later with Edwin J. Houston as the Thomson-Houston Co. and a predecessor of the General Electric Co.

Sprengel had invented in 1865 a mercury vacuum pump which would produce a much higher vacuum than any previous pump. This had been the inspiration behind the efforts of Joseph Swan of England, who probably came closer than the others to achieving the goal finally attained by Edison. But it was Edison coming into the competitive search late, who reviewed the nature of the problem of "sub-dividing the electric light" as it was often called,

who determined the optimum voltages for use for the purpose—substantially that which is in use all over the world today, and it was Edison who established the theory of the high-resistance filament, the necessity of a high vacuum, and constant potentials as requisites to a successful incandescent lighting system, even before beginning the experiments to establish the lamp itself. The first conclusive evidence of the correctness of his theory was the success of the cotton thread, carbonized filament lamp, the last in a series of thousands of Edison experimental lamps, but the first to burn for nearly two days.

One of the chief bugs of the vacuum lamps, Edison's as well as all others, was the fact disclosed in the course of experiments that oxygen was freed by the filament of the lamp when heated after evacuation and sealing, thus oxidizing the filament and shortening its life. The solution finally arrived at by Edison was to heat the filament electrically during the evacuation of the air, which drove off the occluded oxygen, which then would be withdrawn by the pump. Later, treatment of the filaments by gasoline vapor was a method used to "firm up" the filament and to harmlessly combine with the oxygen. The introduction of chemical "getters" came much later in the development of the tungsten filament lamp by engineers of the General Electric Co., chief successor to the earlier Edison General Electric Co.

This oxygen trapped in the material of the filaments was one of the chief "bugs" which the Englishman Swan had failed to discover. However, in common with most of the other competitors in the race for the first commercially practicable lamp, Swan also failed to realize the importance of a high-resistance filament to a complete multiple lamp system—the backbone of the Edison conception of the need to be met. While Edison from the first had in mind the practical demands of a complete distribution system that would compete with illuminating gas, most of the others who were closest to a successful demonstration lamp were confining their attentions to the one element.

Now we are able to see that with a successful incandescent lamp, but one step is necessary to make of it a vacuum tube. An amazing fact is, that with no demand existing for such a device and years before the accomplishment of wireless telegraphy, Thomas A. Edison did just that! In 1883, while experimenting with the carbon filament incandescent lamp, Edison discovered that charged particles were emitted from the heated filament. This was called for a time in scientific circles "The Edison Effect." Regardless of nomenclature, this discovery in pure science provided the basis of what is now termed "electronics." An appropriate coincidence was that the first paper to be published by the American Institute of Electrical Engineers was an article on the "Edison Effect," written by Professor Edwin J. Houston. Mr. Edison introduced a plate into the incandescent lamp to intercept these charged particles for the purpose of regulating voltage and upon the claims for this use he was granted a patent October 21, 1884. Thus U. S. patent No. 307,031 became the foundation patent of the electronics industry.

An associate of Edison, John W. Howell, while experimenting with one of these tubes in his laboratory in the Edison Lamp Works at Harrison, noted that the tube could be used also as a rectifier of alternating current and wrote an article upon this use which also appeared in the Transactions of the American Institute of Electrical Engineers. This immediately stimulated further interest in the "Edison Effect" among scientists. In 1885 Edison made some of these tubes which he gave to Sir William Preece, who had given the first demonstration of the phonograph before a scientific society in England. It was from Preece that Fleming, another British scientist and inventor, secured one or more of the Edison tubes and the result was the "Fleming valve" of 1903. This was identical with the

Edison voltage regulator tube, but was used with a different external circuit for a quite different purpose—the detection of "wireless waves." Now as we have seen, this was not the first detector of wireless waves, for by this time wireless telegraphy had progressed to the iron-filing coherer, electrolytic and crystal detectors, all forms of high-frequency alternating current rectifiers. However, the very first detector of wireless waves had been the "etheroscope" of Thomas Edison, who had invented it to detect the presence of what he had called "etheric force."

The identity of the later Fleming valve with the "Edison Effect" tube was confirmed beyond question by the decision of the Federal Court for the Southern District of New York in the suit of Marconi Co. vs. DeForest Co. (236 Federal Reporter 942), which had been brought on the basis of the Fleming patent by the Marconi Co. on the ground that DeForest's audion tube had infringed it. In the court decision it was stated that in view of the precedence of the Edison patent, which had been used for low frequencies only, that Claim 1 of the Fleming patent alleged to be infringed, was too broad as issued and limited therefore, to the use with high frequencies of the order used in wireless telegraphy. This limitation was effected by filing a statement with the patent office to that effect, known as a "disclaimer." The filing of this disclaimer enabled the court to hold the Fleming patent valid and not anticipated by the prior Edison patent. In other words, the court recognized that the Fleming patent as originally written was too broad in its claims and should never have been approved by the patent examiners.

In any case, Edison was not a party to this suit, so it was a relatively simple matter to secure agreement, as he had not claimed the device as a detector of wireless waves and the original patent had already expired. Fleming had claimed an entirely different functional purpose for the tube than had Edison. Actually, what Fleming had done was

to extend the sphere of usefulness of
the Edison tube by designing for it
a new external circuit. So, one of the
penalties of Edison's multifarious nature was not only to deprive himself in
many cases, of profits from his own
labors, but also indirectly to divert
much of the credit for his scientific
accomplishments, as well. Such was
certainly the case with reference to his
basic discoveries pertaining to wireless
telegraphy and as the inventor of the
fundamental form of the vacuum tube.
This is not to diminish the contributions
of the others. DeForest had converted
the two-element Edison-Fleming rectifier tube into an amplifier by adding a
third element, together with an external plate voltage supply. Variations in
the rectified electron-carried flow from
filament to plate operated to control the
flow of a second circuit supplied by an
external local current supply, thus
operating as an amplifier. The first
plate was later changed to a grid, the
latter comparable to the plate of the
tubes of today, and covered by a subsequent patent.

The suit of the Marconi Co. vs. De-
Forest Co. was countered by a suit of
the DeForest Co. against the Marconi
Co. for infringement of its improvements as mentioned. The Marconi Co.
admitted that the DeForest Co. patents
on these improvements were being infringed upon and that the claims on
these counts were valid. This "confess-
ing judgment" as it is called thus
cleared the way for consideration by
the court of the validity of the Fleming
patent and the question as to whether
it was infringed upon by the audion
three-element tube of DeForest.

During the course of the trial, every
type of detector previously used was
considered by the court, including the
coherer, microphone, magnetic, electrolytic, and crystal types. Each of these
prior methods involved certain restric-
tive defects upon the future development of the art which were removed
only by the advent of the Fleming valve
and the improvements of DeForest. The
verdict of the court in part read,

"The contribution of Fleming was
clearly invention and is entitled to
liberal interpretation and consideration."

The contention of the DeForest attorneys was that the audion operated on a
different principle from that of Fleming in that it was a relay, its unique
feature in providing currents of audio
frequency employing a local energy
source, distinct from the input energy.

It was shown by the attorneys for
the Marconi Co., however, that the use
of a local current, or "B" supply source,
had been used before Fleming and De-
Forest with detectors of earlier types to
secure improved results. As these prior
types of detectors were also rectifiers,
it was maintained that the use of a
local current supply antedated the De-
Forest patents. The court adopted the
view prompted by the expert testimony of Waterman, Armstrong, and
others that the grid and plate combined
with the two circuits of DeForest's
Audion were equivalent to the single
plate with the circuit of Fleming and,
therefore, the audion operated on the
principle of rectification, the "B" battery source used by DeForest only
assisting in this action.

The court's decision, therefore, was
that the three-element audion of De-
Forest, used as a detector, or as an
oscillator, or as an amplifier, infringed
upon the Fleming patent. Even though
the Fleming valve even at this very
time was already obsolete by reason of
DeForest's improvements and upon
which the Marconi Co. had admitted
infringing. In other words, the court
decided the DeForest improvements
were based upon what Fleming had accomplished.

This decision was later affirmed by
the Circuit Court of Appeals, Second
Circuit (243 Federal Reporter 560). The
court said, "DeForest in his three-
electrode audion has undoubtedly made
a contribution of great value to the
art, and by the confession of judgment
in respect thereof, defendant company
may employ the just results of this con-

tribution." But the question remains, with respect to historical accuracy, to whom belongs the major credit for the initial and basic contribution of the first vacuum tube, Fleming or Edison? Edison had built the first tube, Fleming had discovered a new use for it. Would Ambrose Fleming ever have been able to have carried out the organized research and intensive experimentation that produced the first commercial incandescent lamp?

There is revealed a great disparity in the philosophy and reasoning of patent reviewers and of the courts in dealing with the relative merits of basic inventions and of contributory improvements and/or new uses. In this case, although careful distinctions were made between the relative claims of DeForest and Fleming, historic justice was denied Edison, whose research and accomplishment was so unique in this particular instance that the contributions of both Fleming and DeForest are quite secondary. Considered from this viewpoint, which was tacitly admitted by the court, the contribution of DeForest towards the new use in adding the all-important third element, was the greater of the latter two.

If the philosophy of this court had been applied to the patents cases, there is little question but that Edison would have promptly received the rightful credit as inventor of the carbon-button transmitter, which made Bell's telephone practical. This would have detracted in no way from Bell's credit as inventor of the first articulating telephone. Both inventions were essential to successful telephone operation and both, with relatively minor improvements, are in use today.

If the philosophy of this court had been applied to the 1894 case of American Graphophone Co. vs. The North American Phonograph Co., this company as holder of the Edison patents, could not have been adjudged a violator of the Graphophone patents of Bell and Tainter, for the latter were contributory. Fortunately, in the interest of the ultimate establishment of his-

toric truth, the most irrefutable facts are the artifacts of the industry—three dimensional evidence in the shape of the inventions themselves. Barring a world holocaust much of what has been accomplished remains to be examined at will, to prove or refute the claims of inventors, the wisdom of patent examiners or the justice of the courts.

Elsewhere we have noted that except for the use to which they were put, the Fleming valve and the "Edison Effect" tube of 1888 were identical. It is true that the use to which a device is put is in part the subject of the patent. But is it not ironical that Edison, discoverer of "etheric force" and the inventor of the first detector of it should also have designed the basic radio vacuum tube without realizing it? It is also somewhat tragic that by reason of experiments with the "Edison Effect" having ceased before Reginald Fessenden came to work for Edison, Fessenden missed exposure to them. For if Fessenden had become aware of the potentials of this one Edison device in addition to the concepts which he developed subsequently, he might well have become the dominant figure in the future of wireless telephony and radio that his accomplishments otherwise deserved.

However, it is in the nature of things for new uses to be found for old devices. It must be recognized that Howell and Fleming found new uses for the Edison tube. It must be recognized that it was Fleming who first saw its possibilities for use as a detector of wireless waves and made it serve as such by the simple expedient of adding a different type of external circuit to it. Fessenden in the paper previously referred to described this development as follows:

"In 1905 Professor Fleming invented a very efficient detector based on the 'Edison effect' in incandescent lamps, and the observations of Elster and Geitel on the rectifying effect of such an arrangement on Hertzian oscillations."

If this is true, and it must be, for the results of the experiments with the Edison tube by Elster and Geitel had been previously published in Germany, then the patent examiners were incorrect in allowing a patent to Fleming, for he had contributed nothing to what had been previously known and published!

There must have been a great deal of misunderstanding of the various principles involved, or of failure to assimilate new contributions at the time for Fessenden said:

"Virtually nothing was done in Europe in the way of producing sustained oscillations by the arc or high frequency method until recently, possibly because of Duddell's erroneous statement to the effect that frequencies much above 10,000 could not be obtained by the Thomson Elihu arc method, and Fleming's statement that an abrupt impulse was necessary and that high frequency currents, even if of sufficient frequency, could not produce radiation."[17]

In his 1908 paper, Fessenden described the Poulsen arc as an interesting modification of the Elihu Thomson arc, with the arc formed in hydrogen instead of in air or compressed gas, as with the latter. He said that it is not as efficient as the older method and gives rise to stray harmonics, but that he mentioned it because of the interest in it in Europe. The Fessenden description is quite at variance with the description in the historical summary of the development of wireless telephony as given by N. H. Slaughter D.S.M., of the Engineering Dept. of the Western Electric Co. as given in a paper presented before a joint meeting of the Electrical Section

and Philadelphia Section of the American Institute of Electrical Engineers Oct. 30, 1919, in which Slaughter said:

"With the development of the Poulsen arc the first successful attempts at radio telephony were begun."

But we will return to Mr. Slaughter later! Fessenden, by the way, justified his criticism of the Poulsen arc by referring to qualitative tests made of it by Dr. Austin, as recorded in the bulletin of the U. S. Bureau of Standards, Vol. 3, No. 2.

Fessenden stated that as of the time he was speaking in America, June 1908, the development of the sustained oscillation non-microphonic system had progressed steadily and had reached the stage of commercial practicality. To sum up the state of the art then achieved before proceeding to a description of his recent experiments, Fessenden listed some of the later types of detectors. One, a frictional receiver in which the received waves produced a change of friction between two moving surfaces and thus produced an audible signal, was based on the electro-motograph principle. This was a discovery in pure science made by Edison and demonstrated by him before the National Academy of Science in Philadelphia in 1874.[18] Upon this detector Fessenden applied for a patent in 1905. Another was Fessenden's heterodyne receiver, for which application was filed June 28, 1905. Fessenden described this most important invention as follows:

"The heterodyne receiver, in which a local field of force actuated by a continuous source of high-frequency oscillations interacts with a field produced by the received oscillations and creates beats of an audible frequency."

It must be obvious to even the layman that here was propounded one of the great principles of radio, yet who gives

[17] *Proceedings of the International Congress,* St. Louis, 1904; *The Electrician,* Vol. LI, 1903, Duddell.

It would almost seem that the quotation of Fleming's published statement further damns his historical claim to rightful credit for the first vacuum tube, for he obviously did not understand the nature of the oscillations that his tube was designed to detect!

[18] Used in the Edison loud-speaking telephone in England.

a thought to Reginald Fessenden to-day? However, Fessenden must have had a blind spot, as had Edison, when he surveyed the possibilities of the vacuum tubes which were to be utilized by others to bring about the fruition of his dreams. He mentioned favorably the Cooper-Hewitt mercury receiver, but his comments on the audion of DeForest denoted but little interest. He said of it:

"The 'audion' of DeForest, a very interesting and sensitive device, which though superficially resembling Prof. Fleming's rectifier appears to act on a different principle."

Later in the exposition of his experiments, Fessenden said:

"The previously mentioned thermoelectric receivers of Dr. Austin and Mr. Pickard and the vacuum tube receivers of Fleming, DeForest, and Cooper-Hewitt also act very satisfactorily. The fact that the writer has not been able to get as good results from them may be due to greater familiarity with the liquid barretter and heterodyne receiver."

Yet, as we now know, with his heterodyne concept and the yet unrealized amplifying potential of the audion tube he had, within his grasp, all of the essentials of a modern radio circuit!

Fessenden told of the interesting manner in which he discovered the principle of the modulation of a carrier wave by the voice currents in the following words:

"The writer has been asked on several occasions how the wireless telephone came to be invented. In November, 1899, shortly prior to the delivery of my previous paper, while experimenting with the receiver shown in figure 3 of that paper, I made some experiments with a Wehnelt interrupter for operating the induction coil used for sending.

"In the receiver mentioned the ring of a short-period Elihu Thomson os-

cillating current galvanometer rests on three supports, i.e., two pivots and a carbon block, and a telephone receiver is in circuit with the carbon block. A storage battery being used in the receiver circuit, it was noticed that when the sending key was kept down at the sending station for a long dash the peculiar wailing sound of the Wehnelt interrupter was reproduced with absolute fidelity in the receiving telephone. It at once suggested itself that by using a source above audibility wireless telephony could be accomplished."

To achieve a carrier frequency above audibility, Fessenden had his collaborator, Prof. Kintner, design an interrupter to give 10,000 breaks per-second. Experiments were made in the fall of 1900 with transmission over a mile, but with poor speech quality.

By 1904 and 1905 both the arc and a 10,000 cycle alternator were being used with such success that sets were advertised and tendered to the U. S. government.[19] By 1906, the high-frequency alternator was perfected and used for telephony between Brant Rock and Plymouth, a distance of 11 miles. Articulation was excellent as described by telephone experts who witnessed tests. On Dec. 11, 1906, invitations were extended to a number of scientists to witness tests in connection with wire lines. A report was given in the *American Telephone Journal* for Jan. 26 and Feb. 2, 1907, the editor of that publication having been among those present.

In July 1907, the range was extended to 200 miles, conversations being carried on between Brant Rock and Jamaica, L. I. For this purpose an efficient antenna had been erected at Jamaica approximately 180 ft. high. Fessenden said that by this time wireless telephone experiments were also in progress in Europe, some using his earlier arc method, others using the Poulsen arc.

---

[19] *The Electrician*, London, Feb. 22, 1907.

N. H. Slaughter of Western Electric Co., in his paper of 1919 previously mentioned, stated that a chief drawback of the wireless methods of this earlier period was the necessity of inserting the microphone directly in the antenna circuit, or otherwise directly modulating the radio frequency current, which imposed too great a load on the microphone. However, Fessenden said in his 1908 paper that he had developed a new type of microphone which he called a trough transmitter which would carry as much as 15 amperes. This was a water jacketed, carbon granule transmitter with platinum-iridium electrodes. He also designed a relay amplifier embodying this principle for amplifying weak incoming signals.

Fessenden apparently always preferred the liquid barretter receiver, which was quite human, as it was his own invention. Had he been more sensitive to the possibilities of the audion of DeForest in its then used state as a detector, he might have become aware of its future usefulness as an amplifier and as a transmitting oscillator. He very likely would have been led to the same conclusions reached by other later investigators.

Meanwhile, Marconi, the opportunist, had been making the most of the publicity attendant to spanning great distances, using much more primitive equipment for straight wireless telegraphy. Unhampered by the necessity for providing a smooth carrier wave with perfected characteristics essential for voice modulation, Marconi was concerned with distance, not quality. As late as 1911, according to a paper prepared by Marconi and read before the Royal Institute of Great Britain on June 2, 1911, he was still using the rotary spark-gap with a spark frequency of 500 per second. He was utilizing his magnetic detector or vacuum tubes for receiving, but as yet no vacuum tube amplification. Yet with this rather crude apparatus for that late date, he was able to establish regular, commercial communication between Clifden, Ireland and Glace Bay,

Newfoundland. Thus Marconi, with the backing of the British government was able to achieve spectacular results, in this manner reaping the popular acclaim as the "inventor of wireless."

This is not recited to dim the importance of his demonstration of the practicality of wireless telegraphy, but to accord some measure of due recognition to certain others who made much more essential contributions to radio and especially *electrical recording technics*, with which this work is primarily concerned. From the latter standpoint, the contributions of Marconi were negligible; those of Henry, Edison, Thomson, Fessenden, and DeForest were essential. As late as 1911, as we have seen, Marconi had not been interested in voice transmission and considered the chief benefits of wireless telegraphy to be international business communications, ship-to-ship and ship-to-shore communications, particularly as an aid to ships in distress—worthy objectives, but not germane to our subject.

There is no questioning the fact that the work of Fessenden was fundamental to the later development of commercial wireless telephony and radio broadcasting. After the successful demonstration of his devices and methods to the Bell Telephone Co., in 1908, contracts were drawn up by representatives of the Bell Telephone Co. calling for the installation of wireless telephone communication links between Martha's Vineyard and Boston, and for the construction of wireless telephone long-distance lines between Boston, New York, Buffalo, and Washington. However, after a delay these contracts were not signed and the reason given by the representatives of the Bell Telephone Co. was not that there was any doubt of the practicality of Fessenden's methods, but that the banking interests had decided that the company had been expanding too rapidly and therefore they were forced to revise their policy. As a consequence, wireless telephony for commercial use was delayed for about a dozen years.[20]

----

[20] *Radio Broadcast*, July, 1922.

Now Fessenden was a scientist, not a businessman, and after the complete exposition of his equipment and methods before the engineers of the Bell Telephone Co., it is perhaps not too surprising that in 1919 we find a representative of the Western Electric Co., wholly owned subsidiary of the Bell Telephone Co., claiming full credit for the engineers of his company for the development of successful wireless telephony. Despite the evidence of contracts tendered by the Bell representatives to Fessenden, which they later failed to sign, N. H. Slaughter of the Western Electric Co. in a paper delivered before the American Institute of Electrical Engineers, Oct. 30, 1919, managed to deliver what he termed a "Historical Summary" of the development of wireless telephony without even mentioning Fessenden's name!

Among other things Slaughter said: "With the development of the Poulsen arc, the first successful attempts at radio telephony were begun." This we know is quite at variance with the facts previously given. But to be fair to Mr. Slaughter, we will give this quotation complete with context, as given under the heading "Historical Summary."

"The first requirement for any wireless telephone station is a source of radio frequency current whose amplitude from cycle to cycle remains constant, except when varied by the modulation imposed upon it by the voice current. If variations in its amplitude occur, due to other causes, these variations will introduce disturbances which will cause the system to be deficient in the effective transmission of speech. It is at once evident that the original source of radio frequency current used in wireless telegraphy, namely, the oscillatory discharge of a condenser supplied with energy from a low frequency source, is entirely unsuited to the purposes of wireless telephony.

"With the development of the Poulsen arc the first successful attempts at radio telephony were begun. These attempts involved the second factor in a wireless telephone station, namely, that of modulating the radio frequency current in accordance with the currents supplied by a telephone transmitter. The early attempts to accomplish this modulation, by means of microphones inserted directly in the antenna circuit or coupled to the circuit in various manners, were largely unsuccessful, due to the limitations of the microphone devices, such as the low current capacity and the small range of variation of resistance.

"A second source of radio frequency current is the high frequency alternator, which has been developed in various forms and which has been likewise used with limited success for wireless telephone transmission. The same lack of a suitable modulating device handicapped the use of the high frequency alternator until the advent of the audion or vacuum tube. The characteristics of the vacuum tube have been fully described in many recent publications, and will be discussed in this paper only in so far as these characteristics are directly applicable to the problems of wireless telephony. It will be seen from this subsequent discussion that the vacuum tube possesses in a remarkable manner the precise characteristics required for the generation and modulation of radio frequency current for low power wireless telephone stations, and for the detection and amplification of radio signals of any character whatsoever. Its influence on the art of wireless telephony may well be compared with the influence of the gas engine on aviation."

Deftly, you see, Slaughter evades the fact that persons other than Poulsen were largely responsible for the development of the arc method. He also very casually passes right over the fact that these persons were also very much concerned with the development of the high-frequency alternator, which he mentions in an off-hand manner as though it had always existed for a multitude of purposes and had not been laboriously and expressly developed for the purposes of wireless telephony!

Slaughter then described the new use of the vacuum tube as an oscillator. He stated that although the vacuum tube had been invented in 1906, its development into a sufficiently practical form for use in wireless telephony had been comparatively slow. He stated that this development had been accelerated beginning in 1912, when the American Telephone and Telegraph Co. became interested in the vacuum tube for telephone repeaters. He stated that as a result of improvements in tubes and experiments the transmission of speech from Washington, D.C., to Paris and Honolulu by wireless telephone had been accomplished in 1915. In these experiments the vacuum tube had been used as a radio frequency generator, as a modulator, and as an amplifier.

Now for the record, it should be pointed out that without the resources of A.T. & T., and without using vacuum tubes for creating the carrier oscillations, speech had been received in Scotland in Nov. 1906. Conversation between Brant Rock and Plymouth had been picked up by the operators at Michrihanish, Scotland, who sent back reports identifying the voices and repeating the exact words of the conversations, which were subsequently verified by the log books of the station.

That Mr. Slaughter had a guilty feeling about the matter may be indicated by his apparent inability to review the development of wireless telephony factually, or to recognize the contributions of various persons by name so as to give credit where it is due. Perhaps a partial explanation and the sequel to this story is to be found in the next chapter.

CHAPTER 17

THE THEORY OF MATCHED IMPEDANCE

A DRASTIC revolution in attitudes and purposes came over the leaders of the lateral disc phonograph industry during 1924. Confronted with figures showing a precipitous decline in sales, its officials suddenly became aware of their almost total unpreparedness to compete with the burgeoning radio industry. Moreover, it slowly dawned upon them that while they had been attempting blindly to "ride out" the wave of intense popular interest in radio broadcasting, tastes in entertainment had been rapidly changing.

The moment for decision was at hand. Men who have been complacent for years, when suddenly faced with the loss of their personal fortunes, can become amazingly amenable to suggestions that seem to promise a way of averting disaster. Certain Bell representatives meeting with the harassed talking machine men promised to roll them a pill that would cure the ailing industry if they would cooperate and listen to reason. It is said the pill was so bitter that some of the Directors gagged upon it, but all finally swallowed, even the President, although he was made quite ill. It may have been that he was troubled with certain personal ideals which it was made clear would have to be discarded.

To partially explain this allegorical description, it should be recalled that from the earliest days of the phonograph, its mission had been conceived of as the "storing up" of sound. At first

the effort consisted largely of trying to make the various kinds of sounds recognizable. As technics were improved the sights were raised and new goals became evident in the more ambitious claims of the various inventors. Horns were substituted for ear tubes; volume was increased; duets and quartets were recorded. After some years of development, bands and small orchestras were used to provide background for voice or solo instruments instead of the tinkling piano accompaniments. "As loud and clear as the original," was the caption on an Edison Concert Grand advertisement of 1900.

Records came to be evaluated as more or less faithful reproductions of the original performance. The culmination of this trend came with the Edison diamond disc "Re-Creations" of 1915 and thereafter. Realism had become the generally accepted ideal of the recording industry of that time. The reproduction of overtones had been made the subject of intensive study in the Edison Laboratory and elsewhere. Absolute definition had become a fetish with the "old man," himself. Reflected sounds were looked upon by him as "muddying up" the reproduction. In the Victor Laboratories and those of its affiliates in Europe, as well as certain others such as Fonotipia in Italy, emphasis had been laid from the first on the securing of a "brilliant" reproduction, as near to the original in volume and quality as possible. It is true, therefore, that some room resonance was generally permitted in the recording practice of these studios in order to facilitate the recording of the instruments farther away from the recording horn. In the United States the Columbia recording experts for a long period endeavored to collect more reflected sound as a means of getting more bass. Nevertheless, the ideal in common was to secure accurate voice and solo instrument reproduction. A factor in this was that there was a focus to the old method of horn recording, just as there was a focus to the reproducing system. Sometimes when, by careful calculation, or perhaps more often by a fortunate chance placement and combination of circumstances, a highly desired "forward" effect would be achieved, giving the feeling of the actual presence of the artist.

Now however, in 1924, a new purpose enters. Instead of the old idea of "storing up" sound, or of re-creating it, the capturing of sound was to be considered as a synthesis, the projection of it as an illusion. It is true that illusion is inherent in the methods of the motion picture, dependent as they are upon the psychological phenomenon of the retention of vision. Nothing in the methods essential to the reproduction of sound waves are of that nature. Even so, the old idea of preserving, or storing up of the human voice or musical performance for repetition at will now gave way to the creation of calculated effects, of a specious and spurious type of reproduction. Proof of this statement lies in the fact that the chief creator of the Western Electric system, J. P. Maxfield, was to acknowledge in his own writings within a few years that he and his collaborators had, in a somewhat exaggerated sense, constructed a Frankenstein monster. This is not to question the sincerity and intent of Mr. Maxfield, who in 1924 quite evidently had not realized what the ultimate effects of his innovations were to be. However, be that as it may, there is no denying that the acts of the Bell executives and engineers, individually and collectively, were largely responsi-

ble for the establishing of new recording industry attitudes that are present today.

It must be conceded that these new attitudes made it possible for the ailing industry to adopt methods which by their facility and versatility placed it in a position of being able to accept the status quo of public taste as it had become conditioned by exposure to radio. Not only this, but as Maxfield was so soon to deplore, the adoption of radio methods by performers in their recording sessions was to accentuate the trends in popular taste towards acceptance of the unreal. Viewing this situation in retrospect, we may excuse Maxfield, but the ultimate purposes of his superiors to overwhelm the talking machine industry with plausible new viewpoints and technics can scarcely be doubted.

During the acoustic period, the discussion of "realism" versus "romanticism" had been confined to the province of the listener. He often liked what he heard from his talking machine even though technically it was often woefully deficient. The recording expert, on the other hand, was always striving mightily and against seemingly insuperable odds to attain absolute realism. Now, at long last, a new set of values was to be offered to the public. In the guise of science, the illusion of hearing as though in a distant concert hall was to be presented as a great advance in the technics of sound reproduction. It was new, it was different; and at first, at least in the United States, it seemed that nearly everyone was greatly impressed with this newly discovered attribute of the phonograph— to transport the concert hall into the living room, or vice versa. However, as time went on, this illusion began to pall, and to stimulate the sales of records, other and more subtle forms of distortion were introduced. The insinuating sotto voce, over amplified sounds made by "Whispering" Jack Smith and Little Jack Little represented only the more obvious misuses of the microphonic technics eventually to be foisted on the public. Rudy Vallee was to popularize the term "crooner" and open the doors of the recording studios to a flood of trick stylists from radio. This trend became epidemic. Soon stage appearances had to be bolstered with public address systems for without amplification the crooning Mills brothers and Miss Poop-poop-a-do could not have been heard beyond the third row!

It was not long before most persons had but the slightest conception, between radio and records, of what the singers or instrumentalists of either media really sounded like. New likes and dislikes without reference to the reality of the originating sounds became prevalent. New criteria for the evaluation of recorded performances became established. What average listener today knows or cares about "accuracy of reproduction?" He knows what he likes and dislikes, the fact that he seldom has reference to an original performance bothers him not in the least. To understand what has happened in a cultural sense, as well as technologically, it is necessary to know these facts pertaining to the way in which electrical recording and reproduction methods came into use. It should be somewhat humbling to the proponents of uncontrolled license in the use of these methods to realize that Thomas A. Edison, who established most of the basic elements essential to electrical recording, was the last of the pioneer record manufacturers to employ it. Morally he was right, even though his own phonographic enterprise was soon to be overwhelmed by the avalanche brought forth by the introduction of the Western Electric system by Maxfield. The standard which the latter set up in the acoustic Orthophonic Victrola (Fig. 15-1) was swept away in the same flood of radio-generated public demand for more bass, more volume, and unrestricted license in both recording and reproduction technics.

In another chapter there has been recounted the extraordinary role that chance played in the early history of

the development of the phonograph through the award of a cash prize to Alexander Graham Bell by the French government. As a result of this circumstance Bell had been enabled to organize the Volta Laboratory Association for the stated purpose of engaging in telephone and acoustical research. This series of events culminated in that colossus and terror of the early phonographic world, the American Graphophone Co. At that time the parent telephone company, the American Bell Telephone Company, had its collective hands full of its own technical difficulties and at the same time was engaged in waging its life-and-death struggle with Western Union. It wanted no part of its stepchild, the Graphophone. The men interested primarily in establishing the Bell telephone on a profitable basis could see no commercial possibilities in the Messrs. Bells' and Tainter's version of the phonograph. But within a few years, with the Western Union settlement behind and financial security of the telephone enterprise assured, opportunity again knocked at the doors of the telephone men. This time it was the doors of the Board Room of the Directors of the company, in meeting at the Boston headquarters. Through the door came a representative of Emile Berliner, who had previously assisted them with a tactically convenient telephone patent. This time Berliner had sent to them his new talking machine, named the Gramophone. To his discomfiture the board members regarded his new disc machine as a toy, for which they can hardly be blamed. Also, knowing full well the actual functional worthlessness of his telephone patent which they had purchased, the directors had further reason for skepticism regarding Berliner's inventive abilities. Yet, before them at the moment was the opportunity to buy for a pittance the same talking machine that Eldridge R. Johnson was within a few years to build up into a multi-million dollar empire!

Eldridge R. Johnson was primarily a mechanic, turned businessman. His development of Berliner's crude Gramophone into the Victor Talking Machine had been along strict evolutionary and expedient lines. Down through the years, such research as was done was under the heavy hand of Johnson who, like Edison, had little use for academic theory and mathematical formulae. He early sought to surround himself with men who thought as he did, in contrast with the practice of Edison who often employed well-known mathematicians and university professors if he felt that their training and skills would help him, even though he enjoyed ridiculing their efforts from time to time.[1] Contrasted with the turnover at the Edison laboratories, the situation at the Victor plant was quite different, most of the officials and his board of directors were with Johnson for years. Johnson's comparatively easy triumphs in the markets over his arch rivals over the years eventually rendered him quite insensitive to the possibility of a possible encroachment upon his empirical domain by theorists and experimenters. He and his board felt secure in the possession of certain basic patents and a proven formula for doing business. Although the amazing accomplishment of Edison in achieving precision reproduction of voice and solo instruments with his new disc machine had given the Victor executives some temporary concern, the business ineptitude of the Edison organization together with the surface noise problem which began to plague the Edison records increasingly through the war years, soon calmed their fears. Anyway, as always, Victor had the great artists, had she not?

Thus, head in the sand of his own accomplishments and surrounded by satisfied, trustworthy men of his own choosing, the usually imperturbable Mr. Johnson found himself suddenly unprepared to deal on equal terms with these outsiders who were bringing before him what was purported to be a revolu-

---

[1] One of these mathematicians was Samuel Insull, another A. E. Kennelly, the latter is referred to elsewhere and in the latter part of this chapter.

tionary concept of recording and reproduction. The Victor men, confident in their impregnable position, had been accustomed for years to giving aspiring inventors from outside the realm a courteous but firm brush-off. But here were men speaking glibly and confidently the jargon of science who came from a corporate group too large and powerful to be dismissed lightly. Moreover, the more their proposal was examined, the less it appeared in the nature of an opportunity and the more it appeared as an ultimatum. What if this were to be placed in the hands of their competitors? Agreeing with their philosophy or not, the Bell engineers had succeeded in advancing the theory and technics of lateral recording by electrical means to a point from which there could be no turning back. Eldridge R. Johnson and his laboratory men had carried the improvement of the acoustical recording methods as far as they had been able with their strictly empirical approach, but without knowledge of theoretical acoustics and electronics they had neither the talent nor the time to duplicate the advantages offered by the new Western Electric process.

The basis for electrical recording had been laid in quite early days by a number of theorists and experimenters. Most of the important laws regarding resistances, inductances, capacitances, etc. had been worked out in the development of the telegraph. The necessity of equalizing resistance and capacity by the use of higher voltages and "high intensity" electromagnets in receiving telegraph instruments had been outlined by Joseph Henry even before the first commercial telegraph and as incorporated in Morse's first successful telegraph by Vail. Edison's quadruplex telegraph and his introduction of the induction coil in telephone circuits very early in that field is ample evidence of his understanding of these properties. The relationships of electrical to mechanical energy, of electrical capacity to kinetic energy, of electrical resistance to mechanical friction had all been well established years before in the designing of many types of electrical devices, particularly dynamos and motors, which because of the application of these known principles, soon reached high efficiencies even today not attained in steam turbines and the internal combustion engine. Most of this research was done by men who were not telephone men.

The origin of the phonograph concept in Edison's mind was that of producing a telephone repeater similar to his telegraph repeater, as his published statements, patents and laboratory notes attest. From the day the first phonograph was built it was possible to record and reproduce articulate speech electrically. The very first description of Edison's idea, as published in a letter to the Editor of the *Scientific American* in November 1877, outlined the device as a telephone repeater, with both the recording and reproducing styli attached to telephone diaphragms. This was electrical recording! However, the first phonograph actually built was entirely mechanical, for the furore over the news that Edison had created a machine that would speak made it desirable to produce it in such a form that it could be demonstrated anywhere. The demand for the phonograph for exhibition purposes resulted in the shelving of it as an adjunct of the telephone for a considerable number of years.

Electrical recording was done experimentally from the time of the introduction of wax cylinders forward. Except for the recording of telephone conversations it was not used commercially for the making of records for two reasons; first, because in the earlier stages of these arts the quality of reproduction of both the telephone and phonograph was so low as to preclude a truly successful combination; second, because of the lack of suitably developed mechanical or electrical amplifiers. Such experiments as were made quite often made use of some form of tubular air coupling between a telephone receiver and the recording dia-phragm, which, incidentally, fits the bandpass filter theory propounded many years later by the theorists responsible for the Western Electric system. In some cases a recording stylus was attached directly to the telephone diaphragm, as originally proposed by Edison. A number of patents were issued in the early days upon such devices. One of the chief reasons for the failure of these attempts at electrical recording was that the telephone designers were quite content with receivers of poor quality and limited frequency range, which sufficed for telephone conversation but were entirely unsuited for the reproduction of music. After competition in the telephone field had been practically eliminated by the victory in the courts of the Bell interests over Western Union, improvement of telephonic quality was very slow and the quality of reproduction of the entirely mechanical phonograph soon far outstripped it. Only a limited sensitivity is desirable in telephony. Too sensitive a transmitter or receiver is a hindrance to voice communication because of extraneous sounds. A wide range of frequencies is also undesirable.

The closest approach to an actual commercial application of electrical recording in the early period was the Telegraphone of Valdemar Poulsen, invented by him in Denmark in 1898. This was the first wire recorder. He also later developed a flat steel disc with a raised spiral ridge which was magnetized by a recording head very similar to that later used to actuate the armature of the wax-incising recording heads. Again, it was principally the lack of a suitable means of amplification that prevented the successful development of these devices at that time.

However, in all branches of the electrical industries the knowledge of electrical circuits and their relationships to mechanical equivalents continued to grow. One of the principle contributors to the formulation of discovered properties was A. G. Webster, who wrote "Theory of Electricity and Magnetism" in 1897 and "Dynamics of Partials and of Rigid, Elastic and Fluid Bodies" in 1904. A contemporary engaged in telephone research, G. A. Campbell, in 1903 wrote "On Loaded Lines in Telephone Transmission." In the meantime a one-time Edison associate, Reginald Fessenden, was demonstrating the feasibility of the wireless telephone. Moreover, he was establishing the modulated carrier wave principle and other elements which were to make successful radio broadcasting possible, even without vacuum tubes. It was Fessenden who focussed the attention of the Bell officials on the great potential of wireless communication and placed his methods at their disposal, as stated elsewhere. A contract had been drawn up providing for the construction of a number of stations by Fessenden for the Bell company for long distance communication by wireless telephone, but negotiations were broken off. However, it is noteworthy that Bell research was not restricted by this decision—in fact it was expanded rapidly. About this time the Bell Telephone Laboratories became very much interested in Lee DeForest's audion tube. The end result of this sequence of events was the first successful transmission of speech by wireless from the U. S. to Honolulu and return in 1915, and also the accomplishment of the first successful transcontinental telephone conversations. An ironic note in this connection is that the voice of Metropolitan soprano Anna Case, demonstrating the achievement of Edison in the re-creating of her voice by singing in direct comparison with the phonographic reproduction for the first time, had her voice carried to Thomas A. Edison at the Pan-American Exposition in San Francisco from his library at Orange by long distance telephone by means of vacuum tube amplification at the same time.

It was this same year of 1915 that A. G. Webster wrote a paper which was read before the National Academy of Science entitled, "A New Instrument for Absolute Acoustical Measurements." This described his Phonometer, based on the principle of resonance, for measuring intensities of pure sounds. However, about a year before, in December of 1914, Webster had written another paper which was read before the American Physical Society which was not published in the Proceedings of the society until 1919. In an accompanying note it was stated that publication had been withheld because of continuing development of experimental apparatus by Webster. The title of this highly important paper was "Acoustical Impedance and the Theory of Horns and Phonograph." The effect of this delay on the subsequent development of the phonograph industry may be compared in some ways with the delay in the issuance of the patent to Thomas A. Edison on large diameter cylinder recording, which may have belatedly inspired Thomas Macdonald to build the Graphophone Grand in 1898.

Arthur Gordon Webster was at that time a member of the staff of Clark University, Worcester, Mass. With a colleague, L. T. E. Thompson, he had published in the same journal a paper on "A New Instrument for Measuring Pressures in a Gun." The caption accompanying the article described both Thompson and Webster as of the "Ballistic Institute" of the University, which may account for the delay in publication of other of the articles as perhaps due to security reasons. In view of the importance of Webster's theories and data to the concepts later evolved by Maxfield and Harrison, it would seem that modern electrical recording owes something to the field of ballistics.

There is no doubt that the article by Webster on "Acoustical Impedance and the Theory of Horns and Phonograph" inspired the Bell scientists to go to work on the problem. Webster had called attention to the fact that the British scientist, Oliver Heaviside, had introduced the term "impedance" in dealing with the alternating currents theory of electricity. He also had noted that engineers had failed to observe that this concept would be useful in the study of mechanics and acoustics. Webster established the analogy between mechanical impedance and a condenser in an electrical circuit. He also stated that this analogical theory had been incorporated into formulae which had received practical application by Professor G. W. Stewart in designing horns for use for war purposes. In this now classic treatise, Webster wrote that he had found that it was untrue that the profiles of brass musical instruments were hyperbolic, even though so stated by various texts. He said that he had established that the bell of every instrument could, for all intents and purposes, be represented by one of three formulas which he had developed. Published with the paper was a chart showing response curves for a trombone, coach horn, and a phonograph horn. It showed but little difference between the trombone and a phonograph horn. Webster stated also that he had discovered that a plaster cast of a trombone of the same air cavity dimensions as the trombone would have the same tone quality, thus showing that the notions of musicians and others that the quality of brass of which a horn was constructed was responsible for its tone quality was a myth. It is quite possible that Webster's interest in the property of horns had been prompted by the accomplishment by Edison of precision reproduction of the human voice at about the same time. Edison had used a heavy iron horn, which was considered an entirely inappropriate material by other talking machine manufacturers.

The Webster paper attracted the attention of others than the Bell technicians, however. Among these were Hanna and Slepian, who together wrote a paper published in the *Transactions of the A.I.E.E.* for 1924 entitled, "The Function and Design of Horns for Loud Speakers." These men were also not Bell engineers as later developments will make clear. However, about this time the technical journals began to be fairly well padded with articles by various Bell scientists, revealing the intensive research which was now under way in the Bell laboratories.

During 1924, a large group of engineers of the Western Electric Co., under the direction of J. P. Maxfield and H. C. Harrison were engaged in electrical recording experiments. After a preliminary period of seclusion it became necessary to send wax master records out of the laboratory for processing. These were sent to the Pathe plant in New York City. According to Fred Gaisberg in "*The Music Goes Round*," veterans of the phonograph industry Frank Capps and Russell Hunting were there and becoming curious, played over some of the test pressings. They were amazed at the increased volume and the sibillant sounds recorded. Hunting was then American manager of the Pathe-Freres Co. Capps was an inventor and former associate of Edison, and he had been retained by Louis Sterling, President of the English Columbia Phonograph Co., Ltd., to send him reports on the developments in the phonograph industry in the United States. Capps certainly earned his fee in this case, for he sent sample pressings to Sterling, informing him that he understood that negotiations were already underway with the Victor Co. for exclusive use of the new process. Sterling cabled the Western Electric Co. to delay any decision until his arrival and boarded ship for the United States.

He later found that a draft of an agreement which would have given the Victor Talking Machine Co. exclusive control of the Western Electric method for phonographic purposes had been in the hands of the Victor executives for over a month, but that consummation of the agreement had not been possible because of the illness of Eldridge R. Johnson, who was then President of the Board. Whether his illness was induced or aggravated by the terms demanded can only be conjectured. However, it is known that at the same time the laboratory experts of the Victor Co. were frantically trying to find some way of escaping the necessity of acceding to the demands of the A. T. & T.—

Western Electric representatives. The arrival of Sterling put an end to the delaying tactics. He worked furiously and sold the telephone men on the wisdom of not restricting the process to just one company. The exclusive offer to Victor was withdrawn and both companies were subsequently licensed on an equal basis, thus resulting in the introduction of electrical recording and new types of acoustic reproducing instruments by them in 1925. In the United States these were advertised as the Orthophonic Victrola and the Columbia Viva-tonal Phonograph. The visit of Sterling to this country was of paramount importance, for with such interest being manifested on the part of a formidible competitor any disinclination of the Victor men to take their pill had vanished. At this time the American Columbia Phonograph Co. was owned by the English Columbia Co.

According to Gaisberg's account, Emile Berliner, father of the Gramophone, had also figured in the devious maneuvering that had preceded the adoption of the electrical methods.[2] It seems that he was visiting some old associates at the Bell Laboratories one day when some of the experimental electrical recordings were played over for him. Gaisberg said that Berliner then told some of his friends at the Victor plant about the new method being developed and that this resulted in the opening of the negotiations. Later it was disclosed that experiments in electrical recording had been in progress in the English Columbia studios for a year previously, but were abandoned upon acquisition of rights to the Western Electric process. This to a large extent explains Sterling's alertness to the news from America, for his engineers had been working along similar lines but had thus far failed to come up with a commercially practicable method.

To give proper credit, there is no questioning that Maxfield and his associates had revolutionized the science of sound reproduction. The facility and

[2] *The Music Goes Round,* F. W. Gaisberg, The Macmillan Co., New York, 1943.

opportunities for doing things in recording which had never been done before are also beyond question. There is also no doubt but that the new methods provided a thoroughly practical answer to the situation which then existed in the lateral recording branch of the industry. Radio had captivated the public, the record industry was in a slump, sales of talking machines were at low ebb. However, to maintain a proper perspective on the contributions technically of Harrison and his colleagues, it must be remembered that the average quality of radio reproduction at that time was very low. Commercial receiving "sets" of the 1924-25 period seldom had reproduction quality equivalent to even that of the old Victrola. Nevertheless, the lure of free entertainment and the novel feeling that one was actually listening to persons playing or singing in distant places was extremely potent. Since the establishment of the first broadcasting station on a regular schedule in 1920, hundreds of commercial stations had come into being and truly tremendous audiences tuned in every night. A minor factor in the competitive situation was that after the introduction of new, smoother surface records with readable white labels, the sales of Edison phonographs and records had again begun to cut into the rapidly declining disc market for the inferior lateral records. In the face of Edison's undeniable quality and the free entertainment offered by radio, the new Western Electric process seemed to offer the only hope for the ailing lateral disc industry.

To properly evaluate the historic importance of the Western Electric process and the new concepts which accompanied it make it imperative that a fairly complete and critical analysis of it should be given at this point. In the *Transactions of the American Institute of Electrical Engineers* for 1926 a paper was published by Maxfield and Harrison which explains their theories and the methods which they chose to employ. Illustrated are the particular devices which were commercially employed in the Victor recording studios and in the Orthophonic Victrola. Beginning with a brief introduction to the elemental purposes and prior methods of recording by the acoustic method, which it is unnecessary to review here, the authors then launched into their departures from previous practice. In our analysis of the Western Electric process only as much of the Maxfield-Harrison paper will be quoted as is necessary to a comprehension of the points of major importance.

The title of the article by J. P. Maxfield and H. C. Harrison is "Methods of High Quality Recording and Reproducing of Music and Speech based on Telephone Research." After the introductory discussion of previous methods the first sub-heading was "Studio Characteristics and Transients." [3] In this the authors claimed that perfect reproduction requires that the components of the reproduced sound reaching the ears of the listener should have the same relative intensity and phase relationship as the sound reaching the ears of an imaginary listener to the original performance would have. With this statement there is no quarrel, in fact this had been the goal of former methods until upset by the conquest of the old recorders by the new, as will be disclosed. The authors then went on to state that it was difficult, if not impossible to attain this goal with a single channel system, that two would be required. Despite the popularity binaural sound has since acquired, this statement of the authors is to a great extent fallacious. There is at any one instant but a single wave front reaching the ears almost simultaneously. Actually, the ears are unable to distinguish phase differences except under highly regulated laboratory conditions. Due to the rapid and continuously shifting patterns of direct and reflected sounds as in orchestral performances, the ears even in the presence of the instruments are

unable to distinguish depth and the relative location of individual instruments to any appreciable extent during ensemble playing.

Maxfield and Harrison dismissed the dual channel, or binaural method as impractical. However, they claimed to have achieved a certain effect of depth with the single channel system which they were introducing. They ascribed this spatial effect as perhaps due to the increased apparent vibration of the instruments situated at the far end of the recording room as compared with those in the foreground. This, then, was the illusion to be made use of by the authors to enhance the effect of realism. This might perhaps have been better described as follows;

"The delayed reception of sound direct from voices or instruments in the background against an aura of brilliance from the still further delayed echo is contrasted in varying degree with the quality of sound from the nearer voices or instruments, which record with more body and fundamental resonance and with much less echo, thus producing an artificial effect of placement."

The authors stressed the importance of the acoustical qualities of rooms to adequate musical performances. They quoted Sabine's figures on the period of reverberation which had been found to give optimum results in recording musical performances with the room resonance by the binaural method. The authors stated that they had found it advisable to reduce Sabine's figures for their single channel system.

Aside from room resonance, Maxfield and Harrison stated that transients set up by the recording or reproducing system constituted a secondary source of apparent increased reverberation. The authors said that the system they were describing was relatively free of violent phase shifts within most of the frequency range covered, but that there were some undesirable phase shift characteristics with small accompanying

---

[3] Webster's International Dictionary, 1971, "transient—a temporary electrical oscillation that occurs in a circuit because of a sudden change of voltage or of load."

transients near its limiting cut-off frequencies. This means distortion. By noting the range claimed by the authors in the following quotation and bearing in mind that a normal person can hear up to 12,000 cps, the effect upon naturalness of voice reproduction may be appreciated.

"The frequency range which it will be desirable to cover, if it were possible, with relative uniform intensity for the transmission of speech and all types of music including a pipe organ is from about 16 cycles per second to approximately 10,000.

"It may be interesting to examine the record requirements for a band of frequencies this great. For the purpose of this illustration, a lateral record will be assumed although in all factors except the time the record will run, the arguments apply in a similar manner to the hill-and-dale cut."

Yet read what Maxfield wrote in 1933.[4]

"It is only recently that we have been able to record frequencies above 5,000 or 6,000 cycles with any degree of faithfulness, but now the engineers of the Bell Telephone Laboratories and Electrical Research Products, Inc., have developed, in commercial form, the vertical cut method of recording to such a high degree of perfection that they are able to both record and reproduce frequencies up to 9,000 or 10,000 cycles and direct electrical reproduction up to and even above 15,000 cycles has been accomplished."

Note that the above quotation contradicts the earlier statement by Maxfield that the arguments applied in a similar manner to the hill-and-dale cut. It should be observed that in 1925, when the earlier statement was made, Edison was still in the phonograph field and a force to be reckoned with. In 1933, when the contradictory statement was made, the Edison company had with-

[4] The Voice, Its Production and Reproduction, Stanley and Maxfield, 1933.

drawn from the home phonograph market and Thomas A. Edison was dead.

The authors then went on to state that for a given intensity of sound the amplitude of the cut is inversely proportional to the frequency of the tone, and that a point will be reached somewhere at the low end of the sound spectrum where this amplitude will become great enough to cut from one groove into the adjacent groove, or in the case of the vertical cut, to cut so deeply that with the present·methods the wax would tear instead of cut away with a smooth surface. However, it can be demonstrated yet today that Edison was then cutting pipe organ records with fundamental notes much lower than that possible with the lateral records of that time, and by the acoustic method. The authors also discussed the limitations on the upper register imposed by the relationship of the diameter of the tip of the stylus to the groove dimensions, speed of travel, etc. The weakness of the Maxfield-Harrison approach to the problem was in their failure to recognize the essential importance of utilizing a permanent, nondeformable stylus tip as a means of extending the upper register. The hill-and-dale industry had discarded the steel needle in the early 1890's as unreliable and unscientific. The balance of the information given under the heading "Studio Characteristics and Transients" was devoted largely to these limitations of the lateral method.

The next sub-heading was "Mechanical Versus Electrical Recording." The authors pointed out the small amount of power obtainable from the soundwaves, and of the difficulties and unnatural conditions imposed by acoustic, or horn recording. They directed attention to the subterfuge resorted to of using violins with diaphragms and horns, or "Stroh" violins, in order to get enough power from the strings to cut the wax. The crowding of the musicians around the recording horns and the unconventional arrangement of the orchestra due to the relative insensitivity of the recording mechanism was

Edison Tinfoil Phonograph, built by the London Stereoscopic Company in London —probably by Charles Stroh. It was made in 1878 and was the first commercial phonograph having a motor (gravity type) and a governor. (Electric & Musical Industries, Limited Museum—Hayes, Middlesex, England.)

Edison Phonograph of 1887 had "electric motor works." The recording and reproducing diaphragms were arranged on a swivel for interchange. It was known as the "Spectacle" model because it resembled a pair of eyeglasses. (Handbook of the Phonograph.)

PLATE II   IMPROVED EDISON PHONOGRAPHS

Edison "Improved Spectacle" phonograph of 1889. This type used a six- to eight-volt DC motor. A rheostat permitted operation from 110-volt DC lighting circuit. (Edison National Historic Site Museum.)

Edison battery-operated "Spectacle" phonograph of 1889 was mounted on a sewing machine stand. Box contained four wet cells (Edison-Lalande) to supply about five amperes current to the DC motor. (Edison National Historic Site Museum.)

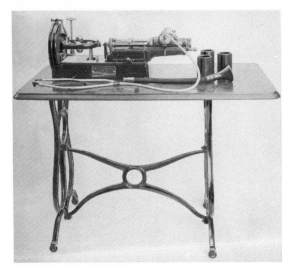

Edison "Water Power" phonograph of 1889–1890 used a combination recorder-reproducer. A flexible hose was connected to a water faucet and to the paddle assembly on the left. Speed was controlled by a 3-ball governor. (Edison National Historic Site Museum.)

Edison "Hand Treadle" phonograph of 1889 used the spectacle recorder-reproducer. Motive power was achieved by pumping a small paddle coupled to flywheels and a governor. (Edison National Historic Site Museum.)

PLATE IV   **EDISON "HOME" AND "STANDARD" PHONOGRAPHS**

Edison "Home" phonograph, 2nd model, produced in 1901. It had a New Style cabinet, played standard two-minute records, and sold for $30.00 with a 14" polished brass horn. (O. Read collection.)

Edison "Standard" phonograph of 1897 had an interchangeable recorder or reproducer. The latter could be adjusted to track the record grooves. Built-in shaver removed thin coating from cylinder for re-use. (O. Read collection.)

Edison "Standard" phonograph, 1909, was designed to play the new four-minute records. Accessory gears could be added for playing the two-minute records. Sold for $30.00 as shown. (Edison National Historic Site Museum.)

Edison "Home" phonograph of 1911 had an open-ended mandrel. The machine played both two- or four-minute records by means of a turnover Type O reproducer. Proper gear pitch was selected by a manual gear changer. (Clark-Welch Collection.)

Edison "Standard" phonograph of 1911 with cygnet horn and supporting crane. Reproducer was Type O turnover. Played both two- and four-minute records. (Edison National Historic Site Museum.)

Edison "Gem" phono-graph of 1898. First of four compact models. Played the two-minute brown wax cylinder. Knob turned to control speed of governor and moved in and out for braking. (O. Read collection.)

Edison "Triumph" pho-nograph of 1898 could play fourteen two-min-ute records per winding of its triple-spring mo-tor. It was supplied with a 14-inch brass bell horn and sold for $50.00. (O. Read collection.)

Edison "Gem" phono-graph, 1901, with im-proved spring motor and start-stop-regulating de-vice. A gear-change at-tachment (added later) reduced rotation speed of feed screw so that four-minute records could be played. (O. Read collection.)

Edison "Gem" phonograph, 1908, played both two- and four-minute records, using a Type K combination reproducer and a Fireside horn supported by a crane. (Edison National Historic Site Museum.)

Edison "Triumph" phonograph of 1908 played the new four-minute records. Heavy crane supported a morning glory horn. Sold for $60.00 complete. (Clark-Welch Collection.)

Edison "Triumph" phonograph of 1911 was equipped with Type O reproducer, triple-spring motor, and laminated oak bell horn. This model is probably the most rugged of all cylinder phono-graphs. (Edison National Historic Site Museum.)

PLATE VI   EDISON "FIRESIDE" AND "OPERA" PHONOGRAPHS

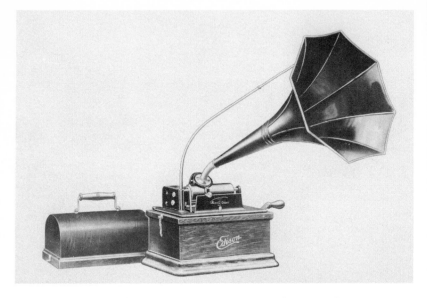

Edison "Fireside" phonograph of 1909 met the demand for an inexpensive model to play the new four-minute records. A two-piece morning glory horn with 11-inch bell was provided. (Edison National Historic Site Museum.)

Edison "Fireside" phonograph of 1911 used an improved spring motor, could play both two- and four-minute records, and was furnished with a cygnet-type black japanned horn. (Edison National Historic Site Museum.)

Edison "Opera" phonograph of 1911 featured a sliding mandrel and an automatic stopping device. A lever raised the combination K reproducer to clear the record automatically. (Edison National Historic Site Museum).

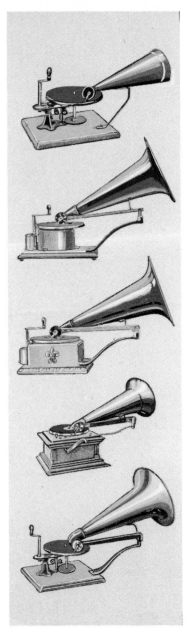

Eldridge Johnson "Toy" talking machine, introduced in October, 1900. It operated by hand and played a seven-inch, single-sided Berliner record. Sold with metal horn for $3.00. (RCA Victor.)

Eldridge Johnson Type "A" Victor, 1900, had a flat wooden tone arm. A leather elbow coupled the reproducer to neck of brass horn. Spring is in housing under crank. Price was $12.00. (RCA Victor.)

Eldridge Johnson Type "B" Victor, 1900, became the Victor "Trade Mark" model (with Nipper, the dog). It sold for $18.00 with spring motor, brass horn, and Johnson reproducer. Played seven-inch lateral records. (RCA Victor.)

Eldridge Johnson Type "C," made late in 1900. Had wooden tone arm mounted vertically. Spring motor was altered so that crank protruded from side of oak cabinet. Sold for $25.00. (RCA Victor.)

Eldridge Johnson Type "D" Victor machine of 1901 used mechanism of "Toy," but was furnished with a large brass horn mounted on a wooden tone arm. It sold for $6.00. (RCA Victor.)

PLATE VIII   VICTOR TALKING MACHINES

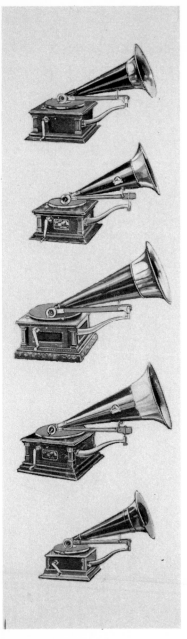

Victor "Monarch" of 1901. Had a seven-inch turntable, wooden tone arm, and Improved Johnson reproducer. Sold for $40.00 with brass bell horn. Known as Model M. (RCA Victor.)

Victor "Monarch Junior" Type E, made in 1901, used a new metal, ribbed tone arm. Brass-finished elbow replaced leather for horn coupling. Turntable was seven inches in diameter. Sold for $25.00. (RCA Victor.)

Victor "Monarch Special" Type MS of 1901 featured a ten-inch turntable and heavy spring motor. This model could mount a larger horn than other models. Price, $45.00. (RCA Victor.)

Victor "Improved Monarch" of 1902 featured new spring motor, rigid metal tone arm, and larger horn. Mounted in a heavy oak case—it was priced at $35.00 with a ten-inch turntable. (RCA Victor.)

Victor "Royal" was introduced in 1902 as a low-priced talking machine for playing the Berliner-type, seven-inch records. It sold for $15.00 with metal horn with brass bell. (RCA Victor.)

Edison "Premium" phonograph of 1911. Cabinet front swung open for easy access to mandrel and reproducer. Very few of these were made, and are now sought by collectors. (Edison National Historic Site Museum.)

Edison "Amberola," 1910, with home recording attachment, employed the early wax cylinders and recorder. Larger horns were sold for "louder" recordings or for groups. (Edison National Historic Site Museum.)

Edison "Amberola" phonograph of 1913, designed to play the Blue Amberola celluloid records. One of the first models to use a diamond stylus. (Edison National Historic Site Museum.)

Edison "Diamond Disc" phonograph of 1915, equipped with a "Loud Speaking Attachment." Device clamped to cabinet front to support the horn. (Edison National Historic Site Museum.)

Edison Disc phonograph, made in 1911. Horn had a continuous taper from reproducer to bell. The mica-diaphragmed reproducer is positioned to respond to vertically-cut records. (Edison National Historic Site Museum.)

PLATE X   VICTOR DISC TALKING MACHINES

The "Victor I" was introduced late in 1902 and featured the new "tapering hollow arm." Supplied with eight-inch turntable, single-spring motor, and choice of Exhibition or Concert sound box (reproducer). Sold for $25.00. (Victor 1908 catalogue.)

The "Victor II" of 1902 had extra-heavy single spring, a ten-inch turntable, and was furnished with black - japanned steel horn having a 13¾-inch bell. It sold for $32.50 with choice of Concert or Exhibition sound box. (Victor 1908 catalogue.)

The "Victor III" of 1902 had improved double spring motor. It played five 10-inch records with one winding. Equipped with No. 19 Victor flower horn, ebony finish with gold stripes. Sold for $40.00. (Victor 1908 catalogue.)

The "Victor IV" of 1902 had polished mahogany cabinet with hinged top measuring 14 × 14 × 7¼ inches. It featured an improved speed adjustment that indicated rpm of the 10-inch turntable. Choice of two horns—sold for $50.00. (Victor 1908 catalogue.)

The "Victor V" was introduced in 1903 with 12-inch turntable, heavy-duty triple springs, and choice of horns. Like previous models in this series, choice of either Exhibition or Concert sound box was optional. This model sold for $60.00. (Victor 1908 catalogue.)

The "Victor VI," made in 1904, was of a handsome mahogany. Metal parts were 14-carat triple gold-plated. Horn was also of mahogany cross-banded veneers. Motor was nickel-plated and had triple springs. Price was $100.00. (Victor 1908 catalogue.)

The "Victor Junior" of 1906 was the lowest-priced Victor of the period. Had oak cabinet with nickel trimming. Horn was dark red with gold stripes. Had combination brake and speed regulator for eight-inch turntable. It sold for $10.00. (Victor 1908 catalogue.)

The "New Victor O" of 1908 was an inexpensive mahogany-finished model with eight-inch turntable, speed regulator, single-spring drive, and flowered metal horn with "soft amber hue." Horn was 16-inches long with a 14-inch bell. Sold for $17.50. (Victor 1908 catalogue.)

The "Toy Graphophone" of 1898 sold for a mere $1.50 and included reproducer, six-inch tin horn, and five special disc records. Also called "Child's Talking Machine."

The "Five Dollar Graphophone" of 1898 was equipped with a 10-inch black tin horn. Type Q sold for $5.00; Type QC (in bent-wood cabinet) sold for $7.50.

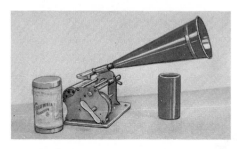

The Columbia "Twentieth Century" 1901 Type BC played both standard and the new six-inch long Columbia Gold-Moulded Twentieth Century records. Style "Premier" sold for $100.00; horn extra. (Clark-Welch Collection.)

The "Eagle Graphophone" of 1898 had a spring motor, 10-inch japanned tin horn, and oak cabinet. Price was $12.00; recorder, $5.00 extra. Known as Type BX.

The "Columbia Leader" of 1906 used the Lyric Spring Contact reproducer. Type BE came in oak cabinet, had triple spring motor, and sold for $30.00, with horn.

The "Ten Dollar Graphophone" of 1898 had clockwork motor. Known as Type Q-Q, it sold for $10.00, complete with 10-inch horn and bentwood cabinet.

PLATE XII   OTHER COLUMBIA MODELS

(A) Columbia "Jewel" Type BK sold for $20.00 in 1906 with aluminum horn and spring contact reproducer. It came in an oak cabinet and had a tandem spring motor.

(B) The Columbia "Jewel" offered a choice of red or blue enameled horn and support crane and sold for $25.00 as shown.

(C) Columbia "Peerless" Graphophone of 1906, known as Type BF. It featured a quadruple spring motor that "could be wound while playing." It sold for $40.00 with an aluminum horn and for $43.20 with a larger horn and crane.

(D) Columbia "New Leader" Type BKT of 1906 had an attachment for playing both two- and four-minute records. It sold for $35.00 as shown or $40.00 with a wooden horn.

(E) Columbia "New Invincible" of 1906 had heavy-duty motor and two- and four-minute attachment. The Type BET sold for $45.00. Wooden horn was $5.00 extra; "oak symphony" horn was $10.00 extra.

(F) Columbia "Sovereign" Type BG had a hand-polished mahogany cabinet and featured a quadruple-spring motor. Had aluminum horn and sold for $50.00.

(G) Columbia "Aluminum Tone Arm Graphophone," 1907, for disc records. Made in five models—the BN sold for $25.00, the BH for $30.00, the BI for $45.00, the BJ for $75.00, and the BD for $100.00. Models BN, BH, and BI had oak cabinets; Models BD and BJ had mahogany cabinets. Ten-inch turntables for BH and BI; 12-inch for BD and BJ.

Produced in England under Patents Granted by Edison in the United States

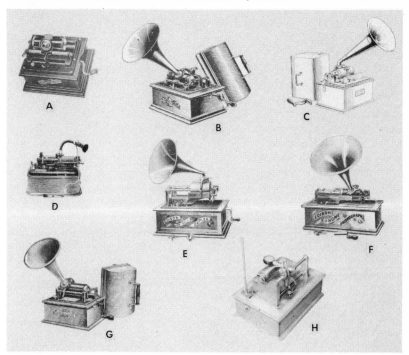

(A) Edison Bell "Elf" and "Imp" phonographs both had the same "upper works." The difference between the two models was in the motor and better cabinet of the "Imp." The "Elf" sold for 15s. 0d., the "Imp," 10s. 0d.

(B) Edison Bell "Standard" had an aluminum horn, polished sapphire stylus, and nickel oil can and shaving attachment. Fitted with a spring motor. Finished in black and gold. The body was of polished oak. The reproducer sold for £4 4s. 0d. (£4 10s. 0d. with deluxe cabinet); the recorder, for 12s. 6d.

(C) Edison Bell "New Empire" phonograph, circa 1903, was supplied with a fantail reproducer, sapphire stylus, polished aluminum horn, nickel elbow, and winding key. Nickelled throughout, had a spring motor, and was enclosed in a French polished oak case with nickel fastenings. Sold for £1 15s. 0d.; the recorder was extra, 12s. 6d.

(D) Edison Bell "Commercial" dictating machine advertised that "correspondence may be dictated and thoughts registered at times when a stenographer is not available." The cylinder could record twice as much dictation, seven minutes, as other machine of the period, up to 1,400 words on one cylinder.

Contained a flexible speaking and hearing tube, and by pressing a button, could be stopped and started at will. Sold for £17 0s. 0d.

(E) Edison Bell "Concert Duplex" phonograph. Supplied with a large polished aluminum horn, new fantail reproducer, nickel elbow, and double mandrel. Fitted with a triple-spring clockwork motor. Finished in black and gold enamel. Sold for £17 5s. 0d.

(F) Edison "Home" phonograph. Manufactured in the United States. Similar to the "Home" phonograph illustrated on Plate IV. Sold for £6 6s. 0d.

(G) Edison Bell "Gem" phonograph. Fitted with an aluminum horn, fantail reproducer, and oiler. Had a right-hand crank wind instead of a clock key, separate starting lever, and speed regulator. Sold for £2 5s. 0d. in fumed oak case with glazed finish; £2 10s. 0d. in deluxe case.

(H) This Edison Bell phonograph played any record from two to five inches in diameter.

PLATE XIV   OTHER PHONOGRAPHS, CIRCA 1905

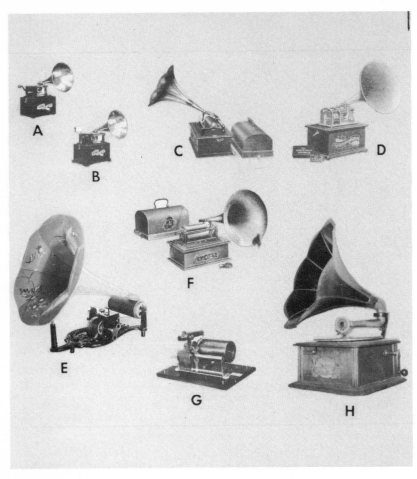

(A) Lambertphone "Companion" retailed at £2 10s.

(B) Lambertphone "Entertainer" retailed at £3 10s.

(C) Excelsior "Ruby" talking machines
had a sapphire stylus and solid brass
flower horn 12¼ × 10¼ inches in diameter. It retailed at 45/—.

(D) Microphonograph "Henry Seymour"
(1905 Model) Microphonic reproducer
fitted all Graphophone types and could
be fitted to the Edison machines with
special carrier arms. The Type A played
two records at one winding and sold
for £2 10s; the Type B played four

records at one winding and was priced
at £3 7s. 6d., including the recorder.

(E) The "Puck," an English-made talking machine, had a clockwork motor.

(F) Pathé "Coquet" reproducer.

(G) Microphonograph reproducer, the
old Pathé "Perfecta" phonograph with
the Henry Seymour improved attachment, sold at 10/6. It was made of brass
and highly nickelled. It could take
either the Seymour or Pathé reproducer and could be converted to take
any other make.

(H) Pathé "Actuelle" talking machine.

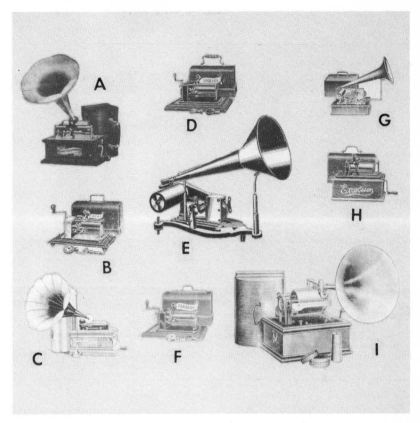

(A) "Trump" Graph-o-phone had a flower horn that came in assorted colors. The motor could be wound while running. Housed in an oak cabinet. Retailed for £2 2s and was advertised as "giving a tone as sweet and pure as a £10 10s. instrument."

(B) Murdoch "Sylvia C" featured a top crank wind.

(C) Columbia "Home Premier" Graphophone had a reduced diaphragm to soften and mellow the volume without impairing the quality of tone. It sold for £16/16/—.

(D) Murdoch "Angelica" had a top-crank wind, sapphire styli.

(E) New Century phonographs retailed for 4/—. New Century Gold Moulded records sold for 1/— each.

(F) Murdoch "Pandora" had a top crank wind, black enameled base and cover, all other parts nickelled.

(G) Murdoch "Magnet" was mounted on imitation satin wood. It had a molded metal bed plate, nickel mandrel and fittings, nickel horn with patent rest and adjustable support, dome reproducer, stop and start lever, etc. It was advertised as a "cheap machine."

(H) Murdoch "Excelsoir" could be fitted with a green flower horn.

(I) Pathé "Duplex" Grand Concert phonograph was advertised as a "triumph—all squeakiness and nasal twang overcome." Pathé reproducers ranged from 27/6 to £30. Pathé was apparently bothered by imitators; they advertised that "the name Pathé is embossed on each record—none others are genuine."

PLATE XVI   **UNUSUAL TALKING MACHINES, CIRCA 1898**

(A) "Polyphone," made by the Talking Machine Company, was advertised as being "guaranteed more than twice as loud and many times more musical, sweet and natural as the original orchestra, band or singer. No other talking machine will do this." It featured two horns, could be called one of the forerunners of our modern two-speaker system.

(B) Dupliphone talking machine played both small and large records, combining two machines into one. The Graphophone Dupliphone sold for $41.00; the Phonograph Dupliphone, for $46.00.
  The Dupliphone Attachment could be attached to any Columbia Graphophone, A.T. Graphophone, or Home Phonograph. Concert or Grand records could be played without interfering with the running of the smaller records. The Graphophone Dupliphone Attachment sold for $16.00, the Phonograph Dupliphone Attachment, for the same amount.

(C) "Double Bell Wonder," circa 1900, like the Talking Machine "Polyphone," gave twice the volume because of its two horns. In addition, the double horn, according to the advertiser, gave greater quality and purity of tone. The machine, with two records, was priced at $20.00.

(D) Talking Machine "Polyphone," 1899, used with the Edison Phonograph. Any talking machine could be made into a "Polyphone." Again, the advertisement stated: "Guaranteed more than twice as loud as any other talking machine; sweet and natural as the original orchestra, band or singer."

(E) This talking machine was offered free with the purchase of three dozen Columbia records at the regular price of twenty-five cents each. It was an imported machine with a clockwork motor. In addition to offering the machine at no additional charge with the purchase of records, a supply of tickets was also furnished so the owner could "earn money giving entertainments in public."

(F) "Echophone" talking machine featured a clockwork motor and an all-glass tone arm. At the end of the tone arm, the stylus was formed. A glass tube terminated in a crude bellows coupled to ear tubes or a horn.

(G) Standard Talking Machine, Style X, one of two disc phonographs produced by American Talking Machine Company. The turntable was 10 inches in diameter and had a one-half inch center stud so that only special records having a one-half inch diameter center hole could be played.

stated to make it difficult to secure the spontaneous enthusiasm and the best efforts so essential for inspired performance. These limitations of the acoustic lateral recording methods as they existed at that time are undeniable. The new method of recording employing a microphone would permit more natural positions for singers and musicians, the authors stated, which would be conducive to a more relaxed and artistic performance.

That the adapting of radio methods to the business of recording failed to some extent of meeting his ideal may be gained by the following quotation from what Maxfield wrote in 1933 in "The Voice, Its Production and Reproduction":

"With the dead pick-up the only method of balancing the component parts of a musical ensemble or a soloist against his accompaniment is, therefore, by means of control of the relative distances of the various instruments from the pick-up. Even when a proper balance has been obtained, it is lost if any instrument changes its loudness materially compared with that of the other instruments. Also, since there is no sense of acoustic perspective, the loud instruments tend to drown out the weaker instruments, and thereby destroy the artistic balance. As a result of this a large majority of the artists have developed what is known as a 'radio (or a recording) technic'. In the case of singers it has developed the 'mezzo voce' or crooning type of singing, even for classical numbers of a character where a large part of the emotional content resides in the volume range, and in the full, free power and color which characterizes real operatic, or concert singing.

"This radio technic has become so firmly ingrained in the natures of our present day radio and recording musicians, that many of them cannot conceive of attending a recording 'date' without bringing either modified instruments or intentionally disregarding the instructions to play or sing as they normally do in concert. This was well illustrated in a recent recording 'date' of a forty-piece orchestra when the musicians were requested to bring standard instruments and to play as if they were playing to an audience. It should have been easy for them to follow these instructions, since most of them were members of a large symphony orchestra, and they were asked to report at a full size theater for the recording 'date'. In spite of these facts, several of the men arrived with instruments which they said recorded better than did their concert instruments, and it was with great difficulty that we were able to induce the players of the louder instruments, such as the brasses and tympani, to play with anything like normal power. In fact, in the case of the brasses, it was only after they had been told three times that the violins were outplaying them that they became angry enough to really produce the volume necessary for the proper natural balance."

Maxfield was entirely right in so commenting on the falseness of the methods of playing and singing which had become firmly inculcated by the inherent propensities of radio microphonic methods. However, he errs in blaming it entirely on the influence of the dead studio. He and his associated Bell engineers had provided unlimited opportunities for tonal modulation made possible by supersensitive microphones and unlimited amplification. Compared with the limitations of the old acoustic process, the cure had proven to even its chief sponsor to have become worse than the disease. However, these abuses of his Western Electric recording method which he so deplored were in part due to a natural desire on the part of listeners. It is quite normal for the music lover to wish to hear as much of the full, close-up, undistorted tone of the voice or instrument as possible. Unfortunately the listener to a recorded or broadcast performance has access to no criteria with which to distinguish the true from the false, except for his memory.

No matter how important reflected sound may be in the securing of adequate record or radio reproduction of the larger orchestras or ensembles, the fact remains that the complex interference patterns set up by the walls, floors, ceilings, etc. of even the most perfect auditorium constitutes a distorting vibrational screen through which the original tones must penetrate in sufficient volume to be acceptable to the ears of the listener. The novelty of being able to hear singers and instrumentalists without the heretofore inevitable difficulties associated with theater and auditorium conditions was one of the valid reasons for the employment of so-called "dead" studio recording. Technically the dead studio technic is correct. Since when has it been considered natural to superimpose the acoustical qualities of one room upon that of another? What is wrong with the desire to hear the singer as though he were present in your living room, singing just to you, your family, and guests? Why do orchestra seats cost more? Why are not artificial reverberation devices attached to pianos, or violins, when played in the salon or home?

Under the heading "Mechanical Versus Electrical Reproducing," the authors made the following statement:

"Where the question of reproduction is concerned, the same two alternatives mentioned for recording present themselves, namely, direct use of power derived from the record itself versus the use of electromagnetic equipment with an amplifier. In this case, however, the situation is a little different as the power which can be drawn directly from the record is more than sufficient for home use. Since any method of reproducing from mechanical records by electrical means involves the use of a mechanical device for transferring from mechanical to electrical power and a

second such device for transferring from electrical back to mechanical power, that is, sound, it is necessary to use two mechanical systems, one at each end of an electrical system. Where the power which can be supplied by the record is sufficient to produce the necessary sound intensity, as in the case of home use, it is in general simpler to design one single mechanical transmission system than it is to add the unnecessary complications of amplifiers, power supply and associated circuits. In case where music is to be reproduced in large auditoriums, the power which can be drawn from the record may be insufficient and some form of electric reproduction using amplifiers becomes necessary."

Except for the laterally cut LP and the 45 rpm lateral discs, this is as true today as it was then. Actually, if other principles had been employed and developed, it would be possible to dispense with electrical reproduction of records for home use today. The capacity for easily producing floor-shaking bass, generated a demand for an unbalanced kind of reproduction which, because of the resulting competitive situation, was in large part responsible for the withdrawal of Edison from the phonograph field, and which in turn accentuated the public demands for all-electric reproduction. The one restraint upon license in the lateral disc industry and the only criterion of what might be considered proper reproduction was swept away with the abandonment of the acoustic Orthophonic Victrola. Records no longer had to be cut to meet the requirements of a standard instrument.

Under the sub-heading "Brief Description of Recording System," Maxfield and Harrison outlined the principal elements of their apparatus as consisting of a condenser transmitter, a high quality vacuum-tube amplifier and a magnetic recorder. It may be of interest to recall that the first condenser transmitter had been made by Thomas

A. Edison in 1877, before the phonograph had been invented. As we have seen, many years before he had discovered the scientific principle upon which vacuum tube amplification was evolved—the flow of electrons from the heated filament of his then new incandescent lamp. Joseph Henry had supplied the principles of the electromagnetic recorder and methods of balancing electrical and mechanical components which made possible the magnetic telegraph. The authors concluded this part of their exposition with the following pertinent comment:

"In the design of the recording and reproducing systems each part of the system has been made as nearly perfect as possible. Errors of one part have not been designed to compensate for errors in another part. Although this method is more difficult, its flexibility, particularly as regards the commercial possibilities of future improvement, justifies the extra effort. There is, therefore, no distortion in the record whose purpose is to compensate for errors in the reproducing equipment; the only intended distortion in the record being that required by the inherent limitations mentioned above."

Unfortunately, this statement represented an ideal which was not long adhered to. After the renaissance of the phonograph industry in the 1930's, recorded characteristics varied from one make (label) to another and even in the output of one manufacturer from time to time.[5] There was no way in which the record purchaser could be certain of matching the characteristic of a given record with his reproducing equipment.

The next sub-heading was "General Basis of Design." The authors stated that their design was based on the development of the mechanical and electromechanical portions of the recording

and reproducing system as the mechanical analogs of electrical circuits. They paid tribute to the prior work of Campbell, Zobel and others, principally telephone research men, as having provided the basis for such a design procedure. In particular, they ascribed much of the success of their method to the development of filter circuits for telephone transmission. However, the many references to telephone men and scientific papers by them to the exclusion of others of equal or greater importance seems quite obvious.

Of more interest is the information given under the next sub-heading, "Detailed Analysis of Mechanical and Electrical Analogs." Preceding the exposition of the method of application to sound recording and reproduction, the authors gave a list of the corresponding mechanical and electrical quantities, with the symbols used, as follows:

"Mechanical

Force	F (dynes)
Velocity	U (cm./sec.)
Displacement	S (cm.)
Impedance (or mechanical ohms)	z (dyne sec./cm.)
Resistance	r (dyne sec./cm.)
Reactance	x (dyne sec./cm.)
Mass	m (grams)
Compliance	c (cm./dyne)

Electrical

Voltage	E (volts)
Current	i (amperes)
Charge	q (coulombs)
Impedance	Z (ohms)
Resistance	R (ohms)
Reactance	X (ohms)
Inductance	L (henries)
*Capacity	C (farads)

* H. W. Nichols, 'Theory of Variable Dynamical Systems' — *Phys. Review,* Vol. 10, 1917."

The authors also gave credit to E. L. Norton for working out the mathematics of mechanical and electrical analogs. They also mentioned Hanna and Slepian as having provided data on force equations for the air-chambers of loudspeakers. In this connection, Hanna

[5] Characteristics have been agreed upon since by most companies, but there are still variations which will be discussed elsewhere.

arose after the delivery of the paper before the society and stated that the authors had failed to credit the exponential horn principle sufficiently in assigning reasons for the improved results achieved.

Having set up this table of equivalent quantities, the authors proceeded to set up design formulae covering the functions of the components of their mechanical reproducing system. With most of these there is no quarrel in principle, but because of the relative complexity of the system and the number involved the total error could be quite large, as an examination will reveal. Moreover, although the analogy of a transformer with a primary-secondary reciprocal to the corresponding lengths of the arms of the stylus lever is obviously valid, the complicated stress pattern of the spider in alternately pushing and pulling the diaphragm at six points does not permit of such a simple and convenient analogy. The reason for the six point attachment is not given, nor is the resultant eddy current problem which it creates in the diaphragm dealt with in any way. If any of the individual analogies are invalid, or if certain analogical factors are left out, as seems to have occurred in this instance, then the entire design explanation becomes to some extent just an interesting fiction.

The next sub-heading was entitled "General Design of Mechanical Systems." The first and last paragraphs are important to our analysis. The first has to do with the arrangement of the masses and compliances so that they form repeated filter sections, determining the magnitude of these quantities so that all have the same cut-off frequencies and characteristic impedances, and providing the proper (horn) resistance termination. Credit was given for the methods which had been developed for measuring mechanical impedance. The last paragraph was in part as follows:

"Such a method has been developed which at the present time covers a range of frequencies from somewhere below 50 to about 4,500 c.p.s. Work is still being continued to extend this method to higher frequencies. This method of measurement has been very useful not only in determining the magnitudes of the impedances in the degree of freedom in which it is desired that they shall operate, but in designing the impedances to motion of the various parts in directions in which they should not be permitted to vibrate. - - -"

Note that although the authors offer this as a thoroughly practicable method that they neglect the severe and extremely variable limitations upon high frequency response imposed by the steel needle, which both audibly and visually deteriorated during the course of one trip through the lateral abrasive containing groove to the extent that it could not be safely used again. The position of the authors was that regardless of such undesirable factors the band-pass filter method use in balancing electrical circuit design could be confidently extended to include the mechanical portions of electromechanical systems.

Maxfield and Harrison next described the electromagnetic recorders. These resembled the later electromagnetic pickups of the horseshoe type in principle and construction. One model utilized bundles of aluminum foil to provide mechanical impedance to match the calculated resistance of the acoustical reproducing system. A later model employed a split rubber ring to serve this purpose which functioned better, according to the authors. In the older acoustical method of recording, such mechanical damping of the recording stylus had not been required as the resistance of the wax to the weaker motivating forces supplied a more or less proportional damping, depending upon the efficiency of design of cutters and waxes, angle of cutting, etc.

The next sub-heading, "Design of the Reproducing Apparatus," is of special importance. Maxfield and Harrison claimed that the analogy between the mechanical and electrical filter was more perfectly shown in the case of the reproducing equipment. If this were true, would the acoustical method of reproduction which they sponsored have been displaced by electrical methods within a few years? The fact is that in several important respects the equations set up as a basis for the Western Electric method of acoustical reproduction were faulty. Errors were introduced at several points by assigning values to elements which were not proper analogues of elements of electrical circuits. Although projected as a 'scientific' method, as contrasted with previous design methods, much was still empirical and contingent upon existing practices. The adoption of sound-box weight (the old No. 2 Victor) and that of the new Orthophonic sound-box was the result of such an empirical decision, as was the acceptance of the shellac base disc and the number of threads per inch, rpm speed, and the steel needle. Moreover, in eliminating the bottle-neck of the old style goose-neck, the empirical adoption of the weight of the former sound-box was compounded into an error, for more weight became placed on the needle point resulting in excessive wear on both needles and records. As with electrical recording, it became much simpler to secure maximum deformation of the record groove under any and all performance conditions. So was the average reactance forces against the needle and the sidewalls of the grooves increased, resulting in greater wear of both needles and records.

A most ingenious feature of the system set up by Maxfield and Harrison for the design of their reproducing mechanism was the incorporation of the exponential horn theory of Hanna and Slepian as an integral termination. The authors calculated the resistance termination needed in mechanical ohms. According to the quantities assigned to the various components of the diaphragm-stylus assembly this was found to be 533 mechanical ohms. This, they said, was entirely insufficient so an air-chamber transformer was necessary. As stated before, the air-chamber transformer is an acceptable analogy to that of an electrical transformer. However, the shape of the primary and secondary areas has a most important effect on the validity of the analogy—it may be that these do not match the corresponding elements of the other side. In discussing the horn design, the authors stated that they were using a logarithmic formula to provide the proper resistance termination for their mechanical filter circuit. They stated that the general properties of logarithmic horns had been understood for some time and referred to Webster's "Acoustical Impedance and Theory of Horns and Phonograph." [6] Regarding this the authors said,

"There are two fundamental constants of such a horn,—the first is the area of the large end and the second the rate of taper. The area of the mouth determines the lowest frequency which is radiated satisfactorily. The energy of the frequencies below this are largely reflected if it is permitted to reach the mouth."

However, the original source of this concept which Webster had carried forward in his researches was Lord Rayleigh, who in 1878 had written,

"If the diameter of the large end of a speaking trumpet be small in comparison with the wave-length, the waves on arrival suffer copious reflection. - - - But by sufficiently prolonging the cone, this reflection will be diminished, and it will tend to cease when the diameter of the open end includes a large number of wave-lengths. Apart from friction it would therefore be possible, by diminishing the angle of the cone, to obtain from a given source any desired amount of energy, and at the same time by lengthening the cone to secure the unimpeded transference of this en-

---

[6] *Proceedings National Academy of Science,* 1919.

ergy from the tube to the surrounding air." [7]

Hanna and Slepian had provided the latest data upon the energy characteristics of horns of the logarithmic, or exponential type. These horns, as we have shown elsewhere, were the result of an evolutionary course of empirical development, first appearing in musical instruments, rather than the invention of any one person. Horns that were approximately exponential in rate of expansion of curvature from the small end to the mouth had been used by Edison for his cylinder Amberola as early as 1908. The idea of formulation of the exponentially expanding cross-section of this type of horn came after they had already been sucessfully employed in musical instruments and the phonograph.

In order to secure a horn with a maximum bass response within a reasonable compass, Maxfield and Harrison designed a folded horn, or re-entrant type. As was later discovered, the folding introduced certain periodicities, or distortions, which were not anticipated in the design. These horns had a constantly expanding bore from the neck of the tone-arm at the sound-box, through a heavy cast-iron mounting terminating in the wood chamber, like the prior Victor Victrola. The rate of taper and area of the mouth opening placed the low cutoff at about 115 cycles, according to a chart which purported to give a comparison with the characteristic of one of the best of the old style "phonographs." If the machine referred to was one of the best of the prior Victors, such as the model VI, the use of the word "phonographs" was misleading. Phonographs were then being produced (standard commercial instruments) which could improve the curve given. Moreover, the Victor Talking Machine Co. never to that time had referred to its product as a phonograph. Presented in a scientific paper this inaccuracy is especially deplorable.

There was a discussion period following the presentation of this historically important Maxfield-Harrison paper. This was opened with comments by C. R. Hanna, which were published in full in the *Transactions of the American Institute of Electrical Engineers* for 1926. It was quite evident that Hanna felt that the successful reproduction of lower registers by the new Orthophonic Victrola was due much more to the exponential horn than it was to the theory of matched impedance to which the authors had attributed major credit. Hanna claimed that the impedance of the mechanical system did not have to be uniform over a wide band of frequencies for it to be forced to vibrate in the low frequency range. He pointed out that this could be done by reducing the stiffness of the diaphragm, as Maxfield and Harrison had done. Hanna clearly indicated that he placed little credence in the validity of the Maxfield-Harrison bandpass electromechanical system of analogs.

E. W. Kellog also read some comments on the new system. He discussed the "spider" in particular, attempting to explain its complex functions in words other than those of the authors. He considered that it acted somewhat as a spring. Elsewhere it had been suggested that its chief function was to cause a larger area of the diaphragm to act as a piston. There is no doubt but that it combined these functions and others. Therefore, it performed in other than a purely unilateral fashion and an analog to a portion of an electrical circuit could not be set up for it logically. Kellog also expressed surprise at the substitution of magnetized ball bearings for the customary knife-edge fulcrum of the stylus bar. Actually this use of ball bearings athough continued for years was subsequently proven to provide no advantage. In fact, if they had been dispensed with, the sound-box assembly could have been lightened and the excessive wear upon the early

---

[7] *Sound*, Rayleigh, (Art. 280).

electrically recorded records could have been somewhat minimized.

L. T. Robinson next made a few comments, opening with a very significant statement, as follows:

"I am in agreement with the statement of the authors that 'There is therefore no distortion in the record whose purpose is to compensate for errors in the reproducing equipment.' In employing so many elements, some of which can be so readily modified in performance the temptation is very strong to look only at the final result and not be too critical as to where any corrective treatment is to be administered. I hope that the stand taken by the authors will be firmly adhered to by them and others who are working along similar lines. In this way, any progress that has been made, or will be made, becomes permanent."

Mr. Robinson's concern for the maintenance of the avowed integrity of approach of the authors in not designing errors into the recording method to compensate for deficiencies in the reproducing system was well founded, as witnessed by the later developments in the industry. Within a few years there was not one record manufacturer in the United States adhering to the concept that the characteristic of the record should not be deformed. Mr. Robinson also scored in his prediction that the full realization of the potentials of the electrically cut record would come through electrical reproduction. However, he also made a statement that the volume at which music was reproduced was important and that to be satisfactory it should be about equal to that of the original sounds. He pointed out that a loud sound from a given instrument is quite different in quality from that of a soft sound from the same instrument when reproduced with great volume. This is a very significant truth which is generally not fully appreciated even today.

Maxfield admitted and deplored the existence of this propensity of the microphonic technics for encouraging purposeful distortions in "The Voice, Its Production and Reproduction." Paradoxically, the very freedom which Robinson said was to be achieved by the combination of electrical recording with electrical reproduction served to remove the last natural restraint upon distorting the waveform as impressed in the record. With the demise of the acoustic Credenza Orthophonic Victrola the listening public lost its last official criterion as to the proper volume and quality of any given Victor recording of voice or instrument. What would Mr. Robinson or Mr. Kellog say today about the use of echo-chambers in recording, which are cut in or out like the grand swell of the pipe organ; or of the laying of one recording over another recording repeatedly to simulate echo and orchestral effects with but one voice and/or instrument? What would these gentlemen say about Montovani? Suppose the instrument to begin with is an already electrically amplified guitar and the alleged singer is crooning softly into the microphone—perhaps using a throat contact mike—just what is reality?

In conclusion a short statement was read by A. E. Kennelly, one time Edison associate, as follows:

"We have here presented to us the wonderful analogy which underlies mechanical and electrical phenomena, with mechanical phenomena interpreted in electrical terms. We have long known that mechanical inertia was really electrical, and we are now finding that all these mechanical phenomena are primarily electrical quantities."

In the ultimate sense, Kennelly's statement is very likely true. Later writers have carried these analogies even further. Yet, regardless of the increased range and improved tonal reproduction of the Orthophonic Victrola over the prior Victor talking machine, it was never to dare the test of direct comparison with the living voice or instrument, as Edison's purely acoustic phonograph had been doing successfully since 1915.

On the positive side, Maxfield and Harrison had introduced elements into phonograph design practice which could be calculated and adjusted by information secured from measurement devices. What before had been entirely empirical and hence indeterminate, now could be reduced to theory and determinable quantities. Probably it had to come in this way, but why the least perfect recording method should have been the one with which they were to start experimenting is somewhat of a mystery. There was a great deal of emphasis on push-pull amplification at the time and it may have been that because the lateral disc record was a push-pull device it seemed to fit in better with the system envisioned.

Needless to say in view of the foregoing, Maxfield and Harrison were not phonograph experts and in the application of their matched impedance theory to the lateral disc talking machine, several important facts were neglected, leaving much further work to others. The chief neglected fact was that precision reproduction of voices and solo instruments had been achieved by Edison as early as 1915. It would seem that from a scientific viewpoint this would have been the place to start to improve. Maxfield in 1933 admitted the hill-and-dale method of recording was superior to the lateral.

It is paradoxical that the same engineers who brought scientific measuring devices to the aid of the bumbling talking machine industry should have perpetuated at the same time the unscientific, replaceable steel stylus and abrasive-carrying record surfaces.

CHAPTER 18

END OF THE ACOUSTIC ERA --
ANALYSIS OF METHODS

THE inauguration of regularly scheduled radio broadcasting in the latter part of 1919 by the opening of the first commercially operated radio station KDKA, Pittsburgh, by the Westinghouse Electric and Manufacturing Co. marked the beginning of an era and foreshadowed the close of another—that of acoustical recording. There was little intimation or evidence of this in the first months with audiences numbered perhaps in thousands consisting largely of confirmed "wireless hams" listening with earphones glued to their ears. But soon the rest of the family became just as interested and the radio "bug" spread to thousands of other homes, as well. Within a year or so radio stations sprang up all over U. S. and Canada and in that time the nightly audience increased from estimated thousands to millions.

Crystal sets gave way to one "peanut" tube sets, then to two-tube, and detector-amplifier multi-tube radios that would operate loudspeakers. Naturally enough, the use of loudspeakers at once multiplied the number of potential listeners. During the first few years of the rapid expansion of the radio audience, the policy of the leading manufacturers of phonographs was precisely alike—especially that of the three leaders, Victor, Edison, and Columbia. They were like the three Hindu monkeys—they could see no radio, could hear no radio, and refused as far as they were able to do so to permit the recording artists to engage in any radio broadcasting.

For this reason, in these formative years, radio had developed musicians from force of necessity and vocal soloists who had not generally been known to the public as recording artists. There were exceptions, of course, such as Jones and Hare, who became known as the "Happiness Boys," but like these they were generally popular artists who recorded for all of the companies and hence were not bound by exclusive contracts. For the most part, the greater artists, such as the red seal Victor artists and those of similar stature who recorded for the other leading companies, were engaged on an exclusive basis with contracts providing for payment of royalties which could be interpreted by the legal counsel of the companies as forbidding their appearance, without special permission, on radio programs.

By 1924 the formation of the chains was under way, one with WGY, General Electric's station at Schenectady as a nucleus, another with KDKA as its leading station and WEAF, New York as the originating station for most chain programs of the new American Telephone and Telegraph Co. network. Obviously, as the sales of radio time came to be "big business" especially to the contract sales organizations of the chains, the matter of securing adequate talent became a matter of great importance. This fact, together with the very evident interest that A. T. & T. would have in expanding the profitable use of its long distance telephone lines for chain program transmission was the principal reason for the decisions of the various leaders of the electrical and communications industry not only to enlarge their activities in radio manufacturing and broadcasting, but to attempt a conquest of the recording field, as well.

Radio columnists of the early 1920's commented occasionally on the refusal of the leading phonograph companies, notably Victor, to permit their artists to broadcast. Therefore, the indications of a reversal of attitude in February of 1925 in this respect by the Victor Talking Machine Co. might well have seemed to some to portend the changes in the recording industry about to come. Renee Chemet, violinist and exclusive Victor artist, played on a radio network program sponsored by the Victor Co. from WEAF's studio in New York. The April 1st Victor record supplement listed a recording of one of the numbers played by Chemet on this program with the following comments:

"Chemet has made a beautiful record of the Rondo she played at the Victor broadcast concert on Feb. 12,—swift, impetuous, scintillating with life. All the resources of the violin are called into play. With it are coupled, on the other side, a beautiful broad, majestic adagio from a Handel Sonata, and an allegro of almost Olympian jollity, somewhat in the rhythm of the classical rigadoon. Both numbers are played with amazing spirit,—and with that unconscious completeness and perfection of style which is the mark of greatness in the technical side of an art."

It is only a speculation that the engineers of A. T. & T. very likely made an electrical recording of this number which may have been used for illustrating to the Victor executives the benefits of the new Western Electric process, as it seems that experiments by the Bell engineers at the Victor plant were already highly advanced. In any event, the fact that Victor was consorting with radio in any way should have been indicative of such a possibility. However, the record as issued was recorded by the standard Victor acoustic method. This record, No. 6497 was to be one of the last of its series to be recorded by that process. The very next month witnessed the issuance of the first commercial record to have been electrically recorded by the new Western Electric process.

Within the next few months a considerable number were issued, but no announcement was made to distributors, dealers, or the public of the change in method. Store buyers of record stocks were the first to note the changed qualities which denoted the new records, even when played on the conventional store demonstration instruments. There was a definite increase in the sharpness of the sibilant sounds, such as "s," which had always seemed difficult to record previously. There was generally an increase in volume, which the mica diaphragms of the current Victor instruments failed to tolerate well. Dance records, in particular, were strident and raucous. Naturally, this caused an unfavorable reaction on the part of the buying public as the proportion of these new electrically recorded records was increased until by the end of the summer all releases were of this type.

Dealers and distributors became uneasy and by September it became necessary to disclose to them the impending developments. Distributors were furnished with a single sample, in most cases, of one of the models of the new Orthophonic Victrola, and meetings were held of representatives of dealers in each territory to advise them of the plans for its introduction to the public. At this time, distributors' warehouses and the salesrooms of the stores were glutted with Victor merchandise. Public interest in radio and the prior failure of Victor to keep up with its principal competition, especially in respect to the reproduction quality of its own records, was in large part responsible. A survey of the releases of the past year or so prior to this time also reveals that many of the older artists of the Victor galaxy were no longer recording the more important operatic and concert selections as they had originally done, but had descended to recording popular songs of little appeal to lovers of classical music.

Perhaps in some cases, older artists were no longer willing to entrust their interpretations of the more demanding works to the intense scrutiny which recordings permitted. Whatever the explanation, the result was that the tremendous drift in this direction, together with a failure to keep up with shifting public tastes in other respects, had resulted in serious accumulations of unsold records. The doubling of the Victor red seal series sold in 1923 also had the effect of convincing a large part of the buying public that all single-face records were obsolete, although it is true that the greater part of the doubled records in the new series were from the same stampers used previously. However, an eccentric groove had been added to operate an automatic stop, which was not on the previous single-sided discs, which may have also operated to influence the public. Many of the single-face records had been on dealers' shelves for years, many demonstration worn, and the war-time records had an abnormal amount of surface noise as well.

Failure to keep pace with changing public taste, stimulated in earlier days to a great extent by its own activities, was in part responsible for the dilemma of the Victor Co., its distributors and dealers at this particular time. It must be pointed out that recording of the greater artists was not originated by the Victor Co.—that it had begun on an extensive commercial basis in Europe even before 1900, though accomplished to be sure by means of American inventions. Somewhat abridged editions of operas and operettas had been recorded in England, France, and Italy as early as 1906. The first uncut symphonies and concerts were also recorded in Europe before this was achieved in the U. S. The first complete symphony to be recorded in the U. S. by Victor was paradoxically the Schubert Unfinished Symphony, recorded by Leopold Stokowski and the Philadelphia Symphony Orchestra. It was issued in Nov. 1924 as one of a group of six albums comprising the first releases of the new "Music Arts Library of Victor Records." Included with the Schubert symphony was the Schumann Quintette, Opus 67, played by the Flonzaley Quartet, with pianist Ossip Gabrilowitsch. The remainder of the six albums, the first to be issued as a series by the Victor Co., were simply collections of isolated items of sacred music, operatic arias, concert songs, light overtures, and violin selections gleaned from the catalog.

Accompanying this most inauspicious beginning of its album library, which was to become a major trend in record merchandising, the following announcement was printed in the monthly release bulletin:

" - - - the Victor Company has searched its great library of immortalized music,—the most comprehensive of the world,—and from it has carefully selected a group of records of representative music, interpreted by great musicians; these it has gathered into an anthology of music,— The Music Arts Library of Victor Records."

As usual, the advertising staff of the Victor Co. was not troubled by false modesty. The fact is that this was a pitiful beginning. In February of that same year—(1924), Victor had announced a special group of European recordings with masters imported from its English affiliate, The Gramophone Co., Ltd., which much more fittingly could have been dignified by having been made the cornerstone of such an ambitious project as "an anthology of music." This special release was described in a brochure corresponding to the format of the usual Victor supplement. It was entitled, "A Special List of Wagnerian Masterpieces." This list of recordings had been, with few exceptions, recorded in England. The great importance of the English and European recordings represented was that they were recorded by a large symphony orchestra with vocal soloists, with score as written. This was the first time that this had been successfully accomplished. Most Wagnerian recordings had been inadequately recorded with smaller orchestras than required, and with revised orchestrations. Also, these European recordings had been directed by foremost conductors, such as Albert Coates, Percy Pitt, and Eugene Goosens.

Indicative of perhaps a somewhat jaundiced view of this evidence of British enterprise was the neglect of Victor to regularly list this significant group of recordings in its subsequent monthly bulletins, as was the custom with regularly issued records. However, indicating that there was perhaps good reason for professional jealousy was the rapid addition of other English recordings to the "Music Arts Library." One of these was the Gilbert & Sullivan Mikado recorded by the D'Oyly Carte Opera Co. complete on eleven 12" records, with libretto, which was announced in the March 1st 1925 Victor supplement. There was a rather cute, but sly attempt to deny the British credit justly due for the accomplishment represented in this accompanying announcement:

"The music is just what you would expect under the Victor imprint. As England is the home and the great shrine of Gilbert & Sullivan Opera, it was to England that we went for an authoritative interpretation of this most enjoyable work."

The fact is that various European companies and particularly The Gramophone Co., Ltd., and the English Columbia Co., had been outstripping the American lateral record producing companies in developing recording technics and in creating new markets, such as that which desired recordings of the longer classical works. The Columbia Phonograph Co., Inc. owned by Columbia Graphophone Co., Ltd. of London, had initiated its first album sets, known as the "Columbia Fine Art Series of Musical Masterworks," also in 1924, with all European recordings. The next symphony to appear in what had been projected as a Victor enterprise was also an English recording, the Pathetique Symphony, No. 6 of Tschaikovsky, which comprised five 12" records in an album. In the next succeeding months, complete recordings of Petrouchka by the Royal Albert Hall Orchestra and Beethoven's Fifth Symphony, both directed by Sir Landon Ronald, were also announced. Even after the development of electrical recording, the same trend continued, with a great part of the recordings of the Victor album sets originating in Europe, and an even greater percentage of the Columbia Masterworks Series.

For the first time in its history, in July of 1925, Victor announced officially drastically reduced prices on single-face red seal records. The prices of $1 records were reduced to 65¢, $1.50 records were reduced to 90¢, etc. Actually, many dealers went beyond these authorized cuts and threw their stocks out for half-price.

This much seems clear. Either Victor had used the English masters to fill in until the electric recording method was perfected, thus saving the heavy investments necessary to the recording of longer works by large organizations, or the threat represented by these European accomplishments was an influence in promoting its receptivity to the opportunity to make all existing lateral-type talking machines and records obsolete.

From the earliest days, the policy of the Edison companies, undoubtedly determined by the personal decision of Thomas A. Edison, had been always to extend the benefits of progressive phonographic improvements to existing owners of Edison phonographs wherever possible. The American Graphophone

Co., on the other hand, several times introduced radical innovations inapplicable to their existing instruments. One of these had been the Graphophone Grand, copied from a machine invented by Edison, but which he had withheld from the market probably in part because it might tend to make obsolete the standard size cylinders; another had been the 20th century Graphophone, which utilized longer cylinders which could not be played on standard machines. But this definitely had not been true in the Victor Co. practice up to the time of the change to electrical recording. It is true that there had been little over-all increase in knowledge or application of acoustical science for a considerable length of time in the Victor laboratory. Such improvements as were made were in details rather than the result of the application of strikingly new principles. At any rate, up to May of 1925, the latest records made at the Victor plant would play as well on the earliest machines of their manufacture as any records they ever had produced.

But this was changed virtually overnight by the introduction of the Western Electric process. Not knowing of the impending developments, many buyers of records for the music shops were astounded at the cacaphony that ensued in trying out some of the advance releases on the regular store demonstration instruments. This was especially true of dance records which when played on the standard Victor machines were uncomfortably strident and almost unbearable to listen to. It has since been found that certain electrically recorded records of a later period may be played on the old mica diaphragm instruments without such a raucous effect; therefore, it is entirely conceivable that had they wished to do so that records entirely acceptable for the older instruments could have been produced. Had it been determined that the proper policy to pursue was to make all existing phonographs obsolete?

Making records which would not play acceptably on the older machines but which could be reproduced with an astounding improvement in breadth of tone range and new quality on an entirely new series of instruments was a possibility. The idea of creating intentional obsolescence had earlier been inaugurated and confirmed as a commercial success by the motor-car industry, with its great automobile shows and yearly introduction of new models. After the successful introduction of the Orthophonic Victrola this seemed to set, for years to come, the pattern for the phonograph and radio industry: lessened concern for permanence and reliability—always introducing something new and sparkling, even though shining only with a transitory brilliance like the firefly in the night.

But there is no gainsaying that the Orthophonic Victrola symbolizes the closing epoch of the acoustic phonograph period. Introduced by special demonstrations held in the ballrooms of the country's leading hotels to audiencies of selected guests, the ties that obligated the world's largest manufacturer of phonograph records to further faithfully serve past-purchasers were severed in the name of science by the overwhelming advances vouchsafed in the name of the new Orthophonic Victrola. How could anyone ask that it be otherwise—after hearing the miracle of a record before them transformed from a squawky, strident sounding distortion as played on one of the old style Victrolas to a thing of beauty and broad tonal balance as played on the superb new Credenza model Orthophonic Victrola? November 2, 1925 was publicized as "Victor Day" and throughout the country demonstrations were given in the display rooms of the dealers of the new acoustic reproducing instrument.

The story of the Orthophonic Victrola and the Columbia Viva-tonal Phonograph is the Bell Telephone Laboratories—Western Electric story. A comparative analysis of these and other methods is required. The conclusions which have been reached are based on the writings of those concerned in this development and upon the three dimensional evidence still available in the

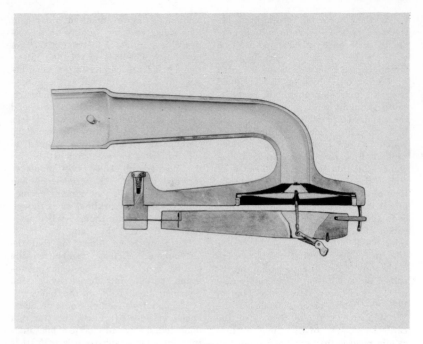

Edison

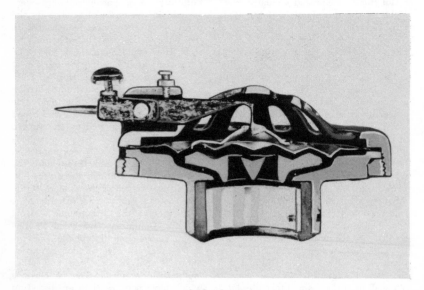

Orthophonic

Fig. 18-1. A comparison of the Victor Orthophonic reproducer and the Edison diamond disc reproducer.

form of records and reproducing instruments. One of the most important conclusions that must be reached by anyone who cares to investigate both classes of information thoroughly is that there would seem to have been in existence, at least at that time, a tacit understanding among certain leading engineers and acousticians of the scientific societies that scientific knowledge should be accepted to consist only of the "literature" of these fields, ignoring quite altogether the three-dimensional evidence left by those who did not choose to contribute learned papers upon their accomplishments!

For instance, Webster's work on the logarithmic or exponential horn was not submitted until 1914, several years after a practical prototype of this type of horn had been introduced by Edison commercially, yet no credit is given to Edison for this prior use.[1] The later paper of Hanna and Slepian extended the work of Webster to include radio applications, but again without giving any credit to Edison. How Maxfield and Harrison were able to write a resume of phonograph development without once mentioning the name of Thomas A. Edison may well be marvelled at. Maxfield and Harrison said:

" - - - reproduction may be termed
perfect when the components of the
reproduced sound reaching the ears
of the actual listener have the same
relative intensity and phase relations
as the sound reaching the ears of an
imaginary listener to the original
performance would have had."

Maxfield thought so well of this definition of perfect reproduction that he

---

[1] U. S. Patent No. 943,663, applied for May 24, 1905, issued Dec. 21, 1909 for a horn with varying thickness, showing a bore of constantly increasing cross section, diameter, not necessarily logarithmic. Essentially the same curve was used in the improved "Triumph" external horn Edison phonograph of 1911. This horn was made by S & V, called Music Master, for Edison and its characteristics were so good that it was used in identical dimensions with the first dynamic speakers of Magnavox. Virtually the same design is used for exterior type P. A. speakers today.

quoted it again in his 1933 work with Stanley. However, in the latter publication he proved, by his own words, that this goal was impossible of attainment with his own process, which involves the recording of reflected sound, in the following words:

"Conditions under which records are
made for phonograph purposes fail to
meet these requirements. (Measurement of intensity range and vibrato
of voices.) Both the old acoustic
record and also the newer electric
records have been made under conditions where a considerable amount
of reverberation has been included
with the direct sound from singer to
pick-up. Under these conditions, any
intensity variation occurring in the
record may be due either to a fluctua-
tion of the direct sound, or to intensity change due to the shifting
interference pattern."

As has been suggested not too subtly, the chief indictment of Maxfield and Harrison as scientists is their complete ignoring of the work of a greater scientist, Thomas A. Edison. More than a decade before the advent of the Orthophonic Victrola, Edison had incontrovertably demonstrated the accomplishment of precision reproduction of the human voice and of various solo instruments. The uncoerced and unbiased judgment of hundreds of music critics, as reported and published in leading newspapers all over the United States, attest to the success of the Edison direct comparison tone-tests. Despite various unacknowledged borrowings from the work of Edison and others, there never was a direct comparison made between the Orthophonic Victrola and a performance by any singer or other artist as far as is known. None was possible, not only because of the lack of accurate high-frequency overtone response essential, for reasons to be given shortly, but also because it is manifestly improper to superimpose the acoustical qualities of one room upon that of another. That is, to put it another way, for the singer to come before you with his or her voice submerged in the echo pattern of another room or auditorium. But there are other contributory factors which thus far have been neglected.

The weakest point in the electro-mechanical analogy of Maxfield's theory of the mechanical system of the Orthophonic Victrola is the spider of the reproducer. Bettini had used the spider principle for vertical-cut cylinder recorders and reproducers as early as 1889.[2] If this is to be considered an essential element of the system, then Bettini should have been given credit. Strangely enough, although his chain of electrical analogs breaks down at the spider because of the complex nature of its function as applied in the lateral method, it seems to fit much more logically if applied to the Edison acoustic system. On a side by side basis (See Fig. 18-1) sections through the Victor Orthophonic reproducer and the Edison diamond-disc reproducer would reveal that the diaphragm of the Edison reproducer has a stiffening pyramidal element on the air chamber side. This is of porcelain, low in weight, high in resistance to compression. This compelled the central area of the diaphragm to function in plunger fashion, the precise purpose of the metallic spider somewhat similarly shaped in the Orthophonic reproducer. But there is this essential difference, there was no bending possible in the Edison element, it was rigidly attached to the diaphragm. The bending, or spring action of the six legs of the metallic spider introduce what Maxfield terms "compliance," but the various forces grouped under this one heading make it impossible to concede that this is a usable analogy. The lateral stylus vibrates with a push-pull effect on the spider, which means that the legs of the spider are not only acting as a spring, but rigidly attached at the ends to the cone of the spider and to the one piece diaphragm, must alternately be pushing and pulling in a plane parallel

to the diaphragm as well. The whole pattern of alternate tension and compression of both spider and diaphragm is too complex to be thus simply reduced to a workable analogical design basis. It comprises what is known to physicists as an indeterminate structure, difficult to analyze except on an empirical basis and hence not amenable to a design solution by formula.

Another feature of the Edison reproducer which will be noted is the graduated layer of cork which extends from the center area to within one-half inch of the perimeter damping rings, which, incidentally are also of rubber or cork-faced with paper. This graduated cork lamination on the diaphragm served to permit concentric ring vibrations in an even scale from the highest frequencies to the lowest in the true lineal relationship essential to correct reproduction and which can never be produced by a corrugated diaphragm. An integral feature of the continuity of the cork was in the damping action it supplied, an essential feature also neglected in the design of the orthophonic diaphragm assembly, which is damped at the edges only. Note also the small mass of the lever and stylus assembly, an important feature in transmitting relatively undistorted higher frequencies to the diaphragm. Extremely important is the flexible connecting link between the diaphragm and stylus lever. This resembles a piece of silk fishline which supplies exactly the sort of pure filter action, or "compliance" envisioned for the spider of the Orthophonic reproducer, but which was not achieved, for reasons already stated. It must be obvious that the action of any spring in series with a reproducing system is to alter to some extent the nature of the vibrations. Maximilian Weil later made a definite improvement on the Orthophonic reproducer idea in his "Audak," by replacing the spider with a piece of mica which was riveted to the corrugated diaphragm and which greatly reduced the distortion of the higher registers caused by the spider, and extended the upper range, although not

[2] U. S. Patent Gazette, Vol. 48, p. 921 "Recording and Reproducing Sounds" filed by G. Bettini April 11, 1889, issued Aug. 13, 1889.

eliminating certain other objectionable features.

The essential rightness of approach of the Edison method may be appreciated by reflecting for a moment on the ease with which acceptable articulation is achieved by making a "lover's telephone" with a pair of any old cylindrical ice cream cartons or coffee cans and a piece of string. As is perhaps well known to most readers a hole is punched in the center of the bottoms with a taut string through the holes held by knots on the insides of the containers, which serve to collect the sound, or to assist in the hearing, as the case may be. With such primitive materials conversation can be carried on in a normal tone of voice over several hundred feet. As this idea was known before the telephone, it is obvious that the mechanical-wave transmission theory did not have to originate with the electricians of the Bell Telephone Co. It must also be clear that in the spider an attempt was made to combine this kind of action with the driving action of a spring or lever, which, if it may be done, was not accomplished successfully in this attempt. To decisively prove that the effect of the spider was to alter the harmonics of the recorded frequencies, the following is quoted from Maxfield's own statements in his 1933 work, under the heading "Effect of Mechanical Systems on Sound."

"We have now discussed briefly, the nature of sound and some of its characteristics which are important from the point of view of music and speech. We will next consider the effect of a limited number of mechanical systems on sound. A most important class of these systems is the resonance group, and it might be interesting to digress for a moment and consider the nature and effect of resonance by itself. Most people are familiar with the simple experiment of a weight suspended by a spring. If the weight is lifted a small distance from the position in which it is hanging at rest and then is allowed to fall, it will start to return to its original position of rest. By the time it reaches this position, it is travelling so rapidly that it overshoots, thereby stretching the spring to a point where the weight will no longer balance its tension. This increased tension gradually brings the weight to momentary rest at a point below its normal position of equilibrium and then starts lifting the weight again. By the time it has reached its point of normal equilibrium, it is going so fast that it once more overshoots. This process would be repeated indefinitely if it were not for the fact that the motion is gradually stopped by the friction of the air and the friction in the spring itself. The frequency, i.e., the number of complete up and down vibrations per second, is called the natural frequency of the resonant system. This natural frequency depends upon the mass of the weight and the stiffness of the spring."

In the case of the spider, instead of a fixed point spring-suspended weight relationship, we have two inertia elements with a spring between, which also has a calculated weight, or inertia and the three together constitute a resonant system. The interposition of a spring provides a high-frequency resonance element which inevitably alters the character of transmitted vibrations in the higher frequency range. Contrast this to the linkage of the Edison diaphragm-stylus assembly and it will be seen that the latter is in the nature of what Maxfield termed a pure compliance and that it conforms to the demands of his band-pass filter theory, whereas his own device does not.

As evidence, consider the fact, demonstrated with standard, unaltered instruments, that the Edison phonograph of 1915 or later will play the electrically recorded Edison discs of 1927 to 1930 with excellent fidelity and without distortion, although with some attenuation of the extreme lower frequencies which also occurs in the reproduction of the acoustic records. Whatever the validity of the band-pass filter analogy of Max-field, the principles applying to the mechanical system must have been well established by Edison before the development of the terminology applied by Maxfield and Harrison.

Now let us deal with some of the other changes introduced into the reproducing equipment and analyze them purely in terms we know to be thoroughly applicable; those of acoustics and mechanics. To begin with, the Orthophonic reproducer had been obviously designed to impose the same weight on the record as the precedent No. 2 Victor reproducer, or "sound-box," as they were more commonly referred to in the talking machine industry. This weight of the sound-box alone in both cases was exactly 151.5 grams. However, in modifying the Johnson goose-neck to provide for a constant taper instead of the former uniform diameter cross-section and also to eliminate the abrupt angle formerly introduced in the joint at the tone-arm proper, the distance from reproducer to this vertical joint was increased. Thus the pressure was increased on the record from the former approximately 122 grams with the Victor No. 2 reproducer to approximately 142 grams in the Orthophonic assembly. This, together with the increased amplitude of the vibrations cut into the records over a wider range by the new process, resulted in the excessive wear experienced with many of the new records, despite the steps taken to reduce resistance internally in the vibratory train. These facts would seem to indicate that the sound-box of the Orthophonic had been designed before and independently of the design of the rest of the mechanical reproducing system, instead of upon an electrical analogy of the entire system.

A goal of the Johnson regime in development of the Victor had been the capturing of the elusive overtones—the achievement of "brilliant" quality in reproduction. This was undoubtedly nurtured by the "star" system, probably as much responsible for Victor design

policy as for its prestige success on an advertising campaign basis. The influence of the voice of Caruso alone in this respect is perhaps incalculable. This design philosophy was undoubtedly responsible for the change in the stylus ratio from 1.44 which had been established for the older "exhibition" sound-box, to the 1.66 ratio adopted for the Victor No. 2. This change in ratio accentuated the "ringing" tones of Enrico Caruso and others of the Victor opera and concert artists, reinforced in part somewhat unnaturally by certain resonance periodicities of the mica diaphragm, steel needle, and other parts. This ratio change also had made considerably more difficult the proper transmission of lower fundamental register tones due to the stiffness of the mica diaphragm. In other words, the frequency range of the reproducer had been shifted upwards to favor the higher registers. Now, coming to the Orthophonic, this was reversed. The ratio was established at 1.25. This may have represented a decision at that time that it was time to drop the star system, or that the time was ripe to cultivate the market for recordings of orchestral and other types of music than that of soloists, as had been decided by the leading European companies. At any rate, it did nevertheless represent the time of shift of emphasis in these categories. The demonstration and sales value of the Victor galaxy of great operatic artists and concert soloists dropped like a plummet after the introduction of the Orthophonic Victrola.

The strangest fact of the entire Maxfield-Harrison paper is the way in which this most important fact of the re-design of the Victrola was left unexplained. However, it is known that this change facilitated the passage of the lower registers, which could be radiated without the increased resistance encountered with any given type of diaphragm as the mechanical advantage ratio is increased. Conversely, this change in ratios explains succinctly why the new electrically recorded discs sounded so abominable when played on any of the millions of old Victrolas, the greater number and the latest models of which were all equipped with the No. 2 reproducer. Naturally the amplitude of cut of the upper registers had to be increased to compensate for the lower ratio of mechanical advantage of the Orthophonic reproducer. Quite incidentally and conversely, the old acoustically recorded records lost their former incisiveness and sounded pallid and weak when played on the new Orthophonic Victrola.

In extending the width of the frequency range of the diaphragm, spider and stylus assembly, several already known and previously utilized concepts essential to correct reproduction were ignored, perhaps because of a sincere but mistaken confidence in the correctness of the analogical basis for design which had been set up. One of these was the already known shortcomings of the common steel phonograph needle, not only because of the wear and tear on the records, but more importantly because of the diminution in high-frequency response that occurred in just one playing as a result of needle wear towards the end of a selection. There were also other distortional influences introduced which apply in varying degree to all removable styli. As a matter of justice, a former medium steel needle with constant taper from point to shank was probably the most uniform transmitter of vibrations of all frequencies to the stylus bar of all the removable type needles with perhaps the exception of the tapered, cactus-type needle, which had certain other undesirable characteristics such as breaking down on loud passages; and by picking up particles, acting as a lapping medium.

All needles with constant cylindrical sections below the thumb screw socket have resonance values which affect the quality of reproduction in the higher frequencies. The necessity of providing a socket with thumb screw to hold removable styli in itself provided a need for stiffness and mass which also increased the moment of inertia of the stylus bar assembly to a point which definitely imposed a low ceiling on high-frequency response. In attempting to reconcile these conflicting resonance factors a "compliance" had been built into the Victor tungsten stylus by means of a narrowed section just below the needle socket. These needles had been developed several years before the introduction of the Orthophonic and their sale was promoted even more vigorously thereafter. However, the tungsten wire which protruded from the tip of the needle had a cylindrical section which cut into the lower radius curve of the record groove until it was ground to conformity by the abrasive which was mixed with the record surface material. Theoretically, the steel needles came properly shaped to fit the groove. Actually the final polishing of the steel needles was accomplished by turning them in steel barrels, much as pebbles are self polished by the churning of the surf. Needless to say, the predicating of an entirely new system of recording upon the basis of needles of these unreliable and unscientific types, more than thirty years after the use of temporary styli had been dropped by the hill-and-dale phonograph industry, was a major mistake. The defects of the removable styli were perpetuated by Maxfield and Harrison, perhaps at the insistence of the Victor Co., but with the end result that the acoustic Victrola was eventually to be eliminated as a satisfactory reproducing instrument.

The primary reason that the hill-and-dale industry had discarded the use of changeable needles so much earlier was the softness of the wax record. The making of records by the many original phonograph companies licensed by Lippincott for the local entertainment trade was in large part dependent on this critical factor. The use of soft wax blanks for purposes of reproduction as well as recording, made efficiency in the transmission of the weakly incised vibrations absolutely essential. In an earlier chapter the story of the reasons duplicating methods were not used in

the early days of the cylinder phonograph has been covered thoroughly.
The design conflict was between having
blanks soft enough to record satisfactorily and a reproducing system light
enough and responsive enough to permit a sufficiently large number of playings of the original record. Obviously,
efficiency in the transmission of the
recorded vibrations was a must from
the very beginnings of the cylinder
industry.

In the course of development of the
cylinder phonograph it was early
learned that it was the imposed weight
and inertia of the vibratory chain that
caused undue wear to the soft wax
cylinders. Long before Maxfield and
Harrison it had become axiomatic to
reduce stylus and diaphragm inertia to
the irreducible minimum. More than
this, it had been proved by countless
experiments by trial and error, as witnessed by innumerable surviving design examples, that abrupt changes in
cross section and mass in the design of
moving parts must be avoided to facilitate reproduction of all of the recorded
frequency range as well as to mitigate
record wear to undulations at certain
frequencies. It would have been logically expected that in view of the
ostensibly scientific basis upon which
Maxfield and Harrison were expound-
ing their views before a learned scientific society that these simple truths,
discovered years before, would be reflected in the subsequent literature of
the art, but not so. Comparisons in
these respects between the new Orthophonic system and the precedent Victor
reveal little recognition of these important but previously neglected factors. For instance, the stylus bar of the
Victor No. 2 sound-box weighs 4.6
grams, which is admittedly inordinately
heavy. But the Orthophonic sound-box
stylus although shorter, still was reduced to only 3.9 grams with a spider.
This may be contrasted with the stylus
bar with linkage for the Amberola cylinder reproducer of .7 gram, or the
Edison disc reproducer stylus bar with
linkage of .9 gram. Despite the ex-

tremely light weight of the aluminum
alloy diaphragm of the Orthophonic,
weighing but .3 gram, the total weight of
the vibratory train of the sound-box
was 4.2 grams as against a total of 2.2
grams for the Edison disc reproducer.

This inertia was not the only difficulty. A great deal of the upper register
distortion in the Orthophonic was
caused by the way in which this weight
was disposed. Already mentioned is the
abrupt change in section caused at
the low end of the needle socket by the
use of removable needles. Another
(immediately above the pivot spindle)
was occasioned by an abrupt change in
mass, where the solid section of the
stylus abruptly is changed to a thin U
section continuing to the attachment to
the center of the spider. This U section
was appropriately tapered but the
abrupt changes mentioned, plus the imposition of another vibratory mass concentrated at one point, namely the
thumb screw, each introduced distortion to some part of the frequency band
transmitted. The history of the development of the gramophone by Berliner,
carried forward by Johnson, illustrates
well that the very nature of the lateral
method, which used stampers and hard
surfaced records from the start, was
responsible for the ignoring of these
principles which had to be recognized
in sheer self defense by those using
the soft wax cylinders. This in turn
was probably responsible for the ignoring of these factors vital to absolute
precision of reproduction by Maxfield
and Harrison. Some of these design
fallacies were again perpetuated later
in the design of the stylus and armature
assemblies of the early electric pickups,
which were also notoriously hard on
records.

Hanna's discussion of the Maxfield-
Harrison paper was, of course, a quite
obvious attempt to claim that the larger
share of the credit for the improvement to lateral reproduction achieved
through the new means was due to the
adoption of the exponential horn theory,
as expounded previously by himself and
Slepian. However, the change in dia-

phragm stylus bar ratio mentioned was at least as important. Also a considerable part of the improvement in more uniform transmission was due to the elimination of the bottle neck of the old Victor, rather appropriately entitled the gooseneck, which had a uniform cross section, an abrupt turn at its juncture with the tone-arm proper, with sharp edges and a leaky joint. But the greater part of the improvement came from the adoption of the constantly expanding cross section of tone chamber as a whole starting from the smallest diameter at the neck of the reproducer to the outermost lip of the horn. This idea had not originated with Hanna and Slepian, although they had collected experimental data upon the performance of such horns. Edison had utilized this principle quite fully in his Triumph model Amberola cygnet horn of 1911. As has been stated, this horn was the prototype of many of the overhead radio horns of the mid 1920's, such as the Magnavox. This design was also utilized in a modified form in the DeLuxe Amberola, as a cabinet enclosed horn. Incidentally, but not less important, was the fact that these phonographs in common with the later Edison diamond disc phonographs, had an absolutely air-tight tone passage from reproducer diaphragm to the outer rim of the horn. To be fair, it must be conceded that in the Orthophonic system steps were taken to make this passage as air tight as possible, but it was at best only partially achieved. The Credenza Orthophonic model represented the highest development commercially of the new system. It was provided with a 72" long re-entrant exponential horn with a large aperture. This horn was also furnished with the later DeLuxe automatic record changer for $1,000. A complete line of instruments with shorter horns and smaller cabinets was also provided. The interesting feature of this was the fact that although the Maxfield-Harrison theory of matched impedance would call for a different sound-box for each one of these widely varying tone chambers, such was not the case—the same reproducer being used for each.

The effect of the introduction of the Orthophonic Victrola upon the record business was profound. In 1924, Victor dealers had spent enormous sums advertising Victor Records, particularly in the autumn pre-holiday season, half the cost being borne by the Victor Co. as customary. Due to the changeover and the reaction to the new records as played on the old machines, as noted, advertising of Victor records dropped to a very low level during 1925. Single-face Victor records were offered at reduced prices and all Victors, except for certain later period models, were offered at half price early in the fall of 1925. Even after the appearance of the Orthophonic Victrolas, old model Victors were still being advertised at half-price during 1926, and large supplies of the old records were still on the market.

Within a year or so, backed by tremendous advertising campaigns, the displacement of the Victor Victrola by the Orthophonic Victrola became an established fact. For some reason, Columbia was never able in the U. S. to match the advertising effort of the Victor Co. and consequently the Columbia Viva-Tonal phonographs are now somewhat of a rarity. However, the new-process laminated Columbia records, first introduced in 1922, had proven to be very successful in combination with the Western Electric recording method. The smoother surface proved to be superior to that of the solid stock Victor record in resisting the reaction of the new reproducing systems. Within a short time independent manufacturers had developed reproducers to replace those of the older Victor, Sonora, and Columbia machines which would often play the new records quite satisfactorily despite the inadequacies of their horns and tone arm assemblies, again illustrating that there were fallacies in the concept that long horns were a necessity.

As previously stated, album sets had made their appearance on the American market in 1924, shortly before the inauguration of electrical recording. Nearly all of these album sets by both companies had apparently originated in Europe. But it is interesting that this primarily European cultural development stimulated American invention in respect to both recording and in developing automatic record-playing equipment. The new found facility in recording the larger orchestras which the electric process afforded, certainly accelerated this trend. Also the auditorium resonance recorded through the use of the microphone added a feeling of life to orchestral reproduction which it had quite lacked before and which added immeasurably to the public response to the new symphonic recordings. Through the combination of all of the influences mentioned, technical as well as psychological, a new class of record buyers came into the market—those interested primarily in the recordings of the major works of the great composers, as played by the world's leading musical organizations. This new and important group of record buyers constituted a latent market for automatic record-changing phonographs.

At first the major companies paid slight heed, although there had been numbers of such devices patented. In fact, the automatic record player was really forced upon the leading recording companies by developments quite outside their field. In a sense, it all began with the Brunswick-Balke-Collender Co. which had been left out in the cold when the deal had been consummated between Western Electric and the representatives of Victor and Columbia for the use of the new process. Brunswick, because of this, decided to meet this competition by being the first to bring out an all-electric reproducing instrument. This they did with the cooperation of engineers of RCA , General Electric Co., and the Westinghouse Electric & Mfg. Co.; it was called the Brunswick Panatrope. This used a horseshoe magnet pick-up, similar to those used by most other of the early models, a vacuum tube amplifier, and

the first dynamic speaker to be used on any home equipment. It is interesting to note that the dynamic speaker is the reverse of the dynamic microphone, invented by Edison. However, perhaps due to the rush to get the new instrument on the market, the components were not well balanced and while the volume was virtually unlimited, the tone reproduction was not as good as that of the Orthophonic Victrola, or the Viva-Tonal Columbia. Within a short time, however, the Panatrope was improved and Brunswick put out a complete line of radio combinations with Panatrope and also a line of improved acoustic phonographs, as well. It is important to note that Brunswick did not consider it necessary to use the oversize horns used in the Credenza, or in fact, to use re-entrant horns of any type. It is true, however, that the reproducer was quite closely patterned after that of the Orthophonic. Brunswick records were made by a light-ray microphone system originally developed for sound-film recording by the General Electric Co., based on the principle of the 1879 Photophone of Alexander Graham Bell, which like Poulsen's magnetic wire recording method was not commercially practicable at the time for reason of a lack of a suitable means of electrical amplification. As modified for use in disc recording, with an amplifier and recording head comparable to that of Maxfield and Harrison, this was called the Pallatrope. The name "Panatrope" was adopted for the Brunswick all-electric reproducing instrument.

Even before the advent of electrical recording various radio-phonograph combinations had been offered to the public. At first panels were made removable in certain models of Victrola, Sonora, Brunswick, Columbia and others, to permit optional installation of a standard-make radio chassis. Soon this market became absorbed almost completely by the Radio Corporation of America, with its Radiola. Speaker heads were provided with the earlier models to be affixed instead of the sound-box when radio reproduction was desired. Later, internal connections to the horn were provided with an external knob to control a valve in the sound chamber. The secondary phase of the Orthophonic promotion period was one of selling combination radio-phonographs. "Victor with Radiola," "Brunswick Panatrope with Radiola Super-Heterodyne" were familiar terms in the advertising of the day. As radio reproduction improved, it became evident in the higher priced combinations that radio reproduction was often freer of distortion without this new acoustic system and was being hampered by it. This impelled other manufacturers to follow the lead of Brunswick in developing all-electric reproducing instruments.

Even before its acquisition by the Radio Corporation of America, Victor had introduced the "Electrola" and combination instruments which played records through the electrical reproducing system. Columbia developed a line of electric reproducing instruments assisted by the Kolster Radio Corporation, in which the horseshoe magnet of the pick-up was positioned horizontally in relation to the record surface, an idea used later by Capehart. This assisted in reducing the tendency of the tone-arm to twist, in responding to the lateral action of the stylus. Victor later attempted to solve this by extending cobra-headed wings on either side of the pick-up head and the affixing of weights on the under side—a much more devious way of solving the same problem! But Brunswick, by pioneering the all-electric phonograph (from the first equipped with a plug-in power supply, electric-motor turntable, and rugged pick-up), had supplied the elements necessary to provide a market for the record-changing mechanisms.

The public had revelled in the new found propensity of the new type phonographs and the dynamic speakers for producing great volume and thundering bass. It was as a secondary result in the chain of events begun by Maxfield and Harrison in changing the sound-box ratio that this came about as we have shown. Now the poor inventors who had been chased away repeatedly from the plush waiting rooms of the executives of the big recording companies suddenly found a new market for their contrivances. One of the first of the new all electric coin-operated phonographs was produced by the Automatic Music Instrument Co. of Grand Rapids, in 1927. By the mid 1930's there were others by Capehart, Seeburg, and Wurlitzer. Soon it became the rage of the grilles and taverns.

The term "juke box" is said to have originated in the south, where the fad really had its first great impetus. Rightfully or not, this sort of indoctrination tended to set the popular taste for reproduction in home phonographs as well. Capehart, sensing that the home phonograph market was the more important, deserted the "joints" and began the production of its later series of Capeharts with elaborate, large-size cabinets with oversize dynamic speakers and a new type turnover changer. The sound of a majestic symphony booming from the Capehart was most impressive, but actually, the high frequency end of its reproduction spectrum was entirely inadequate. Some improvement in balance was made in some models of later years, but the lack of a proper criterion was quite evident. Later, the Capehart Co. became "a financial associate of ITT." But Homer Capehart, who went into politics, had long since ceased to have any interest in the company bearing his name.

As is well known, the Radio Corporation of America had succeeded in the mid 1920's in gaining complete control of the radio industry through the acquisition of the DeForest, Hazeltine, Armstrong, and LaTour patents. The evidence of the success of the total program of this patent group including A. T. & T. was in the acquisition of the Victor Talking Machine Co. by a group of New York bankers in 1927 for $30,000,000. This subsequently resulted in the merger of R C A and the Victor Talking Machine Co. as the R C A Victor Co. The effect upon the Columbia Phonograph Co. was even more pronounced. It resulted in the dictated withdrawal of that company from the phonograph and radio business and its acquisition in 1932 by Grigsby-Grunow, for the purpose of record manufacture only. Various other companies had made great progress in the radio industry, including Atwater Kent, Majestic, Stromberg-Carlson, Fada, Freed-Eisemann, Zenith and many others, all of whom paid tribute to the radio trust. A. Atwater Kent, who made a huge fortune before the fetters had been made ready, pulled out while still ahead. Majestic "Mighty Monarch of the Air" made the fatal mistake of trying to compete with the very companies to which it was paying heavy royalties, embarking on great and costly advertising campaigns on popular priced radios and radio-phonographs. Well-known through the depression, Majestic finally folded after an abortive try at the record business in the mid 1940's like Sonora. Stromberg-Carlson, makers of specialty telephone apparatus and Zenith managed to persist, perhaps because of special connections. Many, many names formerly prominent, Federal, DeForest, and Ware, disappeared one by one.

Radio had done more than to create world-shaking shifts in the balance of power among great corporations even to proving itself a potent weapon in deciding national elections—it also served to change the standards of public taste in music and its idea of what were desirable qualities in reproduction. Before radio, the average purchaser of a phonograph had wanted a soft-toned quality of reproduction. Many used piano-tone steel needles and fibers, often with the doors on the tone chamber partially closed, as well. After radio the demand was for greater volume. Whether this was a reaction from the necessity of using ear phones with the elementary crystal sets, or because of the desire to have a louder loudspeaker than that of the neighbors is a problem for the psychologists. In any case, those who remember this nostalgic era (the competing loudspeakers of the business streets and residential neighborhoods) recall the increasing loudness.

As the most constant criterion with which to estimate this phenomenon over this critical and formative period of development of public taste, consider the Edison (disc) phonograph. In the first years after its introduction in 1912, the most common complaint of prospective customers was that the reproduction was too loud. This was partly due, no doubt, to the fact that a much broader band of frequencies was being reproduced than was obtainable from the talking machines of the time. This, of course, corresponds to the impression of greater loudness which the engineers revealed in their discussions of the Orthophonic Victrola in comparison with the former instruments. For this reason the Edison phonograph had been equipped with a tone modulator consisting of a large ball of sound absorbing material which could be pushed by a lever into the throat of the horn. By 1925, this complaint had been totally reversed—many prospective customers said that the Edison phonograph was not loud enough, even with the modulator all the way out from the throat.

Quite typical of the Edison faculty for doing the right thing at the wrong time, was the decision made to attempt to meet the crowding competition of greater volume instruments by the production of a long-playing phonograph. Again quite typically, Edison decided quite empirically that what he would do to achieve this was to multiply the playing time of the existing Edison record by three. This meant that instead of 150 grooves to the inch, the new record would have 450. (Present LP's average about 250.) This 1/450 appeared to be an almost impossible fine groove to process satisfactorily, to say nothing of producing a record which would stand up in service.

Ultimately this proved to be true, even with the extraordinarily hard Edison phenolin surface. The record walls would break down in a short time when played with the special reproducer with the extremely fine diamond point required. However, the Victor attempt at a successful long-playing record at 33⅓ rpm made several years later, with a groove size about that of the standard Edison groove, or about 150 to the inch, was likewise a technical failure, and was also withdrawn from the market a few years later. Consider also the fact that the Edison long-playing disc was reproduced at 80 rpm! Although not a commercial success it is also important to observe, in relation to a consideration of the relative merits of the two general types of reproduction (vertical versus lateral), that the Edison long-playing record with a groove of only 1/450 of an inch wide, was reproduced acoustically by a reproducer that was varied only in the stylus and in the floating weight from that of the standard Edison disc reproducer as used since 1912. Consider too, that this new record-playing equipment was made available to all former users of Edison phonographs, as well as being incorporated into new models. There is here a great contrast in ethics with that displayed by the lateral industry.

From the standpoint of timing, this Edison move was all wrong. In the first place it did not provide an answer to the demand for more volume. The new long-playing records, which offered up to twenty minutes of music on a side were not louder, but somewhat reduced in volume from the standard Edison discs. Also the Edison catalog contained no complete operas, symphonies, or concertos demanding longer playing time. Edison record buyers were not particularly interested in continuous playing. Moreover, the Edison records could only be played with spring-wind motors and only the official laboratory models had a playing time equal to the demands of the longer playing records.

But this abortive introduction of long playing records was apparently somewhat an act of desperation, for experiments had been under way for some time in electrical recording. Walter

Miller, Recording Director; and Charles Edison, then Vice-President; both had urged Thomas A. Edison to get into electrical recording even before it was obvious that the Western Electric process was going to be a commercial success. However, for quite a time, Edison would have none of it because of his unfavorable experiences with electro-acoustical devices in the telephone development era. He predicted distortion would be inevitable in all electrical recording methods.

As in the belated entrance of Edison into the disc field, the pattern repeated itself. Experiments were begun by some of the Edison men before Edison's consent was finally won. Walsh, General Manager of the Phonograph Division, proposed that an electrical radio-phonograph be developed that would play the conventional lateral disc records with quality which would equal the best obtainable from the Orthophonic, or the Panatrope, but which would play Edison discs better. The hopelessness of trying to restrict buyers of new instruments to the limited Edison disc repertoire was now apparent to everyone.

Meanwhile, Walter Miller and Holland, who also had tried to persuade Edison to go into electrical recording, were working independently in the Edison recording studio in New York, and a few electrical recordings were made there as early as 1926.

At this time the laboratory at West Orange lacked measuring devices to establish corresponding acoustical and electrical impedances, such as had been used by the Bell engineers in developing the Western Electric process. As more than a decade of public tone-testing had demonstrated the accuracy of his acoustic process, Edison felt there was something wrong with the claims made for the electric process on the basis of acoustical measurements—that these results were not comparable with what one could hear. Therefore, he sought for a way to determine the amount of distortion involved in each method without recourse to measuring devices.

Theodore Edison suggested this might be done by going through the entire recording-reproduction cycle repeatedly; the first record produced would be played by its standard phonograph to make a second; the second record to make a third, etc. This would intensify defects in any part of the cycle, whether in the cutting of the wax, in the plating, making stampers, pressing, or in phonograph design. While this was not done at the time because of lack of access to the complete processes of others, it was later tried and it was found that after a certain number of times through, only the spurious resonances would remain!

A great deal of time and costly experiment was required to electrify the Edison method. Up to the beginning of these experiments there was not an alternating current power line in the Edison laboratory—a last vestige of the famous conflict between Edison's direct current system and the alternating current of Tesla and Westinghouse!

Once a satisfactory method of making records electrically was found, there still remained the problem of developing a combination instrument which would also play the conventional lateral-cut records.

But another hurdle had to be cleared, that of getting into the radio field without paying excessive royalties to the radio trust. This was finally accomplished by the purchase of the already licensed Splitdorf Radio Corporation of Newark, N. J. Imagine,—the founder of the electric lighting industry, granter of the first degree in electrical engineering, and grantee of the basic patent in electronics, being compelled to get into the radio industry by way of the back door! Actually, this serves to show what a long way Edison was prepared to go to save his favorite invention, the phonograph.

During the many months of experimentation, the Edison monthly disc record release folders had borne the caption "No Distortion on Edison Records." There is no doubt that this "fidelity to an ideal" was largely responsible for the failure of Edison to keep up with his competition in other respects. By the time Edison was satisfied to switch all recording over to the new electric process, the other companies were far in the lead in programs of recording the major orchestral works of the great composers in album sets. Album sets were quite impossible to the Edison phonograph, for each of the Edison discs, made in ten-inch diameter only, weighed ten ounces each and was a quarter of an inch thick. A short time after the introduction of electrical recording, but after the dropping of the Edison long-playing records, some superb complete recordings were made on the standard Edison discs of chamber music works by Schubert and others by the New York Trio and the Roth String Quartet. One of the most tragic aspects of the Edison story is that there was never a complete symphony recorded. One of the old man's greatest ambitions was to achieve a successful recording of the Beethoven's Fifth Symphony. It was recorded; however, the records were not approved for release, probably rejected by Mr. Edison.

Shortly after the introduction of the new recording process, the answer to the demand for greater volume was met by the introduction of a new line of acoustic phonographs known as the "Edisonic." These had a somewhat larger horn than those of the previous laboratory models and were also equipped with an improved reproducer, which was estimated to provide 2½ times the volume of the standard reproducer. Prior to the introduction of electrical recording, a louder reproducer had been supplied to owners of Edison instruments which was named the "dance reproducer." However, this was not only louder, but also rather strident, lacking the smooth balance of the standard reproducer. The new Edisonic reproducer, however, had the same reproductive capacity of the standard reproducer, but with much greater volume. These were made available to Edison owners on a nominal exchange basis, continuing a policy towards purchasers of Edison goods that had been in effect for many years. Actually, most collectors of Edison records indicate their preference for the former laboratory model phonographs with either the standard or the Edisonic reproducer. The fact that the standard reproducers, with few exceptions, would play the most demanding of the new electrical recordings with complete facility and breadth of tone, is a tremendous tribute to the basic correctness of the original design principles.

After the acquisition of the Splitdorf Radio Corporation in 1928, production of an all-electric radio-phonograph was begun. The Splitdorf radio with a regenerative Armstrong circuit and a Peerless single-turn voice coil dynamic speaker was revised and renamed the Edison radio. Three models were introduced in 1929, one a straight radio, a radio-phonograph combination at $495, and a DeLuxe push-pull circuit combination for $1,000. The combination instruments were equipped with a unique, well-designed pick-up, patented by the son of the inventor, Theodore Edison. This pick-up had an offset diamond stylus which was made available for playing the diamond-disc records simply by leaving out the steel needle or other removable stylus used for playing the lateral-disc records. In the light of present "hi-fi" tastes, the amplifier-speaker characteristics were weak in the higher frequency range and over heavy in the bass. Thus, the voice and solo instrument fidelity of the Edison acoustically recorded discs was to some extent lost and the well recorded Edison electrical discs seemed to take on some of the exaggerated bass then characteristic of the competition products.

After 1929, succeeding lines of instruments were made to play only the laterally-recorded discs. For a short time before the withdrawal of Edison from the record field, laterally-recorded discs were issued. For a time the same Edison recordings were issued on diamond disc records, the new needle-type discs, and the blue amberol cylinders—such was his loyalty to his old customers!

Recently, the writer of a popularized treatment of the phonograph saga had the Edison Phonograph Works closing down at the end of the tin-foil phonograph demonstration period, in October of 1878. He asserted that Edison had deserted the phonograph at that time, when he had merely put it aside to work on the electric light. Actually, as a matter of historic accuracy, there was no "Edison Phonograph Works" until 1888. But this author also has Edison "deserting" the phonograph not only early, but late—in 1929. What is the record? Edison was the last of the founders of the original phonograph enterprises to be in control of his business. It was he, personally, who gave the order November 1, 1929, that production of musical phonographs and records was to cease. But the company which Thomas A. Edison founded continued to produce the Voicewriter which performs the same useful functions in the business world that his improved phonograph of 1888 was designed for.[3]

Mr. Edison gave the order in 1929, before the full impact of the great depression had been felt in all its fury. These were the days when Arthur Brisbane was exhorting his readers of the front page of the Hearst papers and others from coast to coast "Don't Sell America Short!" Years before Eldridge Johnson had sold out his Victor Talking Machine Co. to a banking syndicate, later merged with R C A. The American Graphophone Co. and the Columbia Phonograph had long before crashed as a result of stock market manipulations, the latter company having been finally reorganized with new management and capital. Who deserted? Against the advice of many of his business associates, Mr. Edison made this decision, which must have been a bitter one. He did

---

[3] Amalgamated in 1956 with the McGraw Electric Company; Max McGraw, President; Hon. Charles Edison, Chairman of the Board.

so because he knew what had to be done to save his enterprise. Those who were later employed by the Thomas A. Edison Industries Division of the Mc-Graw-Edison Company, whether producing storage batteries, Voicewriters, testing equipment, or other products, may rightfully respect the sagacity and courage of Mr. Edison in sacrificing his favorite interest to the welfare of his employees and associates. Unfortunately, the decision was reached to close down the Thomas A. Edison Division in 1973, and most of the buildings were demolished. With one or two exceptions, only the restored original manufacturing buildings, with the Library and offices, including the home of Mr. Edison, Glenmont, in nearby Llewellyn Park remain as charges of the Edison National Historic Site, operated as a museum complex by the U.S. Park Service, Department of the Interior.

CHAPTER 19

THE MOTION PICTURES AND SOUND RECORDING

NINEVEH, of Biblical fame, was destroyed in 606 B.C. In the ruins during archaeological excavations, a coarse lens of quartz and an inscription too fine to be read with the unaided eye were found. Aristotle in his writings noted the optical effect of after-images, evidence of the persistence of vision phenomenon essential to the illusion made use of in motion pictures. In 750 A.D. Geber, an Arabian alchemist, discovered the effect of light upon silver nitrate, the basis of photographic processes. Thus, some of the principal elements of motion pictures have been known since ancient times.

Friar Roger Bacon, sometimes called "Doctor Mirabilis," wrote extensively of the uses of mirrors and lenses in 1267, and deplored their employment in the practice of "black magic" to deceive the people. In 1450, Lenone Battista Alberti, Italian cleric and architect, invented the camera lucida, which combined the principles of lense and prism, used by artists for sketching to this day. In 1500, the noted Leonardo da Vinci, artist, sculptor, architect, and inventor, gave the first complete written description of the portable camera obscura—the elemental box-type pinhole camera familiar to all experimenters in photography. He was the first to accurately explain its relationship to visual perception. The principle of the camera obscura had been known long before da Vinci, however. It may have been first noticed by the cave dwellers

that a hole in the skin across the entrance would project a reversed, upside down image of the exterior upon the opposite wall!

In 1558, Giambattista della Porta (1543-1615) of Naples wrote of making a number of light and shadow devices for entertainment purposes, thus becoming the first picture showman. A decade later, Monsignor Daniello Barbaro introduced the lens into the opening of the camera obscura.

The next important step was the invention of the magic lantern by Athenasius Kircher, a German priest then in residence at Sacred College in Rome. He published a book, "Ars Magna Lucis et Umbrae,"—"The Great Art of Light and Shadow," in 1646, a second edition in 1671. Kircher experimented, improved and demonstrated continuously, over a long period, and many others were incited to emulate his experiments in various countries. The number of experimenters from this time forward became so numerous that this account will attempt to deal only with those who made the more significant contributions. For instance, Johann Zahn in 1685 had developed Kircher's lantern to a high efficiency, improved only in principle by the addition of better illuminants as time went on. Motion was introduced into magic lantern projection technics by Pieter van Musschenbrock in 1736, by means of a multiple slide system. By 1780, Jacques Alexander Cesar Charles, retained by Louis XVI to do optical research, had developed a device which would project images of living persons, and from this the Magnascope—a projection microscope.

Etienne Gaspard Robertson in France originated the Phantasmagoria in 1798, by which moving visions were projected upon a screen of smoke by means of magic lanterns on wheels. Shortly after the inception of the 19th century, Tom Wedgewood was making profile pictures in silver nitrate on glass, by the action of light. In 1814, Joseph Nicephore Niepce began actual experiments in photography. Knowledge of motion and color was carried forward by Daniel Brewster, Scotch scientist, who invented about this time the Kaleidoscope, the mirror device for producing an innumerable number of colorful and symmetrical designs, which is still made and sold as an educational toy throughout the world.

It was Peter Mark Roget who first gave the scientific explanation of persistence of vision to the world, in 1824. He proved it by a card with a picture of a bird on one side, a cage on the other, which when whirled rapidly produced the illusion of the bird within the cage. John Ayrlon Paris developed a toy on the same principle which he called the Thaumatrope, which is also made yet today.

Another important event was the association of Niepce, pioneer of photography, with Louis Jacques Daguerre, in 1829. Daguerreotypes in a few years made their work famous throughout the world. But many sincere and indefatigable investigators worked along this and other lines pertinent to the final issue—motion pictures, without financial success or acclaim. One of these was Joseph Plateau, Belgian scientist, who sacrificed his eyesight by overexposure to the sun in performing optical experiments relative to the persistence of vision. Plateau and Simon Ritter von Stampfer, an Austrian geometrician and geologist, independently conceived of the idea of the "magic discs," by which a series of progressively altered designs upon the discs,

when whirled and viewed through a series of slots would give the effect of motion. Variations of the Plateau-Stampfer discs were called the Fantascope, Phenakistoscope, or Stroboscope. Two years later, William Horner in England improved on the idea by arranging the designs on a horizontal instead of a vertical wheel, thus permitting several persons to observe the action, instead of one. Ebenezer Small, a professor at Amherst, introduced the magic discs to the U. S.

Wheatstone, the well-known English scientist, invented the stereoscope in 1838. The following year both Talbot in England and Daguerre in France announced the achievement of success in producing photographs by means of the camera obscura. Hippolyte Bayard at this time also was experimenting with paper photo prints. In 1849, Brewster introduced a binocular camera, which was copied in France by M. Quinet, a photographer who named it the "Quinetoscope," from which some believe the term "cinema" was ultimately derived. The year following Frederick and William Langenheim, of Philadelphia, patented the Hyalotype, a process for producing positives on glass slides for use with the magic lantern—a most important development.

This accelerated the tempo and by 1852, Wheatstone, in England, Jules Duboscq and Antoine Claudet in France, were experimenting with photos instead of drawings on the magic discs. The year following, Franz von Uchatius, an Austrian army officer, developed a device combining the Plateau-Stampfer discs with the magic lantern—the first true motion picture projector.

However, in the general enthusiasm for the effect of perspective produced by the stereoscope, there was much effort wasted in the attempt to combine stereovision with motion. In other words, the attempt to combine unperfected elements was premature. For example, William Thomas Shaw in 1861 invented the Stereostrope, which consisted principally of eight stereoscopic photos mounted on an octagonal drum, which were viewed with the Wheatstone stereoscope. Others on the same general order were the "Motorscope," by James Laing; the "Stereofantascope," or "Bioscope," by Leon Foncauld, the French astronomer; and the "Photobioscope," by Cook and Bonelli. It is rather obvious to us now that they were attempting too much with too little information.

But little by little progress was being made. Coleman Sellers in the United States patented the "Kinematoscope," a toy using a paddle wheel action which produced motion pictures. Perhaps the only important still missing element of modern motion pictures was supplied by John Wesley Hyatt of New York, who invented celluloid in 1868. Another toy, with which everyone is familiar, is the little book of pictures which when "riffled" through rapidly, produce a motion picture. This also was invented about this time and was called the "Kineograph." A scientist, James Clerk Maxwell, mentioned elsewhere in another chapter of this book for his electromagnetic wave theory, which contributed to the understanding of electro-acoustical relationships, also was interested in optics and perfected a device known earlier as the "Zoetrope," which operated on the magic discs principle, by substituting concave lenses for the slots, eliminating the distortion caused by the curved surfaces of the pictures.

An over-publicized phase of movie development, in view of the previously cited work of many others, was the photographing of a horse in motion, obtained by Edouard Muybridge in California. He had been employed by Governor Leland Stanford of California to establish whether or not all four feet of a trotting horse were off the ground at one time. This was done by multiple cameras, electrically controlled by threads actuated by the wheels of the sulky. This work was brought to the attention of Etienne Jules Marey, French physiologist, who was much interested in the possibilities of motion photography as an aid to science in his field. Muybridge visited Marey in Paris and Marey used the Muybridge photos mounted in one of the magic disc devices to study muscular action in motion.

In 1877, Charles Emile Reynard developed the "Praxinoscope," another variation of the Plateau-Stampfer discs, with a mirror set in the center for viewing, a definite improvement. Two years later he produced a projection model. It was also in 1877 that Edison invented the phonograph, by a simple, uncomplicated act of disassociation—a miracle when contrasted with the slow, painful course of development of photography, not to mention motion pictures! Busy with both the electric light and the telephone at that time, in view of the zeal for development of other devices of all kinds, it is astounding that he was not somehow deprived of all credit for this most important invention, to say nothing of living to receive commercial remuneration.

In 1884, George Eastman of Rochester, N. Y., began the manufacture of roll paper film for his Kodak camera. Just three years later, Hannibal Williston Goodwin, an Episcopalian minister, obtained a patent on photographic pellicle, a material similar to celluloid. He had become interested in photography through the use of slides and the magic lantern in entertaining his congregation, it is said. His patents led to the formation of the firm of Anthony and Scovill, from which came the trade name "Ansco." Marey, in France, also achieved some success about this time in producing motion pictures by using slips of coated paper film. This was indeed the crucial year, for Edison now began experiments with the stated objective of doing visually what his phonograph did aurally, and even of greater importance, of combining both to produce motion pictures with sound.

In 1889, Ottomar Anschutz invented the "Tachyscope," which used the luminous Geissler tube to intermittently illuminate translucent pictures mounted around the circumference of a wheel.

This simple expedient eliminated the need of slots, shutters, or lenses. However, as with Marey's work, the "Tachyscope" pictures were individually made and assembled in sequence only through the most laborious and exacting work. There was no motion picture camera. Meanwhile experiments were going forward at the Edison laboratory under the direction of Edison and William Kennedy Laurie Dickson, an expert amateur photographer who had been with Edison since 1883. Edison went to Paris in 1889, but before leaving, a motion picture camera had been designed and an order for film stock to his specifications had been sent to George Eastman in Rochester by Mr. Edison. While in Europe, Edison visited Marey in Paris, who showed him his latest device based on the magic discs principle, but which he had now arranged to illuminate by a method similar to the "Tachyscope."

Upon his return to the United States, Mr. Edison was given a demonstration of *talking pictures* projected on a four foot square screen in the Edison Laboratory at West Orange, on Oct. 6, 1889. This projector employed the film stock made to Edison's specifications by Eastman and upon which the first true motion picture photographs had been made by means of the Edison camera. The sound was supplied by synchronized wax-type cylinder recordings. In connection with these events it is interesting to note that it was on Dec. 10, 1889 that George Eastman applied for a patent on flexible photo film. This was not issued until 1898, however, after which a long legal battle ensued with the estate of the late Rev. Goodwin. A compromise settlement was finally agreed upon which left the motion picture uses of film entirely in the hands of Eastman. Eastman certainly knew a good thing when he saw it!

To dispel any lingering doubts as to the breadth of Edison's concept of the ultimate field of motion pictures, the following is quoted from a letter written by Edison to the Pittsburgh Press, published Sept. 20, 1896.

"In the year of 1887 the idea occurred to me that it was possible to devise an instrument which should do for the eye what the phonograph does for the ear, and that by a combination of the two all motion and sound could be recorded and reproduced simultaneously. This idea, the germ of which came from the little toy called the Zoetrope, and the work of Muybridge, Marie (sic) and others has now been accomplished, so that every change of facial expression can be recorded and reproduced life size. The kinetoscope is only a small model illustrating the present stage of progress, but with each month new possibilities are brought into view. I believe that in coming years, by my own work and that of Dickson, Muybridge, Marie (sic), and others who will doubtless enter the field that grand opera can be given at the Metropolitan Opera House at New York without any material change from the original, and with artists and musicians long since dead."

In 1891, Edison applied for patents on the Kinetograph camera, and the Kinetoscope viewing apparatus. To complete the picture of the existing state of the art elsewhere, it should be noted that in Paris, Reynard had opened the Theatre Optique, using films with hand drawn pictures, progenitor of our modern cartoon pictures! It is important to note that before the Kinetograph, there had been absolutely no motion picture camera, however, *of any description*. On April 14th, the year of 1894, at 1155 Broadway, New York City, the first ten of Edison's Kinetoscopes went into operation, using 50 ft. reels of film. Later in the year, they were introduced in London and Paris, where they were the principal incentive to his competitors, for he had failed to apply for foreign patents. From this time forward, there was not a day when motion pictures were not shown somewhere in the world.

In 1895, successful projection of motion pictures on a screen was achieved in Paris by Louis and August Lumiere with a machine which they called the Cinematograph. In England it was also done by Robert W. Paul, with the Bioscope, and in America by Thomas Armat, C. Francis Jenkins, the Lathams, and others. Edison at first sold the films outright, also the Kinetoscopes. His attitude towards projection was that the showing of pictures to large audiences would quickly kill the usefulness of the films. Without the experience now familiar to all of us, it is hard to understand that this was a perfectly rational conclusion, yet Edison has been ridiculed in more than a few stories on the movies because of it. However, his agents advised him that the public wanted projection equipment and would certainly obtain it from unlicensed sources if he did not supply it.

The result was that on April 23, 1896, the first gala showing of Edison pictures was made in Koster & Bial's Music Hall, Herald Square in New York City, which was situated where R. H. Macy's store is now located. An Armat designed projector was used, built by Edison. Befitting the importance of the occasion, the affair was a formal dress function, to the probable disgust of Edison, who disdained formality, but who nevertheless was seated in a box. The projection was superintended by Armat. As a prelude to this first of motion picture premieres, six acts of vaudeville were presented by Albert Bial, manager of the theater, but the motion pictures stole the show. Twelve of the short fifty-foot length skits were shown, such as were standard for the Kinetoscopes. Among the titles were, "Sea Waves," "Umbrella Dance," "The Barber Shop," "A Boxing Bout," "Venice, Showing Gondoliers," and "Kaiser Wilhelm Reviewing His Troops." The shadow stage was ready, the novelty of picture in motion sufficed for the moment, but the development of a film art was yet to come.

As noted previously, Dickson had demonstrated successfully motion picture projection with sound in October of 1889. However, Dickson left the employ of Edison about 1894 to associate with one of the numerous competitors who were then springing up in the motion picture field. This may have been connected with the decision to shelve projection and sound pictures due to many technical difficulties which still remained to be solved before commercialization would be practical. This decision also permitted concentration on the production and improvement of the Kinetoscopes which were already in large demand as a means of securing the necessary revenue to continue experimentation with the larger idea. Instead of having the temerity to criticize Edison for his failure to push projection and sound pictures manifested by some authors, it would seem that some consideration should be given to the fact that Edison's practical mind had suggested a means of launching both the phonograph and motion pictures on a basis which afforded a financial basis for extending the search for improvements. It is an undeniable fact that a great many scientists in all periods have had to be subsidized by royalty, philanthropists and foundations—or by teaching school. Only in late years have we had industrial laboratories for financing scientific research. *Edison always found ways and means of paying his own way.*

As we have pointed out elsewhere in another chapter, the failure of Edison to have established the phonograph on as firm a financial basis as was quickly achieved in the motion picture field, was largely due to the greed and chicanery of others, who would destroy what they could not control. However, the same sort of piratical influences were in evidence again in these formative days of the motion picture industry. Edison had spent literally millions of dollars on experiments, attorney's fees, and patents. He now found his patents infringed and circumvented on all sides. By his own error, he had failed to have his basic motion picture devices patented in Europe. Hence others were enabled to take out European patents on similar devices and even to market certain products in the U. S. As Edison was personally very busy with development work, he was too occupied personally to spend time in long drawn out court cases against the many outright infringements by men who now publicly and ostentatiously claimed credit for the invention of motion pictures. However, despite this situation, the Edison Co. delivered 80 projectors of the Armat design from April to November of 1896, illustrating the tremendous public interest that was being manifested. Edison also resumed work on his projecting Kinetoscope, independent of the Armat device, which had been called the Vitascope.

In 1897, George W. Brown claimed the invention of a device for synchronizing the projector and the phonograph. Three years later, Gaumont received patent on a sync motor method. Others who confined their attention to screen projectors were much more numerous, as there was a ready-made market awaiting. These included many names later familiar in the industry, including Owen A. Eames of Boston; Edwin Hill Amet, of Chicago; W. C. Hughes; Warner; Gossart; Perret & Lacroix; Sulle & Mazo; Gauthier; Messager; Baxter & Wray and almost innumerable others.

In 1903 Eugen Lauste invented and demonstrated a method of producing sound from film, by means of photographed sound waves. This was done by means of light projected through the film onto a selenium cell. The fact that light affected the conductivity of selenium had been known for many years; in fact, Alexander Graham Bell had invented a method of projecting sound by means of this principle over a beam of light, which he called the Photophone.

Meanwhile the Edison enterprise was establishing a commercial foundation for the development of a new medium of art expression, entertainment, and education. This same year the first film exchange was opened by Miles Brothers, San Francisco exhibitors. Films at this time were sold outright to the exhibitors, so this represented an advance in the more economic use of the films. It marked the beginning of the end of the "tent-show" or barnstorming period, in which an exhibitor traveled with one set of films until they were worn out. This was much the same basis on which the tin-foil phonograph had been first launched—traveling exhibitors.

In this same year, Edison produced many films in the famous "Black Maria" at West Orange. However, the film "The Great Train Robbery," the first film to tell a complete story, was an outdoor picture made in the hills around Orange.

The improvement in the content of the films led to the development of the motion picture theater. Davis and Harris, Pittsburgh demonstrators, redesigned an empty shed which they had been using on the usual temporary basis into a permanent, luxurious show place which they named "The Nickelodeon." This to our sophisticated tastes may not seem to be much of an advance, but this original "Nickelodeon," or nickel theater, was the prototype of today's picture palaces. Within two years there were some 5,000 such permanent motion picture theaters in operation all over the U. S.

Meanwhile, in 1906, Dr. Lee DeForest had combined Lauste's sound on film principle with the photo-electric cell and was experimenting with amplification by means of his new three element vacuum tube. Also of future importance in the exploitation of talking pictures, but purely incidental at that time, was the fact that the four Warner brothers were establishing their first motion picture theater, the "Cascade," in a converted store in New Castle, Pa.

By 1907 all of the get-rich-quick opportunists of the country were apparently trying to "get in the act." Edison and the other licensed producers could not keep up with the mounting demand for films and illegitimate producers sprang up right and left. There being no legal way to secure motion picture cameras or film in the

United States, where the incontestibly basic Edison patents were presumably in effect, most of the more careful entrepreneurs bought European-made copies of the Edison camera—others, with everything to gain and nothing to lose, just went right ahead, patents or not and made their own. To illustrate just how flagrant this was, consider for a moment the fact that the first successful motion picture film had been made to the specifications of Thomas A. Edison by George Eastman. It was Edison who determined the width of the film (35 mm), and designed the four notches per frame for the ratchet feed device—both of which are standard yet today. In fact, a large box of punchings from film, found in the chemical storeroom at West Orange proves that the sprocket holes were punched at the Edison Laboratory. All of Edison's early competitors had been dependent upon Edison films in the development of projectors and cameras. By now even another dodge had been discovered to avoid even the necessity of paying for copies of the Edison films. Bootleg film was produced and used for copying, or "duping," as it was called, the original films, thus removing the profit from the producing of these original films.

This situation led to the formation of the Motion Picture Patents Corporation in 1908, which at first was intended to embrace only those companies which were considered to possess legitimate, operable patents. These companies were Edison, Biograph and Vitagraph. Later others were found desirous of also operating on a legitimate basis and the roster was increased to also include Essany, Selig, Lubin and Kalem, in the U. S.; and Melies and Pathe, in France. One of the reasons some foreign companies found it desirable to come into the fold, even though the basic Edison inventions had not received foreign patents, was that Edison had improved the shutter mechanism and other important elements considerably in perfecting his projection Kinetoscope.

To implement this, the Motion Picture Patents Corp. in 1910 established a nation-wide film exchange which was named the General Film Co. to act as sole distributors for the member producers. The General Film Co. acquired 57 of the then 58 existing distributing exchanges. Only one of these exchanges refused to become a member and this was owned by William Fox, powerful independent producer and owner of a chain of theaters, who was thus in a position to buck what he called "the trust." In 1911, in order to assist in bringing order out of chaos which had prevailed prior to the formation of the Motion Picture Patents Corp., George Eastman, friend of Edison, who also had a great stake in the founding of the industry, gave Jules Brulatour the exclusive distributorship of all cinematograph positive film to be produced by the Eastman Kodak Company. Brulatour then proceeded to acquire all of his prior legitimate competitors.[1] Years later, Eastman's right to do so was upheld by the U. S. Supreme Court, despite the dissolution of the Motion Picture Patents Corp. by order of the same august body, which is certainly indicative of a tremendous inconsistency.

In 1912, William Fox brought suit against the Motion Picture Patents Corp. presenting the charge that it represented an illegal monopoly operating in restraint of trade in violation of the Sherman anti-trust laws. Back of him, of course, were the thousand and one scoundrels who had been making a killing by piracy of patented devices, operating in most cases without patents or licenses of any kind. Some of the independents other than Fox were also powerful and clever, even though not possessed of the strategic position occupied by Fox, who was producer, distributor, and theater chain operator. One of these was Adolph Zukor, who, in the drought occasioned by the drying up of the supply of unlicensed films by the operation of the patents pool and Brulatour, imported a French-made picture starring Sarah Bernhardt which

---

[1] Federal Trade Commission Docket No. 977.

was shown through independent theaters with great success. Encouraged by this, Zukor had the rather colossal nerve, in view of the circumstances to attempt to secure the approval and backing of the legitimate members of the Motion Picture Patents Corp., for an extension of his activities, which was refused. However, Zukor was determined to stay in the industry and organized the Famous Players in Famous Plays Co. and employed the then best-known director in the industry outside of D. W. Griffith—Edwin S. Porter.

One of the important factors in this situation which enabled this sort of outright flaunting of the patent rights which had been granted to inventors was the then current popular uprising against the "interests" and "trusts." Chief incitement to this popular wave of indignation was the trust busting activities of President Theodore Roosevelt. The elements allied with Fox were exceedingly active in engaging newspaper support and in spreading propaganda. As usual in these situations, the pioneer inventors were poor publicity men and the net result was that the public was entirely unable to differentiate between the legitimate monopoly which is conferred upon inventors by the granting of letters patent, and the type of monopoly that is represented by financial interests gaining control of formerly competing manufacturers or dealers in staple necessities of life. There is a vast difference between cornering a commodity market and the monopoly granted to an inventor for a specified length of time in which to reap the rewards of his efforts.

During these turbulent years when strong men often failed in meeting the demands of directing some one phase of the hectic industrial or technological metamorphosis, Edison was directing dozens of industrial operations including mining, storage battery manufacture, electric generating and distribution system designing, electric locomotives, cement manufacture, and plastics. Besides a full program of research in a

number of lines always going ahead simultaneously, Edison would turn to the problems of the phonograph and motion pictures for relaxation. As we know, he perfected many features of each, but the proper combination of the two seemed to elude him.

By 1912 a number of other producers and distributors of motion pictures had decided also to buck "the trust," emboldened by the stand of William Fox. Whether in reaction to this situation or not, in 1913, Edison gave demonstrations in many cities of the U. S. of his latest talking picture device, the Kinetophone. For this he employed a 5½-inch diameter celluloid cylinder record, similar to the blue amberol record. A mechanical advantage amplifier was used to step up the volume and synchronization was managed by a long pulley system connecting the projector in one end of the theater with the mandrel of the phonograph behind the screen at the other end. Here the damage done to Edison's legitimate interests in the motion-picture industry by the trust-busting activities of Theodore Roosevelt was equalled by an edict of the labor unions. This edict was that the Edison technicians trained to operate the complicated projection and sound synchronization equipment were not to be permitted to do so and that the local union projectionists should handle all equipment. The upshot was that as the mechanism at that stage of development was far from foolproof, the sound often got out of step with the pictures, film breaks were not spliced in the manner required and the results while at times hilariously funny, were disastrous to the enterprise. This failure, together with the decision of the Federal Court ordering the dissolution of the Motion Picture Patents Corporation, handed down in 1915, marked the termination of Edison's attempts to coordinate sound with pictures.

However, another element in this situation was the great fire which destroyed most of the Edison plant in December of 1914, which had started in the film building. Also Thomas A.

Edison was busy in Washington, Fort Myers, Key West, or on shipboard much of the time as Chairman of the Naval Consulting Board. The people of the United States are quite generally unaware of the value of Edison's contributions to his country in World War I, or of the cost to his commercial enterprises which this service entailed.

The independent producers were responsible for the institution of the "star" system which the industry has never quite outgrown. Adolph Zukor, for instance, in 1914 contracted with Mary Pickford at the then unheard of figure of $104,000 per year. Charles Chaplin, the later celebrated comedian was probably the first screen personality to achieve sufficiently high personal popularity as to engender a trend towards the star system based on estimations of "box-office" value. When chided with this by the critics, it became a favorite rationalization of these producers to maintain that they were creating new aesthetic standards. Nevertheless, the yet celebrated film, "The Birth of a Nation," produced under the direction of David Wark Griffith in 1915, had been produced by one of the pioneer companies, Biograph, a member of the Motion Picture Patents Corporation. Its cost was $110,000, the largest amount spent on any feature picture to that date and it grossed over 2½ million dollars. To be fair to the viewpoint of the independents it must be conceded that only the determination of D. W. Griffith was responsible for its completion as a feature picture and in preventing its being parcelled out as a serial. For more than a decade, however, it retained distinction as the most successful screen accomplishment, and since has had numerous revivals.

This year of 1915 found a number of the "states' rights" distributors and independents grouping together to form the Paramount Pictures Corp., for the purpose of financing and distributing feature length pictures to be produced by affiliated members. Unquestionably the success of the "Birth of a Nation"

had a great deal to do with this development. By the following year, most of the independents had begun the movement to Hollywood, now the world's film capitol. Partly this was because of the ideal sunny climate and pure air, of great importance to the filming of outdoor scenes, but partly also to get away from the environment of the members of the Motion Picture Patents Corp., which had their studios in and near New York City. The following year the U. S. Supreme Court upheld the Federal Court decision of 1915, which had ordered the dissolution of the Motion Picture Patents Corp. However, Eastman still retained his monopoly on the film. Except for Eastman, the inventors of the essential motion picture devices were thus deprived of the protection of their patents.

Edison had conducted demonstrations of talking pictures on a country-wide basis all during 1913 and his company produced 19 talking pictures that year. This rather determined effort to launch sound with motion pictures failed for two principal reasons; first, because of the lack of positive synchronization between speed of the film and the cylinder record speed; and secondly, neither projectors nor the film itself were perfected to the point where breaks would not occasionally occur in the film, which needless to say prevented use of the sound with that portion, at least. Ludicrous effects were produced when the film got out of step with the record, which prejudiced the public and the producers against the system. It is pathetic to consider that at this very time Lee DeForest was demonstrating for Western Electric his audion amplifier system. Dr. Harold D. Arnold was interested in it, saw its possibilities in telephony and was later involved in perfecting it. Meanwhile, other investigators had also been carrying on extensive research and experiments designed to solve these problems. Prominent among these had been Theodore W. Case, of Auburn, N. Y., who worked for a number of years upon the idea of using a tiny mirror attached to a diaphragm vibrated by the sound waves as a means of registering sound simultaneously with the sight on a margin of the same film—the sound track idea now in use. The first of a long series of patents upon elements of this process was granted to him in 1919. It seems altogether too obvious now that this should have proven to be the ultimate method. But those who know of the innumerable "bugs" that afflicted this system and the disheartening results even after years of work can readily understand why it was that the synchronized record approach was the first to receive the enthusiastic acclaim of the public. Satisfactory and consistent results from the sound on film proved to be a will-o'-the-wisp for a number of years. At times, results were good enough to seem to promise that success was just around the corner, but not good enough to convince the moving picture magnates that they might possibly be able to do something with it. It was very difficult for the developers of the process to get theaters to book the short specialties which were produced on an experimental basis, first because of the need to install special equipment, and second, because of the unreliable quality of the sound. Meanwhile we must not lose sight of the Warner brothers, who after ups and downs as exhibitors and distributors, had incorporated and entered the production field. In 1917, they scored with "My Four Years in Germany" by former ambassador James W. Gerard.

Actually, in state of technical development, talking pictures were about on a par with radio, in 1920, and for reasons that were similar. However, there was a vast difference in the rate of commercial development for reasons that may be easily understood. A chief reason for the rapid progress in radio technology in the early 1920's was the fact that the thousands of wireless "hams" provided an immediate audience and a potential market upon which to launch the immature, partial, and rather tentative experiments in commercially sponsored broadcasting.

Almost immediately it became apparent that here was a vast new field for advertising exploitation with virtually no competition, promising almost immediate returns for relatively small investments. The amazing phenomenon of wireless telephony was that equipment designed to receive only dots and dashes would receive sound-modulated carrier waves within its frequency range just as well. Thus by a miracle the advent of radio broadcasting found many thousands of homes equipped with earphone receivers—a ready-made audience to which entertainment and advertising could be directed. This supplied a nucleus of immediately available revenues with which to provide for financing of broadcasting stations and to plan sales and operating organizations on a stable basis.

No such opportunity was presented to the inventors of talking pictures. The methods of presentation of silent pictures with subtitles and musical scores played by orchestras and pipe organ had been developed to a point where this mutation and synthetic substitutions for the normal sounds had been accepted by a large share of the public as a fine art of great merit. In fact, this may be rediscovered some day to have been true, but be that as it may, the pertinent fact is that change was not sought for by the public at large. Also, at that time the motion picture industry was still in a rapid state of expansion. This meant that the available motion picture theater demand was filled by the silent picture output of the studios—no change was demanded by the theater owners. In fact the "block-booking" and close control of outlets by producing companies precluded change. It is true that some sporadic bookings were made here and there of Case's Movietone pictures. In 1920, for instance, pictures were shown of the presidential candidates, due to popular interest in the elections and this seemed to provide a temporary interest that enabled the promoters to secure scattered showings of other of the Movietone "shorts." But again, theater managers and the theater patrons reacted indifferently, bookings became fewer and fewer. Without a doubt, the same difficulties in dealing with the hidebound projectionists and their union leaders which had been partially responsible for the Edison talking picture failure also dogged the Case efforts.

Here we come to another of the interesting and recurring tangencies of the associated fields of investigation. Dr. Lee DeForest, inventor of the three element radio vacuum tube and who had sold his rights to his tube and other radio patents to RCA, became interested in the possibilities of the Case invention. He acquired the rights to the Case patents, including the "Tellafide" photo-electric cell, the heart of the projector unit which transforms the variations in light of the sound-track into variable electric currents, which when amplified, operated the loudspeakers, which were located in back of the screen. DeForest succeeded in making a considerable improvement in the quality of voice and music reproduction. Understanding the principles of electronic amplifiers and especially the need of more scientifically designed loudspeakers, this is quite understandable. He also had an idea of building up a library of short subjects which would not depend too much on release dates at a particular time, so that a market might be gradually built up and as new outlets were provided with equipment, the existing material could be used again in areas where it had not been used previously. Meanwhile, Case continued his research and beginning with 1925 all Case patents were assigned to "Case Research Laboratory, Auburn, New York."

By November of 1925, DeForest had added to the Phonofilm library, sound pictures by the following groups and artists: Eddie Cantor, Weber & Fields, Sissle & Blake, Balieff and his Chauve-Souris, Raymond Hitchcock, Puck & White; the Ben Bernie, Ray Miller and Paul Specht bands; Roy Smeck, Monroe Silver, Harry Hirshfield, opera singers; Bernice DePasquale, Leon Rothier, and Mme. Marie Rappold; Anna Pavlowa, Max Rosen, Roger Wolfe Kahn's band, Chauncey M. Depew and Dr. Frank Crane. Al Jolson was announced about this time as the latest new recruit of Phonofilm, and in a publicity blurb it was stated that he was to receive a fee in excess of the highest he had previously received in making phonograph records. It was stated that he received $15,000 for two sides of a phonograph record from Brunswick, but that he received $10,000 for a single song on Phonofilm. There is no question that the Jolson name was magic in those days. In 1929 he was to set the all-time high for the early period of copies of "Sonny Boy," which he had also recorded for Brunswick. The acquisition of the services of Jolson by DeForest seems to indicate that sound-on-film was receiving considerable acceptance at that time.

But again, just as the expenditure of the efforts of many men and the investment of millions of dollars seems about ready to pay off, the Bell Telephone men became interested in the talking picture field. Having developed the Western Electric system, by which the conquest of the phonograph industry was then about consummated, it was found that by certain relatively minor changes this method could be adapted to secure considerably improved results acoustically over that of the then existing sound-film technic. This was done by reducing the recording speed from 78 rpm to 33⅓ rpm to secure longer playing time, which was again increased by the employment of larger discs. Positive synchronization of record with projector was achieved by employment of synchronous motors (pioneered by Gaumont in 1897). Starting points of both film and record were marked to make absolute synchronization easily controlled. With the improvement of films as well as in the film projection mechanisms, breakdowns were no longer frequent and duplicate prints would take care of any emergency. A high-quality amplifier was provided, the same kind as used for the new recording process. Folded, re-entrant horns of the same type developed by Harrison for the Orthophonic Victrola were used in back of the screen, with powerful dynamic-type driving units.

However, the same fallacy of the steel needle was perpetuated again in this new film process, which was called the Vitaphone. Incidentally, some ignorance of the history of phonograph development by the sponsors was indicated by the fact that this same corporate name had been used by a former phonograph manufacturer in New Jersey as recently as 1920. The new discs were made up to 20 inches in diameter and in order to reduce surface noise to a tolerable level with the high amplification necessary, the former practice of putting abrasive in the surface material, as was still done in the commercial Victor records, was eliminated, resulting in a much smoother, but also less durable surface. These records were provided with a space on the label to indicate the number of playings, which was strictly limited. These records, incidentally, were processed and pressed in the Victor plant. Warner Brothers, then in a critical financial condition, saw the possibilities of the new Western Electric process and decided to gamble everything on it, signing a contract on June 25, 1925. Stanley Watkins of Maxfield's Western Electric sound staff moved a crew and equipment into the old Vitagraph studio in Brooklyn, which then belonged to Warner Brothers. Here experimentation was carried on until most of the more obvious difficulties were ironed out.

For the debut of the new talking pictures a series of "shorts" were recorded by some artists with names well known to record buyers, but with the exception of Anna Case, Metropolitan Opera soprano, who had made a full length feature motion picture in 1915, quite unknown to motion picture audiences. These included Giovanni Martinelli, also of the Metropolitan; violinists Mischa Elman and Efrem Zimbalist; Harold

Bauer, pianist, and soprano Marion Talley. These great artists were presented by Will S. Hays, then arbiter of the film industry. The world premiere was a gala occasion at Warner Brothers New York theater, on Broadway between 51st and 52nd Streets. Also shown was the latest Warner Brothers feature picture, "Don Juan," with John Barrymore, which was specially provided with a symphonic score on the Vitaphone discs. This event occurred on February 19, 1927. On Oct. 6, 1927, Warners presented the first full length talking picture, "The Jazz Singer," featuring Al Jolson. This was the picture that sounded the death knell of the silent pictures.

By this time William Fox had purchased the Movietone rights and was issuing travel and news pictures, which, however, did not nearly equal the quality of sound reproduction of the Vitaphone. The first of the Fox Movietone shorts had been shown on June 21, 1927, at the Roxie, and the first all-Movietone newsreel was shown on October 28th, with King George V, Crown Prince Edward, Marshal Foch, Poincare, the Crown Prince of Sweden, David Lloyd George and Ramsey MacDonald.

At first, talking pictures only had a few talking sequences, to permit movie audiences to become accustomed to the change. Also technics had to be perfected—the demands of the microphone suddenly immobilized what had been formerly visually a very active medium, owing to the inherent requirements for motion to sustain interest in the silent films. Traveling booms for keeping the microphone over the principals had not yet been devised, nor rapidly traveling sound trucks to keep up with outdoor action. There also was considerable difficulty in solving the acoustic problems in many theaters so that the sound was uniformly acceptable in definition and quality. During this transitional period many pictures which had already been in the course of production were equipped with "goat glands," as they were facetiously called in the industry—talking sequences so that they might be advertised as "talking pictures."

William Fox had been enabled to produce sound pictures by accepting a sub-license from Warner Brothers, who had, as stated, an exclusive contract for the Western Electric process. However, even though hit hard by falling box-office receipts, the other large producers demurred. The "Jazz Singer" had cost the record sum of $500,000 to produce but had brought in $2,500,000 gross, although this had been only partially a sound picture. Money was not the principal reason, however, but the other powerful figures of the movie industry just refused to have it said that they were paying tribute to the Warner brothers.

When the "Jazz Singer" was released there were only about 100 theaters wired for sound in the U. S., although Warner Brothers at that time had some 7,500 outlets for their pictures. After the New York opening, bookings were arranged on a road show basis, which permitted time to make installations of sound equipment in advance of each showing. Warner Brothers assumed the financial risk of the installations, to be repaid out of profits. The cost ran from $5,000 to $20,000 per theater depending on size and certain other variables. Many of the theater owners paid for their equipment installations on the earnings from the "Jazz Singer" alone. Warner Brothers bought the Stanley Co. of America in the summer of 1928, getting 250 theaters and a third of First National Pictures. They then proceeded to buy control of the latter and so acquired an additional 500 theaters.

In order to overcome the objections of the other large producers to doing business through the Warners, Western Electric and its parent company, A. T. & T. organized a new corporation, Electrical Research Products, Inc. to furnish engineering service and to license the use of equipment manufactured by Western Electric. To effect this program, the patent rights to Vitaphone and Movietone were recovered from Warner Brothers and the Fox Film

Corp. and pooled with other patents with E. R. P. I. Now all of the major producers expressed willingness to go ahead and were licensed. Then began the mammoth, but profitable, job of equipping the sound stages of Hollywood and thousands of theaters across the country. By the end of 1929, over 4,000 theaters had received sound installations and $37,000,000 had been taken in from the sale of equipment and services.

Outside of a few unimportant producing studios, this left only RCA outside, which, as a subsidiary of General Electric, had felt secure in its exclusive possession of the patents to the Photophone sound-on-film method, which had been perfected by GE engineers.[2] But time was running out, by this time virtually all of the first-run theaters of the country had been secured by either Paramount-Famous Players-Lasky Corp., Loew's Inc. (MGM) and the large circuits affiliated with First National, which now had been absorbed by Warner Brothers. Fox and Universal had also been gaining outlets steadily and Warners continued its spectacular rise.

Faced with this situation, the GE-RCA interests, Rockefeller backed, founded Radio-Keith-Orpheum, comprised of RCA, American Pathe, and the Keith-Albee-Orpheum theater chain, for the purpose of producing sound pictures. The Warner Brothers-E. R. P. I.-Western Electric-A. T. & T. aggregation was a Morgan financed operation. The financial importance of these alignments may be appreciated by considering that from a state of virtual insolvency in 1925, Warner's assets had expanded to $16,-000,000 by the close of 1928 and by the end of another year to $230,000,000.

Then came the stock market crash, but the movie business somewhat miraculously held up. Wall Street financiers were amazed at what seemed to be a depression proof industry. Meanwhile the top strata battle for control

[2] Fed. Communications Commission, Report on Investigation of Telephone Developments in the U. S.—House Document No. 340 (1939).

of the talking picture industry continued between the Morgan and the Rockefeller interests. Recovery was predicted to be just around the corner by the financial columnists in 1931, again in 1932. Arthur Brisbane, famous Hearst columnist continued to exhort his readers "not to sell America short." But the "bears" kept after the market while breadlines grew and the unemployed walked the streets.

However, by 1933 attendance began to fall off in the theaters. The novelty of the sound pictures had worn off, money was tighter than ever, savings had been dissipated, employment was at a new low. Even the magic spell of the flickering films failed to give solace. The result of the prolonged depression and the belated recession in theater business was that in 1937 Paramount was bankrupt, R. K. O. and Universal in receivership. Fox Film had to undergo reorganization. The battle of the giants was over—the internal feud had been resolved with the Morgan-A. T. & T. faction in complete control, not only of the motion picture industry, but in overall command of recording and communications by wire or through the air.

Yet the basic elements for both sight and sound had been supplied by the inventive genius of earlier generations. The use of selenium in a photo-electric cell had been patented by Alexander Graham Bell in 1886. The phonograph and motion picture had been invented separately by Thomas A. Edison, most of the essential improvements in processes involved had been made by him. The microphones used had been invented by him. The essentials of the vacuum tube, the incandescent lamp, and the "Edison effect" were Edison contributions. Edison's dynamic microphone, reversed, became the dynamic driving unit for the Vitaphone and other types of theater speakers. Incidentally, a dynamic moving-coil speaker had been patented as early as 1877 in England by Sir W. Siemans, within a year after the development of the telephone. The Movietone microphone was the condenser microphone, invented by Edison, improved by Dr. Edward G. Wente.

CHAPTER 20

SOUND PICTURES AND THE PHONOGRAPH INDUSTRY

THE conquest of the motion picture industry by the electrical tycoons has left certain definite marks on both the radio and phonograph fields, which are now, of course, subject to the same top level domination. The 33⅓ rpm lateral disc record, developed for Vitaphone, also suggested the recording of radio programs for distribution to local stations, which would fill the needs of advertisers of products which had distribution outlets only in certain areas, or who might wish to try out radio promotion on more modest budgets than would be possible with chain programs. These records were named "program transcriptions" and so described when broadcast, because of the then prevalent prejudice against records—"canned music" as it was called. The complete conquest of the Victor Talking Machine empire by the Rockefeller wing of the A. T. & T.-RCA-Westinghouse-GE trust had been made evident by the complete merger of the two companies, Radio Corporation of America and Victor in 1930, when the RCA offices were moved to Camden. In July 1930, the Brunswick Radio Corp. became a subsidiary of Warner Brothers.

It is just a coincidence that this year in nearby Philadelphia there was being issued the first copy of a new monthly magazine *Disques,* published by H. Royer Smith, music merchant and a pioneer Victor dealer. It was indicative of a subtle, but eventually very important shift in emphasis of the interests of recorded music enthusiasts. This was not the first monthly publication which had been devoted exclusively to the interest of the record collector, for the *Phonograph Monthly Review* had been first issued in October of 1926, just at the inception of the electrical recording era. It is interesting to note that in the review of the currently issued discs in *Disques* there were reviewed records by not only the American companies, Brunswick, Columbia and Victor, but also imported recordings by Edison-Bell, Fonotipia, the English National Gramophonic Society, Odeon, Homocord, Parlophone, Polydor, and the English Regal Co.

A symptomatic fact was that of the domestic records reviewed, all of the classical and celebrity records issued by Brunswick and Columbia had been recorded in Europe, as well as a majority of those of Victor. Nor was this the exception, but rather the rule. The new electrical monarchs of the American recording industry had not been one wit more sensitive to detect the changing public taste than their mechanical predecessors. As early as 1928, the new trend had been correctly sensed by W. H. Tyler and J. F. Brogan who on the basis of their evaluation of the prospects of the future, had founded the Gramophone Shop in New York City. A strong impetus to the new movement was supplied by these same men who published the *Gramophone*

Shop Encyclopedia, edited by R. D. Darrell, editor of the *Phonograph Monthly Review,* who had received a Guggenheim fellowship to write about records. A large share of the business of the *Gramophone Shop* was built on the sale of imported recordings. One of the chief functions of the *Gramophone Shop Encyclopedia* from the standpoint of its immediate effect on the music lovers of America interested in records was to disabuse them of any misconception they might have entertained as to the leadership of recorded art being in this country. By far the greater part of the comprehensive and virtually complete listing of classical recordings in the Encyclopedia as recorded by the new electric processes were from other countries, most of them unavailable on domestically issued discs. Other entrepreneurs also saw the light and began to cater to the new class of record buyers, among these the Liberty Music Shops of New York. These along with Royer Smith's of Philadelphia also developed a considerable mail order business, circulating lists of imported recordings to a rapidly growing clientele.

But the new barons of the industry in America paid slight heed. Except for portable phonograph, all-electric radio phonographs had virtually displaced acoustic phonographs by 1930—in the U. S. It is interesting that acoustic machines continued to be developed and sold in England well into the 1940's. Some of the finest of these were more or less custom-built, open-horn instruments which were preferred by some British connoisseurs to the last. The American record industry produced some 65 million records in 1931, of which Victor produced about 30 million. The American Record Co., owner of Columbia and maker of most of the chain store discs, accounted for about 17 million and Brunswick for about 12½ million of the balance.

There seemed to have been at the time a curious disparity between the thinking of the engineers of the leading American companies and the trend which we have noted. One of the evidences of this was a curious novelty offered by Victor in 1931 with some of its radio combinations. This was an attachment by which pre-grooved black plastic discs could be used for direct recordings of radio programs or for home recording of voice or instrumental music with a small microphone which was provided. This was accomplished by switching part of the output of the amplifier through the magnetic pickup, which thus served as a recording head. Up to this time there had been virtually no attempt to sell home-recording equipment since the all-purpose cylinder machines of Edison of about 1906. The material of the blank discs was similar to that of the later acetate blanks, but the recording was done with special needles which indented, instead of incising. The resistance of the sides of the pre-formed grooves to the blunt recording stylus provided was too great and the resulting reproduction quality was not good, in fact, musically it was quite ineffective.

It was also in 1931 in England, that English Columbia and H. M. V. were merged into E. M. I. Capitalization was established at £6,266,000. Announcement was made by Alfred Clark, Chairman of the Board of The Gramophone Co., Ltd., and Louis Sterling, Managing Director of the Columbia Gramophone Co., Ltd. It was stated in the announcement that the companies would continue in competition as before, but that unnecessary and costly duplication of recordings would be avoided.

In America, not long after the introduction of electrical recording, professional recording equipment had been developed using aluminum discs, such as the Talk-O-Phone, and recording studios sprang up in the principal cities of the country. The quality provided with the best discs and equipment was often excellent and this innovation proved a boon to music students and radio stations. Without doubt, these developments paved the way for the acetate base recording blanks which displaced them. Also important was the introduction of piezo-electric pickups. The property of various crystals of developing electric currents when a varying pressure was applied had been known for a number of years. With Rochelle salt crystals it was found that electric currents were produced almost in direct ratio to the changes in pressure. Rothermel, in England, and Charles Brush, in the U.S., were the first to successfully "grow" these crystals in such a way that they could be successfully applied to commercial uses. The Brush Development Corp. was then organized by Brush and began manufacturing commercial pickups.

These new crystal pickups not only had the advantage of being cheap, they also were actually better in quality of output than many of the magnetic units then being produced and generally were more stable. The chief advantage, however, was that the weight on the record could be drastically reduced. It was this that permitted the use of acetate blanks for instantaneous recordings **and also the subsequent introduction of the LP or Microgroove records. It** was also the crystal pickup that ultimately focussed the attention of engineers and connoisseurs alike on the manifest absurdity of the removable needles, and especially of the steel needle.

With these new acetate discs and improved cutting styli, quality was excellent and surface noise negligible. The discs were made of aluminum, coated with layers of acetate varnish. Later, paper discs were made with a vellum paper base, by the Wilcox-Gay Co. and others for sale at low prices for use with home recording equipment. During the Second World War and the aluminum shortage, professional blanks were also made with a glass core. Needless to say, these were very fragile, whereas the other types were not breakable, although the surfaces were sensitive to injury. A considerable number of manufacturers made machines for both professional and home-recording use. Radio station equipment using acetate blanks became invaluable for recording statements of persons in the news for later broadcasting, and for taking off chain programs for broadcasting at another time, as well as for special program recording. Generally, these discs were recorded at 78 rpm for musical reproduction, or at $33\frac{1}{3}$, for speeches.

Record sales in 1931 had not actually reached low ebb, but almost. The commercial phonograph record seemed to many to be on the way to extinction. Sales, industry-wise, had dropped from a high of over 100 million discs per year to about 10 million, and from a gross of $250,000,000 to $5,000,000 by the end of 1932. This was the year of the banking holiday, the beginning of the Franklin D. Roosevelt era. The depression had brought all retail business excepting absolute necessities to almost a standstill. Columbia had gambled heavily on radio, announcing a line of "Tele-Focal" radios and combination instruments, but buyers were not forthcoming.

This was the year that the Columbia Phonograph Co. was bought by Grigsby-Grunow, manufacturer of the Majestic radio, from Warner Brothers. But radio continued in a slump. RCA, weary of the fruitless experiment with home recording, decided to make longer playing "transcriptions" for the public. Executives of all record producing companies were desperate, those of Victor no less than the others. Logically, Victor was in a good position to try long playing records, for in the Victor vaults there was a considerable quantity of recordings of the longer works which would benefit by uninterrupted playing. So in 1932, Victor announced its $33\frac{1}{3}$ rpm longer playing "transcriptions," produced in 10-inch and 12-inch diameters, which just about doubled the playing time of the standard discs.

In the front of the Victor catalog issued that year, the following statements were made:

"The quality of Victor records has been steadily advancing since the very beginning of the electrical recording, and within the past few months has made enormous strides. Developments in the laboratory indicate that, while there is, scientifically speaking, no room for further radical development in recording, there will be a steady although gradually diminishing improvement in the art as it approaches the limit of perfection. Continuous improvement in fidelity, sonority and surface quality can even now be noted almost from month to month, and Victor records have reached such a point in development as to make it reasonable to assume that it will never be necessary to remake records dating from 1931 onward, because of any possible future progress in recording."

Ah, these Victor dreamers! More than seven years later Compton Mackenzie, editor of the *Gramophone*, closed a review of records and record playing equipment of that date with the following statement:

"I have just heard a remarkable new H.M.V. pick-up, and when I write remarkable, I mean remarkable. However, I can say no more of that at present because it has not yet been played to the public. I wonder if we can persuade the various makers of pick-ups and loudspeakers to challenge the verdict of an audience from a concert platform as once upon a time the acoustical instruments challenged that verdict."

But to continue with the Victor catalog, under the heading "Long-Playing Victor Records," was the following:

"Long-playing records were first presented by Victor, not as a completed achievement, but more accurately, as an experiment in public reaction."

This was certainly a bold-faced attempt to steal from Edison the popular American credit for the first production of the long-playing record. The weasel wording to achieve this result, however, had a strong backlash, as the new Victor "transcriptions" proved not much more successful than the long-playing records of Edison. But to continue the copy from the catalog:

"That reaction was so definite that the work of developing this interesting type of record has been intensively developed (*sic*) and now the long-playing record takes its place in the Victor General Catalog. A policy of recording all major works on both standard and $33\frac{1}{3}$ rpm records has been adopted. The playing time has been fixed at such length that no sacrifice of musical quality - - - inevitable if the grooves are carried too near the center of the record, - - - need be made. The musical quality of the long-playing record has been brought to a point not only comparable, but absolutely equal to that of the standard record. Standard and long-playing records are now made simultaneously, and are identical in every musical detail except duration and volume. The latter quality is compensated fully and without the slightest alteration in musical character, by the modern electrical R. C. A. Victor phonograph, which has a power of amplification without distortion beyond any reasonable need."

Actually, there was no listing of these records in the catalog, although a brochure was issued simultaneously containing only a very small portion of the album set material then available on standard records. The statement as to the policy established to record both standard and long-playing records may have been true at the moment, but if so, it was in effect only for a short time. The statement as to the equality of quality of the long-playing records and the standard discs was false. Again, the fallacy of the steel needle had been perpetuated, although this time "sugar-coated" with chromium. The effect of the flaking chrome, ground into the surface of the discs by the heavy weight of the then standard horseshoe pickup was disastrous. Some of the 10-inch discs were pressed in shellac, most of the 12-inch discs and the album sets of long-playing discs were pressed in a flexible plastic. However, contrary to the statement quoted, the quality of these records was not equivalent to the standard discs at any time.

The electric turntables for playing them were equipped, of course, with a speed shift device to reduce the rpm from 78 to $33\frac{1}{3}$, whereas the earlier spring-wind Edison acoustic long-playing phonograph had a shift to change the rate of feed across the record from 150 threads per inch to 450. Both systems were technical failures. The Victor fiasco seemed to have been the greater one in a sense because of the extent of its commitments, and the extravagant advertising claims made for it. For example, the Guerre-Lieder by Schonberg, recorded by the Philadelphia Orchestra was listed at $28 for the album set of 14 standard 12-inch discs, or $21 for the same performance on 7 of the new discs, including the album. Not long after, it was impossible to secure the special chrome needles for playing the latter, long-playing set. This is certainly in violent conflict with the claim made that "- - - It will never be necessary to remake records dating from 1931 forward, because of any possible future progress in recording."

The next year Grigsby-Grunow collapsed and the Columbia Phonograph Co. assets were purchased by the American Record Co. which had been getting along on the chain store sales of low-priced discs and the sales to "juke box" operators. With millions of unemployed roaming the streets, many with savings and many who had none spent idle hours in the saloons. The nickels, dimes, and quarters of the patrons of the grilles served to assist materially in priming the pump of the record industry just about as it seemed doomed to many of its veterans. By 1934 it has been estimated there were some 25,000 juke boxes in operation.

But that is the dismal American picture. England had never lost its love for the Gramophone, even though its origins had been across the sea. The term "canned music," reputedly originated by American bandmaster Sousa, never became popularized in England. Had it not been for the successful weathering of the world financial crisis by the now stronger English companies who continued to supply the bulk of the longer symphonic recordings and the classical repertoire that graced the catalogs of Victor and the bulk of the recordings in these categories issued in the U. S. by Columbia and Brunswick, there would have been little basis for the cultural renaissance of the phonograph in America. However, to be perfectly objective, it must be conceded that as always the bread and butter of the industry was the popular record. Without the "pops" there would be no classics. But more was owed to England for the basis for the new trend towards the recording and reproduction of the larger musical forms, the symphonies, concertos, oratorios, etc. The founding and financing of the London Philharmonic Orchestra from 1930 to 1940 was done largely by the English Columbia Graphophone, Ltd. The enthusiasm and optimism of the English leaders of the industry served by the operation of certain tangent cycles of activity to inspire certain leaders in this country as to the possibilities of a revival of popular interest in recordings.

During the summer of 1934, E. R. Lewis of the British Decca Company came to the U. S. and in the course of his visit engaged in a series of conferences with Jack Kapp of Brunswick, and E. F. Stevens, Jr. of Columbia. The upshot was that these latter men left their former connections and associated themselves with Lewis in forming the American Decca Company. Financial backing was provided by Lewis and authority was given the new company to use English Decca masters for sale to the American trade. The English Decca Co. had a fairly good celebrity list which could be drawn upon, if desired, but the intent of the organizers was primarily to cultivate the popular demand, with particular emphasis on the juke box trade.

Now although this development served to give heart to the American record trade, it cannot be chalked up as a very large contribution, in itself, to the development of the musical taste of the American public. The radios of the period were afflicted generally with a "tubby" bass and to avoid the surface noise from the records when used as a phonograph, the treble was generally turned down. That the claims made for improvement in accuracy of reproduction by the adoption of electrical recording were somewhat fictitious was pointed out in an article in the *American Music Lover* on needles and their effect upon fidelity. It stated that most commercial recordings cut off at 6,000 cps, which obviously was not much better than many of the acoustically recorded needle-type records. The article discussed tests made with a variety of types of needles then available, including the new Victor chrome needles, also the steel, fibres, thorn and cactus needles, and the then new Walco sapphire stylus. The introduction of sapphire needles is of interest in that they were not sponsored first by a record producing company yet represented a step in the direction in which the lateral industry was to have to turn if there was to be progress. Indeed, this situation seems to have been symptomatic of the technical leadership in that branch of the record industry from the earliest days—new ideas generally seemed to be brought in from the outside.

One of the factors in the trend towards the use of more durable needles in this country was the juke box. The operators had to have styli that would stand up under rough treatment and that would play a large number of records. This led to the development of alloy tipped needles, which were insensitive to shock, would play a considerable number of discs and most important, were economical. It was

really a good thing for the sinking disc business that outsiders gave some attention to the needle question, which the record makers themselves had not, for it was the sudden increase in the amusement machine business that began to "bail out" the all important popular record sales and put their producers on an even keel. By 1936, Decca, which deliberately aimed its new product for this market, began to show a profit. Victor about this time began to advertise "higher fidelity," using a new piezo-electric crystal, featherweight pickup. This reduced record wear, but as the recording was not in truth as high in fidelity as the ads would have the public believe, results were not particularly astounding.

American leadership in the field of classical recording is a myth fostered by American advertising men and publishers for the benefit of the American public. It has never been believed elsewhere. Consider this fact; even in "pre-electric" 1923 there were flourishing Gramophone Societies in England. By 1936 the Gramophone society movement had grown to such an extent in England that there was formed a National Association of Gramophone Societies. There were member societies in India, South Africa, Egypt, and Singapore, as well as those of the British Isles. In Sweden, the Gramophone Society at Lund insisted also upon joining the English National Association, which threatened to make it imperative to change its title to "International." In England there were Beethoven and Mozart societies and various local Gramophone societies. Many of these groups sponsored special recordings made available by subscription, which were generally prepared by the major companies. Nothing comparable to these societies then existed in the United States. The nearest thing in this country was the cut-out record collectors movement of a later period which resulted in the issue of rerecordings by individuals or private collectors' clubs, or of the issuance of records made but never issued—mostly from the acoustic era.

But a promise of brighter things to come was seen in the emergence of a new recording company, Musicraft, which in 1937 celebrated the tercentenary of Buxtehude's birth by a specially recorded edition of the works of this composer. This encouraged others, such as "Gamut" and "Timely," who arrived on the record producing scene to sponsor such composers as William Boyce (18th century). It was characteristic of the trend of the new generation of record buyers to seek out works of the type quite familiar to students of music, but which had been heretofore utterly neglected by the phonograph industry. Needless to say, this trend had been nurtured by the examples which appeared from time to time in the domestic catalogs which were pressed from imported masters.

Amongst its dead timber, Victor discovered that it had one live vice-president, Thomas F. Joyce. Given a free hand with an inspiration of his own, he founded this year the Victor Record Society. He had developed an inexpensive, portable record player, with a synchronous electric motor that had to be started with the hand and a new, lighter-weight electromagnetic pickup. This permitted the use of a small turntable about 8″ in diameter so that a removable cover of small size could enclose the entire unit when not in use. The 10″ and 12″ standard records would overlap the turntable, but with the lighter pickups the weight of the discs was sufficient to allow this. A cord with plug was provided for attachment to the radio chassis equipped to receive them. Devices were also supplied for attachment in other ways to sets not so equipped.

These players were made available to "members" who joined the Victor Record Society, together with a number of discs and a subscription to the *Victor Record Society Review* for $14.95. Very likely the company lost money on the initial promotion, but this project placed about 150,000 record players

within a year with the result that a new generation of record playing enthusiasts was born. Record business began to pick up very noticeably, so much so that the next year the Columbia Broadcasting Co. bought the American Record Co., including the Columbia Phonograph Co., for the sum of $700,000. The latter was renamed the Columbia Recording Co. and Edward Wallerstein, who had previously been in charge of Victor recording activities, was made president.

By this time there were an estimated 225,000 juke boxes grinding out the bumps and consuming with a ferocious appetite for the latest hits, some 13 million discs a year. Popular record sales in the U. S. accounted for 88% to 90% of the number of discs and about 70% of the dollar volume. Decca sold this year 12 million discs, Victor 13 million, and Columbia about 7 million. Thus, since these figures include classical as well as popular records, it may be easily seen that a very important part of the total production was due to the popularity of the juke box. Victor also produced about a million classical discs in special albums without the Victor label as a sort of newspaper promotion, which also stimulated the public interest in classical music on records. However, 95% of the Decca records were sold at 35¢ each. This, plus the chain-store record competition of Columbia had virtually forced Victor to put out a line of records at the same price, which were named "Bluebird." One of the earlier low-priced chain-store records had been named "Grey Gull"—perhaps that is where the idea came from!

Victor still retained the bulk of the celebrity record business and its Victor Record Society deal served to increase its popular record sales, as well. Up to this time the rather limited amount of classical music recorded in the U. S. had been largely done by Victor. But now, with Columbia Broadcasting resources behind it, Columbia Records, Inc., began a more ambitious schedule of classical repertoire recording, launching it with the Columbia Broadcasting Co. Orchestra, directed by Howard Barlow and Walter Gieseking, pianist. To get away from the cheap record competition, a new series of red label popular records was issued featuring leading dance bands and soloists for sale at 50¢. Columbia had in their laminated record used for this new series a product superior technically to that of Victor or Decca, with a smooth surface. These records stood up well to the punishment of the juke boxes and the new automatic record players which were becoming popular about this time.

Both Columbia and Victor began to expand the production of album sets, which in turn, had the effect of stimulating the demand for radio-phonographs and for automatic record playing equipment. The Victor long-playing record was quietly dropped. The development of compact, drop-type record changers seemed to many to be the answer to the problem of securing continuous, (or virtually continuous) performance of the kind of music that demanded such continuity. Human nature played a part in this—it became a hobby with many lazy individuals to stack up the record changer with a motley assortment of favorite records and then sit down to read the paper, or take a nap. Of course these are not our confirmed phonophiles, to whom such conduct would be most unseemly —but these trends all boosted record sales. More than that, these rather indifferent record buyers were largely responsible for the idea of putting out record albums of popular music, which reached great heights in the 1940's. Albums made it easy for these comfort loving record fans to buy groups of records which had been already arranged to suit particular fancies.

Probably one of the greatest factors in the rebuilding of the prestige of the phonograph and records was the spectacular success of Capehart. Beginning as a de luxe juke box, the acquisition of a superior type turn-over record changer by Homer Capehart

gave him the idea of producing a high-priced home phonograph, a sort of "Steinway," of home phonographs. As the promotion of this sort of an instrument would conflict with the juke box, the latter was dropped and all effort was concentrated on the new "Capehart," intended for America's finest homes. For a number of years, the Capehart was sold exclusively as a phonograph. It was well engineered, played records with almost human care. The record changing mechanism would play 10" or 12" records, intermixed, if desired, unwanted records could be rejected by a push of a button. However, producing no records, catering not at all to the radio public, disaster was predicted for the operation by moguls of the record companies. Instead, sales of the Capehart grew year by year and leading music stores in the leading cities vied for the highly valued Capehart franchise. Capehart became a leading advertiser in the more exclusive, as well as some of the popular magazines. As intended, it became the ne plus ultra, the phonographic equivalent of the Steinway in the homes of Mr. and Mrs. prosperous American. Moreover, it exercised a sobering influence on even those who could not afford to buy it and no longer was it fashionable to poke fun at those who were bold enough to admit their preferences for recorded music. Unquestionably, after the Capehart had begun to achieve widespread attention, it would have paid the phonograph industry to have doubled the Capehart profit on each sale! However, Homer Capehart had long since lost control of his company which was taken over by Farnsworth Radio and Television Co. Capehart, as is well known, decided to go in for politics and was elected U. S. Senator from Indiana. Even before this, radio had been incorporated, which to the purists represented a departure from the highest ideals, such as had been represented by the old de Luxe, all wood tone passage phonographs of Sonora and that of the first Brunswick Panatrope—all without radio.

By 1939 there were an estimated 300,-000 juke boxes in operation, absorbing some 30 million discs a year. This year Decca supplied about 19 million of these records valued at almost $4,000,000 gross. Decca had also secured the fabulous Bing Crosby, who had been just one of the nameless "Rhythm Boys" when introduced by "Pops" Whiteman. Some say now that it is a question of who secured whom, Decca or Crosby, but in any case it was and is one of the most highly successful partnerships of the record industry. At times it has been asserted that in our larger cities during certain hours of the day, there have been times when it has been impossible to get out of reach of Bing Crosby's voice!

Crosby was so unbelievably popular that many of the so-called record stations, those which depend almost entirely upon records for broadcasting, found it expedient to feature programs of Crosby records twice a day and sometimes even more often. Daily Crosby record programs have been carried by some stations for many years. This inevitably led to the featuring of records in similar daily periods by other crooners and dance bands, which in turn, stimulated the sales of album sets by these stars. It was found by the record manufacturers that the popularity of the record programs was a sure guide to sales potential and afforded an excellent means of determining the kind of album sets of popular music that would have a ready sale. This fact also tended to mitigate the opposition of the recording companies to the broadcasting of popular records, which in the early days of electrical recording had been quite pronounced, leading to the printing on the label of the warning, "not for broadcast purposes."

The entertainment record business, meanwhile continued to grow. An article in *Fortune* [1] estimated that by 1940 there would be 500,000 of the gaudy, illuminated monsters consuming some 50 million discs per year. The importance of this market to the industry was responsible for many of its technological conflicts. Actually, the Capehart had been developed from the juke box idea into a home entertainment instrument without solving some of the more serious problems. The newly found facility in reproducing a smooth, full-bass register with the electrically recorded records, audio amplification, and oversize dynamic speakers germane to what was then the new sound, had also been made the basis of the Capehart. In order to suppress the needle noise, heritage of the mistake in perpetuating the steel and other changeable needles, little or no effort was made to extend the frequency range into the upper registers. Actually, the Capehart promotion was largely stylistic, rather than representing any sort of striving for the goal of true high fidelity. It is true that the use of large heavy cabinets permitted fairly ample baffle-areas for the speakers, used with high-quality amplifiers, gave a rich, full effect to the reproduction of records of symphony orchestras or pipe organ, but was quite unsuited to solo instrument and voice reproduction. However, the sales of many hundreds of these instruments served to stimulate the manufacturers of radio combinations to somewhat emulate the bass-heavy reproduction of the Capehart with the result that ultimately questions were aroused, especially among the more musical, as to whether this kind of reproduction was adequate. As Capehart made no records, it was powerless to set up reproduction standards for the industry even if it so desired. Sonora in an earlier acoustic period had been faced with the same dilemma.

Perhaps the best analysis of the situation as it then existed was made by the author of an article which appeared in *Fortune* in September, 1939, entitled "Phonograph Records." The sub-heading outlined the scope of the story succinctly as "From fat to lean and halfway back again: for its current boom the record industry can thank

---

[1] Fortune, "Phonograph Records," Sept. 1939.

the juke boxes, light- and heavy-music lovers, and technology." The writer had noted that failure to keep up with technological progress had been responsible for the slump in the record business that had virtually wiped out the then existing industry in the 1920's. In summing up the situation as he saw it, he said quite prophetically:

"- - - But it is obvious that the future belongs to the companies most hospitable to new ideas and best equipped to do something with them. The record is far from perfect, and its imperfections may alienate its customers again. As in the early twenties, improving the fidelity of reproduction is less altruism than common sense.

"Record materials are much the same as they were twenty-five years ago. Surface noise is more vexatious than ever, especially as background for sounds in the higher frequencies, which therefore often are suppressed in phonographs, almost invariably in juke-boxes. It is caused partly by abrasives in the materials to wear the steel needle down. The thing has been, with heavy pick-ups, that either the needle or the record had to wear; and consumers preferred to throw away needles rather than records. But the combination of extremely light pick-up, diamond stylus, and a new record manufacturing process involving a light plastic has reduced surface noise immensely. Such a record as used by broadcasting companies for transcriptions is being played 500 to 2,000 times without noticeable wear, whereas the average home record is usually in bad shape after 100 to 150 playings.

"The old controversy between lateral-cut and vertical-cut or hill-and-dale records is coming up again. With the heavy tone arm of the mechanical phonograph, the lateral cut was and is superior. The hill-and-dale cut, which, like the improvements of the early twenties, has been perfected in the Bell Laboratories (under H. A. Frederick), now seems better."

The author undoubtedly accepted the demise of the vertically-recorded record as evidence of the superiority of the lateral method, as far as acoustically-recorded records were concerned. Ample evidence has been given elsewhere in this book to disprove that conclusion. However, his revelation that the Bell engineers were experimenting with vertical recording is of interest, especially in respect to the comparative advantages and disadvantages of the two methods at that time, so the quotation from the *Fortune* article will be continued, as follows:

"In the grooves of a lateral record the needle vibrates from side to side, held in between the waves and ripples of the groove walls. A vertical record is one in whose grooves the stylus vibrates up and down, riding the waves like a boat. The chief disadvantage of the lateral groove is that the needle does not track down its center as it should, but flounders from side to side as it takes the curves. This action causes a muddiness, a lack of separation of the instruments or voices. To anyone who has heard a lateral and a vertical record of the same range, both made at the same time with the same orchestra, played on a good phonograph, the difference is impressive. At present, moreover, the vertical record has a slightly wider frequency range. And since potential amplitude (or extent of vibration) of a lateral record depends upon the space between grooves (if too narrow the graver will vibrate over into the next groove), a lateral record takes more space to play the same music.

"- - - It may be that the practical objections to the hill-and-dale record have been exaggerated. It would cost comparatively little to cut vertical duplicates of the lateral records when recording. The masters could be stored away for two or three years, while the standard and classical catalog was being built up, and then issued along with the announcement of a radically new phonograph playing both the old and the new types of records. A pick-up for such a machine is already in use. This course, exploited for all it is worth, might be just the shot in the arm the record industry will be needing.

"There are now no home records of true high fidelity, that is, with an undistorted range extending up to 8,000 or more and down to say 40 cycles. Neither are there any phonographs widely available that would do such records justice. But there are such records and phonographs, and they are being played every day. The World Broadcasting System, for instance, has a big library of them, which are let out to broadcasting stations to fill in between programs. Some of them are capable of reproducing over a range of 30 to 10,000 cycles, — of encompassing every fundamental and overtone casually discernible by ninety-nine out of a hundred human beings. They come closer than anything ever has to fulfilling Mr. Edison's claim for his early phonograph: 'Just as loud, just as clear, just as sweet.' But the reaction of the companies to arguments for the vertical cut is one of disapproval, tempered with the statement that a lateral record can be produced to equal the best hill-and-dale disk. In either case the consumer would be justified in looking forward to considerable improvement in records and the machines that play them."

Until Muzak converted to tape, the Western Electric vertical-cut system was used. The discs were made of Vinylite and were processed by RCA. When played with the best equipment, many of these Muzak discs reveal a quality that is unsurpassed. Before writing off the vertical-disc permanently, the reader should keep the following in mind:

1. The last fundamental contribution to the vertical-cut method was the inverse-feedback recording head, which was designed in 1938.
2. The Western Electric vertical-cut record was a compromise, because the shape and dimensions of the groove had been based on the "V"-shaped lateral groove established by Victor and carried over into the $33\frac{1}{3}$-rpm Vitaphone and radio transcription discs.
3. The Western Electric transcription pickup was a hybrid, designed to play both vertically and laterally recorded discs.
4. There has always been an unused vertical resultant force from all lateral records, due to the "V"-shaped groove. This is still true with monophonic LP's played with standard pickups, and also accounts for some of the improvement when a monophonic LP record is played through a stereo cartridge.
5. Stereo discs owe much of their superiority to the fact that they now are partially vertical.

CHAPTER 21

THE MODERN AUTOMATIC PHONOGRAPH INDUSTRY

IT WAS not until the late 1930's that the colloquial expression "juke box" came into general use. The term had its immediate origin in an old southern word of African origins used among the Negros, "jook," meaning to dance. Therefore, the rather widespread popularity of coin-operated phonographs in the earlier acoustic period of cylinders and discs antedated the introduction of the descriptive term "juke box" by many years.

As recounted elsewhere, the first coin-operated phonographs had employed the improved electric motor-driven wax cylinder mechanism that Edison had designed primarily as a business machine. These converted Edison phonographs played a single cylinder only. A repeating device sent the reproducer back in position to start the record over when another coin was deposited. In the earliest models introduced on the West coast, a separate coin chute was furnished for each of the several pairs of ear tubes through which the patrons listened. With this system, it was possible to garner thirty cents or more in nickels from a single playing. Thus, the idea of the "override" is hardly new!

Lest present day operators should be tempted to scoff at the primitive machines of the earlier day, evidence of fabulous profits by some of the early phonograph companies was submitted to a convention of these companies in 1891. The Missouri Phonograph Com-

pany had some fifty multiple tube machines in locations in June of that year and one alone returned $100 in one week. The Louisiana Phonograph Co. reported collecting about $1,000 from one machine in April and May, 1891. None of this was paid out to the location owners, as the phonograph was considered to be a business attraction!

Naturally, this abnormal profit situation did not continue for long, for the patrons could not select the tunes unless several machines were installed. In fact, by 1897 this had become standard practice and there were phonograph "parlors" in most larger cities in the United States and abroad. At this time, the United States Phonograph Co. of Newark, N. J., then closely allied with the Edison interests, were the principal manufacturers of the return mechanisms and coin-slot control devices. In "A Complete Manual of the Edison Phonograph" published by that company in 1897, the following was said about them under the heading "Nickel-in-the-slot Phonographs."

"Nickel-in-the-slot Phonographs are adaptations of the standard M Phonograph, with omissions and changes to meet the requirements of a coin-operated machine. The omissions are of parts that have no service to perform, such as the body box, speaking tube, turning rest, etc., and the changes relate to the details of combination with another device. This device is required to enable the nickel dropped in the slot to start and stop the Phonograph, and to return it automatically to operative position after one reproduction. The first is generally called the nickel action, and the second the return mechanism. The Phonograph and automatic mechanism thus combined and set in a cabinet, together form what is known as the nickel-in-the-slot Phonograph. "Many devices for automatic service were exploited some years ago when the idea was first conceived, but so far as the writer is aware only one of them has survived, and only one is manufactured now. This mechanism has made the nickel-in-the-slot business practical. The principle is the closing of the electrical circuit by means of a nickel, not through the nickel or by its weight, but by the action of its diameter. The weight principle was tried and found wanting, being too delicate a method, as any light balancing action must be when subjected to rough usage and varying levels. The idea of a slot machine being to provide a single reproduction for the coin deposited, it necessarily must be equipped with a reliable device to stop the machine when through playing and return it to operative position for the next coin. - - -

"Cleanliness about the machines and their accessories cannot be enforced too rigidly. The most successful parlors are those where in addition to the hearing of good musical selections on the Phonographs, the cabinets are kept highly polished, the glass clean, the machines bright, the announcement cards fresh and interesting, the tubing white, etc., and in this particular way it may be said that the Phonograph slot business does not differ from other enterprises that appeal to and depend upon the patronage of a scrupulous public whom it is well not to offend.

"Any slot device to be effective must be thoroughly automatic, simple and reliable in action. Nothing is so in-

jurious to the business as the failure of a machine to respond to the nickel. These points have been clearly set forth by Mr. Andem, the organizer and manager of several successful parlors. He enumerates the following as among the requisites of a good attachment. It should raise and lower the speaker arm gently at the beginning and end of the record, without jar or friction. Moreover, it should do this accurately. It should allow the Phonograph an opportunity of a second or more for the motor to gain full speed and come under control of the governor, before reproduction begins. It should be so constructed as to raise the speaker arm and stop the reproduction before the electric current is shut off and the speed diminishes, to prevent the gradual dying down of the sound. It should be so attached to the Phonograph as not to put extra work upon the motor that will prevent the free starting of the machine. It is also equally important that during the entire forward travel of the speaker arm during the period of reproduction, there should be no mechanical resistance from weights or springs, for besides the waste of power the drag will interfere with reproduction by binding the speaker arm and crowding the speaker out of track."

How many present day operators would care to have lived through those days? Eventually it became customary to install other coin-operated machines along with the phonographs in the parlors, such as scales, electric shockers and Edison Kinetoscopes. These augmented establishments became known as "penny arcades." However, this was a misnomer as far as the phonograph was concerned. A nickel was the coin nearly always required and a nickel would buy then as much as a quarter buys today.

Actually, four- and five-cylinder attachments had been introduced before 1900. They permitted playing each cylinder in sequence, but without a choice.

These were originally sold for use with ear tubes, but later some were equipped with short horns. Both the National Phonograph Company and the American Graphophone Company manufactured coin-operated phonographs well into the 1900's; some were equipped to play the large five-inch diameter concert cylinders, first introduced in 1898. **The English Lambert Company made this size of molded celluloid cylinders for a time; these should have been ideal for automatic coin machine operation.**

The Regina Music Box Company in 1905 introduced a six-cylinder, coin-operated phonograph named the Automatic Reginaphone. It played the records in sequence only and was equipped with either ear tubes or a horn extending from the cabinet top. This same year, the Multiphone had appeared on the market. It was a monstrosity with a large Ferris wheel carrying twenty-four cylinders on individual mandrels around the periphery from which the patron had free choice—provided he furnished the motive power as well as the nickel! The only automatic disc coin machine of any consequence then on the market was made by Julius Wilner in Philadelphia. This played twelve ten-inch discs in sequence only. Upon deposit of a coin, the lowest disc in the magazine was lifted into playing position and a fresh needle fed automatically to the sound box before it reached the record.

The Automatic Machine and Tool Company of Chicago manufactured the first truly selective disc mechanism. Although spring motor-operated, it was automatic, permitting a choice of twenty-four selections stored in racks at either side of the turntable. The mechanism was enclosed in a five-foot high cabinet with glass panels on three sides to permit viewing the operation, similar to the cylinder Multiphone. A forty-inch long horn protruded from the top. As in the earlier cylinder mechanisms, Gabel's device had a screw feed mechanism to carry the sound box across the record; it also was equipped with a magnetic slug-detector. The en-

tire operation by the patron was confined to one handle at the front of the cabinet that changed the record, the needle, and wound the motor all in one turn. In the industry, the John Gabel Automatic Entertainer is recognized as the true progenitor of the modern juke box, yet this was only 1906!

The same year, another cylinder machine was produced by the Skelly Manufacturing Company of Chicago. This was a coin-machine adaptation of the Columbia Twentieth Century Graphophone, using wax-type cylinders six inches long—the same size as the dictating machine cylinders used into the 1940's. The mechanism contained a revolving wheel offering a choice from twenty-five of the longer-playing three-minute cylinders. This machine was named the Concertophone. Selection was made by a dial; aside from being hand-wound, improved models like the Entertainer and most others of the time, were fully automatic. As the patron wound the motor, the record selected would automatically shift into playing position and be restored at the end of the playing. These models also had a glass front and a reflecting mirror to expose the ingenious operation. A similar, improved model with a different cabinet was designed for homes, thus being probably the first wide-choice home automatic phonograph. Incorporating as it did the patented Higham friction amplifier, these machines provided ample volume for noisy locations, the one needed feature the John Gabel Entertainer lacked. The quality and efficiency of the Higham friction amplifier device may be judged by the fact that Edison in 1912 adopted it for use with talking motion pictures.

As evidence that the cylinders were by no means out of the running was the introduction in 1908 of an improved six-cylinder machine by Regina, named the Regina Hexaphone. This was enclosed in a well-designed, compact little cabinet, with a built-in wooden horn of excellent acoustic quality, similar to the Edison cygnet horn of the same period. The Hexaphone was electric motor-operated and fully automatic, though obviously the choice was limited.

The earlier development of the phonograph "parlor" was an attempt to meet a recognized need for automatic operation and selectivity. It seems rather ironic that just as the phonograph parlors had begun to develop a clientele, another of Thomas Edison's brain children had moved in to set up competition—the nickelodeon, the early nickel motion picture theater. By 1907, Chicago had 116 nickelodeons in operation and only 19 of the so-called penny arcades, into which the parlors had degenerated, were left. Obviously, the nickelodeons were offering considerably more entertainment for the same price. The novelty of listening through ear tubes had long since worn off. Sound from the early cylinders and discs, through such acoustic systems as were generally available, was too thin and deficient in range and volume to install in noisy locations. The Concertophone with the Higham mechanical amplifier was an abortive step in the right direction, failing primarily because the longer Twentieth Century cylinders were available for only a year or so. However, it proved quite sensational because of its volume and attracted crowds, earning as much as ten dollars a day.

As a result of these early inventive efforts, manufacturers and operators became aware of the potential existing for better-engineered mechanical musical instruments with sufficient volume for restaurants, ice-cream parlors, bars and other places where people congregated. The Regina people earlier had shown the way with their large, deluxe coin-operated music boxes offering patrons a choice of up to twelve of the thirty-inch diameter punched metal tune-discs, automatically fed into position. The automatic Reginas were enclosed in beautifully built and finished cabinets of rosewood, oak or mahogany. They accommodated the twelve- to thirty-inch diameter metal discs in the various models. One or more of these also dispensed a candy bar, delivered at the close of the musical selection. Although hand wound, prices of the larger automatic Reginas ranged from $500 upwards. Hence, from a prestige standpoint, they occupied a position comparable to the finest automatic phonograph systems today. Many of these were sold by the Wurlitzer organization after 1897, as the result of a contractual relationship entered into that year. Electrical operation was the one desirable feature the Regina lacked. That this might have been accomplished seems indicated by the appearance of the coin-controlled Peerless Piano about the same time. This was the first electric motor-driven, pneumatic player roll piano.

The Pianorchestra of Wurlitzer represents the next progressive step in development, combining piano with other instruments. This also operated pneumatically from perforated paper rolls containing from two to seven selections. Especially significant is the fact that not only was there a nickel slot on the instrument, but it also could be operated from remote control wall boxes. These were introduced in the early 1900's.

There have been four distinct phases of coin-operated musical instruments. First was that of the non-electrically amplified cylinder and disc phonographs, for the most part non-selective; second was that of automatic pianos and other mechanical instruments, or combinations thereof, a few with selective mechanisms; the third phase was that of electrically-amplified phonographs, the later ones being completely selective; and fourth, the modern phase of multiple-selection, high-fidelity, with remote control and multiple-speaker systems. The four phases of coin operation were separated by three periods of transition: the first from about 1908 to 1912, the second from about 1925 to 1930, and the third from about 1939 to 1948. The latter transition period covers the intensive growth in electronic science extending through World War II. During the war, most companies produced defense equipment, even before many of the foremost electronic experts had been siphoned off from industry to develop radar and other electronic gear.

Despite the vicissitudes of competition, the mortality of men and their fictional corporate bodies, a strong line of continuity of purpose seems to be running through and connecting these four phases through the difficult transition periods. Consider that no less than three of the present four American manufacturers were active in the second phase and through the third, despite differences in the products they were placing before the public. The fourth company, coming into the field later, acquired the patents of the John Gabel Co. that had been active in the latter part of the first phase and had again entered the lists in the last phase.

The John Gabel Co. had persisted longer than the other early pioneers of coin-operated phonographs, because it had been working along what is known now to be the proper approach —providing selectivity. However, it had ceased producing the Entertainer during the automatic piano phase and had again re-entered the field in 1933 with the Starlite, an electrically-amplified, coin-operated selective phonograph. Here it should be observed that in the third phase, except for the Automatic Musical Instrument Company and Seeburg, the present companies were not first in the field with selective instruments. Mention should be made of some earlier pioneers.

Homer E. Capehart, later a U. S. Senator from Indiana, had introduced the Capehart Orchestrope in 1928. This was a coin-operated phonograph that played fifty-six selections, but was non-selective. In 1929, the Mills Novelty Company of Chicago introduced the Dance Master, a twelve-selection, coin-operated automatic. This had a mechanism with twelve separate turntables arranged with the playing plane radial to the center of the large Ferris wheel arrangement to which they were attached. The wheel carried the turntable

with the required disc into the playing position, similar in a way to the action of the earlier cylinder-playing Multiphone. There was sufficient space between the turntables for the pickup arm to swing in and operate. A dynamic speaker was employed, typical of most units of this period.

Wilcox "Ampliphone," Mid-West Automatic Phonograph Co., 1932, 10 selections. (Courtesy of The Wurlitzer Company.)

Edward A. Link, Binghamton, N. Y., a former manufacturer of orchestrions, in 1929 introduced a quite different mechanism with a twin pie-plate stack arrangement for changing records. This was a selective coin-operated phonograph similar to the later Wilcox "Ampliphone," more economical of space than the Dance Master, also playing only one side of each record. E. A. Link is now renowned as head of Link Aviation, Inc., makers of the world famous Link Trainer. Another early entry was the Concert-trope, coin-operated, made in Indianapolis, playing thirty-three selections both sides, only in sequence.

Dependence of the acoustic phonograph upon telegraphic research was detailed in an earlier chapter, as was the dependence of electrical recording upon telegraphy, wireless telephony and radio. In addition to the above, the automatic coin-controlled phonograph enterprises owe a great deal to the technics developed in the prior phases of automatic musical instruments, especially to the piano industry. Three of the four surviving companies in the juke box field were formerly in that business; one, Wurlitzer, still manufactures pianos.

It should be noted that the continual purpose of some of the chief executives of these companies has been rather consistently directed toward developing automatic mechanisms for coin operation. This is considerably contrasted to the motivations of certain other piano manufacturers who, at one time or another, made phonographs for the home market. The latter group includes the Kimball Piano Co., the Starr Piano Co. (makers of Gennett phonograph and records) and The Aeolian Company, which made phonographs and records in the United States and England. These companies made the conventional single play machines and as far as is known, never attempted to develop automatic phonograph mechanisms. Therefore, the third phase of the automatic phonograph industry seems to have developed partially from certain already well-established personal behavior and corporate situations. Inventive opportunity and market needs were envisioned by men who were masters of factory technics and merchandising methods, rather than from chance experimentation. Possession of certain basic patents or patent rights was unquestionably important. But the fact remains that the original inventors of many of the fundamental devices essential to the various automatic selective phonograph mechanisms had seldom been able to commercialize them.

The story of how the present companies happen to be in the field is largely the story of the transitional period between 1925 and 1930. To get hold of the far end of the thread of consistent purpose and determination leading to the present leadership of the industry, one must go back into the pre-phonograph history of each one.

AMI Incorporated is one of the pioneer coin-operated phonograph manufacturers of the modern era that had

National Automatic Selective Phonograph, 1927, 20 selections (affiliated company of Automatic Musical Instrument Co.)

its roots nourished in the piano industry. It was founded in 1909 as the National Piano Manufacturing Co., on the basis of one electric piano plus two U. S. patents; neither to that time had been granted. However, the conception was a good one, for it covered a selecting device by which any desired music roll from a magazine might be played automatically. This mechanism was successfully developed and produced. During the early years, the operation was divided into two corporations to facilitate administration. The earlier corporate entity continued to manufacture, and another corporation owned and operated the instruments in

National Automatic Selective Phonograph mechanism, 1927, 20 selections (affiliated company of Automatic Musical Instrument Co.)

the locations. The latter company was named the National Automatic Music Co. By 1925, it had some 4,200 pianos in location in the United States. In a way, this separation of manufacture from ownership and operation somewhat resembles the situation existing in the early days of the coin-operated phonograph under Lippincott's North American Phonograph Co. For somewhat different reasons, this latter day plan also failed to be flexible enough to meet competitive necessities; in 1925, the two companies were again merged as divisions of the Automatic Musical Instrument Co. By this time, it had become apparent to management that with the advent of electronic methods, the electric piano would eventually have to give way to the automatic, electrically-amplified disc phonograph. Corporate changes cleared the way for appropriate action.

About this time, a crude model of an automatic selective disc phonograph mechanism was brought before the executives by its inventor, B. C. Kenyon. Kenyon's device transferred the discs from a vertical storage rack to a horizontal turntable. The company acquired exclusive use and sales rights and its

engineers, under Clifford H. Green, assumed the task of developing the mechanism commercially and combining with it completely automatic, coin-controlled electrical operation and amplification. As perfected, the record changing device seized the record between two fingers, much like a human hand, and transferred it through an arc to the turntable, rotating in transit so the desired side would be up in the playing position. Because of the limited life of the phonograph needles, an automatic needle changing device replaced the needle after each ten plays. Theoretically, the number of records handled by this system was limited only by the storage space of the discs. For practical reasons, the capacity of these earliest of modern juke boxes was limited to ten discs, providing a choice of twenty selections. It must be remembered that the 78-rpm shellac discs were much bulkier than the present vinylite 45's and often varied in thickness, diameter and location of the starting groove. Current for the sound system was supplied by a built-in generator. The engineering was so successful that by the end of the first year some 8,500 of the new instruments had been placed in locations. By 1930, most of the company's coin-operated pianos had been replaced by these phonographs, with about 12,000 in use.

The outlook seemed bright for the Automatic Musical Instrument Company in 1930. As yet, there was little competition in the coin-operated phonograph business. The thousands of machines out were earning a steady income and being serviced by a widespread service organization. Its automatic record selector was being adapted for use with home instruments. New companies were being formed in foreign countries to exploit its products. General Motors Radio Corporation, owned jointly by General Motors and RCA, was licensed by Automatic to use its devices in the home instrument field. But the depression was at hand; as with so many other flourishing enterprises, Automatic Musical Instruments Co. found its earnings decreasing and a corporate reorganization eventually was necessary. However, before turning from the early history of this company to others, this is the place to highlight another significant contribution of this company, because of its far-reaching portent of things to come. In 1931, before the reorganization, Automatic had installed the first remote control system, by which selections from various stations could be made. The electrical selecting mechanism utilized a coil for each selection; when energized by an electric current, it magnetically moved a mechanical finger —a prototype of today's marvelous remote control devices.

The story of Justus P. Seeburg could well have been made the plot for one of the success stories by Horatio Alger. Born in Gothenburg, Sweden in 1871, he was the son of a wealthy tobacco goods manufacturer. However, his father met with financial reverses and at the time of his dealth, the family fortunes had been exhausted. Justus was then nine years old. After completing his education at the Chalmer's Technical Institute in Gothenburg, he emigrated to America in 1886 to make his fortune.

Justus' first job in America was with the C. S. Smith & Co. piano factory in Chicago. He was ambitious and his interest in his work led him to attend courses in adult education in a Chicago night school, later studying technical subjects at the Lewis Institute. He also studied drawing and designing at the Chicago Art Institute. In 1892 he became a naturalized citizen. He married a Swedish girl in 1896 and the following year, a son, N. Marshall Seeburg, was born. In later years, this son assumed the presidency of the company his father was to found.

Within a few years after arriving in this country, Justus P. Seeburg was superintendent of the Cable Piano Co. of Chicago. Later, he was co-founder of the Kurz-Seeburg Co., Rockford, Illinois, organized to produce piano actions. However, Mr. Seeburg sold his interest in that firm and in 1902 returned to Chicago, where he organized the J. P. Seeburg Piano Co., incorporated in 1907. That year, the company began manufacturing coin-operated automatic pianos. These utilized electric motor-driven bellows controlled by perforated paper music rolls.

A line of "Orchestrions" was introduced in 1910, in which various other instruments, principally of the percussion family, were added to the piano. Popularity of the up and coming "nickelodeons," the five-cent motion picture theaters, had led Seeburg to develop the "photo-player." This was a combination piano, organ and traps operated by player roll action, and produced music and sound effects to accompany the silent films.

As the years went on, Seeburg also developed electric motor-operated pipe organs for churches, mortuaries and theaters, as well as manufacturing special music rolls for each type. The pipe organ business was sold in 1921. Seeburg also manufactured player pianos for a number of years, discontinuing this line in 1923. Production was then concentrated on the coin-operated Orchestrions, which had been developed into highly reliable, versatile instru-

Seeburg Audiophone Senior, 1928, 8 selections.

ments; some of them provided for selection of tunes by the patrons. Wall
boxes were also furnished as an extra,
some shaped like the Orchestrion they
operated, but in miniature. However,
these wall boxes were not selective.

That Justus P. Seeburg and his engineers were fully aware of the impact
of electrical recording and amplification
would have upon the coin-operated
musical instrument industry is indicated by their promptness in develop-

ing a coin-operated phonograph. Although the first all-electric home phonograph, the Brunswick Panatrope, had
been introduced in 1926, the following
year Seeburg began to manufacture all-
electric, coin-controlled phonographs.
The same year, the company discontinued the Orchestrions. Almost from
the first, Seeburg mechanisms provided
for selection. The Seeburg Audiophone,
first introduced in 1928, was equipped
with eight individual turntables ar-

ranged on a Ferris wheel, similar in principle to the early cylinder Multiphone. However, the plane of the turntables carrying the discs was tangent to the circumference of the carrier, so only eight discs could be carried and only one side of each could be played. What a contrast to the marvelous Seeburg Select-O-Matic of the present, offering a choice of 200 selections!

Other audiophones were developed in which the plane of the turntables on the carrier was maintained in a constant horizontal position, with some economy in space. But it was not until the Seeburg Melophone was introduced in 1930 that the number of selections possible was increased to twelve, playable sequentially only. During the early 1930's, Seeburg, along with many others, was in receivership. It turned to manufacturing "Ray-Gun" targets, refrigerator and washing machine meters and kindred products. Ingenuity, product diversification and applying manufacturing skills to other fields enabled

Seeburg as well as others to weather the depression. [1]

Another interesting story is how Wurlitzer came into the industry. Rudolph Wurlitzer, born in 1831, was the son of a prosperous music merchant in Schoeneck, Germany. For generations, his ancestors had made and sold musical instruments. One was made Master Violinmaker by the Saxon guild. Rudolph was of an independent nature. Although he could have continued in his father's footsteps, he chose instead to emigrate to the United States in

[1] How well this was accomplished is evident in the subsequent history of the company. In 1937, although continuing as chairman of the Board of Directors, J. P. Seeburg turned over the presidency to his son, N. Marshall Seeburg. J. P. Seeburg became well-known for his philanthropies, particularly to educational and Swedish-American organizations. He had conferred upon him the knighthood of the Royal Order of Vasa by King Gustav of Sweden, as well as numerous other decorations and citations. In 1956, the Seeburg family sold controlling interest to Fort Pitt Industries, Inc., since renamed The Seeburg Corporation.

Seeburg Audiophone Jr., 1930, 8 selections, open to show mechanism.

Seeburg Audiophone Model E, 1931, choice of 8 selections.

1853, without parental assistance. Landing in Hoboken, he made his way to Philadelphia and eventually Cincinnati —wherever he could find work. Saving a large portion of his frugal earnings, within a few years he began a part-time business importing handmade musical instruments made by craftsmen from his native Germany. In 1861, Rudolph established a factory in Cincinnati to manufacture drums and bugles; many were used in the War between the States. By 1865, Wurlitzer was the largest band instrument retailer in the United States; a branch store was opened in Chicago. It was some years later before the situation developed that explains the presence of Wurlitzer in the automatic coin instrument business today.

The Rudolph Wurlitzer Company in 1893 became one of the distributors of the Regina Music Box Company, Rahway, N. J. Soon Wurlitzer was the largest single outlet, selling disc music boxes through its mail order department and music dealers, as well as its own stores, throughout the United States. The first Wurlitzer experience in selling coin-operated musical instruments was with the Selective Regina. In the first decade of its association with Regina, Wurlitzer annually purchased from Regina products valued at $100,000 to $150,000, but the inroads of the home phonograph caused a sharp decline in succeeding years.

In time, Wurlitzer became the largest distributor of Victor talking machines. Hence, this company has been doubly tied in with the phonograph industry. Rudolph H. Wurlitzer, one of the three sons of the founder, became a personal friend of Eldridge R. Johnson, who had improved Berliner's Gramophone until it was commercially successful. The close relationship of Victor and Wurlitzer continued into the RCA-Victor era. Though of little importance financially, it is worthy to note that for a number of years prior to World War II, Wurlitzer coin-operated phonographs and accessories for export were distributed by RCA Victor.

But these events occurred much later than the gestative period of the Wurlitzer interest in coin-operated musical instruments, which began with the Automatic Reginaphone. The Regina Music Box Company, as well as the Wurlitzer enterprise, had its inceptions in European craftsmen and craftsmanship. It began with one Eugene DeKleist, also destined to enjoy a long and profitable association with Wurlitzer. DeKleist had been born "von" Kleist in Dusseldorf about 1867. Well-educated, he became an accomplished pianist and organist. While a relatively young man, he became associated with Limonaire Freres in Paris, manufacturers of merry-go-round organs and music cylinders, later being transferred to the London office. DeKleist emigrated to the United States, and by 1897 was the largest manufacturer of barrel organs for carrousels and carnival rides in the United States. His factory was located at the manufacturing center of carnival equipment, North Tonawanda, N. Y.

DeKleist that year offered Wurlitzer the distributorship of his barrel organs. Wurlitzer declined, but urged DeKleist to develop a coin-operated electric piano. As a result, the Wurlitzer Tonophone won the Gold Medal award at the Pan-American Exposition in 1901. The Tonophone operated on the barrel organ principle, with pegs inserted in a large diameter cylinder similar to the Swiss music box cylinders, but much larger. It was the first of a number of several Wurlitzer-inspired, coin-operated instruments such as the Orches-

trion, automatic reed, flute and trumpet organs, and the Wurlitzer Military Band Organ. Examples of many of these and other automatic musical instruments can still be found in operating order. There is an especially fine collection at the Musical Museum, Deansboro, New York; another at the Cliff House in San Francisco.

In 1908, the Rudolph Wurlitzer Company acquired the plant and business of DeKleist. It became the nucleus of the present North Tonawanda Division. Shortly after, Wurlitzer added the manufacture of pianos and player pianos. By acquiring the Hope-Jones Organ Company in 1910, it could develop what later became famed as "The Mighty Wurlitzer." This operation was also transferred to North Tonawanda. In 1914, the Melville Clark Piano Co. of Chicago arranged for Wurlitzer to act as exclusive agents in certain domestic territories and abroad. An eventual result was that the Melville Clark Piano Co. was acquired in 1919 and its plant at DeKalb, Illinois converted to the manufacture of Wurlitzer grand pianos. Expansion of Wurlitzer manufacturing facilities and retail operations continued through the 1920's. However, the stock market crash and resulting depression hit the far flung Wurlitzer operations as it did so many others. Even before 1929, full-length sound pictures had pulled the rug out from under the mammoth Wurlitzer cinema organ business. It will be recalled that before full-length sound films, all feature pictures, short subjects and even newsreels for many years had been accompanied by musical scores for piano, orchestra and pipe organ. The inevitable retrenchment and elimination of unprofitable manufacturing items soon left available vast areas of plant space at North Tonawanda for the opportunity with which this account is primarily concerned.

In 1933, Homer E. Capehart, after an exchange of correspondence, met with Farny R. Wurlitzer, then manager of the North Tonawanda plant. Mr. Capehart had just taken an option to purchase the assets of the

Wurlitzer Simplex mechanism, 1934, played top side only of 24, 78-rpm discs.

bankrupt Simplex Manufacturing Company of Chicago. However, the Simplex mechanism was a good one, one Capehart knew could be successfully developed. Thus, Wurlitzer had the plant space, an organization and the means to produce, together with a background in coin-operated musical instruments; Capehart had a good mechanism. The two came to terms. The result was the Wurlitzer Simplex.

The prospect of repeal of the prohibition amendment portended the opening of a vast new market, so planning for the new venture was on a commensurate scale. Homer Capehart was engaged to supervise the conversion of a large part of the North Tonawanda plant to produce the new instrument. Demand soon exceeded the predictions; in 1935, transfer of all piano manufacturing to DeKalb became necessary. Thus, the Rudolph Wurlitzer Company, a name long famed in musical circles, was committed to play a prominent role in the modern automatic coin-operated phonograph industry.

For several years, Homer E. Capehart, who later became United States Senator from Indiana, was a vice-president of the Rudolph Wurlitzer Company. Capehart was a farm boy, entering the army in World War I at the age of 18. After receiving his discharge, he sold farm machinery for the J. I. Case Plow Company. Later, he was employed by the Holcomb & Hoke Manufacturing Company as a salesman, rising to branch manager and eventually sales manager. Holcomb & Hoke originally made popcorn machines, later pioneering in the manufacture of refrigerated food display cases. More pertinent to our story, Holcomb & Hoke were also the manufacturers of an early electrically amplified coin-operated phonograph called the "Electromuse," with a non-selective mechanism. This probably influenced Homer Capehart considerably and led to his subsequently keen interest in the coin-operated phonograph industry to which he contributed so much.

After resigning as sales manager of Holcomb & Hoke Manufacturing Company, Homer Capehart founded in 1927 the Capehart Corporation at Huntington, Indiana to manufacture high quality automatic coin-operated phonographs. Various mechanisms were developed and sold. One of these operated like an elevator; the records were arranged in a vertical stack conveyor, and ran up or down to leave the proper record exposed at the playing level, somewhat like cutting a deck of cards. Obviously, with the pickups then available, this mechanism would play only one side of each disc.

The best remembered coin-operated Capehart is the "Orchestrope," a huge console instrument with a horizontal deck-type changing mechanism. The records were slid from a magazine at one side over the central turntable and after playing slid to a similar magazine at the other side. Although the Orchestrope was a well-engineered instrument of pleasing appearance and exceptionally good sound reproduction quality for the time, it was non-selective. Successful from the start, the Capehart business expanded and it was necessary to move into a new factory in Fort Wayne, Indiana in 1929.

Homer Capehart also could foresee a splendid opportunity for a dependable, high quality home phonograph with automatic changer. He bought the patents on a turnover-type changer from the Columbia Phonograph Company, and in 1930 his engineers perfected it. As a result, the Capehart Deluxe automatic home phonograph was placed into production the following year. The changer was an ingenious mechanism that would automatically turn over and play the reverse sides of the records after playing the sides stacked toward the turntable. It would play ten- and twelve-inch discs intermixed. Later, a device was added so that any selection could be immediately rejected at the push of a button. Furnished in massive, well-built cabinets in modified period designs, the Capehart in the 1930's became the largest-selling, higher-priced home automatic; and exclusive dealer franchises were much sought after for years.

A sanguine enterprise, the Capehart Corporation had run into difficulties that had toppled older and more strongly entrenched companies during the depression. As a result, just as the Capehart Deluxe automatic home phonograph was beginning to pay off, Homer Capehart found himself pushed out of control. In 1932, Capehart founded the Packard Manufacturing Corporation, later owned by him. The following year, he became associated with the Wurlitzer Company. He instituted a policy of selling which was of great importance in the development of the coin-operated phonograph industry. He had independent businessmen buy and operate phonographs, rather than selling them directly to the owners of the locations, as had been done formerly. Senator Capehart has said with respect to this policy:

"It is my best judgement — had we adopted the policy of selling direct to locations, the industry would not have succeeded because the individual owner would not have kept the machines working, would not have changed records often, etc. Once we adopted the above mentioned policy at Wurlitzer—all others followed suit."

After leaving the Wurlitzer organization, Homer E. Capehart again became identified with the Packard Manufacturing Corporation, which subsequently engaged for a number of years in manufacturing automatic coin-operated phonographs. He was elected United States Senator from Indiana in 1944, and was re-elected several times.

Capehart did not make the first home record changer of the new electronic era. The first to receive considerable attention was offered in combination with the Orthophonic Victrola in 1927. The phonograph was entirely acoustic, utilizing the twelve-foot folded reentrant Maxfield-Harrison tone passage, but the turntable and changing mechanism were electrically operated. Since this model in its necessarily huge cabinet sold for $1,000, sales understandably were not large. Aside from lacking suitable semipermanent styli, early inventors of home record changers faced the same problems as the manufacturers of coin-operated instruments. There was no uniformity in the physical characteristics of the various makes of records, such as thickness, outside diameter, weight, location of the starting turn, and most important, no uniform stopping groove to actuate the cycling mechanism. Since the introduction of its double disc Red Seal series of celebrity recordings in 1922, Victor had pressed an eccentric stopping groove in its discs to actuate the patented brake henceforth installed on all Victrolas. Earlier, others had developed various automatic stopping devices that had to be preset for each record; obviously no help to the designers of automatic mechanisms. Hundreds of patents were issued during the transitional period for devices that could not be made to work reliably because of no uniformly applied stopping groove, or no standardization of records. Suitable styli was another bugaboo; the first semipermanent needles were merely plated with gold or other metals. Treated and untreated cactus spines and thorns were also used. But for automatic use these were quite impossible, for they frequently failed unexpectedly. The Victor tungsten stylus, with a slender cylindrical filament of tungsten imbedded in the tip, was likewise too fragile for automatic mechanisms. Coin machine operators changed the needle each time the machine was serviced; in the interest of record longevity, this had to be done quite frequently.

During the shellac disc period, the home phonograph market required sequential operation only, and ideally provided for handling both ten- and twelve-inch discs. To be successful, the commercial changer had to provide for a completely free choice of a fairly large number of selections. Ideally, it should play either side of any disc in the machine, but it was necessary to design for ten-inch discs only.

The earliest album sets had been designed for manual playing only; part one and two of a series would be on opposite sides of the same disc, part three and four on the next disc, etc. Understandably, designing changers to perform in this sequence for home use would be uneconomical in terms of a suitable selling price for the larger share of the market, although practical for higher priced home and commercial units. As a result, for use with the Automatic Orthophonic Victrola, the Capehart, and other early home automatic instruments, the AM (automatic machine) sets were introduced by the record producing companies. The first half of the symphony, concerto, or other programmed material would be on the R side of discs in an album, the remaining half on the L sides, the latter in reverse order. Thus, with even the least expensive changing mechanisms, the listener reloaded the changer only upon completion of the first half. In view of the different requirements for coin operation and home automatic phonographs, it is interesting to note that Capehart had pioneered in both fields. Success of the Capehart home phonograph with the turnover changer was so marked that for years the company could turn a deaf ear to the plebeian demand that radio be included! These deluxe phonographs sold for around $600. Not until the sale of the much less expensive drop-type changers became important in the home phonograph market did Capehart offer a line of lower priced units with changers of this type, also introducing AM and FM radios into its deluxe line.

As noted previously, Homer E. Capehart left the Wurlitzer organization in 1940 and became chairman of the board of the Packard Manufacturing Company in Indianapolis, which he had founded. Packard also produced coin-operated phonographs for a few years following World War II. About this time, the Capehart Company amalgamated with the Farnsworth Radio & Television Corporation. This, in turn, became a satellite of International Telephone & Telegraph Corporation, but has since ceased to orbit.

The selective coin-operated disc mechanisms went through a process of evolution and perfection similar to the home changers. Because the operation could not be kept under the watchful eye of the owner, the need for absolute reliability was that much greater. Research and development were continuous throughout the electronic era to the present. New models were introduced as rapidly as improvements were proved—sometimes earlier, to the regret of the producing companies! Seeburg had introduced a new type called the Melophone in 1930 (twelve tunes, no selection), as well as variants of its original Audiophone (eight tunes, selective) in a succeeding three-year period. The Automatic Musical Instrument Company was then making instruments for both home and commercial use, either coin-controlled or push-button operation. The phonographs would play either ten- or twelve-inch records. This company as early as 1930 was also installing automatic distance control mechanisms for musical instruments and radio, as well as automatic selecting devices for playing rolls for the piano and pipe organ. Notable among innovations introduced by this company, predecessor of AMI Incorporated, was the first electrostatic speaker, used in their coin-operated phonographs as early as 1930.

However, the depression adversely affected this company as it had the others, and on January 1, 1932 a successor company of the same name was organized. Engineers Lloyd J. Andres and Clifford H. Green were authorized to develop a new line of improved coin-operated phonographs, which were first introduced in 1934. The new instruments offered a choice of twenty selections. These also employed a multiple coin entry system. In addition, an individual coin entrance device was developed for each selection with an electrical system utilizing a coil for each choice, as had been used in some installations since 1930.

Repeal of the prohibition amendment on December 5, 1933 almost overnight multiplied the opportunities of operators for profitable locations. Within months, thousands of restaurants, bars and taverns were being opened from coast to coast and the automatic coin-operated phonograph soon became a factor in the competition for patronage. Logically, this was the year the industry witnessed its greatest gains since the '29 crash had knocked the props from under the entire economy. Naturally, other manufacturers were eager to get in the business and several did so. Of these, the only survivor is Rock-Ola.

In 1934, the National Association of Coin-Operated Machine Manufacturers, with headquarters in Chicago, had an industry code approved by the National Recovery Administration. Only a part of the production of these manufacturers was devoted to coin-operated phonographs. However, since the days of the formation of this association and the N. R. A. code, the industry has remained rather tightly controlled by relatively few manufacturers, even though the National Recovery Act long ago was declared unconstitutional by the United States Supreme Court. On the other hand, without question the phonograph record business was saved for the second time in its short fifty-year history by a phase of coin operation. It was in 1933, following the lowest point in record sales, that Wurlitzer had decided to put into production the Simplex mechanism brought to it by Homer Capehart. To illustrate the uphill climb to the present, in the 40th Anniversary issue of *Billboard,* December 29, 1934, only one coin-operated phonograph was advertised, the Wurlitzer Simplex, and there were only two ads of record manufacturers, one for Perfect Records (25¢) of the American Record Co., and one of the Vocalion Records of Brunswick Record Corp. However, Mills, Gabel, Seeburg and the Automatic Musical Instruments Co. were already producing large numbers of juke boxes. Rock-Ola also began the production of automatic phonographs in 1934.

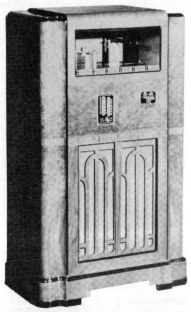

Rock-Ola Multi-Selector, 12 selection phonograph of 1935.

Although the Rock-Ola Manufacturing Co. had not been incorporated under that name until 1932, it also had earlier antecedents in coin operation, though not in the piano business.

Mr. David C. Rockola, president of the company, was born in Verden, Manitoba, Canada. When fourteen years of age, he was obliged to leave school to make his own way. By the age of twenty, he owned and operated a concession and food processing business, also engaging in the manufacture of coolers. Recognizing the potential of the coin-operated machine industry, Mr. Rockola obtained a position with one of the leading manufacturers in Chicago, his capabilities securing for him rapid promotion. In 1924, he became a distributor and operator of vending machines and weighing scales. Mr. Rockola invented and patented a new scale mechanism, which formed the basis for his founding the Rock-Ola Scale Company in 1927.

Therefore, coin operation also gave this company some continuity with the earlier transitional period. Rock-Ola also manufactured some fine games that received wide distribution and established a basis for entering the automatic coin-phonograph business. The Rock-Ola Manufacturing Corporation (now registered in Delaware) has the further distinction of having acquired all patents issued to the John Gabel Co., the earliest pioneer of a selective, coin-operated disc phonograph. The first Rock-Ola instruments were placed in

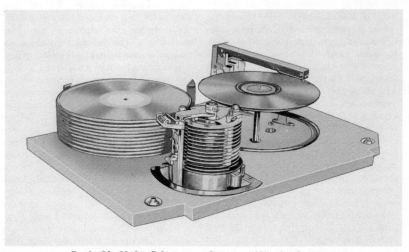

Rock-Ola Multi-Selector mechanism, 1935, 12 selections.

locations in 1934. They featured the Multi-Selector mechanism and a slug-proof coin chute.

Rock-Ola later introduced a Dial-A-Tune device; records were selected by dialing, like a telephone. This company also introduced "Mystic Music," a central station-type operation wired to the locations for selection. However, telephone line charges the staff needed plus turnover of the girl switchboard operators, (who were alternately kidded and solicited by the patrons), resulted in abandoning this venture. All the surviving companies had similar experiences they would prefer to forget! Undaunted, Rock-Ola went on to develop other devices that were completely successful, as attested by its being one of the four surviving manufacturers.

Five years after repeal, the record business was well on the way to recovery. Not only had the automatic coin-operated phonograph industry reversed the downward trend, but aided by the introduction of higher quality home phonographs and plug-in portable record players, the past prejudice against "canned music" had begun to disappear. Moreover, the juke box provided a new way for record dealers to assess the probable demand for popular records without depending on the word of manufacturers' sales representatives. Reports printed in *Variety*, *Billboard* and such periodicals from week to week cited the popularity of the various records as played on the juke boxes, and also gave rise to the Saturday night radio program "Hit Parade." Terms such as "sleepers" and "comers" became part of record industry jargon. It is more than coincidence that record sales for the home market began to show a marked increase. In part, it was because the omnipresent coin-operated phonograph had begun to change popular attitudes toward recorded music. The popularity of the phonograph today is such that younger people have difficulty believing the low esteem into which it had sunk in the late 20's and early 30's. To illustrate

the gloom and pessimism pervading the industry at the low point, a statement by Walter U. Hurd, then editor of the Amusement section of *Billboard*, Sept. 23, 1934, is quoted as follows:

"In 1933, I suggested to the advertising staffs of two prominent manufacturers of phonograph records that it was time to plan a record merchandising program, which would get phonograph music into the home as soon as economic conditions made it possible for the people to buy. One said that television would complete the finality which radio had given the phonograph; another said there was no new appeal which would bring the phonograph back into popularity; a manufacturer of coin-operated phonographs had told me there would never be a real comeback in that field."

Few manufacturers of coin-controlled phonographs ever lost confidence in the future. Within five years from the introduction of the Wurlitzer Simplex in 1934, sales by this one company had jumped from 5,000 to 30,000 units. Seeburg in 1935 brought forth the Selectophone, developed by its engineer Wilcox, who also had been responsible for the Audiophone. The Selectophone had a selection system of individual turntables on a common revolving shaft, replacing the cumbersome Ferris wheel mechanism. The record turntables remained stationary while the pickup arm assembly was raised or lowered to play the proper selection. Seeburg also introduced a quite different instrument called the Symphonola. This provided a choice of twelve selections by setting a mechanical dial. Its capacity was expanded to twenty selections in following models. This mechanism controlled a sliding tray containing the record slide. The turntable alternately rose and descended with each selection, coming up under the record to support it as the pickup moved into playing position. A model was also made that was equipped with a new coin slide to accommodate nickels, dimes and quarters. This model also presented a new method of selection by individual levers.

Though new to the phonograph field, Rock-Ola Manufacturing Company also expanded rapidly. In 1934, Mr. David C. Rockola, founder and president, acquired the present huge plant in the heart of Chicago. One reason for the purchase was to provide factory facilities to manufacture coin-operated phonographs under patents acquired from the Holmes Manufacturing Co., as well as to expand Rock-Ola production of other types of equipment. Its initial entry in the phonograph field was the Rock-Ola Multi-Selector. As the name implies, it provided for making more than one selection at a time, a popular and desirable feature.

The industry continued to expand rapidly from 1935 to 1939, as did the revitalized home phonograph business. In 1939, Seeburg introduced the "Playboy." This unit was made up in two sections. The top section was the industry's first selective remote control wall box. It was a "wireless" type, so called because electrical impulses were sent along the power lines already in the location as a means of making the selection. The lower part of the unit was a stand containing a remote speaker. Prior to this, remote speakers had required a special primary current to energize the field coils of the dynamic speaker units necessary then for high-level sound reproduction. With the introduction of the high-flux Alnico magnet PM speakers throughout the radio and phonograph industry, auxiliary speakers were no longer a problem. During the years before 1939, color and lighting effects in the design of floor cabinets to attract attention had flourished. The contrast between some of the newer models and older models was so pronounced that many companies offered auxiliary lighting attachments to be added to earlier models. Seeburg also had developed sequential-type record changers for sale to home phonograph manufacturers. For some years prior to World War II, their output

averaged about 2,000 per day, in addition to normal coin-operated phonograph production.

Electronically operated remote control units were developed further by Seeburg in 1940. That year, the first 20-selection Seeburg Symphonola with electrical selection, as well as the first three-wire type control box, was introduced. The latter was a most practical innovation that has since been adopted as standard by the rest of the industry. Just prior to World War II, all companies had been busy bringing out improved models. Rock-Ola had introduced "Dial-A-Tune," described previously, and "Mystic Music," wired to a central station that serviced the selections; otherwise, it had a sound distribution system similar to the "Muzak." This was a development also made possible by the availability of PM speakers. The last prewar Seeburg was the 1942 "Hitone," a victory model 20-selection phonograph. Wurlitzer also produced a victory model that played 24 selections.

During the war, all phonograph manufacturing plants were occupied with war production work. In the meantime, ideas and possible improvements were mulled over in spare hours by engineers of various companies. Shipment of thousands of automatic phonographs to various PX's around the world at that time did much to popularize phonograph music with the men and women of the military services.

By the end of the war, Rock-Ola had readied for production a new remote control system to replace the former Dial-A-Tune. Dial-A-Tune had failed because of abuse by the public rather than any technical problems. Another interesting Rock-Ola development was the Carrousel Line-O-Selector. In a way, this seems to be somewhat of a misnomer, for the basket carrier is really in the Ferris wheel position, although the records are brought forward vertically for playing. Other features include a record lock mechanism and automatic volume control.

Introduction of the LP records in 1948, followed by the 45's early in 1949, resulted in chaos in the entire phono-graph industry. At first, the big question was how successful the 33⅓ rpm microgroove record would be. Then the problem became which of the two new types would survive. This hectic period became known as "the war of the speeds;" utmost confusion prevailed as the two record producing giants, Columbia and RCA, grappled for industry domination.

The 45-rpm disc introduced and licensed to others by RCA was then, as now, manufactured only in the seven-inch diameter. RCA also introduced at the same time a rapid action drop-type changer for these discs. These records had a large center hole and the changer had a large spindle of the same diameter through which the mechanism operated to change the records. Columbia countered by introducing a seven-inch 33⅓-rpm microgroove disc. Since it had only the conventional small hole in the center and a different speed, it could not be played on the speedy and efficient new RCA changer. Nor was there a record changer on the market that handled the new seven-inch Columbia discs satisfactorily.

The initial battle resulted in an expensive draw for both companies, especially RCA. After spending millions promoting the 45-rpm disc and running down the LP's, based on its own prior disastrous experience with them, RCA was forced to adopt the 33⅓-rpm microgroove disc, pioneered by Columbia for its longer classical selections. On the other hand, because of the obvious practicality of the RCA center spindle-operated, drop-type changer and the records designed for it, Columbia eventually had to adopt the 45-rpm disc for its popular and shorter selections. Within two years, authorities conceded that it was neither the LP nor the 45-, but the 78-rpm discs that would have to go.

Actually, the juke box industry had a great deal to do with the survival of the 45-rpm record, for its engineers readily saw the advantages of multiple selection from the new, smaller-diameter discs offering equal playing time. The large hole in the center also offered opportunities for better changer design for automatic coin-operation. Moreover, had the ten- and twelve-inch LP records vanquished the 45-rpm discs, it might have been the death knell of the juke box, for selectivity and frequent change of selections were proven to be requisites of successful coin-operation.

Other factors, such as permanent styli and the weights imposed upon the records, also interested the engineers. With the newer pickups and lighter tracking pressures upon the records, record wear would obviously be minimized. This in turn permitted the designers of coin-operated phonographs to provide for better high-frequency response than had ever before been practical. Earlier attempts at higher fidelity invariably had incurred the danger of inviting a high level of surface noise from certain records due to variations in the shellac discs, their abrasive content and the semipermanent styli previously employed.

As late as 1948, automatic coin machines had not been equipped with anything approaching permanence in styli. Except in radio and broadcast transcription service, diamond styli were practically unknown in the lateral disc industry. In this transitional period, Walco introduced a replaceable sapphire stylus for automatic coin phonographs. With the advent of the 45's in 1949, the dilemma was solved; standardization was possible at last. Today, an estimated 5,000 plays may be heard from a modern juke box record without audible distortion.

A brief survey of the situation existing in 1948 will indicate by contrast the marvelous progress made in the years since then. In 1948, Wurlitzer was fighting record wear by adopting the Zenith-developed Cobra pickup. In advertising this step to the trade, a chart was shown indicating a definite falling off of fidelity in from 50 to 300 plays with the old-type magnetic pickups. With the Cobra lightweight pickup, the

AMI, Incorporated, 200 selection phonograph, 1958.

AMI, Incorporated, 200 selection phonograph mechanism, 1958.

chart showed it possible to treble the number of satisfactory plays. Lighter pickups and more compliance were needed for technical improvement! Even before adoption of the 45's, introduction of lighter weight magnetic pickups of the variable reluctance type, and of improved crystal and ceramic cartridges, pointed out the way to conserve records and increase fidelity. Other companies soon adopted one or another of the lighter pickups. To illustrate how far the lateral disc industry had lagged behind the vertical in this respect, cylinder records as early as 1910 had rolled up a score unequalled today for number of plays! In *Variety*, October 11, 1952, an article by Jim Walsh stated that the probable longplay champion of all time was a U. S. Everlasting cylinder entitled "Peter Piper," a xylophone solo by Albert Benzler. Walsh said this record had been played on a machine in a Cleveland penny arcade for seven months, and by automatic count had been heard 40,444 times! This was a celluloid cylinder played by a sapphire stylus.

Postwar expansion proceeded at a breakneck pace. AMI (in 1946, the corporate title had been shortened to AMI Incorporated), Aireon, Mills, Packard, Wurlitzer, Seeburg and Rock-Ola found it necessary to conduct schools for training operators. Filben, a newcomer, introduced its first floor models, having previously manufactured mirror cabinet and hideaway units only. Another name before the public was Pantages Maestro Company of Hollywood, which attempted to revive the telephone talkback studio system. Aireon introduced the Coronet, also manufacturing wall boxes and hideaway units as well as remote speaker installations. Mills Industries, Inc., of Mills Violano fame, introduced the 20-record, 40-selection Constellation. Packard, which Homer E. Capehart now owned, introduced its Manhattan model, offering 24 selections. Rock-Ola's Magic-Glo was among the big sellers at this time. Seeburg's Wall-O-Matics also became familiar to the public through thousands of installations from coast to coast. A novel combination of television with the automatic phonograph was offered by the Telejuke Corporation, a sudsidiary of Speedway Products, Inc. This was built as one unit with joint amplifier and speaker, with a reflector-type TV screen at the top. It was provided with a coin chute and push-button selection. The H. C. Evans Company acquired the patents and equipment of the Mills phonograph in 1948; manufacturing began in 1949.

Automatic Musical Instrument Company had withdrawn from owning and operating instruments before the war, concluding that such equipment could be operated better by independent businessmen rather than by salaried employees. Following World War II, a new management was instituted, headed by John W. Haddock, a manufacturer experienced in the heavy machine industry. The corporate title of the company was also abbreviated to AMI Incorporated. Retaining the basic and time-tested AMI principle of transporting the record from storage to turntable, a completely new and improved automatic changer was developed, storing twenty records and providing forty selections. Despite the introduction of the 7-inch, 45-rpm disc, this company continued to produce a 78-rpm phonograph from 1946 to 1956. Thus, juke boxes were introduced into many countries before the 45-rpm records had been established internationally.

In 1951, a record changer to handle 45-rpm discs was introduced by AMI, in models providing a choice of 40, 80 or 120 selections. Another model with a capacity of 200 selections was introduced in 1955. The later type is more compact and substantially simpler in principle. For the "memory," a simple pin for each selection was used instead of the solenoid and mechanical finger action standard in all previous automatic selective changer designs. These postwar advances were made under the direction of Mr. H. H. Vanderzee, who had been brought into the organization by Mr. Haddock from the heavy ma-

Seeburg M100A Select-O-Matic phonograph, 1948. The first 100 selection automatic coin-phonograph (78-rpm discs).

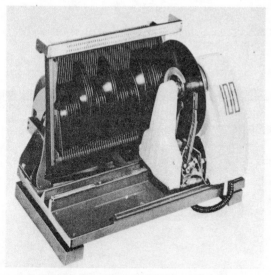

Seeburg Select-O-Matic M100A mechanism.

chinery field. From 1952 on, the engineering activities have been directed by Mr. George S. Brown, Jr. The names of Kenyon, Green, Andres, Vanderzee and Brown are prominent in the development of the automatic phonograph and are in large measure responsible for the strong patent position AMI enjoys. One of the later developments is a high-fidelity sound system utilizing the exponential horn principle, introduced in 1954.

In 1948, Seeburg installed its first SICM (Seeburg Industrial and Com-

Seeburg "SICM" (Seeburg Industrial Commercial Music system), 1948. System played 100 ten- or twelve-inch 78-rpm discs, both sides.

Seeburg Select-O-Matic Library Unit, 1957, 200 selections, 45-rpm discs.

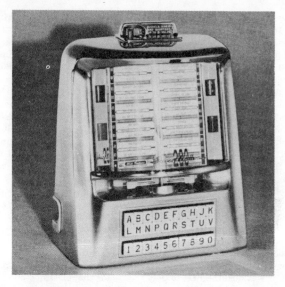

Seeburg 200 selection wall box, 1955.

Seeburg 200 Select-O-Matic, 1957, 200 selections.

mercial Music) system. It played 100 intermixed 10″ and 12″ 78-rpm records on both sides. This was the world's first 100-selection automatic phonograph and the first to store and play phonograph records vertically; the ideal position for automatic operation, as the records shed dust and abraded particles as they play. In this system, the "Select-O-Matic" mechanism runs horizontally along a track in front of the discs, pulling out and playing the desired selections. The SICM units were designed primarily to provide background music for banks, offices, factories, etc. Within a year, the Select-O-Matic mechanism was adapted for the Seeburg M100A, the coin industry's first 100-selection coin-operated phonograph; some were placed in locations in December, 1948. This was not only the first multiselection phonograph, it was also the first to play records vertically.

Ultimately, the multiselection phonograph had a profound effect on the industry. Prior to this time, the juke box had been looked upon primarily as a "hit tune" phonograph. Multiselection made it possible to program music appealing to a variety of tastes. Standard favorites, show tunes, jazz and semiclassics, as well as hit tunes, could be made available. It also came at a propitious time for Seeburg. In the postwar period, twelve manufacturers were turning out equipment at top speed; within a year or so, overproduction resulted. Eight of the twelve manufacturers went out of business in a short time. There was good reason for this. Although normally there are 400,000 to 500,000 locations in the United States suitable for coin-operated music equipment, only about 15% can produce enough income to justify the cost of a new phonograph every year or so. When new models are introduced, the operators customarily put them in the better locations and move the older ones down to the secondary locations. In 1948, the market was so glutted from overproduction, new equipment was being promotionally financed and put into secondary locations. As a result,

the equipment was not taking in enough money to justify the cost. Therefore, opportunity for increased revenue through broader programming came at an opportune time for those operators in a position to take advantage of it.

The Seeburg Select-O-Matic mechanism was a natural for the 45-rpm discs and the first of these was introduced in October, 1950; it also offered a choice of 100 selections. In August 1955, Seeburg brought out the first 200-selection Select-O-Matic with the following original features:

1. A new matrix memory system with no moving parts, utilizing small ferrite memory cores known as Toroids instead of the previous electromechanical solenoids.
2. A revolving drum program selector that classified and separated the 200 selections into five different categories of forty selections each.
3. A dual pricing system to enable profitable use of both 45-rpm singles and Extended Play (EP album) 45's.

The dual pricing system completed the opportunity for increased profit, enabling operators to offer longer-playing selections at a proportionately increased price.

The guiding genius of Seeburg progress during this period was Carl T. McKelvy, its top sales executive, assisted by an able engineering staff.

Wurlitzer automatic coin-phonographs employing 45-rpm records were also offered for the first time in 1950. This was done at a time when the "war of the speeds" had not yet been resolved; therefore, it became a factor in the decision. Succeeding Wurlitzer models offer a choice of 104 or 200 selections by means of a carrousel mechanism. Another feature is the new "Playrak" coin register, optionally equipped with a single-coin entry to accept nickels, dimes and quarters, or with double-coin entry to accept half dollars. These instruments were introduced in Wurlitzer's centennial year,

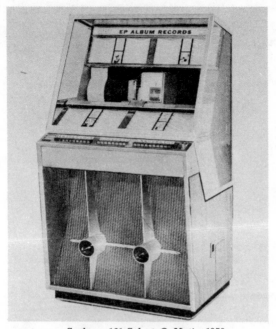

Seeburg 161 Select-O-Matic, 1958.

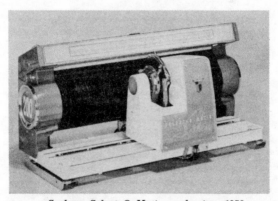

Seeburg Select-O-Matic mechanism, 1958.

1956. The following year, Wurlitzer also introduced half-dollar play wall boxes.

Rock-Ola was the first to reintroduce the revolving record carrier. It meets so well the needs of the 45-rpm discs that two other companies use it. Among patents in the portfolio of this company, the most recent and important is upon the revolving record drum.

To truly appreciate the high level of perfection and the amazing versatility of modern automatic phonographs, reflect on the long and tortuous path of progress since the first coin-operated

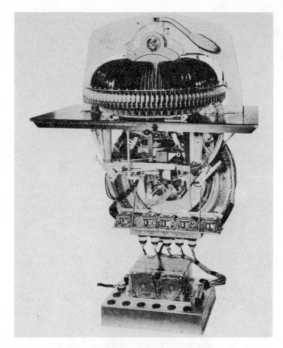

Wurlitzer 200 selection phonograph mechanism, 1958.

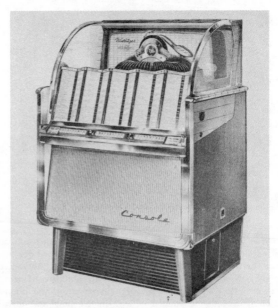

Wurlitzer 200 selection phonograph, 1958.

Rock-Ola, 50 selection phonograph, 1958.

Rock-Ola, 120 selection phonograph, 1958.

phonograph was put on location in the Palais Royal Saloon in San Francisco, November 23, 1889. The earliest era of the cylinder industry ended in the crash of the Lippincott empire, costing investors millions. Hundreds of other investors lost millions more in successive efforts to establish the coin-operated Multiphone and other immature devices. The present four manufacturers in the United States are the remainder of a dozen or more that sprang up before or after repeal.

The rise in popularity of the juke box coinciding with the repeal of the prohibition amendment has had a tendency to cloud the legitimacy of this industry in the minds of many otherwise fair-minded people. Some writers have taken advantage of this to write about alleged racketeering in the juke box business. What are the facts?

Today, the cost of equipment for an average installation is well over a thousand dollars. Increasing the number of selections from twenty, to forty, and finally from one hundred to two hundred, also means greater expenditures for records and a great deal more study of his patrons' tastes by the operator. One operator can only service so many locations; he must be a trained electronic expert and an engineer as well.

The organizations to which most operators and service technicians belong are committed to policies of legitimate competition as being in the interest of the thousands who make their livelihood in what has become a great industry. The operators have an organization, The Music Operators of America, of which Frederick M. Granger is national president and managing director. The production and service engineers, as well as the majority of electronics experts, also are generally members of technical societies. The manufacturers in the United States are represented by their own organization, the Automatic Phonograph Manufacturers Association, with headquarters in Evanston, Illinois.

Rock-Ola, 200 selection phonograph, 1958.

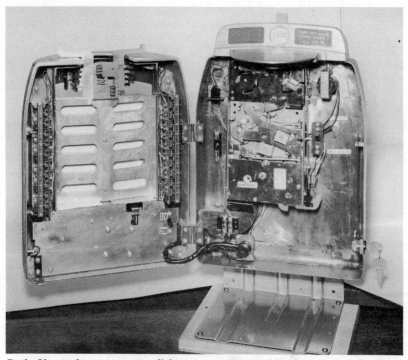

Rock-Ola single-coin entry wall box, interior view, 1957. Accepts nickels, dimes, quarters and half dollars, 120 selections.

In closing this chapter, another facet of the export situation should be mentioned. AMI Incorporated and others have licensed producers of automatic coin phonographs in England, France, Denmark, Mexico and other foreign countries. So far, these licensees have successfully met the competition that has sprung up in these countries. Among the foreign competitors not licensed by one or another of the American companies, Germany has several producing manufacturers, including Bergmann, Wiegandt and Tonomat. Wurlitzer also has juke box assembly plants in Germany and Mexico. Some larger distributors make a practice of taking in trade the older machines, reconditioning them for export. This is in itself a business grossing several million dollars annually.

Increasing the number of selections to 200 from a single compact mechanism, plus the longer playing time of the EP 7″ discs, has again made some of the products of this branch of industry a factor in the home phonograph market. For those more casual listeners who prefer semiclassical and popular music, it is perhaps the ideal type of record changing mechanism. Seeburg is already bidding for its share of the potential home market. It should be noted that the AMI mechanism automatically plays the 45-rpm album sets in the proper sequence.

A prospect thus far undeveloped lies in extending the capacity of modern automatic changers to handle conventional 12″ LP discs. One important future use may be the installation of automatic phonographs in libraries and educational institutions. Adaptations of remote control devices already in use would permit selecting a work of any length almost instantaneously. The present inefficient and costly methods inherent when using a library staff, and indiscriminate handling of record resources by users would be largely supplanted by automation. Irreplaceable and expensive records would be conserved, handled only on rare occasions by a trained technician. Accredited students would be permitted to transcribe excerpts on tape for study, under proper restrictions.

With great interest, the automatic phonograph industry observed the development of stereophonic sound. Within months after the adoption by the record producing industry of the Westrex system, the companies had ready for the market stereophonic instruments and complete sound systems. Engineered to the needs of special locations, the illusions were almost spectacular but in general stereo has not proven to be the attraction it promised to be. Costs of plays have gone much too high.

Not foreseen has been considerable opposition to "rock" music by many patrons and to the loudness and repetitiousness of much music of this type by others. Some locations are said to make provisions for a period of silence by deposit of an appropriate coin!

Perhaps these considerations may have had something to do with the decision of Wurlitzer to discontinue the manufacture of automatic coin phonographs in 1974.

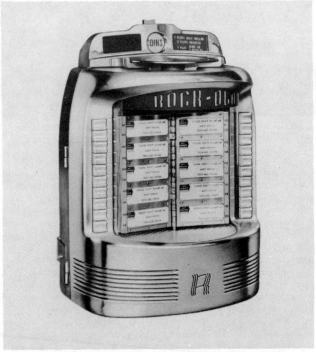

Rock-Ola single-coin entry wall box, 1957. Accepts nickels, dimes, quarters and half dollars, 120 selections.

CHAPTER 22

THE WAR OF THE SPEEDS

THE outbreak of hostilities in Europe in 1939 brought to a virtual stop the travel of artists from Europe to America and vice versa. The exportation of master records to America also was greatly diminished as recording activities in Europe became severely curtailed, especially of the great symphony organizations which had been depleted by calls to the various armed forces. This resulted in the isolation, musically speaking, of America, which was suddenly thrown upon its own immature resources. Victor, Columbia, and Decca, faced with this cutting off of the source of supply of the majority of their classical orchestral masters just as the demand for this type of recorded music was reaching new heights, competed in signing up the available American symphony orchestras for recording contracts.

As Robert Gelatt said some years later in the *Saturday Review of Recordings:*

"Around 1940 enforced musical isolation forced R. C. A. Victor and Columbia to place virtually every major symphony orchestra under contract, with the result that only too often a superlative European waxing of the 30's was cast aside to make room for a mediocre American product of the 40's."

This statement of Mr. Gelatt's clearly indicates the technical discrepancy between the average European recording and the American, as well as comparative musical proficiency. It was about this time that Decca began the recording of originals upon acetate blanks instead of wax. To begin with, as in many process changes, results were not uniformly good and this fact is clearly evident in many of the Decca American recordings of that period. Edward Wallerstein, new president of Columbia, also instituted the use of the acetate blanks, but with considerably better success. The principal reason for the use of the new process was economic—it was cheaper. Also, the acetate blanks could be played back with a light-weight pickup without ruining them, which was not always true of wax, thus facilitating the entire recording operation.

As the "cold war" in Europe suddenly exploded into fury, France crushed and England faced with invasion, supplies of many essential materials to the U. S. were completely shut off. Shellac, principal ingredient of records to this time, was processed from "lac" imported from India. To stretch the available supply, the older manufacturers ground up tons of slow moving records from factory and distributors' stocks, mixing the re-worked material with the virgin shellac. Eventually, all dealers were required to gather up old records from purchasers, paying two or three cents apiece for them in what were called "scrap drives."

Columbia, with its coarse center filler and laminated process, was in the best position to withstand the worst effects of this situation, for its supply of virgin shellac could be saved entirely for the surfaces, where most essential. Victor, Decca, and other manufacturers, however, using a homogenous mixture, were forced to use larger proportions of new material and so the playing quality of their records suffered. Surface noise to volume ratio was increased and pressings often failed to bring out the more delicate nuances present in the masters and the stampers. Quite understandably, this industry dependence on one strategic, imported material stimulated experiments with substitutes, particularly with the new synthetic resins and other plastics which were then being developed. About this time, Frank B. Walker, executive vice-president of RCA Victor, predicted that after the war there would be new materials used for records, such as Vinylite, but that the price would be perhaps double that of the standard shellac record. Walker also predicted the possibility of records with finer grooves. He said, however, that this was impractical at that time because of the predominance of heavy pickups then in use. He also pointed out that the existing automatic record players would not handle these lighter records. This prediction is of considerable interest in relation to the subsequent unfolding of events.

But now another event occurred to even more completely upset the industry. James Caesar Petrillo, czar of the American Federation of Musicians, knowing of the spot the recording companies were in for talent, delivered an ultimatum to the recording companies demanding an increase in recording fees and a royalty payment on every record produced. As the recording companies absolutely refused to entertain such a proposal, Petrillo ordered a 100% ban on all recording in August of 1942. The effects of the ban were not immediately noticed by the public, for the recording studios had been kept busy laying in a supply of recordings in every category

for which there was expected to be a demand, especially of the latest hit tunes. Releases of this more perishable material were held back and staggered so as to minimize the effects of the drouth. But the weeks lengthened into months and soon it became apparent to everyone that Petrillo held the whip and was prepared to outwait the leaders of the industry.

Nearly a year after the imposition of the ban, the U. S. Conciliation Service certified the dispute to the National War Labor Board, but Petrillo refused to recognize the latter as having any authority in the matter. Now, the hardhit smaller recording companies, seeing that there was no settlement in prospect, acceded to Petrillo's demands as the only alternative to going out of business. In September, the National War Labor Board issued a direct order to Petrillo to lift the ban on recording but he promptly refused to comply. The order of the War Labor Board was backed by President Roosevelt, but Petrillo remained adamant and refused to accede.

As recourse to the highest authorities had failed, the major companies now submitted to the principal demands, that involving the royalty arrangement. In accepting the terms dictated by Petrillo, Edward Wallerstein, president of the Columbia Recording Corporation sent a telegram to Judge Vinson, Office of Economic Stabilization, as follows:

"It is now more than sixteen months since July 5, 1943, when the United States Conciliation Service certified to the National War Labor Board the dispute between Mr. Petrillo and the recording companies. We have waited those sixteen months for action by one or more branches of the Government. We have waited sixteen months since the first hearing before the War Labor Board on July 9th; ten months since the end of the protracted hearings before the Panel appointed by the War Labor Board; eight months since the filing of the Opinion by the Panel recommending that the War Labor Board 'exercise its power to terminate the strike to the end that the conditions prevailing on July 31, 1942, be restored'; seven months since the argument before the War Labor Board on the confirmation of its Panel's Report; almost five months since the issuance by the War Labor Board of an Order directing Mr. Petrillo to lift his ban on recordings; three months since the issuance by the War Labor Board of an Order directing Mr. Petrillo to show cause why its previous Order had not been complied with and almost three months since the hearing on August 17th on the return of that order to show cause. We have waited more than two months and a half since the War Labor Board, apparently unable in any other way to enforce its order, certified the question to the President of the United States through your office and we have waited almost another six weeks since October 4th, when, as a result of your recommendation to the President, he requested Mr. Petrillo by telegram to end the strike. It is over a month since Mr. Petrillo replied to the President and refused to comply with his request. Despite that action by Mr. Petrillo which apparently disposed of Government action, we have waited another month since our telegram of October 12th to the President pointing out that the statement in his telegram to Mr. Petrillo that the strike did not affect the war effort was inconsistent with the repeated findings of the War Labor Board and its Panel as a result of which, on the following day, October 13th, the President at his press conference publicly stated that he would study the laws to determine what could be done to enforce the War Labor Board's Order. We have waited over three weeks since the Report on October 18th that the President had referred the matter back to you to investigate the laws and since our telegram to you of October 20th referring to the report that the matter was back in your hands and ending with the statement that unless you act quickly, we will be forced to accept Mr. Petrillo's terms. The economic pressures on us are such that we can wait no longer and must now either sign or go out of business. Since no action has been taken by the Government, we have today entered into a contract with Mr. Petrillo's union which will include provision for payments by us directly to the Union, the principle which we have resisted for more than 27 months, which we contested before Government bureaus for sixteen months and which, although successful in our contests, we are finally accepting because of the Government's unwillingness or incapacity to enforce its orders."

(Signed) Edward Wallerstein
President, Columbia
Recording Corp.

The settlement resulted in no increase to the musicians of recording fees, but the royalty payments to the union were used to set up a fund to be administered by a trustee for "organizing and arranging the presentation of personal performances by instrumental musicians on a regional basis." The manufacturers of records were required to pay into the fund a 1% royalty on records under $1., 1½% on records up to $1.25, and so on up to 2½% on those above $2. In justifying the position of the musicians' union and Mr. Petrillo, Milton Diamond, his counsel, stated that the estimated "take" of the industrialists from the juke boxes alone was somewhere around $250,000,000 per year. This is not presented as a brief for Mr. Petrillo, but only to indicate the extent of the stakes involved. On the total record business, it was estimated that payments into the union fund would be around $2,000,000 per year.

The passing of more than two years without any recording worthy of mention in the United States is, of course, a matter of major importance in the history of the development of the art. One major effect was to still further increase the disparity between the foreign accomplishments and the domestic, both in respect to content and technics. It should also be noted here that the fact that the major producers of records were able to hang together and maintain a unified position seems also to indicate that the competition between these major producers was more or less "in the family." It is probably true that there was some "bad blood" between the Rockefeller and the Morgan branches of the family, and there would be other family squabbles, but this threat from outside was another matter.

In any case, within hours after RCA Victor had also signed the settlement agreement, its New York studio was busily engaged in recording Vaughan Monroe in the "Trolley Song." This was particularly apropos, for considering that before the ban European recording had been technically about ten years in advance of American recording, the processes then employed were yet in the trolley-car period. But work had been going on in the laboratories and changes were being contemplated, without question. The March *American Record Guide* had an editorial on "Records and Reproduction — After the War," which was in some ways quite accurate in its prophesies. Editor Peter Hugh Reed predicted built-in styli, probably of harder metallic alloys, and the use of sapphire and diamond points. He also suggested the possibility of a trend towards custom-built combinations and higher fidelity in sound reproduction, all of which materialized.

Fortune for October 1946 contained a feature story on "Music for the Home," which disclosed how well or how poorly its own earlier predictions of an article of 1939 had been fulfilled. The title of the story was "Music for the Home" and the theme was the "golden" ear versus the "tin" ear. These terms were described as having originated in radio engineering circles, the first associated with those who like their music pure; and the others, perhaps in a great majority, who seem to prefer their music distorted.

The general background of the article was supplied by reference to certain radio industry conducted tests which were purported to prove that the public at large rejected high-fidelity music reproduction. By ostensibly deploring this allegedly proven fact, the article tended to rally support for the sponsors of high-priced, complicated radio combinations and custom-built equipment who were specializing in developing the prideful satisfactions that the readers of a class publication might have in reflecting on the lack of taste and discrimination of the masses.

The choice of "exhibit A," the person acclaimed by *Fortune* as one possessed, as described, of a "Golden Ear of the Richest Sheen," is of interest in assessing the motivations behind what was presented as a disinterested analysis. This person was described as follows:

"- - - he is one of that small band who have dedicated a good part of their lives to extending the range of reproduced sounds to the limits of human hearing. Merely reproducing the highs and lows to which most pre-war instruments are deaf will not satisfy Tom Kennedy or any other golden ear. A purist, he insists that the tones be noise-free and undistorted, sharp, clear, and full from treble to bass. The only damper his enthusiasm seems to know—so far not very effective—is the fact that when fidelity even approaches the degree achieved in his laboratory, the cost graph rises like a helicopter.

"Kennedy has gone to fantastic lengths. His receiver is well designed and, of course, has an FM circuit. His main amplifier was built at the Bell Telephone Laboratories. His speaker has three units. To forestall phonograph vibration, the motor is mounted separately, while a dental-machine belt carries the rotary motion to a turntable anchored in 600 pounds of sand. The pickup arm sports a featherlight sapphire needle, kept at even temperature and humidity in an airtight container until just before it is used. Kennedy makes his own superior recordings of broadcast music.

As a result, his parlor concerts are unsurpassed for fidelity. He has been accused of making a fetish of it, of listening to tone rather than to music. 'Listen!' he says, 'Compare music from my equipment with what the average combination gives. You'll go home and throw rocks at your set.'"

Reading between the lines, there is no doubt but that the effect of this article was to build up the market for the high-priced radio-phonographs and the makers of custom-built installations, which had been given its initial impetus by Homer Capehart and his deLuxe turnover record changer and super-dynamic speakers.

The article explains that there were many manufacturers of radio-phonographs whose standards were years behind practically attainable levels, which was undeniable, as it is today. But in illustrating the extensive, as well as ponderous, equipment of Mr. Kennedy, there was being built up the same "small-boy-grown-up" interest in things mechanical and electrical that may be found latent in magnates of commerce and industry, no less than in other men. This is often manifested in these men who can afford to indulge these propensities by their avidity for model railroads, expensive cameras, yachts, and custom-built cars. This then, represented a more or less full-fledged attempt to open a new luxury market. The Kennedy equipment was sufficient to prove that the best was costly, as true a maxim as ever, and sufficient to the discerning possessor of "golden ears" and the wherewithal, as well. High fidelity, talked about for years, was at last to be made available for those who would be willing, or able, to pay for it!

This business of exploiting the exploiter is highly stratified. That which is published in a dollar-a-copy, $10-a-year magazine is not going to have much, if any, effect upon the buying decisions of Mr. & Mrs. John Q. Public, but is quite likely to have some bearing on the attitudes of Mr. & Mrs. Hi

Tycoon. Thus, *Life* at the bottom, *Time* in the middle, and *Fortune* at the top were able to deal separately with different levels of the populace. *Fortune* did not reach the mass market—it was never intended to. It was not a proper medium, therefore, for the manufacturers of medium- and low-priced merchandise of widespread distribution. The answer is that at that time there were two powerful factors working towards the building of a restricted, high-price market for higher fidelity equipment. One of these factors was FM (frequency modulation) which increased the range of possible frequency coverage from a maximum of 10,000 cycles with AM, to 15,000 cps. Most often, amplitude-modulation stations broadcast considerably less than the 10,000 cps to avoid overlapping and interference between stations. The other factor was the high-fidelity phonograph trend, developed principally by radio experimenters who were not content with the commercial equipment generally supplied. Many of these in various localities began the production of custom-built units; however, the parts came from licensed manufacturers, and these sales had begun to assume interesting proportions.

Therefore, the higher the price for high fidelity, the higher the profits for the holders of the essential patents. The leaders of the industry, A. T. & T., the General Electric Co., Westinghouse, and RCA Records, completely assembled sets and parts; it was all the same. In the *Phonograph Monthly Review* of July 1931, A. J. Franck of the International Records Agency, record importer and dealer, said:

"Of course it is hard to impress an industry which is not much troubled with competition. I mean by that, according to my estimate, over 90% of all record sales accrue to the benefit of the same world-wide corporate family."

Actually, the idea that super-amplification and massive equipment was essential to high-quality electrical reproduction was being disproven in England even while the presses were printing the article. If anyone thinks for just a moment, he will realize the fallacy of the notion that the greater the number of times of amplification of the initial wave pattern, the more accurate the result. Just as in the magnification of a tiny portion of a negative, the greater the magnification, the more the picture is enlarged, the more distortion occurs. With a powerful, multi-tube amplifier, each successive stage of amplification changes to some slight degree the pattern being amplified. The need for great power with exceedingly weak incoming radio signals in modern radios operating without benefit of an outside antenna is understandable. It would be foolish to suggest that any improvement in quality arises from this necessity! It had been demonstrated by Maxfield and Harrison that the mechanical power produced by the standard 78-rpm, lateral-cut disc record was sufficient with even their rather elementary equipment to meet the volume needs of the average household without any additional amplification.

The English radio-gram designers, as they were called over there, proved this point because of the necessity of providing electric gramophones for a price conscious clientele, but which was at the same time somewhat discerning. Perhaps the *Fortune* article was right to the extent that the medium- and low-price buyers in America were not as critical as those of England. If so, then the attitude of the author was callous in not deploring the fact. Shortly after the *Fortune* article was published, the London Decca Company introduced a low-priced, portable record player which they called the Piccadilly. This was equipped with a new type, lightweight magnetic pickup with a sapphire stylus. The amplifier only employed three tubes, including the rectifier, and would reproduce a frequency range from 50 to 14,000 cps. With the new Decca FFRR records (full frequency range recordings), this light, inexpensive record player would outperform American

combinations costing ten times as much. Decca sent this together with some of its deluxe models, minus radios, to the New York salesrooms of its American affiliate, the London Gramophone Corp., with the plan of equipping them with American-built radios, as different bands of frequencies would be required than in England.

Experts who heard these new record players at the London Gramophone Corporation showrooms on West 22nd street were, almost without exception, of the opinion that these were the finest ever produced. There is little doubt that if they had been placed on the American market in quantity that the equilibrium of that market would have been upset. For some strange reason that has never been satisfactorily explained, it was found impossible to find American manufacturers to supply the radios and the plan of selling them in America was dropped. However, the records caught on in a big way. Even played on American equipment, the superior range and definition of the London Decca records was apparent, and sales zoomed from coast to coast. Considering the reaction of the record buying public to the FFRR records, which was almost immediate, and certainly spontaneous, as they were higher priced because of the import duty, what becomes of the "tin ear" concept of the American radio men?

It seems apparent that some deal must have been made to permit the importation of the London Decca records without interference, provided importation of the playing equipment was stopped. As Franck stated in 1931, there was no real competition. A portion of all record and equipment sales eventually went to the same top echelon corporations; therefore, it was expedient to deny Americans superior equipment at lower prices because they were willing to pay more for less efficient equipment.

There is definitely a great deal more to a qualified analysis of distortion in electrical recording and reproducing equipment than is told in the supposedly authoritative *Fortune* article. Some of these have been touched upon in previous chapters, such as the varying speed beneath the stylus, the cramping effect upon the stylus action towards the center of any laterally recorded record, and the inherent defects of the replaceable stylus. We have now added another frequent contributor to distortion, that of employing inordinately large amplifiers for the volume required. There is no denying that the output from these super-amplifiers was often smooth, full, and rich in breadth of tone; nevertheless, it often was far from accurate and fooled the listener by its very facility. All of the crispness and brilliant dissonant characteristics of certain instruments had been rounded off and the result was a syrupy lushness.

Meanwhile, RCA Victor's vice-president had seen his prediction of the postwar use of Vinylite confirmed, when his company issued "Till Eulenspiegel" on transparent, red Vinylite in October of 1946, at a premium price. Sample pressings were also circulated to Victor dealers everywhere for demonstration purposes. The policy was to make the Vinylite records available on an optional basis at a somewhat higher price in the classical series only. The next year the company began a new series of revivals of acoustic and early electrical records by the greater artists, also pressed on the red Vinylite, to be known as the "Heritage Series." The masters were processed with great care for this purpose, but the price of $3.50 failed to meet with the approval of the collectors. Also, some of the recordings selected were not too well chosen, according to authorities. Belatedly, the price was dropped to $2.50, but this was still considered too high. One commentator succinctly remarked, that because these recordings had presumably paid for themselves years ago, it would have been more in the nature of common sense to have offered them at a price below the regular Red Seal records, rather than above.

The relations between the collectors of cut-out records and the Victor company had for years been strained. Ever since the inception of the electrical-recording era, American collectors had been sending to England and getting records with superb surfaces by artists long out of the American catalogs, such as those of the great tenor, Francesco Tamagno, whereas excepting through privately arranged special releases through clubs, the old acoustic records and cut-out electrical recordings were almost entirely unavailable. The pre-electric arrangement whereby a special pressing of any record for which the master existed might be obtained had long been discontinued in America. Understandably, many collectors regarded the Heritage series as a hold-up and refused to buy at what they considered to be inflated prices.

The extension of recording into heretofore unexplored fields was being done mostly by the smaller companies. In 1947, Disc, one of the new companies, featured compositions of Hovhaness and Ceyr; Keynote, music of Stravinski and Vivaldi; Ultraphone issued excerpts of Alban Berg's Wozzeck. Inflation began to affect costs and Columbia raised the price of all records 25%. Victor raised the price of album sets, as the cost of paper products had increased greatly. The use of Vinylite and other plastic records increased. Sales of children's records zoomed as unbreakable records made this outlet a "natural."

Suddenly, with little advance notice to the trade, Columbia announced its new long-playing records, designated as "LP," in the spring of 1948. The player for these records was made to Columbia specifications by Philco Radio and Television Co. of Philadelphia, deep in the heart of the enemy territory. These new 33⅓-rpm records, pressed in black Vinylite, had been developed by Messrs. Goldmark and Backmann of the Columbia research staff. At first glance, these new LP's seemed but little different from those of the abortive RCA Victor attempt of 1931—which were also 33⅓ rpm and pressed in 10″ and 12″ diameters. However, the earlier

Victor long-playing record groove had a width a little less than that of the standard 78-rpm disc. This permitted a playing time of little more than double the standard disc of the same diameter. However, the Columbia LP disc had a groove considerably finer, which could be spaced from 190 to 225 to the inch, or double that of the standard disc, giving at the reduced speed three to four times the playing time. The 12″ Columbia LP would contain up to 20 minutes of music to a side, as against a maximum of about 10 minutes of the earlier Victor long-playing record. The Columbia microgroove was the first lateral-cut record designed for a permanent stylus only—this was essential if a smaller tip radius was to be employed.

The difference between success and failure developed upon that point—no pun intended. Tin-ears or not, the public had rejected the earlier Victor long-playing program transcriptions just because of this fact. The "highs" were not in them, and the sound became especially fuzzy toward the center of the discs. Edward Wallerstein, the president of Columbia, was with Victor at the time of the long-playing record fiasco. He stated to a friend later that he had been requested to do something about the dilemma—to either have something done to make these records satisfactory or to wind up the program. Wallerstein said that Fred Barton, an engineer, after considerable study, felt that the problem would be solved with a 1-mil groove. However, with the heavy pickups then in use and the unreliable replaceable styli, this was considered impractical; hence, the production of the Victor long-playing records was dropped.

That in 1948 Victor had been caught unawares by the announcement of the Columbia LP records, may be assumed by its still backward position in respect to needles. Semipermanent metallic alloy and jewelled styli were rapidly becoming standard equipment with many manufacturers by this time; yet, in the same issue of the *Saturday*

Review of Records, in which the first announcement of the Columbia LP records appeared, which were dependent on the employment of a permanent, precision stylus, Victor was still advertising its replaceable "new Multi-play needle." Moreover, within a month after the announcement, rumors began to be circulated in trade circles that a certain large company was about to issue a new disc and record-playing equipment, to have a turntable speed of 40 plus rpm, but that it was not to be a microgroove, as the Columbia groove had been called by its inventors. It is interesting to note that this rumor began to be circulated *after* a number of other recording companies had signified their intention to make use of Columbia's microgroove system under a licensing arrangement.

Irving Kolodin called attention of the record buying public to this "gossip," as he termed it, in the November 1948 *Saturday Review* and condemned in advance any possible infliction of yet another speed on the public. Very likely Kolodin had also heard the statement made that this new speed record player was in the nature of a reprisal, but he was eminently fair and if he was familiar with it he did not say so. However, an engineer on the Victor staff mentioned that an order had been given to produce any new type of record of good reproducing quality, as long as it had a different speed and was not interchangeable. He also stated that a record player was to be developed to go with it which would not play the Columbia or any other standard LP record. That this was probably true is indicated by the fact that this was precisely what the RCA Victor engineers produced.

In the February 1949 issue of the *Saturday Review,* the publishers gave free editorial space to an article by James W. Murray of RCA Victor to explain its position in respect to the disclosed intention of his company to produce 45 rpm records and a new type record player that would only play this type disc. Murray began by referring to

Kolodin's editorial to which we have already directed your attention, stating that he regretted that at the time, RCA Victor was not in a position to place before the writers of the *Saturday Review* (Kolodin and Canby) information which might have altered their conclusions. Murray then referred to the new 45-rpm system as "the first integrated program of record and player planning and design in the fifty-year history of the industry." Thus he started off his discussion with a profound mistatement, for there had been several. Included among those which would fit Mr. Murray's definition were the first Edison Home Phonograph and records, of 1896; the Columbia Concert Grand, of 1898; the Neophone, London, 1903; the Edison Diamond Disc Phonograph, 1913; the World Gramophone, 1923; and the Columbia LP of 1948. Murray stated that the articles in the *Saturday Review* had caused considerable discussion, that this might have a salutary effect in further emphasizing to record purchasers and dealers the importance of standardization in the industry. Standardization, he argued, could be approached from different viewpoints. He maintained that Victor was more desirous than any other manufacturer for standardization because RCA Victor was the only company producing both records and instruments. In attempting to justify this position, Murray stated that newspaper accounts had not done justice to the fact that an entirely new system of recording and reproduction had been demonstrated which was radically different from anything that had previously been in use and that this new system offered the greatest promise of future standardization for the entire industry.

Actually, considering the Columbia microgroove system as having been established, an analysis of the Victor 45-rpm system reveals nothing new except the speed and the record changing mechanism. The material of the record was the same, the 6 oz. pickup cartridge was virtually the same, the stylus was so nearly the same that they may be used on either Columbia LP or Victor 45, as the grooves were almost identical in cross section. Seven-inch diameter records had been made in the early days of the industry by the corporate ancestors of both companies. In fact, Columbia's predecessor, the American Graphophone Co. had made seven-inch discs with a large center hole years before for the Standard Talking Machine Co. of Chicago.

Knowing these facts, it will be of interest to record historians to note the reason which Mr. Murray gave for choosing the speed of 45 rpm. He said:

"The speed, for record and turntable, was 45 revolutions per minute, arrived at mathematically by using the quotient of 100 as the figure for an optimum, distortion-free record in which the maximum permissible intermodulation distortion figure did not exceed ten percent.

"By establishing a ratio between reproducing stylus, playing time which would equal or exceed the longest playing twelve-inch conventional record, and a record size which would be conveniently small for storage and handling, a turntable speed of 45 rpm emerged as the mathematical answer. At this speed engineers could guarantee five and one-third minutes of distortion-free performance, and the finest quality record in RCA Victor's history."

This explanation offered nothing new in respect to the requisites for producing "distortion-free" records. It does reveal, contrary to his statement, that this was "the first integrated program of record and player planning and design," that this new record was tied most definitely to the maximum playing time of the then existing 12″ Victor record. Mr. Murray also stated that the research project which had culminated in the 45-rpm system had been under way since 1939, which would have been about the same time that Wallerstein had left RCA Victor to become the president of Columbia Records, Inc. He also said that between 1942 and 1948, the new record player had become known to the research staff as "Madame X," and that both the machine and records had been subjected to continual test. He said that Victor had been in a position to introduce the revolutionary new system since 1946, but had not done so partly because of the shortage of Vinylite and partly by considerations involving the record-buying public, as well as the retail record dealer.

Several million dollars were spent by RCA Victor the first year to "put over" the 45's and every device in the book was used to persuade other record manufacturers to go along. The acceptance of the LP by other manufacturers had been almost 100%. Not all of the originally issued LP records by Columbia and other companies had been completely successful. However, comparisons of the LP's with the standard discs of the same performances as to reproduction quality, as published in the *Saturday Review,* revealed that for the most part, the LP's very quickly assumed a position of general superiority as to quieter playing surface, frequency range, and clarity. This being true, the magnitude of the RCA Victor efforts to achieve acceptance for its system which provided on the average no improvement in reproduction over the LP's and which by the statements of its representative was tied to the old conventional record in playing time, may be appreciated. Newspapers and record columnists in a variety of monthly and weekly publications discussed the "war of the speeds" and the public and the record dealers were generally viewed as being caught in the middle with everything to lose and nothing to gain.

In February of 1950, Victor issued the first LP's, which were immediately acclaimed for their excellent quality, even though by this demonstration the Victor engineers were upsetting its published criticism of the LP's of not so long before. Although this represented the first capitulation, the war of the giants continued. LP's spread to England in July of 1950, after what seems like a long delay for such a thoroughly proved improvement. The first of these were produced by Decca, whose American subsidiary had been among the first to embrace LP in America. There was some doubt with the first few issues as to whether the successful high fidelity of "FFRR" of the 78-rpm London Decca records was to be successfully transferred to LP's, but again, within a short time it was to be seen that these records would continue to challenge the best that could be produced on LP's, as they had been doing for a number of years on the standard discs.

In the early stages of the battle of the speeds, Columbia had issued a 7" LP disc for short play material, to meet the challenge of the 45. To illustrate that the bitterness continued even after the decision of Victor to produce LP's, as late as August of 1950, Columbia was still advertising "Originator of $33\frac{1}{3}$-rpm LP Records—One Speed is All You Need." But in February of 1951, the first 45's by Columbia were being issued. The denouement came in the almost simultaneous announcement of the retirement of Edward Wallerstein as president of Columbia Records, Inc.

It is obvious that the 45-rpm system did work out well, especially for short-duration selections; however, its introduction at the time worked incalculable mischief in the industry. The necessity of having recordings available in three forms also meant great hardship to dealers and the loss of thousands of important items which were not in sufficient demand to warrant rerecording in the new speeds.

CHAPTER 23

GROWTH OF THE COMPONENT SYSTEM

THE multimillion dollar high-fidelity component manufacturing business has been built up within a few short years from its basis in a minor hobby interest, involving comparatively few persons. Its foundation requires a bit of analysis to be understood, especially as many of the later proponents of "hi-fi" have come to consider it almost as a cult with many pseudo-scientific and esoteric connotations and who are quite likely to roundly denounce anyone so rash as to label it as a mere hobby movement. However, Webster defines a hobby as:

"A subject or plan to which one is constantly reverting in discourse, thought, or effort; a topic, theme, or the like (considered as) unduly occupying one's attention or interest."

The decision as to whether this properly applies to the usual "hi-fi" addict and his favorite subject will be left to the reader!

Actually, many persons of certain age groups came into their interest in what is now called "hi-fi" quite naturally, as a logical outgrowth of association with related activities and interests. Persons who tinkered with telegraphs and telephones in their boyhood days, or who were perhaps the wireless "hams" of a few years back, are particularly susceptible to the "hi-fi" virus. This is not to say that otherwise these persons are not normal, nor to imply that the pursuit of high fidelity is not a meritorious pastime. Certainly, it is not less worthwhile to try to secure the utmost in faithful results from phonograph records by experimenting with various types of equipment, than it is to try to get better photographs by trying various combinations of lenses, filters, and films. Photography as a hobby has left its infancy far behind. Many camera fans are now able to recognize the degree of their abnormality, but not enough time has elapsed for more than a few of our "hi-fi" addicts to gain such personal insight and perspective.

Anyone who prefers to put together carefully chosen components to suit his own ideas of what high-fidelity sound should be has every right to do so. However, he will enjoy the results of his efforts much more if he will relax and not expect every visitor to his home to agree with his conception of what proper sound reproduction should be. Those who can hark back to the satisfactions gained in putting together "peanut tube" sets and in logging the greatest distances in receptions will recognize that the greater pleasure came from the doing, rather than the boasting about the results. For these reasons, many of those who have given the most to the high-fidelity movement have also gotten much out of it. More than a few of the pioneer high-fidelity men graduated from wireless experimenting to the assembling of radio and amplifier kits, thence to the building of improved "sets" as they were then called, and finally to higher, fidelity phonographic reproduction.

The true beginning of the component system of parts especially designed for sale directly to the public and for assembly by the purchaser was in the radio kits offered by a few small mail-order houses in the 1920's. But it was not until the introduction of portable record-playing attachments around 1934 that the phonograph became involved. Victor inaugurated the "Victor Record Club," offering an electric motor-operated record player with a magnetic pickup at a very low price, in combination with a subscription plan by which the purchaser would agree to buy at least one record a month for a year. These record players could be coupled to almost any console radio of the time. As most records were still cut with approximately constant velocity, except for constant amplitude in the bass end, magnetic pickups would function reasonably well within the limited frequency limits of the recordings of the time, which had a maximum top range of from 6,000 to 8,000 cps. The radios varied greatly in quality of reproduction and the matching was obviously only approximate. The additive nature of a device to be attached to radios of varying characteristics in this way promoted questions as to possible improvements. Often, the results were so poor that remedial measures had to be taken, perhaps with the assistance of the local radio service man. The growth in sales of replacement parts to stores and radio service men led to the development of improved and more reliable parts, some of which became recognized "components" as time went on.

The early, mass-produced magnetic-pickup record players were not well engineered, with arms too short for proper tracking, noisy motors, and other difficulties too numerous to mention. The obvious lack provided an opportunity for manufacturers to make better record players. The introduction of the lighter weight piezoelectric pickup cartridge by Brush gave an added impetus to the movement back to rec-

ords. As the crystal had a high impedance, it required special provision for matching. Although low in cost in itself and much lighter in weight than the previous magnetic pickups, these advantages caused attention to be concentrated on the needs for better arms, greater compliance, and better design for alignment and tracking. The manufacturers of complete phonographs began almost immediately to use the new crystals as standard equipment, but the ball was now rolling—a growing number of inveterate experimenters were not to be denied and more and more separate record players, tone arms, cartridges, speakers, kits of radio tuners, amplifiers, and other parts began to appear on the market.

Further impetus was given to the trend back to the playing of records by a nationwide campaign organized in 1939 under the name of Publisher's Service Co., Inc., which involved the cooperation of a local newspaper in each community. A series of full-page ads was run in the cooperating newspaper with the details of the offer. To all who would agree to purchase all of the ten albums, one a week with a coupon from the paper, a record player with a crystal pickup would be sold for $3.00. Each album consisted of three or four twelve-inch symphonic recordings of the better known master composers, and sold for $2.99—a low price for that much music at that time. The records were processed by one of the larger manufacturers bearing the label "World's Greatest Music—Philharmonic Transcription." The name of the performing organization was not given, although obviously competent and well recorded. The label also carried the message "by arrangement with the sponsor of 'World's Greatest Music' presentation licensed by manufacturer only for non-commercial use in homes."

The use of crystal pickups often required special matching, especially as most records were now recorded with treble pre-emphasis. The distortion was particularly annoying when the record players were attached to the older sets which had been designed to receive the output of the earlier magnetic-type pickups. By now it was apparent to many record connoiseurs that greater flexibility was needed to play the records of various makes and periods of manufacture properly, and that the use of bass and treble controls alone did not suffice. With the gradual introduction of treble pre-emphasis to assist in suppressing surface noise and of constant amplitude in the bass end to prevent overcutting, each recording company had arrived at its own decisions as to where the crossover should be and the shape its recording curve should take. A period of absolute anarchy ensued as far as the characteristics of records were concerned. It is a little difficult to fathom why each of the engineers making these decisions should feel that he had a right to disregard what others in the industry were doing. However, when some manufacturers decided to keep the characteristic they were employing a trade secret, the situation became so ludicrous as to be fantastic. How could anyone know how to play the records assuredly to the best advantage without this information?

This was the situation technically when World War II came along. Many will remember the record scrap drives in which dealers allowed two or three cents apiece on every old disc turned in, so that the manufacturers might reclaim the shellac which was then in short supply. The training of thousands of young men in the fundamentals of electronics during the war by industry for the manufacture of radar and communication equipment, and by the armed forces for the installation, servicing, and operation of such equipment, resulted in a vast new group of young men who became aware of interesting possibilities. The development of compact, efficient record-changing mechanisms, before and during the war, accelerated the growing interest of the younger generation in the playing of records of any type. Men stationed in other countries, England in particular, were often amazed to see how much

further ahead in sound engineering some of the equipment developed abroad was over similar equipment then in general use in most of the commercial phonographs sold in the United States. Quite a few brought back with them components with which to make their own sound systems, or learned the names of superior brands of pickups, turntables, amplifiers, and speakers which they would import when they were available.

At the close of the war, many kinds of surplus amplifiers and other electronic gear were a further stimulus to both the new and older groups of experimenters. But, as a whole, the more firmly entrenched manufacturers of factory assembled radio-phonographs remained quite indifferent to the possibilities for improvement in fidelity. No less an authority than *Fortune,* a magazine devoted to industry and management, testified to this fact in October, 1946—two years after the close of the war. In an article entitled "Music for the Home," the thesis was outlined in a subheading as follows:

"What's what with the radio-phonograph combination . . . which sometimes approaches high fidelity, but more often does not. The industry's theme: the public isn't interested."

Two statements in the article were especially pertinent to the situation which the *Fortune* article so convincingly described,

". . . the quality of the instrument's music is often just not very good. Tones are weak or blurred or unintentionally strident. The bass booms like a juke-box, making an innocent string-bass section sound like a cave of the winds. The various elements of the music are far out of balance—hundreds of dollars of investment do not do very well by W. A. Mozart.

"The live question, therefore, is just how good such reproduced music is—and can be. The radio networks seem self-satisfied as usual. The record and radio-phonograph manufacturers are advertising their postwar products with a swoon of words. But if one thing in the whole field is certain, it is that large elements in the industries mentioned are getting very fancy prices for very inferior musical reproduction."

The article dealt with the problems of bass compensation and treble pre-emphasis, stating with respect to the latter:

"Because de-emphasizing units would add appreciably to the cost of the radio-phonograph, pre-emphasized records are used almost entirely for broadcasting."

Although this was true with respect to the relative amount of pre-emphasis then employed in most of the standard phonograph records made for home use, it was not true of others. The reference to "unintentionally strident" made by the author, as quoted in the foregoing, seems indicative of records made with considerable treble pre-emphasis as reproduced through a reasonably good phonograph of the time equipped with a magnetic pickup. Some records of the period beginning in 1938 had the treble so highly pre-emphasized that they were almost intolerable to listen to on any standard phonograph. This situation inevitably led to investigation on the part of many of the better informed record fans and resulted in much productive experimentation.

The writer of the *Fortune* article cited an example of this individualistic effort which formed the basis of the strong trend towards high fidelity by certain connoiseurs whom he labelled collectively as "golden ears." His example was Thomas R. Kennedy, Jr. of New York, who, in his private quest for higher fidelity, had put together a very complex combination of commercial components and laboratory apparatus, including special amplifiers built by the Bell Telephone Laboratories. In a caption under his photograph, Kennedy was described as possessing a "golden ear of the richest sheen." The antithesis of Kennedy in the eyes of the author was the majority of the radio-phonograph manufacturers, about whom he had this to say:

"On the other side of the argument are many radio-phonograph manufacturers, whose standards of fidelity are years behind practicable levels. They are known as 'tin ears' in high-fidelity circles. Their position is understandable enough—if not exactly admirable. They have heavy investments in plants, patents, and franchises. High fidelity threatens the value of many of these commitments. Cagily, they have moved out of the defensive position with an attack on what they term 'unreasonable' high fidelity. Their thesis is simple: the public neither wants nor likes wide-range reception or wide-range instruments."

Industry leaders were said to have justified their position that the public did not want high fidelity by pointing to surveys which had been made, in particular one which had been conducted by Howard A. Chinn and Philip Eisenberg of the Columbia Broadcasting System. In tests conducted by these men, audiences had chosen standard broadcasts (up to 5,000 cycles) over wide-range programs (up to 10,000 cycles) by more than two to one. Owners of FM sets, who were presumed to have been better conditioned to wide-range reproduction, surprisingly, rejected the wider range by more than four to one. Professional musicians, even more surprisingly, had voted fifteen to one against the wider ranges.

The writer for *Fortune* supplied his answer to this poll by the broadcasters in the fact which he presented that most listeners had become habituated to boomy bass, mellow treble, and lack of tonal clarity. While this seems pertinent to the general listeners, it is illogical when applied to the other groups, those of the FM set owners and the musicians. A better reason is probably to be found in a technical paper written by Louis A. DeRosa of the Federal Communications Laboratory of Nutley, N. J. in 1949 entitled "Distortion in Audio Systems." Mr. DeRosa ascribed the quite general lack of acceptance of wide-range sound reproduction to phase distortion, a factor which many engineers had thought unrecognizable to the human ear. This theory accounts very well for the contradictory results of the poll, as well as for the phenomenon described as "listener's fatigue." Eventually it was found necessary to employ amplifiers which had ranges greatly in excess of the actual hearing range in order to eliminate this difficulty.

The interest of Kennedy in high fidelity was perhaps not altogether typical of the subsurface revolt which was then brewing against the quality ceiling which had been imposed by the policies of the larger manufacturers, but it was symptomatic. As the authors disclosed with reference to Avery Fisher, there were some smaller manufacturers who did not subscribe to the apathy and contentment with lack of progress evidenced by the others. Another strong influence not mentioned was the competition for business on the part of smaller manufacturers who specialized in such parts as pickups, amplifiers, and speakers; or even in such smaller components as resistors, volume controls, etc. In their zeal, they were often forced to demonstrate the superiorities of equipment by assembling complete sound reproducing systems incorporating in them the requisite high-quality apparatus made by others. When the larger manufacturers refused to buy superior parts as a result of such demonstrations—which became frequent after the war, the answers were obvious. Consequently, many smaller manufacturers of improved components either went into the manufacture of more complete units, by acquiring licenses to manufacture other needed parts from other patent holders, or went into the business of selling directly to the public.

It has often been noted that wars tend to stimulate cultural and technical progress. World War I was at least partially responsible for the development of accurate sound measuring devices which later became important in the improvement of microphones used for broadcasting and recording. The end of that war found A. T. & T., the General Electric Co., Westinghouse, and the United Fruit Co. gathering up patent rights from private inventors, from the Alien Property Custodian, and others which eventually resulted in the organization of RCA and the initiation of commercial broadcasting. World War II had a similar effect, the science of electronics having been pushed ahead rapidly by unlimited expenditures by the government upon radar and other such devices. The principal corporate "loot" brought back from abroad in this war included magnetic tape, tape recorders, and microphones surpassing our previous best, and record processing improvements which indicated that even with the 78-rpm lateral disc, high fidelity was possible.

The ground swell which was eventually to overcome the apathy of the large manufacturers can also be partially attributed to the "war effort." Herbert Brean wrote an interesting article on this aspect which appeared in *Life,* June 15, 1953. Brean credited an Air Force communications sergeant, Irving Greene, with having started the "hi-fi" movement in at least one group of men while with the troops in New Guinea. Out of relatively primitive materials, Greene is said to have assembled a record playing outfit of such fine tonal qualities that many of his soldier friends were greatly impressed. Educated by Greene as to what could be extracted from records, the author stated that some of these later sought his assistance in converting to "hi-fi" some expensive commercial radio-phonographs which had been "liberated."

Among servicemen stationed throughout the world were a considerable number who were already record collectors. Many of these stationed in England or the continent were able to pick up records to add to their collections. Some were most surprised to learn of the superior surfaces and fidelity of many of the leading European records as compared with those then being sold in the United States. It became particularly noted that records processed in England from masters exported from the states were generally superior to those sold in the states.

However, this led almost immediately into increased importations of records and the realization on the part of certain English manufacturers that the American market was vulnerable. In fact, it was the export of large quantities of London Decca records to the United States and the establishment of a distributing organization in 1948 that finally brought the American record manufacturers to the realization that higher fidelity was not only salable, but was being demanded by a fair share of the American public. Within months, the frequency range of the recordings of most of the domestic companies was stepped up and improvements were introduced in processing and surfaces. The "Hi-fi Bandwagon" was at last on the way!

The introduction of the LP record by Columbia and others in 1948 may well have been a calculated maneuver to dispose of the threat of the European invasion, rather than just a logical step forward in the domestic competition for business. Perhaps it was recognized that with the greater dislocations which had afflicted the industry abroad, it would require a considerable time for the foreign companies to also get set to produce the new microgroove records. At any rate, this is precisely the way in which it worked out. To many listeners, the first LP's issued seemed not to have reproduction quality to warrant the full-scale effort which was put behind them. Some observers believe that the great success of the Columbia promotion was in inducing most of the smaller companies to agree to use the process which had been developed by Dr. Goldmark. Columbia experts processed most of the early releases by the smaller companies and it may be that this cooperative

effort was really responsible for the notable improvements which soon came about in both the cutting and the processing of these records. At any rate, connoiseurs who at first hearing had dismissed the Columbia microgroove record as another attempt which would probably be as abortive as the English "World" records of 1923, the Edison 40-minute discs of 1927, and the Victor long-playing "transcriptions" of 1931, soon found that they were compelled to listen to later issues with respect.

The successful promotion of the LP microgroove record by Columbia was also a notable achievement in that Columbia Records, Inc., was not a manufacturer of record playing equipment. For this reason, Philco made for Columbia the first $33\frac{1}{3}$-rpm turntable attachments with which to launch their sale to the public. Columbia freely furnished information to all of the several cooperating manufacturers who agreed to produce radio-phonographs and record players of their own for playing the new discs. This offered a new and golden opportunity for the various companies to develop and to introduce record players which would play both the new discs and the older 78-rpm records. Especially, this seemed a wonderful opportunity to the smaller manufacturers, for the largest one, RCA Victor, had said officially that it was going to have nothing to do with Columbia's LP. Within a short time, news leaked out that Victor was going to introduce a new record with yet another speed, 45 rpm, and would be offered to the industry on the same basis as had the Columbia LP.

Instead of stopping the successful promotion of the LP, the news seemed only to stimulate the eagerness of the inventors of record changers and record-playing equipment to produce units which would handle any or all proposed speeds, including the $16\frac{2}{3}$-rpm, talking-book records. Almost immediately the possibilities of designing new low-inertia, high-compliance cartridges for use with the new LP records became evident to a number of inventors.

Several types had been developed for use with broadcast transcriptions which could easily be adapted for use with LP's; however, some of these types, such as the moving-coil pickup, were expensive to manufacture. A G. E. engineer had developed an inexpensive moving-iron pickup, light in weight because of the use of Alnico magnets, but requiring the use of a preamplifier because of the low-voltage output. This was the variable-reluctance cartridge, and when redesigned for the new LP records, became the first large-selling special pickup component.

The willingness of some of the more enthusiastic adherents of the LP records and "hi-fi" to spend money soon led to the adaptation of even more difficult moving-coil type pickups to LP use by Pickering, Fairchild, and others, who thus found themselves in the high-fidelity business almost overnight. Maximilian Weil of the Audak Co. had been one of the pioneers in reproducer sound-box design as far back as the Orthophonic Victrola, and he now designed a highly compliant, tuned-ribbon pickup for use with the new records. Except for the crystal cartridges, nearly all pickups required preamplifiers. The better the cartridge, the more apparent was the need of preamplifier controls, in order to secure a proper matching with the characteristics of the various records. G. E. and others had supplied small one-tube preamplifiers, but the matching was approximate and did not allow through the usual tone controls sufficient flexibility to meet the increasing disparities in the characteristics of the various improved LP records, which were so rapidly coming into the market. Without a doubt, the perversity of human nature being what it is, the very difficulties which confronted converts in their pursuit of the elusive quality called high fidelity seemed to whet their appetites. To many, cost was no longer an insuperable obstacle, and it was this zeal for perfection which encouraged the development of special preamplifiers with elaborate and highly flexible controls.

As they were inexpensive, many manufacturers of pickups continued to develop the crystal type. Within a year or so, because of improved design and the need of replacing styli, replacement cartridges became an important item in sales. The use of sapphire and diamond styli became important to the record connoiseur, not only to the securing of higher fidelity, but as an essential to the preservation of his investment in records. The necessity of replacing sapphire and even diamond styli after a period led to the introduction of a variety of pickups of all types with replaceable styli. The earlier crystals had been of the Rochelle salt type. Brush later introduced the PN cartridge, utilizing a crystal of ammonium phosphate, which would withstand higher temperatures and humidity than the Rochelle salt type without impairment of its functions. One unusual pickup employed the FM principle (frequency modulation), in which capacitor plates mounted in close proximity would have the space between them altered by the stylus action. The varying capacity would in turn modulate the circuit of a miniature FM transmitter.

The strain-sensitive pickup, while a more recent development, is in theory related to the oldest type of pickup introduced back in the pre-electric recording period, utilizing the carbon grain principle of the telephone transmitter. The strain-sensitive pickup also used carbon as a variable resistance element, but in this case the carbon was coated over the strain member. Like its prototype, the carbon transmitter, this type of transducer generates no voltage, so requires a polarizing voltage source and a special preamplifier designed to provide complete compensation for the various recording characteristics.

Another unusual type of transducer is the "Cobra," designed by Zenith engineers. In this type, a round flat vane is attached to the top of the stylus with a small coil adjacent to the vane. The coil is connected to an oscillator so that the movement of the vane induces changes in the coil and oscillator, which are amplified in the usual manner.

RCA Victor had further accelerated the trend towards component sales when it introduced the 45-rpm record in 1949, with the companion rapid-drop changer. As Victor only reluctantly again began the manufacture of LP records in 1950, the feud between the leaders of the industry created golden opportunities for the independent inventors and the smaller manufacturers. Within a year or so, hundreds of new manufacturers of records, high-fidelity components, and subassembled or complete (package) units, came into existence. Numbers of tape recorders for both home and commercial use were put before the public and stereophonic sound became a frequent subject of discussion. Wire recorders had received a considerable play before and right after the war, but the limited frequency range and other difficulties had prevented any serious development except for utilitarian purposes where sound quality was not of major importance. Tape was a far different matter. German electronics experts had brought tape recording to a point of excellence, so that they had been enabled to substitute it for wax originals even before the close of the war. In 1948, tape recording was adopted as the standard initial step by all of the major American recording companies. At that time, however, professional tape equipment was exceedingly costly, and several years of development work was required before good tape decks with reasonably high-frequency response and dependability were offered to the public for moderate prices.

Perhaps the first serious attempt to introduce true multiple-channel stereophonic sound to the home record market was that by Emory Cook. The basis of his system was a record with two spiral grooves, one for each of two channels. One spiral groove was on the outer portion of the recorded area and the other on the inner half, next to the label. The corresponding point in the outer groove would always be in line with the same place in the performance on the inner groove. The radial distance between these corresponding points would also be always the same, so the playback could be managed (with some careful adjusting) by two pickups attached to the same arm. The output from each pickup would, of course, be fed into a separate amplifier and speaker system. Three-channel stereophonic systems were developed experimentally by others, and with the development of multiple-channel tape machines by Ampex for industrial purposes (automation), there seems to be no limit to the possibilities in this respect. It remained for English Decca, however, to first launch a type of stereophonic record which might conceivably have a considerable commercial potential. This involves the recording of two channels of sound in one record groove. This is done by modulating the groove from the spiral norm both laterally and vertically; in other words, by recording one signal in the now customary lateral movement and the other signal hill-and-dale, or up and down. In the playback, the pickup action is so arranged that the lateral movements of the stylus generate a current in one coil which is responsive only to such movements, and the vertical movements generate a current in another coil. This is very similar to the moving-coil pickup designed by Western Electric for playing both lateral and vertical transcriptions back in the 1930 period. In the United States, the dual-track, stereophonic tape systems, such as that of Ampex, had a considerable sale.

In retrospect, perhaps the greatest boom to the postwar development of high-fidelity equipment was the hassle over record speeds. Second in importance was the development of various kinds of exceedingly accurate test equipment. It was the latter which enabled the setting up of standards of performance for the various parts of electroacoustical systems, so that these components might be assembled with predictable quality of performance. Before the war and even for a time after, the quality standards of most manufacturers producing radio-phonographs had been very low. Perhaps one reason FM had made so little headway at the time when it logically should have gained the most (before TV) was because the barons of the industry were fully cognizant of the comparisons which would be made in the homes between record reproduction and FM, as well as between AM and FM! The understandable reluctance of the radio-phonograph manufacturers to install FM tuners in reasonably priced units also played a decisive part in the picture which in turn tended to delay the extension of FM broadcasting, which had remained virtually static for years, despite its universally conceded superiority to AM. This factor in the over-all situation without question delayed the recognition by the public of the advantages of wider range phonographic sound reproduction. When persons cannot make direct comparisons, they seldom realize just how deficient the quality of reproduction may be.

Inherent in manufacturing practice since the introduction of electrical recording and reproduction had been the expedient practice of balancing off the deficiencies of one part of the sound reproducing system against those of others. If the amplifier output had a peak in its output, a speaker would be used which had a dip in its curve in the same frequency area, or it might be taken care of by the design of the baffling enclosure or damping, etc. The altering of the characteristics of the records from constant velocity to constant amplitude under 500 cps, and the introduction of varying amounts of preemphasis at the other end of the spectrum were all consistent with a pattern of making compromises to get the best results through expedient means, some of which at times were quite at variance with accepted theory.   ·

It must be conceded that the empirical changes in recording characteristics, which were introduced to offset the inherent limitations of the lateral recording method, did provide the answers

to extending the frequency range and in reducing the surface noise problem to a reasonable minimum. The fallacy in the situation was that each recording company was going its own way in setting up what it considered to be the optimum curve. For a considerable period, it appeared that the leading companies were going to be adamant in adhering to their own standards. This narrow and reactionary policy would enable each manufacturer to build cheap compensatory devices in his phonographs so that his own records would sound best on these instruments which were provided with proper matching, but the records of other manufacturers could not be played quite so well. Delightful competition! The smaller independent manufacturer of phonographs who attempted to provide built-in compensation units to play all records equally well found it difficult to compete, as quality had to be cut elsewhere to meet a given price range. This situation naturally played into the hands of the component manufacturers, who did not need to concern themselves with the ultimate cost of a complete system, but could concentrate on the superiorities of their particular specialty.

Some of the pioneer companies had progressed from the manufacture of certain components, such as loudspeakers, to the manufacture of complete radio-phonographs, such as Magnavox. It has not been until comparatively recently, however, that one company has been able to successfully straddle both fields, that of component sales and the manufacture and sale of complete radio-phonographs. One reason lies in the fact that entirely different sales and distributing organizations have evolved for each field. An exception to this rule throughout the entire high-fidelity period has been the Fisher Radio Corporation. *Fortune* in 1946 had singled out Fisher as a notable exception to the general indifference of the manufacturers of complete radio-phonographs to the opportunities which existed for achieving high fidelity in commercial production. Fisher was also one of the first to make highly flexible preamplifier units for sale as a component to the public, so as to provide record connoisseurs with the ability to secure proper matching for any record.

Fisher's early success was attributed to precision engineering, handwork, rigid inspection, and extensive testing.

Another organization of special significance was the McIntosh Laboratories, of Binghamton, N.Y., which specialized in the manufacture of preamplifiers of professional quality for matching the curves of the various companies, both in the U.S. and abroad. These were made as input units for a line of high quality push-pull amplifiers. Research by the company's engineers produced charts by which the high fidelity enthusiast could accurately contour the curve from the record for optimum reproduction without guesswork.

The McIntosh organization is still functioning in the production of high-quality solid-state amplifiers and, in addition, manufacturers loudspeaker systems.

The anomaly in the situation is that it was largely in the laboratories of the large manufacturers in which most of the precision industrial electronic testing equipment had been developed. These included the Bell Telephone Laboratories, Westinghouse, General Electric, and RCA. It was the intelligent application of such testing equipment to commercial manufacturing procedures which made predictive results and the component system possible. It was not the larger companies, but the smaller independents, many of whom had their principal interests in but one specialty or component, such as Electro-Voice and University in speakers, Brush and Rothermel in piezo-electric devices, Pickering and Fairchild in studio pickups, and Garrard and Collaro in turntables and changers, which utilized to the greatest creative advantage the various kinds of marvelous testing equipment which had first come from the laboratories of the larger manufacturers.

On the recording side of the picture, it was also the smaller independents, many of which sprang into existence with the introduction of the LP, who soon initiated important improvements in recorded range and quality, notably Capitol and Westminster. The first high-fidelity test and demonstration records by these companies created a furor—soon everyone was in the act.

The ability of the specializing manufacturers to produce large quantities of components, which would deliver results within extremely close limits and at reasonable prices, not only made a tremendous business in selling by mail, through distributors, and through retail outlets, but also made possible the rejuvenation of the factory-assembly industry. High fidelity now is widely available in either complete package units or in the form of selected components. New international alignments of leading corporations in the electronic and recording fields have also produced some interesting changes in policies. The divorce of RCA Victor from its long-time ties with The Gramophone Co., Ltd., the latter a subsidiary of E. M. I., became responsible for the direct advertising of RCA Victor components to the English market. This is indeed carrying "coals to Newcastle" with a vengeance, for if any place is the birthplace of "high fidelity," it is England, home of the Williamson amplifier. Many of the finest high-fidelity components had been imported to America from England for years before RCA recognized the importance of the movement. In America, the names of Goodmans, Collaro, Garrard, Ferranti, Williamson, Briggs, Wharfedale, Tannoy, and Quad are at least as well known to most "hi-fi" enthusiasts as are those of Jensen, Zenith, Magnavox, and Rek-O-Kut. Germany, France, and Holland have also contributed to the progress in high-fidelity recording and reproduction. Holland is particularly noteworthy as the place of origin of Philips—now a world-wide organization ranking with RCA, Columbia, and E. M. I.

CHAPTER 24

RECORDING STANDARDS

SURPRISINGLY enough, in England (where it is now recognized that much of the best early period electrical recording of orchestras was being done), there was not nearly the same rapid trend towards all-electric reproduction in the years 1930 to 1940 as in America. As late as the spring of 1935, the editor of the *Gramophone*, Compton Mackenzie, had let loose a blast at the growing incursion of all-electric reproducing instruments, as follows:

"Of one thing only am I completely certain at this moment, which is that the really passionate devotee of the gramophone for a long time to come will get more pleasure out of his instrument if it is acoustical, and I am even going to add hand-wound, than if it is electrical. This is not a question of sour grapes. I challenge any reader who possesses the finest electrical gramophone to capture the spirit of the music as successfully as the owner of a Mark Xb, an Expert Senior or a Cascade."

These mentioned instruments were the leading acoustic reproducing instruments, equipped with open horns, but designed expressly for acoustical reproduction of the new electrical records. They were custom built, having reproducers especially attuned for the best possible reproduction of the types of records the purchaser preferred. In many cases, different reproducers were sup-

plied for reproducing different types of records, a situation quite analogous to the use of the different types of microphones for their varying requirements.

The development of these highly scientific acoustical reproducing instruments in England, plus the economic limitations imposed by the size of the country, average purchasing power, etc., resulted in a much more protracted period in which acoustical reproducing instruments were more predominant than in America. Then too, the "juke box" craze never hit England as it did the United States in the early '30's; so there was not the cultivation of a taste for the experience of the "booming" bass so common to early all-electric radiophonographs in America. This delay in England in adopting all-electric reproduction generally is reflected in the English recordings which were made during the 1930-40 period. The heavy predominance of acoustical reproducers in England and British trading areas meant that the manufacturers were forced to adhere to a tonal balance in recording. This was not true in America where, during the greater part of this period, most records were being reproduced electrically.

Mr. P. Wilson, technical expert for the *Gramophone*, took exception to his editor's askance attitude towards the oncoming electric gramophones. It is recorded that he said in his column of May 1935:

"Mr. Mackenzie has an uncanny knack of expressing right judgements in a provocative way, while at the same time being profoundly wrong in his reasons and his explanations."

In regard to the challenge thrown down to his readers by the editor, Mr. Wilson expressed his viewpoint as follows:

"The first question I ask myself is where can one find 'a really passionate devotee of the gramophone' nowadays. Although I have spent, and still spend, a large proportion of my leisure time in matters phonographic, I should hesitate to call myself a passionate devotee, and in point of fact most of my pleasure is obtained electrically. But I suppose the Editor would rule me out of court for that reason. I have, however, a large circle of friends who would not dream, as things are at present, of exchanging their large horn gramophones for an electric gramophone. Not one of them, however, would prefer a hand-wound to an electric motor and all would change over immediately to a radio-gramophone if they were satisfied that by that means they could retain that peculiar quality which Mr. Mackenzie so aptly terms 'the spirit of the music,' while gaining something of the flesh and blood and body.

"Whatever our views about the standard we should aim at in reproduction, there can be no two opinions on the question whether either method has achieved perfection. We may delude ourselves in our most expansive moments that 'really it is just the same as listening to the real thing,' but if we are honest, actively honest I mean, we know in our heart of hearts that our reproduction is not within measurable distance of producing the same sensation as massed strings, for example. We can get a very close approximation in the case of a few voices (but not a choir) and we can produce a most effective illusion to a person listening in the next room in

the case of chamber music. Even the piano is now very nearly conquered. But mass effects are quite another matter."

Here, Mr. Wilson discloses the chief difference in over-all quality of acoustic versus electrical reproduction as it was at that time. The electrical reproduction was more solid, convincing in the timbre of the middle and lower registers. Thus, even though the upper register was comparatively thin and weak, the floor shaking bass and sonorous breadth of the middle register gave a resounding conviction to the full orchestra that the relatively weak, unamplified energy of the acoustical instruments could not equal. On the other hand, the diffuse nature of dynamic speaker reproduction failed to afford that definition, clarity, and freedom from intrusive transients afforded by the best acoustic reproducing instruments. Mr. Wilson emphasized the basic nature of the technical conflict then going on, in the following words:

"I would gladly take up the Editor's challenge and introduce him to not one but quite a number of radio-gramophones which would give him the 'spirit of the music' in full measure, but I cannot do it in the Outer Hebrides. (The Editor's home.)

"Unfortunately, an answer of this sort does not dispose of the whole question. In my view, the precise terms of the challenge are not nearly so important as the feeling that lies behind them, and with this feeling I have very great sympathy. I do not like many of the radio-gramophones that are on the market today. I find it intolerable to listen to some of them even for half an hour, let alone to live with them for an extended period. The cult of the bass has been going on for some ten years now, and until recently things were going steadily from bad to worse. And in this connection I must remind the Editor that the 'Expert Committee' was almost alone at the beginning in their protests against the growing fashion. What in the world is the good of having bass if it is a boomy, or a plummy or a fluffy or a slushy bass? (I might well add, what is the use of having an extended treble if it is a keen, piercing, penetrating, ear-splitting noise; but that is another story.) The cause of good reproduction was set back for years when the quality of tone produced by some of the dumped American instruments became the rage over here. It is not unusual for British journalists to speak patronizingly, even sneeringly, of the standard of quality of American instruments. They would be better advised to turn their eyes inwards, for in almost every case the judgment is based on the fact that America found it possible to get enhanced prices over here for goods which were regarded as tenth-rate over there. I believe that our dealers have been mainly to blame for the cultivation of this lotus quality. Certainly, it was they who pressed on our manufacturers the necessity for producing instruments which would surpass these dumped Americans in soporific effect.

"Thank goodness that stage is about all over. I have abundant evidence, not merely from my connection with this magazine, but from several other sources as well, that there is a large and growing demand for electrical instruments with not merely less bass, but a different quality of bass; and with that spirit of the music, that delicacy and refinement which is a characteristic of the three mighty acoustical gramophones of which the Editor wrote.

"It can be done, and that without much trouble. The only difficulty is to persuade our salesmen that it will pay them to have it done, and to get our technical folk to disregard for a while their theories about response curves and such-like things. I am all for scientific method in these matters. But I must protest that it is the negation of scientific method to hypnotize oneself with theories based on

a priori assumptions, and to shut one's eyes to the evidence which shows these theories to be inadequate because the assumptions ignored important facts, sometimes deliberately in order to simplify the problem. "This worship of response curves is foul idolatry. The functions and limitations of such standards must be clearly recognized before real progress can be made."

Mr. Wilson scored heavily on this latter point. Response curves were, and still are a particular fetish of American engineers. Mr. Wilson then went on to tell of a lengthy argument which he had with a distinguished loudspeaker designer, in which he had attempted to point out to him the unreal, fruity quality of the bass. The designer's only defense was to point to the response curve as indicating that there could not possibly be any "plumminess" as alleged. Mr. Wilson completed his account of the episode, as follows:

"He seemed surprised when I insisted that the response curve did not tell the full story. My suggestion that in any case the method of taking a response curve of an instrument with a low decrement (or damping factor) by measuring the acoustic output picked up by a microphone from a note of continuously varying pitch was one which was open to grave suspicion, appeared to be new to him. Yet, it seems clear that a speaker of low decrement would give a smoother response curve by this method of measurement, than one in which each separate note is quickly damped out, while in actual reproduction it would have a smearing or blurring effect on the quality of tone."

Mr. Wilson also called attention to another factor commonly ignored in reproduction research, namely the variable tolerance of the human ear to different irregularities in a response curve. He said, "I greatly fear that in recent years an insidious form of what he calls romanticism has been taking hold of the Editor's mind."

However, certain other writings of Mr. Wilson seem to indicate that he also was afflicted with a romantic viewpoint of a rather different type. These expressions came about as a result of some opinions voiced by Mr. P. G. Hurst in this same issue of the *Gramophone*, from which the foregoing quotations were taken. Incidentally, the ideas of Mr. Hurst at that time seemed also to be in considerable conformity to those of the Editor. Hurst, conductor of *"Collectors' Corner,"* said that he had received a request to discuss relative merits of past and present singers and that he considered this a provocative subject. He said that in particular he had been asked to say whether in his opinion Galli-Curci was the Tetrazzini of today; whether Rethberg and Giannini were the equals of Destinn, and what he thought of Korjus and Rosa Ponselle. Hurst, in his columns, said that he disliked personal comparisons and felt that he was wise in avoiding them, and he pointed up another important factor tending towards the drawing of invidious comparisons in the following words:

"There is the further difficulty that reproduction has become so commercialized and standardized that it is not an easy matter even to recognize a singer's voice; and further, that the technique of the recording studio makes it possible for almost anybody who can give tongue, however crudely, to have his or her voice so dressed up with overtones and resonances as to produce the sort of noise that today is such a commercial success.

"In the old days there was the 'Exhibition' sound-box, and no other of any importance; so although the results were not comparable with the living voice, they were, at least, comparable with each other; and that was valuable. Consider the difference today; the microphone makes everything possible, and even after the laboratory workers have produced their synthetic 'stars,' we are faced with a very considerable choice of reproducing apparatus; so unless we keep our heads, we are in danger of falling victims to something which is merely meretricious and quite unmusical, which we, in our turn, may torture into a roar or strangle to a trickle, as taste may dictate. And then I am asked to compare this singer of thirty years ago with that singer of today! What singer of today? The robot, or the living?"

So the next month the busy Mr. Wilson found it necessary to take on his brother columnist, Mr. Hurst, in addition to his editor, Compton Mackenzie, as follows:

"When I unburdened my soul last month on the misdirection of ideas that has led to our present commercial standard of electrical reproduction, I hardly expected to be driven so soon to discourse on the same subject from a different point of view. The sad thing is not so much that a higher standard has not been achieved, as that it is difficult to persuade the powers that be that the public wants something different. They believe, and not without good reason, that the larger public have what Mr. Mackenzie would call 'romantic' tastes; that they like a resonant bass and a sugary middle register; and that above all they hate anything in the way of harsh sounds, whether these be characteristic of the original instruments or merely adventitious extras—surface noise, atmospherics, heterodyne, whistles, side-band splash and the rest.

"I was so disturbed, however, when I read some of the remarks in 'Collectors' Corner' last month that I felt I must try to make it clear that when Mr. Hurst departs from his historical discussions and wanders off into technical comments on the quality produced by different pieces of apparatus he invariably talks through his hat. . . .

"Like Jack Horner in his own little corner, Mr. Hurst may prate as long as he likes about his preferences amongst historic records. But to suggest that the recording of ancient days was in any way comparable to modern electrical recordings in the matter of faithfulness, freedom from distortion or, in short, of realism, is just sheer nonsense. The technique of the modern recording studio makes many things possible which were previously impossible; in particular, the 'dressing up of voices with overtones and resonances,' which was an inevitable feature of acoustic recording, can now largely be avoided. And it is!

"The microphone does *not* make everything possible, and laboratory workers do not produce 'synthetic stars.' If I may borrow a political phrase of yesterday, every time Mr. Hurst opens his mouth on technical matters he puts his foot into it.

"He apparently has an impression, and here I must admit some of the Editor's words have lent him support, that voices were recorded more faithfully by the acoustic method than by the microphone method. I have no hesitation in describing that view as a complete illusion. It may be that in some cases the very nervous tension of the older system, and the fact that many failures preceded a success in the final product, led, as the Editor has suggested, to better performances before the recording instrument. It may be also that the old vocal recording reproduced by a particular instrument, will appear more faithful than an electrical recording by the same singer reproduced on the same instrument. In the one case, attenuation in recording may be partly compensated by resonance in the reproducer, whereas that same resonance would completely mar a good electrical recording. Those of us who experimented extensively with the design and tuning of soundboxes in the old days, deliberately took advantage of this possibility and used different sound-boxes for different types of records. There is no doubt, however, that only one pickup, if it is a good one, is necessary for reproducing modern electrical recordings at their best. . . .

"Another example may be chosen from quite a different sphere of sound recording: the film 'One Night of Love': most people who saw that picture must have been impressed not only by the singing of Miss Grace Moore, but also the excellence of the sound recording generally. It is not generally known, however, that the sound was recorded on disc records dubbed on to the film. The recording was hill-and-dale and some people have attributed the excellence to that fact. I am told, however, that the experts themselves hold the view that the main reason for the success was that the sound recording was done in a studio properly designed from an acoustic point of view, rather than being dependent on the chances of a film studio.

"I do not propose, on this occasion, to enter into any long discussion on the so-called 'over-amplification of voices' in recording, about which so much has been said. And this for a very good reason; I have never been able to find out exactly what is meant by the term. I have taken many records that have been pronounced to be faulty in this respect, played them through, both privately and to my friends, and have found no cause for complaint. My reproduction, mind you, has been electrical under which a better balance between singer and accompaniment is secured and volume can be satisfactorily adjusted. The same records reproduced acoustically have shown a lack of balance, but that could hardly be said to be the fault of the records. I am still awaiting conviction that 'over-amplification of voices' is anything more than an incidental feature of some particular reproducing systems: usually the inability of an acoustic reproducer to portray the energy content of the bass notes in an orchestra, or the failure of most electrical reproducers to exhibit definition in the bass as well as fundamental energy."

The reader will probably sense the temperature aroused in Mr. Wilson by Mr. Hurst's remarks. Let it be said here that Mr. Hurst's views on this particular subject have been found applicable right up to the present, including the LP's which were not on the market at the time he made the comments to which Mr. Wilson took exception. In evidence, let us refer to a review given by Editor Irving Kolodin in the *Saturday Review of Recordings* in June 1951, quoted as follows:

"As most everyone knows, M-G-M is offering a film called 'The Great Caruso,' in which Mario Lanza, Philadelphia-born tenor, is impersonating as much of Caruso as the film ventures. The question naturally arises: Will anyone ever make a film called 'The Great Lanza'? To judge from this sampling of his talents, the nays have it. "Lanza's normally robust and fine-textured voice has been tricked up by every device known to the acoustic trade—open, echoey hall, built-up volume level, uncommonly close microphoning—to make him more Caruso-like. What has been overlooked, however, is the matter of giving the young man a grounding in the style which Caruso eventually learned from Toscanini (for Verdi), from Puccini (for Puccini), and even from some respected coaches in New York for his great Eleazar in 'La Juive.' What we have in Lanza is a free-swinging, high-balling warbler who telegraphs all his punches and depends on the knock-em-dead technique for all his effects. "Under some circumstances he might have come along to serious consideration—his high C could really blow out the gas, to recall a comparison of earlier days—but he seems destined for a glorious splurge of fame, fortune and forgetting. I shed no tears for Lanza, but the memory of Caruso—and his art—deserves better. It's hardly possible to turn down the record to a point of ordinary audibility, which makes it fine for tracing down rattles in a speaker, anyway."

In reviewing an LP rerecording of an early acoustic disc, Aida Favia-Artsay said in *Hobbies* for June, 1958 with respect to the French tenor Escalais:

"While listening to ODX 145, one can't help wondering about what sort of metamorphosis this colossus of a voice would undergo in the electrical recording process, with its controls and boosting gadgets. Somehow, a feeling of gratitude then comes over for the impossibility of changing the voice or its individuality on early records."

One of the things that the "more passionate devotees of the gramophone" had found so enjoyable about the acoustic reproducing instrument was its utmost dependability. Every time a favorite voice was reproduced it sounded the same. It must be recognized in this connection that Compton Mackenzie and P. G. Hurst knew their artists as well as their records, as well does Irving Kolodin and Aida Favia-Artsay.

In the later years of electrical recording, it became quite generally realized that violence could be done to the finer nuances and especially to pianissimo by the alteration of volume alone, whether in recording or in reproducing. This, Mr. Wilson seems to deny. During the latter half of the acoustic period there were quite successful attempts to record softly. Among examples which will be remembered by the greater number of record collectors are the German Odeon recordings by Dajos Bela and his orchestra, in which admirable balance was achieved, including capture of some of the finest gradations of orchestral subtlety. Despite surface noise, many early German recordings of Lieder exhibit this same striving to secure accurate reflection of true mezzo-voice quality and timbre.

Many of the acoustically recorded accompaniments of HMV and other continental companies also began to reflect a true tonal balance and lack of forcing that was more or less characteristic of the earlier period. In the United States, the Edison Diamond Disc records very early demonstrated that acoustical recording could be amazingly effective in re-creating the composer's intent in the mood appropriate by means of smooth, low-volume recording. Many of the Edison records of instrumental and vocal quartets and salon music ensembles were played and reproduced under controlled conditions now unknown to the industry, adding immeasurably to their enjoyment. The realism of the Edison records was attested to by the side-by-side comparison tests often offered. What was not realized by the critics of the electrical period is that unlimited manipulation of the characteristics of the recording, whether in the recording or in the reproducing, destroys not only reality but the subtleties as well. Even despite the technical backwardness of the Victor Co., Paul Whiteman in 1919 precipitated a major revolution in its recording technics when he proceeded to play "jazz" in a suave, relaxed fashion instead of in the unrestrained, furious manner always theretofore considered necessary to secure a good "cutting." It was Whiteman's example which resulted in the later Victor Salon Orchestra, directed by Nathaniel Shilkret, which was a direct effort to capitalize on this new found propensity for recording the finer nuances and subtle effects in contrast.

It was found by many collectors of the acoustic period that these products of the conscientious efforts of many of the early recording experts could have their effectiveness heightened by the employment of the right sound-boxes and certain needles. Oftentimes the very defects introduced by the relative deafness of the acoustic medium seemed to contribute a mystical and ephemeral quality to the reproduction comparable perhaps to the blurred, unreal, out-of-focus quality of many art photographs. That this element is romantic is undeniable, yet it resulted from the searching for the more elusive and intangible qualities of musical performance of whatever type in which the true spirit of the music is to be found.

That these qualities had been quite lost in early electrical gramophone recording was indicated quite clearly by Cedric Wallis in his article entitled "The Future of Recorded Romanticism." The sum total of these facts should bring both the romantics and the realists to understand that the desires of both schools of thought are to a great extent dependent upon the establishment of certain standards of reproduction, upon which proper attention should have been directed long ago. It is true that the realist is more generally of the group primarily concerned with high fidelity, watts of undistorted output, and secondarily concerned with the subtleties lost through indiscriminate use of the volume control. It is also true that the romanticist is more concerned with the obtaining of a mood, and with the maintenance of certain more or less intangible and indescribable qualities. Therefore, he is the one who insists on predictivity and reliability. He is the one who wishes always to be assured of that which he has tasted and found good, whether it be real or a chance illusion smacking of unreality.

The point which has thus far eluded the protagonists of both groups is that there can be no absolute reality without recording *and matching reproduction standards* any more than there can be predictive realization of illusive effects, without recording standards. The needs at both extremes of the continuum along which all of us gravitate in our changing tastes and moods can only be fully met by the provision of standards. What progress has been made towards this unknown but essential objective?

In England,[1] lateral electrical recording methods were stabilized to a considerable extent by the lengthened period,

---

[1] *Gramophone,* March, 1936, p. 385.

during which the preponderance of all records produced were being reproduced acoustically. The early use in England of "tweeter" speakers in the 1930's by the treble-conscious experimenters and engineers was a direct result. By such means, it was made possible, to some extent, to enjoy the extension of the fundamental bass range afforded by the electrical reproducers and dynamic speakers, and at the same time retain and to extend the upper register. Even in "tin-ear" America, there was eventually a revolt against the "boomy" bass and a considerable interest in "higher fidelity." Nevertheless, there now has been agreed upon by the industry a standard of recorded characteristics which would permit the designing of "ideal" reproducing instruments. Without such standards being unequivocally set by even any one manufacturer for the reproduction of its own records, the criticisms and comparisons made by record critics are diminished greatly in value, in some cases made meaningless. Very seldom, a critic will qualify a review of a particular group of recordings by stating the kind of equipment which he is using.

C. G. Burke writing for the *Saturday Review of Recordings,* July 1950, without particular intent to do so, painted a word picture of the anomalous situation in a humorous story entitled "The Dethronement of Queene Anne." In the opening paragraph he says:

"When two hearers disagree about the technical qualities of a recording familiar to both—and they do very often—the difference may be caused by unequal human perceptions, temperaments, or experiences, but it is more probably the result of the incompatibility of two phonographs. If the disputants exchanged instruments it is quite likely that they would swap opinions too. Human perceptions vary but machines vary more, and both are also mutable. Only the record, before age or injury subdues it, is changeless and complete at its birth. A record is engraved with a complexity of sound

and no phonograph available to us now can coax from the grooves all their latent complexities exactly as they were received there. The best records sound magnificent but they would sound better if we had better instruments on which to play them. A residue of silent sound lies in every disc. When the reproducing apparatus is of the best the residue is comparatively small; when the apparatus is poor the residue can exceed the output."

Burke points out that some listeners are content with very inadequate reproduction from obsolete portable phonographs, while others are dissatisfied with the finest, custom-built equipment. He says that between these two extremes are the great majority of phonophiles with countless gradations in taste and sensitivity to distortions. Constantly, the majority in between is being augmented with recruits brought in from the portable substratum and losing graduates to the cult of so-called high fidelity. As Burke states it:

"The last, by the unwavering fanaticism of their demands and the influence a learned clamor can exert, affect imposingly the course of recording policy. They want exact realism. They want the continuous splendor of the Boston Symphony Orchestra audibly present in their living rooms, indistinguishable from the orchestra in Symphony Hall, without the loss of a single overtone from cymbal or triangle. The great improvements of the last few years—ffrr and microgroove—stimulate a fiercer hunger for glories newer still. They are inescapably and forever damned, a perfectionist elite in sight of and approaching a culmination that can never be quite attained.

"Once their zeal has infected others previously contented with the placid issuance of a gentle musical entertainment from a comfy, reassuring phonograph incapable of parading the dazzle of the new records, the neophytes undergo the breathless excitement of discovery and revelation, renewed and renewed again as equipment is discarded and replaced by more elaborate or more accurate components. New values of reproduction are sought and eventually found, bit by bit, after disappointment, exasperation and expense. The original germ of discontent, cultivated, will produce progressively improved blooms, each bearing fertile seeds of untoward dissatisfaction.

"The typical convert to the dogma of perfectionism begins in discontent, with little valid information and dubious assistance. He has a box (not improbably mounted on Queen Anne legs) which, through the magic of an electric current, emits music. Once complacent about the quality of the issuing sound, he has despised it since hearing an enviably richer complexity burst forth from a box owned by a friend. The friend's box (bleached modern) cost $800, his own $250, so the audible return is honestly proportionate. But knowledge of this does not stifle dissatisfaction. At a phonograph shop he is told what he already knows, that equality with his friend can be had for $800."

Burke continues on with his humorous presentation to show that the more one wishes to spend on special equipment to secure maximum fidelity, the more he may. His imaginary convert to the "dogma of perfectionism," as he terms it, makes a call at a radio supply store and hears for the first time, but not the last, a "promising patter of decibels, cycles per second, the audible spectrum, response curves," and the like.

After initial investments in a pair of variable-reluctance pickups and a preamplifier to replace his older crystals and bring his "Queene Anne" up to date, he is satisfied for a few weeks. Then he begins to note the shrillness of the violins on LP's, which he later corrects by adding an equalizer to the circuit. This reduced the treble scream and refined the bass; however, this directed his attention to the deficiencies of the speaker, which of course had to be replaced. The extended range thus obtained in turn revealed by the thud and wow that the turntable was uneven—also that the sapphire styli now showing signs of wear produced distortions inaudible in the older speaker. So now Mr. Burke's high-fidelity convert bought new pickups, a turntable, and a new amplifier. This combination of more ideal equipment revealed that the speaker recently purchased was not delivering all that it should. So, another was purchased with separate high- and low-frequency drivers, directional horn, six-pound magnet, infinite baffle, and absorbent packing. Since inferior preamplifiers can be injurious to the quality of sound, he purchased a new and better one. He then found that a single-radius point would not deliver satisfactory results for all records so he supplemented his .003 diamond point with others of .0025 and .0027, also .002 and .0022, each mounted on cartridges of the variable-reluctance type. He also purchased an oscillograph to study the results obtained from each.

As if this were not enough, he had also discovered the stereophonic possibilities from the use of multiple speakers at different distances and heights, so he purchased others. At a cost of about $2,000, Mr. Burke's imaginary neophyte (whom the editor infers is Mr. Burke) has himself about as fine a phonograph as he could put together, outside of a professional laboratory. Mr. Burke concluded his story with two paragraphs, as follows:

"Expert guidance would have deprived the former neophyte of a succession of triumphs but would have saved for him nearly two-thirds of his expense. There are many audio experts and there are many audio quacks. Music lovers should entrust a high-fidelity project only to audio men with distinguished credentials.

"A basic manual explaining the principles and functions of high-fidelity reproduction of sound, with the technical jargon thoroughly glossed and tabulated, would obviate the costly empiricism of retarded correction and personal discovery. It is curious that a fundamental manual, focused brightly and exclusively on the constructional aspects of the finest reproduction of music from records does not exist. It would help." [2]

Elsewhere in this work, the *Fortune* story of a similar person, but an engineer with ears of "Golden sheen," is given. What is the truth about this elusive and costly high fidelity? Will a high-fidelity amplifier increase the maximum spacing of 10,000 modules per second toward the center of an LP disc, or equalize the different degrees of dynamic range from different recordings? Will unlimited expenditures for equipment enable any purchaser to know that the records he is playing will withstand comparison with the artist or artists? The answer is obvious. The next question which involves high fidelity, but which is far from the whole story, is whether or not, in respect to precision in reproduction, are we moving forward or backward? In this connection David Hall wrote in his "Records" in 1950:

"Since 1948 the record picture here in America has undergone the most drastic and far-reaching change in its history, the result being that the non-breakable fine-groove 33⅓-RPM long playing and 45-RPM 7-inch discs are rapidly taking the place of 78-RPM shellac records as a medium for recorded sound."

However, Mr. Hall stated unequivocally that in terms of absolute sound quality the 33⅓ long-playing record does not and could not bring to the listener the 30 to 14,000 cycles per second frequency range or 50 decibel dynamic range offered by the best 78-rpm discs.[3] The

limitation on the LP record with respect to range is that with 33⅓-rpm, the record is turning a bit faster than one revolution in two seconds, which means that at the inner grooves which have a diameter of about 4½ inches there has to be 10,000 back and forth undulations in the 9 inches of travel per second to produce a note of that frequency, which is therefore limited by the diameter of the tip of the stylus. Hall also said:

"At any rate, the year 1950 will almost surely decide whether the 45-RPM disc and its associated playing mechanism are merely 'an improvement on the obsolete' or whether it has real advantages to offer over the more cumbersome and more costly 78-RPM shellac and plastic discs, as well as over the 10- and 12-inch 33⅓-RPM discs with their preselected repertoire. The same applies in some degree to the Columbia 7-inch 33⅓-RPM disc. I myself feel very strongly that the production and sale of three record types is wasteful and uneconomical for both the industry and the buying public. Present indications seem to be that the 45-RPM disc will serve best in the popular music category and in purchasing cost, weight, durability, and ease of storage; one could scarcely ask for anything better, especially when used in conjunction with the Victor changer mechanism, which is of excellent quality and a buy comparable to the newer-type Columbia 33⅓-RPM record-player."

Hall had earlier stated that 78-rpm turntables and record changers formed the major current market for records, and that the range of reproduction for the fine-groove records was limited to 10,000 cps, whereas the best 78's would deliver up to 14,000 cps. At any rate, it is directly opposed to that of *Saturday Review of Recordings* editor, Irving Kolodin, who had opposed the introduction of the third speed, 45-rpm, most heartily.

However, David Hall brings up some other challenging information. He states

---

[2] Since, such a manual has been written, *The Recording and Reproduction of Sound* by Oliver Read—Howard W. Sams, Inc., Indianapolis, 1952.

[3] The introduction of the ½ mil. radius stylus is directed at this problem.

that, in his opinion, there is need of overhauling the "jerrybuilt" price structure of the 33⅓-rpm discs. He recommended a sale price based on 5-minute time segments. He stated that average savings in buying LP's over the standard album sets were 25%. Illustrating the new economies in cost and space, Hall said:

"Recorded music that at current prices would cost about $130 on 78-RPM shellac records and occupy 15 inches of shelf space, costs about $97 in the 33-RPM format, taking only 3½ inches of shelf space. The equivalent repertoire on 45-RPM discs would total to approximately $102 and occupy 10 inches of shelf space."

The 45's, however, did sell by the millions and pop tunes poured from juke boxes in every town and hamlet.

The musical historians' Eldorado had been pushed farther away by the necessity of maintaining production in three speeds. The specter of unavailability of by far the greater number of recordings of all periods and types looms greater than ever before. The need of record merchants to spread their inventory over three current types of records meant that at a time when the number of companies and the number of different recordings issued approach all-time highs, that the freedom of choice in any one store was about a third what it was before the LP's and 45's appeared. But more than this, over a period of more than fifty years of recording by the lateral method, several hundred recording companies have come and gone. Many of the masters of these companies have been wantonly destroyed, others lie moldering in the vaults of various and sundry successors.

Collectors' clubs and private initiative have resulted in the recording onto standard discs and LP's of a comparatively few of the millions of these now commercially unavailable discs and cylinders of other days. The possibility of many of the remainder ever again being made available is remote under the existing conditions of the industry.

A somewhat analagous situation exists in the book publishing, periodical, and library fields. Here the exponentially expanding volume of material is said to make it necessary to double the size of university libraries every ten years. However, many large libraries have found it possible to keep down inordinate and costly expansion of physical facilities by utilizing a modern invention, namely the microfilm. In this way, space consuming files of newspapers, weekly and monthly periodicals can be reduced to an unbelievably compact minimum. Not only this, but much material too rare and fragile to be entrusted to student handling, such as rare books and manuscripts, may be microfilmed and made available most completely.

The demand for similar availability of the recorded heritage has been becoming more and more apparent. Editor Compton Mackenzie of the *Gramophone* in August 1936 stated that he had received from Mr. Hurst a series of articles by Reynaldo Hahn deploring the destruction of historic matrices in France of the voices of many famous singers. Mr. Mackenzie expressed the thought that in case there was any danger of a similar wholesale destruction threatened in England, that there should be steps taken to found a gramophonic museum which had been proposed by Gordon Bottomley. The latter had written an open letter to the editor of the *Gramophone* which had been so highly thought of that it had been published as a feature article in the February 1936 issue.

In his letter, Mr. Bottomley deplored the tendency of other writers of the *Gramophone* to make gentle—though sometimes sympathetic—fun of Mr. Hurst and his ardent, ingenuous collaborators of "*Collectors' Corner.*" He had come to believe, he said, that they were right in taking their hobby of preserving the voices of great artists of the past seriously and that posterity was going to be concerned about it. He stated that the monthly appearance of *"Collectors' Corner"* was a symptom of an important problem and if its significance had been grasped earlier, the hardest part of Mr. Hurst's self-imposed task might have been unnecessary. They would, he said, at any rate have received informed furtherance and recognition. The problem which the situation presented he placed to the editor in the form of this question:

"Does there exist anywhere any institution—or even the embryo of an institution—which is doing for gramophone records even a little of what our great libraries do for books, our museums for antiquities, or—in a different way—our Zoological Society for animals, and our Kew Gardens for vegetables?

"Possibly one of our libraries *is* willing that gramophone and phonograph records should be deposited with it for the benefit of posterity. All the same, if that is so, it is not sufficient. We need to know how and when they can be heard; if they are in charge of an assistant as skilled as a demonstrator in physics, who knows how to care for them expertly and play them without injury; and if there is an adequate organization for keeping the collection up to date and for filling in the blanks in early issues.

"If most of these things are still not being done, it is urgent time that a commencement should be made; and it is right that we should begin asking if someone is not going to make it— and someone with the necessary impetus to get things done.

"Something is already lost. The first systematic recordings of great singers were soon out-moded by technical improvements, and so passed quickly out of knowledge. But some of those singers were never recorded again. We know already, from Mr. Hurst's useful exploration and experience, that their records are already at remarkable premiums—and that in spite

of an interim of rough usage, little care, and half ruination from playing with bad needles. In another thirty years those that are left will be fetching the prices of jewels of the finest quality, and we shall have libraries of records then that will be spending large incomes in filling up 'incunabulous' blanks that need not exist if something were done even now. . . .

"By now there are probably, in this island alone, several dozen private record-libraries that have been long enough in the making to have definite historic as well as artistic value. It is more than likely that their creators and owners think regretfully of the time when they can foster them no more—or protect them from dispersal or, still worse, rough usage; so that there would be a liklihood of at least some of these being bequeathed intact to the commonweal's ownership, if there were any suitable organization in existence that could take charge of them competently.

"These would be invaluable now, and presently invaluable, but the immediate prospects are not encouraging. The present alternatives seem to be some school of music, though most probably could not afford a qualified custodian and would give the students in their gayest moods open access to them; or some city public library, where the 'Silence' notices in the rooms open to the public would present difficulties in the way of the records being heard at all—while also the size of the section would, for a considerable time, make the engagement of a whole-time qualified custodian unlikely. In both these cases, the records would sometimes suffer—either through light-heartedness or the routine that permits a man to say 'I always change all the needles every morning.'

"This kind of care and possibility is a deterrent thought in considering a collection that has cost many hundreds of pounds, and that contains records some of which are memorable and some miraculous—and all brought into perfect condition with various types of vegetable needles, ensuring a practical permanency. From all points of view, an organization (or a separate section of an existing organization) for the preservation of the finer kinds of gramophone records is an inevitable necessity. The future is certain to supply it; but if that is left to the future, the expense will be infinitely greater, and the result far more incomplete. Before now the *Gramophone* has changed the course of the gramophone's development: I wish you could use its influence to foster the foundation of a National Record Library—and I trust you will prove to have other readers who also feel that this should be done before too much is lost."

This was the situation in record-conscious England, where there were several enterprising Gramophone Societies. In America the situation was at that time even more deplorable and, of course, has deteriorated most rapidly since. The pioneer American companies never did take the care that most English companies yet in existence have, and the mortality of record manufacturers here has been greater. However, well-meaning as Mr. Hurst's pioneer efforts were, he considered the collectors of rare vocal records as a "cult" and later attempted to define the area within which they should operate. In

attempting to lay down rules of conduct and to delineate the period of "great singing" and to limit the field in which the "true" collector would be interested, Mr. Hurst aroused the ire of many with other viewpoints and was ultimately displaced by the editors. Nevertheless, his knowledge of the great singers of early days and their records had proven a stimulus which promoted the search for hidden vocal treasures all over the world and for which one day posterity will have occasion to be grateful. It is quite certain, among other things, that without *"Collectors' Corner"* and the co-operation of Mr. Hurst, that there would not have been published before World War II the compilation of historic vocal recordings of the period from 1895 to 1908 as published by Robert Bauer in Milan, Italy, and which was instrumental in the saving of much valuable recorded material which surely would not have been located after the war. This listing of the recordings under the names of artists from all countries gave the titles, name of recording companies, and the year recorded, as well as the catalog numbers. Attention was thus focused for the first time on the vast number of important vocal performances which had been registered in wax during the first decade of the lateral disc record industry alone.

From this source of information (the Bauer catalog has since been revised) and other available data, the following statistical table has been set up to

PERIOD OF 1898 TO 1909 (Inclusive)

Vocal Classical Records by Recognized Artists	No. of Individual Recordings	Available in Some Form	Masters Yet Existing	Rerecordings by Others
Cylinder Records	3,500	0	Unknown	75–100
Hill-and-dale discs	1,200	0	Unknown	50–75
Laterally recorded discs	15,500	2,500	7,000	500–600

PERIOD OF 1910 TO 1924 (Inclusive)

Vocal Classical Records by Recognized Artists	No. of Individual Recordings	Available in Some Form	Masters Yet Existing	Rerecordings by Others
Cylinder Records	2,500	0	Unknown	12–25
Hill-and-dale discs	2,700	0	750	24–50
Laterally recorded discs	22,500	2,500	15,000	200–300

illustrate the lamentable state of availability of our recorded heritage in the field of operatic and concert singing only. This, of course, represents only the minor part of all recordings which have been issued.

Of this total of about 47,000 estimated vocal classical recordings of all types recorded during the entire acoustic period, well over one-half were operatic selections. Less than 10% of these are available in any form from the manufacturers. Knowing that this category of vocal classicals was only a small part of all the recorded repertoire during all those years and as these artists were the highest priced and that consequently better care was taken of these masters than of others, one can sense what a shibboleth the phrase oft repeated in advertising was, "now recorded for posterity." This is further emphasized by the estimate that less than one-third of these most valuable matrices are in existence. This means that if the remainder of the records issued for which no matrices exist are to be saved for posterity, efforts will have to be made to locate copies in suitable condition for rerecording. The possibilities of finding these have been constantly lessened with the passage of the years. One of the most important reasons was the complete elimination of the cylinder and hill-and-dale disc branches of the industry. Not only did this result in wholesale destruction of the masters, but because of the stigma of obsolescence, the greater share of these instruments and the records produced for them have been destroyed.

Another factor which operated to decrease the possibility of finding in America lateral discs by certain artists was the ridiculous ban on German recordings during World War I. Practically all German recordings were also withdrawn from the catalogs and most were never replaced. The acts of the leading manufacturers of the laterally-recorded discs in America at the time of the introduction of electrical recording in 1925 also prejudiced a great majority against the older records—the

people were deliberately led to believe that there was no truth in the older method, which led to the wholesale destruction of millions of acoustically recorded discs. Technological changes and the use of the changeable needle accounted for the destruction of millions more, extending even into the electrical period.

The shortage of shellac during World War II, resulting in record scrap drives, accounted again for a wholesale wave of destruction in the frenzied attempts to secure new lamps for old. Now, again, the swing to the microgroove records has resulted in the discarding and destruction of many fine recordings by the general public. Sad to relate, this trend has also been manifested by supposedly intelligent record collectors who should know better, but who are apparently more interested in the convenience of standardization of their collections than in the art represented.

During the expansion of 78-rpm album sets during the 1940's, many libraries over the country installed record rental libraries. During this period, many music schools and fine arts colleges had also expanded their record libraries and listening facilities. Now, however, with the lack of standardization, the very real dangers from indiscriminate handling became multiplied; and consequently, free access to collections has been almost totally eliminated. Of what use would a library be if students could only have access to books through the faculty?

Many of the college and library collections had their inception with the Carnegie Foundation grants for this purpose made in the 1930's. Even as things were with one type of record, the wear and tear occasioned through ordinary use, most of it traceable directly to the inherent faults of changeable needles and the known inherent defects of the lateral method, had resulted in a loss of usefulness of a larger part of these recordings. Most of these recordings of the early electric period were unavailable from the manufacturers within a comparatively few years.

Besides these nuclei furnished by the foundation, some libraries had been given collections of rare recordings of the acoustic period. The disastrous deterioration of these recordings of all kinds has resulted in a large part of the contents of many of these libraries being marked "restricted—for faculty use only."

In March of 1949, C. G. Burke stated in the *Saturday Review of Recordings* that tests which he had made of the wearing quality of the LP's versus the standard 78-rpm shellac discs showed the former to be much more durable. He warned, however, that the LP's should be used only with a jeweled point with the lowest possible pressure. But here it should be pointed out that stores have had a great deal of trouble with damage to LP records through the careless handling in the listening booths by patrons—which is precisely the sort of handling that one would expect from college students.

But aside from the complexities of dealing with three different types of recordings, any of which can be ruined by playing with the wrong equipment, there are other factors in the reproduction qualities of the LP records which indicate that while the inherent defects of the method may be minimized, they are never going to be eliminated. In *Radio and Television News* for October 1948, there appeared an article by Norman C. Pickering and John D. Goodell, from which the following is quoted:

"It should be borne in mind that an engineering staff concerned with micro-discs faces all the not inconsiderable problems involved in recording and pressing under standard conditions multiplied by a dimensional factor of approximately 2, in addition to certain special considerations. To establish a reference for this, it may be pointed out that at 33⅓-rpm using a .0025 spherical radius for the playback stylus tip, the 7-inch diameter groove will be down about 20 decibels in frequency response at 10,000 cycles per second. The smaller the diameter

(the lower the relative velocity of the groove with respect to the stylus), the shorter is the wave length at a given frequency and the more abrupt are the corners the stylus is required to travel. When a half wave length is comparable to the dimensions of the stylus, it can bounce only slightly in greatly distorted saw-tooth waveforms. If the stylus radius is reduced to .001, it should be able to track a shorter wavelength successfully. This is true only if proper coupling to the groove is obtained, which requires proportional scaling down of groove dimensions. This leaves an excessive amount of land between the grooves and makes it possible to close up the pitch. (Loading effects of the cutter are neglected here since they may be properly compensated with little difficulty.) The amplitude of the cutter drive must also be lower in proportion. Note too, that the diameter at which the 20 decibel loss appears for 10,000 cycles per second becomes proportionately smaller.

" . . . In all disc recording the excursion amplitude is limited by groove spacing at low frequencies, (note—true of lateral recording only) which is the principal reason for constant amplitude recording below a turnover frequency around 300 to 500 cycles per second. This limitation does not appear at high frequencies recorded at constant velocity, hence, the excursion amplitude at constant velocity is inversely proportional to frequency. In microgroove recording, the maximum amplitude of low frequencies is about half the amplitude possible with standard grooves. This introduces the advantage that high frequencies may be recorded at higher relative amplitudes (with respect to low frequencies), with microgroove techniques. It is common practice to *attempt to compensate for losses at high frequencies* in the relatively small diameter portion of the records with equalization that boosts the high frequency range. It has also been deemed desirable to use recording curves such as the NAB and Orthocoustic curves with considerable high frequency pre-emphasis to allow noise reduction with de-emphasis networks in the playback system."

Thus, it can be seen that the wave-forms indelibly produced in the lateral recordings of today of whatever speed or type are not only subject to the distortional effects associated with the limitations of the method, but to the ca-prices of the engineers. Popular under-standing of the deficiencies of the lateral recording method is very limited, par-ticularly because of the not inconsider-able progress made despite them. There is also a definite lack of general appre-ciation of the fact that the larger part of the recorded heritage of the first 75 years of the phonograph is unavailable and in danger of being lost altogether. The lack of standards by which an in-telligent appraisal of recordings can be made is also a serious matter.

The process of making records in a new, but impermanent medium, of in-adequate range and unpredictive qual-ity of reproduction, to be played on equipment of a constantly transitional and stylistic order, is part and parcel of a program of continuous change and obsolescence for that which was sold just yesterday. Needless to say, this commercial concept of the phonograph as an entertainment device which should have its tonal qualities scaled down in ratio with the selling price, and the record as something ephemeral, to be consumed and discarded, has had the most disastrous effects upon its use as a medium of education.

This stylistic and transitory approach to recording and reproduction also has had a most destructive effect on the heritage of recordings for posterity, not only because of the continuous and enormous losses of masters and records in the hands of the public, but also be-cause of the questionable validity of what is left. The person who purchases a given recording today knows nothing of its recorded characteristic and knows of no instrument upon which it is de-signed to play with any assurance of reproduction fidelity. What then of the music lovers and record historians of the future?

That is the situation and here are the needs:

1. Standards of reproduction for spe-cific records which indicate clearly the type of instrument and the proper settings to provide the most accurate reproduction possible.
2. Research to establish the best meth-ods of the past or present which are not being employed because of the exigencies of commercial de-velopment or the misuse of mo-nopoly.
3. Reform of the patent system to provide monopoly only to the true inventor and to deny monopoly to the commercial opportunists who more often than not deprive the real inventors of their rights.
4. The setting up of a phonographic archive, perhaps government spon-sored, as a repository for master records no longer of commercial value, to also function as an agency for restoring for educational use and posterity the recordings of the past.
5. The provision of high-quality, low-cost equipment for educational and library use, with or without the cooperation of the existing industry.

The solutions to the problems pre-sented in filling these needs will be dif-ficult only because of the overweening power of the present leaders of the industry. This book has shown that most of the best principles brought out in the course of the industrial develop-ment of the phonograph have been abandoned along the way for a variety of reasons which no longer apply. The comments of many present-day experts could be quoted to the effect that the hill-and-dale method, for example, is superior. None could be more convinc-ing, as the statement of Bell engineer Maxfield in 1933 in which he admitted that at that time they were recording then by the lateral method only up to 6,000 cps, but that by the hill-and-dale process, the Bell engineers had been able to record commercially up to 14,000 and 15,000 cps.

Dealers had resented the continuous barrage of high-sounding technical terms and formulae used by the recording engineers. These had changed and been added to from year to year since the innovation of electrical recording in 1925. As far as fidelity was concerned, dealers felt that engineers were retrogressing, not progressing. All the most highly involved reasoning no longer served to cover up the fact that in many cases the engineers were seeking to justify the continuation of development of inherently inferior methods.

The complete anarchy existing in the retail field caused by the pseudo-competitive tactics of the American producing companies had saddled the dealers, who had no part in the conspiracy with the necessity of stocking three types of records, restricting the choice of the consumers by two-thirds. According to experts, this meant the eventual elimination of the 78-rpm discs, the only one of the three types of lateral discs capable of reproducing up to 15,000 cps. Therefore, dealers felt that the time was ripe for a return to the superior vertical-cut method wherein longplay could be combined with high fidelity. The perfecting of recording on both magnetic tape and sound film to a high degree would seemingly operate to insure the use of the best possible methods for disc recording, for competitive reasons. So it might, but as we have shown, these fields of recording and reproducing were not competitive. In any case, the disc record was the most convenient and practical way of storing up musical performance, especially for unlimited and economical duplication, ease of handling and storage.

A paramount need was that of making our accumulation of recorded art truly available for educational purposes. Neither conventional record playing equipment nor the types of records available were suitable for library or educational uses. The new records, although unbreakable, were easily soiled and damaged. Only a limited repertoire was available in any one place in any one of the three existing commercial types of records. As to the valuable recordings of former years, if one were to travel from one music library to another from coast to coast, he would not be able to find more than 10% of just the vocal classical records of the past 70 years, for reasons which are probably very obvious to those who have read this book.

Lack of standardization of recording methods with reproducing mechanisms had always plagued the industry, and contributed to widespread confusion. Lack of storage space and cost were also important elements in the non-availability of records for educational institutions and libraries. Space requirements were always troublesome to libraries, even when confined to books and manuscripts. However, a great boon to the librarian and historian had been the introduction of the microfilm method. This conserved valuable space and was also used to preserve irreplaceable material from unnecessary handling. Something of the sort was also needed for the library collection of recorded music. The segregation of valuable recordings which it is impossible to replace and restriction of the use of such items to the faculty had become customary in the music libraries of schools. The fact that the best performances generally produce the greatest demand and hence, the most rapid wear, meant that the greatest loss always occurs where it can be afforded the least. Therefore, one of the greatest needs is for some special provision for the preservation of those more important recorded performances, while at the same time providing a means of keeping them available, not only to the faculty, but to the students.

The general public should be able to order, at some reasonable price, copies of recordings which are no longer commercially available. If the masters are no longer available and the recording was of importance, there should be some agency interested in rerecording from an existing pressing, if possible. There is no reason why this cannot be done on a virtually self-sustaining basis.

So much for the needs; the industry itself, during its first seventy-five years, has supplied the answers. It remains only to seek them out and re-combine them in the best possible manner. The wealth of our recorded heritage must somehow be freed of commercial restrictions. What would our libraries amount to if their contents were dictated by a tight monopoly of book publishers?

Aside from the hill-and-dale method, the most important of the discarded methods which it seems obvious should be employed is that of the variable speed, constant-groove velocity beneath the stylus turntable, as first covered by Bell and Tainter in their patents, but never used by them. It was demonstrated successfully by the World Record Co. in England in the 1920's, but circumstances prevented this company from getting the necessary financial foothold to keep going. The Edison hill-and-dale disc of 1913-29, if combined with this method, would have been highly efficient. The Edison disc had 150 grooves to the inch as compared with the 90 to 100 grooves of the lateral discs and the playing time would have been doubled by keeping the minimum groove speed as the new constant. However, if this variable-speed turntable were to be combined with the Edison long-playing record of 450 grooves to the inch, with slow speed electrical recording and reproducing, a true "microrecording" method is presented. If a groove speed equal to about 40 rpm on the interior grooves of a standard disc were to be adopted as a constant-groove speed, it would be possible to store up a total of one and one-half hours on one side of a 12-inch record, or three hours to each disc!

In this connection, it is important to observe that the amplitude of recording on the hill-and-dale disc is not limited by the groove width as in the lateral method. This means a much greater

dynamic range. Neither is the stylus point cramped in responding to the higher frequencies towards the center of the spiral, which is important to high fidelity. The voltage output for a given type of pickup would be greater with the vertical-cut, long-playing record. This is succinctly demonstrated by the fact that the original 450 groove-to-the-inch Edison long-playing records were reproduced acoustically! This added initial increment of energy direct from the recording means that less amplification would be required. Less amplification means fewer components, lower cost, less distortion.

Moreover, with the Edison-cut and a surface equal to or better than that developed by Edison for use with the diamond stylus, the question of record wear becomes negligible. Neither is there any noticeable wear of the diamond stylus. This is not true of the diamond when used with the inherently faulty lateral-groove principle. Even with the vinylite, the eccentric lapping action ultimately alters the bearing surface of even a diamond stylus to a degree that it may damage records.[4]

Now, assuming that research has been done to establish the optimum methods of cutting the records, of securing the best surfaces, and of establishing standards for the creation of equipment which will predictively re-create the original performances with accuracy, there remains the problem of availability. What is the greatest cause of record destruction and consequent lack of availability? Aside from the variations in records of different manufacturers and periods, of playing equipment and needles, the greatest cause of record damage and destruction is the human handling. Here again, in a more recent period of phonographic development, there is to be found a method of dealing with this problem. The new three-hour record which we have assumed, a true microrecording method of full frequency range and dynamic

4 "Reproduction of Microgroove Recordings," Norman C. Pickering and John D. Goodell— *Radio & Television News*, Oct. 1948.

range, provides the primary means of assembling a great quantity of musical performances within a small space. Certain other technics developed in the Ediphone and in the juke-box industry will serve to make any part of this storehouse of music available quickly and easily without human handling. The dictating and transcribing phonographic devices have determining mechanisms so that the stenographer can locate any desired part of a recording at once, or may repeat as often as is desired any required portion. Everyone, we are certain, is familiar with the Seeburg automatic phonographs which will play any one of 200 selections. Is it any less important to provide such convenience to the students of fine music?

By combining these two control methods, the problem of human handling is largely solved. By assembling banks of selective mechanisms of this sort, the entire rerecorded repertoire, historical and modern, could be compressed into a space not larger than a neighborhood library. The losses of records could be made negligible by this plan. The output of these banks of phonographs could be wired to soundproof listening booths (preferably with living room acoustics) where the controls would also be placed. It would be possible for any listener in any booth to draw upon any bank not then in use. Outlets could be provided in the booths so that students could plug in portable tape recorders to take off selections to be studied at home. Classrooms could also be provided with similar speakers and controls. The widest possible availability would be thus provided without any handling except by the expert in charge.

Now this is just part of a comprehensive scheme to provide access to our now largely unavailable resources of already recorded music. The late Melville Clark, president of the Clark Music Co., Syracuse, N.Y., pioneer merchant of phonographs and records, has long ago had an idea that merits serious consideration. Mr. Clark, incidentally, was a well-known harpist and assisted pioneer recorders at the Edison Labora-

tory, the Victor Talking Machine Co. and the Columbia Phonograph Co. in early experiments in recording the difficult harp tone. He was the inventor of the Clark Irish harp and of a new glass harp, which is impervious to moisture. His idea was the formation of a national "Perpetuation of Recorded Art Association." His idea was to enlist behind this the merchants of the United States who have seen the growth of the recording industry and who have also noted the indifference of the manufacturers, of musicians and public alike, to the losses occasioned by changing methods and the vicissitudes of competition. He also felt that the recording industry should back such an organization and contribute to it such masters that no longer have commercial value, for the purpose of ensuring their preservation for future generations.

But a greater opportunity seems to lie in the making available, as well as preserving, and with this Mr. Clark agreed. Certainly Mr. Clark's plan should receive support and perhaps congressional attention. The Library of Congress has already done a wonderful job in both the preservation of American folk songs and in making them available. How important it is also to save the evidence of the greatness of our musical artists of the past half century and more, and to make generally available a great musical heritage already paid for by the public!

It would seem that intelligent and organized efforts should be brought to bear, perhaps through such an organization as Mr. Clark proposed, to rerecord everything of merit that has ever been done, to the extent that this is yet possible. Such corrections should be made in pitch in rerecording the older records which were often erratic in this respect so as to make the reproduction accurate. Of great importance also would be the analysis of the methods by which the original recording was made, so as to compensate as far as is historically justifiable for the lack of balance known to exist in the original recording. Tabulations of the characteristics of the recordings of the electrical period should be made, as this information is yet to be found, and corrections made to fit the standards set up. The records made by artists on types of records of which the characteristic is known, whether acoustic or electric, would provide a guide to other records in which this knowledge is lacking.[5]

With the reduced cutting resistance offered by the best waxes to the slower speed and finer incising tool, it may be that the Edison acoustic method of recording should be re-investigated for some purposes. Certainly, the fact that this has been the only method which has thus far been able to sustain the supreme test of side-by-side comparison with the living artist would seem to indicate that research should be extended from where Edison left off. Regardless of whether electrical methods of recording and reproduction are used or not, the objective should be the same as that all-but-forgotten ideal of Thomas A. Edison—absolute fidelity to the original performance.

_____

[5] Since the writing of this chapter, new developments such as the Sennheiser Binaural Recording System (*High Fidelity*, Jan., 1975) makes possible new methods of recording and reproducing actual music performances for binaural listening, provided suitable padded earphones are used and not the Sennheiser type which for other reasons avoids this exclusion of the ambience of the listening area. The author of the article, who also wrote the technical report on the Sennheiser system for *High Fidelity*, correctly noted the need for separation of the ambience patterns collected in using the Sennheiser system from the interfering and distorting ambience of a differing listening situation.

The improved results noted by the *High Fidelity* expert provides the separation necessary between performance area ambience and listening area ambience at the headset, whereas in the equally valid Edison tone-test recording system, the ambience of the recording studio was reduced by acoustical treatment below a cognizable threshold. The author also states that the Sennheiser system produces results superior to quadrasonics, which is no surprise to the authors of *From Tin Foil to Stereo*.

CHAPTER 25

REALISM, ROMANTICISM, AND HI-FI

THE advent of electrical recording in 1925 found few qualified critics of the phonograph record prepared to cope with an unprecedented situation. Especially was this true in the United States, where the musical writers had failed to wholeheartedly accept the phonograph, judging the entire field by the extent of its failures rather than by its accomplishments. Consequently, there was neither a rationale nor a body of disciplinary thought to serve as a guide to proper criticism of the new found facility in recording afforded by the adoption of electrical methods.

As Harry Alan Potamkin said in the *Phonograph Monthly Review*, July 1930:

> "We in America have never really looked upon the gramophone as much more than a piece of furniture or a mechanism, seldom as a means of expression. Only now is there any appearance of a disc-critic, although the radio from its start has been included in the journalistic enterprise."

Without sympathetic and enlightened criticism to discipline the inclinations of the engineers and promoters, excesses were bound to result. Exaggerations reflecting the reaction from the limitations of the acoustic methods were a feature and selling point of the records of the early Orthophonic period. Many musicians who should have known better, as well as the greater part of the uninformed lay public, accepted the products as an achievement of "science" and their performances as a triumph of realism.

It was several years before tentative questions began to be raised. Generally, the slump in the record industry which occurred following the stock market crash of 1929 is altogether attributed to that event and to the tremendous popular interest then manifested in radio and talking pictures. However, in retrospect, it seems evident from the statistical picture that there also was operative a psychological reaction against certain inherent deficiencies in the quality of the electrical recordings of the 1925 to 1930 period. In other words, unqualified acceptance had given way to subconscious rejection. Even the engineers, who now seem so blind to the present limitations and defects of current recordings, are quite willing now to point out those shortcomings of the earlier period, so it is quite unnecessary to waste space discussing all of the sources of distortion involved.

The principal problem of the acoustical method of recording had been one of providing enough energy to the cutting stylus to make possible adequate volume in the entirely mechanical method of reproduction. Except for the Auxetophone and the 20th Century Graphophone, there had never been any form of amplification employed in the commercially produced reproducing instruments. Therefore, when the Western Electric process was introduced through

Victor's Orthophonic Victrola and Columbia's Viva-tonal Phonograph, the recording engineers revelled in the new found latitude in forming the grooves of the record. However, because of the inherent limitations of the lateral method, it was almost immediately found expedient to alter the recorded waveform, thus the groove technically must be considered to be deformed, rather than formed. Some of the deformation introduced in these early electric records was intended to offset deficiencies in the reproducing system, some to purposely exaggerate the new ability to reproduce lower fundamental tones.

The Brunswick Panatrope followed these acoustic instruments almost immediately (the first all-electric phonograph) which thus permitted amplification at both ends, and now for the first time it became possible to reproduce a symphony orchestra with full volume, if not with complete fidelity. With the natural restraints imposed by the former acoustical methods removed, the competition between the recording engineers quite logically resolved into seeing who could get the utmost from the new technics. Unfortunately, for the most part, the new electrical recording experts were not musicians. Unfortunately also, these new radio-trained recording experts had little use for the advice and counsel of the old acoustical recording experts, who were generally relegated to the background with their archaic views on the necessity of sublimating accompaniments to the soloists.

Actually, technics were changing much more rapidly during this period than the ability to master them and the radio experts would have done well to have paid more heed to the acoustical experts and to the musicians around them. Due to these rapid changes and conflicting attitudes, the rare opportunity to set up new standards for record sound reproduction was lost, perpetuating the chaos of the acoustic period. It should be noted that we have offered proof elsewhere that the reproduction system of the Orthophonic Victrola had been calculated to insure

the obsolescence of the prior Victor acoustic record, and that all possibility of making valid comparisons using the new instrument of records produced before and after the introduction of the new methods had been lost. This might possibly have been justified if there had been a sincere effort to set up new standards, but sad to relate, such was not the case.

It was really only a short time after the introduction of the Orthophonic Victrola that it was apparent to almost everyone in the American industry that the all-electric reproducer would be the ultimate home instrument. Many had recognized it from the first. This is not to say that this eventuality was by any means a technical necessity, but that the course of the industry was following the nature of its new sponsorship. Now the failure of the engineers to set up standards of recorded characteristics at the time of the abrupt changeover from acoustic to electrical recording becomes apparent. For a number of years, the recorded characteristics of the discs gravitated between the dissimilar demands of the all-electric and acoustic reproducing mechanisms in the hands of the public. The strivings of the engineers for improvement was therefore largely misdirected and conflicting —a situation which has continued almost to the present day.

Recognition of these facts on the part of the record-buying public have been partial and groping. Information has come not from the engineers or musicians, where one would expect it, but chiefly from a few record collectors who had maintained a thread of continuity with the past into the then rapidly changing present. Baffled perhaps by the dizzy speed of the changing technological situation, certain connoisseur collectors were the first to detect that there was something wrong with the theretofore unqualified claims of the publicists of the industry as to the perfection of the new methods and the entire inadequacy of the old.

For the *Phonograph Monthly Review* of December 1930, Riccardo M. Aleman of Cuba, noted connoisseur of recordings, wrote an article on "Vocal Recording Standards." In this, Mr. Aleman sought answer to the then heretic question, "Do electrical recordings invariably sound better than acoustical ones?" Mr. Aleman's comments on this question are of unusual importance, for not only was he perhaps the greatest authority on the recordings of the entire world of the acoustic period and of the electrical recordings to that point, but he was personally acquainted with many of the great artists and knew their voices well. Moreover, he stated the instrument upon which he was making the comparisons was a Credenza Orthophonic Victrola. Due to the varying recorded characteristics of the records of the acoustic and electric periods, as well as within each, this is essential information. The published criticisms and comparisons of various recordings as published in numerous periodicals today are quite valueless from a technical standpoint without information as to the type of equipment being used by the critic.

Bearing in mind then that the great body of the acoustic recordings did not correspond to the reproducing characteristics of Mr. Aleman's Orthophonic Victrola and making due allowances for the fact, let us consider what he had discovered by that comparatively early date. He says, in part:

"Certainly, most of my readers will be surprised when reading the question of headlining this article. Some of them, rather many of them, who are great lovers of the new electrical system of reproducing the human sounds, will be alarmed. Surely they are thinking of what I am going to answer to myself; and it will not take a long time before all my readers know the solution of this problem. Most phonophiles think that the new electrical records are very good from every point of view; and they have not hesitated to withdraw from their record libraries all their acoustic records, thinking there is no use to keep them after the new process has been invented. Some have sold their old records at a very cheap price, and others have given them to some friend. Well, I am an admirer of the new electrical records, but not in a general way, and with some reservations.

"Not all electrical records are at the same height of perfection. I shall set apart the artistic side of the records, which belongs to another matter; I shall limit this article to what may be called the mechanical side of the record-making. Not all the electrical records, as I said before, have the same clarity, the same sonority. We may find many and many splendid records; but there are numerous records that sound very opaque, very weak; some of them almost inaudible; others, such as those belonging to the *Marina* set, which have been reviewed with his usual competence by my distinguished friend Mr. William S. Marsh, in the July edition of this magazine, are too loud and with very noticeable vibration. In the *Marina* set all the artists excepting the baritone, Marcos Redondo, seem to have sung their roles extremely loudly. If you compare these *Marina* records to other selections made by the same artists (Capsir, Lazaro, and Mardones), you will notice that their voices are entirely different. However, I think that it is better to have a very loud selection than an almost inaudible record.

"One of the latest releases of the Victor Company has been the 'concertato' 'O Sommo Carlo,' from Verdi's *Ernani*, - - -. It is sung by Giuseppe De Luca, Grace Anthony, and Alfio Tedesco, with the Metropolitan Opera Chorus and orchestra. The phrases allotted to the baritone De Luca are sung in a classical way, with real unction and delicacy (it must not be forgotten that 'O Sommo Carlo' is a very humble invocation to the soul of Charlemagne); but his voice is very weak, and it looks as if De Luca had put a piece of cloth or heavy paper on his mouth. The timbre of his voice seems to have lost its natural brilliancy, for De Luca's voice has always been characterized by its sonority and mellow timbre, always full of peculiar sweetness, which differentiates him from any other baritone. So, it is really a great surprise to hear that record. Of course, we cannot think that De Luca's voice has been diminished, for on the other side of the record there is the 'Barcarola' from Ponchielli's 'La Gioconda,' sung by De Luca and the Metropolitan Opera Chorus, which is surely superbly sung by the mentioned baritone, showing the freshness and the beauty of his voice.

"In my record library I have some other 'concertati,' 'O Sommo Carlo,' which sound very well. There is one performed by Fregosi, Fullin, Poli-Randacio, Righetti, Nessi and Baracchi (Fonotipia record); one sung by Stracciari, a soprano and a tenor whose names do not appear on the label (Columbia record). I have two records of Mattia Battistini; one of them is sung with soprano De Witt, tenor Taccani and La Scala Chorus; the other with Emilia Corsi, Luigi Colazza, Aristodemo Sillich and La Scala Chorus. Mario Sammarco, the soprano Bohuss and the tenor Jose Palet, made the same piece for the Fonotipia. They are accompanied by La Scala Chorus and pianoforte. Benvenuto Franci has sung the mentioned 'concertato' for electrical recording, as have Fregosi and Stracciari. Both Battistini records and that of Mario Sammarco are acoustical, and they sound as well as any electrical record. Besides those I have referred to, I have one 'concertato' 'O Sommo Carlo' sung by Alfred Gandolfi (now at the Metropolitan), the tenor Ballin and the soprano Signora Agostoni, always with La Scala Chorus. And finally, there is the oldest of all, the one sung by Francesco Cigada, Maria Grisi and Remo Sangiorgi and the same Chorus. This record appears in the 1906 catalog of H. M. V. It sounds better than any electrical recording of the same piece."

Mr. Aleman cited a number of other interesting comparisons showing the utter falsity of the industry-inspired conception that adequate reproduction could only be obtained from the new electrically-recorded records. More than this, Mr. Aleman's comparisons reveal the varying characteristics of the new recordings when played on the one instrument which is indicative of the lack of standards and the indecision of the recording engineers as to whether the records should meet the requirements of the Orthophonic Victrola or the new Electrola.

Mr. Aleman was exceptionally well-informed. He was one of the very few who did not accept the statements of the publicists of the new era at face value and who made tests with the three-dimensional evidence. He was one of the few of the old-time collectors who did not dispose of valuable collections of the old acoustical recordings. Consider in this respect that not only had the industrialists relegated into oblivion the very great fruits of the first 25 years of professional disc recording in 1925, but now in Mr. Aleman's article is contained the evidence that only five years later they were already proceeding to make obsolete the investments of millions of persons throughout the world in the Orthophonic Victrolas which they had so recently sold them.

A most important fact also revealed is that even with the lateral recording method, acoustic methods of recording might possibly have been developed for use with matching acoustical reproducing instruments of improved design. But the greatest lesson of Mr. Aleman's 1930 comparisons is that the setting up of adequate standards is an essential to the most intelligent evaluation of the records of any or all periods.

The preoccupation of the recording engineers of the early electric period with radio methods was a great obstacle in the way of recognizing the need of such standards at that time. Two quite contrary philosophies of recording had developed as a consequence. One of these derived from exposure to the "close-up" radio broadcast where small groups of singers or instrumental ensembles would use a small, dead studio and work close to the microphone. Carried to its ultimate end, this technic resulted in the popularity of the vocal distortions of the "crooner" and of the heavy, lush background music. The effect of this method was to provide an effect of intimacy, the orchestra and soloist being transported into the living room, the singer or soloist singing or playing just for you. The contrary philosophy was based on the conception of bringing the listener into the studio or auditorium. In this method, the natural room resonance of the studio, or acoustical reflections of the auditorium, were broadcast along with the sound directly received by the microphones to give that illusion to the radio audience. Quite naturally, this was an almost unavoidable characteristic of broadcasts of actual performances of symphonies and operas.

As noted elsewhere, Maxfield and Harrison, principal designers of the Western Electric method, were protagonists of the latter school of thought. However, many of the recorders imported from the radio field had been working with the less aloof radio dance bands and their "mike" embracing "thrushes" and crooners. One of the results was the early electric-era phenomena of such characters as "Whispering Jack Smith" on the Orthophonic records and Little Jack Little who recorded for Columbia. They have been followed by countless others, many of whom, like them, could not dare a public appearance without the aid of at least a PA system to amplify their voices or instruments. Obviously, this sort of thing may be enjoyable, but it does not constitute accurate sound reproduction. It may do no harm but should be recognized for what it is, an unnatural distortion. On the other hand, the recording of large orchestras, vocal ensembles, operatic performances, etc., where room resonance was recorded, also involved technical and distortional difficulties. It was soon found, for instance, that broadcast quality was not good enough for permanent recordings where indefinite repetition would soon reveal the slightest defects. A single false note, or coughing from the audience, could ruin for recording purposes what had seemed to have been an exceptionally good performance. Now, with most original recording being done on tape, this difficulty has been somewhat obviated, as a few blemishes can be edited out of the tape and corrections dubbed in. This had not been possible in the early electrical recording period. However, the most grievous source of difficulties in the recording in resonant halls or studios was the multiple reflections, resulting in complex wave formations which "muddied" rapidly played passages.

The selective qualities of the reflection characteristics of individual auditoriums would also reinforce certain tones while reducing others to inaudibility. In an endeavor to meet this problem, many sound engineers resorted to the use of multiple microphones, enabling them to bring out passages that had been too weak with a single microphone. This method, however, produced unnatural side effects which plagued broadcasts and recordings for years, as was confessed at the Gramophone Conference of technical experts held in England in November, 1938. At this conference, Mr. A. C. Haddy, senior recording engineer to the Decca Record Co. Ltd., said in respect to the pioneer work of Voight in England in the design and use of moving-coil recording heads as early as 1926 that it was unfortunate that the bad acoustics and factory processing at that time had offset the excellent quality of his recordings.

The *Phonograph Monthly Review* in 1931 carried a story on a new method which had been employed in the broadcast of the music drama "Wozzeck," using a new type of parabolic microphone. This composition by Alban Berg is filled with dissonances and was considered an exceptionally difficult assignment. The article was written as an interview with engineer O. B. Hanson, in charge of plant operation and engineering for NBC. The broadcast took place from the Philadelphia Metropolitan Opera House with what the interviewer described as "a remarkable degree' of success." Engineer Hanson explained that the secret of the unusually fine results had been in the elimination of the use of a number of variously placed microphones and in the employment of a single "parabolic reflector" type of condenser microphone. This microphone was described as having a parabolic bowl with the condenser microphone at its center from which protruded four long rods. Hanson explained to the interviewer his theory of the single "pick-up" as follows:

"Additional microphones create a condition very similar to bad acoustics. That is, there are several different sound pick-ups and several different sets of reverberations. This generally means hearing a 'fuzzy,' or distorted transmission and not a clean-cut tone.

"This was generally the complication during broadcasts in which the carbon type was used. Several of these were often used in a single radio broadcast to bring out or 'spot' different orchestral selections or sections of a chorus. Acoustical interference noticeable as a fuzziness in quality was the frequent result.

"Now with the condenser type of microphone, NBC engineers have found they can work over a larger range and eliminate audible aberrations up to a certain size orchestra.

"With the great symphony orchestra broadcasts, however, these microphones were so far away from the instruments that room noise crept into the transmission.

"The development and application of the parabolic reflector microphone by the NBC solved the problem. This device employs a directional sound reflection principle utilized during the late world war for combatting enemy air raids.

"The new microphone may be regulated to assimilate sound waves within a certain radius, just as a focussed camera or a spot light's rays cover a specific area. It is placed farther away from orchestral instruments, or singers, than the ordinary condenser-type microphone. The result is a more harmonious blending of instruments and voices."

Actually, the one-point pickup for orchestral recording had been early recognized by others as the correct one, and for similar reasons, including Maxfield, the chief designer of the Western Electric process of recording. However, it had been found expedient to "spread the risk" by utilizing multiple microphones, combining them, or cutting them in or out as necessary. One of the elements that worked against the establishment of accurate indices as to what constituted good reproduction was the lack of personal responsibility engendered by the divided duties and pressures of scheduled radio broadcasting technics.

The statement of Hanson that the several different sound pickups create a condition very similar to that of bad acoustics is a very valid one. This corresponds in a way, although for a slightly different reason, with the observations of Maxfield in respect to "transients" occasioned by the interference patterns of auditorium acoustics. Even today, many "authorities" are quite completely confused as to the relationship of room resonance in the recording room to that of the listening room. In the *Saturday Review of Recordings* of June 1951, Edward Tatnall Canby wrote on "Liveness in the Listening," as follows:

" 'Liveness,' the compound effect of multiple room reflection upon played music, is—if you wish—a distortion of 'pure' music; but it happens to be a distortion essential to naturalness of sound. Without it music is most graphically described as 'dead.' Liveness fertilizes musical performance, seasons and blends and rounds out the sound, assembles the raw materials of overtone and fundamental into that somewhat blurred and softened actuality that is normal, in its varying degrees, for all music. Disastrous experiments in 'cleaning up' music by removing the all-essential blur long since proved to most recording engineering that musicians do like their music muddied up with itself, reflected. Today recording companies go to extraordinary lengths to acquire studios, churches, and auditoriums, (not to mention an assortment of artificial, after-the-recording liveness makers) in order to package that illusively perfect liveness."

Mr. Canby's reference to "disastrous experiments in 'cleaning up' music by removing the all-essential blur" is merely the recitation of defeat in attempting to secure exactitude of reproduction by the lateral recording method. Does anyone complain that the sound of a violin or piano sounds 'dead' when played in their presence, because of the absence of the multiple reflection pattern of another auditorium? Does anyone complain because the voice of the singer before them is not clothed with the echoes of Carnegie Hall? The answer is given in Mr. Canby's last quoted sentence, lateral recording practice has had to resort to artifice and illusion—failing to capture the essence of reality. Mr. Canby says, a little further on in this article:

"What, then, of reproduced music? Liveness being essential for music in any form, somehow or other we must approximate it in our own homes. Simple you say. Just set up a mike and record it, along with the music. That's what is done, of course. But there are complications, you already can see. What of the listening room's own reflective power? Clearly, music

from the phonograph is subject to the same sort of reflection in your room that made the original liveness. If it is of significant proportions (and it often is), then we have liveness compounded upon liveness. Double liveness, double trouble. The musical balance is upset, the sound is unnatural—and we blame the record."

Here note that Mr. Canby admits the technical incorrectness of superimposing the acoustic qualities of one room upon another, also that the liveness of many living rooms is of significant proportions. Let us see what he proposes:

"Then perhaps a 'dead' listening room, well cushioned, draped and rugged, is the answer? The sound would then reach you direct from the speaker, liveness and all, unharmed by predatory room reflections. But, alas, it doesn't work. For, remember, liveness in its natural state never comes direct from the musical source itself. Therefore, a so-called 'point source,' such as a loudspeaker, turns the recorded liveness — however faithfully transcribed—into a meaningless contradiction that the ear is utterly loath to accept. Sounds terrible. And again we blame the record."

Just one comment here—such a 'dead' living or music room as Mr. Canby suggests would be untenable—even for conversation, to say nothing of listening to a musical performance of any kind. But let us see what other alternative Mr. Canby suggests:

"What to do then? One quick mind suggests the ideal solution—record all music in padded-cell studios, entirely 'dead.' Play all records in specially chosen listening rooms with fine musical acoustics thus adding all the liveness in its natural form (coming from all directions) at the moment of reproduction. Wonderful, if impractical! With such a plan music could be seasoned to taste with liveness; each room would impart its peculiar flavor, and the same recording could take on as many different guises as music-in-the-flesh in our varied halls and studios. Results would in truth be extraordinarily interesting. I can guarantee, though, no home short of the baronial would do for the avid collector's liveness needs."

Mr. Canby's conclusion does not agree with his previous statement that the liveness of the listening room "is often of significant proportions." Any room adequate for use as a music room will have a reverberation pattern suitable for music reproduction — if not, then liveness introduced in the recording can only be considered as an expedient—not as an essential to absolute fidelity. The only reasonable exception to this is the case of the full symphony orchestra, pipe organ, or operatic performance where, for the average listening room the volume has to be considerably lower than the original performance. Here, the "projection," or capturing of the acoustical quality of the originating auditorium may be condoned, but should nevertheless be recognized for what it is.

But let us see what Mr. Canby offers in proof of his contention that the recording of room resonance is always essential and desirable. He continues as follows:

"Indeed, I heard by accident (and was tricked by) just such an effect. A test recording, submitted for approval, was played with gorgeous results in a large public room containing a convenient machine. Every listener there — as would you — assumed that the quality of the sound was in the recording; whereas in point of fact, as we later discovered, it was entirely in the room! The record itself was horribly 'dead'."

Every reader has by this time, no doubt, been subjected at one time or another to one of those restless periods when phonograph records have been played over the PA system, to fill in while waiting for the main attraction. Who is

there who is not aware of the cacophony resulting from "liveness" of artificially brilliant recordings being thus mixed with the reverberations of the listening hall? Mr. Canby was not tricked by hearing a recording of the music alone plus the reflection pattern of the room in which he heard it—he was simply unprepared philosophically to recognize the truth when he heard it. It may be that Mr. Canby's own listening room is deficient in normal acoustic responsiveness, for he closes the article with this paragraph:

"What's happening to your records in your own living room? Better investigate."

Now that both sides of this question of "Liveness in the Listening" have been presented, the question of recording standards in regard to the extent to which the recording of room resonance is permissible or desirable becomes properly posed. It would seem to be true that perfectly reproduced music would contain nothing but the sounds of the originating voice or instrument. It would seem that the collection of reflected sounds implies either an inadequacy in accomplishing the feat of precision in reproduction, or in the physical limitations of the listening room. On the one hand, in 'dead' facsimile recording, we have the ideal of reality, on the other, the projection of illusion. The impossibility of bringing the full symphony orchestra into the average living room with satisfactory acoustical effectiveness, even in miniature, must be conceded, but that is no reason why every singer and instrumentalist that visits your living room via recorded performance should sound as though they were singing somewhere else miles away. Without any absolute standard of reproduction, how can any search for recorded truth reveal it?

The fact is that since the inception of electrical recording, a certain group of recording engineers have made a fetish of recording the acoustical background. It was found that doing so in connection with the recording of larger groups and ensembles assisted materially in concealing the lack of high-frequency range and gave a spurious effect of brilliance to the recordings. In other words, the use of room resonance recording was in large measures an expedient to offset certain limitations of the lateral recording method.

As the technical writers of the trade papers are concerned with the maintenance of cordial relationships with the advertisers who support the publications of their writers, it is quite to be expected that rationalizations should be made about the deficiencies of methods and equipment. However, infrequently individual writers come forth with a truly candid disclosure. Such was one written by D. J. Julian which appeared in *American Music Lover* of July 1944. Under the heading "Looking Ahead," Mr. Julian said in regard to recording characteristics:

"The utter absence of agreement as to recording characteristics before the war has been most disconcerting. It is noticeable that all the blatant, shrill experimentation by the engineers has been directed to the classical repertoire (surely, *not* the dance tune, which finds its way into the juke box, where experimentation would not be tolerated). How long suffering is the lover of good music!

"Since record publication from the early days of recording has been international in scope, technical advances should be more or less synchronized by important manufacturers throughout the world. It is a strange fact that, on the whole, Great Britain has lagged behind the rest of the field in putting into production some of the technical achievements consummated during the thirties. Why? Not because of the disinclination of the companies there to progress; for nowhere will be found such alertness and sensible cooperation by the industry with its customers. In England many of the most enthusiastic puchasers of records still cling to acoustic machines;

and this bloc of the market must be reckoned with. The balance between bass and treble is unfavorable enough at best when a record is reproduced mechanically, without further robbing the low register to bloat the 'highs.'

"We should keep this point in mind; frequency range is *not* the most important single element in making records.

"From the early experimental days of electrical recording until 1935, standards of groove shapes, depth of cut, and 'Characteristics' remained substantially stable all over the world. The system was called 'constant velocity'; and in practice frequencies above 250 cps were engraved in a pure constant velocity characteristic (i. e., amplitude frequency equalled constant). Below 250 cps—called the 'turnover' or 'crossover' point—the cut was constant amplitude (all frequencies being limited to the same amplitude, instead of the amplitude increasing with a decrease in frequency).

"Beginning about 1935 the 'crossover' point was moved up to 500 or 600 cps in America, with the result that larger signals could be inscribed (so that the *dynamic range* was extended). This was all to the good. True, there was some loss in bass response, but reproducing instruments were coming off the lines with bass tone controls to compensate for this.

"All too soon the recording characteristic fell into disrepute in this country: each engineer had his own ideas. Some wished to extend the 'crossover' point to 800 cps . . . to 1,000 cps . . . and perhaps even higher. What appeared to be a friendly rivalry sprang up among the brethren: to see who could make the *loudest* record.

"About this time, 'phony high fidelity' reared its monstrous head, when someone decided that increasing the intensity of frequencies in the 3,000 cps region would impart a spurious brilliance that sounded 'nice' on the cheap sets where the output transformers took a nose dive on frequencies above that point. The effect was ear-splitting enough to cut through the noise of a boiler plate works, on a good machine, unless the treble tone control was jammed down hard to maximum attenuation.

"There is a definite advantage to be gained if 'peaking' is skillfully executed, because the signal-to-noise ratio will be better. But to a specified 'curve' be reached by all companies; and then *only* if it appears that the advantage gained is sufficient to offset the obvious drawback; fussing with the tone controls every time we change from the London Philharmonic to the New York Philharmonic Symphony.

"I question the wisdom of the thrusting upon the patient classical record buyer the capricious and whimsical babel of languages spoken by the companies' engineers. Experimentation should be done in the laboratory —not on the public. A certain measure of sanity is desirable in recording. If *frequency range alone is sought,* this could be more effectively carried out with a 33-rpm motor and vertically recorded transcriptions.

"When production of reproducing instruments is begun after the war, it is hoped that the amount of pickup equalization will be in harmony with what the engineers will put down in the wax."

The advice of Mr. Julian to his fellow engineers was not followed. In fact the situation with respect to recorded characteristics became much worse than at the time he wrote his copy. The recorded characteristics of the current LP's varied from company to company. There was even a difference in the diameter of the styli used to play them.

The absence of informed and disinterested critics to deal with this situation was pathetic. Ridiculous positions had been assumed by those writing for the phonograph publications. Canby, for instance, in the *Saturday Review of Recordings* for January 1948 said,

"- - - people don't like 'high fidelity'" and essayed to explain why, in the following words:

"It seems that people don't like high fidelity. There have been numerous tests given recently which indicates that, given a choice between limited-range and true, undistorted, wide-range reproduction, most people immediately pick that which is the *least* faithful to the original sound."

He went on to justify this conclusion as the result of a psychological conditioning resulting from the long exposure to reproducing instruments of limited volume and tonal range. In part he ascribed this to the lesser demands upon the attentiveness of the listener to a less brilliant reproduction. There is undoubtedly a modicum of truth in this, but Canby carries it to a ridiculous extreme. He says:

"Our reaction to any higher tones issuing from a loudspeaker is powerfully conditioned. So much so that, as the psychologist will understand, we automatically wince *even when we hear correct, undistorted tones.* This seems to me a prime reason, to add to the others, for the summary rejection of 'high fidelity' by those who have casually taken the various listener tests (and by those who sample good FM radio for the first time.)"

The assumption that the "wincing" of the listeners was due to the high fidelity and that there was no distortion may be explained by a discovery made since that time. From the *Asbury Park Evening News* of April 18, 1949, the following is quoted:

"The Monmouth County sub-section of the Institute of Radio Engineers will meet - - - Louis A. DeRosa of Federal Communications Laboratory, Nutley, will speak on 'Distortion in Audio Systems.' He will show how a study of the functions of the ear in detecting distortion has given importance to a previously ignored criterion of audio amplifier performance, phase distortion.

"For years 'high fidelity' has been a controversial subject among radio engineers. At first many believed that a flat frequency response, where all tones from the lowest to the highest audible could be reproduced with equal input levels would represent the ultimate in re-recording the original sound. As laboratory equipment began to approach the ideal, radios sold to the public improved, but one moot question led to a raging question that is not yet settled. It began simply enough; these new radio sets had better response to low notes and high notes, but many of them also had knobs marked 'tone control' that muffled the higher tones.

"Then it was discovered that almost every set owner turned his tone control part or all the way down, throwing away the 'high fidelity' that the radio engineers had striven to put there. Some radio men said, 'The public won't appreciate high fidelity until they have been educated to it. They have been listening to phonographs, sound movies, and $9.95 radios so long they have forgotten what a live orchestra sounds like.'

"To others, this appraisement of the situation didn't ring true. They suggested that something might still be wrong with radio sets of modern design. Noise (crackling and hissing) and distortion (the scratchy sound a radio makes when the volume is set too high), both are unpleasant to listen to and both are reduced by turning the tone-control down. After the war several radio engineers began independent experiments in an attempt to discover whether the average radio listener did or did not like full range in music and speech.

"Results are inconclusive as yet, but have indicated that even the very best reproducing systems may have defects, perhaps not even recognized as defects previously, that cause discomfort to the listener. Mr. DeRosa will discuss a type of distortion called 'phase distortion' that has been known to exist but was thought to be undetectable by ear. Mr. DeRosa will show that it is detectable and deteriorates the quality of reproduction."

Thus "pop" goes one attempt to rationalize the easy assumption of radio and recording engineers that the average listener is possessed of "tin ears." One might well say the only "tin ears" the public has are the ones the industry has sold them!

However, there is a romantic attachment that is often formed by listeners for recordings that are far from perfect. Everyone has probably experienced a love for an object of art that exists despite knowledge of its shortcomings. One does get used to the "tone" of one's favorite radio or phonograph. An extreme example of this was once cited by P. Wilson, technical advisor for the *Gramophone*. He told of a friend of his who, after having attended a symphony concert at the Queen's Hall, said to him that he much preferred the tone of his gramophone. The real orchestra was too loud and coarse, he said, and irritated him after the refinement of his gramophone. This, of course, is an extraordinary case. However, in the *Sunday London Times* of September 23, 1934, no less a person than the eminent music critic Ernest Newman had predicted an eventual "Musician's Eldorado." He said that would be, when all the great music of the world will have been recorded by "the one artist in the world who is best qualified" for its performance. When those conditions are fulfilled, Mr. Newman said, the "best musicians" would no longer have to attend concerts but would be freed from the maddening distractions of the concert room and from the disturbing influence of the "personality" of the conductor. Then the music lover would be able to study and re-study in the intimacy of their chambers "the great works that are an eternal joy, an eternal challenge, and an eternal mystery" to them. Impossible though such a thought may seem to be, there is no question but that such romantic notions have a basis in psychological fact.

Patric Stevenson, in writing to the *Gramophone* on Mr. Newman's philosophical conjecture of a "Musician's Eldorado," thought that the idea presented a hazard. He feels that the ability to repeat a performance *ad infinitum* is fraught with implications. In referring to a statement made by Compton Mackenzie that the effort required to "think out" the scratch of the old records that Nikisch had made of the Fifth Symphony had increased his attention to and consequent enjoyment of the music; Mr. Stevenson said:

"If this is true, as I believe it to be, Mr. Newman's Eldorado is not quite such an enchanting, danger-free land as it appears at first sight. This ability to repeat indefinitely one interpretation, no matter how 'ideal' it may be, is full of traps for the unwary, and I fear even good musicians would become unwary in a gramophonic Eldorado of perfect recordings. No, let us ever be ready to listen with open minds to new interpretations of familiar works and not switch off or dismiss them curtly because they do not conform to the 'ideal' to which our reference records have accustomed us."

Pertinent to the subject of standards is the article "Reproduction and the Real Thing," which P. Wilson wrote for the *Gramophone,* presumably as a result of the remark of his friend that he preferred the sound of the reproduced orchestra on his gramophone to the real performance. Mr. Wilson said:

"At the time, I remember that I fully shared the views of my friend that the object of all reproduction was to simulate the real thing—to create the illusion of reality, if you will, but the contact with reality was the important thing and the closer that contact the greater the illusion. I have

held that view for many years now and my endeavours have been directed towards making the contact closer.

"Let me confess at once that my mind is full of doubts; not indeed as to what should be the immediate object of our endeavours, but rather as to what will be their real value in the result. I still think we should strive after an illusion of reality, but I am clear that the particular reality of which we may have an illusion is not likely to be the same reality as that from which our records or our broadcast transmission was derived.

"I can perhaps make my point clear by illustration. By good fortune, and the kindness of our operatic record reviewer, I was able to be present at Covent Garden for the first performance of *La Cenerentola.* Like most others of those present, I was enchanted—by Rossini, by Mme. Supervia, by Ezio Pinza, by the orchestra, by the ensembles—in fact, by everything. It all left a very vivid impression on my mind. The following evening I listened to the broadcast performances of Acts II and III. **The reception was magnificent; everything was behaving itself as it should** do but does not always do. Again I was enchanted, and retained a very vivid impression of what I had heard. It was, in fact, an excellent illusion of reality. But the vivid impression and the reality were not the same as those I had on the previous evening. It does not much matter to my argument whether they were better or worse, whatever those words may mean in this connection; they were real and they were different."

Mr. Wilson then proceeds to try to analyze the differences, such as that at home he was concentrating on the hearing alone, that he was comfortably at ease and similar factors. He also mentioned that he was hearing from more or less a point source, which may have robbed him of some of the effect of perspective of the original. However, in respect to this point and its relation to Mr. Canby's quotes on the same subject from "Liveness in the Listening" this is quoted:

"I got quite a good illusion of perspective and I could make the volume level about the same all over as that which actually reached my ears at the theater. Incidentally, although some of my technical friends sometimes tell me that I could do with a stronger bass, I found that, on the contrary, my musical friends were right in suggesting that the bass is a little too strong—not much, but a little."

Also of interest, of course, is Mr. Wilson's conclusions, as follows:

"Although my illusion of the Friday evening did not, therefore, correspond exactly with the reality I had experienced on the Thursday, I claim that it was definitely an illusion of a possible reality and had even greater value.

"Normally, of course, when one listens to a broadcast, or plays a record, one has no clear idea of what the actual reality was. And it may be thought that the suggestion of a different reality which I am now making is fraught with the danger of giving sanction to any standard of reproduction as long as it is not unpleasant. Such, however, is not the case. The more one soaks oneself in original performances, the more sure one's judgement becomes of the value of pieces of reproduction as illusions of some reality or other. My suggestion is not mere word-spinning, I am sure. I am not an expert either in psychology or in artistic criticism; but I am becoming expert in the art of listening and it is this which prompts me to suggest that more careful analysis of the purpose of musical reproduction is required. As a technician I can say with confidence that the results of such an analysis may be of far-reaching consequence. For at the mo-

ment our technical, and so-called scientific, standards are in something of a mess. Will not our expert music critics come in and help? This is a job for them and not for either the executive musician or the technical expert."

Mr. Wilson's conclusions that "our technical and so-called scientific standards were in something of a mess" at the time is heartily agreed with by your authors. Otherwise, the article was simply an interesting piece of rationalization. Anyone who would expect that the phonographic reproduction of an operatic performance in the home would be productive of identical reactions to that of a phonographic reproduction in the theater would not be thinking realistically. Would you expect a singer in your home to sound exactly the same as if she were singing in a concert hall? Such attempts to discuss realities under totally differing acoustic conditions do not point towards the solution of the problems of proper standards of reproduction. The concept of two different kinds of "reality," is a purely romantic one.

This "romantic" viewpoint towards the phonograph record was expressed quite completely by Cedric Wallis about two years later in March, 1936 in an article in the *Gramophone* entitled "The Future of Recorded Romanticism." This also appeared later in the *American Music Lover*.

Mr. Wallis stated that the romantic viewpoint towards records had its origins in the acoustic recording period. He said:

"In those days battle raged between two schools of opinion, who called themselves, respectively, Realists and Romantics. The Realists stood out strongly for as accurate a reproduction as possible of the actual sounds recorded, but the Romantics held that a certain sacrifice of accuracy was permissible, nay, even desirable, if it induced a quality more pleasing to the ear. To a Romantic, realistic records were always 'shrill' or 'thin,' or both. To a Realist, a romantic record would appear 'wooly' or 'foggy.'

"- - - With the advent of the electrical recording process of recording, it may be said that the dispute ended. The Romantics were drummed off the battlefield. - - -

"Mr. P. G. Hurst has crystallized for most of us the cult of the old record as a collector's piece, but it is not quite from his point of view that I visualize the future of obsolete, romantic recordings. - - -

"Play over, if you can, one of the Gerhardt-Nikisch *lieder* records. Realistically speaking, the resultant sound is probably not much like Gerhardt, and it is certainly very little like Nikisch. In the hard light of realism the Beethoven C Minor Symphony, which still adorns the HMV Historical List, bears singularly little resemblance to the Berlin Philharmonic, or for that matter, any other first class orchestra. In a word, these records are not phonographic.

"Now that I have admitted so much, your modern, efficient realist will feel more than ever justified dismissing all our cherished evergreens as useful only to any crank who may wish to play the boring, and in this case ineffective, role of *laudator temporis acti*. But let your modern, efficient Realist hold his hand for just one minute. While he does so, we will take a glimpse at the sister art of painting.

"Why does one catch one's breath before a Madonna of Luini, or an improbable-looking bunch of sunflowers by Van Gogh? Certainly not because of the realistic accuracy with which either painter has represented his subject. The Virgin may be quite out of drawing, according to the shape of modern femininity—her hands are probably too large, and even her face is not strikingly beautiful, as the Society weeklies measure that term. As for Van Gogh—any gardener will tell you that his sunflowers would never take a prize at the Royal Show.

- - - In a word, once again—these pictures are not photographic!

"Let us attempt to draw our analogy. To be phonographic is good—but to be photographic is regrettable. Why the discrepancy? Why shouldn't the sauce that so excellently sets off the painter's goose season equally well the record-maker's gander? There is only one answer to such a question. The record-connoisseur's standards of taste has not yet had time to mellow sufficiently and to evolve.

"It is therefore the purpose of this article to suggest that many (I would not dream of saying all) outdated recordings by their very unrealism, have the quality which goes to make a great painting transcend its subject-matter. By this I wish to claim for them a value which I think in time will come to be rated higher than the strictly phonographic realism of our more efficient modern recordings. When the art of the gramophone is as old as that of painting is today, who knows what evolutionary miracles of taste may not have taken place? Where will your loves lie then —with the Rembrandts, or with the brilliantly efficient fruits of a modern, fool-proof Kodak?"

Mr. Wallis has something there, even though he leaves out the fact that photographers also take "romantic" pictures with blurred outlines, or other purposeful variations from absolute truth. Exhibitions are held frequently of photographs which reveal the sort of emphasis and intentional distortions which once were held to be the exclusive province of the artist. The chief difference, and one which we fear invalidates Mr. Wallis' analogy is that the distortions in the old phonograph records were not intentional. His feeling that the field to which his "romantic" label can be properly applied terminated with the inauguration of electrical methods is also faulty.

Many early period electrical recordings now seem as unrealistic, or more so, than many of the acoustically recorded records when played on suitable equipment, or when properly rerecorded by experts. Now, however, by playing over and over again the same passage onto a recording tape, experimenters such as Les Paul with his "The New Sound" are creating purposeful distortions of the recorded groove to which they are transferred. This procedure, then, would conform to Mr. Wallis' criterion. Perhaps too, the singers who have sung duets on phonograph records with themselves, such as Richard Tauber and Lawrence Tibbett, fit the descriptive title of "Romantics." But of more importance to our discussion of recording standards is the distortions which are purposely created by the use of echo chambers and electrical circuits which accomplish the same end.

In the February 1950 *Saturday Review of Recordings,* Edward Tatnall Canby expressed his surprise in learning that many popular songs with accompaniment were recorded in two sessions. First the instrumentalists would record their performance on tape. Then, perhaps weeks later, the vocalist would listen to the recorded accompaniment (probably by earphones) and record a separate vocal tape or sound track. Then the engineers would rerecord both, juggling the volume levels for background and emphasis. Canby points out that sound editing has been going on for years in the movies, and, to some extent, tape has also been edited for broadcasting. He quite reasonably asks what protection we can have against the abuse of this editorial privilege. Illustrating the dangers that existed, he recited the following story:

"A very well-known soprano of the Met—so the story goes among tape recording folk—recently hit a whale of a false high note in a broadcast opera performance. It was all over in an instant and nobody minded. The trouble was that the opera was to be rebroadcast later from tape. That, the lady couldn't take. The tape editors were called in, the squawk was snipped out; a search was made through the opera for another high note of the same pitch which was patched into place—and a 'perfect' performance went on the air."

The story could have been improved by substituting the voice of another singer—and later was, in the case of a famous Wagnerian soprano.

However, this ultimate step is just one more in a long series stemming from the failure to establish recording standards. A member of a record collectors' club in Washington, D. C. protested the practice of 'dubbing' or copying as a fraud. He referred to the Capitol rerecordings from German Telefunken records in particular. He felt that original recordings should be issued just as they were made. Canby took notice of this complaint in his column "Some Highs and Lows" in the *Saturday Review of Recordings* in August, 1949. He defended the modern practice of rerecording, stating that it was his understanding that many of the Telefunken recordings would have been unusable in the form received after the war. He admitted that there may be passages in the older records that may sound better in the originals, but that other bad passages had received necessary corrective treatment. Canby also stated that many LP's showed distinct improvement over the earlier 78-rpm versions of the same performances. He noted that even before the war, Columbia had begun copying all records from high fidelity transcriptions and that at the time of his writing, the LP's were being rerecorded with better quality than was possible at the time the tapes were recorded, because of subsequent advances in the electronic art. Canby concluded, saying:

"Yes, some of the finest European recordings are still made without copying. No doubt an ideal recording is at its best and cleanest when pressed direct. But few recordings are perfect! In most manufacturers' minds,

the benefits of copying easily out-
weigh that outside chance for first-
off perfection—and in any case the
record war has made re-recording a
necessity."

In other words, expediency is of more
importance than accuracy! Mr.
Canby had mentioned the utility of one technical procedure in changing of the recorded "characteristic," the balance of
high and low tones, to suit differing
needs, in February 1948. In his quoted
article in the foregoing, he also stated
that various special troubles such as a
recording with a harsh upper register
must be toned down in rerecording, "to
give a nicer sound." However, there is
no limit when the bars have been let
down. He also says:

"Artificial echo (another hush-hush
operation now widely performed)
may be added to give resonance and
brilliance to recordings that seem too
dry and close in sound. (You may
note that some LP reissues, benefiting
from such treatment, are distinctly
different in sound from the standard
versions.)"

Not once in several articles does Canby
refer to the impossibility of knowing
where the truth leaves off and the "improving" begins. If agreeable listening
quality is to be the only reliable criterion left for evaluation of recorded
music, then we are far from being realists and are floundering in the depths
of romanticism. The prognosis of such
a possible development had been given
as early as 1930 in an article in the
Phonograph Monthly Review by Harry
Alan Potamkin entitled "The Progress
of Mechanical Entertainment in Europe."
In discussing the esthetics of mechanical
musical accompaniments, for motion
picture sound films, he quotes from a
French magazine, the *Nouvelle Revue
Francaise,* some remarks by Paul
Deharme, who was proposing the creation of a Radiphonic Art. This is re-
quoted as having a bearing on the
rerecording problem:

"Deharme believes that the contemporary intelligence is in need of
'imagination, of lyric transformation,
such as is not offered by the classic
forms, nor even by the new art-
forms, and which radio may satisfy.'
"Among these prime necessities he
places 'the taste for the unreal,' as
is evinced in the willingness of the
popular mind to believe in a succession of images lacking color projected
upon a screen lacking relief, and in
such a contradiction of ordinary
logic as the animated cartoon of Max
Fleisher, where real personages par-
ticipate with designs. He believes that
the radio can create its analogy to
these visions, by putting in place of
a spectator of images an auditor of
images."

Potamkin also said that Deharme's concept of unreality had been anticipated
by one London critic who in commenting upon a radio production of Maeter-
linck's "The Bluebird," had spoken of
the successful presentation of the unreal nature of that work through the
microphone. Potamkin quotes Sabaneev,
founder of the Russian Institute of
Musical Science as having said:

"Our age is the triumph of technics.
We see their invasion of the musical
art—an art essentially remote from
the material plane. As a matter of
fact there is nothing abnormal in this;
music has always been developed in
very close contrast with technics, and
its whole evolution has depended upon
material causes. Examples are not far
to seek: the expansion of music, its
beginning, corresponds with the invention of the mensural system, which
is a contrivance of a purely technical,
and not of a musical or creative order.
Then we see a fresh outburst of creative fertility coinciding with the invention of music-printing, another
technical phenomenon. What would
music have been if the organ and
keyed instruments had not been invented? The keyboard in combination
with the tempered scale alone made

Bach possible, and there is nothing 'creative' in these."

In Mr. Potamkin's stimulating article, Professor Sabaneev is quoted as having made these prophesies concerning the further mechanization in the musical art; that there will be an increasing differentiation between the active creator and the passive listener; and that there will be created an instrument in which the artistic will would exercise control over properties of every note. The first prophesy has been realized in the phonograph and recordings; the second prophesy is the electronic organ.

CHAPTER 26

COPYRIGHTS AND
PERFORMANCE RIGHTS

EUROPE, home of the great classical authors and composers, was logically the first to recognize the principle of ownership by the enactment of copyright laws in the various countries. Originally, these copyright laws protected the author, composer, or the publisher from the unauthorized copying and sale of copyrighted material only and gave them but little control over the performance of these works for profit, except for the rights to produce complete plays or operas, etc.

In January of 1851, there was organized in France the Societe des Auteurs, Compositeurs et Editeurs de Musiques, to work for more effective recognition of the rights of the authors, composers, and publishers in performance rights as well as to assist in the prosecution of infringers under the existing laws. The idea spread to other European Countries and similar organizations were formed in the leading countries such as Germany, Italy, Austria, France, and England.

The first copyright statute of the United States was passed by the Congress in 1790. This granted to the copyright holder protection for twenty-eight years, with provision for renewal. As these early laws were passed long before the invention of the various types of coin-slot musical instruments and the phonograph, the question of rights to the mechanical reproduction of copyrighted music or words did not have to be considered. Hence, in the early

days of the phonograph, the only persons paid for their music recorded on the cylinders were the performers. For a long period of time, the phonograph was looked upon as a toy by most musicians. For this reason, little importance was attached by composers and authors to the precedent which was then being established of permitting records to be made and sold for profit, without the necessity of securing permission of the copyright holders. In the United States, the effects of this precedent have not been completely eradicated to the present day.

Even when the popularity of the phonograph became well-established, the use of copyrighted material was not generally frowned upon by the publishers, who generally thought the records to be good advertising which would result in increased sale of sheet music. However, by the 1900's some authors and composers began to entertain doubts as to the wisdom of permitting indiscriminate performing and recording for home reproduction of their works. One of these was John Philip Sousa, the "March King," whose famous band had ostensibly made recordings from the earliest days of the cylinders. Actually, what had happened was that Sousa had permitted a few of his musicians to go to the recording studios to make the records. These were then issued and he was paid a fee for the use of his name in the catalogs and advertising. There was some legitimate excuse for using only a few of the musicians, for more would not record well in the primitive stage of the art of recording.

After leaving the conductorship of the U. S. Marine Band, Sousa's reputation was largely built on his famous marches, which were, of course, played by the many local bands from coast to coast. The Sousa band records, first issued on Columbia cylinders and later on the Edison cylinders, were large sellers and served greatly to augment his popularity with the many lovers of band music, and throngs waited expectantly to hear the famous band on its many triumphant tours. The fame of Sousa soon eclipsed that of the theretofore almost equally famous Patrick Gilmore, whose band under other leadership also had made cylinders for Columbia. Sousa's band also recorded for the Berliner hard rubber discs, and here to make his imprimatur more obviously authentic, he permitted the use of his signature as well as his name, which was engraved in the surface of each disc.

Although he profited financially from the phonograph, Sousa really had only contempt for the medium. It has been said that he was first to use the derisive term "canned music." So great was his disdain that when Eldridge R. Johnson sought from Sousa an exclusive contract to record with the newly-formed Victor Talking Machine Company, Sousa agreed to the contract but sent his concertmaster Arthur Pryor to serve as the actual director with the musicians necessary to make the records. Pryor did not share Sousa's antipathy for the talking machine and soon became so proficient in arranging the band music for recording, in positioning the performers before the recording horns for the best results, and in conducting for recording, that he was invited to form his own band. This he did with the result that for years Arthur Pryor's Band was second only to that of Sousa in the United States and was accorded considerable recognition abroad. Today he is probably remembered principally as the composer of "The Whistler and his Dog."

Sousa was one of the prime movers for stronger copyright laws, both to cover the performances of copyrighted music by others and the use of such music for mechanical reproduction. Victor Herbert was another composer and conductor who agreed with Sousa and who also made his opinions on the subject known.

As in the establishment of the basic copyright laws, Europe led in the extension of the principle to cover performances by others and the mechanical reproduction of copyrighted material. The *Talking Machine World* (London), of February 15, 1905 told of the ruling of a French court against the unauthorized reproduction of copyrighted songs or music. Naturally, there was opposition from the record manufacturers and M. Pathe of Pathe-Freres was reported to have said that the Societe des Auteurs, Compositeurs et Editeurs de Musiques was demanding a royalty of seven cents on every record sold. M. Freres was quoted as having offered ten per cent of gross sales, but that this offer had been refused. This successful suit in France attracted much attention in the United States, for a similar suit brought by the John Church Company in the United States eight years before against a phonograph record manufacturer had been defeated so decisively that no publisher had dared such a suit since.

In February 1906, *The Talking Machine World* reported another important decision in Brussels, Belgium; that of the Compagnie Generale des Phonographes, Pathe-Freres, and Societe Ullman v. Marcenet and Puccini. This was one of the more important cases, due to the effects upon the conventions of international copyright agreements and by precedent upon the laws of signatory nations. One of the key passages in the article is as follows:

"The defendants in this action were the complainants in a previous action in the Lower Court, where they were successful in having the recording of copyright music by record manufacturers recognized as a breach of copyright. The talking machine manufacturers appealed against this decision, and the decree just handed down upholds their objection."

However, the court made it clear that this reversal of the decision of the lower court was made on a point of law and recognized the justice of the rights of the composers in the following statement:

"In matters of literary and artistic property the relations of Belgium with France and Italy are regulated by the International Convention of Berne of 1886. By the terms of this Convention it seems that only foreign authors have the right to reproduce their works or to authorize their reproduction in any manner whatsoever. This is subject to the exception as follows:

'The manufacture and sale of instruments reproducing mechanically airs of music does not constitute musical infringement.' "

The Talking Machine World article further quoted the court decision as follows:

"- - - It seemed inequitable that the authors could not, except in the case of public execution, receive any profit from the reproduction of their works, nor oppose such reproduction except in certain conditions; but that the Court was forced to decide that the authors were without right so long as the Convention of Berne had not been modified or denounced."

But in August of the same year as the foregoing decision, the Italian Society of Authors and Composers won a suit in Italy for royalties on record sales. This case established a firm precedent governing the rights of the music and song writers. However, comparatively speaking, the interpreters of music and

script had at the time made little progress in bargaining collectively with the users of their talents. In September of 1906, it was announced that M. Note was forming an association of singers and actors in France. While this was more in the nature of a labor union, it may have seemed reasonable that if the composers and authors could expect royalties from records, so should the singers and the interpreters of the music.

These events stimulated Sousa, Victor Herbert, and their friends in America to push for revision of the laws and the formation of an organization to secure enforcement. As a result, the Copyright Act of 1909 included provisions covering the performance of copyrighted works by others, and also covered mechanical reproduction. Moreover, it implemented enforcement of the unauthorized performance clause by providing for a minimum infringement damage claim of $250 for anyone proven of violation. A set price of 2¢ royalty on each record was also included.

That Edison was entirely in accord with the securing of proper compensation to authors, composers, and publishers seems indicated by the fact that it was at this time he employed Victor Herbert as Director of Recording. Later, Herbert was engaged in a similar capacity by Victor, suggesting that Johnson was of a similarly fair-minded disposition with respect to the recompense of authors, composers, and publishers. As has been noted elsewhere, both Edison and Johnson generally conducted themselves as businessmen, which always was not quite true of others at this time.

Except for artists engaged on an exclusive contract, it was generally customary to pay artists a flat fee for a recording session. C. G. Childs had initiated the royalty basis of payment in order to secure the great artists exclusively to Victor, such as Caruso, Melba, Plancon, Homer, Eames, and many others. In later years, the royalty basis was adopted by other companies and extended also to popular stars with established reputations. For the most part, the matter of payment to performing artists was competitive and still remains so. To a beginning artist, the fact that he has been engaged to make records by a leading phonograph company is much more important than the remuneration. Hence, the amount actually paid to many artists for making records generally had been considered a private contractual matter.

Performing rights to copyrighted material is something else, for it is difficult to ascertain where and when all of the performances for profit take place. The problems of arranging for consent, correspondence, and bookkeeping are enormous. Naturally it irked well-known authors and composers to visit theaters, hotels, and other places of amusement to find others profiting greatly from performances of their works for which they may have received only the royalty on a single sheet of music! Many of the New York composers and publishers were accustomed to meeting at the Lamb's Club and Kean's Chop House to discuss this problem. George Maxwell, then managing director of G. Ricordi & Company, pointed out to his colleagues the successful efforts of the performing rights societies abroad. An amendment was made to the copyright statute by Congress in 1912, but which still did not serve to solve the problem of enforcement which rested largely upon those whose rights were infringed.

Formal organization of the American Society of Composers, Authors, and Publishers (ASCAP) was finally achieved in 1914. George Maxwell was elected president; Victor Herbert, vice-president; Glen McDonough, secretary; and John L. Golden, treasurer. This for the first time provided an appropriate bargaining and licensing agency to deal with all types of performances of the copyrighted material of members. However, under the law as it existed, this applied only to performances for which a special admission fee was charged and excepted musical performances in the home as well as music that was reproduced mechanically. As soon as the organization of ASCAP was accomplished, within a week, 135 publishers had joined. One of the oldest, Joseph W. Stern and Company, abstained. It was reported in the February 21, 1914 issue of *Billboard* that practically every composer and lyric writer in the profession had become members. The board of directors included Rudolph Schirmer, Henry Waterson, Fred Belcher, Irving Berlin, and E. Ray Goetz.

Plans were laid to begin an enforcement campaign with the hotel orchestras, to be followed by the cafes and cabarets. A test case with the Hotel Men's Association resulted in an adverse decision for ASCAP in 1915. Victor Herbert personally brought the next suit against an infringer on the basis of plagiarism. The United States District Court in New York dismissed the action and the Circuit Court of Appeals sustained the decision. However, the United States Supreme Court reversed the lower courts on January 22, 1917. The result was that a package deal was proposed by the Hotel Men's Association which was accepted by ASCAP. The motion picture houses (large employers of musicians in those days of the silent films) were next put in the courts. The exhibitors defended their position by a countersuit alleging restraint of trade, but lost in a decision rendered by Judge Goff, April 4, 1918.

At this time, a number of important publishers were not members of ASCAP. They felt that the equal splitting of income among the authors, composers, and publishers, one-third going to each, was inequitable, as the publishers had to assume the commercial risks. Therefore a change was made, with one-half of the ASCAP income to go to the publishers and one-fourth to each of the others, the authors and composers. As a result, many of the dissident publishers joined.

Royalties shortly thereafter passed the $100,000 mark for the first time, with the motion picture houses contributing more than half. Until 1921, the officers of ASCAP drew no salaries. In this year Maxwell was still president; J. C. Rosenthal was the general manager; and Nathan Burkan, who had been the attorney from the first, still continued to represent ASCAP in the courts.

A sequence of events now occurred which eventually was to vitally affect radio (and indirectly the phonograph), for ASCAP now became allied with the Vaudeville Managers Protective Association. The latter organization was then headed by Pat Casey, who had Edwin Claude Mills as his assistant. In 1919, Mills had been with the Music Publishers Protective Association at $15,000 per year and had been made chairman of the board in March of 1920 at $20,000 per year. Both protective organizations were located then in the same building on West 45th Street in the same offices used by ASCAP. Due to the mutual membership in the organizations by the publishers, Mills was named chairman of the administration committee of ASCAP, which also included, among others, Gene Buck and Silvio Heine.

In 1923 Gene Buck was elected president of ASCAP. The Paramount Building was erected in New York about this time and Buck gave Paramount an opportunity to get some of its royalties back by renting the entire 25th floor as headquarters for ASCAP. This also seemed to establish the rapport that existed between ASCAP and the motion picture exhibitors. Now radio performance rights began to assume importance and radio station WOR in nearby Newark was made a party in a test case. However, WEAF in New York decided to take a license without a contest. In 1929 Mills left the MPPA and ASCAP to form the Radio Music Company for NBC. Three years later ASCAP hired him back.

A result of the mergers was the filing of an anti-trust suit against ASCAP, which was now taking in over two million dollars annually. In 1934, the headquarters of ASCAP was moved to the RCA Building in Rockefeller Center. This latter move seemed to indicate that a peaceful settlement of ASCAP's negotiations with the broadcasters was possible. However, in the September 28, 1940 issue of *Billboard*, there appeared a full page advertisement as follows:

"An open letter to all band leaders:
"As you know the radio chains have announced that they will bar ASCAP music from the air beginning New Year's Day.

"As you know, the purpose is to monopolize the air with the music of the chain-organized, chain controlled BMI.

"We believe the bandleaders will have something to say about it. We believe the FCC will have something to say about it.

"We believe that the chains might just as well take away musicians' instruments as take away their music.

"Boycott or no boycott, the public will still want to hear its favorite tunes, by its favorite writers, played by its favorite bands. And our composers, authors and publishers will continue to give it the music it wants.

"If the public cannot get the music it wants from the chains, it will get it from the individual stations, such as those operated by Elliot Roosevelt, Warner Brothers, and many who have signed with ASCAP.

"It will get it from sheet music and records. It will get it from the bands in hotels, ballrooms, night clubs, dance halls and theaters.

"Music gets around. So does the public.

"Don't let anyone pick your material for you. Don't gamble with your following. Don't gamble with your reputation.

American Society of Composers, Authors & Publishers.

John G. Paine, General Manager September 21, 1940."

This major disagreement was one of considerable importance to the record industry, for by 1940 much of the time of many radio stations throughout the country was being taken up in the play-

ing of phonograph records and transcriptions—the latter was simply a more
palatable euphemism coined by the radio industry to designate records especially prepared for broadcast purposes. The principal purpose in doing
this was to combat the public aversion to records which had been created
by such derogatory terms as "canned
music."

The musicians were also vitally interested in the radio chains ASCAP
controversy and not particularly because of the restrictions upon the music
which could be played. Mass unemployment of musicians had resulted from
the introduction of talking pictures into
the movie houses and the decline of
popular interest in vaudeville. The stay-
ing at home of thousands to listen to
radio and the displacement of live entertainment in many smaller bistros and
taverns by "juke boxes" also were important factors in the declining employment of musicians, which was at low
ebb. The situation being as it was,
James Caesar Petrillo, president of the
American Federation of Musicians, realized that his union was then in no
position to battle the broadcasters or
the record manufacturers, so patiently
bided his time. As far as the musicians
and Petrillo were concerned, the industrialists then held all of the cards, for
the Copyright law specifically covered
only the rights of the authors, composers, and publishers and not those of
the interpreters of music. As far as the
juke box was concerned, the situation
was even weaker, for in the law there
was a special exemption clause, as
follows:

"The reproduction or rendition of a
    musical composition by or upon coin-
    operated machines shall not be deemed
    a public performance for profit unless
    a fee is charged for admission to the
    place where such reproduction or ren-
    dition occurs."

The picture was considerably different
with respect to the rights of the inter-
preter, or performing artist, and the
record manufacturer, however. In the
highest court of Pennsylvania (Waring
vs. WADS) and in a U.S. District Court
in New York (RCA vs. Whiteman), it
had been decided in both instances that
the performing artist had a property
right in his rendition as recorded and
might restrict the use of that record.
It was further held by those courts that
the commercial use of a record without
the authority of the artist constituted
unfair competition with the artist. The
New York Court also held that the
broadcasting of the record without the
consent of the manufacturer also constituted unfair competition with the
record manufacturer. It should be noted
that in these cases the principle of their
use for commercial purposes was involved.

These court decisions prefaced a period in which the records of many recording artists bore the legend "not
licensed for radio broadcast." Meanwhile, the battle raged between ASCAP
and the big broadcasting chains, who
had organized "Broadcast Music, Inc."
(BMI), gathering up such non-ASCAP
copyrights as they were able and signing up authors and composers who were
not ASCAP members, as well. Although
the cases mentioned previously concerned only the radio broadcasting of
phonograph records, the principles involved were considered to be possibly
applicable to any commercial use, including coin-operated phonographs by
some authorities, including Andre D.
Weinberger, who wrote an opinion to
this effect for Billboard. Weinberger
pointed out, however, that most band
leaders and singers did not consider the
music machine industry as unfair competition, but as a market for their
talent.

By another year, it was evident that
the music offered by BMI was insufficient to satisfy the public, who for
twelve months in many areas had been
unable to hear anything on a chain
program by Victor Herbert, Gene Buck,
Irving Berlin, and many other favorite
composers, both classical and popular.
The break came with the signing with

ASCAP by the Mutual Broadcasting System in May of 1941. A poll was taken later in the year which revealed that 65% of all the music played over MBS was ASCAP. The stalemate with respect to the other chains continued for a few more months, but the major networks finally knuckled down and signed. As recently as 1957 Bing Crosby issued a statement to the press blaming the major networks for favoring BMI compositions as against the better music offered by ASCAP, which indicates that a "cold war" had been continually in progress through those many years.

As has been noted, Petrillo bided his time and when the time was ripe, he decided to attack. Not the operators nor owners of locations, or with the broadcast stations, his principal target; instead he went to the headwaters, the record manufacturers. Patiently, during the depression years, Petrillo had cemented his control over his local organizations of musicians. His principal weapon had been in the form of advice and legal assistance to the locals with the result that by the time he was ready to go after the record manufacturers, not a live performance at which an admission was to be charged could be given in any community of the country—even by high school and amateur musicians, without the consent of the American Federation of Musicians.

When Petrillo approached the leaders of the recording industry early in 1942 asking for a flat rate to be paid to his union on each record pressed, these industrialists did not believe it possible that he could make good on his threat to keep all of the musicians out of the recording studios. These men knew full well that the technological changes fostered by their companies through radio, phonograph records, and talking pictures had displaced thousands of musicians all over the country and that the unlimited duplication of one performance through pictures and records had made good music accessible to all, as well as vast profits to all—except the musician. This had all occurred with hardly a protest from AFM,

yet here stood James Caesar Petrillo telling them that unless they came across not a recording turntable would turn.

Nevertheless, the recording industry was forced to live for twenty-seven months on its fat of accumulated recordings not yet issued, or by re-issues of older recordings. From August of 1942 to November of 1944, the only new records which were made were by a few singers with harmonica accompaniment, or by harmonica bands, such as the Harmonicats. Petrillo, it seems, had ruled that the harmonica was not considered a musical instrument! However, so tight was his control over the musicians that even well-known artists who might have dared his wrath were unable to find even suitable piano accompanists. The public has long forgotten the unkind remarks written and spoken about Petrillo during this period, during which he even defied the intercession of the President of the United States.

In this contest, the break occurred when some of the smaller record companies signed with Petrillo late in 1943, but as stated previously, Columbia and Victor remained steadfast until November of the following year. Columbia was the first to surrender, and a telegram sent by Edward Wallerstein, president of Columbia Recording Corp. to Judge Fred M. Vinson, Office of Economic Stabilization, Washington, D. C. stated well the position of the recording companies, as well as indicating the heat the controversy had aroused, as quoted in full on pages 334 and 335.

This telegram, while expensive in terms of what it cost to send, is actually most economical with respect to summing up the case for the recording companies. Wallerstein is revealed by this to have been a worthy pleader to follow in the footsteps of his Columbia Graphophone Company and American Graphophone Company predecessors, Col. Payne, Edward Easton, and Philip Mauro.

The signing by Columbia Recording Corp. was followed by the immediate capitulation of RCA Victor.

To be fair to Petrillo, the case of the musicians in view of the problems of technological unemployment which had been created by the introduction of mechanical sound reproduction instruments during the decade prior to 1942 was a just one. One result of Wallerstein's final telegram of protest was that Petrillo agreed to the setting up of a trust fund to be administered by a trustee to be appointed by the record manufacturers. The Music Performance Fund, as it was called, was to be used to finance concerts to be given by musicians in the various communities for the purpose of music appreciation, to give local musicians needed employment and for charitable work in entertaining in hospitals, etc. All such projects were to be submitted by the locals of the AFM for approval and then submitted to the trustee for review and his approval. No admission charge or other commercialization of these concerts was to be permitted. Although this was a clear-cut victory for Petrillo, it has actually done little except to give temporary help to unemployed musicians. It must be observed that this contract between AFM and the recording companies does not have anything to do with royalties to be paid to individual musicians, nor does it invest him with a continuing interest in the infinitely repeated performances of his interpretative efforts, as do the contracts with ASCAP for the authors and composers.

Within a few hours after RCA Victor signed, Vaughan Monroe was recording the "Trolley Song" and "The Very Thought of You." Meanwhile, José Iturbi was busy recording selections composed by the popular band leader, Morton Gould. Thus the two-year hunger of the American public for the music so long denied them was assuaged by great performances of immortal music!

The jumping of the gun in signing with AFM by Wallerstein of Columbia and the leaving of his former employers RCA Victor, is of interest when compared with his action in introducing the improved 33⅓-rpm LP record in 1948 and the reaction of RCA Victor, which decided not to follow suit but to introduce a 45-rpm disc instead. Is it true that Victor had planned to introduce virtually the same 33⅓-rpm improved LP but Wallerstein had beaten them to it? In any case, it cost RCA Victor millions of dollars to popularize the 45-rpm disc and it was only the further and technically contradictory improvement of extended play that saved the 45 rpm disc from complete relegation to the juke-box field.

CHAPTER 27

CORPORATE GENEALOGY

CORPORATIONS are inventions of men. A number of men may associate for almost any legitimate purpose and apply for a charter. This charter grants the group as a body certain legal rights, privileges, and obligations of an individual as distinguished from their original and separate status as citizens. In other words, a new superorganic entity is created. With due respect to its particular kind of charter, it may buy and sell property, engage in business, or do many of the things an individual can do—and even some things a person cannot do. For instance, a corporation may possibly outlive not only one of its founders, but perhaps all of them, and many have. On the other hand, corporations cannot vote, even though they may rule. Many of our governmental entities, including some states which grant certificates of incorporation, are corporations and its citizens are its stockholders.

An outgrowth of the Renaissance and nourished by the Industrial Revolution, corporate growth and activity has been responsible to a great extent for the tremendous expansion of industry and commerce in the Western world, especially in the past three centuries. Free enterprise and individual initiative alone could never have accomplished so much in such a comparatively short time without corporate organizations. Almost of equal importance has been the granting of letters patent for inventions. Recognizing that creative thought can only be a product of the human mind, pat-

ents for inventions have been granted only to individuals, though they may be assigned by those individuals to the ownership of corporations.

Corporations are of manifold types, ranging from governmental entities, church societies, educational institutions, banks, and insurance companies on down to virtually one-man enterprises which may have been organized to legitimately lose money for tax purposes. Some of our larger industrial corporations, including one or more of those with which this text is concerned, have more stockholders than there are residents in some states! As the legal climate of some of these states, such as Delaware, has proven to be especially healthful and conducive to corporate growth, the political power of our larger corporations may easily be appreciated.

Corporations and the granting of letters patent may therefore be said to share, though somewhat disproportionately, the credit for the phenomenal development of our phonograph industry, among many others. Logically, two classes of specialists in law have been prominent in this development, patent and corporation attorneys. Within the eighty-year span of the industry, a marked deviation has come about between these two classes of law practice with respect to the industry. Corporation lawyers have been important from the beginning in the organization of the phonograph enterprises and in the devious maneuverings for control of the industry. True, the earlier companies were organized around a person or persons in possession of one or more important patents, but individuals and individual patents have become progressively less important as the corporations have increased in size.

Aside from more intense specialization, the relationship of corporation lawyers to the phonograph industry has remained about the same. However, the relationships of patent attorneys to this and other industries have been markedly changed within the period of eighty years. Prior to the turn of the century, nearly all patent attorneys were free agents, offering their professional services to any inventor who wished to engage them. Now, the greater number of patent law specialists are "house attorneys" who work for a single corporate employer on a salary basis. This, in itself, serves to indicate the relatively decreasing importance of patents.

The changed status of the patent attorney is symptomatic of a parallel and fundamental change in the status of the inventor. Now, most inventors are "engineers" who work on a salary basis for corporations. Although, as has been said, law forbids granting patents to corporations, the obligation to assign individual patents to the corporation is often made a provision of the employment contract. Questions have been raised in the press lately as to the loss of prestige occasioned by the mass employment of professional engineers by the automotive, plastics, electronics, and aircraft industries. This has progressed to the point where large numbers of such employees have been seeking to safeguard their interests by joining unions. It's obvious that, when hundreds of engineers are put to work side by side in the laboratories of the large corporations, their status ceases to be managerial or, perhaps, even professional. The reality of the individual and his special creative abilities within the history of the phonograph have become submerged in the welter of collective cycles of activity created for the most part by others. Will there ever again be such ruggedly individual inventors as Morse, Bell, Whitney, McCormick, and Tesla?

Important in the change which has come about is the commercial use of the monopoly granted to the independent inventor in return for full and complete publication of information about his device or process, which is often quite dependent upon resources other than those usually available to him. Many inventors of phonographic devices, in common with many others, have often fought unsuccessfully for years to reap some profit from the monopoly ostensibly granted them by letters patent. Often, an inventor has lived to see his inventions utilized through the corporate devices to create a monopoly for others, which he knows by the basic intent of the patent laws, should have been reserved to himself. Thus, the fictional corporate devices have proven more important in shaping our *available* commercial phonographs than the collective contributions of countless innovators.

The span of phonographic history has neatly bridged the era beginning with the high-flying, fiercely independent and competitive inventors of the period between 1880-1910 to the research and industrial engineers of today. Organized industry needs resources for quickly putting new ideas to work. Granting this, there is some question of the stifling of incentive to invent by the very size and complexity of our modern industrial giants. Also, the restive, inventive type of person is one seldom equipped to deal realistically with the prosaic problems of factory methods and economics. Edison was probably the only one of the master inventors of the early era who was also adept in organizing factory processes and marketing his own products. He proved this not only with the phonograph, but in a dozen other fields. A classic example of his versatility was in successfully converting a tremendously expensive iron extraction plant he had built in New Jersey into a new type for cement manufacturing, when the discovery of the vast Masabi iron ore deposits in the Midwest made the former operation unprofitable.

Edison also had an uncanny knack for being practical in his inventing. The tinfoil phonograph was exactly what was needed at the moment. It was the simplest possible device for demonstrating the principle involved and it served that purpose beautifully. Has anyone ever produced a simpler one? Being simple, it was also cheap and practical to build in any shop without special tools. It paid its way handsomely from the start. An equally simple corporate device accompanied it, the Edison Speaking Phonograph Co. When the profits from the exhibition period for which this phonograph had been designed had been garnered, the books were balanced and the corporation became dormant until Edison could find time from his commitments to Edison Electric Light Co. to carry the phonograph into its next stage of usefulness.

As discussed earlier, Gardiner G. Hubbard, father-in-law of Alexander Graham Bell and his chief financial backer, was one of the directors of the Edison Speaking Phonograph Co. Despite the surface good relations that always prevailed between the Bell and Edison families, some questions have never been satisfactorily answered. Is it possible that Gardiner G. Hubbard was unhappy about the failure of Edison to carry on the development work on the phonograph sooner? Was he perhaps a bit irked because of Edison's continued loyalty to the Western Union interests who were then preparing to set up competition to the Bells in the telephone field? Could this possibly explain why Alexander Bell and his colleagues of the Volta Laboratory Association in Washington, D. C. in 1880 rather suddenly switched their investigative and inventive efforts from the telephone to the phonograph?

Regardless of the answers, Tainter's notes in the Smithsonian Institution clearly reveal a complete change of research direction occurring in that year. Another interesting question is posed

by the lag in filing applications for patents. However, Dr. Chichester A. Bell, Alexander Graham Bell, and Charles Sumner Tainter in 1885 and 1886 applied for the famous patents which provided the basis for formation of the Volta Graphophone Co. to act as as a patent holding corporation. A little later, the Supreme Court reporters, including Andrew Devine and James Clephane, who became the financial backers of the Volta group, organized the American Graphophone Co. to engage in the manufacture and rental of the Bell-Tainter Graphophone for dictating purposes. Here, the reader should carefully note, were two of the three essentials for inventive success . . . money and the services of competent attorneys. The reader may well say, "Yes, but you have left out the most important essential, the inventions themselves." Rest assured, this omission is intentional. Years after the ozocerite cylinder record and the Bell-Tainter Graphophone had passed into the limbo with the Edison tinfoil phonograph, the American Graphophone Co. was still doing business at the old stand!

"But," the reader may object, "wasn't this also true of Edison?" The answer is that the corporate device originated to commercialize the Edison demonstration tinfoil phonograph was not accompanied by the two requisites above, nor were they needed in view of the different purpose served. Other types of corporate devices had to be set up to give the new Edison phonograph designed for business and commercial use a proper environment for manufacture, sales, and service. The Edison Phonograph Co. organized in 1887 for development, the Edison Phonograph Works for manufacturing in 1888, and Lippincott's North American Phonograph Co., with its numerous local phonograph company satellites, were the legalistic devices intended to meet these needs. If Lippincott had not tried to eliminate possible competition by trying to bring both the phonograph and graphophone together under his aegis, his corporate invention, the North American Phono-

graph Co., might still be in business today! In this interesting speculation, it
should be observed that as far as the
basic functional elements were concerned, the Edison Home Phonograph
of 1896 was virtually the same instrument as the improved Edison phonograph of 1888. However, the Graphophone of 1896 was a totally different instrument than the Bell-Tainter
Graphophone of 1888.

Even during the collapse of Lippincott's empire, caused largely by the
machinations of the Graphophone group,
growth of the slot-machine phonographs, penny arcades, and use of improved phonographs for entertainment
was showing a great profit potential.
Survival of many of the local companies
for a number of years, despite the leasing plan which was unsuited to the new
purposes, indicates the entire corporate
system could have been reorganized
along proper lines if the attorneys of
the defunct Graphophone enterprise
would have permitted it.

Forced to it, Edison organized the National Phonograph Co. to succeed the
Edison Phonograph Works and to have
the additional functions of distribution
and sales. Several of the old "state's
rights" companies which had been organized by Lippincott were still enabled to carry on as before, but not on
an exclusive basis. One of these companies was the Columbia Phonograph
Co., which had been organized by
Edward Easton and others of the Washington reporters, to operate in Washington, D. C., Maryland, and Delaware
under Lippincott's North American
Phonograph Co. Some of the organizers
were also connected with the American
Graphophone Co. In view of subsequent
events, was this all part of an exceedingly diabolical plot? If not, it was
certainly a most provident coincidence
that the founders of the American
Graphophone Co. had in the Columbia
Phonograph Co. just the right kind of
corporate device needed to tide them
over the impoverished years from 1889
to 1893 so that Thomas H. Macdonald
might come to them from the North

American Phonograph Co. and reorganize the Graphophone factory to produce Edison type instruments. More
than this, the maintenance for several
years of the fiction that the Columbia
Phonograph Co. was an entirely independent company and therefore still entitled to act under the franchise originally granted by the North American
Phonograph Co. enabled them to continue to advertise Edison Phonographs
and records at the combination penny
arcades and sales depots they were organizing in Atlantic City, New York,
Baltimore, Philadelphia, and eventually
in St. Louis, Paris, London, and other
European cities.

How tenuous this legal supposition
was and how inept the Edison attorneys
is illustrated by this fact. The Edison
Phonograph Works in 1896 had been
enjoined from producing phonographs
on the basis that the rights given by the
American Graphophone Co. to act as
sales agent had not given the Edison
Phonograph Works permanent rights to
produce instruments of the Graphophone type. Actually, a perusal of the
original phonograph contracts reveals
no consideration of patent rights. While
Lippincott's agreement with the Graphophone Co. was a personal one, the
agreement with Edison extended to the
company which Edison knew Lippincott intended to form. Ultimately, this
legal action resulted in a cross licensing
agreement. From the time the National
Phonograph Co. was organized in 1896
to the present writing, the Edison corporate development has had a strict
lineal continuity, although in 1911 a
consolidation of the Edison enterprises
was made under the title "Thomas A.
Edison, Inc." The Phonograph Division
was discontinued after the cessation of
phonograph and record production in
1929, but the Ediphone Division, later
named the "Voicewriter Division," continued to operate.

The American Graphophone Co., incorporated in January 1886, was primarily a manufacturing company. For
a short time it attempted to lease the
Bell-Tainter Graphophone directly in

Washington, D. C. where most of its founders were located. After the organization of the North American Phonograph Co. and the Columbia Phonograph Co., the former was the distributing company and the latter the local company in the home territory. At this time, the Graphophone Co. located its factory in Bridgeport, Conn.

After the Lippincott enterprise collapsed, the American Graphophone Co. plant in Bridgeport was cleared of the old foot-treadle Bell-Tainter machines by Thomas Macdonald. Preparations were made to make instruments of the Edison type for demonstration purpose, for penny arcades, and ultimately for the home market. As soon as these new type instruments were in production, a new company, Columbia Phonograph Co., General, was organized to open and operate combination penny arcades and sales depots. The first of these were opened on the Boardwalk at Atlantic City. The Edison name was used freely. The original Columbia Phonograph Co., licensed under the North American Phonograph Co. to sell Edison Phonographs in the District of Columbia, West Virginia, and Delaware, continued its claim on that franchise. At that time, the Columbia name was practically unknown to the general public. The Columbia Phonograph Co., General was made the exclusive distributor of American Graphophone Co. products for the world.

In 1906, the American Graphophone Co. was reorganized as the Columbia Graphophone Co., thus recognizing the identity known to have existed from the first, even though obscured by titular difference. In 1918, the manufacturing operation was made the basis of a banking and stock promotion scheme as the Columbia Graphophone Manufacturing Co. This financial expansion was not matched by the requisite product improvement, and coupled with the advent of radio, the American companies were bankrupt in 1923. Meanwhile, Louis Sterling, who had some years before organized the Columbia Phonograph Co., Ltd. in London, now put up the money to reorganize the American companies as Columbia Phonograph Co., Inc. This new company, now English-owned, in 1926 purchased the Okeh Phonograph Co., formerly the General Phonograph Co., importers and pressers of Odeon and Fonotipia records for the American trade. The Columbia Phonograph Co., Inc. in 1928 assisted in the reorganization of Independent Broadcasters, Inc. into the present Columbia Broadcasting System.

However, an international shakedown occurred after the 1929 stock market collapse. In 1932, Grigsby-Grunow, Inc., temporarily fat with the accumulated profits of its successes with Majestic's "Mighty Monarch of the Air" radio receivers, was able to purchase the Columbia Phonograph Co., Inc. from Columbia Phonograph Co., Ltd. Just two more years of continual recession and its totally dependent patent status was sufficient to reduce the once "Mighty Monarch" to bankruptcy and the Columbia Phonograph Co., Inc. was sold to a banking syndicate called Sacro Enterprises.

In 1938, the Columbia Broadcasting System purchased the American Record Co. plant, formerly the Scranton Button Works and used by the Columbia group for pressing records for the five and ten cent store trade in the halcyon days. CBS organized the Columbia Recording Corporation and prepared to go into the transcription business. This was followed by the acquisition of Columbia Phonograph Co., Inc., which consummated as nice an example of corporate vitality and regeneration as anyone could ask for! Columbia Records, Inc., is the present corporate name of this company and it is a wholly-owned Columbia Broadcasting System subsidiary.

RCA Victor's story is a similarly complex one. Founded on the basis of Emile Berliner's Gramophone patents, the U. S. Gramophone Co. was organized in Washington, D. C. in 1893, and the Berliner Gramophone Co. the following year. How Gaisberg brought Eldridge R. Johnson and Berliner together shortly after this, with Johnson improving the Gramophone and becoming its first manufacturer, has been recounted elsewhere. Frank Seamon organized the National Gramophone Co. in 1896 to act as exclusive distributor of Gramophone products in the United States. There is some reason to suspect that from the first, Seamon may have had an understanding with the officials of the American Graphophone Co., for within three years his company was endorsing the products of a competing disc company. This was the American Talking Machine Co., which, by interesting coincidence, had been organized in 1896 also, to produce cylinder records. Now this company had suddenly begun the production of gramophone-type machines called the "Vitaphone" and red disc records similar to the Gramophone records, except for their color. Another strange coincidence was that a young man by the name of Jones was in charge of recording for this company. Quickly stopped by Berliner on the basis of patent infringement, National Gramophone reorganized itself as the National Gramophone Corporation and another corporation was organized as the Universal Talking Machine Co. to manufacture a gramophone-type instrument, the Zonophone, and records. These developments occurred between 1897 and 1900.

Prevented by an injunction from marketing "Gramophones" and "Gramophone Records" in the United States, because of the exclusive contract his company had given Seamon, Berliner turned his attention to Europe. He sent William Barry Owen and the Gaisbergs to Europe with the results explained in more detail elsewhere. In the United States, Eldridge R. Johnson continued to produce the Gramophones, but sans the name and "Eldridge R. Johnson" records, were made by his improved process, now for the first time with paper labels. Perhaps a temporary split had occurred between Berliner and Johnson, for neither patent information nor any reference to Berliner appeared on these goods. Johnson also organized

an independent company which he named the Consolidated Talking Machine Co. to carry on his commercial distribution. That there was no rift between Johnson and William Barry Owen seems to be indicated by the fact that Johnson registered the famous "His Master's Voice" trademark at this time, and it was first used in advertisements of the Consolidated Talking Machine Co.

In September of 1901, an agreement having been reached between the litigants, Johnson organized the Victor Talking Machine Co. to manufacture improved instruments under the Berliner patents as well as his own. In the meantime, Prescott, Hawthorne, Leeds, and others had organized the International Talking Machine Co., which proceeded to establish the Zonophone as the earliest world-wide disc competitor for Berliner, and it also immediately began recording an extensive classical repertoire, as well.

Victor, with C. G. Childs as its recording director, continued to make spectacular gains in sales each year until 1920, when the postwar slump and the popularity of radio began to take effect. By 1924, business was down more than 50%. In 1926, introduction of the Western Electric recording process and the Orthophonic Victrola, plus a tremendous advertising campaign, turned the sales sharply upward again, but only for a year or so. The organization of the National Broadcasting Co. by RCA that year will indicate to the reader that the full competitive power of chain broadcasting had not yet been reached. In February of 1929, RCA acquired the common stock of the Victor Talking Machine Co. from a banking syndicate. Eldridge R. Johnson had owned the stock previously. Other corporate changes of no great importance have since taken place, including a period as RCA Victor Manufacturing Co. to its later status as RCA Victor Division of the Radio Corporation of America.

The only other earlier lateral disc companies whose genealogy has not been traced are Brunswick, Aeolian, and Decca. The Aeolian Company, manufacturers of pianos and organs, entered the phonograph lists in 1915. Vertical records were made for a time, but by 1918, all production was lateral. Records and phonographs were also manufactured by this company in England. In the 1920's, the Aeolian Company discovered that the phonograph was not going to be the bonanza anticipated, even though the Vocalian red records were introduced and promoted towards the end of its phonographic career. Eventually, its recorded repertoire and the Vocalian label were taken over by Brunswick and ultimately found its way into the company of other lost causes represented in the collections of the American Record Co. and Columbia.

The Brunswick-Balke-Collender Co., of billiard table and bowling ball fame, began the production of universal-type, enclosed horn cabinet phonographs in 1920, as well as lateral-cut records. An attempt to establish competition with Victor in the field of classical music was made, both with domestic celebrity recordings and by pressing imported matrices from Polydor. Needless to say, timing of the Brunswick effort to get into the phonograph business was wrong, for this was the beginning year of the steady decline which was to last for nearly fifteen years. By combining efforts with General Electric Co. in 1926, the Brunswick Panatrope and the Palliotrope recording method was introduced. At any rate, the Brunswick Panatrope, first all-electric reproducing phonograph with dynamic speaker, made little headway against the all-acoustic Orthophonic Victrola. Brunswick also introduced improved acoustic reproducing instruments but these also had a limited sale. By 1929 the Brunswick-Balke-Collender Co. also had had enough of the phonograph business and sold their radio-phonograph and record business to Warner Brothers. In 1938, Columbia acquired the Brunswick catalog along with others mentioned previously.

The Decca Record Co., organized in this country partially with European capital in 1934, was about the only significant development of permanent importance to have come out of the depression years, except perhaps the juke-box renaissance. Concentrating on recording and pressing records rather than producing radios or phonographs, the foresight of its founders seems now to have been little less than psychic. By focusing its attention on the popular record market and cultivating Hollywood talent for the then mushrooming juke-box business, this company avoided most of the headaches being experienced by others. Decca was among the first to realize the potential market being created by the disc jockeys and used them to its advantage instead of fighting them, as had been the custom. The success of Decca and its ace, Bing Crosby, whom this company had lured away from Columbia, was one of the influences which prompted Metro-Goldwyn-Mayer to attempt to do much the same thing, but not nearly as successfully. Decca also pressed imported matrices, particularly vocal classicals by leading European orchestras. Decca also did some local celebrity recording, but this was secondary to its main purpose.

A few other companies had limited careers in the United States during the acoustic era, such as Emerson, Cheney, and the Starr Piano Co. The latter produced the Gennett records, particularly important to the jazz collectors of a later period. However, except for comments which have been made about them elsewhere, there is little reason to dwell on their careers. But the European companies founded in the acoustic era have descendants of considerable importance. The genealogy of the E. M. I., Ltd. and the Phillips group and their present relationships to the American companies will be of special interest.

In July, 1897, at the request of Emile Berliner, William Barry Owen embarked for England to seek capital to back the Gramophone enterprise. In December of that year, The Gramophone Co. was formed and an order sent to

Berliner in the United States for a shipment of machines and records. In May of the following year Joseph Berliner, brother of Emile, was sent to Hanover, Germany to open a plant for manufacturing records and assembling machines from parts imported from the United States. August 25, 1899, the company was reorganized as The Gramophone Co., Ltd. with a capital of £150,000. Mr. Trevor Lloyd Williams was named chairman and William Barry Owen, managing Director. The trademark registered by the company was "The Angel," which has recently made its reappearance after a long lapse in use. It was in September, 1899 that Mr. Owen purchased the later famous "His Master's Voice" picture from artist Barraud. This explains why The Gramophone Co., Ltd. failed to use this valuable piece of artwork for several years. Evidently Owen was quite aware of its potential importance, for he obviously lost no time in getting it off to America. Companies were organized the same year in France, Italy, and Germany, all to operate under the patents of Emile Berliner.

Following a decision to also engage in making typewriters, the company was reorganized on December 10, 1900 as The Gramophone & Typewriter Co., Ltd., with a capital of £600,000. Joseph Berliner was one of the directors. The following year, the company opened a branch in India. In 1902, a branch and factory were opened in Russia. In close succession, branches were also opened in Denmark and Sweden. In 1906, a branch was opened in Persia and foundations were begun for the first record pressing plant on the present site at Hayes, Middlesex. Nellie Melba laid the cornerstone and production of records began in 1908. Other factories were built in Spain, India, and France. In November of 1907, the name of the company was changed back to The Gramophone Co., Ltd. By 1912, beside the countries already mentioned, the company had plants in Austria, Spain, and Poland, and branches in Belgium, Hungary, and

Egypt. There also were agencies in Australia, South Africa, Ceylon, Holland, New Zealand, and other Eastern Countries.

The first World War resulted in the loss of the German business, and a long, protracted suit by the company against the German government resulted. Eventually, The Gramophone Co., Ltd. was forced to form a new company and a new trademark in Germany. One of the side results of this situation was the illegal release of Caruso and other celebrity records in the United States under the Operadisc label—some from masters which had been shipped to the Gramophone Co. or its affiliates by the Victor Talking Machine Co.

In 1929, The Gramophone Co., Ltd. purchased The Marconiphone, Ltd. and was thus able to enter the radio field. It also made a brief venture into talking pictures. The capitalization was increased about this time to £3,340,000. In 1936, the company entered the television field. Mr. Trevor Williams was the first chairman of The Gramophone Co., Ltd., and remained so until his retirement in September 1930, when he was succeeded by Mr. Alfred Clark, who had made one of the earliest improvements to the Berliner Gramophone in 1897 in the United States. Mr. Clark held this post until he retired in 1946.

The Gramophone Co., Ltd. was reorganized as a private limited company and merged with the Columbia Graphophone Co., Ltd. in 1931 as a unit of Electrical & Musical Industries, Limited.

The European history of the Columbia-Graphophone companies began with the sending to Paris of Mr. Frank Dorian by the Columbia Phonograph Co., General in 1889 to open a depot similar to those his company had opened in various American cities. It wasn't until a decade later, however, that a similar depot was opened in Berlin. In May, 1900, the company opened its first office in London and transferred its head office there from Paris. Recording of English artists was begun immediately and by 1903 were being manufactured at the rate of 50,000 per month. However, the bulk of the records sold came from the Bridgeport plant in the United States, comprising both cylinders and discs, perhaps several hundred thousand monthly.

In 1908, Louis Sterling, who had been associated with Russell Hunting, as has been discussed, began a business in selected records from the Columbia Phonograph Co. lists. Later, Columbia acquired his business and Sterling was employed as its manager. On February 13, 1917, the Columbia Graphophone Co., Ltd. was registered in England as a private company with a capital of £200,000 to acquire the European business of the Columbia Graphophone Co., Ltd. of West Virginia. Ownership was by the American parent company, thus really changing only its country of registration. This paved the way, however, for English ownership, for in 1923 an English syndicate purchased the entire shareholdings from the American owners and converted it into a stock company. Sir George Croydon Marks was made chairman and Louis Sterling, managing director. In considerable contrast to the American Columbia picture, the English company subsequently enjoyed a phenomenal growth, and in 1926 and 1927 respectively, capitalization was increased, first to £600,000 and then to £800,000. This growth and ample capital enabled Columbia Graphophone Co., Ltd. to acquire control of its American parent company, the Columbia Graphophone Co., Inc. The company also purchased the Nipponophone Co. of Japan and the Pathe Co., including Pathe Orient and its other Far Eastern branches. Later, the company also purchased the Lindstrom and Transoceanic Trading Companies, both with worldwide ramifications.

By 1928, Columbia Phonograph Co., Ltd. had nineteen factories operating or under construction. In 1930, the now

Lord Marks stated the company was nearly as large as The Gramophone Co., Ltd. By 1931, these two companies were operating fifty factories in nineteen different countries. Both were new in the radio business. With increasing competition and shrinking markets due to the world-wide recession, the possibility and desirability of amalgamation became obvious. Negotiations were undertaken. As a result, The Electric & Musical Industries, Limited was incorporated in April, 1931. Directors were Alfred Clark, Louis Sterling, John Broad, George Croydon (Lord Marks), Edward DeStein, Michael George Herbert, David Sarnoff, and Edmund Trevor Lloyd Williams.

From the autumn of 1930, world conditions had progressively worsened. After the merger, therefore, in all countries where duplication of plant facilities existed, manufacturing where practical would be consolidated into one. This offered great economies and enabled the participating companies to weather the crisis. As in the United States, the upward climb did not begin until mid-1933. In 1934, capitalization of the companies was adjusted to conform to the shrinkage in assets. In 1934, as a result of a continuous research program and product development, E. M. I. organized Marconi-E. M. I. Television, Ltd. to develop transmission facilities for high-definition television. The following year, equipment was ordered from the company by the British Broadcasting Co. for the new television station at Alexandra Palace. In 1936, through The Gramophone Co., Ltd. and its subsidiary, Marconiphone, Ltd., television sets were placed on the market.

Always leaders in high-quality recording and the development of sensitive record processing methods resulting in records of superior quality and silent surfaces, introduction of the LP record in the United States in 1948 was followed within a year or so by its adoption by the E. M. I.

CHAPTER 28

A NATIONAL ARCHIVE OF RECORDED SOUND

FAILURE of the phonograph record to attain an unquestioned cultural acceptance equivalent to the printed page is an enigma which thus far defies logical explanation. As a purveyor of truth in a literal sense, the phonograph record has never been second to the printed word. As a medium for artistic expression, it far surpasses printing in its potentialities for entertaining and communicating. Emotion can be expressed directly and the depth of feeling sensed by the listener. The capacity for verbal articulation, pauses for effect, sublimation of some things, accentuation of others — may immeasurably assist the author in his purpose—enable him to convey his meaning with crystal clarity. Stilted conventions of literary style which exist in every written language and which vary from one era to another are formidable impediments to accurate verbal communication. Tones and manner of speaking provide rectifying context for language symbolism and the difficulties of literary style, or perhaps even the lack of it.

Directly spoken words of any man, even though he may only be reading what he has written, are vastly superior to an access to his written works as a means of understanding him and his message. Next to a direct confrontation, the recorded word offers the best index to assessing him as a living, articulate individual. The spoken word is often vibrant with emotion, or cool and dispassionate, or bellowing in rage. Does the printed page convey these qualities accurately? Does "Mein Kampf" tell us as much about what kind of a man Adolph Hitler was as the accumulated recordings of his ranting and raving in public speeches?

Next to sound motion pictures, phonograph records of voices of famous persons which have been recorded since the introduction of the improved phonograph of 1888 constitute biographical material of the greatest importance. Yet where in the world has there been a consistent effort to bring together and preserve these recordings of the voices of important persons?

Strangely enough, there seems to have been a much greater cognizance of this potential of the recorded word in the early days of the phonograph when it was still in a comparatively undeveloped state. In the meantime, there seems to have arisen some sort of psychological block against accepting the superior capacities of the phonograph as a means of intellectual communication. Very likely this is the same block which has defeated so many well-intentioned efforts to bring to fruition the glowing predictions for audio-visual education.

A factor in this climate of non-acceptance, if it may be so termed, is probably the adamant, though often denied, stubborn resistance and opposition to all sound (and sight) reproducing instruments by the larger number of professional musicians and music critics, especially those who are en-

8888888

gaged in teaching. Though many professional musicians have profited greatly from exploiting these media, it has only been within the past few years that more than a handful of the more serious musicians and actors have expressed an appreciation for records and talking pictures.

Delay in maturation of the phonograph record as a vehicle for cultural communication, if a passable maturity may now be assumed, has generally been laid on the doorsteps of leaders of the phonographic enterprises by spokesmen for our cultural groups, notably the music editors and critics.[1]

Particularly, a great deal of criticism was leveled at Mr. Edison in this respect. Isn't this somewhat like condemning Gutenberg for the present difficulties with objectionable literature? Since the earliest days, music educators have likewise nourished the habit of calling attention to deficiencies of the "talking machines" of whatever period or type, as an excuse for failing to make use of its potential as an aid to music and speech instruction, or even for its obvious utility for stimulating music appreciation. From 1912 to 1922, Victor Talking Machine Company spent millions of dollars and wasted a great deal of effort in trying to break down this inborn opposition of educators who could see no good in the new medium. Even though Victor's intentions must be conceded as not altogether altruistic, neither were those of book publishers!

Yet, almost from the beginning, as early as the 1890's, some astute businessmen had welcomed the phonograph into their offices despite the relative crudity of the instrument. They welcomed it, not only because of its obvious advantages in permitting dictation at pleasure and transcribing at leisure, but also because they soon discovered that it encouraged, nay demanded, better thinking, better enunciation, and better speech habits on the part of the executive staff. They also discovered that the business phonograph

[1] *Edison's Phonograph*, R. D. Darrell, Sewanee Review XLI, January-March 1933.

promoted alertness, accuracy, and dependability on the part of clerks and stenographers. It was not the opposition of management which gave the early entrepreneurs of the local companies such a hard time. It was employees who were afraid of technological unemployment and who humanly resisted any change in what we now recognize as slovenly habits.

Even today, however, outside of stenographic or secretarial schools which deal directly with the need of properly trained personnel to use dictating and transcribing equipment, few schools or colleges use these or similar devices for the beneficial, self-correcting potential they possess.

From the beginning, the phonograph had a definite capacity, which was seldom used, for assisting in training the speaking or singing voice. Range of the human voice is not wide and limitations were not nearly as serious as with much instrumental music. Paradoxically, an instrumentalist, Josef Hofmann, famous pianist-composer, was the first among notable musicians to express an active interest in the phonograph and to personally encourage Edison in his desire to improve it. Josef Hofmann wrote to Edison from Germany and Edison shipped him one of the improved wax cylinder phonographs with a quantity of blank cylinders in 1890. He was delighted with the results and sent Mr. Edison a number of records of his own compositions. The handwritten letters from Josef Hofmann to Mr. Edison are in a file in the vault of the Edison National Historic Site at West Orange. Some of the records may also be there. Perhaps Mr. Hofmann, being a child prodigy, had not yet been taught to practice discrimination!

Generally speaking, physicists and acousticians did not underrate the potential of the improved phonograph Edison had introduced in 1888. Helmholz, Germany's famous acoustician, dropped everything in 1890 and 1891 to assist Mr. Wangemann, Edison's representative, in demonstrating possibilities of the new phonograph before leading scientific societies in Germany and Austria. As mentioned elsewhere, Sir William Preece had done the same in England with the earlier tinfoil phonograph, but now Edison had complete promotional facilities in England in charge of Col. George E. Gouraud.

Mail correspondence schools were not slow to recognize the educational value of the phonograph. As early as 1898, Rosenthal and Cortina in the United States were selling language courses complete with textbooks and cylinders keyed to the text. Blank records were supplied with special mailing containers for the student to register his recitation on, to be returned to the school for grading and correction. The phonograph method had certain advantages over classroom instruction. One may not easily halt or turn back the lecturer to have repeated something that may have been missed, or worse yet, misunderstood. This was absurdly simple with the record! Nor does one, in classroom recitation, hear one's self as another hears him. This is just as true, as psychological tests have proven, of the singing voice. It is only through the medium of the recorded voice, whether on a record, tape, or film, that true objectivity in criticizing one's own voice may be attained. The well-known International Correspondence Schools of Scranton, Pennsylvania also adopted the phonograph method of instruction early in the wax cylinder period and continued its use well into the Blue Amberol era. As a matter of fact, Edison continued the 100 groove/in. cut on the durable and unbreakable Blue Amberol cylinders prepared for the International courses, so the wax cylinders might still be used as before for recording by the student. Many disc language courses are now on sale to the public, but a valuable instructional asset was lost when the use of student recitation records was dropped, being somewhat incompatible with the disc method. There is no reason why home language courses could not be returned to the former effectiveness

with the modern disc or belt-type dictating equipment. Obviously this would add to the selling price of the course. Phonographs used in the early period probably represented not more than $5 to $7.50 of the cost to the manufacturer. A modern disc or belt dictating machine sells for perhaps twenty times this amount.

The point is, if musicians and educators of that time had been equally conscious of the opportunities offered by the phonograph in the declining years of vocal opulence, perhaps not so many of them would now be mourning the passing of the art of "bel canto," or bewailing the poor musical tastes of our young people for wanting nothing but microphone crooning and "rock and roll." Neither the professional musicians, nor their arbiters of what is good and acceptable in music, the music critics, have anyone to blame but themselves for failing to properly appreciate and preserve more of such mementos as have been willy nilly preserved from what is now being recognized as a great period in world music and history. Where had there been written by any famous writer on the subject of music or by any music critic of the early days words of prediction of a great place in the future of music for the phonograph? One looks in vain for any statement or prediction by any of the well-known writers in the field of music, or by the music critics of the early period of the phonograph, which would indicate they felt it was either useful or even desirable.

To be fair, musicians and critics were not altogether alone in their myopia. The author of a paper delivered before the Franklin Institute and which appeared in the *Journal of the Franklin Institute* for April 1878 selected as his subject "This Wonderful Instrument— The Phonograph." However, in it he said he found it quite impossible to conjecture the uses to which this new invention might be put! Doubtless, Thomas A. Edison had thought a great deal more about it than others would be expected to. Two months later, in an article published in the *North American Review,* he listed a variety of purposes for which he felt the phonograph would be useful. Under the heading of "probabilities," he listed the following:

Letter writing and dictation.
Records of books, as read by elocutionists.
Educational purposes, for teaching languages and elocution.
Musical and entertainment records.
Family albums of voices.
Toys, musical boxes.
Annunciators for clocks, etc.
Advertising.
Preserving voices of the great.

Within Mr. Edison's lifetime, all these prophesies came true. Omission of voice and instrumental training by means of the phonograph may be significant. Did Edison sense the impending opposition by the musical fraternity? In this article, Edison also predicted the phonograph would perfect the telephone and revolutionize telegraphy. He also predicted telephone messages would be automatically recorded, as they later were by his Telescribe of 1914, and in devices now leased by the telephone companies for this purpose.

Most pertinent to the subject of this chapter was the last item on Mr. Edison's list, "Preserving the voices of the great." He elaborated on this as follows:

"It will henceforth be possible to preserve for future generations the voices as well as the words of our Washingtons, our Lincolns and our Gladstones and to have them give us their greatest efforts in every town and hamlet in the country."

Edison did his part. He made this possible. He, himself, sought for and had the voice of Gladstone recorded. We have somewhere on records the voice of Franklin D. Roosevelt reviving hope in leadership with his statement that "we have nothing to fear, but fear itself." We have Winston Churchill proclaiming many immortal phrases, including the one about not having been appointed Prime Minister to liquidate the British Empire and the need of the British people to endure "blood, sweat and tears." A long list of records of the voices and messages of famous men have been recorded. Yet, except for perhaps the two just mentioned, most people would not have the remotest idea where they might go to hear them. Certainly they are not available, as they should be, "in every town and hamlet in the country."

Edison was indeed the first to try to make his phonograph perform these functions. The improved Edison phonograph of 1888, using the first solid wax-type blanks, was designed primarily as an instrument of communication, to be introduced first as a business machine for "letter writing and dictation." However, there was nothing to prevent it from being used for other purposes, except perhaps its bulk. So, other cultural connotations became attached to it almost immediately, particularly in the recording of voices of famous persons. So unlimited was Edison's enthusiastic confidence in the practicality of substituting recorded dictation for shorthand, he believed it might be possible to go a step further and send the dictated cylinder to the person to whom the correspondence was directed. Use of the phonograph for dictation has been fully realized, of course. But the idea of sending records in lieu of letters, though promoted several times in various forms, has always failed. With the latter purpose in mind, Edison devoted considerable time and secured patents on designs for cylinder blanks which could be folded flat for mailing and hence would also be unbreakable. However, none proved commercially practicable. The American Graphophone Company's lineal descendant, the Dictaphone Corporation, developed a flexible vinyl belt with the properties Edison was seeking. Records of whatever type used for dictation and correspondence purposes, Edison called "phonograms."

Col. George E. Gouraud was Edison's representative in England. He maintained quarters in a large Victorian house which he named "Little Menlo," in Upper Norwood, Surrey. At Piermont on the Hudson, in New York State, lived The Reverend Horatio Nelson Powers, is reputed to have been a cousin of Col. Gouraud. While on a visit to Mr. Edison on June 16th, 1888, he recited a poem he had written entitled "The Phonograph's Salutation" into the phonograph to be sent to Col. Gouraud with the first of the improved machines then being readied for shipment to England. It was dedicated to Mr. Edison and addressed to Col. Gouraud as follows:

Edison's Library
June 16, 1888

Dear Colonel Gouraud:

Mr. Edison has kindly honoured me with an invitation to give, in the phonograph, an opinion of its merits.

The contemplation of its wonderful character and performances is overwhelming, and my feelings naturally seek vent in verse. But the Phonograph will speak for itself. Now listen to its voice:—

The Phonograph's Salutation
I seize the palpitating air. I hoard
Music and Speech. All lips that breathe are mine
I speak, and the inviolable word
Authenticates its origin and sign.

I am a tomb, a Paradise, a throne;
An angel, prophet, slave, immortal friend:
My living records, in their native tone,
Convict the knave, and disputations end.

In me are souls embalmed. I am an ear
Flawless as truth, and truth's own tongue am I.
I am a resurrection; men may hear
The quick and dead converse, as I reply.

Hail English shores, and homes, and marts of peace!
New Trophies, Gouraud, yet are to be won.
May "sweetness, light," and brotherhood increase!
I am the latest-born of Edison.

HORATIO NELSON POWERS

Along with this dedicatory poem, Edison dictated a phonogram addressed to Col. Gouraud, which concluded with the following jingle:

"Gouraud, agent of my choice
Bid my balance sheets rejoice
Send me Mr. Gladstone's voice"

Results of this somewhat mercenary suggestion of Mr. Edison was a private exhibition of the improved phonograph, arranged at "Little Menlo" at Norwood by Col. Gouraud. Among the guests were Sir Morell Mackenzie. Lord Rowton, Sir John Fowler, the Earl of Aberdeen and Prime Minister Gladstone. This information was obtained from the archives of the Edison National Historic Site at West Orange, New Jersey. Years later, a controversy arose in England as to whether Gladstone and the late King Edward had ever recorded their voices. On July 7, 1910, the editor of *The Sound Wave and Talking Machine Record*, published in London, wrote to Edison, asking whether the late King Edward had made a record. Edison replied as follows:

"If I remember right, one of my assistants took a record of King Edward and also of Gladstone, Kelvin and Bismark. These records were in his possession for many years. Some three years ago he was killed on a railway and I have never been able to locate the records, which is a great pity, as we could now by making masters, preserve them for all time."
(signed) T. A. Edison

Now these were evidently not made at the demonstration at Little Menlo referred to above, but do serve to illustrate the need for agencies to see to the preservation of such rare verbal documents. However, corroboration of the fact that Gladstone was at the demonstration and permitted his voice to be recorded came from another letter to the editor of *The Sound Wave and Talking Machine Record,* written by J. E. Hough, one of the pioneer phonograph men in England, whose part in the early days has been touched upon in Chapter XI, "The International Situation." Pertinency of his remarks to the subject of this part of the story makes its inclusion imperative, as follows:

To the Editor of the Sound Wave
Edisonia Works, Peckham
June 21, 1910

"Sir, I observe in the *Sound Wave and Talking Machine News* for June conflicting statements in respect to a phonograph record having been taken of His late Majesty's voice. Your contemporary states "it is not generally known" etc. The *Sound Wave* 'regrets that no record was ever taken.' I am rather inclined to think that your version of the matter is correct. It is one of these things that common sense would seem to render imperative, and that scientific developments should not be entirely lost. I have made researches and find that in January, 1899, records were sent to Mr. Edison of the voices of Mr. Gladstone, Sir Morell Mackenzie, Mr. James Knowlton, the Earl of Aberdeen, Earl of Meath, Lord Rowton, Sir John Fowler, Sir William Hunter, and Sir Roland Prothero, and it is interesting to know that the record delivered by Mr. Gladstone was sent to Mr. Edison in response to his specific request to Col. Gouraud, who was Mr. Edison's agent or partner in London at that time. This request became known, and elicited a stanza in the London *Globe,* of which the following is a copy of the first verse:

EDISON TO GOURAUD

Send me Mr. Gladstone's Voice

'Send me the secret, send it on,
To the Land of Washington;
Ere the profit others make,
Send it me for Humbug's sake
All the electric box of tricks,
How to split a hair in six;
How to patch a tattered lie,
Facts forget and deeds deny—
Send me, agent of my choice,
Send me, oh send me, Gladstone's voice!'

"At the Paris Exhibition of 1889 we find amongst the visitors to see the phonograph were the late President Carnot, Mr. Gladstone, Prince and Princess of Wales, Prince of Monaco, Buffalo Bill, and various others, but we do not find it stated that the Prince of Wales or any of the personages mentioned made records at the time.

"As to whether they did or not is a matter of comparative insignificance, if the registered tones are reserved for private use and withheld from any public utility.

"Some few years ago, after the death of Mr. Gladstone, I made strenuous efforts with the authorities of the British Museum, offering to provide the Institution with records made by any important personages, provided they would keep them as mementos. At that time the road seemed perfectly open for that purpose, to have obtained a record from the Kaiser, King Edward (then Prince of Wales), and many other celebrities, provided it could have been done with the national object of retaining so valuable a memento of the respective individualism of each. It is too tiresome and annoying to go through the details of the efforts made, only to find they were all blocked by crass official hostility, without result, simply that it was 'not a subject which could be entertained by the British Museum.'

"The conclusion seems inevitable, therefore, that an old buckle from William the Conqueror's armour would be prized immensely, whilst an authentic reproduction of his voice would be no earthly use or benefit to the present generation.

"At that time the Edison-Bell Company were manufacturing indestructible records, and my offer was to deposit the original wax records for preservation and to make as many duplicated copies as the Museum desired in indestructible material so that they could be heard by applicants upon payment of a small fee, which I thought would have been sufficient to have borne the expenses of such an organization.

"As small beginnings lead to important ends, I think it is a great pity that so little enterprise was shown by those in charge of this most magnificent institution; the time of which I am speaking is some 7 or 8 years ago, and during the interval so many men of eminence have passed away, of whom so precious a relic as that under discussion might have been retained in the possession of the nation, and amongst them that of the beloved monarch whose passage has excited such deep regret throughout the civilized world.

"I feel in this connection that it is not sufficient to have merely a record of the voice of eminent persons in some private collections, because it is difficult to realize what public benefit could be derived, unless some such principle as I have suggested could be adopted for their possession on behalf of the public. I am in possession of vocal records delivered in 1890, which might be considered priceless if they could be put to public use, for instance, three by Alfred Lord Tennyson, 'The Charge of the Light Brigade,' 'Bury the Great Duke' and 'Let the Tale be Told,' and Mr. Gladstone, March 15, 1890, 'A message to a Meeting in New York.' I regret to say, however, that this record has been so much used and worn as to be unintelligible. Florence Nightingale, Prince Napoleon, H. M. Stanley, Phineas T. Barnum, but these records are merely venerated relics, and so far as any public use is made of them

they might as well be buried in oblivion.

"I also have quite a long record delivered by the late Dr. Talmage when in London, and I suppose we shall still go on as one eminent person after another passes away after another, still regretting that we have not availed ourselves of opportunities open to us, and it is sad to think how much might have been preserved, how much has been lost! Gladstone, Salisbury, Victoria, Edward, and hosts of others, eminent in science, statesmanship, art and war. We have with us yet our dear old 'Bobs,' and there are many whose memento, properly preserved, would I feel quite sure be welcomed by hosts of our fellow countrymen.

"I believe the only record rendered by Mr. Gladstone, except the one of which I have just spoken, is the one which was sent to Mr. Edison, and I am afraid the publicity given to that particular record, and the developments which followed have not been conducive to a generous compliance with requests which may have to be made to eminent personages to entrust their vocal records to those who have applied, and this may possibly have been the cause why Her Most Gracious Majesty, Queen Victoria, imposed a drastic condition, when she made a speech upon a record to be forwarded to Menelik, the King of Abyssinia. It may be remembered that some years ago, closely following upon the Italian defeat at Addis-Abeba, the favour of the Ethiopian Emperor was sought by both the French and the English. A special envoy was sent to the Abyssinian Court, and by the influence of the Earl of Denbigh (at that time chairman of the Edison-Bell Company), the company furnished a phonograph which formed one of the presents to the Emperor, and Her Majesty the Queen spoke a diplomatic message, dictated by the late Lord Salisbury, in which the name of Menelik, his Queen was embodied, but the drastic condition was that after Menelik, his Queen, and others at the Court had listened to the message, the record was to be destroyed, and the injunction was imposed upon the honour of the Earl of Denbigh, which injunction was faithfully carried out—the record was destroyed and no copies of any kind, or any publication of the matter it contained, was made.

"Thus the nation has been deprived of what might have been considered a valuable memento of her late Majesty.

"Surely some arrangement could be made by which a museum or a section of a museum could be devoted to valuable relics of this kind. It would be interesting, for instance, if amongst other things, Mr. Roosevelt, on his recent visit, had amongst his own energies left behind a virile record of his voice; it might have been preserved at the British Museum or elsewhere, and I can see no real objection to such a scheme being carried to a fruitful and successful issue, but I am afraid there is a good deal of prejudice and red-tape to be overcome before a corresponding estimation is rendered to a 'photograph' of the voice as is yielded to that of the outward form."

Yours truly,
J. E. Hough

Although he was not then considering the even more highly important art aspects of phonography, Mr. Hough stated the case for the government sponsored archive better than anyone else. Periodically, pleas for such a public sponsored repository for valuable recordings have been made in various countries.

Mr. Hough also clarified some of the questions with respect to the records of Gladstone and others. It was thus authenticated in 1910 that a record of Gladstone's voice had been sent to the United States in 1890. (In the magazine article the date, by a presumed typographical error, had been incorrectly given as 1899.) Hough's letter

infers that the publicity about the Gladstone record and subsequent developments had been responsible for the reluctance of the Queen and other illustrious persons to permit their voices to be recorded. This was probably true. However, most of the unfortunate publicity, such as the purposely distorted versions of what Edison said on the phonogram to Col. Gouraud also affected Edison adversely. The "developments which followed" probably alludes to the commercial offering of "authentic records by the Hon. William H. Gladstone" which had been put on sale in the United States by a New Jersey phonograph company. With the state of the art as it was in 1890, Gladstone would have had to make his speeches by the "round." One original would permit making only a limited number of copies. Although the Gladstone records were almost immediately denounced as fakes, probably thousands were sold. A cylinder record by Gladstone was advertised for sale by a collector in England in the *Gramophone* a few years ago. Was it an original, or a fake from the United States? Probably the only way to find out would be to compare it with the only authenticated recordings of Gladstone known—those now in the vault at West Orange, New Jersey.

For years after Mr. Edison's death, whereabouts of the shipment of cylinders from Gouraud to Edison was unknown. Edison is known to have loaned some of them for rerecording to Robert Vincent. They were subsequently returned. Some of these were used for a special radio broadcast series entitled "Voices of Yesterday" and on the Harvard Vocarian series of 78 rpm disc records also prepared by Vincent.

Probably one of the most fascinating records sent to Edison by Gouraud was that of the trumpeter, Kenneth Landfrey, who had sounded the bugle call for the charge of the light brigade at Balaclava in 1854. Using the battle-battered original bugle, Landfrey again sounded the call in 1890 for the phonograph. He also made a brief speech commemorating the occasion. Landfrey, now an old man, was introduced on the record by the clear tones of a woman's voice, saying, "Record made at Edison House, Northumberland Avenue, London, August 2, 1890." Nurse Florence Nightingale was 70 years of age when she made a companion record contained in the same shipment. She spoke affectionately of her former comrades of Balaclava. The voice of P. T. Barnum, the famous showman, speaking from England, was another and with the two above was featured on "Hark, the Years!", a well-known documentary LP record prepared by Capitol Records with the cooperation of Robert Vincent.

It was not until June of 1953 that Mrs. Kathleen McGuirk, secretary and assistant to Mr. Norman Speiden, curator of the Edison Museum at West Orange, discovered the box of cylinders in a cupboard in the Edison Library directly back of the cot on which Mr. Edison occasionally took a nap. Among interesting records found in the box were some of a later date, such as the voice of John Wanamaker, taken in 1908; Count Leo Tolstoy, recorded by an Edison representative in Russia; and one by President Diaz of the Republic of Mexico, who addressed a talk to Thomas A. Edison. Also found in the box was a record by Col. Gouraud introducing Mr. Gladstone on the occasion of the memorable gathering at "Little Menlo" and Gladstone greeting Mr. Edison through the phonograph. This was in addition to the speech of Mr. Gladstone contained on another cylinder.

Many other famous persons are known to have recorded their voices on visits to the Edison laboratory, including ambassadors and rulers of foreign lands, but only a precious few remain. Others which have been gathered by Edison's representatives included the voices of Robert Browning, Alfred Lord Tennyson, Sir Henry Irving, Sir Arthur Sullivan, Count von Bismark, and the Emperor Franz Josef of Austria. What has become of these?

When the box was opened, about ten of the early white wax cylinders of the 1890 period had deteriorated or were so feebly recorded they could not be identified. Perhaps development of more sensitive and critical rerecording methods may make them again available.

It is significant that even before a realization of the potential of the phonograph as a musical instrument for the home had occurred, and before its promise as a business machine had developed, or a coin-slot phonograph had even been conceived, its importance as a repository of history was being demonstrated by its inventor and his representatives. Even before introduction of the solid wax blank records which made preservation for posterity possible, Edison had recorded the voices of many famous persons on the perishable tinfoil. However, like the Bell-Tainter small diameter ozocerite coated cardboard cylinders, the Edison tinfoil record period will have to be written off as a "lost decade." Some of the recorded tinfoil sheets are in the Smithsonian Institution and the Edison Museum at West Orange. Perhaps one day a safe way will be discovered to transfer these incalculably delicate undulations to a surface from which they may be safely converted back to sound!

After adoption of the solid wax blank and sloping mandrel by the American Graphophone Company, both the phonograph and the graphophone began to be employed for accumulating historic and ethnological recordings. Almost immediately, students of languages, tribal customs, and folk lore realized that here was an instrument of great value. Enthusiastically, leading universities and museums sent out recording expeditions to the heart of darkest Africa, to the wilds of the Amazon, and to reservations of vanishing Indian tribes of the South and West. Unfortunately, metallic soap blanks were prone to deteriorate in excessive heat and humidity, and working without advantages of laboratory conditions and with primitive equipment proved quite discouraging. Such worthwhile recordings as were obtained later deteriorated to the point of uselessness because of fungi, which

corroded the delicate recorded undulations. Because of these disastrous results, similar efforts lagged and for a
number of years such expeditions were
few and far between.

In Chapter VI, "The Bettini Story"
has informed the reader about the
amazing collection of great voices
gathered by Lieut. Bettini on the fragile
wax cylinders during this same period,
of which but a few copies have survived. Also touched upon was use of
the phonograph for the purpose of analyzing functioning of the vocal chords
by a prominent surgeon of New York,
Dr. J. Mount Bleyer, who also collected
the voices of a great many famous
opera and concert singers. Not one of
these records is believed to have been
saved.

Even though Mr. Edison's primary
objective in 1889 was to perfect the
phonograph as a business machine in accordance with his obligations to Lippincott's North American Phonograph Company and the many local phonograph
companies which had been organized,
he did not lose sight of its potential
usefulness in the field of music, as has
been alleged on more than one occasion. Early in 1889, Edison sent Mr.
Theodore E. Wangemann to Boston to
record a concert by Hans von Buelow,
the famous German pianist and conductor. According to an article in the
American Art Journal of April 27, 1889,
the intent was to record the entire concert on cylinders. It is not known if this
was actually done, or what became of
the complete set, if so. It is known that
Mr. Wangemann did supervise recording the coda of the first movement of
Goldmark's Symphony, as played by
Garrick's Orchestra, complete with the
applause of the audience. He also made
a recording of the Listemann Quartet
and another of a harp solo by Schuecker.
All three were recorded in Apollo Hall,
Boston.

Edison's energies were diverted from
his interest in cultural aspects by difficulties into which the Lippincott enterprise was plunged. However, after gaining back control of his phonograph pat-

ents, he showed his continued interest
by sending an improved phonograph to
Lionel Mapleson, librarian of the Metropolitan Opera Company. Mapleson immediately set out to secure recordings
of actual performances of the Metropolitan from the stage. At first he went
about this by concealing the recording
phonograph in the prompter's box near
the footlights. However, the large horn
he was using to collect the sound protruded from the prompter's box so
much the view of some seat holders
was obstructed and complaints resulted.
Mapleson then rigged up the phonograph on the catwalk, just behind the
proscenium arch, high above the stage
with the horn hanging below, concealed
by the scenic borders.

Thus, snatches of authentic historic
performances were secured, including
some by artists never available on commercial records, such as Jean DeReszke.
Due to the height from the stage, many
of these recordings are technically very
poor and some have suffered from fungi
and the ravages of time. Geraldine
Farrar, famous Metropolitan soprano of
a somewhat later era, learned of the
existence of these recordings and had
them turned over to William H. Seltsam
of the International Record Collectors'
Club, to be rerecorded onto the standard 78-rpm discs. This occurred during
the 1930's. Among the first of these
issued by IRRC was one with the voice
of Jean DeReszke, which was seriously
afflicted with surface noise due to deterioration of the cylinder, as were
many of the others. However, the
Mapleson cylinders provide the only
access to the peerless tenor of the
golden age, and according to those priv-
ileged to have heard him, give a fair
impression of his voice. In an article in
the *American Music Lover,* the editor
said with respect to the Mapleson rerecordings:

"I cannot avoid mention at this time
of the impressions of great singers
of the past that many of us have
gained from Mr. Seltsam's rerecordings of the Mapleson cylinders. Both

Mr. Fassett and I have discussed the recordings of Mme. Eames in these pages. When Mr. Seltsam issued two short excerpts from the second act of Puccini's La Tosca, featuring the voice of Emma Eames, Emilio De Marchi and Antonio Scotti, which Mapleson recorded at the Metropolitan Opera performances of January, 1903, many of us heard for the first time the true magnificence of Mme. Eames' voice. In no other recording has the thrilling dramatic intensity of her upper tones been so realistically conveyed."

Since then, many of the Mapleson cylinders have been transferred to the LP's by Mr. Seltsam. A dozen Mapleson cylinders are owned by the Music Division of the New York Public Library, according to its chief, Philip L. Miller. In this library, due largely to the diligence of Mr. Miller, are many other rare, irreplaceable records, both cylinders and discs, including a complete set of the 1903 Columbia Grand Opera Series. Here also is to be found perhaps the finest collection of early catalogs, manuscripts, and other literature of the industry available to the public anywhere.

In the United States, however, hardly a serious musician of the earlier period envisioned a cultural place for the phonograph in the field of music, even after introduction of studio recording by Columbia, Edison, and Berliner. Early day recording enthusiasts to whom we owe what little has been salvaged were looked upon as being quite "balmy," to use the parlance of the time. In America, potential of the phonograph record as a medium of cultural communication was slightly appreciated by musicians, musical writers, and critics.

In Europe, the situation was quite the reverse. In those countries where the cylinders obtained a foothold, such as France, England, Belgium, Holland, and to a lesser extent Germany, Austria, and Russia, many fine performances of worthwhile music were recorded on commercially issued cylinders prior to perfection of the molding process in 1901. In Europe too, reaction to the initial recording expedition of the Gaisbergs for the Gramophone Company to Italy, Germany, and Russia had been sensational. However, it must be observed Caruso had already recorded for the cylinder phonograph and for discs of the International Zonophone Company before the Gramophone Company secured its initial list of ten titles issued in England and in America the **following year, with such far reaching consequences.**

Continental view of the failure of Americans to have earlier realized possibilities of the phonograph is that it was a natural concomitant of American lack of culture. This may yet be true today, to a degree. Improvement in music appreciation of the American public today over the 1900's may be attributed to many things. Chief among these are the cumulative and regenerative effects of music well performed and conveyed through phonograph records, radio, and a very few fine sound pictures. Television so far has offered a promise that remains largely unfulfilled.

Now we are in a paradoxical situation. On one hand we have interest in good music to an unprecedented extent. Recording companies are issuing thousands of great performances of music by competent artists each year. But where are the historic performances of yesteryear? Where may one go to hear them?

In 1947, Robert Bauer published a catalog entitled "Historical Records," listing lateral cut disc records by famous or well known vocal artists from the year 1898 through 1909. In this partial compendium, Mr. Bauer listed over 15,300 titles of selections sung by several hundred artists, covering a span of about ten years of the acoustic recording era. Of all the classical vocal records issued during that twilight period of the "golden age," these are the most available and most easily transferred to LP discs. However, in the period since the inception of LP recordings in 1948, not over 300 of these 15,300 performances have been so transferred. Already, some of those rerecorded discs are no longer available to the public. This is also the fate of a great many newly recorded performances of merit each year. It is safe to say not half of one per cent of all vocal classical records of all kinds, vertical and lateral, cylinder and disc, are available for purchase in any form by the public, nor is there any one place where one may go and hear more than a small fraction of selections by the world's greatest singers.

Yet, down through the years, eminent persons here and abroad had contributed a great deal of effort that should have led to attaining at least one relatively complete archive in at least one country of the world. Some aproached the problem from that of ethnology, others from that of music and speech as an art. Certainly they are mutually compatible. J. W. Fewkes in May, 1890 wrote for *Scientific American* about preserving the languages of the Indians, referring particularly to the recording of the Passanoquaddy Indians in Maine. In the *Talking Machine World,* June 15, 1905, an article by Dr. Wangemann, chief assistant to T. A. Edison, stressed the potential of phonograph records for voice culture. In the same issue, an item appeared on Columbia cylinder records which had been recorded at the Vatican by the late Pope Leo XIII. (Lieut. Bettini had also made three records of prayers by the Pope.) The August 15, 1905 issue of the same magazine announced that Professor E. W. Scripture of New York, a member of the Carnegie Research Society, had secured a record of Kaiser Wilhelm's voice. A copy was deposited in the Library of Congress, one in the National Museum, and one with Harvard University. Is it possible one of the three copies has survived?

Francis Densmore was the pioneer recorder of Indian and folklore for the Library of Congress, accumulating over the years of her service more than 3,000 cylinders. Many of these fell prey to the fungus, but some have been trans-

ferred to LP's for use in the Bureau of Ethnology. John and his son Alan Lomax later gathered on wax and aluminum recording discs many folk songs of the early settlers as recorded by surviving singers linked by custom and tradition to a past that had all but slipped away. Many of these fine and sensitive renditions of native folk songs were released on 78-rpm discs and later transferred to LP's by the Music Division of the Library of Congress.[2] However, though folklore was being saved, much great talent of foremost opera and concert artists then being offered to the public has been dissipated by competition and time. For instance, in 1906, Leeds & Catlin, long in ambition but short in patents, offered in a full-page ad in the *Talking Machine World* records by such well-known artists as Mlles. Agussul, DeMoregest, Elise Elizza, Marie Dietrich, Messrs. Constantino, Alberti, Note, Berti, Luria, Inre, Braun, Weber, Aumonier, Milbran, Piccaluga, Marechal, and Corbelli. Almost immediately, they were enjoined for infringement of patents, and the records were never released.

For a time it appeared the ethnologists would win out in one or another of the attempts to form an archive. In September of 1906, Professor A. L. Kroeber, secretary of the Anthropological Department of the University of California reported on a month's exploration among the Indians of North Humboldt County, bringing back 100 graphophone records of songs, myths, and traditions of the Yurok tribe. In December of the same year, the Academy of Science of Vienna reported 41 cylinders of various German dialects had been gathered by Dr. J. Schultz. Also, the Academy announced that Dr. Park had obtained 32 native recordings from New Guinea and Dr. Felix Exner had brought back 68 Sanscrit songs. Several other expeditions were also mentioned. That in Vienna efforts persisted in this direction is indicated by an article in the *Gramophone,* April 1925, entitled "Archives in

[2] *Adventure of a Ballad Hunter,* John A. Lomax.

Sound" by Hans Pollak, Ph.D. This was described as an account of the work of the Phonogram Archives in Vienna. A selected quotation from this report will most succinctly convey its purpose and scope:

"The idea of founding this unusual kind of scientific collection came from the Vienna physiologist Sigmund Exner, who is now head of the Vienna Phonogram Archives Committee. The special instrument used in Vienna for making records for the archive is called the 'Archive Phonograph' and is similar to Edison's. The main difference is that the records are made on discs and not on cylinders, but the instrument is no gramophone as the method of recording is Edison's, that is to say, the sound waves are recorded vertically in the thickness of the wax, and their ordinates are at right angles to the surface of the wax to which the oscillating diaphragm is parallel. By a galvanic process a copper negative is made from the original record and then nickelled over; and from this matrix, as many positives as wanted can be made. - - -

"Today the Phonogram Archives contain more than 3,000 records of which a careful catalog up to the number 2,000 has already been published.

"There are four main groups; records of philogical interest, records of musical interest, voice-portraits of famous persons, and records of special interest to students of music and physics."

The above represents the most consistent effort anywhere. Despite the letter of Mr. Hough to the editor of the *Sound Wave and Talking Machine News* referred to earlier, a few matrices of disc records had been deposited with the British Museum on four separate occasions from December, 1906 to July, 1911, a total of 27 discs, including one of the voice of Lord Kelvin. In 1921, 13 more matrices were added. In connection with the notable article on the Vienna Phonogram Archives which appeared in the April 1925 *Gramophone,* and reflecting on these few deposits left with the British Museum, a writer asked:

"- - - is it conceivable that this represents the sole collection of memorable records in a public and permanent institution in this country?"

In 1948, the late Melville A. Clark, of Syracuse, New York, former president of the National Association of Music Merchants, proposed to the music industry the formation of a Perpetuation of Recorded Art Association. One of its functions would be to preserve the masters of records deemed no longer of commercial value, so they would indeed be preserved for posterity. Articles upon this suggestion appeared in several trade papers, including *Radio Retailing.* However, only one of the smaller companies offered to assist in the endeavor.

Although little or nothing has been done to meet the need for a safe repository for valuable recordings of the past, even less has been done about making them available. Most of the important recordings no longer on sale by the manufacturers are unobtainable, even on special order. A comparative few are available in the form of repressings or rerecordings from sources which supply collectors' records. Most of the large manufacturers now send copies of all releases to the Music Division of the Library of Congress. While this seemingly represents a great contribution, it actually does little or nothing to insure these recordings will still be available fifty years from now.

Necessity for handling delicate records properly renders the keeping of archive material for posterity and making truly available their content quite impossibly inconsistent. Every lending library of records, of which there are now several hundred in the United States, can testify to this. The fate of the Carnegie grant record libraries of the 1930's given to various colleges and institutions is further proof. The vinylite record, though not as easily broken by impact as the shellac, is even more vulnerable to wear, dirt, and scratching.

It will not be until methods developed by the juke-box industry are applied to the phonograph archive problem that a solution will be found. This would solve the problem of indiscriminate handling of records. Dubbed tapes or discs could then be taken without laying a hand on the archive discs, which would be in banks of selective-type automatic record players operating under the guidance of an expert. When masters have ceased to have commercial value, their records should go into the public domain and be sent to an institution for permanent preservation. Why should the composer have only a limited tenure to his ownership and the manufacturer of a recorded performance an ownership in perpetuity?

CHAPTER 29

DISC VERSUS TAPE—
A LOOK INTO THE FUTURE

WHEN *From Tin Foil to Stereo* was first published in 1959, the stereo disc of the present type had been introduced by Columbia only the year before. By international agreement, the Westrex 45-45 system, developed and patented in 1937, was to be used by all leading companies for reasons of compatability and standardization. Founded on the early work of A. D. Blumlein, who designed a stereo cutter for the conventional 78-rpm disc, the successful development of minigroove recording by RCA for the 45-rpm discs, and Columbia's Peter Goldmark for the LP's, plus lightweight pickups, the use of vinylite and other smooth synthetics made successful stereophonic systems not only possible, but inevitable.

A review of this development is essential to a clear understanding of the difficulties in making a prognosis in 1959, as well as to the verification of what was said by your authors about stereo at that time. Therefore we have retained only that part of the preceding edition of this chapter that describes contributions that were important to the development of stereophonic recording and reproduction from discs. It is well to note that commercial exploitation of stereophonic sound of quality, which encouraged the resumption of work to produce a viable disc system, was with stereo tapes. Also, the broadcasting of stereo tapes over the air created a cult of listeners and indicated a base for a new market.

To recap the technical innovation essential to a viable stereo disc system it is necessary to credit Edison for his prescience in determining that permanent styli were necessary for virtually noise-free recording and reproduction, as early as 1890, a dozen years before his company was able to successfully mold cylinders. His chief assistant and partner in the Menlo Park days developed a method of making hard synthetic sapphire which pointed the way that the entire industry followed in the cutting of records in the decades to follow.

Eldridge R. Johnson, who created the basis for the Victor Talking Machine Co. and the world-wide Gramophonic enterprises by improving Berliner's crude Gramophone, astutely adopted Edison's ideas of cutting into solid wax blanks with precision sapphire styli, actuated by glass diaphragms. The art of shaping the cutting tools of sapphire styli with burnishing surfaces to reduce the tendencies to tear was further aided as early as 1892 by the hot-stylus technic of W. Bruening. Another early development pertinent to both the LP high-fidelity capability, as well as stereo technology, was the first knob-shaped sapphire styli for reproducing high frequencies more accurately with the new, high-speed wax cylinders which were produced by Edison beginning in 1902. This was really the first elliptical stylus and reveals the early mastery of groove-stylus relationships as very important then in view of the materials available to Edison for cylinders as a result of an adverse patent decision.

The flat disc record became a sizable industry after 1900. Even though cylinder records had sold by the millions, people became style conscious and showed more and more interest in the newer instruments produced by the Victor Talking Machine Company. The era of electrical recording starting in 1925 was made possible by the radio receiver and its amplifier, thus providing two vital ingredients for successful recording. First, sound could be amplified to any required degree. Microphones replaced the acoustical recording trumpet or horn; the tiny currents in the microphone could be amplified to drive a cutter under controlled conditions. This meant that orchestras, for example, could be more widely dispersed during a recording session, and by careful microphone placement, instruments could be arranged for the most satisfactory and pleasing balance. The second advantage of electrical recording was the removal of some of the mechanical recording and reproducing elements where forced mechanical vibration hindered an original recording. Because the new electrical technic had neither weight or mass, it responded more accurately to sound picked up by the microphone and subsequently pressed into the grooves of the record.

The history of the microphone is a separate story. Since its carbon button version appeared, the microphone has been perfected to where it is largely responsible for the high-fidelity LP's and tapes produced today. Companies manufacturing disc records steadily perfected microphoning and at the same time continually improved amplification and cutting equipment.

Another great contribution was made by an engineer, Isabel Capps. She had spent many years experimenting with groove shapes and cutting styli that would result in the cleanest removal of recording surface material and the least distortion to a record groove. She

eventually developed a new technic of producing extremely accurate jewel faces. These, in turn, substantially reduced surface noise.

Further quieting of disc recording resulted from the "hot stylus" technic patented by W. Bruening in 1892. A small coil of wire wrapped around the cutting stylus and fed with a suitable current heated the stylus to a predetermined temperature. The softening effect as the stylus cut into its groove left the walls free of ragged or minute torn materials. This technic is still used today.

The familiar 78-rpm shellac record was for many years a world-wide standard, and if it were not for the blockade of the Malayan Peninsula by the Japanese, resulting in a shellac shortage, we might still be producing records having a shellac base. Because of the blockade, a new, synthetic material was immediately required. The Office of War Information needed immediately an unbreakable plastic-type material that could be easily shipped throughout the world and on which propaganda programs could be recorded and distributed with least possible delay.

Vinyl interested RCA Victor, and they immediately experimented with pressings using the new material. The recordings were surprisingly quiet, and the frequency response was outstanding compared with the shellac record. Above all, this new material was practically unbreakable; even though quite costly when compared to the shellac disc, Vinyl would practically guarantee its safe arrival to any part of the world.

Engineers at Columbia, in the meantime, looked upon the Vinyl record as a medium on which to record a wider range of audio frequencies than had been heretofore possible. This, they felt, could be done with less noise and under better control. The diamond stylus had reached some popularity and, with records made on the new Vinyl, resulted in greatly improved disc records that could be played over and over without apparent deterioration. At last, engineers had come up with a material, groove, and stylus mated to one another—a truly compatible record technic.

A major contribution was made by Peter Goldmark and other engineers at Columbia, working with personnel at Philco, who developed special equipment to produce the popular Columbia microgroove LP record used almost extensively today. It provided: (1) longer playing time, (2) improved dynamic range, (3) high fidelity frequency response, (4) light needle pressures, (5) longer record life, and (6) no needle scratch and background noise.

While it is true that machines having a speed of 33⅓ rpm were used in the home recording market many years before, these did not possess the quality of the new Vinylite pressings. Earlier attempts to employ slow speed and to attain greater playing time failed because the groove pitch could not be made fine enough to substantially increase the recording time, and the distortion and noise were excessive. Because of these limitations, the early phonographs operating at 33⅓ rpm displayed excessive wows at slow speeds, and as a result, the public rejected them.

As stated in previous chapters, Columbia had developed special equipment to record the new LP record, using its microgroove system. Originally, 50 minutes could be recorded on both sides of a 12″ disc at 33⅓ rpm. This compared to 8 or 9 minutes on one side of a standard 33⅓-rpm disc and 4 to 5 minutes on a standard 78-rpm disc. Columbia used 224 to 300 lines per inch instead of the conventional 96 to 120.

The new groove widths were only one-third those of the standard type. This necessitated developing light pressure playback cartridges using a stylus tip radius of approximately 1 mil. Today's high-fidelity records were the direct result of these Vinylite records first produced by Columbia. The terms "shellac" and "wax" are still popular today when referring to record materials. Actually, pure shellac without additives would be extremely brittle because shellac is simply natural resin. More correctly, the material is a thermoplastic, meaning it will melt. To the lac were added various fillers, including carbon black, producing the familiar black associated with the 78-rpm record. On the other hand, Vinylite is a synthetic resin plastic developed in the United States by Union Carbide and Carbon Corporation, the developers of Bakelite. As LP recording improved, average playback stylus tip dimensions were reduced to 0.7 mil.

The story of record development would not be complete without briefly discussing the disc commonly called a "transcription." These 33⅓-rpm discs had been used for many, many years in the broadcasting industry. These are 16″ in diameter and similar to the old standard 78-rpm disc except the grooves are slightly narrower and closer together. Playback styli for these transcriptions usually used a tip radius of 2.5 mils.

The first talking pictures employed the transcription-type record synchronized mechanically with a film projector, as mentioned earlier. For many years, master discs have been cut at various "pitches." A close pitch permitted longer playing time. Later, "variable pitch" was used, and bass frequencies of large amplitudes could be controlled from cutting through to adjacent grooves by deliberately widening the groove pitch during these heavy sound modulations. Having less violent characteristics, the weaker high frequencies could be properly cut into closely-spaced grooves. With greater control, a cleaner master was produced, resulting in a far greater number of clean copies.

Prior to 1946, high-quality recording was done on perfected lacquer-coated recording discs. Today, they have practically replaced wax for professional recording.

During the middle of World War II, magnetic wire recording reached the experimental stage. At the end of the war, American GI's learned of the magnetic tape developments that had been made in Germany. Magnetophon had been producing its paper-backed magnetic tape for broadcast purposes. A few machines were brought back to the United States following the war. Engineers soon found the new method possessed distinct advantages for recording because the tape could be edited and otherwise controlled, which was impossible with instantaneous disc recording. Recordings containing flaws could be rerecorded with slight delay, as against the costly technic used heretofore requiring destruction of master discs. Tape made its greatest impression in broadcasting and rapidly replaced the disc transcription in radio stations throughout the country. Programs recorded on magnetic tape could not, as a rule, be distinguished from live programs. This was not true, of course, with the disc record, where any imperfections would be heard.

Recognizing the versatility of magnetic tape, the film makers in Hollywood were among the first quantity users of tape for recording sound to accompany motion pictures. As in broadcasting, the film producers found economies with tape and were quick to take advantage of its editing and mastering possibilities.

Dubbing of duplicate sound was simplified with tape. No longer must a disc be played into a recording machine to make a direct copy. Having been removed from tape, inaccuracies in the original did not appear on these copies. This was not true with the disc, where the slightest inaccuracies would be rerecorded onto the duplicate. All sound for motion pictures has for many years been recorded originally on magnetic tape.

The first commercial tape machines designed specifically for binaural or two-track recording appeared early in 1949. Third dimension in music was demonstrated at the Audio Fair in New York that same year. Binaural then was touted as a new development. History records, however, that approxi-

mately 25 years ago an Englishman, A. D. Blumlein, patented a system of stereo sound on disc. This British patent [1] outlines the very principles of our modern stereo discs. Blumlein employed a conventional lateral cut for one sound channel and a vertical or "hill-and-dale" for the other. He used a cutter incorporating two armatures linked to the common cutting stylus. Sound energy from two microphone-amplifier channels was fed separately to the coils of the two armatures controlling the magnitude of the vertical and lateral cuts. The stylus was pivoted, allowing the point to move either vertically or laterally. The two coils responded to each motion, reproducing the trace cut in the groove as two separate outputs. A conventional 78-rpm disc was employed for the pressing.

Emory Cook, of Stamford, Connecticut, introduced another technic of stereo disc recording in recent years whereby a disc could be cut using a double sound track. Cook employed two channel recordings—one on the inner half of the record and the other on the outer half. To play such discs, two playback cartridges were needed. It was mandatory, of course, to start each of the two styli in the proper groove to produce the desired effect. Another technic was shown at the London Audio Fair sponsored by the British Sound Recording Association. A two-channel, single-groove LP based on the experiments of Arnold Sugden was demonstrated. This technic employed a combined vertical and lateral cut in a single groove.

The Decca Company, at their Hempstead Laboratories in England, was experimenting with stereo, using the "carrier system." Two sound channels were separated electronically from a supersonic carrier frequency. Due to high costs, the idea was later abandoned.

Meanwhile, magnetic stereo tape developed to where many suppliers sold prerecorded symphonics and other recordings through regular retail record

[1] No. 394,325.

outlets. Many excellent tapes available today and embracing classical, "pops," mood music, and other selections are capable of hi-fi stereo reproduction of the finest quality. The number of releases grows larger each month despite recent developments with the stereo disc.

Introduction of the stereo tape recorder for the home in 1955 heralded the most dramatic increase ever seen for a single product in home entertainment. Sales figures show that it took only two years for the tape recorder sales pattern to shift from monaural to stereo.

The tape recorder industry has indeed kept pace with the stereo disc. To provide more playing time per dollar, engineers have constantly improved the tape machine in order to compete with the upsurging interest in the phonograph and its stereo disc.

A new four-channel recording and playback head for magnetic tape was announced early in 1958 by Shure Brothers. This multichannel head, designed specifically for the home tape recorder, doubled the playing time of previous two-channel machines. Having twice the recording time on a reel of tape, the multichannel head could play the "stacked" prerecorded tapes then being sold. It also would play regular dual- or single-track tapes produced for the older machines. This cartridge plays both forwards and backwards, and a speed of 3.75 inches per second provided outstanding stereo reproduction quality. Tracks A and C record and play back in one direction and tracks B and D, in the opposite direction.

The Stereo Disc

With the advent of the stereo disc, the phonograph has bounced back as a permanent fixture in the American home. Just who invented the stereo disc is controversial. The utter confusion in the minds of the public had incited editors of the trade press early in 1958 to strike back at the unfavorable publicity and misstatements that had been made in the daily press.

Record and Sound Retailing in its February 1958 issue lashed back at these critics with an editorial titled "The Stereo Disc Today!", written by editor Neil F. Harrison. This editorial follows in its entirety:

"The stereo disc today, and the impact it can have on the entire recorded sound industry, is like a twin-edged sword: it can be used to hew out a new and exciting market that will supplement and add to the growing billion dollar recorded sound field, or it can be used to create a confused situation that could possibly be disastrous. The marketing of a stereophonic record is by all means a desirable and exciting development. Almost every segment of this industry will benefit since it will give the retailers something new to offer the public, the record manufacturers will have a new product to sell, phonograph and component manufacturers will be able to broaden their markets, and even tape and tape instrument manufacturers will benefit from the expanded interest in stereo. It is because there is so very much to be gained from the proper development of the stereo disc that we feel compelled to throw some light on a situation that has already done harm, and may do a great deal more damage if it is not brought under control, and immediately. . . .

"Almost all of the responsible elements of this business have seen the problems involved in bringing out the stereo disc as a mass product, and have refrained from making early claims for the sake of obtaining publicity. Most of the trade papers and consumer press have been careful and realistic in their approach to the stereo disc. Unfortunately, however, there is a vocal minority, which either because of personal motives, carelessness, or just plain irresponsibility, have been giving the impression that the stereo disc is already perfected, that all the problems of compatibility, equipment requirements and marketing have been resolved, and that the stereo disc will leap on the market full-grown within a matter of weeks. The result of this fairy tale has been that a growing number of dealers are becoming apprehensive about their LP inventory and their phonograph inventory. The public, which is quick to hear about these things, is starting to think about waiting for the stereo disc, and to stop building their record libraries. . . .

"In the trade press, *Billboard* and *Home Furnishings Daily* have both been guilty of giving the stereo disc the green light one time, and then doing a complete about face the next. For example, in the *Billboard* issue of December 23, there is a story with the following lead paragraph: 'The stereophonic disc as a mass market item will really arrive sometime in 1958. That's the opinion of Mr. R. E. Warn, vice president of Westrex, the firm that has pioneered the development of the stereo disk in the U.S.' Continuing with the story it said, 'It could hit the market in force in the first quarter of the year or the last quarter,' Mr. Warn stated. 'It's hard to estimate any closer than that. But it is safe to say that stereophonic disks will be a factor in the business during 1958.' Directly alongside there was a box giving the details of a story concerning itself with a record manufacturer who 'says his entire record output will be stereophonic.'

"Exactly seven days after these stories appeared, the December 30th edition of *Billboard* ran a lengthy lead article which stated in its opening paragraph —'Despite the presence of at least one so-called compatible stereo disk on the commercial market, and despite the apparent readiness of some cartridge manufacturers to mass produce stereo pick-up units, the advent of the stereo disk for Mr. Average Citizen's living room may be further off than many have been lately led to believe.' Directly alongside this article, was an editorial which closed

with the following: 'To sum up: Every important phonograph and disk manufacturer is working at producing a good stereo disk and playing system. They face specific problems and they are trying to solve them. In time—not next month or perhaps even this year —they may be expected to produce a workable system that dealers can safely and profitably sell.'

"As for *Home Furnishings Daily*, on October 8, 1957 there was a page one headline which said, 'Discs Seen Beating Tape For Stereo.' The accompanying story included the following:

'Stereo discs will eventually "knock the pins out from under" magnetic tapes as a principal source for stereophonic sound, in the opinion of most high fidelity components manufacturers. They predict that this will begin to happen in the fall of 1958 . . . The fate of stereophonic tape in the home would seem to be doomed.'

"This story goes on to say, 'six companies are planning to market stereo discs before the end of 1957.' Actually no stereo discs were marketed in 1957, and for all practical purposes there are still no stereo discs on the market. . . .

"In October, *Home Furnishings Daily* carried this article—'Magnetic tape not only will be able to hold its own in the stereophonic playback field even with the introduction of the stereo discs, but will prosper because of them.'

"How it is possible to say the future of tape in the home appears to be 'doomed' because of the stereo disc on October 8, and then three days later state that stereo on tape will 'prosper' because of the stereo disc, is a bit difficult to understand.

"Taking another jump, HFD carried this cheery bit of 'news' on October 16 —'Already Sam Goody, one of the nation's largest record distributors who has heard the stereo disc demonstrations, is talking about taking measures to prevent getting stuck with a large, obsolete inventory of monaural discs.'

"The argument that a trade paper must tell both sides of the story does not exactly hold true in this situation. In every industry there is always a small element which attempts to prematurely profit from a new development to the detriment of all concerned. To give editorial space, most of which is guesswork and personal opinion, to this element is neither good journalism, nor very good sense. The harm done by these articles cannot be erased by a later more realistic appraisal of the situation.

"Perhaps the most flagrant disregard for both facts and a sense of responsibility to its readership appeared in the December 29, 1957 issue of the *New York Times*.

"A lengthy article by the chief record critic of the *Times* included this bit of fantasy, 'All of the major record companies are planning initial stereo disk releases during 1958.' The fact of the matter is that NO major record company has announced that it will release stereo records in 1958, although all of them are working to perfect the disc. We wonder how many readers who saw that statement have stopped purchasing LPs? This article in the *New York Times* goes on to say, 'Many qualified observers feel that in two or three years the conventional disk will be on its way out.' That this statement is sheer nonsense can be seen in the fact that the disc itself still is not perfected; there is no equipment upon which to play the stereo disc; the purchaser of the stereo disc will still have to obtain a second amplifier and speaker, in addition to the special needle and cartridge, and finally the public will have to be sold. Quite a number of things to be accomplished 'in two or three years.'

"As if the above were not enough, this article which appeared in the newspaper that bears as its slogan 'All the news that's fit to print' closed with this well-aimed, if undeserved low-blow: ' .`. . something tells this writer bargains are going to be easier

and easier to find as 1958 progresses. As stereo disk and stereo tape begin to make a dent in the record industry, manufacturers and dealers might be looking for a way to get rid of their LP stocks. They won't pay you to take them away, but they may offer you some mighty impressive inducements.' We believe any comment about the possible effects of this statement on the industry is not necessary.

"Before the entire structure of this business is weakened by these irresponsible and misleading stories, and by tiny independents attempting to 'get in on the ground floor' with stereo discs that can only be played in laboratories, something must be done to allay the fears of the retailers and the growing confusion of the buying public. As we stated previously, the vast majority of those concerned with these questions are anxious to see the stereo disc develop as it should—and that is as an addition to the LP and 45, not a substitute. . . .

"A wholesome and realistic approach to this situation was found in a statement from Pickering and Company, which recently developed and demonstrated a stereo cartridge. We would like to quote from this statement, and ask you to remember, this is from a source which would have much to gain from the early appearance of a stereo disc.

'Recent events and activity with stereo discs could easily be construed by the public as an indication that stereo discs are here, and can be purchased in the near future. Such a belief can lead to confusion. The public must realize that in this age of rapid communication such activity is always widely publicized, and is not a definite indication that stereo discs are soon to be on the shelves in record shops. The truth of the matter is that no one in the industry knows, or can offer, more than a personal opinion as to the progress of the stereo disc. Much lies ahead in the development of the production techniques to produce a stereo record and quality play-back equipment for such a record. The very nature of the stereo record makes it in itself more complex than a conventional one, and the mechanical equipment to record and play back a stereo record is also more complex than conventional equipment.

'Despite the recent enthusiastic publicity, the next step in this business of stereophonic record reproduction must be taken with extreme seriousness and precise development so that the stereo disc and associated mechanical equipment can rightfully take their place on a true level with high quality music reproduction.'

"We believe this to be a sane approach to the subject, and one which should have been widely circulated. However, we have been unable to find a record of its being published either in the trade or lay press. . . .

"As a result of the distorted picture that has been painted, dealers will in coming weeks be called upon to explain to their customers the true status of the stereo disc. In order to do this, and thus help avert a dangerous situation, the dealer must himself be made aware of the status of the stereo record.

"The Westrex 45/45 method has been selected for the American market, at least. A few stereo cartridges have been made available in limited quantities, but most manufacturers admit that there is still room for improvement. As for product, only one manufacturer has actually brought out a few test stereo discs. The question of exactly how compatible the stereo disc is, and what sort of reproduction you will get from a stereo disc when it is played monaurally is still very fuzzy. The problem of rumble and distortion is still unresolved. Whether or not standard phonograph equipment is suitable for stereo reproduction also is clouded. And one very important consideration that certainly has not been given enough publicity, is the fact

that the consumer will have to purchase a second speaker and amplifier, in addition to the stereo cartridge.

"Too many people, even in the industry itself, seem to have the impression that the stereo disc is merely a modification of the LP, and that conversion is a matter of minutes and a few dollars. The truth of the matter is that the stereo disc is a complicated and as yet unproved new development, and it will take more than minutes and a few dollars to equip for stereo discs. It will also take quite a while before there is enough real product on the market to make it a factor in this business. The July N.A.M.M. Trade Show may see a few pieces of stereo disc equipment, and some of the major record manufacturers may bring out some stereo discs in late fall. All seem to agree, however, that the stereo disc will not be much of a factor for at least 12 to 18 months, and possibly longer.

"Mr. Dealer, these are the true stereo facts of life! Pass it along to your customers. The outlook for the new year is excellent. Don't let irresponsible talk and actions threaten that outlook."

We think Mr. Harrison did an excellent job analyzing the situation facing the industry. The LP market did not suffer from the unfavorable newspaper publicity. Record releases in ever-increasing number found their way to the dealers' shelves. Phonograph sales in all categories continued to find new customers. Binaural tapes also enjoyed a lively sale, and stereo demonstrations were given throughout the U.S., using prototypes of the newly developed stereo cartridges and playback system.

The Record Industry Association of America, Inc., known as the RIAA, on March 25, 1958 approved standards recommended by the Engineering Committee for stereophonic disc records:

1. In stereophonic disc phonograph records, the two channels shall be orthogonal modulations of a single groove.

2. In the 45°-45° stereophonic disc phonograph recording, the two axes of displacement modulation are inclined 45° to the disc surface.

3. In 45°-45° stereophonic disc phonograph records, the right-hand information, as viewed by the listener, shall appear as modulation of the outer sidewall of the groove.

4. In 45°-45° stereophonic disc phonograph records, equal in-phase signals in the two channels shall result in lateral modulation of the groove.

5. Lateral modulation of the stereophonic disc record shall produce equal in-phase acoustical signals at the loudspeakers.

6. The 45°-45° system is recommended as a standard for stereophonic disc phonograph records.

It was further recommended that:

1. The desirable tip radius for reproducing stereophonic disc phonograph records be .5 mils.

2. The included angle of the groove be 90°.

3. The bottom radius of the groove of the finished record be .2 mils maximum.

Also approved for stereophonic disc records were the same recording and reproducing characteristics and the same dimensional standards that had previously been adopted for 45-rpm and 33⅓-rpm records.

Conditions in Britain early in 1958 apparently were no better than those in America. The pioneer developments that had led to the stereo disc had apparently been ignored and had suddenly reappeared in the British press in much the same manner encountered in the United States. In rebuttal to claims made by American inventors, *The Gramophone*, April 1958, printed the following editorial, which reveals the contributions made by the English in stereo disc technics. The technical editor of *The Gramophone* in his editorial gives evidence that many developments covered in the United States press were not of American origin, but on the contrary were claimed to be those of the British scientists. This editorial, we think, is important enough to be reproduced entirely. This is what Mr. Wilson had to say:

" . . . In 1492, we are told, Columbus discovered the continent of America; and since that date the inhabitants of that wonderful land have from time to time discovered Europe. But only occasionally, it seems, do they discover what the Europeans have been doing —or at any rate, give them credit for it. "We in *The Gramophone* have had that American insularity (or should we now call it sputnikality?) brought home to us on several occasions. The latest fables that are being spread, however, both in America and over here, about the American triumphs in stereo disc recording are amongst the most fantastic. Even our usually well-informed contemporary, *High Fidelity,* has fallen for them, as witness the article in the February issue commenting on the difference between the hill-and-dale-cum-lateral system (hereinafter called the V/L system) and the 45/45 system which it calls the 'Westrex System' because Westrex happened to give a demonstration of it at Los Angeles last September. "What the fables do not reveal is that following on the Westrex demonstration, Decca (or 'London Records' as the description goes in America) gave, in the opinion of many, a superior demonstration of Stereophony from discs made on the V/L system and asked that international agreement should be reached as to which system should be pursued. It was left to America to choose, because Decca, with their German Associate, Teldec, had already fully developed both systems! They were, in fact, in the fortunate position of Prime Minister Lord Melbourne, who, it is recalled, once closed the door of the Cabinet room and told his colleagues that he didn't care a damn what they decided so long as they all said the same thing. We ourselves have had demonstrations of both V/L and 45/45 systems at the Decca Recording Studios and have no doubt whatever of the excellence of the Decca recording. . . .

"That was the position last October/November when we introduced our readers to the subject. Since then agreement has been reached that the 45/45 system shall become the International Standard, and that the recording characteristic for each of the two channels shall be the same as for our present LP discs.

"But it is now being said that Decca have recognised the superiority of the American system and have changed over from their V/L system to the Westrex system so that manufacturers of reproducing apparatus can get busy designing new pickups and new control units and so on in anticipation of the issue of stereo discs at the end of the year!

"We must therefore lift the curtain a little higher and disclose something more of what has been going on behind the scenes and, in particular, what we had in mind when at the close of our report (p. 551, May 1955) on the first demonstration by E.M.I. of 'Stereosonic' Tapes, we commented on the presence of Mr. Schwarz and Mr. Haddy of Decca and said: 'Rumour has it that they, too, have something startling to reveal before long. And rumour is not always a lying jade.' . . .

"At that time Decca had three systems of stereo disc recording in advanced stages of development and could have marketed first-class stereo discs according to any one of them, had it been commercially politic to do so. But of course very few people would have been able to play them and they might well have become museum pieces or, alternatively, have done untold damage to a great industry. It will stand to the lasting credit of Mr. E. R. Lewis that he has consistently refused to allow Decca to be stampeded into premature dis-

closures which could have this effect, even though they might have been to the immediate prestige of his company.

"Now, however, the issue of stereo discs can begin as soon as ever the reproducing equipment is generally available. All the major recordings of recent years have been done stereophonically at the same time as they were recorded for our present 'Monaural' system (as it is rather inaptly called); and all that is necessary now is to transfer from the stereophonic tapes to discs. It may come as a surprise, by the way, that though the stereophonic reproduction is considerably more realistic than that from LP records made at the same time, the monaural reproduction from one channel of stereo is not so satisfactory as the LP.

"Of the three alternative systems that Decca have developed, two were foreshadowed by A. D. Blumlein in his E.M.I. patent of 1931 (394,325). These are the V/L and 45/45 systems. The third is what is known as a modulation system, in which two discrete frequency bands are arranged to modulate a carrier frequency simultaneously. It seems that a patent covering this system was granted to Mr. W. H. Livy, of Edgware, Middlesex, in 1948 (612,163 with application date in 1946). He proposed to use a 13 kc/s carrier and one frequency band up to 6 kc/s and the other from 6 kc/s to 13 kc/s. The Decca system was developed independently and used frequency bands 0 to 13 kc/s and 15 kc/s to 28 kc/s with a carrier frequency of 14 kc/s. As we have said, it was developed to a successful conclusion, though it appeared that the cost of the reproducing apparatus would be considerably greater than that for the Blumlein systems. Still, even though it has now been put aside, one considerable advantage remains from its development; it has taught Decca how to make a recording cutter which will be operative up to at least 28 kc/s. . . .

"Blumlein's patent dealt not only with the principles underlying stereophony but also with the placing of microphones and the recording of the two channels, whether on film or on a disc. It showed, too, that the V/L and the 45/45 systems are equivalent, 'since channels recorded at 45 degrees to the wax surface give their sum and difference as the effective lateral and hill-and-dale amplitudes.' Moreover, Blumlein specifically says: 'If the two channels being recorded are directly picked up from two microphones or are intended to work unmodified into two speakers, that is with intensities and qualities similar, it is preferred not to cut one track as lateral cut and the other as hill-and-dale, but to cut them as two tracks whose movement axes lie at 45 degrees to the waxed surface. And when I visited Hayes last month to have a discussion of the subject with Mr. H. A. M. Clark and Dr. G. F. Dutton, I learned that in his internal departmental memoranda Blumlein had elaborated his analysis and his preferences, though he does not appear to have worked out fully (as has now been done, mathematically) that, other things being equal, there will be less tracing distortion with the 45/45 system than with the V/L. "It is interesting to note, too, that Blumlein described possible designs for both variable reluctance and moving-coil types of apparatus for the two systems and invented transformer arrangements to convert from one system to the other. He also remarked, prophetically enough, that 'it would appear that for such a record, a material other than that now used for lateral-cut records would be desirable, and a material of the nature of cellulose acetate is indicated.' How true that is was demonstrated by Mr. Clark and Dr. Dutton at an informal discussion at the Institute of Electrical Engineers on February 24th. They actually played a record that Blumlein had recorded at 78 rpm and had been pressed in standard shellac material.

It was adequate to show that true stereophony was produced by Blumlein's instruments; but the background noise was too great, and the frequency range too small, for the result to come up to what is possible with modern methods. "The patent includes no fewer than 70 claims and is a wonderful example of scientific insight. I only met Blumlein casually in the old days when he was working at the Columbia studio in Petty France; but those who knew him well, and particularly those who worked with him, all assert that he had one of those rare minds that seem to work by flashes of illumination: they know the answer at a glance, even though proof may cost them laborious nights. It was a real tragedy for this country that he should have lost his life in a plane crash, whilst testing out a Radar system during the war. What might he have done with modern techniques and materials? "His microphone system became the basis for recording Stereosonic Tapes; but it now appears that it was not the only stereophonic system possible, and in fact Decca and other recording companies use a different arrangement. His stereo disc ideas were not developed, however, until Mr. Haddy, the Chief Recording Engineer of Decca, got to work on them. That is an interesting story which cannot yet be told. But this much must be said. When questioned about it, Mr. Haddy has just replied, with characteristic modesty, 'Pure Blumlein!' . . ."

The Bell Telephone Laboratories (about 1937) patented a vertical-lateral disc system in which one sound channel was carried by motion 45° to the right and the other 45° to the left of vertical, producing a balanced system. After the smoke of battle clears, we think both the tape and the disc recording industry will realize that tape and disc will probably be used for years. Each medium has its advantages and disadvantages. With the rapid development in the stereo disc and in new tape technics, the future for both should be secure. The requirements of the two media are well known. In a phonograph recording, listeners demand the utmost in mechanical perfection and performance. They demand that all notes must be played, and played correctly.

Tape editing, on the other hand, has so corrupted many modern musicians that a flawless performance before a recording microphone is now a rarity. Even if engineers and producers could give up tape editing today, we doubt they ever would. Tape editing has become so complex that companies have literally forced the use of tape as an original recording medium.

Tape has effectively replaced the disc in schools, homes, church recordings, etc., because few people like to carry an 80-lb. disc recorder when they can do the job better and easier with a 20-lb. tape recorder. Chip removal has long been a bugaboo of the disc record fancier—and even with tape, reels using easy tape threading have been developed to simplify matters for the novice. Duplicating tape recordings has had its appeal too. Duplicating equipment for the dubbing of discs is relatively expensive, and there are not enough users of home disc machines to find one handy for dubbing.

C. J. LeBel, an expert with both disc and tape, writing for *High Fidelity* magazine, October 1957, states:

"For home nonstereo listening, disc will always have a place, since high-quality single-channel reproduction is less expensive on disc than on tape. (Tape cost has diminished a third in six years, though.) Also, a whole evening of background music (3½ hours) can be loaded on a changer; the equivalent in tape would require a fourteen-inch reel (using 7½ ips, dual track) to handle 4,100 feet of tape. This is not the last word, for the disc time could be stretched to 4.7 hours without loss of quality, if

disc manufacturers chose to push the variable-pitch technique to its maximum. Tape time can be stretched only by reducing tape speed or adding more tracks, both of which reduce quality. . . ."

Requirements for stereo tape are not as severe as those for monaural. Stereo masks deficiencies heard in monaural reproduction. With the two-channel stereo head, manufacturers have discovered they can get good quality despite the crowding of four channels on a one-quarter-inch tape.

Even though most recordings for radio broadcasters have been made on tape for many years, because of the cost, transcriptions made from the tape masters are still on discs.

Mr. LeBel goes on to state that two unlikely improvements could create a technological revolution: First, a universal shift to ½-mil playback styli, combined with intensive use of variable recording pitch, to put about an hour of recording on each side of a twelve-inch disc; second, an improved magnetic head with a $\frac{1}{10}$-mil effective gap, making possible a 15,000-cycle frequency range at 3¾ ips.

On a comparative basis, both tape and disc can yield good response from 40 to 15,000 cps when new. However, the range above 10,000 cycles can be wiped right off a disc with one pass of a stylus from the wrong pickup. Of course, this is unlikely with modern cartridges and diamond styli. On the other hand, the reproduction of tape above 8,000 or 10,000 cycles depends upon the azimuth alignment accuracy of the reproducing head. ". . . The tape counterpart," says Mr. LeBel, "to disc high-frequency deterioration is the effect of a magnetized head, which can erase the high frequencies and add 10 db of hiss, all in one pass of the tape. This is particularly serious with home recorders, in which the chance of magnetizing the head during recording is appreciable. . . ."

This chapter was written as the interest in the stereo disc was reaching a peak. In an editorial, *HiFi & Music Review,* June 1958, forecast the status of the disc-stereo bandwagon and its effect on the high fidelity industry:

"Stereophonic sound will enhance the performance of every hi-fi system. In small living rooms, in large living rooms, in acoustically bad sounding rooms; stereo makes all music sound better. It adds life, in the form of directionality and depth illusion. But, it demands (1) an additional investment upon the part of the hi-fi enthusiast- and (2) the availability of equipment and good recorded material. If these two factors are taken into account, the enthusiast can get started with stereo without worry. The disc stereo bubble is not likely to burst—rather, it is going to solidify."

Mercury Records' Irving Green had drawn an apt analogy between razors and blades to express the relationship between record companies and manufacturers of hi-fi stereo playback equipment. Without a supply of blades (the stereo LPs) and razors (cartridges and preamplifier switching), home stereo from records would be impractical. However, in late April 1958, at least nine independent record companies were known to be producing stereo LPs. All were cutting their records by the same method.

The equipment front was being led by Electro-Voice's VP Larry LeKashman, who aroused widespread acceptance of the E-V ceramic stereo cartridge. Undeniably of good hi-fi quality, its low cost and easy installation plus a high output made the ceramic cartridge attractive to the manufacturers of packaged hi-fi. Do-it-yourself fans with home-grown hi-fi systems were also becoming an active market for the ceramic. Rapidly developing ceramic cartridges of their own, but outdistanced by E-V, were Webster of Racine, Erie Resistor (a newcomer), Ronette, and several others.

For optimum quality when playing monaural LP's, six out of seven hi-fi enthusiasts prefer magnetic cartridges. Complex and delicately constructed, the stereo magnetic cartridge proved to be a costly device. Qualitywise, various models sampled by the *HiFi & Music Review* staff performed excellently, and several were during 1958. Costwise, they cost two or three times the best diamond stylus ceramic. Fairchild, Pickering, Shure, Stereotwin, Rek-O-Kut, General Electric, and Weathers had assembled prototypes late in 1958.

Almost every manufacturer of a professional-type tone arm had either modified or did modify his product to accept stereo cartridges, for a slight additional charge. The Shure Studio Dynetic arm and cartridge were converted for about 50% of the original purchase price. Record changers with built-on tone arms were the easiest to convert to stereo. By mid-June the entire Garrard changer line (RC-98, RC-121-II, etc.) converted stereo magnetic or ceramic cartridges through a simple wiring change.

Besides the cartridge, the home hi-fi system needed another speaker and amplifier or amplifier/preamplifier combination. Fisher, Pilot and Harman-Kardon made special preamplifiers to accept disc stereo as well as tape stereo inputs. H. H. Scott then introduced a "Stereo-Daptor" as a small accessory to simultaneously control the switching and volume level of both stereo channels.

The major manufacturers of packaged phonographs (some of it so-called hi-fi) had announced their intention of concentrating on stereo packaged phonographs for the home (first in the game —Paramount Enterprises). Prices would start at $150, up to $2,000. Several manufacturers were ready to add to or convert their existing monaural systems to stereo playback for prices starting around $65. Admiral, Magnavox, Philco, and Zenith had all planned on heavy stereo package promotion in the early fall of 1958.

The first six stereo LP releases had been extensively tested by the staff of

HiFi & Music Review. These included Audio-Fidelity's "Marching Along with the Dukes of Dixieland," "Bullring," "Johnny Puleo and His Harmonica Gang," and "Railroad Sounds"; Counterpoint's "Juanita Hall Sings the Blues"; and Urania's version of "Saint-Saens' Third ('Organ') Symphony."

The stereo effect was comparable to that previously achieved with stereo tape. Directionality was frequently pronounced, and some recordings tended toward distortion of dynamics—most of the defects were undoubtedly due to the inexperience of the recording companies when "mastering" the discs. Comparisons of identical selections (stereo discs vs. stereo tape) showed the slight hiss in prerecorded tapes was largely absent in the LP version.

Playback of monaural LP records with various stereo cartridges showed quality in no way inferior to that of a good monaural cartridge. However, poor quality resulted when stereo discs were played with a standard monaural cartridge, regardless of the cartridge's construction or price. Stereo discs should be played only with a stereo cartridge, although a stereo cartridge will play monaural recordings.

Audio-Fidelity, during 1958, had more stereo disc releases on the market— "Lionel Hampton," "Leon Berry on the Giant Wurlitzer—Vol. III," "Bagpipes and Drums," and "Mardi Gras Time with the Dukes of Dixieland." Urania, in addition to its "Saint-Saens Third Symphony," added Offenbach's "Gaite Parisienne Ballet," Strauss' "Sparkles in Hi-Fi," and Rossini-Respighi's ballet "Boutique Fantasque" with Sir Eugene Goosens conducting the London Philharmonic, Phil Moody's "Razz-Ma-Tazz" album, and "Society Dance at the St. Regis" with Milt Shaw's Orchestra. Five more releases were scheduled by September 1958. ABC-Paramount had six stereo discs on record shop shelves, including "Strauss in Hi-Fi," "Eyde Gorme Vamps the Roaring Twenties," "More College Drinking Songs," "Heavenly Sound" featuring the duo-piano team of Ferrante and Teicher, "Songs of

World War II," and "Hi-Fi in an Oriental Garden."

Contempory records, on the West coast, had announced the Shelley Manne jazz treatment of "My Fair Lady" for stereo disc. Counterpoints later cut a stereo disc of cello concertos by Boccherini and Vivaldi with the Baltimore Conservatory Orchestra, Reginald Stewart conducting, and Aldo Parisot, soloist. Concertapes and Hallmark were among the other labels in 1958 introducing stereo LP's. To help beginners in stereo get started quickly and economically, Electro-Voice had a special demonstration disc available at $1. A New Jersey mail order club, the Stereophonic Music Society, made a tempting offer for those starting in stereo by way of the disc. An initial investment of under twenty-five dollars brought with it an E-V stereo cartridge, a choice of three stereo discs, and a year's membership in the Society, with future stereo discs available at a 25% discount.

Thus far the stereo disc show had appeared to be strictly an independent record label affair, but, as expected, the majors — RCA Victor, Columbia, Capitol and the rest—eventually flooded the stores with an enormous variety of classical, popular, and jazz LP's by top-notch artists. RCA Victor was first of the majors, with its initial stereo disc releases appearing in July 1958. Capitol had promised its product for early fall of that year. Columbia had been delayed because of its attempt to produce a "compatible" stereo disc. Now that it had decided to go along with the universally adopted system, it was assured its stereo LP's would also be on the market by fall. In short, 200-plus stereo discs were available in the stores by September 1958—and after that, the deluge!

The major record companies, however, then planned to issue standard monaural LP's as usual. Stereo discs, like stereo tapes, were regarded for the time being as an "extra." Since stereo cartridges can play monaural discs, there is no obsolescence problem with present collections of monaural discs.

Stereo, after the initial impact had worn off, was another question. Those who had had tape stereo in their homes stoutly maintained that it was the only way to listen to electronically reproduced music. This is undoubtedly true with first-rate stereo recordings—whether on tape or disc.

The technics have long since been displaced as a result of incompatible philosophies. Yet, we might reflect occasionally on the following fact. In the hands of the inventor of the phonograph, facsimile reproduction of solo voices and instruments by purely acoustical means had been demonstrated as early as 1915!

By the same token, errors of microphone placement and other recording faults, when heard as stereo, are compounded. This was already evident in the flood of stereo discs that had deluged the market during 1958-59. A new mass medium for musical enjoyment had come into being, and was forcing music lovers and audio engineers to listen with new and ever more critical ears.

In the realm of tape, RCA Victor developed a magazine-loading cartridge which offered twin-track stereo at a 3¾ ips speed. The present stage of the art has now permitted mass production of eight-track, 3¾ ips tapes and machines capable of sound reproduction quality on a par with the best 7½ ips tape. The cartridge sound quality is now good enough for most homes, and the ease of handling the tape cartridge marks a genuine step forward in creating a mass market for the prere-

corded tape. Meanwhile, intensive work is being done toward refining stereophonic recording and playback technics, so that the maximum illusion of sonic realism can be produced under normal living-room conditions.

The two-channel stereophonic microphone pickup and playback pattern (two separate microphones, A-B, for recording; and two separate speakers 6 to 10 feet apart, A'-B' for playback) has undergone considerable modification. To eliminate the "hole in the middle" effect, recording has been done with three microphones feeding and recording onto three-channel tape. The middle channel is then "blended" into the two-channel tape or disc. Britain's Electric and Musical Industries Ltd. (EMI) and other European producers have experimented with two-channel stereo miking in coaxial fashion, achieving the proper directional effect by means of sum-and-difference matrixing. Corresponding experiments have been made in the field of loudspeaker design—such as feeding all stereo program content below 700 cps to a common center enclosure while feeding program material above 700 cps to separate "satellite" speakers. This and similar designs have been directed toward gaining a broader area of stereo illusion while eliminating the "hole in the middle."

Yes, Mr. Edison's phonograph has certainly come a long way since his original tinfoil machine of 1877; and it is clear that today's high-fidelity stereophonic listening in the home is still just a forerunner of things to come.

CHAPTER 30

FROM TIN-FOIL TO STEREO -- AND BACK AGAIN!

The remarkable empathy of Thomas A. Edison with nature and his consequent sensitivity to natural phenomena have never been adequately appreciated. An announcement in 1970 of the results of a collaborative effort by five German engineers to put both sight and sound onto a single disc heavily underscores the prescience in the early pioneering by Edison. He was the first to devise and to demonstrate, even before the end of the nineteenth century, means for uniting in recording and reproducing the video and audio capabilities of his separately developed phonograph and motion picture devices.

Even the first means employed by Edison to isolate and demonstrate in the simplest possible fashion the basic phonographic principle seems to indicate, in the light of most recent developments in the art, the uncanny ability of Mr. Edison to abstract a scientific principle and to isolate it for patent purposes. Consider that even before the granting of a U.S. patent to Edison of what is generally considered to be the first phonograph, he had already been granted a British patent on a device using paper tape employing the phonographic principle in a telephone repeater, although hopelessly involved in electromagnetic complications.[1] Therefore, to get a firm, definitive patent he

chose, of all things, to indent tin foil vertically into a pre-grooved cylinder to register, and with a somewhat different stylus, to reproduce sounds.

This was in the latter part of 1877, and in early 1878 he had already developed a demonstration disc recorder which indented vertically a spiral groove into a copper foil disc, which showed remarkable promise.[2] This definitely proves that Edison was the first to make a recording lathe for discs with mechanical feed, and the first to design a playback instrument equipped with a spring motor and governor. He also pointed out to reporters from the *New York World* and the *New York Graphic* that these copper foil discs could be removed from the phonograph and "multiplied to any extent by electrotyping." He estimated that it would be possible to record voices, piano, and even orchestras and described possible means. He predicted that it would be possible to put an ordinary 50-cent novel on one of the foil discs, about six inches in diameter.[3]

Almost a century later, Horst, Redlich, Hans-Joachim Klemp, Gehard Dickopp, and Eduard Schüller of Germany, in a collaboration transcending corporate lines, reminiscent of the glorious days of Menlo Park, adopted Edison's basic

---

[1] Described in text of letter by Edward H. Johnson to the Editor of *Scientific American*, pp. 13 & 14 of this book.

[2] See illustrations pp. 466, 467 of the "improved phonograph" from *The Daily Graphic*, New York; April 2, 1878.

[3] From text of "The Papa of the Phonograph," *The Daily Graphic*, New York; April 2, 1878.

and unique approach to sound recording and put both sight and sound onto synthetic foil discs (Figs. 30-1 and 30-2).[4] Their system employs the recording and reproducing action in the vertical plane perpendicular to the record surface as in Edison's tin foil cylinders or copper foil discs. This is not the Scott-

Phonautograph-inspired, Berliner-developed lateral disc technic of recording and reproducing which in effect lays sound on its side. The Teldec disc, so-called because this initial commercial effort was sponsored jointly by German Telefunken and English Decca, proves that Edison's intuitive rapport with na-

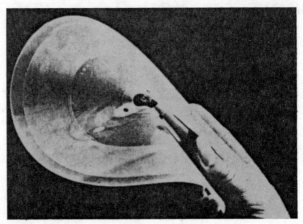

Fig. 30-1. The virtually indestructible PVC foil disc used in the video disc process invented by Teldec.

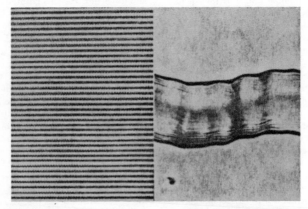

Fig. 30-2. This microphotograph compares the relative densities of the video grooves (on the left) with those on a standard lateral audio LP. The video disc is vertically modulated and contains both video and audio information.

[4] See Figures 1 & 2, from article "Three Views of the Teldec Disc," by Martin Dickstein; *db, The Sound Engineering Magazine,* December 1970.

ture resulted in his correctly choosing between the options of recording vertically or laterally, both mentioned in his first U.S. patent. The feat of recording the breadth of the video spectrum on top of the audio spectrum and reproducing both with quality to best European TV standards, and to do this with a plastic foil disc, is almost unbelievable.

A comparative chart showing the relative state of development of the several classes of video player equipment accompanied an article by Arnold Schwartz entitled "The Video Disc" in *db, The Sound Engineering Magazine* for December 1970. The basic systems were video tape, EVR of CBS Laboratories, Selectavision of RCA, and 8-mm film by ABC and Sylvania. On the basis of simplicity, low cost of producing and reproducing apparatus, the chart shows that Teldec was far ahead. The story of differing systems was told at the time by others in other publications, and the drawbacks of the Teldec system were cited. The only serious one at that time seems to have been the inability to stop one frame at a time; the skipping of grooves by holding the stylus-record position around to the spiral would not damage the disc but occasionally would produce ludicrous effects visually. Also there were demonstration problems with the original playback equipment in the U.S. because of the difference between the 50-Hz European and 60-Hz U.S. power supplies.[5] The fundamental point is that the vertical mode was proven by the Teldec system the right way to apply Edison's phonographic principle and Edison knew it from the start, and never deviated from his confidence in it. It is true that in 1929 he permitted his associates to produce lateral disc records as well as vertical-cut in order to tap the market which had been created by the success of the Orthophonic Victrola, and the increasing number of combination radio-phonographs by Victor and others, none of

which could play the Edison diamond discs.

Since *From Tin Foil to Stereo* was written in its entirety prior to 1960, it is obviously necessary for us to review to some extent the developments in sound recording which have occurred since that time and prior to the demonstration of the first Teldec video discs. Maxfield and Harrison's exposition of their Western Electric process sounded the knell for vertical recording in 1926. Strangely, in 1970, the demonstration in the U.S. of the amazing Teldec system, though perhaps never to be adopted commercially by the American industry, at least convinced most competent engineers that vertical recording was eventually to triumph.

RCA Victor for the first time, in 1954, began to issue high quality reel-to-reel magnetic tapes for sale to the public. Many had looked upon this as signalling the beginning of a grand new era in the seventy-five-year history of sound recording. To others, concerned sentimentally or financially with the existing disc industry, it seemed more like the portent of doom.

In the preface of *From Tin Foil to Stereo* in 1959, the question was posed "Is it likely that one day all present disc records will be obsolete?" Coupled with this were other questions such as "Are there never to be any truly permanent and unchanging values in this always somewhat hectic and unstable multimillion dollar industry?" and "Is the oft advertised expression 'now recorded for posterity' just a will-o'-the-wisp?" and "Is a present generation never to find the recorded art of a prior generation truly accessible?"

Answers to these questions must be found. In industrial development as in world politics, situations of reasonable similarity occur again and again. The solution for a new crisis can often be found by analyzing the mistakes made in dealing with similar earlier crises. The lessons of history may often be profitably applied to the problems of the present.

---

[5] Since the original publication of *From Tin Foil to Stereo* in 1959, the U.S. National Bureau of Standards has adopted the SI (for Système International) system of units in which the basic unit for frequency is the *hertz* (abbr. Hz) in honor of the German physicist Heinrich R. Hertz. The term *cycles per second* (cps) for frequency has been deprecated. (1 Hz = 1 cps)

In the more than two decades which have elapsed since the introduction of high quality reel-to-reel magnetic tape recordings of original performances, it seems that for several reasons phonograph records are here to stay. First is the unity and simplicity of the phonographic disc. The printed information on the central label is an essential part of that unity and is inseparable from it. Moreover, the art of packaging discs has advanced to a point where record production combines pictorial beauty with typographic information about the recording (or recordings) enclosed. Neither reel-to-reel tapes, nor cassettes, nor cartridges, combine so ideally these attributes. Moreover, a reason that is unique is a high degree of immutability. Accidental erasures, damage from playing with magnetized heads, and print-through, for example, often experienced with tape recordings, have no parallel in the kinds of deterioration that affect discs of various types. Historically, well-preserved disc and cylinder records have often retained their original capabilities over many years, and with due respect for the system by which they were recorded, with suitable re-recording methods, it is surprisingly possible to recover more truth than was available from them in the year of their manufacture.

Acceptance of stereo discs by the American public in the early months of 1958 was so rapid that within a year the publishers of Schwann's catalogs found it necessary to integrate the new stereo discs as they were issued with the monophonic releases. Then began a period in which the major companies issued nearly all new releases in both mono and stereo versions. This certainly was a costly business, yet to the major producers it had the desirable effect of reducing the competition from numerous smaller companies, who could not afford it. Ultimately, however, it became obvious to all that such duplication had to be eliminated and thus the erstwhile-titled *Schwann Long Playing Record Catalog* reflected firm decisions by the industry leaders when it published a special announcement in the November *Stereo Record Guide* for 1970. This stated that "Mono records will be listed in the monthly Schwann for the last time in the December issue (excepting those issued during the past year)."

In addition, and again reflecting decisions made by industry leaders, Schwann informed readers "The 1970 Country and Western Schwann Catalog for the first time contains 8-track cartridge numbers in addition to the LP Stereo record numbers." Also included in the announcement was this: "Cartridge and Cassette numbers will be added to the monthly Schwann gradually during the early months of 1971, making the Schwann Catalogs of even greater reference value to the tape and record customer in his home and to the tape and record dealer in the store."

Obviously, the complications and expense of producing both mono and stereo discs were merely being switched to other forms of duplication. Of course, reel-to-reel tapes also were available, but never seemed to be a competitive threat to the discs as did the 8-track cartridges and the cassettes. These latter devices were both adaptable for new uses, as in automobiles, home recordings, or for dictation, where discs were not. However, the matter of making pre-recorded cartridges and cassettes competitive in quality to the best discs, or to reel-to-reel tape, required much technological development.

Quite understandably, a great deal of competitive development of stereo tape and disc recording went on in the principal laboratories of Europe and America. Much was expected from the men who had been successful in developing the LP records, and the stereo discs which all but completely supplanted the mono discs in such a short time.

One of the most important inventions in the search for ways of improving tape recording, aside from the refinement initially introduced into the early series of studio Ampex units and its various competitors, was the Dolby Audio Noise Reduction System, invented by Dr. Ray Dolby of England. This had been presented before the A.E.S. Convention in the U.S. on April 25, 1967, for the first time. Many articles subsequently described the merits of the Dolby system. Although there had been somewhat related technics for compression and expansion in reducing noise, as used in direct disc recording for instance, the Dolby system was better. Scott's system was perhaps better known for the dynamic noise suppressor, but Dolby's system was inherently different. The best exposition of these differences was in an article in *db, The Sound Engineering Magazine* by John Borwick, who first had visited Dolby in his laboratory in 1966.[6]

Borwick states that it was Arthur Haddy, the technical director of the Decca Record Company of London, who was the first key man in the industry to recognize the importance of the Dolby system. By 1969, over a hundred recording studios were using it. The Dolby system is used by many broadcast companies, including BBC, Canadian Broadcasting Corporation, Swedish Radio, and even VNIIRT in Moscow. Many tape recorders now manufactured also are "Dolbyized," even some made in Japan. Without a doubt, cassettes would never have been as useful as they are proving to be, without the Dolby system. Dynamic ranges of all media are enhanced and transmission noise in radio applications is reduced. Competitive systems have also been developed, the sincerest tribute to the Dolby success.

Peter Goldmark, the innovative genius largely responsible for the success of the Columbia long-playing record, adopted as standard by the world-wide industry and which paved the way for the stereo disc, for some years worked on EVR (electronic video recording). As early as September of 1968, Edward Tatnall Canby was heralding the approach of "this radical TV recording and playback

system." He said that it was "a product of long gestation behind the scenes," citing a collaboration between CBS Laboratories, Imperial Chemical Industries, Ltd. of England, and CIBA, Ltd, in Switzerland. Canby confidently stated that "the same master mind that blockbusted the ancient 78-rpm disc with the LP is responsible for the integrated EVR concept, Mr. Peter Goldmark."[7] He stated, however, that "It takes a large team and many brains to launch an overall communications system today" and that as EVR is part electronic and part photographic, the European firms were the photographic arm of the combine.

However, in an introductory paragraph prefacing Canby's article of September 1968, *db, The Sound Engineering Magazine* had printed this:

"Rumors run wild on this remarkable recording system. Frustratingly little information has been made available by the developers. Our author has collected facts and conjectures."

Quite consistently, in connection with another story almost two years later in *db, The Sound Engineering Magazine*, by the same author, the editors placed this prefatory statement:[8]

"Electronic Video Recording is about to spring forth full grown—almost surely before this year is out. The author offers the implications that this medium in its final form will mean."

Canby conceded that at the time of his earlier article the new system seemed hopelessly tied up in back-stage maneuverings, though it had been formally announced more than a year before. He also admitted that but a few months before his second article and almost three years after the original announcement, ". . . the mammoth international

---

[6] "Dolby Revisited," by John Borwick; *db, The Sound Engineering Magazine*, August 1969.

[7] "EVR," by Edward Tatnall Canby; *db, The Sound Engineering Magazine*, September 1968.

[8] "EVR at Take-Off," by Edward Tatnall Canby; *db, The Sound Engineering Magazine*, July 1970.

EVR system, ever growing larger, was still grounded." He further said, "In the U. S. not a cartridge was available on the market, nor a player to convert its miniature film into TV images."

Now, for the first time an EVR player built by Motorola was illustrated as well as a cartridge, showing the pictures, two to a frame, and the sound and sync tracks. At the time, Peter Goldmark was still head of research and development at CBS Laboratories and Edward Tatnall Canby was still full of hope. He said, "Now with bated breath, let us await the launching. Or should I say the take-off?"

But two months before, another smaller consortium had demonstrated its version of a home TV player. The previously mentioned German inventors of Telefunken, in collaboration with Decca engineers, had gone back to Edison's basic concept of recording vertically by indenting tin foil wrapped around a pre-grooved cylinder or a copper foil disc. Edison had considered that all speech and music were capable of being reduced in recording and by reproduction to a series of positive pulses. Of course only a relatively limited range of frequencies was recorded in the days of the demonstration tin foil phonograph, but the basic concept for both audio and video in the Teldec system is based on this Edison principle. As early as 1927, British TV pioneer Baird had recorded 30-line transmissions from a 78-rpm record. Limited by this lateral disc to 5 kHz, he secured 30 frames/sec., which was not up to the present TV standards.

With vertical recording, the Teldec engineers were able to record enough pulses to encompass both the video and audio spectrums by revolving the foil discs at 1500 rpm at 50 Hz in Europe, and 1800 rpm at the 60-Hz standard of the U.S. The rotation of the disc was through three pins through holes around the center of the disc. At the operating speeds, a cushion of air kept the disc from touching the surface of the player unit, gently pressing it

against the stylus. Teldec also borrowed from the Edison technology in that the gearing from the disc drive carried the pick-up across the record at the pitch recorded, which was .008 mm for each revolution.[9]

The simplicity and directness of the Teldec solution would have been admired by Thomas Edison. While not accepted as yet in the U.S., probably for the reason that it is an entirely European-controlled innovation, it may have had much to do with the collapse of the EVR collaboration. Peter Goldmark is no longer connected with CBS Laboratories and the future of the complicated EVR system seems in doubt.

However, since the initial demonstrations of Teldec in the U.S. in 1970, and the publication of articles about it in the popular and audio journals, a revised version under the name of the "TED Videodisk System" has been made available through leading retail stores of the industry in Germany.

The new TED Videodisk is 21 cm in diameter (8"), 0.1 mm thick, of a flexible and unbreakable PVC plastic foil sheet. Information about this latest development is from a talk by Dr. Rolf W. Schiering of Telefunken.[10] Claimed for the disc is that it is produced by a one-step manufacturing system, which takes only a few seconds, and is by far the most economical process for producing video discs. The same advantage would pertain to larger-diameter discs mentioned in earlier publicity about the Teldec discs, but not yet made commercially.

The players (Fig. 30-3) are being distributed through the customary TV-radio and record distribution channels, but the discs are to be available through a number of possible sales outlets, including TV-radio and record shops,

[9] db, The Sound Engineering Magazine, December 1970.
[10] "The TED Videodisk System," Dr. Rolf W. Schiering, Director Audio Visual Department, Telefunken Radio & Television Corporation. Translated and issued by Gotham Audio Corporation, New York, N.Y.

Fig. 30-3. The TED Videodisk player Model TP 1005. (Photo courtesy of Telefunken/Teldec.)

book stores, direct mail, and also for advertising and sales-promotion purposes. As pointed out, the initial commercial effort to exploit the TED system by an 8″ disc player limits the time to ten minutes per side. The sponsors have concluded that there is doubt that feature films could be sold in large enough quantities to be profitable, but suggest the possibility of a Videodisk changer, which is at the demonstration stage of development.

Advantages are also claimed for the simplicity of the playback system made of conventional-type components, with a piezo-electric transducer that uses a diamond stylus, and a record that can be played "many hundreds of times without the slightest damage." Dr. Schiering stated that a worn playback stylus, by contrast with the phonograph record, will not damage a videodisk and can be replaced, when necessary, by the user for less than $25. Also, the servicing can be done by technicians without need for sophisticated testing equipment or special training in optics or laser technology, etc., as in higher-cost equipment contemplated for other systems.

An initial offering of 50 records issued in March has since been doubled, and in Germany, 6,000 units and over 300,000 Videodisks have been made available in about 2,500 retail stores of various types. In Fig. 30-4, a kindergarten class is being entertained as well as educated through the use of cartoon features on TED Videodisks.

Since the development of the TED system for other color-TV standards such as the French SECAM and the

Fig. 30-4. The TED Videodisk system is ideal for short cartoon features for entertaining and educating kindergarten students. (Photo courtesy of Telefunken/Teldec.)

American NTSC system have been completed, it may be available soon in other countries. Dr. Schiering stated that a number of companies in Japan have signed licensing agreements, and it seems likely that this is, as he claims, an important step towards international acceptance.

It is true that audio in all of the projected TV systems thus far is predicated on TV standards—virtually that of FM radio. However, with the present dimensions of TV tubes in the home, ultra-high-fidelity sound is not needed, and would be disproportionate to the video quality and dimensions of the viewing area. Unless a technology is developed wherein the viewer looks through, rather than at the screen, or unless an inexpensive home projection system is developed, there is no need for the auditory stereo illusion. The chief competitive drawback of TED, from the viewpoint of U.S. companies, is that the limiting of playing time to 10 minutes

instead of a minimum of at least 15 minutes, as envisioned earlier, eliminates TV program material as a logical source for records for sale to the public.

There is a definite need for compatability with other media, however. Where projection to large screens is necessary, performances should have adequate speaker systems, and stereo is desirable. In libraries of the future, it is quite likely that the present system of carrels equipped with playback equipment for discs or cassettes will also have TV capabilities with provision for receiving programs either over the air or on closed-circuit TV. Very likely provisions to receive special programs on video tape, and perhaps also for use of information retrieval of slides, for access to computer information, etc., will be provided.

The desirability of a longer-playing disc and the possibility of a way of stopping a given frame are questions now being dealt with in Europe. Meanwhile

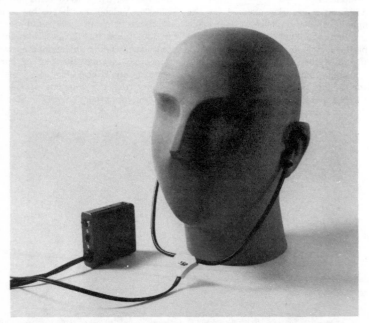

Fig. 30-5. The Sennheiser dummy recording head with external microphones and power supply—also may be worn by a person for recording. (Photo courtesy of Sennheiser Electronic Corporation.)

Fig. 30-6. Recording with the Sennheiser Binaural Recording System. The same sound that reaches the ears is simultaneously collected by the two microphones; there is no redundancy of passing sound through a simulated ear canal once, and a second time from the binaural earphones. (Photo courtesy of Sennheiser Electronic Corporation.)

a new and very practical version of an old idea has been made available in a most convenient form by another German company, and that is the Sennheiser Binaural Recording System.[11]

The Sennheiser system differs from previous versions in that it substitutes externally mounted microphones for those built into the dummy heads (or head simulators) of earlier binaural recording equipment.[12] This permits the microphones also to be worn by a person on his head during recording, where desirable, eliminating the need for earphone monitoring (see Figs. 30-5 and 30-6). Most important of all, the Sennheiser approach also eliminates the redundancy of the impedance of a simulated ear canal before the microphone within the dummy head. This is supplied naturally by the ultimate listener and varies from person to person. The microphones in the Sennheiser system receive whatever any person would

hear, however, in any given listening location, external to the variable physiological differences, but with like separation and orientation.

For educational purposes as well as for library or studio listening purposes, the Sennheiser system seems to offer the simplest and most fool-proof method of hearing a given voice or instrument almost precisely as it sounds without conflict between the ambient conditions of the listening room with that of the performance area. At least in theory it would seem that the fullest realization of the unique ability to put yourself in the studio would be obtained by using headsets sealing off the listening environment.

However, in a report on the Sennheiser binaural recording system which appeared in *High Fidelity* for January 1975, the authors were enthusiastic about the results achieved when the Sennheiser "Open-Aire" headsets were employed. Following is a description of their experience with a pair of conventional headphones with ear-cup seal designed for a maximum rejection of the ambient room sound of the listening area:

---

[11] "Sennheiser's Astonishing Binaural Recording System," *High Fidelity*, January 1975.

[12] "Not Such a Dummy Head," D. J. Meares, B. Sc., BBC Research Department. From *Wireless World*, Vol. 80, pp. 335-336, September 1974.

"The effect improved dramatically. Sound placements—right to left, front to back, near to far, even up to down —appeared more unequivocal, rather like listening to those in particularly fine quadriphonic (read, 'four-channel stereo') reproduction. This is, of course, the claim of binauralism: that *every* nuance of aural sensation is reproduced, not merely simulated or hinted at, as it must be when loudspeakers and standard mikings are used."

Finally, the experts switched to a headset of the open-air type that provides very little seal against ambient noise. The report on this is as follows:

"The verisimilitude was uncanny. Some sounds seemed unequivocally to be in the room—presumably because one *can* hear room sounds and therefore attribute particularly realistic ones to the room, rather than the recording. Spatial ambiences and three-dimensional placements were reproduced with an exactitude that defies even the best of quadriphony." (Sennheiser explains that conventional stereo varies directionally right and left, whereas binaural varies up and down as well.) "When we used the microphone— whether 'worn' by a staff member or by the dummy head—we had no trouble creating tapes that, reproduced on low ambience-seal headsets, delivered the same startling realism. Even in recording on non-Dolby cassettes the quality is, subjectively, superb; the hiss is entirely audible—but at the headphones rather than within the 'space' of the sound reproduced. The listener 'tunes it out' when the recorded content takes over."

In either case, there is little room for questioning as fact the superiority of the binaural principle as being the most efficient and economical way to recover the essential truth of a musical performance as it actually was performed and as it is actually heard by a single individual. With a commercially available high-quality binaural recording system, it is possible for the first time, for any individual with normal hearing, to verify for himself the possible limits of realization of true fidelity, and with simple means.

In the libraries and archives of sound of the future a time will come when questions of authenticity of performances will demand answers. For one thing, in these situations, binaural listening is fast becoming the standard means of retrieval. We are therefore concerned with the availability of simple means for determining the truth of a performance. In the early days of sound recording there were no complicated systems. Therefore, today, there must ever be an alertness to needs for simplification and the provision of means for verification. There was never a better way than an A-B comparison between hearing what goes in with what comes out, but this presupposes a standard playback instrument. In the Sennheiser binaural system, we have such a standard available for archival, library, and research purposes.

This, in effect, would be the opposite of what Edison did in sound-damping the walls of the Fifth Avenue studio designed for recording the voices and instrumental solo performances for the tone-testable diamond disc records. From 1914 to 1927, direct comparison tests were publicly conducted from coast to coast in the United States and Canada in theaters and music halls, large and small, in which the public had opportunity to hear the reproductions from a standard model Edison Laboratory Model Phonograph in side-by-side comparison with the performances of the living artists. Results were published in daily newspapers by music critics and reporters, as covered in a previous chapter.

It is demonstrable that sensitive artists would find it generally quite impossible to perform satisfactorily in an anechoic chamber. In fact, even though the deadening of the reflections in the Edison studio was only to reduce it slightly below the level of cognizability, the effect on the freedom of the artists is obvious when one compares the reproduction from the best of the Blue Amberol cylinders and diamond discs directly recorded for each by the same artists of the same performances, as well as performances dubbed from the discs to the cylinders when this practice was adopted after 1915. There is a considerably greater feeling of relaxed and enjoyable music making by popular artists prior to the diamond discs that was not again in evidence until the Edison discs were recorded electrically beginning in 1927. Edison encouraged the forming of special house organizations, such as the National Promenade Band which recorded really swinging performances of ragtime music on the Amberol and Blue Amberol cylinders, but which seemed tightly recorded and lacking in zest and spontaneity when the same selections were again recorded in the reflection-damped disc studio.

Incidently, but important to our thesis, the enthusiasm of the reviewer for *High Fidelity* led him correctly to explain that the results were better than the best quadrasonic recording. But why not—we have only two ears, not four, despite the development of special earphones which deliver two channels of sound to each ear!

As to the highest quality from discs without distortion, stereo discs recorded from binaural tapes could be used for delivery of the same verifiable high fidelity. One of two things that are still radically wrong with the present stereo discs is that the groove-stylus relationships are prone to produce rapid demodulations in the sides of the groove, as disclosed by the Scanning Electron Microscope photographs shown in an article in the July 1968, *Journal of the Audio Engineering Society.* (See Figs. 30-7, 8, and 9.) The other is the constantly differing speeds under both the recording stylus and playback stylus. There is an optimum surface speed for cutting every type of material used for

record mastering, and there is an optimum speed for playback by every design of playback transducer. Compensations are made for differences in energy needed in cutting, and also in playback modules, and circuitry. These are not necessarily related, for virtually no American company produces a standard playback instrument for its records.

Despite the fact that by international agreement records are made to a certain curve (RIAA), there is no guarantee that the records of the various companies are truly interchangeable. In fact, analyses made at a prominent electronics laboratory with sophisticated half-octave equalizers and time/data analyzers indicates convincingly that each company produces records that have a distinctive and identifiable trademark curve of its own. Therefore, the quest for verifiable high fidelity gets more difficult with increasing complexity of systems.

In order to sum up where we stand sixteen years after the first publication of *From Tin Foil to Stereo,* it seems that a return to simpler systems is necessary if we are to find a way to restore music to its proper dimensions faithfully. In teaching, the voice coach deals individually with the student, and at close range. Learning how to sing, the voice is evaluated and placed by hearing in close-up, usually quite dead, small studios. It seems logical that if the student is to hear his voice as the teacher does, recordings should be made of his voice exactly as the teacher hears it, and reproduced in such a way that they are discussing the same things. It is well-known that in singing (or speaking) the person does not know how his voice sounds to others, and to learn how to use it effectively he has to hear it as others do.

This is not quite so true of performers on other instruments. Yet, to a very considerable extent, the soloist always has a specific relationship in space to his instrument. This factor is a constant which makes it also necessary for his performances to be recorded and reproduced as heard by others if he is to learn to improve the results.

The first series of demonstration phonographs employed tin foil for the recording medium. The nature of the material required indenting rather than incising. Contrary to popular belief, Edison did not invent *the* cylinder phonograph, and Berliner *the* disc counterpart. Edison demonstrated an experimental disc phonograph equipped with a spring motor using an indented copper foil alloy disc in the spring of 1878, only about four months after application for the Edison tin-foil demonstration phonograph patent which had been granted on February 19, 1878. Cylinder and disc lathes of one type or another were already in the arts, and hence, not patentable. The essence of the Edison invention was the design of lathes that provided the novel groove-diaphragm relationships which are central to the phonographic art and which define its essential differences from subsequently developed methods of recording and reproducing sound.

Analyses of the relative economics of storage space made a few years ago disclosed the phonograph disc as being the most efficient. Other advantages of the disc are its unity and immutability. Now the revolutionary breakthrough of video discs indicates that far greater advantages accrue to Edison's original and basic phonographic principle, not only in still greater advantages in ratio of volume of information to storage space required, but also in economy of processing the recordings. Moreover, though vertical-cut modulation has not been the standard of the industry for many years, the recent demonstrations of competing types of video discs indicate conclusively that the often amazingly prescient Mr. Edison was also right in his choice of vertical modulation instead of lateral modulation, which is barely mentioned in his first U.S. phonographic patent.

Now that there are choices of videodisc systems, all employing vertical modulation by one means or another, it seems obvious that eventually there must be a complete reconsideration of the technical anomalies which persist in audio recording. One of these is the variable groove speed under the cutting and reproducing styli. Another is the wasteful nature of the extremely limited stylus groove contact area in present stereo disc recording practice. A third is a lack of symmetry and uniformity in the disc groove as compared to a cylinder groove.

For several years now there has been available the kind of diagnostic tool which reveals succinctly the absolute necessity of eliminating or reducing the effect of these anomolies. This is the Scanning Electron Microscope, revealed in a paper presented April 30, 1968 at the 34th Audio Engineering Society Convention, Hollywood, California.[13]

The authors of the article in the *Journal of the Audio Engineering Society* are J. G. Woodward, M. D. Coutts, and E. R. Levin of the David Sarnoff Research Center, RCA Laboratories, Princeton, New Jersey. An introductory paragraph prefacing the article states:

"The scanning electron microscope (SEM) has only recently become generally available as a commercial device. The combination of high resolution and high magnification with a remarkable depth of focus provided by the SEM, together with simple procedures in specimen preparation, make this instrument admirably suited for use in disc-recording research and development."

Through the courtesy of Dr. J. G. Woodward, we are able to reproduce photographs which show grooves and groove-stylus relationships with amazing clarity. The first figure we have chosen (Fig. 30-7) shows two views of a .7-mil spherical diamond stylus, one

[13] "The Scanning Electron Microscope—A New Tool in Disc-Recording Research," J. G. Woodward, M. D. Coutts, and E. R. Levin. From *Journal of the Audio Engineering Society*, Vol. 16, pp. 258-265, July 1968.

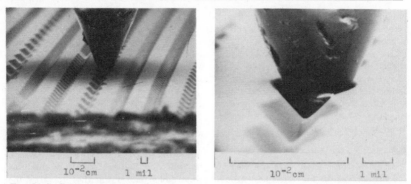

Fig. 30-7. Scanning electron microscope images of a diamond playback stylus in a groove of a vinyl record carrying vertical modulation. (Courtesy of RCA Laboratories.)

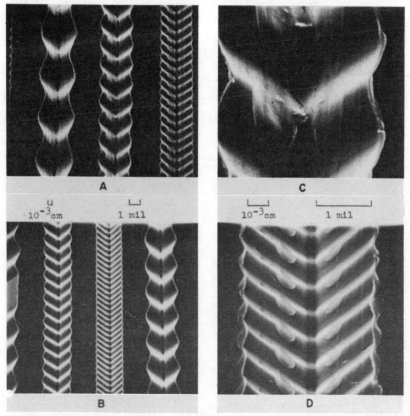

Fig. 30-8. Record wear in a vinyl record viewed along the groove axis following 50 plays of vertical sweep-frequency modulation. **A** and **C**—ceramic pickup; .7 mil spherical stylus; 5 grams tracking pressure. **B** and **D**—high-quality pickup; .2 × .7 mil elliptical stylus; 1.5 grams tracking pressure. (Courtesy of RCA Laboratories.)

showing several adjacent grooves, and one showing a close-up of the stylus in a groove.

The second figure is comprised of four views in a vinyl record viewed along the groove axis. In two instances we are using the captions as published under the *A.E.S. Journal* article. In the case of our Fig. 30-8, we wish also to quote from the text, as follows:

"These pictures show that the wear is more severe on the left-hand groove wall than on the right-hand wall.

The most likely explanation for this is that the stylus-groove contact force was greater on the left-hand wall because of the skating force. No compensation for the skating force was applied to the pickup arm used in these tests."

Skating force can be and is compensated for in many pickup arms, but in combination with the constantly decreasing speed under the stylus which crowds the higher frequency modulations even closer together towards the center of the disc, presents problems

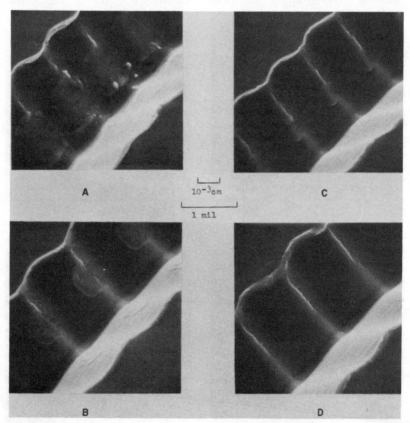

*Fig. 30-9. These photos show groove wear caused by four different pickups following 50 plays. Photo **A** shows the wear produced by a spherical .7 mil stylus tracking at 5 grams; **B** shows the effect of a .2 × .7 mil elliptical stylus at 1.5 grams; **C**, a .2 × .9 mil elliptical stylus at 1.5 grams; and **D**, a .7 mil spherical stylus at 1.5 grams. (Courtesy of RCA Laboratories.)*

which need study and solution. Therefore constant groove speed is not only desirable but most likely inevitable!

The Fig. 30-9 which we present is Fig. 11 in the original *A.E.S. Journal* article, but we have chosen the caption accompanying the article on "Record-Groove Wear," by J. G. Woodward which appeared in *Stereo Review* in October 1968.

Of the three groups of photographs taken with the scanning electron microscope, only Fig. 30-8 shows the comparative wear pattern on both walls with no skating-force compensation employed. By comparing these views with those showing the position of the stylus in the groove (Fig. 30-7), and greatly enlarged views of but one side of the groove (Fig. 30-9), one can appreciate the importance of this recently perfected instrument to the advancement of the art.

Unfortunately, with multichannel tape recording, the recording of tracks at different times, and the use of multimicrophoning technics, the results are often actually sound recordings of nonperformances. The control over what is going to be delivered to the ultimate listener by the authors, composers, and performers becomes vastly lessened. Not only is the control permanently delivered into the hands of the producer, but there are invidious changes in timbre produced by multiple microphoning and the many, many places where mixing distorts quality. As we have said, there is today not even a standard instrument for reproducing a given recording!

Since the startling demonstrations of the Teldec video discs in the U.S. in October 1970, drastic changes in direction of research have occurred. Numerous and unsupported pronouncements about EVR have ceased. That ambitious international collaboration seems to have failed. *db, The Sound Engineering Magazine* later perhaps had gone overboard again in its enthusiasm for Teldec, but at least this was founded on demonstration and not on speculation about a highly touted but inadequately demonstrated system, as admitted by the author of the articles on EVR.

In *TV Guide* for August 16, 1975, we come to an unexpected denouement! The article is the logical sequel to the stories which appeared in *db, The Sound Engineering Magazine* about Teldec, even though not mentioning it. This seemed to indicate that the author, Frank S. Swertlow, was of the opinion that the Teldec system no longer was envisioned as being in prospect for use in the United States. A call to Mr. Swertlow in *TV Guide's* New York offices confirmed this. He informed this author that although Teldec is now in use in Germany, its playing time for an 8-inch disc is only about 10 minutes, whereas earlier articles promised 15 minutes to a side. In any event, the trend since the demonstration of Teldec, has changed the major emphasis from tape cassettes to discs. Mr. Swertlow also said that the availability of program material ready for processing to video discs for the home and educational markets was largely in 30-minute segments and this was an important factor in preliminary decision making, even though it may be two years before home video-disc units can be expected to be generally available in the U.S.

As a preliminary to continuing with the excellent analysis which Frank S. Swertlow has made for the readers of *TV Guide*, we have requested permission to print a paragraph from another writer in the *New York Times Magazine* of May 25, 1975 (with illustrations by Nicholas Fasciano—Fig. 30-10) which sums up the competition to find a videotape or video-disc system that seems now to have reached success with discs, whereas earlier promises seemed to be with tape systems.

Robin Lanier, in his article, "A Home TV Revolution," said:

"In the last eight years, at least 10 companies, among them major electronics firms here and abroad, have worked to develop a practical video disk. These included, besides RCA and

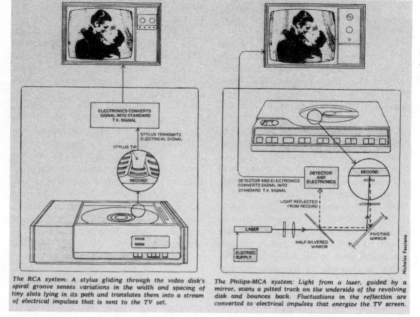

The RCA system: A stylus gliding through the video disk's spiral groove senses variations in the width and spacing of tiny slots lying in its path and translates them into a stream of electrical impulses that is sent to the TV set.

The Philips-MCA system: Light from a laser, guided by a mirror, scans a pitted track on the underside of the revolving disk and bounces back. Fluctuations in the reflection are converted to electrical impulses that energize the TV screen.

Fig. 30-10. Two proposed video-disc systems for use in the U.S. (Courtesy of the New York Times Magazine.)[14]

Philips-MCA, Zenith here in America, Germany's Telefunken, England's Decca, France's Thomson-CSF and some small American companies, notably I/O Metrics in California and Digital Recording in Scarsborough, N.Y. Some of the large companies, preparing for any eventuality, worked on tape cassettes and disks simultaneously. During this period, nearly all of the big organizations succeeded in producing, by one method or another, workable disk systems."[14]

The long and complex mechanical, electrical, and chemical research projects which finally are already producing plastic foil discs in Germany, which store up and reproduce both sight and sound, can best be at least partially appreciated by those who have had the patience to read this present book. We wish to thank Mr. Robin Lanier and The

New York Times Magazine for the excellent summing up of the efforts on a world-wide basis over the past eight years.

Especially at this point we wish to acknowledge the superb digest of the present situation as it affects us in the United States by Frank S. Swertlow and the permission granted by TV Guide for reprinting a major portion of his article, "Giving Television a Spin," in its issue of August 16, 1975, as follows:

"The idea for the video disc was born about a decade ago when researchers felt there was a market for alternatives to commercial television programming. Public and cable television were already available, but these required viewers to sit for regularly scheduled shows—viewers still didn't have the freedom to choose what they wanted and when they wanted to see it.

"Industry observers point out that since Americans spend almost $2 billion a year on phonograph records, a system that offers pictures and sound might reap even more money.

"So for the last decade, electronics firms have tried to develop the technology for such a system. Initially, many devices were examined, including discs, but most of the energy went into magnetic-tape cassette systems.

"Although the technical problems were solved, the engineers could not design a tape system that would be cheap enough. Most video-tape player-recorders were $1000 and up, and even blank cassettes cost $15 a half hour. The cost of producing programmed cassettes boosted the price much higher. (Nevertheless, the cassette market is still a considerable one for such specialized areas as schools and businesses.)

"When it came to low-cost, mass-market systems, the video disc won out. A disc can be stamped out with assembly-line speed for about 60 cents and disc players are cheaper than video-tape decks. The disc system is aimed at the average American family.

" 'The average home is now interested in a broad range of information, and not just entertainment,' says Robert T. Cavanagh, vice president of North American Philips. 'To meet this increased interest, you have to look at the best method of storage. How about video tape? It's too expensive. How about film? That's even more expensive. Now you have to ask is there another medium that is low-cost and can be produced in high volume? The answer is the disc.'

"For the paying customer, the rub is that the RCA and Philips systems are not compatible with each other. An RCA disc cannot be played on a Philips machine, and vice versa, although they operate under the same principle: a vinyl disc is rotated at high speed on a player plugged in to the antenna leads of a TV set. While the disc spins, electronic impulses are picked up and sent to the picture tube. The result is television sight, sound,

color and motion.

"RCA, which calls its system 'Selecta-Vision,' aimed at simplicity in design by using components taken from other products, most notably stereo-record players. The system will cost about $400. Philips reached for more sophisticated 'space-age' technology—the laser. The cost of this system, which does not have a trade name as yet, is expected to be approximately $500.

"The keys to RCA's system are a grooved disc and a sapphire capacitance stylus, a principle similiar to a stereo phonograph and a needle. The disc, which has a number of minute impressions in it, rotates on the player at a speed of 450 rpm (most phonograph records rotate at 45 or $33\frac{1}{3}$ rpm). The stylus glides over the spinning disc, picking up impulses and sending them to the TV screen. Most discs play for 30 minutes on each side and have both stereo and monaural sound tracks.

"The RCA player can be cued to specific sections of a disc for replay (much as you would cue a phonograph needle to a particular song on a stereo record) but it does not have stop-action or slow-motion capabilities. RCA says the disc itself is covered with several protective coatings to withstand dirt, fingerprints, scratches and spills, but it does show wear after several hundred plays. RCA says the average life of a disc is 500 plays. A stylus is said to be good for 300-500 playing hours and replaceable for under $10.

"During a recent demonstration in New York the RCA system worked perfectly. Color, clarity of picture and sound were superb. The machine was as easy to operate as a portable record player. For cleaning or repair work, the device was easy to take apart, and the stylus popped out within seconds.

"The Philips system uses a laser beam and a series of mirrors—called an optical video-disc system—to get the picture off the disc and onto the screen. Philips' laser beam scans the bottom side of the disc while RCA's stylus takes its information off the top.

"In the Philips system, the laser beam —a safe, low-level light beam—is guided by a mirror to the underside of the disc, which rotates at 1800 rpm. The information cn the disc—some 54,000 complete pictures—is then picked up by the laser beam and sent to the TV screen. Thirty pictures are sent every second, the same as in broadcast television. Discs are good for a half hour, although a one-hour disc can be made. A flexible disc for mailing and giveaways will be available.

"The Philips player is more sophisticated than RCA's; it offers slow-motion, stop-action and frame-by-frame sequences. Since each picture will have an index number, which can appear on the screen, the viewer will be able to tune in any frame he desires.

"The Philips disc also has a special protective coating, but since the laser beam does not touch the disc, there is no wear. The laser itself is said to have a life of several thousand hours and a low replacement cost.

"When the two systems are put side by side, their strengths and weaknesses are apparent. Industry observers say RCA may have sacrificed flexibility for simplicity of design and easy repair. Philips has created a more sophisticated machine, but it must still meet the test of everyday use.

"Some have suggested that since the RCA and Philips systems are not compatible, one system must prevail if the discs are to be successful. A top CBS official disagrees. 'The cost of making a disc,' he said, 'is cheap enough to make a disc for both systems. Look, in the recording industry . . . well, you can make a record, either stereo or four-channel, or a tape, which can be eight-track, cassette or open reel.'

"Now that RCA and Philips have settled on their respective systems, the next step seems to be to persuade the public to buy them. Spokesmen for

both firms admit this may be the toughest hurdle: the only reason to buy a system is the programming, but the only way to finance a wide variety of programming is to sell a lot of disc players.

"Both companies, as well as others waiting on the sidelines, recognize the need for varied programming. RCA and Philips may have some special shows at first, but the main source of programming will be movies. Once sales increase, RCA's George Evanoff, vice president for corporate development, says the special programming will increase. 'First, we have to go for mass entertainment, like movies,' he said. 'Later, we will be very specialized, and some of these programs may appeal just to one per cent of the viewers.'

"Cavanagh of Philips agreed, but he stressed the disc will be more than just a medium for entertainment. 'The level of information is constantly going up in the home,' he said. 'There are books, magazines, encyclopedias.'

"Since the disc can store an enormous amount of information, Cavanagh said he expected to see video books, museums and magazines. Students may some day use the disc to augment their classroom lectures and computers may be hooked into the systems.

.   .   .

"The price, industry experts say, will be within the reach of the average family—$400-500 for a disc player and $2-10 for a disc. One disc system is already on the market in Europe, and last march, RCA and N.V. Philips (an international firm based in Holland) demonstrated their systems in New York. Both companies say they are gearing up to put their machines in the American home sometime in 1976."[15]

Also, we now have the video-tape cassettes of Sony and others, with compact players that can be carried any-

[15] Reprinted with permission from *TV Guide®* *Magazine.* Copyright © 1975 by Triangle Publications, Inc., Radnor, Pennsylvania.

where, even stowed under the seats of airliners. These have a usefulness in sales promotion that is self-evident. Likewise, such compact and high-quality systems have proven their worth for traveling lecturers.

Now there are also choices of Kodak Videoplayers that reproduce 8-mm films through television equipment, even for operating many sets over closed-TV circuits. This important new development is made possible by the magnastriping of the film, which has been recognized as superior to the optical track of conventional 8-mm film. This is an important breakthrough, for it makes immediately available a very large and important reservoir of great motion-picture art, plus many educational productions suitable for both home entertainment and educational applications. Moreover, the same soft-wear source materials already processed, such as the super-8 Kodak films in cassette form, may be utilized by conventional projectors equipped with magnetic sound for classrooms or auditoriums. These can also be made individually available to students, scholars, and researchers, through the new Kodak Videoplayers, to carrels in our libraries, or elsewhere. The possibilities of converting such

motion-picture productions to video discs seems most intriguing. This has a potential for making widely available much important material, from what is presently a limited luxury market, to a much broader one with manifold public and educational outlets. The fields of home entertainment, commercial sales, and every educational level from kindergarten to advanced research and continuing education, would benefit.

Regardless of the systems to be adopted, stereo phono discs will continue. Questions about excesses resulting from multi-microphoning, multi-channeling via tape, and quadrasonics on discs are becoming academic. The bringing together of musical performances on video discs, as in TV programming, will impose a natural corrective force on the hideous distortions present in many popular and even some of the classical phonograph discs, since the descent down from the halcyon days of a sincere reaching for "high fidelity." Moreover, the accomplishment of both sight and sound for the compatible 30-minute segments from discs indicates clearly that superior audio and greater economics in storage space are inevitable for the phonographs and records of the future.

APPENDIX

"Methods of High Quality Recording and Reproducing of Music and Speech Based on Telephone Research"

by J. P. Maxfield and H. C. Harrison

(Reprinted from *Transactions of the American Institute of Electrical Engineers, 1926*)

. . . .

"Studio Characteristics and Transients"

"Phonographic reproduction may be termed perfect when the components of the reproduced sound reaching the ears of the listener have the same relative intensity and phase relation as the sound reaching the ears of an imaginary listener to the original performance would have had. Obviously, it is very difficult, if not impossible, to fulfill all of these requirements with a single channel system, that is, with a system which does not have a separate path from each ear of the listener to the sound source.

"The use of two ears, that is, two channel listening, gives the listener a sense of direction for each of the various sources of sound to which at a given moment he may be listening, and, therefore, he apprehends them in their relative distribution in space. It has been found possible with a single channel system however, by controlling the acoustic properties of the room in which the sound is being recorded, to simulate to a considerable degree in the reproduced music the effective space relationships of the original. In this case, with a one-channel system, the directional effect is, of course, entirely absent, and the spatial relationship which is apprehended is probably due to the increased apparent vibration of the instruments situated at the far end of the room as compared with those in the near foreground.

"In recording work, therefore, one of the important acoustic characteristics of a room is its time of reverberation. Although it is probable that this is the most comprehensive single factor, experiment has shown that the shape of the room and the distribution and character of the damping surfaces play a part in the excellence of music in such a room.

"It has been shown by Sabine that for piano music, studios should have a time of reverberation measured by his method of 1.08 seconds. Experience indicates that this figure is also closely correct for other types of music. This figure of Sabine's assumes binaural listening. With single channel systems, such as most of the present reproduction systems, whether for radio or the phonograph, the ability of the listener to separate the reverberations from the direct music by means of the sense of direction is completely removed and there is thrust upon his attention an apparent excess amount of room echo. Experiment has shown that a time of reverberation for the recording room ranging from slightly more than one-half to slightly less than three-quarters of Sabine's figure affords in the reproduced music the effect of a room with proper acoustics. When this effect is accomplished, the person listening to the reproduced music has the consciousness of the music being played in a continuation of the same room in which he is listening and also has a sense of spatial depth.

"Experiment has indicated further that any transients set up by the recording or reproducing system constitute a second cause of apparent increased reverberation. The data obtained thus far are insufficient to permit assignment of quantitative values to the importance of these two factors.

"At the present state of the art, the most important requirement of a recording or reproducing system is its frequency characteristic. This involves two factors, — intensity versus frequency, and phase distortion versus frequency. The effect of the second of these factors is not thoroughly understood but as it is closely related to the production of transients it has to be considered as mentioned above. The system to be described is relatively free, however, from violent phase shifts within most of the range covered, but does have some undesirable phase shift characteristics with small accompanying transients near its limiting cut-off frequencies.

"The frequency range which it will be desirable to cover, if it were possible, with relative uniform intensity for the transmission of speech and all types of music including pipe organ is from about 16 cycles per second to approximately 10,000.

"It may be interesting to examine the record requirements for a band of frequencies this great. For the purpose of this illustration, a lateral-cut record will be assumed although in all factors except the time which the record will run, the arguments apply in a similar manner to the hill-and-dale cut. Since, for mechanical reproduction, the sound at a given pitch is radiated by means of a fixed radiation resistance, it is necessary that the record be cut with a device the square of whose velocity is proportional to the sound power. Under these conditions, it is seen that for a given intensity of sound the amplitude is inversely proportional to the frequency of the tone, and that a point will be reached somewhere at the low end of the sound spectrum where this amplitude will be great enough to cut from one groove into the adjacent groove, or in the case of the vertical cut, to cut so deeply that with present materials the wax will tear instead of cut away with a clean surface. This means that there is an inherent maximum amplitude beyond which it is not commercially feasible to go. Similarly, the minimum radius of curvature of sine waves of various frequencies cut at constant velocity is inversely proportional to the frequency, so that as higher and higher frequencies are reached the radius of curvature becomes smaller and smaller until it becomes too small for the reproducing needle to follow. There is, therefore, an inherent limit set at the upper end.

"In order to extend these limits, it is necessary in the case of the low end to make the spiral coarser and in the case of the high end to run the record at a higher speed. Both of these changes tend to decrease the time which a record of a given size can be made to play. The only alternative of these methods is to cut a record less loud than is the present standard practice and make the reproducing equipment more sensitive. This could be done easily if it were not for the 'record noise' or 'surface noise,' as it is commonly called. Since this surface noise is already loud enough in comparison with the reproduced music to be somewhat objectionable, no appreciable gain in this direction can be made until the technique of record manufacture has been distinctly improved.

"In this connection, there is one other interesting point. It has been suggested that if electrical reproduction were used, it would be possible to cut the record with a characteristic other than uniform velocity sensitiveness and correct for the error by an electrical system whose characteristic is the inverse of the characteristic of the record.* If the change which is made in the recording characteristic tends toward cutting at uniform acceleration sensitiveness, the amplitude varies inversely as the square of the frequency and hence the difficulties at the low end of the scale are greatly enhanced. Similarly, if the records are cut more nearly at constant amplitude, the radius of curvature of the sine waves decreases as the square of the frequencies, hence the difficulties are placed at the upper end. In the process which is being described in this paper, these limitations have been met commercially by having a frequency characteristic of the uniform velocity type between the frequencies of 200 and approximately 4,000 cycles per second. Below 200 it has been necessary to operate at approximately constant amplitude with a resulting loss in intensity which loss increases as the frequency decreases. Above 4,000 it has been necessary to operate at approximate constant acceleration with its consequent slight loss in intensity at the very high overtones. With a characteristic of this type, a range of frequencies from 60 cycles to 6,000** can be recorded with reasonable success although the very low and very high range are slightly deficient. (See Fig. 14.) With a record

* This practice was later adopted by all companies and is one of the points at issue.
** Note that by 1933 Maxfield claimed for his lateral method up to 6,000 cycles only, but that even then above 15,000 cycles were being recorded and reproduced by the Bell laboratories from hill-and-dale discs.

having such a frequency characteristic, the inherent limitations are divided between the two ends of the frequency band and when electrical reproduction methods are used, it is possible to employ a reproduction system whose frequency characteristic compensates for that of the record. "It should be pointed out that an attempt to record notes lower than the low cut-off of the above mentioned apparatus would result in recording only those harmonics of the notes which lie above the cut-off. This in no way prevents the listener from hearing the notes, reproduced by means of the harmonics only, as notes with the pitches of the missing fundamentals although it does somewhat change the quality of the tone. If it were not for this ability of the ear to add the fundamental pitch of a note, of which only the harmonics are being reproduced, most of the older phonographs and loud speakers would have been totally useless for the reproduction of speech and music."

"Mechanical Versus Electrical Recording"

"In attacking the recording part of the problem, two ways at once present themselves: first, the direct use of the power of the sound being recorded to operate the recording instrument; and second, the use of high quality electric apparatus with vacuum tube amplifiers in order to give more freedom to the artists and better control to the process. The amount of power available to operate the recorder directly from the sound in the recording room is so small as to make it extremely difficult to make records under natural conditions of speaking, singing, or instrumental playing. As the use of high quality electric apparatus with associated amplifiers has a very distinct advantage over the acoustic method, they have been adopted for the recording part of the process.

"It will be noticed in Fig. 1A that the artists are grouped very closely about

Fig. 1A. Picture of an orchestra recording for the acoustic process. (This picture was furnished through the courtesy of the Victor Talking Machine Company, Camden, New Jersey.)

the horn. In the case of the weaker instruments such as violins, it has been possible to use only two of standard construction. The rest of the violins are of the type known as the 'Stroh' violin which is a device strung in the manner of a violin but so arranged that the bridge vibrates a diaphragm attached to a horn. This horn is directed towards the recording horn, as shown by the player in the foreground.

"With such an arrangement of musicians, it is very difficult to arouse the spontaneous enthusiasm which is necessary for the production of really artistic music. In Fig. 1B the musicians are sitting at ease more nearly in the usual arrangement and all are using the instruments which they would use if they were playing at a concert. Furthermore, the microphone is now sufficiently far away from the orchestra to receive the

sound in much the manner that the ears of a listener in the audience would receive it. In other words, it picks up the sound after it has been properly blended with the reflections from the walls of the room. It is in this way that the so-called 'atmosphere' or 'room-tone' has been obtained.

"In the old process, it sometimes happened that after the instruments had been arranged in such a manner that the relative loudness of the various parts had been balanced correctly, it was found that the whole selection was either too loud or too weak. This usually meant a complete rearrangement of the players. With the flexibility introduced by the use of electrical apparatus including amplifiers, the control of loudness is obtained by simple manipulation of the amplifier system and is in no way related to the difficulties of the relative loud-

Fig. 1B. Picture of the same orchestra shown in Fig. 1A, but recording for the electric process. (This picture was furnished through the courtesy of the Victor Talking Machine Company, Camden, New Jersey.)

ness of one instrument to another. The only problem for the studio director in this case is to obtain the proper balance among the various musical instruments and artists. The advantages derived from this added ease of control are also made manifest in that it is much easier and less tiresome for the artists and it is usually possible to make more records in a given time."

"Mechanical Versus Electrical Reproducing"

"Where the question of reproduction is concerned, the same two alternatives mentioned for recording present themselves, namely, direct use of power derived from the record itself versus the use of electromagnetic equipment with an amplifier. In this case, however, the situation is a little different as the power which can be drawn directly from the record is

more than sufficient for home use. Since any method of reproducing from mechanical records by electrical means involves the use of a mechanical device for transferring from mechanical to electrical power and a second such device for transferring from electrical back to mechanical power, that is, sound, it is necessary to use two mechanical systems, one at each end of an electrical system. Where the power which can be supplied by the record is sufficient to produce the necessary sound intensity, as in the case of home use, it is in general simpler to design one single mechanical transmission system, than it is to add the unnecessary complications of amplifiers, power supply and associated circuits. In cases where music is to be reproduced in large auditoriums, the power which can be drawn from the record may be insufficient and some form of electric reproduction using amplifiers becomes necessary."

"Brief Description of Recording System" "The system for recording consists of a condenser transmitter, a high quality vacuum tube amplifier and an electromagnetic recorder. Fig. 2 shows the calibration of the condenser transmitter and the associated amplifiers. The condenser transmitter and amplifiers are so designed that the current delivered to the recorder circuit is essentially proportional to the sound pressure at the transmitter diaphragm. The electromagnetic recorder, which will be described later, is designed to work with this type of system. With the exception of this electromagnetic recorder, apparatus of this type has already been described in the literature. (Wente, E. C., 'Condenser Transmitter as a Uniformly Sensitive Instrument for Measuring Sound Intensity' — Phys. Review, Vol. 10, 1917; Crandall, I. B., 'Air-Damped Vibratory Systems'—Phys. Review, Vol. 11, 1918; Martin, W. H., and Fletcher, H., 'High Quality Transmission and Reproduction of Speech and Music' — Trans. A.I.E.E., Vol. 43, 1924; Wente,

E. C., 'Electrostatic Transmitter' — Phys. Review, Vol. 19, 1922; Green, I. W., and Maxfield, J. P., 'Public Address Systems'—Trans. A.I.E.E., Vol. 43, 1923, p. 64.) In addition to this equipment which might be called the recording amplifier system, there is a volume indicator for measuring the power which is being delivered to the recorder and also an audible monitoring system. The monitoring system consists of an amplifier whose input impedance is high compared with the recorder impedance and a suitable loud speaking receiver. The monitoring amplifier is bridged directly across the recorder and operates the loud speaking receiver so that the operators may listen to the record as it is being made.

"In the design of the recording and reproducing systems each part of the system has been made as nearly perfect as possible. Errors of one part have not been designed to compensate for inverse errors in another part. Although this method is the more difficult, its flexibility, particularly as regards the commercial possibilities of future improvements, justifies the extra effort. There is, therefore, no

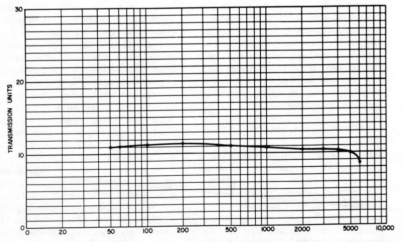

Fig. 2. Calibration of the condenser transmitter and associated amplifiers. This curve shows merely the relative frequency sensitiveness of the system, the zero line having been chosen arbitrarily.

distortion in the record whose purpose is to compensate for errors in the reproducing equipment; the only intended distortion in the record being that required by the inherent limitations mentioned above. See Figs. 2, 14, and 20."

"General Basis of Design"

"An interesting feature of the development of the mechanical and electromagnetic portions of the recording and reproducing system is their quantitative design as mechanical analogs of electric circuits. Both the recording and reproducing systems are good examples of the use of this type of analogy.

"The economic need for the solution of many of the problems connected with electric wave transmission over long distances coupled with the consequent development of accurate electric measuring apparatus has led to a rather complete theoretical and practical knowledge of electrical wave transmission. The advance has been so great that the knowledge of electric systems has surpassed our previous engineering knowledge of mechanical wave transmission systems. The result is, therefore, that mechanical transmission systems can be designed more successfully if they are viewed as analogs of electric circuits.

"While there are mechanical analogs for nearly every form of electric circuit imaginable, there is one particular class of electrical circuits whose study has led to ideas of the utmost value in guiding the course of the present development. This class of circuits consists of infinitely repeated similar sections of one or more lumped capacity and inductance elements in series and shunt and are commonly known as filters. The study of filters began with Campbell. (Campbell, G. A., 'On Loaded Lines in Telephone Transmission'—Phil. Mag., March 1903—do. U. S. Pats. 1,227,113; 1,227,114;—'Physical Theory of the Electric Wave Filter'—Bell System Technical Journal, Nov. 1922;

—Zobel, O. J., 'Theory and Design of Uniform and Composite Electric Wave Filters'—Bell System Technical Journal, Jan. 1923;—Peters, L. J., 'Theory of Electric Wave Filters Built Up of Coupled Circuit Elements'—Trans. A.I.E.E., May 1923; Carson, J. R. and Zobel, O. J., 'Transient Oscillations in Electric Wave Filters,'—Bell System Technical Journal, July 1923; Zobel, O. J. 'Transmission Characteristic of Electric Wave Filters' — Bell System Technical Journal, Oct. 1921;—Johnson, K. S. and Shea, T. E., 'Mutual Inductance in Wave Filters with an Introduction to Filter Design'—Bell System Technical Journal, Jan. 1925; Johnson, K. S., 'Transmission Circuits for Telephonic Communication,'—Van Nostrand, D., 1925) and a recognition of their importance as frequency selection systems in telephone repeaters, carrier systems, radio, signalling systems, etc., led to their extensive study. In the available literature is to be found a fairly complete statement of their properties and details of their design.

"It will be recalled in the case of the telephone circuit that the introduction of inductance coils at regular intervals in the circuit produced a remarkable change in the transmission characteristics. Over a broad band of frequencies the attenuation was reduced and made fairly uniform over that range which beyond a critical frequency called the cut-off frequency, the attenuation becomes very high. In the ideal filters with zero dissipation the transmission characteristics are of the same nature but more clear cut. Structures of this type with infinitely repeated sections will have one or more transmission bands of zero attenuation and one or more bands having infinite attenuation. The impedance characteristics of such a structure measured from certain characteristic points will be pure resistance more or less uniform in the transmission bands, and pure reactance in the attenuation bands. These terminations are mid-series;

that is, the entering element being a series one of half the normal series element; or mid-shunt; that is, the entering element being twice the impedance of the normal, shunt element. The corresponding impedances are called the mid-series and mid-shunt characteristic or iterative impedances.

"If we retain the first few sections of such a structure and terminate them with a resistance which is equal to the resistance impedance of the infinite line from which they were taken, the characteristics are substantially unchanged. It is understood, of course, that this resistance equals approximately the resistance impedance of the remainder of the infinite line at most of the frequencies in the transmission band in which we are interested.

"The presence of small amounts of damping in the various elements also has but slight effect on the general characteristics. These results could in general be readily applied to the various telephone transmission problems because the source and load between which the filter system was inserted generally had, or could be made to have a resistance impedance nearly equalling the mid-series or mid-shunt impedance of the filter within the transmission band. The filter and terminating impedances may then be said to be matched. Where adjacent sections in the filter have impedances similar in character but different in absolute magnitude they may be joined by a suitable transformer.

"Many early attempts were made to design mechanical transmission systems having a wide frequency range in which highly damped single or multi-resonant systems were employed. In these attempts both of the obvious methods of increasing the damping were used, namely that of adding a resistance to the system and that of increasing the value of the compliance and decreasing mass in such proportion as to maintain the same natural frequency. The former of these methods reduces the sensi-

tivity of the system at the point where it is most efficient (See Fig. 9) while the second method increases the response at the points where the system is less sensitive, namely, away from its resonance point. Fig. 9 shows four curves—first, a simple resonant system, Curve A; second, the same system with friction added, Curve B; third, the same system without the added friction but with an increase in compliance and a decrease in mass such that the natural period remains the same, Curve C; and fourth, a band pass type of circuit whose resistance impedance is the same as that of the system in Curve A (See Curve D).

"The results of filter theory have shown how these resonances should be coordinated so that when a proper resistance termination is used, high efficiency and equal sensitivity are obtained over a definite band of frequencies by elimination of response to all frequencies outside the band. With the electrical case of a repeated filter, each section considered by itself resonates at the same frequency but when combined into a short-circuited filter of n sections, there will be n natural frequencies. However, when such a system is terminated with a resistance which equals the nominal characteristic impedance in the transmission band, uniform response in the termination resistance is obtained over the entire band."

"Detailed Analysis of Mechanical and Electrical Analogs"

"Before going on with a detailed treatment of the electrical analogues of the mechanical structures used in the problem of phonographic reproduction, a list of the corresponding quantities used in the two systems will be given, together with the symbols employed.

Mechanical

Force	F (dynes)
Velocity	v (cm./sec.)

Displacement   s (cm.)
Impedance (or
  mechanical ohms) z (dyne sec./cm.)
Resistance   r (dyne sec./cm.)
Reactance   x (dyne sec./cm.)
Mass   m (grams)
Compliance   c (cm. dyne)

Electrical

Voltage   E (volts)
Current   i (amperes)
Charge   q (coulombs)
Impedance   Z (ohms)
Resistance   R (ohms)
Reactance   X (ohms)
Inductance   L (henries)
*Capacity   C (farads)

* H. W. Nichols, 'Theory of Variable Dynamical Electrical Systems'—Phys. Review, Vol. 10, 1917.

(E. L. Norton worked out mathematics of mechanical and electrical analogs.)

"In addition to the above certain other quantities such as angular displacement, pressure and impedance per unit area, and a few others which have no direct electrical analog will be used. These quantities, however, are either standard in the literature or may always be reduced to those given above.

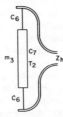

Fig. 3. *Schematic mechanical arrangement of diaphragm and air chamber.*

"As illustrations of the general methods employed certain important portions of the reproducer will be considered in detail. Considering first the electrical analog of the air chamber (1) between the diaphragm and horn, we make use of the following list of Symbols (See Figs. 3, 4, 15, and 16).

(The use of the air chamber to increase the loading effect of the horn on the diaphragm has been appreciated for a number of years. It has been used in telephone receivers, phonographs, and loud speaking receivers since their earliest developments. A treatment of the force equations of the air-chamber was given by Hanna and Slepian, 'The Function and Design of Horns for Loud Speakers'—Trans. A.I.E.E. 1924, p. 393. The equivalent structure, however, was analyzed as a compliance and resistance in series instead of in shunt.)

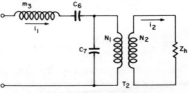

Fig. 4. *Electrical equivalent of mechanical system shown in Fig. 3.*

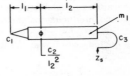

Fig. 5. *Schematic mechanical arrangement of needle arm transformer.*

"m_3 Effective mass of diaphragm in grams

A_1 Equivalent area of diaphragm in cms.

c_6 Compliance of edge of diaphragm

A_2 Area of throat of horn

z_h Impedance of horn—Vector ratio of applied force at the throat of horn to the resultant linear velocity of the air

s_1 Displacement of the diaphragm

v_1 Velocity of diaphragm

s_2 Displacement of air in throat of horn

v_2 Velocity of air in throat of horn

P_o & V_o Initial pressure and volume of air chamber

F   Force applied to the diaphragm

p   Small change of pressure in air-chamber

"For a small change p in the pressure within the air-chamber we have

$$p = \frac{n(A_1 s_1 - A_2 s_2 P_o)}{V_o} \quad (1)$$

where $n = 1$ for an isothermal change and 1.4 for an adiabatic change.

"For the case under consideration, $n = 1.4$ very nearly.

If the horn opening is closed, $S_2 = 0$, and we get for the compliance of the air-chamber as measured from the diaphragm

$$C_7 = \frac{S_1}{p A_1} = \frac{V_o}{n p_o A_1^2} \quad - - - \text{"}$$

(End of direct quotation. By setting up equations for both a schematic case of a mechanical arrangement of diaphragm and air-chamber (Fig. 3) and an equivalent electrical circuit (Fig. 4) the authors offer an elaborate series of computations producing balancing end equations. That for the mechanical series is quoted, as follows: WLW)

$$\text{"}z_m = -j \frac{(A_2)}{(A_1)} \frac{1}{\omega C_7} \text{"}$$

For the electrical analogy

$$\text{"}Z_m = -j \frac{(N_2)}{(N_1)} \frac{1}{\omega C_7} \text{"}$$

Similar analogical computations for the needle arm were made with the following symbols:

"l_1 Distance from pivot point to end of needle

l_2 Distance from pivot point to center of spider

I   Moment of inertia of needle arm

m_1 Apparent or equivalent mass of arm as measured from the center of spider $= \dfrac{I}{l_2^2}$

c_1 Compliance of needle point

c_2 Compliance of bearing to turning of needle arm as measured from end of arm at spider

c_3 Compliance of end of needle arm attached to spider

s_1 Displacement of tip of needle

s_2 Displacement of end of arm at spider

s_3 Displacement of spider

z_3 Mechanical impedance of spider and remainder of structure Vector ratio of applied force to resultant velocity

θ Angular displacement of needle arm

F   Applied force at needle point"

Similar, almost identical matching equations were developed for the mechanical and electrical circuit analogy. The authors then continued:

"The analogy between the two sets of equations is quite obvious. It will be noticed that the effect of the lever arm is to introduce an equivalent transformer of a turn ratio which is the reciprocal of the corresponding lengths of the arms.

"The general method of deducing the equivalent electric circuits should be clear from the above illustrations of the air-chamber and of the needle arm. For example, in the spider section, Fig. 15, the mass is driven directly by the force from the needle-

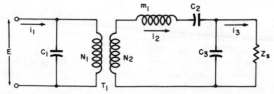

Fig. 6. Electrical equivalent of system shown in Fig. 5 with its termination.

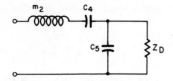

Fig. 7. Electrical equivalent of the spider section.

arm compliance, there being a small series compliance in the connection owing to bending of the connecting rod. The diaphragm is connected through the compliance of the prongs of the spider. The equivalent circuits are shown in Figs. 7 and 16.

"General Design of Mechanical Systems"

"In designing mechanical systems of the band pass type, the problem is three-fold; first, that of arranging the masses and compliances such that they form repeated filter sections; second, determining the magnitude of these quantities so that with or without transformers the separate sections all have the same cut-off frequencies[*] and characteristic impedances; third, to provide the proper resistance termination. Where the transmitted mechanical power has not been radiated as sound this third part has been one of the most difficult to fulfill.

[*] It is permissible to have a section having a higher cut-off than the others provided its characteristic impedance is the same as that of the others over the transmission band of those having the lower cut-off.

"In designing these systems, practical difficulties arose, — first, the difficulty of insuring that the parts vibrated in the desired degrees of freedom only, and second, the difficulty of determining the magnitude of the various effective masses, compliances and resistances. Before the work to be described could be carried out practically, it became necessary to develop a method of measuring mechanical impedances. (Kennelly, A. E., and Affel, H. A., 'The Mechanics of Telephone Receiver Diaphragms, as

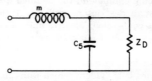

Fig. 8. Electrical equivalent of simple low-pass type of network which occurs frequently in this work.

Derived from Their Motional Impedance Circles.'—Proc. A.A.A.S., Vol. 51, No. 8, Nov. 1915. Kennelly, A. E., and Pierce, G. W., 'The Impedance of Telephone Receivers as Affected by the Motion of Their Diaphragms' — Proc. A.A.A.S., Vol. 48, No. 6, Sept. 1912)

"Such a method has been developed which covers a range of frequencies from somewhere below 50 to about 4,500 c.p.s. Work is still being continued to extend the method to higher

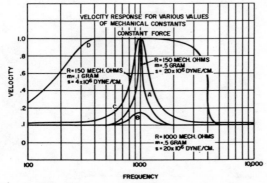

Fig. 9. Velocity response for various values of mechanical constants.

frequencies. This method of measurement has been very useful not only in determining the magnitudes of the impedances in the degree of freedom in which it is desired that they shall operate, but in designing the impedances to motion of the various parts in directions in which they should not be permitted to vibrate. - - - "

"Design of the Reproducing Apparatus"

"As the analogy between the mechanical and electrical filter is more perfectly shown in the case of the reproducing equipment, the detailed quantitative description will be given in this connection. Figs. 15 and 16 show respectively a diagram of the reproducing system and its equivalent electrical circuit. From these diagrams it is evident which units in the mechanical system correspond to the various electrical parts. As the series compliances c_2, c_4 and c_6 have been made so large that the low frequency cut-off caused by them lies well below the low frequency cut-off of the horn, an inappreciable error is introduced in using for design purposes formulas of low pass filters. (Campbell, G. A., 'On Loaded Lines in Telephonic Transmission'—Phil. Mag.,

March 1903.) The two formulas which will be used are as follows:

$$f_c = \frac{1}{\pi} \sqrt{\frac{1}{mc}} \qquad (12)$$

where

$f_c =$ cut-off frequency of a lumped transmission circuit in cycles per second

$c =$ shunt compliance per section in cm. per dyne

$m =$ series mass per section in grams

$$z_o = \sqrt{\frac{m}{c}} \qquad (13)$$

where

z_o is the value of characteristic impedance over the greater part of the band range.

"Equations 12 and 13, which form the basis of the design work contain four variables, f_c, c, m and z_o.

"It is, therefore, necessary to determine two of them by the physical requirements of the problem after which the other two are determined. The upper cut-off frequency f_c was arbitrarily chosen at 5,000 cps as a compromise between the highest frequency occurring on the record and the increase in surface noise as the cut-off is raised. The choice of the other arbitrarily set variable came after considerable preliminary ex-

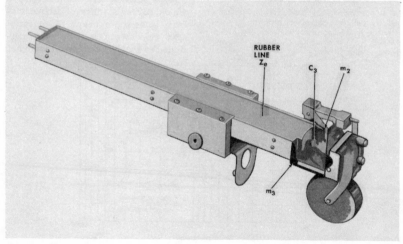

Fig. 10. This figure shows an electromagnetic recorder complete except for the bottom of the case.

perimenting and was fixed by the difficulty of obtaining a diaphragm which is light enough and has a large enough area. Hence the effective mass of the diaphragm m_3 (Figs. 15, 16) was fixed at 0.186 grams which value can be obtained by careful design. The effective area can be made as large as 13 sq. cms. For convenience let the arbitrary value for $f_c = \bar{f}_c$ and the value $m = \overline{m_3}$.

"Solving Equations (12) and (13) for c and z_o, we get

$$c = \frac{1}{\pi^2 \bar{f}_c \overline{m_3}} \qquad (14)$$

$$z_o = \pi \bar{f}_c \overline{m_3} \qquad (15)$$

$$z_o = \frac{1}{\pi^2 c \bar{f}_c} \qquad (16)$$

"In order to obtain the low value of mass mentioned, with a large enough area, it was necessary to make the diaphragm of a very stiff light material. An aluminum alloy sheet 0.0017 in. thick was chosen and concentrically corrugated as shown in Figs. 17 and 18. These corrugations are spaced sufficiently close so that the natural periods of the flat surfaces are all above $\bar{f}_c$. To insure that this central stiffened portion should vibrate with appropriate plunger action, which is more efficient than diaphragm action, it is driven at 6 points near its periphery. Reference to Figs. 15 and 16 and Equation (14) shows that the compliance of the air chamber c_7, of the spider legs c_5 and shunt tip of

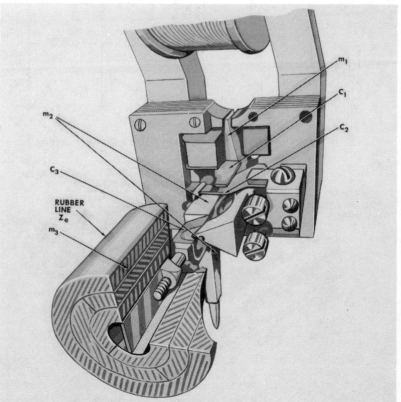

Fig. 11. Detailed drawing of the mechanical filter of an electromagnetic recorder.

the needle arm c_3 are determined. Also the mass of the spider m_2 and the effective mass of the needle arm m_1, as viewed at the point where it is attached to the spider are determined.

"The impedance looking into the system from the record is determined by the rate at which it is necessary to radiate energy in order that the reproduction may be loud enough. The power taken from the record is approximately $V^2 z_0$ since z_0 is the resistance over most of the band. Experiment has shown this value to be approximately 4,500 mechanical ohms. "But substituting in Equation (13) the value of m_3 and from Equation (14) the value of c_5, we find that the impedance is only 2,920 mechanical ohms. It is, therefore, necessary to use a transformer whose impedance

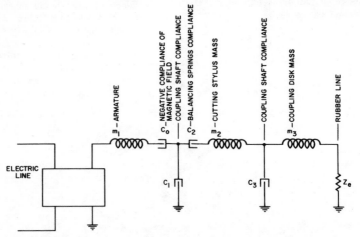

Fig. 12. *Equivalent electric circuit of the electromagnetic recorder.*

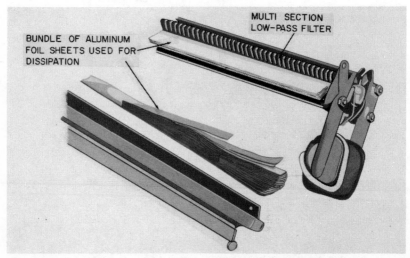

Fig. 13. *Electromagnetic recorder using lumped loaded termination. The method of furnishing dissipation to the lumped loaded line is shown.*

ratio is $\frac{4,500}{2,920}$. From this and a knowledge of filter structures the needle-point compliance can be determined. The value obtained is easily realized with commercial types of needles.

"It will be noted that the record is shown in Fig. 16 as a constant current generator, i.e., a generator whose impedance appears high as viewed from the needle point. That this is necessary is obvious when it is remembered that, if the impedance looking back into the record were to equal the impedance of the filter system, the walls of the record would have to yield an amount comparable with one-half the amplitude of the lateral cut. This would cause a breakdown of the record material with consequent damage.

"The design of the system is complete, therefore, except for the resistance termination which is supplied by the horn for all frequencies above its low frequency cut-off. The characteristics of the horn will be dealt with later. The resistance within the band looking in at the small end of the horn is GA_2 where G = mechanical ohms per sq. cm. of an infinite cylindrical tube of the same area, and A_2 = area in sq. cms. of the small end of the horn.

"Let A_1 = the effective plunger area of the diaphragm (as previously mentioned this is 13 sq. cm.). The impedance looking back at the diaphragm is

$$z_0 = \pi \overline{f_c} \overline{m_3} = 2,920 \text{ mechanical ohms.}$$

from Equation (15), and the impedance looking at a horn whose small end area equals A_2 is

$$z_h = r_0 = A_2G \qquad (17)$$

Substituting
$A_2 = 13$ sq. cm.
$G = 41$ ohms per cm.^{2} we get
$z_h = r_0 = 533$ mechanical ohms.

"This is entirely insufficient so that the air-chamber transformer becomes necessary.

"To calculate the necessary ratio of areas on the two sides of the air-chamber transformer, the following formula is needed. The formula assumes the chamber to be relatively small compared with all wave lengths of the sound to be transmitted, that is, the pressure changes throughout the chamber area substantially in phase.

$$\frac{z_0}{z_h} = \frac{A_1{}^2}{A_2{}^2} \qquad (18)$$

where
z_0 = the impedance of the primary side of the transformer in mechanical ohms
z_h = the impedance on the secondary side of the transformer in mechanical ohms, i.e., the horn impedance

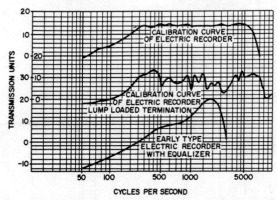

Fig. 14. Calibration curve of three types of electromagnetic recorders.

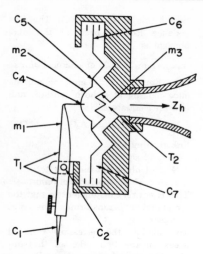

Fig. 15. Diagrammatic sketch of the mechanical system of the phonograph.

v_1 = mechanical current, i.e., velocity on the primary side of the transformer in cms./sec.

v_2 = mechanical current on the secondary side of the transformer in cms./sec.

F_1 = alternating force on primary side of air-chamber transformer in dynes

F_2 = alternating force on secondary side of air-chamber transformer in dynes

A_1 = effective area working into the primary side of the air-chamber in cms.[2]

A_2 = effective area working into the secondary side of the air-chamber in cms.[2]

"The characteristic impedance of the line on the diaphragm or primary side of the air-chamber as shown by Equation (15) is

$$z_o = \pi \overline{f_c} \overline{m_3} \qquad (19)$$

"From Equation (17) the characteristic impedance in the horn or secondary side is

$$z_h = GA_2 \qquad (20)$$

Therefore,

$$\frac{A_2^2}{A_1} = \frac{z_h}{z_o} = \frac{GA_2}{\pi \overline{f_c} \overline{m_3}} \qquad (21)$$

Solving this for A_2, we get

$$A_2 = \frac{GA_1^2}{\pi \overline{f_c} \overline{m_3}} \qquad (22)$$

"The equivalent of the air-chamber to a transformer shunted by a compliance is shown earlier in the paper. "In applying the foregoing method of design to a practical structure, a number of design problems had to be solved. The construction of the diaphragm and the method by which it is actuated have already been described, except for the tangential corrugations constituting the series compliance. The use of these corrugations results in the value of the series compliance being practically independent of the nature of the clamping and has

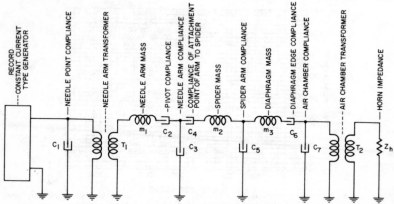

Fig. 16. Electric equivalent of the system shown in Fig. 15.

eliminated a tendency to 'rattle' introduced by unevenness in the clamping surfaces.

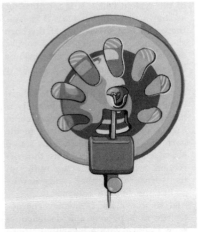

Fig. 17. Mechanical reproducing system without the horn.

"Another feature in connection with the sound box is the needle-arm bearing shown in Figs. 17 and 18. Ordinary knife edge bearings are not sufficiently rigid as fulcrums and the rotational reactance as well as the rotational resistance is undesirably large. A construction which has been found to meet the necessary requirements is the ball bearing type with the steel balls held in position by magnetic pull. By making the ball-containing case of soft steel and magnetizing the shaft, it has been possible to manufacture this bearing reliably and cheaply.

"The horn which has been used as a termination resistance to the mechanical filter structure is a logarithmic one. The general properties of logarithmic horns have been understood for some time. (Webster, A. G., 'Acoustical Impedance and Theory of Horns and Phonograph'—Proc. Nat. Academy of Science, 1919)

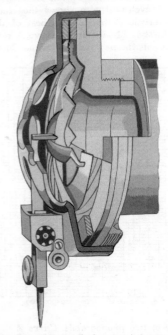

Fig. 18. Sectional drawing showing construction of the system shown in Fig. 17.

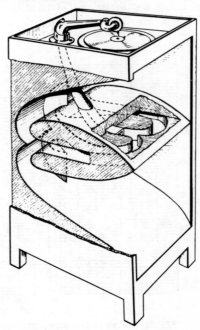

Fig. 19. Sectional view of the folded horn showing the air passage.

"There are two fundamental constants of such a horn—the first is the area of the large end and second, the rate of taper. The area of the mouth determines the lowest frequency which is radiated satisfactorily. The energy of the frequencies below this is largely reflected if it is permitted to reach the mouth.

"From the equations given by Webster, it can be shown that all logarithmic horns have a low frequency cut-off which is determined by the rate of taper, and if the rate of taper is so proportional that its resulting cut-off prevents the lower frequencies from reaching the horn mouth, the horn will then radiate all frequencies reaching its mouth and very little reflection will result.*

"It is possible, therefore, to build a horn having no marked fundamental resonance.

"Since the characteristics of the horn are determined by the area of its mouth and by its rate of taper the

* P. B. Flanders conducted mathematical investigations, checked experimentally by A. L. Thomas.

length of the horn is determined by the area of the small end. This area is determined in turn by the mechanical impedance and effective area of the system which it is terminating, as shown in Equation (22). It is seen, therefore, that the length of the horn should not be considered as a fundamental constant. A paper describing the design of horns based on these principles is being prepared.

"An interesting feature of the horn which has been built commercially is its method of folding. The sketch in Fig. 19 shows a shadow picture of the horn. It will be noticed that the sound passage is folded only in its thin direction, which permits the radius of the turns to be small and thereby makes the folding compact.

"Fig. 20 shows the frequency characteristic of a phonograph designed as shown above with a logarithmic horn whose rate of taper and area of mouth opening place the low cut-off at about 115 cycles. It also shows the characteristic of one of the best of the old style phonographs. Curve A represents the new machine while Curve

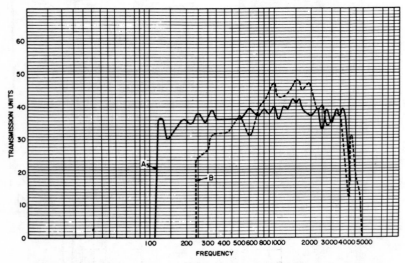

Fig. 20. *Response frequency characteristic of two phonographs. Curve A shows the characteristic of the band pass filter type described. Curve B shows the characteristic of one of the best commercial machines previously on the market.*

B represents the old style standard machine."

Discussion of Maxfield-Harrison paper by C. R. Hanna

"The following discussion applies particularly to that part of the paper dealing with the reproducing mechanism. The relative merits of the several improvements that were made are not clearly brought out in the paper and it is the purpose of the writer to compare the importance of the various developments.

"In listening to reproduction from one of the new-type phonographs, the average person is impressed with just two things; first, the apparent greater volume of sound; and second, the great improvement in the response at low frequencies. The greater volume of sound is due partly to the fact that there are more low frequencies present, and perhaps, in a measure, to the fact that the diaphragm is one which acts like a piston, causing a greater volumetric rate of displacement of air into the horn for a given needle velocity than with the old type of flat diaphragm.

"The improvement in the low-frequency characteristic of the reproducer, as described, could not have been obtained without the use of the slowly expanding logarithmic or exponential horn.

"The authors refer to the work of Arthur Gordon Webster in this connection: the general properties of the exponential horn were given in his National Academy of Science paper of 1919. Webster did not, however, carry his work sufficiently far to show the properties which the authors have stated in their paper; namely that the exponential horn is a uniform radiator of sound down to a certain frequency, known as the cut-off frequency, which is determined by the rate of increase of section and the area of the larger end of the horn.

"The authors cite some work (as yet unpublished), by Messrs. Flanders and Thuras, in which these properties are shown both theoretically and experimentally. I desire to call attention to the fact that the paper by Hanna and Slepian on 'The Function and Design of Horns for Loud Speakers'— (A.I.E.E. Trans. 1924, p. 393) showed these same properties for the exponential horn. The equation for such a horn is

$$A = A_o \epsilon^{Bx}$$

where

A = Area at any point
A_o = Initial area
x = Distance from initial area, cm.
B = Constant which determines the rate of increase.

It was demonstrated that the cut-off frequency is determined by the relation

$$\frac{2\pi f}{B} = \frac{a}{2}$$

where a = velocity of sound. From this it is seen that the smaller B is, the lower will be the cut-off.

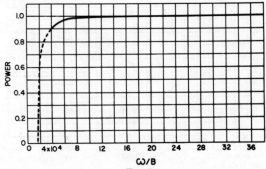

Fig. 1.

"The radiation characteristic of the infinite exponential horn for a fixed velocity of air in its throat was also shown in the paper by Hanna and Slepian. Fig. 1, herewith, shows this curve. The abscissas are $\frac{\omega}{B}$ and the ordinates give the comparison between the exponential horn and the infinite straight pipe which is a uniform radiator down to zero frequency. The cut-off point is seen to be as stated above.

"It was clearly brought out in this paper that an exponential horn could be made with much smaller dimensions than any other shape of horn giving equal performance. A comparison was also shown between a particular exponential horn and a conical horn of equal length and terminal dimensions. This is given in Fig. 2, the superiority of the exponential horn being quite pronounced. Up to this time many persons had advocated the conical horn. It is believed that this paper was the first to show the superiority of the exponential horn.

"Now, taking up the matter of the final or large area of the horn, as is pointed out by Maxfield and Harrison, if this area is large enough to prevent end reflections in the range of frequencies where the horn is a good radiator along its length, a horn will be secured which has very little resonance. The curves of Fig. 3 were presented by Hanna and Slepian to show the variation of reflection with frequency and area. The curves indicate that the smaller the area and the lower the frequency, the greater will be the reflection. It is seen, however, from the curve for the largest area, that the reflection becomes appreciable only in the range of frequencies where the horn ceases to be a good radiator along its length. Hence it follows that a horn of this shape can be designed with no marked fundamental resonance.

"The degree of horn resonance and the position of the cut-off frequency as indicated by Fig. 20 of the Maxfield and Harrison paper agrees very closely with values that can be predicted from the curves of Figs. 1 and 3 in this discussion.

"The very careful proportioning of masses and compliances in the mechanical system of the reproducer has played only a minor part in the securing of a more uniform frequency-response characteristic than in the older types of phonograph. The slight extension of the upper frequency range may be attributed to the accurate design of mechanical parts. It should be pointed out, however, that since the phonograph record is a constant-current (or velocity) generator, the impedance of the mechanical system does not have to be uniform over a wide band of frequencies for it to be forced to vibrate in accordance with the vibrational

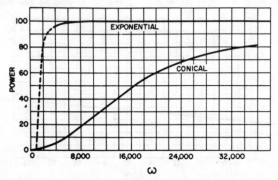

Fig. 2.

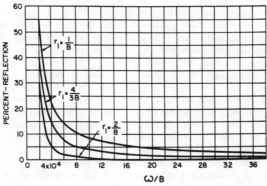

Fig. 3.

velocity of the record. A departure from this fact, not apparent from the electrical analogy given by the authors in their paper, is the ability of the whole arm of the reproducer to vibrate in the low frequency ranges instead of just the diaphragm mechanism. This may be overcome either by increasing the mass of the arm, or as the authors have done, by reducing the stiffness of the diaphragm. "Great credit is due the authors for the design of a mechanical system which is light and resilient, enabling the needle to track the record with small reactive force (and consequent decrease in wear) at the high frequencies where the accelerations are great, and at low frequencies where the deflections are great. The big improvement in the quality of reproduction, however, is due to the use of an exponential horn whose rate of increase of section is small and whose final section is quite large."

Discussion of Maxfield-Harrison Paper by E. W. Kellogg

"I think most of us have thought of the rocking arm, which connects the needle with the diaphragm in a phonograph, as a simple lever, rigid enough so that when the needle moves one way, the diaphragm moves the opposite direction by a corresponding amount. If we could see what is really going on during a high-frequency vibration, we should prob-

ably find that the motion was more nearly like that of a snake. Messrs. Maxfield and Harrison and their associates have accepted the wave-motion picture and based their design upon it. The most striking resultant change in design is the interposition of a flexible link or spring, between the end of the lever and the diaphragm. On first thought, it seems like deliberately throwing away some of the available motion, but the result is quite the opposite. I refer to the spider through which the diaphragm is driven.

"If telephone currents are to be transmitted without distortion over a high-efficiency line of length exceeding a sixth of a wavelength for the highest frequencies, the line must end in a nonconductive resistance of a definite value. A corresponding resistance is required in a mechanical system. In the case of the reproducing system the required resistance is obtained from the sound radiation of the diaphragm. But for the cutting tool, some other resistance must be found. In an electrical system nothing is easier to get than resistance, yet its mechanical counterpart is by no means easy to obtain. Sliding friction is not at all suitable. Motion in viscous fluids and electro-magnetic drag, such as used in wattmeters, are true analogs. I wish to draw an illustration from the case of electromagnetic drag. An aluminum ring, weighing about 4 grams, surrounds a magnet pole, so it is in a radial field of about 10,000 gausses. If one pushes it up and down, it feels as if it were in thick molasses. Yet if this ring is vibrated in an axial direction at 4,000 cycles, its mass so predominates over the resistance that the power factor is only about 40%. Mechanical hysteresis is another means for absorbing energy from vibrations. Rubber has long been used for such purposes. But rubber, so far from being pure in mechanical resistance, is a spring with a power factor of only about 10%. I think the authors of the paper are to be complimented upon the ingenious device by which they obtain with the use of rubber a practically pure resistance with which to load the cutting tool. It should be borne in mind that the damping for the cutting tool is of an altogether different order of magnitude from that which many of us have employed to take out the resonance peaks from loudspeaker diaphragms and similar applications.

"The paper mentions methods of measuring mechanical impedances. I should be much interested to hear something further of the means used, for the problem presents many difficulties, and the results of such measurements would find many applications.

"One statement in the paper causes considerable surprise. The knife edge was discarded because it has too great an elastic yield, and because it brings in too much rotational friction. The knife edge, of course, must work with an initial force exceeding the maximum force on the bearing, due to the vibrations, and is not well adapted to stand forces in more than one direction, but, in the case of the pivot for the reproducing lever, one would expect a well designed knife edge to work satisfactorily."

Discussion of the Maxfield-Harrison Paper by L. T. Robinson

"I am in agreement with the statement of the authors that 'There is therefore no distortion in the record whose

purpose is to compensate for errors in the reproducing equipment.' In employing so many elements, some of which can be so readily modified in performance the temptation is very strong to look only at the final result and not be too critical as to where and why any corrective treatment is to be administered. I hope the stand taken by the authors will be firmly adhered to by them and others who are working along similar lines. In this way, any progress that has been made, or will be made, becomes permanent.

"Speaking of the electrically-cut record in general, we need not, for the moment be concerned with minor details of the process. The results already obtained are so good that we may feel sure that the electrically-cut record has come to stay and will place the phonographic art on an entirely new plane of excellence.

"The mechanical reproducing system described by the authors is a distinct advance over former phonographs. However, I feel that the full realization of the advantage of the electrically-cut record will come through electrical reproduction.

"One great advantage of the electrical method of reproducing is that the control of the sound volume is obtainable quite independently of the cut on the record and the cut on the record is controllable with consideration for the best conditions for the record alone. The advantages of such separation can be learned from the paper if it is read with this point in mind.

"Volume of the sound reproduced is quite important and reproduction to be quite satisfactory must be about equal to the original sounds. A loud tone produced on a given musical instrument is quite different from a soft sound produced on the same instrument and reproduced with great volume."

Comments on the discussion of the Maxfield-Harrison Paper by J. P. Maxfield

"There are one or two technical questions brought out in Mr. Hanna's discussion which are of interest. The first deals with the statement that the new reproducing mechanism has a greater apparent volume of sound. In this connection, it is interesting to note that the response curves of the new and the old machines shown in Fig. 20 indicate that in the frequency region from around 800 to 2,000 c.p./sec. the old machine produced a louder sound from a given needle velocity. It will be seen, therefore, that this apparent increase in volume has been obtained by the widening of the band reproduced rather than by increasing the amount of energy radiated in that frequency band in which the old machine was more efficient.

"The other point of interest refers to his statement that 'The very careful proportioning of the masses and compliances in the mechanical system of the reproducer has played only a minor part in the securing of the more uniform frequency response characteristic than in the older type of phonograph.' In view of the high quality which is obtained and of the commercial requirement that the wear on the record shall not be excessive, the authors do not agree with this statement. It is not necessarily true that because the record is a constant-current generator and, therefore, delivers constant current to the sound-box mechanism, that the diaphragm necessarily delivers constant current to the air. If a relatively stiff, heavy, vibrating system is used, it becomes exceedingly difficult with the con-

stant-current type of generator to obtain good quality and if it is possible to obtain it, the wear on the record becomes excessive. A reference to Fig. 16 indicates that the first part of the system reached is the needle point which has a definite compliance. At the higher frequencies, if the impedance of the reproducing system is too high, the needle will bend instead of moving the rest of the system and the response will be reduced thereby. Similarly, at the low frequency end, if the diaphragm-edge compliance is too small, that is, if the diaphragm is too stiff, the whole tone arm will vibrate and thereby reduce the motion of the diaphragm relative to its case. It is true that, so far as response is concerned, this effect can be corrected by increasing the moment of inertia of the tone arm — a measure which is equivalent to increasing the mutual inductance of the transformer, T_1, (Fig. 16); but if the solution is thus obtained, the wear on the record becomes excessive and in some cases the force becomes so great that the needle will not track in the groove.

"The solution presented in the paper is one in which the mechanical impedance has been made as nearly as possible independent of frequency and is of the nature of a pure mechanical resistance. The result of this type of solution is that a maximum of sound energy at all frequencies within the band is radiated with a minimum of wear on the record."

Edison's Embossing Translator Notes of July 5, 1877, and Translating Embosser Dated June 27, 1877

(Courtesy of Edison National Historic Site,
West Orange, New Jersey)

Edison's Embossing Translator Notes (Cont'd.)

Translating Embosser

June 27 1877

T A Edison

James Adams

I propose in most translate to have the repeating points one line inside the embossing points although it comes to one line outside

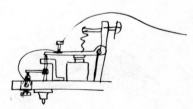

Edison's Embossing Translator Notes (Cont'd.)

Translating Embosser

June 27. 1877

T A Edison

Chas Batchelor

James Adams

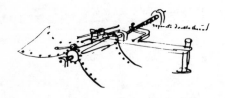

on the Continuous roll embosser I propose for obtaining accurate registration to previously perforate holes either on both edges or on both ⌐ edges also centre or on the centre only and provide the rotating cylinder with pin to pass through the perforations to ensure the feed & registration

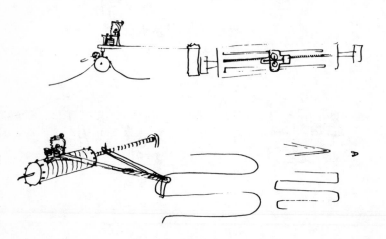

Edison's Embossing Translator Notes (Cont'd.)

Translating Embosser

June 27 1877
Ja Edison

James Adams

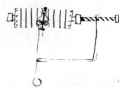

It may be possible that oiled
indenting paper is preferable,
or that the paper should
be paraffined - shellacked or
dipped in plaster paris water =

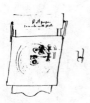

Sketches at Thomas Alva Edison's Laboratory at Menlo Park, New Jersey

(Reprinted from the article "The Papa of the Phonograph,"
The Daily Graphic, April 2, 1878)

Sketches at Thomas Alva Edison's Laboratory (Cont'd.)

The first phonograph

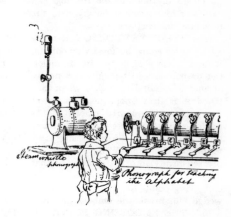

Steam whistle phonograph

Phonograph for teaching the alphabet

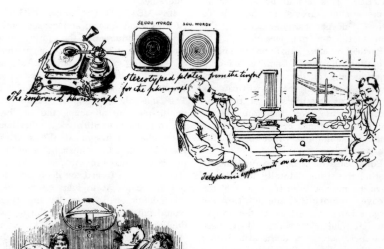

The improved phonograph

50,000 WORDS   500 WORDS

Stereotyped plates from the tinfoil for the phonograph

Telephonic apparatus on a wire 800 miles long

The phonograph at home reading out a novel

RAHWAY! NEXT STATION ELIZABETH CLEAR THE TRACK

The phonograph on the rail, calling out the stations

Edison's Speaking Phonograph

Instructions for Operating

To effectively operate the Phonograph, careful attention must be given to the following instructions: —

1st—TO PUT THE FOIL ON. Remove all wrinkles from the foil by smoothing it upon a piece of glass with a woolen rag or pad—draw it firmly and neatly around the cylinder so that when fastened it is firm upon the cylinder at every part. Improperly placed foil is liable to cause it to be torn, the record to be imperfect, or the embossing point to break. The Foil Wedge should be pressed firmly into the groove, so that no part of it could be touched by the embossing point. An improperly placed wedge will break the embossing point.

2nd—THE EMBOSSING POINT, OR STYLUS. This should be adjusted to make a slight groove in the foil. To adjust it deeper, turn the screw in the arm, to the left, and vice versa.

Particular care must be taken, in operating the Lock Cam, to effect a rigid locking of the arm in position. An arm not firmly locked will cause a variation of the pressure of the embossing point upon the foil, resulting in a skipping, or erasure of the smaller indentations when reproducing the sounds.

Equal care must be observed in adjusting the stylus laterally in order to have it run exactly in the centre of the groove. To move it to the left, turn the large screws at the base of the arm to the left, and vice versa. Always see that these screws hold the arm firmly; if a trifle loose, the stylus will be thrown out of centre.

Be careful not to turn the cylinder backward, or move it laterally while the stylus rests upon the foil. Neglect to remove the stylus, before effecting the reversal or movement of the cylinder, will cause it to be broken.

Always stop the cylinder before the edge of the foil has been reached by the stylus. Failure to do so, may result in a broken stylus, or in straining the carrying nut by jamming the cylinder against the uprights.

3rd—THE DIAPHRAGM DAMPENERS. To dampen the diaphragm, or vibrating plate, no rigid rule can be given, as there are seldom two instruments that require precisely the same degree of dampening. The object of dampening is to prevent the squeaky, metallic sound, caused by a too free vibration of the diaphragm. The usual method of dampening, is to insert small pieces of rubber tubing between the mouthpiece and the diaphragm. The degree of pressure necessary for them to exert upon the diaphragm may be readily determined by a little experimenting—it is, however, never very considerable.

4th—METHOD OF SPEAKING. To effect a good record, and consequently a good reproduction of the sounds, some attention must be given to the method of speaking into the mouth-piece, as well as to the manner of speaking. Chest tones produce the best result. The lips should slightly touch the mouth-piece at all times, the aim being to focus the entire vocal vibrations upon the diaphragm at the shortest possible range. Care must be taken not to press upon the mouth-piece, else the stylus may be forced too deep into the foil and cause it to tear, or to make the indentations so deep that the stylus would fail to reach them in the reproduction. There is considerable knack in the effective use of the voice, and in properly directing it into the mouth-piece, so much, indeed, that a good voice is sometimes rendered ineffective by the lack of it. It is however, readily acquired by a little practice.

5th—REPRODUCTION OF SOUNDS. In reproducing, place the funnel exactly over the small orifice in the mouth-piece, but do not exert any pressure with the hand.

6th—RATE OF CYLINDER ROTATION. The speed at which the cylin-

EDISON'S
PARLOR SPEAKING
PHONOGRAPH.

THE MIRACLE OF THE 19th CENTURY.

It Talks. It Whispers. It Sings. It Laughs. It Cries.
It Coughs. It Whistles. It Records and
Reproduces at Pleasure all
Musical Sounds.

The first recorded attempt to make a Talking Machine was 2600 years ago though diligent efforts have been making ever since. It remained for Prof THOMAS ALVA EDISON, of Menlo Park, New Jersey, to finally solve the problem, and place within the reach of every one a machine that not only talks, but will record sounds of all kinds, and REPRODUCE THEM INSTANTLY, with FIDELITY and DISTINCTNESS.

The adaptation of this wonderful invention to the practical uses of commerce not having, as yet, been completed, in all its mechanical details, this company is now prepared to offer to the public only that design or form of apparatus which has been found best adapted to its exhibition as a novelty.

THE "PARLOR SPEAKING PHONOGRAPH" is intended for use in the parlor or drawing room, and will hold 150 to 200 words. The cylinder is so arranged that the foil can be taken off and replaced at any future time, thereby reproducing the same sounds that have been imprinted upon it. It speaks loud enough to be heard in any ordinary room. We have a limited number now ready which we will sell for $10 cash, packed for shipment, with all needed appliances ready for use.

E. H. JOHNSON, Sec'y,
Edison Speaking Phonograph Co.
P. O. Box 2702, NEW YORK CITY.

Advertisement of Edison's Parlor Speaking Phonograph.

der is rotated is not important. From 60 to 80 per minute is about right. It is highly important, however, that the same speed shall be maintained when reproducing, as was had in making the record; the fidelity with which the tone of voice is reproduced, depends almost wholly upon this. In preserving the key it is essential that the rotation of the cylinder shall be as steady and uniform as clock-work. The hand soon acquires a nice skill in this respect if ordinary effort is made to attain it.

7th — THE SCREW THREADS OR GROOVES. Keep the screw thread on the cylinder and on the shaft free from dirt. A clogging of the thread on the cylinder will catch the Stylus and break it. A clogging of the thread on the shaft will cause the cylinder to turn hard, or make a gritty grinding noise. The carrying nut should be adjusted so as to permit the thread to enter the shaft threads to a point of depth just sufficient to take up all lost motion,—but not to cause a binding of the shaft.

8th—THE STYLUS OR EMBOSSING POINT. The shape of the Stylus is exceedingly important. An improperly shaped point will result in tearing the foil, or in failure to indent the foil, or cause a loud scratching noise, fatal to distinct articulation. The proper shape is as near as possible, that of a chisel with a long bevel. The narrower this chisel can be made on the point of the needle, the clearer and sharper will be the articulation. The chisel should also be very sharp, and the "Wire" or "Feather" edge carefully removed: such edges cause the scratching. The chisel must travel on its bevel—that is to say, with the bevel facing the foil, but not lying flat upon it.

If the Stylus is fixed to the small rubber cushion, so as to stand exactly in the centre of the Diaphragm, and exactly perpendicular to the Diaphragm, the chisel point will then be in proper position on the foil.

No elaborateness of instruction, will be sufficient to enable an operator to become an expert immediately in handling the simplest mechanism. The Phonograph though marvelously simple, considering the work it performs, is no exception to this rule. The general and particular ideas herein set forth will, however, if carefully noted, enable the operator to speedily attain proficiency.

Destructible Parts, and Method of Replacing

1st — THE DIAPHRAGM. This can hardly be classed as destructible, as, with ordinary care, it is practically as durable as any other portion. It may happen, however, by accident or by carelessness in adjustment of the Dampeners or Stylus, that it be given a kink or buckle, in which case a new one must be substituted. To do so, the Stylus must first be removed, then the mouth-piece which is screwed into the frame. The Diaphragm will be found fitted in its place between the paper washers, and fitting the frame neatly, but not so tight as to exert any pressure whatever upon it. The Paper Washers must not be left out; they are important in singing and in other musical reproductions.

2d — THE DAMPENER. These are about one-quarter of an inch long, and soon become "set;" they should therefore be frequently changed. Rubber loses its elasticity so soon, that it is only effective as a spring for a very brief time, where the pressure or strain is a constant one.

3d—THE STYLUS CUSHION. This is also a quarter of an inch bit of rubber tubing, but, by reason of the fact that its elasticity is only brought into play at the moment the instrument is being operated, it is practically indestructible. In placing this Cushion in position, care must be had to prevent the wax from coating any portion of its surface, beyond that essential to holding it in position.

Wherever the wax covers the surface of the rubber, elasticity is lost; and although the Diaphragm is the main "Spring," the rubber cushion is an im-

portant adjunct, causing the Stylus to more "faithfully" follow the record in reproduction.

The neatest method of putting the wax on, is to lay a small piece on the diaphragm resting against the rubber, heat a small wire or screw driver, and hold on the wax until it melts and runs under the rubber, which it will neatly and quickly do if the mouth-piece is held in an upright position.

In fastening the stylus to the rubber, the best method is to place a piece of wax about the size of a mustard seed underneath the spring, hold a heated wire on the tip edge of the spring—not touching the needle—until it melts; continue to hold the spring firmly with the finger or some cool substance until the cooling of the wax has caused it to firmly set. It is important that the stylus should be firmly fixed to the cushion, else the reproduction will not be loud.

4th—THE STYLUS. The importance of this part has led to its very full exposition elsewhere, hence it is only necessary here to call attention to the spring upon which it is fastened, and the clamp in which it is held. The spring should have all its elasticity at the base—that is, close to the clamp. To effect this a moderately stiff watch spring is used, and by filling it nearly through at a point near the clamp, the desired result is obtained.

Care should be had in setting this spring in the clamp, to see that the stylus itself is exactly in the centre of the diaphragm.

For explanation of any practical difficulty, or for a fuller exposition of any of these instructions, address,

E. H. JOHNSON,
General Agent and Expert,

THE EDISON SPEAKING
PHONOGRAPH CO.,
NEW YORK CITY.

The Lioret Phonograph

(Reprinted from *Scientific American,*
Supplement No. 1142, November 20, 1897)

Fig. 1. Exhibition of the Lioret Phonograph in the large hall of The Trocadero.

Fig. 2. General view of the Lioret Phonograph.

Fig. 3. Details of the point and registering cylinder.

Poll of Graphophones and Phonographs under Rental by Local Companies as Reported at 2nd Annual Convention of National Phonograph Association Held in New York City, June 16, 17 and 18, 1891.

Local Companies	Graphophones (business machines)	Phonographs (business machines)	Phonographs (coin-operated)	Total No. of machines
Chicago Central Co.	—	—	—	200
Columbia Phonograph Co.	12 to 15	360 to 363	25	400
Eastern Pennsylvania Phonograph Co.	7	68	25	100 (approx.)
Georgia Phonograph Co.	8	42	—	50 (approx.)
Iowa Phonograph Co.	—	—	—	200 (approx.)
Kansas Phonograph Co.	2	13	41	56
Kentucky Phonograph Co.	0	37	41	78
Louisiana Phonograph Co.	0	10	35	45
Michigan Phonograph Co.	—	—	—	—(no report)
Missouri Phonograph Co.	1	37	96	134
Montana Phonograph Co.	0	5	40	45 (approx.)
Nebraska Phonograph Co.	0	32	48	80
New England Phonograph Co.	17	238	45	300
New Jersey Phonograph Co.	2	13	65 (approx.)	80 (approx.)
New York Phonograph Co.	0	575	175	750
Ohio Phonograph Co.	7	93	61	161
Old Dominion Phonograph Co.	4 or 5	65	155	225
State Phonograph Co. of Illinois	1	59	65	125 (approx.)
Texas Phonograph Co.	0	30	80	110

(Note: Coin-operated phonographs were usually converted Edison Phonographs)

The Multiplex Graphophone Grand

THE LATEST DEVELOPMENT

OF THE

GRAPHOPHONE.

--->+<--

This new instrument was built for exhibition

AT THE

PARIS EXPOSITION.

A Talking Machine having the

Volume of Several Grand Instruments

Reproducing in unison.

--->+<--

The most wonderful sound-reproducing mechanism ever constructed. In volume, the voice of the Multiplex overwhelms the tones of the earlier talking machines as the roar of Niagara's cataract drowns the brook's gurgle.

--->+<--

IT CONTAINS NEW FEATURES IN ADDITION TO THOSE THAT CREATED SUCH A PROFOUND SENSATION WHEN EMBODIED IN THE GRAPHOPHONE GRAND.

IT USES

Three Separate Reproducers

ACTING IN ABSOLUTE UNISON WITH THREE SEPARATE AND DISTINCT RECORDS,

Each one of which gives the same loud, pure tone as that of the Graphophone Grand. The combination of all three in unison gives

AN INTENSITY OF VOLUME

---- AND A ----

SWEETNESS AND RICHNESS OF TONE

Which seem almost beyond belief.

THE tones of the MULTIPLEX are far more faithful to the original rendition of voice or instrument than those of any other talking machine. This fact is due to greater discrimination in the process of recording, rendered possible only by the use of separate recording horns and styluses.

The three reproducers are entirely independent one from another, yet so arranged as to reproduce in unison. Results are obtained that it is difficult to realize are within the possibilities of sound reproducing mechanism.

The Multiplex can be converted in an instant into

A GRAPHOPHONE GRAND OF TRIPLE SIZE

by using only one reproducer to cover the entire length of the cylinder. Special records may be had which will thus give a reproduction ten minutes long.

Designed especially for exhibition purposes at the Paris Exposition, the Multiplex Graphophone Grand is not listed in our catalogue nor carried in our regular stock of machines. But the results obtained from it are so superb, and its reproductions so marvelously faithful, both in volume and tone, to the real voice or instrument, that we have decided to make machines and records of the Multiplex type to order, confidently assuring those who purchase them that they represent the very highest development in the art of sound reproduction.

MULTIPLEX GRAPHOPHONE GRAND

INCLUDING

3 Recorders,	3 56-Inch Brass Horns,	**$1,000**
3 Reproducers,	12 Multiplex Grand Records,	
1 Special Triple Horn Stand,	6 Multiplex Grand Blanks.	

---->+<----

COLUMBIA PHONOGRAPH COMPANY,

NEW YORK, 143, 145 Broadway.
RETAIL BRANCH, 1155, 1157, 1159 Broadway.
CHICAGO, 88 Wabash Ave.

ST. LOUIS, 720-722 Olive St.
PHILADELPHIA, 1032 Chestnut St.
BALTIMORE, 110 E. Baltimore St.
CINCINNATI, 19 E. Fourth St.

WASHINGTON, 919 Pennsylvania Ave.
BUFFALO, 313 Main St.
SAN FRANCISCO, 125 Geary St.

LONDON, 122 Oxford Street, W.

PARIS, 34 Boulevard des Italiens.

BERLIN, 65-A Friedrichstrasse.

THE MULTIPLEX GRAPHOPHONE GRAND

The illustration shown on the facing page was reproduced from the original brochure announcing the "Multiplex Graphophone Grand."

It is significant that a recording group of instrumentalists or singers clustered in front of the horns would, without question, produce three sound tracks. The spacing and the lengths of the directional horns would seem to indicate that a stereophonic playback could be reproduced. Unfortunately, this development was not recognized as "stereo."

It is also significant that the term "multiplex" was applied to this machine. Multiplexing is a current method of FM audio hi-fidelity reproduction.

The machine undoubtedly was made either in 1898 or 1899 because it utilizes mechanical parts produced during those years for other models which employed the 5-inch cylinder. These dates also tie in with the date of the Paris Exposition.

Even though not recognized as such, this machine appears to be the first instrument employing the stereo principle. This was also the first time the term "multiplex" was used, at least in the science of sound.

Speech by Colonel Payne, president of the American Graphophone Company to the representatives of the National Phonograph Association during its second annual convention, New York City, June 16, 17 and 18, 1891.

(Complete text follows introductory remarks.)

"It may not be out of place for me to remind, gentlemen, in this connection, that in 1887 the American Graphophone Company was organized and commenced exploiting the Graphophone in the United States and Canada, and this under a license from the Volta Graphophone Company, holding patents for the United States and Canada. In 1888 Mr. Jesse H. Lippincott made a proposition to us to undertake the introduction of the Graphophone in the United States. After considerable negotiation we entered into a contract with him, the substantial details of which are known, I presume, to every member of this convention.

"The organization of the American (Graphophone) Company and transposition of the name from 'Phonograph' to 'Graphophone,' incited Mr. Edison to renew his efforts towards securing a practical phonograph. Finding this to be the case, the feeling became general among the stockholders that it would be better to harmonize the two interests than to have what might prove an injurious competition. Therefore, through Mr Lippincott, who had then made his first contract with us, an arrangement was made with Mr. Edison which brought about this result. The history of the enterprise from that time is known to you all. Either wisely or unwisely, shortly after the enterprise was fully started, the Graphophone was practically withdrawn from the field by the action of the North American Company; and last summer it was proposed to enter into a new contract. I am not going to discuss the policy of having a single machine. If it can be obtained, it will be very desirable. I think, however, that too much importance has always been attached to that one thing; and that it has tended, more than anything else that has been

done, to retard the general talking machine enterprise. The fact is that there is not another patented invention that has not, at first, been put upon the market in the best way it could be, and then the original machine improved from time to time.

"With regard to our position, I will state that we have never been approached by the North American Company with any suggestion at all as to our policy, our rights, or as to our construction of the contract between Mr. Lippincott and ourselves. We have never been asked by that company for a single machine; nor have we ever been asked by them whether we recognized Mr. Lippincott's assignments to them or not. The only conversation we have ever had on the subject with any gentleman who might be said to be a representative of that company was with Mr. Bush, who himself suggested to me that our contract with Mr. Lippincott was entirely a personal one, one not capable of assignment to anybody in any corporation. This conversation was with Mr. Bush, as the attorney of Mr. Lippincott.

"In view of Mr. Lippincott's financial misfortune, we deemed it important to ascertain just how we stood, and we therefore secured the opinions of gentlemen of eminent standing in the legal profession; and notwithstanding the views of the eminent gentlemen which have been cited here today, I say that no lawyer can read the original contract between the American Graphophone Company and Mr. Lippincott without coming to the conclusion that it is a personal contract with that gentleman. There is not an assignable word in it from beginning to end. It calls for Mr. Lippincott's personal exertions and provides that he is to devote a certain amount of his personal time to the development of the business. I desire, at this time, to correct a statement that has been made as to alleged transactions between the American Graphophone Company and the North American Phonograph Company. I will state, in reply to what has been said in the discussion, that the North American Company has never paid the American Graphophone Company one dollar in any shape or form. Mr. Lippincott did, at times, send us checks of the North American Phonograph Company, explaining that they would answer in place of his own. We have never accepted, and in fact never received, an order from the North American Phonograph Company; we have never had a line of correspondence with that company; we have never shipped a machine at its request or recognized it in any shape or form—not because we did not wish to do so, but simply because we were not asked to do it. Other statements to the contrary are not correct.

"That company has never made an issue with us, has never asked us to recognize any rights it had in any manner, shape, or form. It is perhaps just to the American Graphophone Company to say that we did not know of the contents of the contract or assignment of Mr. Lippincott to the North American Phonograph Company of July 1888, until in January of this year. We knew that there was such a company in existence, and we knew that it was originated after Mr. Lippincott got the rights to introduce the phonograph; but at that time, as you all recollect, that interest was stipulated to be conducted under two heads, namely, The North American Company, under the authority of the North American Company and under the authority of Jesse H. Lippincott, sole licensee of the American Graphophone Co., the two enterprises being kept entirely separate. There is not a letterhead or billhead of any local company printed today that does not bear that conclusive evidence upon its face, recognizing the two separate enterprises. The American Graphophone Company has not said it would not recognize the local companies. It has not taken any position in this matter at all, except in an informal discussion with Mr. Bush; and this discussion was not as the representative of the North American Company, but as the attorney of Mr. Lippincott.

"The present attitude of the American Graphophone Company is that our contracts with Mr. Lippincott are in force. We are acting under them. We are offering him, month by month, the 5,000 Graphophones a year provided for in the contract, and calling upon him to take and pay for them. We are ready to deliver them whenever they are demanded. What he does with them after he receives them, we do not know and do not care, so long as he fulfills his contract with us and does nothing to impair the enterprise.

"I have said to you, I think, about all that it is proper for me to say. We are ready at all times to answer any inquiries that the local companies or that the North American Phonograph Company may see proper to make of us. We only desire that such inquiries may be so presented to us that we can deliberately consider them and prepare full answers."

In response to a question as to whether the American Graphophone Company had a new machine, Col. Payne replied as follows:

"I want to say on that point that we have quite a number of Graphophones at our factory, and recognize the justice of some of the complaints that have been made about them, and are trying to improve them. We have men now at work at Bridgeport on both the Graphophone and the cylinder; and if it becomes a necessity for us to take the field, as it may possibly be, we propose to have a machine that we can offer to local companies or to agents, with some assurance of success."

In response to a question about the option of the American Graphophone Company to purchase Edison Phonograph patents held by Jesse H. Lippincott, Col. Payne replied as follows:

"It was at my suggestion that Mr. Lippincott undertook to buy the Edison rights in 1888, as one means of combining the two interests and getting them all under one management. We did get a contract from Mr. Lippincott of the character to which you refer. Mr. Edison had assigned all of his patents to the Edison Phonograph Company. Years before, Mr. Edison had made an assignment of his fundamental patent to what is known as the Edison Speaking Phonograph Company—a company which did nothing under that assignment, but simply slept on its rights until after the organization of the Edison Phonograph Company and the negotiations between Mr. Edison and Mr. Lippincott had been started. Mr. Lippincott did acquire by purchase the phonograph rights. The contracts are published and are probably known to all of you. There is no reason, therefore, why I should refer to them. Mr. Edison agreed to sell the stock of the Edison Phonograph Company, which was owner of the Edison patents, to Mr. Lippincott for a certain sum of money payable in a certain way. Mr. Lippincott offered that agreement to the American Graphophone Company. The negotiations between Mr. Lippincott and the American Graphophone Company ended in his giving the American Graphophone Company an option to purchase—that is to say, an agreement that they could buy the stock of the Edison Phonograph Company and stock of the Edison Speaking Phonograph Company at any time within five years, at what the stock had cost him. That was in August 1888. Therefore, the American Graphophone Company can, under that agreement, at any time before August 1893, purchase the Edison rights for what they cost Mr. Lippincott. The agreement was that Mr. Lippincott was to take over stock at par or was to be paid in cash. The Edison Phonograph stock went into Mr. Lippincott's possession, was afterwards transferred by him to the North American Company, and by that company redelivered to him, and by him pledged to Mr. Edison as collateral security for a note of his which Mr. Edison holds, and which — I understand — is for part of the purchase money of the same stock. The optional agreement has been recorded in the United States Patent Office. It is known to Mr. Edison, and was known to the North American Phonograph Company at the time it was made."

Reproduction of words and music to "The Song of Mister Phonograph," Copyrighted in 1878.

THE SONG OF MISTER PHONOGRAPH.

WORDS and MUSIC by H.A.H. von OGRAFF.

1: My name is Mister Phono-graph and I'm not so ve ry old;   My Father he's called E....di-
2: In the fruit of mo..dern sci..en..ces, (the   bud was hard to raise);   But sprouts and num'rous Pho..no-

son and I'm worth my weight in gold.   The folks they just yell in-to my mouth and now I'm
grafts are ac...cepted with good...ly praise.   Now silence no longer is gol........den   and words like

..say...ing what's true: For just speak to me I'll speak it back and you'll see I can
Truth shall not fail   and I sing to you, as I make my bow ,   for   E...di...sons

The Song of Mister Phonograph—(cont'd)

The Song of Mister Phonograph—(cont'd)

Edison's Embossing Telegraph—1877.
(Courtesy of *The Edison Institute,* Dearborn, Michigan.)

Thomas A. Edison's intuitive grasp of the shape of things to come was never more in evidence than in this particular instrument.

Designed to record and to repeat Morse code telegraphic messages, it incorporated the basic elements in a surprisingly modern appearing phonograph disc lathe with which suitable changes in groove and pitch dimensions, styli, and recording medium, could be converted to record and reproduce sound.

The embossing telegraph was a highly sophisticated and well-engineered instrument for use with the Edison Automatic Telegraph System, one of three totally different telegraph systems he had developed. Such Edison instruments were in use by the Atlantic and Pacific Telegraph Co. from 1876 to 1879.

According to Edison biographer and Menlo Park pioneer Francis Jehl, one day after Edison had been explaining some of the intricacies of the device, he said, "That machine was the father of the phonograph."

In using the embossing telegraph, circular discs of paper are placed over the turntables with the permanent spiral grooves, and held in place by the hinged outer rings. The two handles at the extreme right and left are used individually to guide each of the two arms to the desired starting position and also to lower or raise the arms which have a solenoid with a stylus attached at the bottom to either indent the paper into the spiral groove, or to trace it in case of a groove already formed.

By an ingenious hinged lever action, the handle action when the solenoid is lowered so that the stylus is in position, also raises an arm under the turntable equipped with a guiding knob which engages with a spiral of the same pitch and exactly parallel to the one above.

In other words, the considerable mass of the two arms, levers, and solenoids are carried by the guide and there is little side pressure in embossing or reproducing the paper recordings—analogical to the TED Videodisk practice 98 years later!

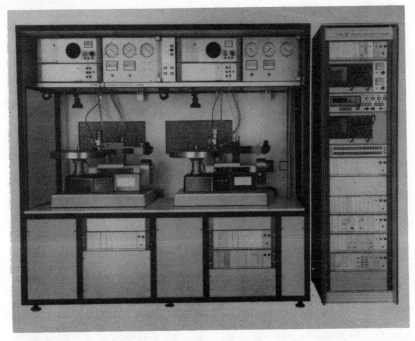

TED Videodisk recording system. (Courtesy of *Gotham Audio Corporation.*)

The first video disc system to reach the consumer market, the result of a collaboration of West Germany's Telefunken and England's Decca companies. In common with two projected alternative video disc systems, TED Videodisk records and reproduces both the audio and visual spectrums in color to European TV standards. However, TED claims to have the least expensive system, foolproof to operate and not requiring specialized training to service.

It is fascinating to compare the dual recording TED turntables with Edison's twin turntable Embossing Telegraph of 1877. Both used paper thin discs of about the same diameter, and both use vertical action perpendicular to the plane of the turntable.

With the TED units are racks of amplifiers, monitoring, and playback units, supplied by George Neumann & Co., also producers of high-quality microphones and pioneers in binaural recording.

Explanation of Corporate Genealogy Chart of Early Companies and Types of Records Produced

The chart shows the relationships of the earlier companies to each other and the more direct lines of descent to some of those of the present. The chart also indicates the comparative longevity of the principal companies and the types of records produced in the various periods. Since there are hundreds of companies and over six hundred labels in the United States alone, it is manifestly impossible to show them all.

Except for the very early period of the "local companies" under the aegis of Lippincott's North American Phonograph Company, there were comparatively few record manufacturers until after World War II. For more than forty years, the two major parent companies of the lateral disc industry, Columbia and Victor, had controlled the Western Hemisphere, and their English affiliates had dominated the rest of the world. The first rift had occurred, however, because of World War I, when the English Gramophone Co., Ltd. lost control of its German subsidiary. Immediately, records pressed from Gramophone and Victor masters under the "Opera Disc Musica" label were sold after the war in the countries of the parent companies, until enjoined by legal action. A new subsidiary company was subsequently organized in Germany by the Gramophone Co., Ltd., but Deutsche Grammophon Gesellschaft continued on its independent way, expanding its operations, first into Austria and then elsewhere in Europe.

The balance of power remained with the original companies, although major financial control shifted from New York City to London in the case of the Columbia interests, and the Gramophone Co., Ltd. eventually gained financial independence from its former colleague, the Victor Talking Machine Co.

Diminishing business due to worldwide business depression beginning in 1929 and the opportunity to effect operating economies resulted in the amalgamation of British Columbia Graphophone Co. and Gramophone Co., Ltd. into Electric & Musical Industries, Ltd. in 1931. E. M. I. also controlled Odeon, Parlophone, Electrola, Voix de son Maitre, Voce de Padrone, and others.

The basic solidarity of the world situation had been established largely by the various contracts that had been in effect between the Gramophone Co., Ltd. and the Victor Talking Machine Co. and its successor, RCA Victor, since 1901. Similar contractual liaison had tied together the opposing Columbia interests for many years, despite the financial difficulties and changes in ownership of the American companies. Therefore, after the formation of E. M. I. in 1931, competition in England was largely a family affair for a time, except for imports and the founding of the Decca Co., Ltd. Acquisition of the American Columbia catalog and the manufacturing facilities at Bridgeport by the Columbia Broadcasting System, itself organized by British Columbian capital, extended this liaison for a number of years.

A potent factor in the breakdown of the status quo, aside from the expiration of patents, was the development of high-quality tape recording shortly after World War II. Control over record archive material and record manufacturing was largely inherent in the laboratory nature of processes theretofore employed. Now this control disappeared, and independent recording companies began to spring up all over the world, as well as independent processing companies to transfer the tapes to discs. In England, Decca had also become a major producer, with plants throughout Europe. Decca also successfully invaded the American market, first through indirect sponsorship and contracts with American Decca Company prior to the war, and after, by the introduction of the Decca FFRR records, later relabeled "London," to avoid confusion with the product of the American Decca Company, with whom relations had been severed. Philips of Holland, electrical equipment manufacturers with world-wide distribution facilities, also entered the phonograph field, manufacturing both playing equipment and records. Soon, both Decca and Philips were contending with E. M. I. in England and elsewhere for the services of leading artists and symphony organizations. Introduction of the LP record, licensed freely by American Columbia, completed the breakdown of the former divided monopoly. Companies were formed to manufacture LP records exclusively, such as Capitol and Westminster in the U. S. Relations were severed between Columbia Records, Inc. and its former affiliate (and indirectly, its founder), Columbia Phonograph Co., Ltd., a unit of E. M. I. In April 1953, Cetra-Soria, an independent Italian company, turned over its masters to Capitol, and Dario Soria, formerly president, assumed charge of a new E. M. I. subsidiary company in the U. S. This subsidiary was to market E. M. I. records under the "Angel" label, which the original British Gramophone Company had registered and used as early as 1898. Philips also entered the American market through a contract with Columbia Records, Inc., some of the records appearing under the Epic label and some, as Columbia. Philips in turn utilized its world organization to market Columbia's American recordings.

RCA Victor in 1956 notified its Gramophone Co., Ltd. associate that it was terminating its long contractual relationships with them in May, 1957. To secure immediate record distribution in England and Europe, a contract was entered into between the Decca Co., Ltd. and RCA Victor. In the meantime, RCA proceeded to build phonograph and record manufacturing plants in Italy, Spain, and Greece and prepared to market records under a new RCA label.

Until January 1956, American Decca had contracted for the rights to the Parlophone name and catalog with E. M. I. This agreement was terminated, and the American Decca Company became affiliated with Deutsche Grammophon Gesellschaft (D. G. G.), which also controlled Polydor and Brunswick catalogs in Europe.

Many newer independent American companies also found it convenient to make contracts with European companies, to secure distribution abroad for their recordings, as well as to gain access to European recordings for marketing in the United States. As an example, in England, Nixa released recordings made in America by Urania, Vanguard, and Westminster. At the present time, the balance of power has shifted to the extent that the Decca Co., Ltd. vies with E. M. I. as the largest European producer, with Philips third. In the United States, although Columbia and RCA are still the largest individual producers, the greater part of the market is now supplied by many independents, including such leaders as Capitol, Decca, and Atlantic.

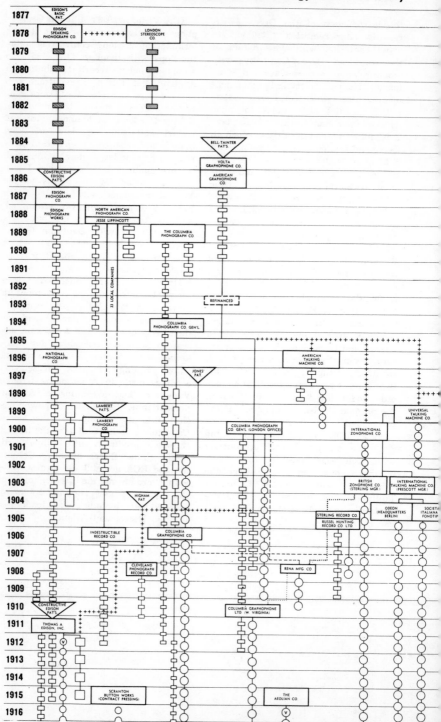

1877	EDISON'S BASIC PAT.
1878	EDISON SPEAKING PHONOGRAPH CO. + + + + + + + LONDON STEREOSCOPE CO.
1879	
1880	
1881	
1882	
1883	
1884	BELL-TAINTER PAT'S
1885	VOLTA GRAPHOPHONE CO.
1886	CONSTRUCTIVE EDISON PAT'S / AMERICAN GRAPHOPHONE CO.
1887	EDISON PHONOGRAPH CO.
1888	EDISON PHONOGRAPH WORKS / NORTH AMERICAN PHONOGRAPH CO. JESSE LIPPINCOTT
1889	THE COLUMBIA PHONOGRAPH CO.
1890	
1891	33 LOCAL COMPANIES
1892	
1893	REFINANCED
1894	COLUMBIA PHONOGRAPH CO. GEN'L
1895	+ +
1896	NATIONAL PHONOGRAPH CO. / AMERICAN TALKING MACHINE CO.
1897	JONES' PAT.
1898	+ + + +
1899	LAMBERT PAT'S / UNIVERSAL TALKING MACHINE CO.
1900	LAMBERT PHONOGRAPH / COLUMBIA PHONOGRAPH CO. GEN'L (LONDON OFFICE) / INTERNATIONAL ZONOPHONE CO
1901	
1902	
1903	BRITISH ZONOPHONE CO (STERLING MGR.) / INTERNATIONAL TALKING MACHINE CO (PRESCOTT MGR.)
1904	HIGHAM PAT. + + + + + + + + + + + + + + +
1905	STERLING RECORD CO. / ODEON (HEADQUARTERS BERLIN) / SOCIETÀ ITALIANA FONOTIP
1906	INDESTRUCTIBLE RECORD CO / COLUMBIA GRAPHOPHONE CO. / RUSSEL HUNTING RECORD CO LTD
1907	+ + + + + +
1908	CLEVELAND PHONOGRAPH RECORD CO. / RENA MFG CO
1909	
1910	CONSTRUCTIVE EDISON PAT'S + + + + + + / COLUMBIA GRAPHOPHONE LTD (W. VIRGINIA)
1911	THOMAS A EDISON, INC
1912	
1913	
1914	
1915	SCRANTON BUTTON WORKS (CONTRACT PRESSING) / THE AEOLIAN CO.
1916	

Companies and Types of Records Produced

Legend

TINFOIL RECORDS	
CYLINDERS, VARIOUS DIAMETERS AND LENGTHS	$1\frac{3}{16}$, $2\frac{1}{4}$, $3\frac{3}{4}$, 5"
DISCS, VARIOUS DIAMETERS, LATERAL CUT	7" 10" 12" 14" 20"
DISCS, VARIOUS DIAMETERS, VERTICAL CUT	
LONG PLAYING DISCS, 45 RPM, AND STEREO DISCS	LP LP LP 45 S EP
DIRECT CORPORATE CONNECTION OR DESCENT	———
LICENSED CORPORATION OR PRODUCT	+ + + + + + + +
CONTRACTUAL CONNECTIONS	- - - - - - - - -
PERSONAL CONNECTIONS OR CONTINUITY	· · · · · · · · · · ·

EDISON HOUSE
(LONDON)

BERLINER
PAT'S

UNITED STATES
GRAMOPHONE CO

BERLINER
GRAMOPHONE CO

NATIONAL
GRAMOPHONE CO

EDISONIA
LIMITED

COMPAGNIE AMERICAINE
DU PHONOGRAPHE
EDISON (PARIS)

THE GRAMOPHONE
COMPANY, LTD.
(ENGLAND)

JOHNSON
PAT'S

EDISON-BELL
CONSOLIDATED LTD.

PATHE-FRERES
(PARIS)

NATIONAL
GRAMOPHONE CORP

CONSOLIDATED
TALKING MACHINE CO

THE GRAMOPHONE &
TYPEWRITER CO. LTD.

VICTOR
TALKING
MACHINE CO

THE
NEOPHONE
CO., LTD.

PATHE-FRERES
(N.Y. OFFICE)

THE GRAMOPHONE
CO. LTD.

PATHE-FRERES
(U.S. CO.)

THE
PARLOPHONE
CO., LTD.

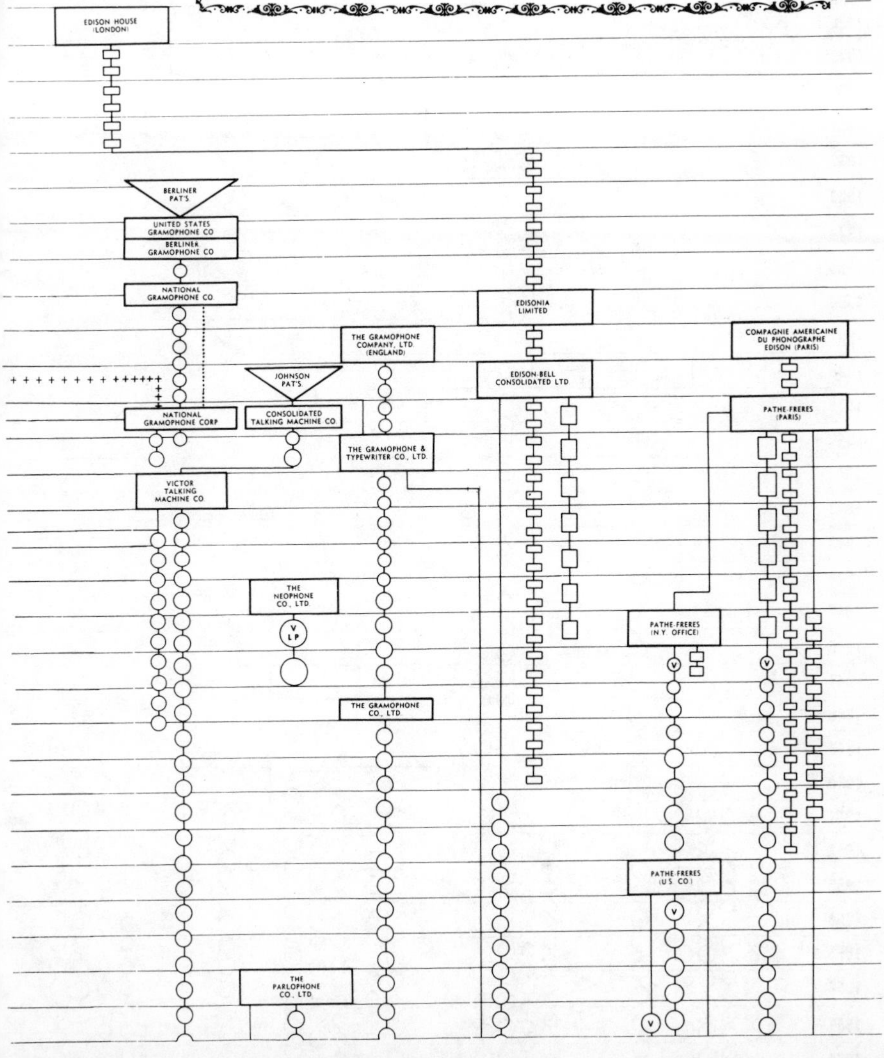

1917					COLUMBIA GRAPHOPHONE LTD (LONDON)		
1918				COLUMBIA GRAPHOPHONE MFG. CO. (USA)			
1919							
1920						BRUNSWICK BALKE COLLENDER CO.	POLYDOR
1921							
1922							
1923				BANKRUPT REORGANIZED AS			
1924			AMERICAN RECORD CO	COLUMBIA PHONOGRAPH CO., INC			
1925					COLUMBIA INTERNATIONAL LTD (HOLDING CO.)		
1926							
1927						BRUNSWICK RADIO CORP	
1928							
1929			CONSOLIDATED FILM INDUSTRIES INC BUYS AMERICAN RECORD CO			WARNER BROS BUYS BRUNSWICK RADIO CORP	
1930							
1931							
1932				GRIGGSBY GRUNOW INC. BUYS COLUMBIA PHONOGRAPH CO, INC			
1933							
1934				SACRO ENTERPRISES BUYS COLUMBIA PHONOGRAPH CO. INC			
1935							
1936							
1937	MUSICRAFT RECORD, INC						
1938			C B S BUYS AMERICAN RECORD CO	C B S BUYS COLUMBIA PHONOGRAPH CO, INC			
1939					C B S ACQUIRES BRUNSWICK RADIO CORP		
1940							
1941							CAPITOL RECORDS
1942					BRUNSWICK CATALOG RELEASED TO DECCA		
1943							
1944							
1945		MERCURY RECORD CORP					
1946							
1947					MGM RECORDS		
1948							
1949							
1950				WESTMINSTER RECORDS	CONCERT HALL		
1951							
1952							
1953							
1954							
1955							
1956							
1957							
1958							

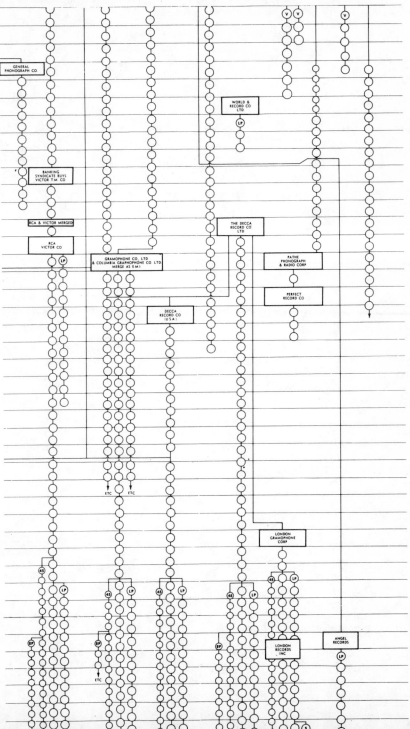

Historical Photographs

Thomas A. Edison in his chemical laboratory in 1906. This building is now a part of the Edison National Historic Site. (Courtesy of U. S. Park Service.)

Historical Photographs

*Eldridge R. Johnson,
1867-1945.*

*Emile Berliner, taken at
about 30 years of age.*

Historical Photographs

Edison's Display at the Paris International Exposition, 1889. Edison Office, Telephone, and Phonograph departments.

Historical Photographs

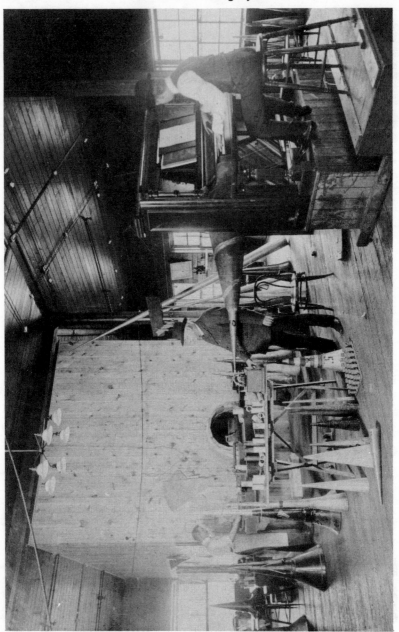

Experimental Recording of Edison Cylinder Records in the Music Room of the Laboratory in West Orange, New Jersey. (Courtesy of U.S. Park Service.)

Historical Photographs

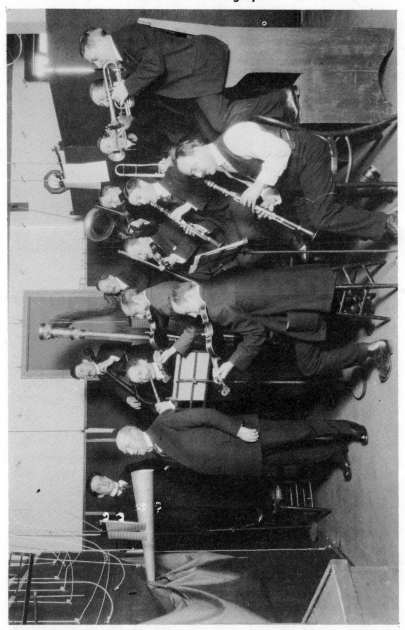

Jacques Urlus making a recording at the Edison Studio, 79 Fifth Ave., New York City, March 30, 1916. Cesare Sodero is conducting the Orchestra. (Courtesy of U.S. Park Service.)

Résumé of R. D. Cortina   Academy of Languages

Thomas A. Edison consistently included the teaching of languages as one of the fundamental functions of the phonograph. Though not the largest branch of the industry, this use has been most persistent and one of the more outstanding success stories.

In 1882, the R. D. Cortina Academy of Languages was founded at 111 West 34th Street in New York City. As early as 1891 and 1892, sets of pre-recorded English and Spanish records with texts were being exported to Central and South America. Blanks and phonographs were also supplied to students. At the Chicago World's Fair of 1893, the Cortina method received first prize in the Department of Liberal Arts, and by 1899, Cortina courses in several languages were widely advertized.*

With but one change of ownership, R. D. Cortina Co., Inc. is also unique in having maintained its headquarters in the same general area of Manhattan from which is now conducted a worldwide operation. In order to meet the varying needs of peoples everywhere,

_____
* From research by Dr. Philip Petersen, Stanford University.

over the years nearly every type of sound recording and reproducing system has been employed. Advanced courses for serious students leading to a degree is as ever a major concern, but there are also special offerings to meet the needs of travelers and more casual requirements in communicating. Today the R. D. Cortina Co., Inc. utilizes not only phonograph records, but also tape cassettes and 8-track cartridges. Their artists have kept up with progress in book and album design with tasteful and effective use of color as well as in uniquely beautiful and practical packaging.

Robert E. Livesey is President and Mrs. Livesey is Editorial Director. Mr. Livesey's father, who worked with R. D. Cortina in the pioneer days, is still active, though semiretired. The family is justly proud of their accomplishments in carrying forward so well the original objective of Cortina and Edison. The history of this 93-year institution merits the attention of the scholars of linguistics, economics, and advertising of our great universities, for it has not only survived, but is a unique example of free enterprise.

BIBLIOGRAPHY

Part A—Texts

Aeolian Co., The. *A New Musical Instrument of the Phonograph Type,* New York; The Aeolian Company, 1915.

Andem, James L. *A Practical Guide to the Use of the Edison Phonograph,* Cincinnati, Ohio; C. J. Krehbiel & Company, 1892.

Barnes, Everette K. *A Treatise on Practical Wax Recording,* Inglewood, California; Universal Microphone Company, Ltd., 1936.

Bauer, Robert. *Historical Records,* London; Sidgewick & Jackson, Ltd., 1947.

Bottone, Selimo Romeo. *Talking Machines and Records,* London; G. Pitman, 1904.

Briggs, G. A. *Sound Reproduction,* Bradford, Yorks, England; Wharfedale Wireless Works, 1950.

Bryan, George S. *Edison, The Man and His Work,* London and New York; Alfred A. Knopf, 1926.

Bryson, H. Courtney. *The Gramophone Record,* London; Earnest Benn, Ltd., 1935.

Clements, Henry B. *Gramophones and Phonographs; Their Construction, Management, and Repair,* London; Cassell & Company, Ltd., 1913.

Cochrane, Ira Lee. *The Phonograph Book,* New York; Rider-Long Company, 1917.

Dearle, D. A. *Plastic Moulding,* Brooklyn, New York; Chemical Publishing Company.

Dickson, W. K. L. *Edison—Life and Inventions of Thomas A. Edison.*

Du Moncel, Theodore Achille Louis. *The Telephone, the Microphone and the Phonograph,* New York; Harper & Brothers, 1879.

Dyer, Frank Lewis; and Martin, Thomas Commerford in collaboration with William Henry Meadowcroft, *Edison, His Life and Inventions,* New York and London; Harper & Brothers, 1919.

Edison, Thomas A. *The Phonograph and Its Future; and the Auriphone and Its Future.* (With "On the Hypothesis That Animals Are Automatic, and Its History," by T. H. Huxley), [Religio-Science Series No. 4], Toronto; Rose-Belford Publishing Company, 1878.

Edison Phonograph Works. *Inventor's Handbook of the Phonograph,* Newark, New Jersey; Ward & Tichenor, 1889.

Fessenden, Helen M. *Fessenden, Builder of Tomorrows,* New York; Coward-McCann, Inc., 1940.

Gaisberg, Fred W. *The Music Goes Round,* New York; The Macmillan Company, 1943.

Garbit, Frederick J. *The Phonograph and Its Inventor, Thomas Alva Edison,* Boston; Gunn, Bliss & Company, 1878.

Gaydon, Harry A. *The Art and Science of the Gramophone,* London; Dunlop & Company, Ltd., 1926.

Gillett, W. *The Phonograph, and How to Construct It,* London; E. & F. N. Spon, 1892.

Goldsmith, Francis H., and Geisel, Victor G. *Techniques of Recording,* Chicago; Gamble Hinged Music Company, 1939.

Gramophone (Publications), Ltd. *Novice Corner: an Elementary Handbook of the Gramophone,* London; Gramophone (Publications), Ltd., 1928.

Hough, J. E., Ltd. *The Story of Edison-Bell to 1924,* London; J. E. Hough Ltd., 1934.

Jehl, Francis. *Menlo Park Reminiscences,* Dearborn, Michigan; 1936 (Vol. 1), 1938 (Vol. 2), 1941 (Vol. 3).

Jones, Francis Arthur. *Thomas Alva Edison—60 Years of an Inventor's Life,* New York; Thomas Y. Crowell & Company, 1907.

Lewkowitsch, J. I. *Chemical Technology and Analysis of Oils, Fats, and Waxes,* New York; Macmillan Company, 1922.

Mackenzie, Compton. *The Gramophone, Its Past; Its Present; Its Future,* London; Musical Association of London (Proceedings at Leeds) Session 51, 1924-25.

McKendrick, John G. *Waves of Sound and Speech as Revealed by the Phonograph,* London; Macmillan Company, 1897.

Mitchell, Ogilvie. *The Talking Machine Industry,* London; Sir I. Pitman & Sons Ltd., 1922.

National Phonograph Association. *Proceedings of Annual Conventions,* National Phonograph Association, 1890, 1891, 1892, 1893.

National Phonograph Company, The. *The Phonograph and How to Use It,* West Orange, New Jersey; The National Phonograph Company, 1900.

Pierce, J. A. and Hunt, F. V. *On Distortion in Sound Reproduction from*

Phonograph Records, Cambridge; Harvard University Graduate School of Engineering Publications, 1938.

Plates (pseud.). *Plastics in Industry*, Brooklyn, New York; Chemical Publishing Company, 1941.

Prescott, George B. *Bell's Electric Speaking Telephone: Its Invention, Construction, Application, Modification and History*, New York; D. Appleton & Company, 1884.

———. *The Speaking Telephone, Electric Light and Other Recent Electrical Inventions*, New York; D. Appleton & Company, 1879.

———. *The Speaking Telephone, Talking Phonograph and other Novelties*, New York; D. Appleton & Company, 1878.

Rayleigh, John William Strutt. *The Theory of Sound*, London; The Macmillan Company, 1877-78.

Rider, John Francis. *Automatic Record Changers and Recorders*, New York; John F. Rider Publications, Inc., 1941.

Rogers, W. *The Gramophone Handbook; a Practical Guide for Gramophone Owners, Etc.*, with Foreword by Compton Mackenzie, London; Sir I. Pitman & Sons, Ltd., 1931.

Rothermel Corporation, Ltd. "A Technical Treatise on the Application of Rochelle Salt Crystals to High Fidelity Sound Reproducers," *Piezo-electricity*, London; Rothermel Corporation, Ltd., 1934.

Seymour, Henry. *The Reproduction of Sound*, London; W. B. Tattersall, Ltd., 1918.

Simonds, William Adams. *Edison, His Life, His Works, His Genius*, Indianapolis and New York; The Bobbs-Merrill Company, 1934.

Stanley, Douglas and Maxfield, J. P. *The Voice, Its Production and Reproduction*, New York; Pitman Publishing Corporation, 1933.

Taylor, Sedley. *Sound and Music*, London and New York; The Macmillan Company, 1883.

Tewksbury, George E. *A Complete Manual of the Edison Phonograph with Introduction by Thomas A. Edison*, Newark, New Jersey; United States Phonograph Company, 1897.

Tyndall, John. *Sound* (5th ed.), New York; D. Appleton & Company, 1895.

Webster, Arthur Gordon. *Theory of Electricity and Magnetism*, New York and London; Macmillan & Company, Ltd., 1897.

Wilson, G. (edited by Compton Mackenzie and Christopher Stone). *Gramophones, Acoustic and Radio*, London; Gramophone (Publications), Ltd., 1932.

Wilson, H. L. *Music and the Gramophone*, London; Gramophone (Publications), Ltd., 1928.

Wilson, P. and Webb, G. W. *Modern Gramophones & Electrical Reproducers*, London, Toronto, Melbourne and Sydney; Cassell and Company, Ltd., 1929.

Part B—Texts and Articles from the Musician's Viewpoint

Alda, Frances. *Men, Women and Tenors*, Boston; Houghton Mifflin Company, 1937.

Bernhardt, Sarah. *Memories of My Life*, New York; D. Appleton & Company, 1923.

Bispham, David. *A Quaker Singer's Recollections*, New York; Macmillan Company, 1920.

Calve, Emma. *My Life*, New York, London; D. Appleton & Company, 1922.

Caruso, Dorothy. *Enrico Caruso, His Life and Death*, New York; Simon & Schuster, 1945.

Culshaw, John. *Serge Rachmaninoff*, London; D. Dobson, 1949.

Dawson, Peter. *Fifty Years of Song*, London; Hutchinson & Company, 1952.

DeTreville, Yvonne. *Musician*, "Making a Phonograph Record"; V. 21, p. 658, Nov., 1916.

Eames, Emma. *Some Memories and Reflections*, New York and London; D. Appleton & Company, 1927.

Farrar, Geraldine, *Such Sweet Compulsion*, New York; Greystone Press, 1938.

Finck, Henry T. *Success in Music and How It Is Won*, New York; C. Scribner's Sons, 1909.

Hall, David. *The Record Book*, New York; Alfred A. Knopf, 1950.

Hamlin, George. *Musician*, "Making of Records"; V. 22, p. 542, July, 1917.

R. Helybut and A. Geber. *Backstage at the Opera*, New York; T. Y. Crowell, 1937.

Hendersen, W. J. *The Art of Singing*, New York; Dial Press, Inc., 1938.

Homer, Sidney. *My Wife and I*, New York; Macmillan Company, 1939.

Hurst, P. G. *The Golden Age Recorded*, Henfield, Sussex; P. G. Hurst, 1946.

Inghelbrecht, D. E. *The Conductor's World*, London and New York; P. Nevell, 1953.

Klein, Herman. *Golden Age of Opera*, London; G. Rutledge & Sons, 1933.

———. *Great Women Singers of My Time*, London; G. Rutledge & Sons, 1931.

———. *The Gramophone*, "The Gramophone and the Singer," June, 1924.

———. *Musicians and Mummers*, London; Cassell & Company, Ltd., 1925.

———. *The Reign of Patti*, New York; Century Company, 1920.

———. *Thirty Years of Musical Life in London*, London; W. Heinemann, 1903.

Kobbe, Gustov. *Opera Singers*, Boston; O. Ditson Company, 1913.

Kolodin, Irving. *The Metropolitan Opera*, New York; Oxford University Press, 1936.

Lahee, Henry C. *The Grand Opera Singers of Today*, Boston; The Page Company, 1922.

Lawton, Mary. *Schumann-Heink—The Last of the Titans*, New York; Macmillan Company, 1928.

Lehmann, Lilli. *My Path Through Life*, New York; G. P. Putnam's Sons, 1914.

Leiser, Clara. *Jean deReszke and the Great Days of Opera*, London; G. Howe, Ltd., 1933.

Lyle, Watson. *Rachmaninoff—a Biography*, London; W. Reeves Booksellers, Ltd., 1939.

Marchesi, Blanche. *Singer's Pilgrimage*, London; G. Richards, Ltd., 1923.

McCormack, Lillie. *I Hear You Calling Me*, Milwaukee; Bruce Publishing Company, 1949.

Melba, Nellie. *Melodies and Memories*, London; T. Butterworth, Ltd., 1925.

Moses, Montrose J. *The Life of Heinrich Conreid*, New York; T. Y. Crowell Company, 1916.

Musician, "A Great Force Needs Your Guidance; a Power for the Development of Musical Taste"; V. 25, p. 5, May, 1920.

Ronald, Sir Landon. *Myself and Others*, London; S. Low, Marston & Company, Ltd., 1931.

Schauffler, R. H. *Century*, "Mission of Mechanized Music"; V. 89, pp. 293-8, December, 1914.

Slezak, Leo. *Song of Motley*, London; W. Hodge & Company, Ltd., 1938.

Tetrazzini, Luisa. *My Life of Song*, London; Cassell & Company, Ltd., 1921.

Thompson, Oscar. *The American Singer*, New York; Dial Press, Inc., 1937.

Wagnalls, Mabel. *Stars of the Opera*, New York; Funk & Wagnalls Company, 1907.

Part C—Articles and Reports

Acoustical Society of America, Journal of, "Effects of Distortion upon Recognition of Speech Sounds"; V. I, p. 132, 1929.

Ibid, "Stereophonic Sound-Film System"; V. XIII, pp. 89-114, October, 1941.

American Institute of Electrical Engineers, Transactions of, "The Audion-Detector and Amplifier"; January, 1914.

August, G. J. *Music Quarterly*, "In Defense of Canned Music"; V. 17, pp. 138-49, January, 1931.

Balmain, C. *The Gramophone*, "Improvements in Gramophones"; V. 1, No. 7, December, 1923.

Banning, Kendall. *System*, "Thomas A. Edison, Manufacturer of Carbolic Acid"; November, 1914.

Barnet, H. T. *The Gramophone*, "Technical Notes"; March, 1924.

Barraud, Francis. *Strand*, "How Nipper Became World Famous"; August, 1916.

Bazzoni, C. B. *Radio News*, "The Piezo-Electric Oscillograph"; August, 1925.

Beard, George M. *Archives of Electrology and Neurology*, "The Newly Discovered Force (etheric)"; V. 2, pp. 257-282, 1875.

———. *Scientific American*, "Nature of the Newly Discovered Force"; V. 33, p. 400, December 25, 1875.

Begun, D. R. *Electronics*, "Magnetic Recording"; September, 1938.

Bell Laboratories Record, "Magnetic Recording and Reproducing"; September, 1937.

Ibid, "The Mirrophone"; V. XX, No. 1, pp. 2-5, September, 1941.

Ibid, "Synchronized Reproduction of Sound and Scene"; November, 1928.

Bell System Technical Journal, "Sound Pictures"; V. VIII, pp. 159-208, January, 1929.

Benson, A. L. *Cosmopolitan*, "Edison's Dream of a New Music"; V. 54, pp. 797-800, May, 1913.

Berliner, Emile. *The Franklin Institute, Journal of*, "The Gramophone"; May 16, 1888.

———. *Ibid*, "The Development of the Talking Machine'; V. 176, pp. 189-202, May 21, 1913.

Bettini, G. *Scientific American*, "The Micro-Graphophone"; V. 15, pp. 281-2, May 9, 1890.

de Boer, K. *Phillips Technical Review*, "Experiments with Stereophonic Records"; V. 5, pp. 182-186, Eindhoven, 1940.

Bond, A. R. *St. Nicholas*, "Talking Thread"; pp. 647-8, May, 1921.

British Plastics Yearbook, "Vinyl Rosins"; September 25, 1925.

Business Week, "Talkie Patent Dispute Ends"; July 23, 1930.

Butler, J. H. *Illustrated World*, "Radio To Make Movies Talk"; V. 37, pp. 373-7, July, 1922.

Caldwell, Orestes H. *Radio Retailing*, "Demonstration of An Original 'Edison Effect' Tube in a Radio Broadcast on 60th Anniversary of Its Invention"; 1943.

Camp, M. E. *American Homes*, "Talking Machine in the Home"; V. 11, Sup. 7.

Campbell, A. G. and Zobel, O. J. *Bell System Technical Journal*, "Electrical Recordings"; 1923.

Child, A. P. *Scientific American*, "Clay Needles for Talking Machine"; V. 123, p. 275, September 18, 1920.

Country Life, "Phonograph as a Decorative Element in the House"; V. 33, pp. 108-10, March, 1918.

Cowley, H. E. *Junior Institute of Engineers, Journal & Record of Transactions*, "The Manufacture of Gramophone Records"; V. 35, pp. 391-411, 1925.

Crawford, R. *Saturday Evening Post*, "Profits and Pirates" (interview with Thomas A. Edison); V. 203, pp. 3-5, September 27, 1930.

Current Literature, "Making Phonograph Music"; V. 33, pp. 169-70, August, 1902.

Current Opinion, "Dehumanizing the Stage"; V. 54, pp. 297-8, April, 1913.

Daily Graphic, "An Interview with Edison"; July 19, 1878.

Ibid. "The Papa of the Phonograph. An Afternoon with Edison"; April 2, 1878.

Ibid. "The Workshop at Menlo Park"; July 13, 1878.

Davis, W. *Science Monthly*, "New Film Phonograph"; n.s. 71 Sup. 10, January 24, 1930.

deForest, Lee. *Scientific American*, "When Light Speaks: Recording and Reproducing Sounds by Means of Light Intensities"; V. 129, p. 94, August, 1923.

Dickson, A. and W. K. L. *Century*, "Edison's Invention of the Kinetophonograph"; V. 206, p. 14, June, 1894.

Dime, Eric A. *Science and Invention*, "The Light Ray Phonograph"; V. 8, pp. 851, 924, 1920.

Dorian, Frank. *Phonograph Monthly Review*, "Reminiscences of the Columbia Cylinder Records"; January, 1930.

Dreher, Carl. *Popular Science*, "What Are Plastics Made of"; p. 58, January, 1944.

———. *Radio Broadcast*, "Phonograph Pick-ups"; V. 13, p. 268, September, 1928.

———. *Ibid*, "Sound Motion Pictures"; V. 13, pp. 352-3, October-November, 1928, V. 14, p. 32, May, 1929.

Duerr, W. A. *Radio Broadcast*, "Will Radio Replace the Phonograph?"; V. 2, pp. 52-4, November, 1922.

Dunlap, O. E. *Scientific American*, "Edison Glimpsed at Radio in 1875: Scintillating Sparks Led to Discovery of Etheric Force"; V. 135, p. 424, December, 1926.

Edholm, C. L. *Scientific American*, "A New Type of Phonograph"; V. 115, p. 553, December 16, 1916.

Edison, Thomas A. *North American Review*, "The Phonograph and its Future"; May-June, 1878.

English Mechanic, "Poulsen Magneto-Telephonograph"; V. 19, pp. 757-8, August, 1900.

Experimenter, "The Evolution of the Vacuum Tube"; pp. 23-6, December, 1925.

Fessenden, Reginald A. *Radio News*, "Wireless Telephony"; January-November, 1925.

Fewkes, J. W. *Scientific American*, "Edison Phonograph in the Preservation of the Languages of the American Indians"; May 2, May 24, 1890.

Foley, A. L. and Souder, W. H. *Scientific American*, "Photographing Sound: A Demonstration of Wave Motion"; Sup. 75, pp. 108-11, 1913.

Fortune, "Music for the Home"; October, 1946.

Ibid, "Phonograph Records"; September, 1939.

Ibid, "Synthetic Crystals"; August, 1950.

Frampton, J. R. *Etude*, "Sound Reproducing Machine Records and the Private Teacher; an Intensive Study in Interpretation"; V. 40, p. 520, August, 1922.

Frank Leslie's Illustrated Newspaper, "The Speaking Phonograph"; March 30, April 10, 1878.

Franklin Institute, Journal of, "Absorption Co-efficients"; March, 1929.

Fyfe, H. C. *Scientific American*, "Telegraphone and the British Post-Office"; V. 83, p. 317, April 25, 1903.

Goodchild, R. *The Gramophone*, "On Fibre Needles"; March, 1924.

Gramophone, "Crede Experts—A Current Survey of Gramophone Progress by the Expert Committee"; January, August, 1926.

Ibid, "Full House at Steinway Hall—Report of Acoustic Gramophone Competition"; July, 1924.

Grau, Robert. *Independent*, "Actors by Proxy"; July 17, 1913.

Hall, C. I. *Scientific American*, "Induction Disc Motors"; V. 4, p. 282, September, 1921.

Hammer, W. J. *Electrical Experimenter*, "Transmitting Sound by Phonograph and Telephone 104 Miles, through 48 Physical Changes"; September, 1917.

Harris, S. *Radio Broadcast*, "How Radio Developments Have Improved Recording and Reproducing"; V. 12, pp. 414-15, April, 1928.

Hayden, E. *International Studio*, "Phonographs as Art Furniture"; V. 78, pp. 249-51, December, 1923.

Henry, O. (pseud.). *McClure's*, "Phonograph and the Graft"; V. 20, pp. 428-34, February, 1903.

Hickman, C. M. *Bell System Technical Journal*, "Sound Recording on Magnetic Tape"; pp. 165-177, April, 1937.

Hopkins, G. M. *Scientific American*, "Scientific Uses of the Phonograph"; V. 62, pp. 155, 248; V. 63, p. 100, March 8, April 19, August 16, 1890.

Houston, Edwin J. *American Institute of Electrical Engineers*, "Notes on Phenomena in Incandescent Lamps (Edison Effect)"; V. 1, No. 1, p. 8, 1884.

Inglis, William, *Harper's Weekly*, "Edison and the New Education"; November 4, 1911.

Institute of Electrical Engineers, Proceedings (London), "Some Aspects of Magnetic Recording and Its Application to Broadcasting"; March, 1938.

Jewett, T. B. *Science*, "Edison's Contributions to Science and Industry"; V. 65, pp. 65-68, January 5, 1932.

Johnson, Edward H. *Scientific American*, "A Wonderful Invention" (letter to the editor describing Edison's telephone repeater); V. 37, p. 304, November 17, 1877.

Jones, Benzel. *British Plastics Yearbook*, "Cellulose"; p. 298, 1932.

Journal of Applied Physics, "On the Electro-Graphic Recording of Fast Electric Phenomena"; October, 1938.

Journal of Scientific Instruments (London), "Progress in the Recording and Reproduction of Sound"; V. 5, pp. 35-41, February, 1928.

Kelley, E. S. *Outlook*, "Library of Living Melody"; V. 99, pp. 283-7, September 30, 1911.

Kesler, C. H. *Radio Broadcast*, "Famous Radio Patents"; V. 2, pp. 207-11, 407-13, January-March, 1923.

Label, C. J. *Electronics*, "Disc-Cutting Problems"; December, 1939.

——. *Ibid*, "Disc Recording"; p. 25, October, 1937; p. 34, November, 1938; p. 17, December, 1939.

Laird, Taylor and Wille. *Acoustical Society of America, Journal of*, "Relationship between Stimulus, Intensity and Loudness"; V. III, p. 383, 1931.

Lane, C. E. *Physical Review*, "Nature of Sound Pitch"; V. 26, p. 401, 1925.

Lanier, Charles D. *Review of Reviews*, "New Phonograph"; V. 73, pp. 99-100, January, 1926.

Larson, E. J. D. *Technical World*,

"Music and Speech on a Tape"; V. 19, pp. 270-1, April, 1913.

Lathrop, George P. *Harper's Weekly*, "Edison's Kinetograph"; V. 25, pp. 444-7, June 13, 1891.

Lescarboura, A. C. *Independent and Weekly Review*, "Art of Canning Music"; V. 105, p. 241, March 5, 1921.

——. *Scientific American*, "At the Other End of the Phonograph"; V. 119, p. 164, August 31, 1918.

Lillington, A. *Living Age*, "Talking Machine"; V. 254, pp. 486-9, August 24, 1907.

Literary Digest, "Colored Films, Talking Movies and Television"; pp. 98-9, August 11, 1928.

Ibid, "Combined Radio and Phonograph"; V. 83, p. 27, October 25, 1924.

Ibid, "Edison's Forty Years of Litigation"; V. 47, p. 449, September 13, 1913.

Ibid, "Edison's Gift to Humanity"; October 2, 1915.

Ibid, "Films that Talk"; V. 71, pp. 20-1, December 3, 1921.

Ibid, "Mr. DeForest's Talking Film"; V. 74, pp. 28-9, September 16, 1922.

Ibid, "Mr. Hoxie's Talking Film"; V. 75, pp. 26-7, December 9, 1922.

Ibid, "New Alliance: Phonograph and Radio"; V. 92, pp. 21-2, February 19, 1927.

Ibid, "Phonograph Built Like an Ear"; September 9, 1922.

Ibid, "Telephone with a Memory: Poulsen's Magneto Phonograph"; V. 101, p. 21, May 18, 1929.

Little, F. B. *Illustrated World*, "Phonograph Made from an Echo"; V. 36, pp. 697-8, January, 1922.

Living Age, "Archive of Voices"; V. 318, pp. 524-5, September 15, 1923.

Lounsberry, J. R. *Radio Broadcast*, "Making Permanent Records of Radio Programs"; V. 5, pp. 363-8, September, 1924.

Lucas, F. F. *Scientific American*, "Looking through the Phonograph Record"; V. 1, pp. 518-20, June, 1920.

Mackenzie, Compton, *The Musical Association, Proceedings*, "The Gramophone, Its Past; Its Present; Its Future"; 1924-25.

Maclaurin, R. C. *Science*, "Edison's Service for Science"; June 4, 1915.

Maitland, J. F. and others. *Bookman* (London), "Musical Taste in England and the Influence of the Gramophone"; V. 60, pp. 38-41, April, 1921.

Mallory, T. J. *Electronics*, "Magnetic Recording"; p. 30, January, 1930.

Mapplebeck, J. *Saturday Evening Post*, "Canning Music the World Over"; V. 195, p. 18, June 23, 1923.

Maranies, H. S. *Annals of the American Academy of Social and Political Science*, "A Day Has Nine Lives (The

Story of the Phonograph)"; September, 1937.

Marcoson, I. F. *Munsey's*, "Coming of the Talking Picture"; V. 48, pp. 956-60, March, 1913.

Marks, G. C. *Etude*, "How the Phonograph Came into Existence"; V. 42, p. 59, January, 1924.

Maxfield, J. P. *Science Monthly*, "Electrical Phonograph Recording"; V. 21, pp. 71-9, January, 1926.

———. *Scientific American*, "Electrical Research Applied to the Phonograph"; V. 134, pp. 104-5, February, 1926.

Maxfield, J. P. and Harrison, H. C. *American Institute of Electrical Engineers — Transactions*, "Methods of High Quality Recording and Reproduction of Sound Based on Telephone Research"; February, 1926.

Maxwell, J. *Living Age*, "Britain's Talkies Come To"; V. 340, pp. 207-8, April, 1931.

McKendrick, John G. *Nature*, "Further Experiments with the Gramophone"; V. 81, pp. 488-90, 1909.

———. *Ibid*, "The Gramophone as a Phonautograph"; V. 80, pp. 188-191, 1909.

———. *Scientific American*, "Further Experiments with the Gramophone"; V. 104, p. 571, June 10, 1911.

Meadowcroft, W. H. *St. Nicholas*, "Story of the Phonograph"; V. 49, pp. 692-9, May, 1922.

Millard, Bailey, *Technical World*, "Pictures That Talk"; V. 19, pp. 16-21, March, 1913.

———. *Ibid*, "Thomas Alva Edison"; October, 1914.

Millen, J. *Radio Broadcast*, "Building an Electrical Phonograph; Combined Radio and Electrical Phonograph"; V. 11, pp. 86-9, June, 1927.

———. *Ibid*, "Electrical Phonograph; Principles Involved in Electrical Recording and Reproduction, the New Panatrope and Electrola; Data for the Home Constructor"; V. 11, pp. 20-3, May, 1927.

Miller, Phillip L. *Opera News*, "Ghosts for Sale, Mapleson Cylinders in the New York Public Library"; V. 6, No. 8, pp. 22, 29, December 8, 1941.

Millikan, R. A. *Science*, "Edison as a Scientist"; V. 75, pp. 68-70, January 15, 1932.

Musician, "What Edison Said About Music and Radio; Interview"; V. 36, p. 7, November, 1931.

Ibid, "Science Again Comes to the Aid of Music"; V. 30, p. 9, November, 1925.

Nernst, W. and R. von Lieben, *Electrician* (London), "A New Phonographic Principle"; V. 47, pp. 260-262, 1901.

Newnes. *Practical Mechanics*, "Storing Speech and Music"; April, 1938.

Outlook, "Talking Movies"; V. 103, p. 517, March 8, 1913.

Parsons, Herbert R. *The Gramophone*, "Phonofilms"; March, 1927.

Peck, A. P. *Scientific American*, "Giving a Voice to Motion Pictures"; V. 136, pp. 378-9, June, 1927.

———. *Ibid*, "Sounds Recorded on Movie Film"; V. 137, pp. 284-6, September, 1927.

Phillips, W. P. *Electrical Review and Western Electrician*, "Edison, Bogardus and Carbolic Acid"; November 14, 1914.

Piazze, T. E. *Radio Broadcast*, "Automatic Record Changers"; V. 16, pp. 310-12, April, 1930.

Plush, S. M. *The Franklin Institute, Journal of*, "Edison's Carbon Button Transmitter and the Speaking Phonograph," April, 1878.

Pollak, Hans. *The Gramophone*, "Archives in Sound—An Account of the Work of the Phonogram Archives in Vienna," April, 1925.

Popular Mechanics, "Amazing Story of the Talkies"; V. 50, pp. 938-45, December, 1928.

Poulsen, V., *Popular Science*, "Telegraphone, Description"; V. 59, p. 413, August, 1901.

———. *Scientific American*, "Telegraphone"; Sup. 50:20616, 51:20944, August 25, 1900, January 19, 1901.

Practical and Amateur Wireless, "The Steel Tape Recorder"; July 2, 1938.

Radio Broadcast, "Talking Movies"; V. 2, pp. 95-6, December, 1922.

Radio Craft, "Sound Recorded on Steel Tape"; April, 1942.

Ibid, Sound Recording on Magnetic Materials"; March, 1936.

Ibid, "Thirty-Seven Hours of Sound on a Single 16-mm. Reel"; May, 1938.

Radio News, "The Life and Work of Lee DeForest"; October, 1924.

Radio & Television, "Records on Paper Tape from Mike or Phone"; March, 1939.

Reddie, Lowell N. *Journal of Society of Arts*, "The Gramophone and the Mechanical Recording and Reproduction of Musical Sounds" (Berliner, Cros, Edison, Bell); V. 56, pp. 637-8, 1908.

———. *Smithsonian Institution—Annual Reports*, "The Gramophone and the Mechanical Recording and Reproduction of Musical Sounds"; pp. 209-231, 1909.

Reed, P. H. *Woman's Home Companion*, "Music in the Modern Home"; V. 55, p. 17, November, 1928.

Reissig, C. C. *Bulletin of the Pan American Union*, "Synchronization of Ac-

tion and Sound in Talking Movies";
V. 63, pp. 139-41.

Rhodes, H. E. *Radio Broadcast*, "Phono-
graph-Radio Amplifiers"; V. 14, pp.
88-90, December, 1928.

Ross, Richardson, *General Psychology*,
F. *NL.*, "Relationship Between Stimulus, Intensity and Loudness"; p. 288,
1930.

Schauffler, R. H. *Collier's*, "Canned
Music; the Phonograph Fan"; V. 67,
pp. 10-11, April 23, 1921.

Schor, George. *Metal Industry*, "Gal-
vano Plastic Reproduction from Metal
Moulds"; September, 1938.

Science Monthly, "New Mechanical
Phonograph"; V. 22, pp. 264-71,
March, 1926.

Ibid, "Principles of the Telephone
Applied to the Phonograph"; V. 21,
pp. 667-8, December, 1925.

Scientific American, "Accuracy in
Talkie Equipment"; V. 143, pp. 102-3,
August, 1930.

Ibid, "Auxetophone for Reinforcing
Gramophone Sounds"; May 13, 1905.

Ibid, "A Wonderful Invention—Speech
Capable of Indefinite Repetition from
Automatic Records"; November 17,
1877.

Ibid, "Canned Music; Processing the
Phonograph Record"; pp. 128-182,
March, 1923.

Ibid, "Celluloid for Phonograph Records"; V. 86, p. 191, March 15, 1902.

Ibid, "Combined Mutoscope and Talking Machine"; V. 98, p. 292, April 25,
1908.

Ibid, "Commercial Graphophone for
Recording Dictation"; Sup. 53:22151,
March 30, 1907.

Ibid, "Edison's Kinetograph and Cos-
mical Telephone"; V. 64, p. 393,
June 20, 1891.

Ibid, "Edison's Use of the Dark Box";
V. 34, p. 33, December 25, 1876.

Ibid, "Electro-Mechanical Phonograph"; V. 90, p. 438, June 4, 1904.

Ibid, "Expiration of the Berliner
Talking Machine Patent"; V. 106, pp.
52-3, January 13, 1912.

Ibid, "Fifteen to 100 Phonograph
Records Without a Stop"; V. 125, p.
242, October 1, 1921.

Ibid, "First Public Exhibition of Edison's Kinetograph"; V. 68, p. 310,
May 20, 1893.

Ibid, "German Law of Copyright on
Phonograph Records"; V. 86, p. 15,
March 8, 1902.

Ibid, "G. H. Herrington's Method of
Recording Sound Vibrations"; January 9, 1902.

Ibid, "The Gramophone"; V. 74, p.
311, May 16, 1896.

Ibid, "Improved Process of Duplicat-

ing Phonograph Records"; V. 86, p.
175, March 8, 1902.

Ibid, "Improving the Reproduction of
Talking Machine Records"; Sup. 27,
V. 109, p. 247, Sept. 27, 1913.

Ibid, "Improving the Tonal Quality of
the Phonograph"; V. 118, p. 121,
February 2, 1918.

Ibid, "Increasing the Power of a
Talking Machine by Compressed
Air"; V. 94, p. 490, December 29,
1906.

Ibid, "Inscribing and Reproducing
Diaphragm for Phonographs"; Sup.
50:20508, July 7, 1900.

Ibid, "Investigations in Phenomena of
the Phonograph"; Sup. 56:23025, July
18, 1903.

Ibid, "Manufacture of Edison Phonograph Records"; V. 83, pp. 389-390,
December 22, 1900.

Ibid, "Motion Pictures That Talk, a
New Method"; V. 135, pp. 53-4, June,
1927.

Ibid, "Moving and Talking Pictures";
V. 108, p. 64, January 18, 1913.

Ibid, "The Multiphone"; V. 86, p. 197,
April 1, 1899.

Ibid, "Multiplex Phonograph with
Five Cylinders"; V. 75, p. 393, November 28, 1896.

Ibid, "Multiplex Telegraphone"; Sup.
53:22151, June 28, 1902.

Ibid, "Museum of Sounds"; V. 134, pp.
185-6, March, 1926.

Ibid, "New Permanent Phonograph
Record"; V. 84, p. 147, March 9, 1901.

Ibid, "New Phonograph"; V. 106, p.
382, April 27, 1912.

Ibid, "New Phonograph"; V. 100, p.
318, April 24, 1909.

Ibid, "New Telegraphone"; V. 89, pp.
237-8, October 3, 1903.

Ibid, "Paper-Weight, Unbreakable
Phonograph Records"; V. 142, pp.
307-8, April, 1930.

Ibid, "Phonograph"; V. 75, pp. 65-6,
July 25, 1896.

Ibid, "Phonograph Appliance for Vis-
ible Record"; V. 100, p. 354, May 8,
1909.

Ibid, "Phonograph Improvements;
G. H. Herrington's Method of Record-
ing Sound Vibrations"; V. 66, p. 20,
June 9, 1892.

Ibid, "Phonograph Needles of Bamboo"; V. 121, p. 6, July 5, 1919.

Ibid, "Phonograph Sound-Box with
a Silk Diaphragm"; V. 120, p. 103,
February 1, 1919.

Ibid, "Phonograph Without Tone-
Arm, Sound-Box and Horn"; V. 120,
p. 322, March 29, 1919.

Ibid, "Pictures That Talk"; V. 128,
p. 19, January, 1923.

Ibid, "The Polyphone; Novel Attachment for Phonographs"; V. 81, p. 100, August 12, 1899.

Ibid, "Poulsen's Telegraphone"; V. 83, pp. 178, 181, September 22, 1900.

Ibid, "Preserving Grand Opera Records for Future Generations"; V. 99, p. 62, July 25, 1908.

Ibid, "Recording Sound on Motion Picture Film"; V. 117, p. 473, December 22, 1917.

Ibid, "Rousselot's Apparatus for Inscribing Speech"; V. 67, pp. 151-2, September 3, 1892.

Ibid, "T. A. Edison's Electro-Chemical Loud-Speaking Telephone"; July 28, 1877.

Ibid, "Talking Motion Pictures"; V. 175, p. 209, September, 1926.

Ibid, "The Talking Phonograph"; V. 37, p. 384, December 22, 1877.

Ibid, "Talking Thread"; V. 128, p. 25, January, 1923.

Ibid, "Telemicro-Phonograph"; Sup. 73:10, January 6, 1912.

Ibid, "Time-Controlled Phonograph"; V. 96, p. 289, April 6, 1907.

Ibid, "Toy Phonograph"; V. 76, p. 230, April 10, 1897.

Scripture, E. W. *Independent and Weekly Review*, "Graphics of the Voice"; V. 63, pp. 969-976, October 24, 1907.

Sharp, Clayton H. *American Institute of Electrical Engineers, Journal of*, "The Edison Effect and Its Modern Applications"; V. 41, pp. 68-78, January, 1922.

Sharp, Clayton H. *Electronic Industries*, "First Milestone in the Electronic Era"; p. 214, September, 1943.

Sherwood, Mabel R. *Bridgeport Life*, "Industrial History of Bridgeport"; December 22, 1934-August 14, 1937.

Skerrett, R. G. *Scientific American*, "A Phonograph That Is Always at Its Best"; V. 124, p. 171, February 26, 1921.

Slosson, E. E. *Science Monthly*, "Talking Motion Pictures"; V. 24, pp. 286-8, March, 1927.

Ibid, "Stereophonic Sound-Film System"; V. XXXVIII, pp. 331-426.

Society of Motion Picture Engineers, Transactions of, "Stereophonic Sound-Film System"; V. XXXVIII, pp. 331-426.

Stirling, W. *Scientific American*, "Gaumont Speaking Kinematograph Films"; Sup. 73:395, June 22, 1912.

Stout, W. B. *Scientific American*, "How To Make a Gramophone"; V. 84, p. 115, February 23, 1901.

Talking Machine News, "The Brussels Decision as to Musical Copyright—Compagnie Generale des Phonographs, Pathe-Freres and Societe

Ullman v. Marcenet and Pascini"; February 1, 1906.

Taylor, J. B. *Scientific American*, "Microscopic Study of the Phonograph"; V. 117, pp. 428-9, November 13, 1915.

U. S. Library of Congress Music Division, Check list of recorded songs in the English language in the Archive of American Folk Song to July 1940, Washington, D.C., 1942.

Viall, Ethan, *American Machinist*, "Making Edison Phonographs"; V. 36, pp. 486-827, 1911.

——. *Ibid*, "Making Victor Talking Machines, etc."; V. 37, pp. 347-52, 726, August 29, 1912.

Wade, H. T. *Scientific American*, "The Transophone and the Telescribe"; September 12, 1914.

Walsh, G. E. *Independent*, "With Edison in His Laboratory"; September 4, 1913.

Watkins, D. E. *Quarterly Journal of Speech Education*, "Apparatus for Recording Speeches"; V. 10, pp. 253-8, June, 1924.

Webster, A. G. *American Physical Society*, "Acoustical Impedance and the Theory of Horns and the Phonograph"; May, 1919 (first read December, 1914).

Wegefarth, W. D. *Lippincott's*, "Talking Machine as a Public Educator"; V. 86, pp. 628-30, May, 1911.

Wente and Bedell. *Acoustical Society of American, Journal of*, "Chronographic Method of Measuring Reverberation Time"; V. 1, No. 3, Part 1, pp. 422-427, April, 1930.

Measurement of Sound"; V. 11, p. 443, 1930.

Westphal, H. F. *Independent Educator*, "Metal Phonographs"; V. 25, p. 25, July 5, 1923.

White, W. C. *General Electric Review*, "Electronics—Its Start from the 'Edison Effect' Sixty Years Ago"; p. 527, October, 1943.

Williams, D. *Illustrated World*, "Motion Pictures that Really Talk"; V. 26, pp. 548-51, December, 1916.

Williams, S. T. *Franklin Institute, Journal of*, "Recent Developments in the Recording and Reproduction of Sound"; October, 1926.

Wireless World, "Recording for Rebroadcasting in Germany"; March 31, 1938.

Wireless World & Radio Review, "The Modern Gramophone. Realistic Reproduction by Means of Valve Amplifiers"; V. 22, pp. 273, 276, March, 1928.

Wylorn, E. J. *The Gramophone*, "The Electrical Reproduction of Gramophone Records"; December, 1926.

INDEX

PART 1

Business Corporations, Firms, and Partnerships

PART 2

Educational Institutions, Government Agencies, and Professional and Scientific Societies

PART 3
Musical Groups, Ensembles, and Orchestras

PART 4

Names of Persons
(Musicians are qualified by voice or instrument.)

PART 5
Publications Directly Referred to or Quoted

A Complete Manual of the Edison Phonograph. Tewkesbury (1897), 130, 301
American Art Journal. (April 27, 1889), 418
American Journal of Science. Silliman (1831), 3
American Mercury. (Sept. 1932), 215
American Music Lover. (July 1938), 294; (July 1944), 381, 418
American Record Guide. (March 1943), 336
American Telephone Journal. (Jan 26. and Feb. 2, 1907), 233
Annual Report of the American Graphophone Co. (Jan. 1900), 60
A Practical Guide to the Use of the Edison Phonograph. Andem (1892), 79
Asbury Park Evening News. (April 18, 1949), 382
Bell's Electric Speaking Telephone. Prescott (1884), 5
Billboard. (Feb. 21, 1914), 394; (Sept. 23, 1934), 318; (Dec. 29, 1934), 316; (Dec. 23 & Dec. 30, 1957), 428
Boston Herald. 203
Bridgeport Connecticut Farmer. (March 26, 1898), 82
Brooklyn Eagle. (Dec. 19, 1896), 65
Bulletin U.S. Bureau of Standards. Vol. 3, No. 2; 232
Country Life. (1918), 215
Daily Graphic, The. (April 2, 1878), 486, 487
Disques. 289
Edison Phonograph News. 64
Edison's Open Door. Tate (1938), 11, 59, 61, 111, 138
Edison, The Man and His Work. Bryan (1926), 38
Egypt. Ebers (Vol. 2), 1

Electrical Engineer. (July 30, 1890, Sept. 12, 1890 and March 11, 1891), 226
Electrical World. (July 1, 1888), 38; (July 12, Aug. 12 and Sept. 16, 1899), 225; (Feb. 20 and 27, 1892); 226
Electrician. (May 5, 1890), 223; (Vol. LI, 1903), 232; (June 24, 1904), 225; (Feb. 22, 1907), 233
Erhaltung der Kraft. Helmholz (1847), 224
Fabulous Phonograph, The. Gelatt (1955), 10
Fortnightly Review. (Feb. 1892), 223
Fortune. (Sept. 1939), 297; (Oct. 1946), 336-339, 345, 346, 362
Gramophone, The. 383, 384; (May, 1935), 353; (March 1936), 385; (April 1958), 431
Gramophone Shop Encyclopedia. Darrell, 290
Great Art of Light and Shadow. Kircher (1646), 275
Harper's Weekly. (March 30, 1878), 21, 22, 45
HiFi & Music Review. (June 1958), 435, 436
High Fidelity. (Oct. 1957), 434
Histoire Comique en Voyage dans la Lune. De Bergerac (1656), 1
Historical Records. Bauer (1947), 419
Hobbies Magazine. 74; (June 1958), 358
Home Furnishings Daily. (Oct. 8 and 16, 1957), 428
Household Journal. (April 1899), 86
Journal of the Franklin Institute. (April 1878), 411; (1899), 86
Journal of Russian Physics-Chemical Society. (Dec. 1895), 223
Life. 337
London Advertiser. 204

PART 6
Topics